PRESS FREEDOM IN CONTEMPORARY ASIA

This book analyzes the constraints on press freedom and the ways in which independent reporting and reporters are at risk in contemporary Asia to provide a barometer of democratic development in the region.

Based on in-depth country case studies written by academics and journalists, and some who straddle both professions, from across the region, this book explores the roles of mainstream and online media, and how they are subject to abuse by the state and vested interests. Specific country chapters provide up-to-date information on Bangladesh, Kashmir, Malaysia, Myanmar, Nepal, Pakistan, Sri Lanka, Taiwan, Thailand and Vietnam, as well as on growing populist and nationalist challenges to media freedom in the Philippines, India, Indonesia and Japan. The book includes a theoretical chapter pulling together trends and common constraints facing newsrooms across Asia and a regional overview on the impact of social media. Three chapters on China provide insights into the country's tightening information environment under President Xi Jinping. Moreover, the legal environment of the media, political and external pressures, economic considerations, audience support and journalists' standards and ethics are explored.

As an international and interdisciplinary study, this book will appeal to undergraduates, graduates and scholars engaged in human rights, media studies, democratization, authoritarianism and Asian Studies, as well as Asia specialists, journalists, legal scholars, historians and political scientists.

Tina Burrett is Associate Professor of Political Science at the Faculty of Liberal Arts, Sophia University, Japan. She is also the author of *Television and Presidential Power in Putin's Russia* (Routledge, 2013).

Jeff Kingston is Professor of History and Director of Asian Studies at Temple University, Japan. His recent publications include *Contemporary Japan 2nd ed.* (Routledge, 2019), *Japan's Foreign Relations with Asia* (Routledge, 2018) and *Press Freedom in Japan* (Routledge, 2017).

PRESS FREEDOM IN CONTEMPORARY ASIA

Edited by Tina Burrett and Jeff Kingston

LONDON AND NEW YORK

First published 2020
by Routledge
2 Park Square, Milton Park, Abingdon, Oxon OX14 4RN

and by Routledge
52 Vanderbilt Avenue, New York, NY 10017

Routledge is an imprint of the Taylor & Francis Group, an informa business

British Library Cataloguing-in-Publication Data
A catalogue record for this book is available from the British Library

Library of Congress Cataloging-in-Publication Data
A catalog record for this book has been requested

ISBN: 978-1-138-58483-9 (hbk)
ISBN: 978-1-138-58484-6 (pbk)
ISBN: 978-0-429-50569-0 (ebk)

Typeset in Bembo
by Apex CoVantage, LLC

CONTENTS

ILLUSTRATIONS

CONTRIBUTORS

Ikhtisad Ahmed is a trained barrister and human rights lawyer turned writer from Bangladesh. Having previously worked within the socio-political sphere of the country, he has since covered it in his non-fiction, fiction and poetry, with a focus on oppression and violations of rights from the perspective of victims.

Tina Burrett is Associate Professor of Political Science at the Faculty of Liberal Arts, Sophia University, Japan. Her recent publications include 'Russian State Television Coverage of the 2016 US Presidential Election,' 'Abe Road: Comparing Japanese Prime Minister Shinzo Abe's Leadership of his First and Second Governments' and 'Mixed Signals: Democratisation and the Myanmar Media.'

Pavin Chachavalpongpun is Associate Professor at the Center for Southeast Asian Studies, Kyoto University. Earning his PhD from the School of Oriental and African Studies, Pavin is the author of several books, including *A Plastic Nation: The Curse of Thainess in Thai-Burmese Relations* and *Reinventing Thailand: Thailand and his Foreign Policy*. Pavin is a chief editor of the online journal *Kyoto Review of Southeast Asia*, in which all articles are translated from English into Japanese, Thai, Bahasa, Filipino and Vietnamese.

Sheila S. Coronel is Academic Dean of the Graduate School of Journalism at Columbia University. She is concurrently also director of the Stabile Center for Investigative Journalism and Stabile professor of professional practice. She began her reporting career in the Philippines and was co-founder of the Philippine Center for Investigative Journalism.

Siddhartha Deb is the author of *The Beautiful and the Damned*. He is the recipient of fellowships from the Radcliffe Institute and the Howard Foundation.

Kevin Evans is an eyewitness as well as participant supporting many of the democratic reforms that were implemented in Indonesia at the end of the 1990s. He continues to support future efforts with the Partnership for Governance Reform.

Farrukh Faheem is presently working as Assistant Professor at the Institute of Kashmir Studies (IKS), University of Kashmir, Srinagar. His research focuses on understanding the protest movement and mobilizations in Kashmir. He is also interested in understanding politics of identity and exclusion among the marginalized. His most recent essay is titled 'Interrogating the Ordinary: Everyday Politics and the Struggle for Azadi in Kashmir,' published in 2018.

Narayan Ghimire has been working as an English news editor for more than 12 years. He is also a media researcher at Freedom Forum Nepal, where he has served for nearly a decade. His work focuses on press freedom, internet governance, digital literacy, freedom of expression and social media.

Elijah Hoole is an engineer by training but has for long retained a keen interest in Sri Lankan politics and society. He previously worked as a consultant analyst for Verité Research, where he monitored the disparities between the Tamil and the Sinhala press for a period of four years. His writings have appeared in both English and Tamil national newspapers.

Rajan Hoole began his career as an electrical engineer and later became a teacher of Mathematics. He was a founder member of the University Teachers for Human Rights (Jaffna) from 1988, which was a co-winner of the Martin Ennals Award for Human Rights Defenders in 2007.

Andrew Horvat teaches Journalism and Modern History at Josai International University. He is co-editor with Gebhard Hielscher of *Sharing the Burden of the Past – Legacies of War in Europe, America and Asia*.

Jaw-Nian Huang is an Assistant Professor of Development Studies at National Chengchi University in Taiwan. He holds a PhD in political science from the University of California, Riverside, and serves as an inaugural Hou Family Fellow at the Fairbank Center for Chinese Studies at Harvard University, as well as a research team member for China Impact Studies at the Institute of Sociology at the Academia Sinica in Taiwan.

Dharmendra Jha is the former chairperson of the Federation of Nepali Journalists (FNJ) and former reserve adviser of the International Federation of Journalists (IFJ). He is currently the General Secretary of Freedom Forum Nepal. He is also a freelance journalist, columnist, freedom of expression advocate, media trainer and right-to-information activist.

Jeff Kingston is co-editor of this volume and the Director of Asian Studies at Temple University Japan. He is author and editor of a dozen books, including *Press Freedom in Japan* (Routledge 2017) and *The Politics of Religion, Nationalism and Identity in Asia.*

Louisa Lim is a Senior Lecturer in Audiovisual Journalism at the University of Melbourne. She is the author of The People's Republic of Amnesia; Tiananmen Revisited, which was shortlisted for the Orwell Prize. She is an award-winning journalist who reported from China for a decade for NPR and the BBC, and she co-hosts the Little Red Podcast.

Justin McCurry is the Japan and Korea correspondent for *The Guardian.* He also reports on Japan and the Koreas for France 24 TV and contributes to publications in Japan and the United Kingdom. Justin has a BSc. (Econ) from the London School of Economics and an MA in Japan Studies from the School of Oriental and African Studies, London University.

David Moser holds a Masters and a PhD in Chinese Studies from the University of Michigan, with a major in Chinese Linguistics and Philosophy. He is currently Associate Dean of the Yenching Academy at Peking University. Moser is author of the book *A Billion Voices: China's Search for a Common Language.*

Syed Javed Nazir teaches Media Writing at Lahore University of Management Sciences (LUMS). He is a veteran of more than 35 years in journalism and media education on four continents. A former newspaper editor, his work has been published in a number of mainstream and academic publications.

Giang Nguyen-Thu is a postdoctoral fellow at the Annenberg School for Communication, University of Pennsylvania. She had many years teaching journalism at the Vietnam National University, Hanoi. Her research interests include media, nationalism, censorship and gender in Vietnam. Her monograph *Television in Post-Reform Vietnam: Nation, Media, Market* was published by Routledge in 2018.

Hyunjin Seo is an associate professor at the University of Kansas and a fellow at Harvard University's Berkman Klein Center for Internet and Society. Her research areas include digital/emerging media, international communication, and collective actions. Before joining academia, Seo was a diplomatic correspondent for South Korean and international media outlets.

Fei Shen is Associate Professor in the Department of Media and Communication, City University of Hong Kong, and Pearl River Scholar at the School of Communication and Design, Sun Yat-sen University. His research interests include public opinion, computational social science methods, and political communication.

Gayathry Venkiteswaran is Assistant Professor of Media and Politics at the University of Nottingham Malaysia, where she is also a PhD candidate. She has 20 years of experience working on media and media freedom advocacy in Malaysia and Southeast Asia. She is co-editor of a volume, *Myanmar Media in Transition: Legacies, Changes and Challenges* (2019).

Chuanli Xia is a Post-doctoral Fellow at the Journalism and Media Studies Centre, The University of Hong Kong. His research interests include political communication, public opinion, and fake news.

1

INTRODUCTION

Jeff Kingston

The twenty-first century may well belong to Asia, as it becomes the nexus of the global economy, but press freedom in the region remains under assault and reporters operate under difficult circumstances due to institutionalized intimidation, government hostility and – in many places – the threat of incarceration, physical violence and death. It is a bleak picture. A press in shackles and limits on freedom of expression erodes democracy, transparency and accountability with major implications for justice, governance, the rule of law and business operating conditions. There is thus a high price to be paid for limiting press freedom, but it is convenient for authoritarian regimes and illiberal democracies wherein the ruling elite don't appreciate scrutiny or challenges to their authority.

At its best, a free press supports tolerance, diversity and secularism without bias or prejudice and provides a space for debate about the critical issues facing a society. But, everywhere, this ideal has proven elusive, and often in Asia we see the worst aspects of a toadying, co-opted or biased press, suffering from self-censorship and inclined towards stoking prejudices and pandering to popular appetites for sensationalism and entertainment. Social media has also been compromised and drafted into culture wars or lobotomized for amusement and diversion in the desperate competition for eyeballs.

This volume covers the media landscapes in Asia navigated, manipulated and consumed in varied societies with a combined population of over three billion people. In our case studies spanning East, Southeast and South Asia, our contributors note that self-censorship is widespread as editors and journalists trim their sails to prevailing political winds and economic realities. Governments wield considerable power to influence the news though regulations and laws and the allocation of licences and advertising budgets that limit autonomy and leverage media dependency on the goodwill and resources of the powers that be. Owners and publishers often have broader business interests that they want to protect from the risks of retribution, should they offend those in power through unfettered reporting about delicate matters or controversial issues. To the extent that media ownership is concentrated in the hands of cronies and pliant entrepreneurs, press freedom suffers. As the state has deregulated the media in line with democratization and privatization, fierce competition and concerns about the bottom line have ignited a race to the bottom, as entertainment and sensationalism attract eyeballs and advertisers. As a result, freedom has not translated into improvement as careful analysis gives way to news-lite. With the exception of Vietnam and China, the case studies presented in this volume involve democracies, but significant democratic backsliding in many of these countries highlights how authoritarian methods are widespread in the region and compromise the freedom of expression. Press freedom also suffers from a lack of judicial autonomy and from judges who fail to uphold the rule of law or bend it to the wishes of the powerful. It is remarkable that reporters still chase hard news and risk much in doing so, knowing as they do, that their colleagues, editors, publishers and the judiciary rarely provide support or protection.

Back in the 1990s, apologists for Singapore's truncated democracy and unfree press tried to assert that there is something called 'Asian values.' These values ostensibly included a preference for strong government and a belief that limits on democratic and human rights were both good and necessary to promote economic development and societal harmony. This attempt to legitimize authoritarian governance in terms of shared cultural norms insisted that Western criticisms of Asian governments for human rights violations and curbs on freedom of expression were actually examples of cultural imperialism. This view has been thoroughly discredited and debunked as the sheer variety of Asian cultures, norms, values, civilizational influences and religions exposed the monolithic thesis as a sham (Li 1999; Jacobsen and Bruun 2000; Kim 2010). Moreover, there are rich liberal traditions in Asia and strong public support for human rights, freedom of expression and democratic accountability. This volume reinforces the consensus that Asian values are diverse, not authoritarian, and that a vibrant press is valued and brave journalists across the region are prepared to risk everything for press freedom. There is nothing to celebrate about the high death toll of reporters in Asia, but this suggests the degree of commitment to the ethos of investigative journalism and the principle of freedom of expression in the region. Of the 503 journalists killed worldwide for practicing their profession between 2006 and 2012, about one-third were in Asia (Occupy Theory 2013). Apparently, they didn't get the Asian values memo. Alas, the deaths and incarceration of journalists and bloggers occurs within a cocoon of impunity, as those who silence the press are rarely held accountable.

The flowering of social media in twenty-first–century Asia has gained momentum, often with grim or malevolent consequences (Funk 2018). It has become the default source for news, bypassing the usual mainstream gatekeepers. In the absence of such gatekeepers, social media is primed for fake news and easily manipulated by those seeking to dupe users, their friends and their followers. Internet trolls, religious zealots and government agents can connect with vast numbers of users on various platforms to promote their agendas, and all too often that involves hate speech and the othering of vulnerable minorities. It is a medium wherein the sensational and provocative hold sway, as clickbait in an echo chamber of virulence, wherein validation is measured in shares and likes. It is often an angry space wherein convention and constraints are shed in a virtual community of shared grievance, untethered umbrage and glowering resentments. Social media has also given rise to the phenomenon of mobocracy whereby self-appointed, unelected leaders seek to influence state policies and agendas by arousing and mobilizing masses of followers to take to the streets as a means of exerting pressure on elected leaders. In Muslim-majority Indonesia, Pakistan and Bangladesh, militant Islamic clerics engage in such tactics to promote intolerance, spread accusations of blasphemy and prosecute targeted individuals in the court of public opinion (Kingston 2019). The ousting and jailing of the ethnic Chinese Christian governor of Jakarta, Basuki Tjahaja Purnama – known as Ahok, on trumped-up blasphemy charges in 2017 is a prime example of mobocracy prevailing over tolerance, leaving a polarizing legacy of distrust. In Muslim-minority societies such as Sri Lanka, India and Myanmar, social media has been mobilized to promote Islamophobia with tragic consequences, most notably the Myanmar military's ethnic clearance operations targeting the Rohingya. Facebook was used by top brass and militant monks to propagate hate speech and to downplay and deny the horrors inflicted on the Rohingya. In the aftermath of the 2019 Easter Sunday suicide bombings in Sri Lanka by Islamic extremists, Bodhu Bala Sena (BBS) – an ultranationalist Buddhist organization – proclaimed vindication on social media for its track record of Islamophobia and inciting communal violence, inspiring more of the same.

Chinese authorities, worried about the potentially subversive influence of social media, have cracked down hard. Enjoying a monopoly on controlling public discourse, deciding policies and setting priorities, the Chinese Communist Party (CCP) has marginalized alternative views and analysis about sensitive issues, ensuring that social media narratives bend to its will and abides by its diktats. As Reporters without Borders notes, 'By relying on the massive use of new technology, President Xi Jinping has succeeded in imposing a social model in China based on control of news and information and online surveillance of its citizens… [Moreover] [u]nder tougher Internet regulations, members of the public can now be jailed for the comments on a news item that they post on a social network or messaging service or even just for sharing content' (Reporters without Borders 2019).

Governments around the region have adopted various social media libel and defamation laws to curb free expression and to enable prosecutions against reporters, activists and ordinary citizens in order to protect the powerful and to limit the spread of ideas and information harmful to their interests. In Thailand, merely sharing an unflattering BBC report on the Thai king can land one in jail for several years. Authorities everywhere now carefully monitor social media to identify 'trouble-makers' and potential threats, but none more so than in China. Beijing spends more money on internal security than on its military budget to ensure that challenges to the CCP are nipped in the bud.

The Chinese government's extensive controls on social media are designed to allow it to shape news narratives in its favour and to eliminate critical views and discordant voices. In doing so, it has become the largest source of fake news, subjecting citizens to a drip feed of regime-supporting propaganda. Of course, Beijing does not have a monopoly on propaganda or fake news, and like everywhere else in Asia, there are ways to evade or overcome the censors. But the Great Firewall of cyber censorship creates a hurdle that most can't be bothered with scaling, a complacency that cedes the right to know.

As Timothy Garton Ash argues, free press is the oxygen of all other freedoms (Garton Ash 2017). It can also be a force for social and legal reforms. For example, the brutal gang rape of a woman on a New Delhi bus in 2012 sparked extensive coverage of this sensitive topic and put pressure on police to improve their victim support and investigative procedures. Suddenly, what had long been ignored was rightly seen as barbaric and out of touch with contemporary norms. Politicians, prosecutors and the police scrambled to adapt to the new climate of intolerance toward rape and the insensitivity toward victims that had prevailed. As the press unearthed horrific stories of child rape, the government enacted tougher penalties to deter rapists, but these have proven ineffective in stemming sexual violence. Rape after all is about power and subjugation. Nevertheless, the press has held up a mirror to society – and people don't like what they see. For example, in 2018 an 8-year-old Muslim girl was held in a Hindu temple where she was tortured and gang raped over several days until the miscreants killed her by repeatedly bashing her with a rock. Such outrages used to be buried, so it is a mark of progress that the public confronts the horrors that others have endured in silence for too long. Reform starts with knowledge.

The *Washington Post*'s motto proclaims that 'Democracy Dies in Darkness,' and so do people. Amartya Sen found that there has never been a famine in a nation with a free press; the news doesn't only set people free but can also mobilize urgently needed support (Sen 1982). Free speech also depends on the ideal of equality whereby everyone – regardless of gender, class, religion or ethnicity – can exercise the right to freedom of expression and all can challenge authority and taboos in the search for truth. It is also the key to shaping a nation's political agenda, giving voice to the powerless, vulnerable and marginalized, while providing a platform to debate poverty, inequality and discrimination. In some parts of Asia, journalists who seek to change the dialogue face the 'assassin's veto,' while others are subject to the chilling influence of threats of violence or denial of access.

The tricky questions are how and where to draw the line on freedom of expression, and the need to ensure it does no harm to others. Hate speech is not sanctioned by freedom of expression, and curbing it is a legitimate right of any society. But there is also the risk of overdoing it as people seem too easily offended, claiming to be affronted to sanction their own indignant denunciations of others, a trait common among the religiously devout. Amos Oz points out in his pithy *How to Cure a Fanatic* (2006) that it helps to have a sense of humour. He observes that fanatics tend not to have one, while those who do are disinclined to fanaticism. Prickly leaders with thin skins are perhaps most in need of a funny bone because they are often the least accommodating of press freedom and the challenges and criticisms involved in free expression. Problematically, they empower others to clamp down on freedom and set the tone for intolerance in diverse societies wherein tolerance and forbearance are in short supply.

Press freedom advocacy and ranking

Reporters without Borders (Reporters sans Frontieres, RSF), Freedom House and the Committee to Protect Journalists (CPJ) all maintain very useful and up-to-date sites about the problems and challenges of freedom of expression. By shining a light in the dark corners of repression and publicizing the risks and harassment that reporters face, these organizations effectively advocate on their behalf. When even the 'leader of the free world' pillories the press as the 'enemy of the people,' the need for advocacy and vigilance is obvious. In addition, the Freedom of the Press Foundation, the Reporters Committee for the Freedom of the Press, the Knight First Amendment Institute at Columbia University and the Index on Censorship also participate in an international network of organizations that collaborate in trying to protect and enlarge the space for reporting and for freedom of expression. These organizations leverage their media connections to maximize coverage and exposure of wrongdoing, but have limited resources to cope with the growing antipathy for journalists whipped up by leaders who are hostile to transparency and the people's right to know.

In the 2019 RSF press freedom rankings, no Asian country is in the top 40 and the highest rank is held by Taiwan at 42 out of 180 countries surveyed (Reporters without Borders 2019). Japan (67) is next, while Hong Kong (73) is the only other entrant in the top 75, while Timor Leste at 84 rounds out the region's top four. Next are Nepal (106), Indonesia (124), Sri Lanka (126), the Philippines (134), Thailand (136), Myanmar (138), India (140), Pakistan (142), Cambodia (143) and Bangladesh (150). In the authoritarian communist league, Laos (171) comes out on top, while Vietnam (176) narrowly edges out China (177).

International rankings of press freedom are problematic, however, because they tend to be subjective snapshots and the comparative rankings sometimes seem skewed because those who are interviewed are not usually in a position to gauge press freedom elsewhere. These respondents don't measure their situation in terms of norms prevailing in other nations, but instead use their own nation's media norms and context as the yardstick for assessing contemporary developments where they work. Moreover, the rankings mask the sometimes rather small differences in numerical scores between nations, meaning the apparent gap between #45 and #55 in the RSF index is less than meets the eye and doesn't necessarily imply a major difference in press freedom. Thus, we view the rankings as broadly indicative and note that they should be interpreted with caution.

Freedom House, a conservative US think tank, conducts its own survey and assigns scores that determine if a country is free, partly free or not free on a scale of 100 points (Freedom House 2019). Among the countries surveyed in our volume, the scores range from China's low of 11 to Japan's high of 96. Freedom of expression and press freedom are not the only criteria, but are metrics used to determine overall scores.

Common challenges

There are some common themes regarding the constraints on and erosion of press freedom in Asia. In many cases, the legal landscape is unfavourable or inadequate, a situation compounded by the lack of judicial autonomy and a climate of intimidation that undermines the rule of law. Although written about Nepal, with a few minor edits, this RSF assessment could apply to many of the Asian media landscapes we survey:

> the new criminal code adopted in August 2018 poses major new threats to press freedom because several of its provisions hamper investigative reporting and restrict criticism of public figures. Another disturbing development was the anti-media rhetoric which government representatives began using and which was widely reproduced in the government's newspapers, radio stations and TV channels. With the threat of prosecution and continuing violence in the field, the environment for journalists working for independent media outlets is extremely difficult.
>
> *(Reporters without Borders 2019)*

The explosion of social media once seemed to offer a way to bypass state censorship and to empower citizen journalists and bloggers, but legal reforms and stepped-up enforcement have, at least in the more authoritarian regimes, shackled this option. The case of Vietnam has parallels in the region, where 'the only sources of independently-reported information are bloggers and citizen-journalists, who are being subjected to ever-harsher forms of persecution including plainclothes police violence. Meanwhile, as Vietnam's citizens become increasingly engaged online, the authorities have been refining their digital repressive methods' (Reporters without Borders 2019). And in some countries, we see that extremists have deployed the internet to attract and mobilize followers and sympathizers, amplifying their voices and stoking the embers of resentment (Mishra 2017). Mobocracy is mobilized from such imagined communities where social media has transcended borders, distance and parochialism to forge common identities on the anvil of shared grievances and anger. Taboos are created and tolerance is pruned back in a climate of orchestrated outrage where religion is weaponized. As Indian intellectual Pratap Bhanu Mehta remarked in March

2019, 'Religion, that very thing that behooves us to transcend our identity, is being reduced to the identity that marks you, for which you will be targeted' (Donthi 2019). The internet is a hothouse for such targeting and for brewing a malevolent, glowering nationalism that is manipulated to divide and arouse angry passions targeting the vulnerable and marginalized.

Violence is the trump card of press censorship. In the Philippines, it is open season on journalists. President Rodrigo Duterte, according to RSF,

> issued this cryptic but grim warning: 'Just because you're a journalist, you are not exempted from assassination, if you're a son of a bitch. Freedom of expression cannot help you if you have done something wrong.' Three Philippine journalists were killed in 2019, most likely by agents working for local politicians, who can have reporters silenced with complete impunity.
>
> *(Reporters without Borders 2019)*

Indonesia also suffers from:

> serious media freedom violations, including drastic restrictions on media access to West Papua (the Indonesian half of the island of New Guinea), where violence against local journalists keeps on growing. Foreign journalists and local fixers are liable to be arrested and prosecuted there, both those who try to document the Indonesian military's abuses and those, such as a BBC correspondent in February 2018, who just cover humanitarian issues.
>
> *(Reporters without Borders 2019).*

Thailand scored a dismal 30 points on the Freedom House index as the military junta has curbed civil liberties and, 'has systematically used censorship, intimidation, and legal action to suppress independent media. Journalists have been detained without charge and questioned . . . in military camps, in an intimidation tactic known as attitude adjustment' (Freedom House 2019).

And in Pakistan, 'Intimidation, physical violence and arrests were used against journalists who crossed the red line by trying to cover stories deemed off limits by the military. After reining in the traditional media, the establishment has set about purging the Internet and social networks of content not to its liking' (Reporters without Borders 2019). The taboo topics vary, but corruption, nepotism, cronyism, military business operations and extrajudicial killings by state security forces are a common foundation across the region.

Bangladesh scored a woeful 41 points on the Freedom House index and earned this damning overview:

> The ruling Awami League (AL) has consolidated political power through sustained harassment of the opposition and those perceived to be allied with it, as well as of critical media and voices in civil society. Corruption is a

serious problem, and anticorruption efforts have been weakened by politicized enforcement. Due process guarantees are poorly upheld and security forces carry out a range of human right abuses with near impunity. The threat posed by Islamist extremists has receded since 2016, when the government enacted a harsh crackdown that saw the arrest of some 15,000 people.

(Freedom House 2019)

In this environment, it is not surprising that,

> Journalists and media outlets face many forms of pressure, including frequent lawsuits, harassment, and serious or deadly physical attacks. The threat of physical reprisals against bloggers and publishers in connection with their work remained high in 2018. A climate of impunity remains the norm, with little progress made on ensuring justice for the series of blogger murders since 2015. Dozens of bloggers remain in hiding or exile.
>
> *(Freedom House 2019)*

Moreover, 'The Digital Security Act, which became law in October 2018 and replaced the ICT Act, allows the [Bangladeshi] government to conduct searches or arrest individuals without a warrant and criminalizes various forms of speech' (Freedom House 2019).

Who owns the media matters, and it is not only regime cronies that pose a threat. For example, regarding Taiwan (93 points), Freedom House (2019) observes that,

> Key media owners have significant business interests in China or rely on advertising by Chinese companies, leaving them vulnerable to pressure and prone to self-censorship on topics considered sensitive by Beijing. In recent years, Taiwanese regulators have resisted proposed mergers that would have concentrated important media companies in the hands of such owners, and the press has been able to report freely on elections.

Freedom House also reported that Beijing has used social media platforms to spread propaganda against the ruling Democratic Progressive Party (DPP) that opposes closer ties with the mainland and funnelled campaign funds to the pro-integration Kuomintang (KMT).

Bias is also a problem, as entrenched powers are often able to rely on a loyal media to project their message and to garner support in the expectation that such favours will be reciprocated. Malaysia experienced a political earthquake in 2018 as the long-ruling Barisan Nasional (BN) was ousted by a coalition of opposition parties that promised significant improvements in lifting press curbs and repealing problematic laws that empowered the state to target its critics. Although the new government has not been able to deliver on many of its pledges because the BN controls the Senate, Freedom House explained that Malaysia merited a higher score of 52 points, 'because mainstream media outlets generally became more politically neutral in their coverage following the change in government, authorities dropped sedition charges against some critics, and certain news sites were unblocked by regulators' (Freedom House 2019).

Self-censorship is common across Asia as the Fourth Estate pulls its punches and doesn't divulge all it knows in order to curry favour and to stay out of trouble. Regarding South Korea, with a score of 83 points,

> The news media are generally free and competitive, reporting aggressively on government policies and allegations of official and corporate wrongdoing. However, a defamation law authorizes sentences of up to seven years in prison, encouraging a certain degree of self-censorship, and journalists at major news outlets often face political interference from managers or the government. News coverage or commentary that is deemed to favor North Korea can be censored and lead to prosecution under the National Security Law.
>
> *(Freedom House 2019)*

Roadmap

Unlike these snapshot reports, our authors provide a deeper analysis and wider context in discussing the problems of press freedom in their respective societies. Our 20 authors come from diverse backgrounds ranging from journalism to academia and civil society. They were born in, live in, have spent considerable time in, or are exiles from, the nations they survey. There are the usual reasons for late submissions, but none more convincing than when the military turned off the internet as in Kashmir. One of our contributors based in China requested anonymity due to fear of retribution. Many of our contributors are vulnerable to harassment, violence and incarceration, and thus we salute their bravery and thank them for shining a light where it is needed. Scrutiny and publicity are the enemies of censorship and repression.

There are few books that navigate across the breadth of Asia in as much depth as this volume. The chapters are organized by region – East Asia, Southeast Asia and South Asia – and alphabetized by nation within those groupings. Tina Burrett presents a theoretical chapter at the outset, while Chuanli Xi and Fei Shen have the last word in their chapter on internet freedom across the region. For East Asia, we have three contributions on China (Anonymous, Lim and Moser) two on Japan (Horvat and McCurry) and one each on South Korea (Seo) and Taiwan (Huang). For Southeast Asia, we cover Indonesia (Evans), Malaysia (Gayathry), the Philippines (Coronel), Thailand (Chachavalpongpun), Vietnam (Nguyen) and offer two chapters on Myanmar (Burrett and Kingston). For South Asia, we cover Bangladesh (Ahmed), Nepal (Jha and Ghimire), Pakistan (Nazir), Sri Lanka (Hoole and Hoole), and have two chapters on India (Deb and Faheem).

We hope readers will learn as much from these succinct essays as we have in editing the volume.

Works cited

Donthi, P. (2019) 'The liberals who loved Modi', *Caravan*. Online. Available HTTP: <https://caravanmagazine.in/politics/the-liberals-who-loved-modi> (accessed 23 May 2019).

Freedom House. (2019) *Freedom in the World*. Online. Available HTTP: <https://freedomhouse.org/report/freedom-world/freedom-world-2019/map> (accessed 23 May 2019).

Funk, A. (2018) 'A grim reality for internet freedom in Asia', *Freedom House*. Online. Available HTTP: <https://freedomhouse.org/blog/grim-reality-internet-freedom-asia> (accessed 23 May 2019).

Garton Ash, T. (2017) *Free Speech: Ten Principles for a Connected World*, New Haven: Yale University Press.

Jacobsen, M. and Bruun, O. (eds.). (2000) *Human Rights and Asian values: Contesting National Identities and Cultural Representations in Asia*, Surrey: Curzon Press.

Kim, S.Y. (2010) 'Do Asian values exist? Empirical tests of the four dimensions of Asian values', *Journal of East Asian Studies*, 10: 315–344.

Kingston, J. (2019) *The Politics of Religion, Nationalism and Identity in Asia*, Boulder, CO: Rowman and Littlefield.

Li, X. (1999) 'Asian values and human rights', *Dissent*, 46: 118–120.

Mishra, P. (2017) *The Age of Anger: A History of the Present*, London: Allen Lane.

Occupy Theory. (2013) 'Most journalist deaths by region'. Online. Available HTTP: <https://occupytheory.org/most-journalist-deaths-by-region/> (accessed 23 May 2019).

Oz, A. (2006) *How to Cure a Fanatic*, Princeton: Princeton University Press.

Reporters without Borders (RSF). (2019) 'World press freedom index'. Online. Available HTTP: <https://rsf.org/en/ranking_table> (accessed 23 May 2019).

Sen, A. (1982) *Poverty and Famines: An Essay on Entitlement and Deprivation*, London: Clarendon Press.

2

THEORIZING MEDIA FREEDOM IN ASIA

Tina Burrett

What is media freedom, why is it important and what are its main impediments? Concepts of media freedom and of the proper conduct of journalism have been mainly theorized with Western democracies in mind (Jiafei 2008: 5; Voltmer and Wasserman 2014: 179). Yet, with the spread of globalization, values such as free speech and an independent media have become almost universal goals. As democratic aspirations proliferate, the forms and functions of media freedom around the world are diverging from practices in the West (Diamond and Plattner 2001; Hallin and Mancini 2012). Even among Western democracies, there is significant variation in interpretations of media freedom and in its contextual constraints (Hallin and Mancini 2004). Innovations in technology and changing political circumstances mean that interpretations of media freedom are always dynamic and open-ended in the West and beyond (Searle 1995). As such, typologies aiming to categorize media systems can quickly become anachronistic. Textbook descriptions of media operations are often undermined by newsroom realities. In Western democracies, for example, scholars identify market competition as the main mechanism guaranteeing media independence and a diversity of opinion in public discourse. A commercialized media supposedly provides a 'marketplace of ideas,' allowing citizens to make the best possible decisions about their lives, communities and government. But in reality, the characteristics of today's mass media often inhibit the free flow of ideas and information. More often than not, Western news organizations belong to large corporations who influence what they cover (Lichtenberg 1990: 103). As news organizations are profit-driven to seek the largest possible audience, opinions and analysis outside the mainstream rarely receive attention (Chomsky and Herman 1988). Although the Western media are conceived as having a watchdog function, they frequently act more like guard dogs for established political and economic elites, granting greater access to public officials than to less powerful groups (Donohue, Tichenor, and Olien 1995). The media are a formidable influence in modern Western societies and ally with other powerful institutions to pursue their mutual interests (Castells 2010).

Clearly, an idealized Western model is not the best lens for analyzing media freedom in other parts of the world. Although many international democracy advocacy programmes promote a framework based on experiences in the West, in non-Western settings, different media forms and practices can be functional and legitimate within their own context (Kumar 2006; Voltmer and Wasserman 2014: 179). Media freedom means different things in different cultural environments, and is contingent on the historical path along which it develops (Bratton 2010; Braizat 2010; Carnaghan 2011). It is shaped not only by legal structures, but also by the preferences, perceptions and performance of those working in the media sector (Benson 2004). Public expectations and the needs of political leaders seeking to influence reporting also affect the practice of media freedom in any society.

To argue that understanding and functioning of media freedom is influenced by culture and history is not to support the essentialism employed by some authoritarian governments to maintain that free speech and democracy are incompatible with local conditions. China's government, for example, cites the nation's 'Asian values' to justify censorship and one-party rule (Shi and Lu 2010; Voltmer and Wasserman 2014: 180; see Moser, Chapter 5). The idea that media freedom and individual expression are alien concepts outside the West has been strongly contested (Sen 2001). All cultures include a concept of freedom, even if it is based on traditions that lead to different interpretations than those found in the West (Taylor 2002). In Myanmar, for example, the notion of freedom has a spiritual as well as political component, emphasizing control over one's personal desires alongside civil liberties (Wells 2018; Walton 2016).

Evidence can be found to show that political history, as well as culture, also influences how media freedom functions. In post-authoritarian contexts, for example, newly elected democratic governments often avoid constructing legal frameworks to regulate the media, fearing that they will be accused of reintroducing state control. Media systems that suddenly go from being tightly controlled to almost completely free often suffer from an excess of sensationalism and the waning of journalistic ethics. Following the fall of the Marcos regime, for example, journalists in the Philippines were often 'rowdy,' pursuing their watchdog role to the detriment of truth and accuracy (Jiafei 2008: 18). A similar no-holds-barred media culture developed in post-authoritarian Indonesia, Taiwan and Russia (see Coronel, Chapter 14; Nuribaiti 2005; Rawnsley 2004: 211; Zassoursky 2004).

Perceptions and practices of media freedom are socially constructed phenomena, influenced by the wider social, political and economic systems in which they are embedded. Since different Asian states are the products of different cultures and histories, their media systems and normative assumptions inevitably differ – not only from those found in Western democracies, but also from each other. Although typologies have been a fundamental tool of comparative analysis in Western Europe and North America, Asia is too vast, dynamic and diverse to make categorizing Asian media systems by 'type' a practical endeavour (Esser and Umbricht 2013; Albaek et al. 2014). Although there are common features among Asian national media systems – especially within subregions – chapters in this volume show that systems that are similar in some ways frequently deviate from one another in other important aspects. On the other hand, research presented in this volume also shows that globalization, in the form of new communication technologies, is posing common challenges to media freedom across the continent.

Rather than presenting a grand theory or typological model of media freedom in Asia, this chapter assesses how existing theories relate to freedom's functioning in contemporary Asian states. It also analyzes common factors constraining that freedom across multiple countries. Constraints are discussed under four subheadings: state actors and institutions, economics and ownership, journalistic norms and ethics, and new technologies and social media. The chapter aims to identify common challenges facing clusters of countries that could inform future comparative research.

What is media freedom?

Give me liberty to know, to utter, and to argue freely according to conscience, above all liberties.
John Milton

A long line of liberal theorists, stretching back to John Milton through John Stuart Mill, have argued for an unfettered and independent media within each state as a guarantee of democracy and of free expression, thought and conscience (Milton 2014; Mill 1989). Freedom of expression and information are recognized as basic human rights in the 1948 UN Universal Declaration. In the modern era, media freedom is generally conceived as the media's right to present and circulate a diversity of ideas and information without censorship by the state, corporate owners or other actors.

John Street (2001: 253) defines a free media as 'a medium which allows for a diversity of ideas and opinion; it is not an agent of a single view or of state propaganda.' Doris Graber (1986: 258) similarly suggests that a free media reflects 'the diversity of opinions throughout the country,' serving as 'the public's agent in communicating with government officials.' Graber argues that while the media should serve the public interest, she warns that 'media freedom includes freedom from control by the public, along with freedom from governmental controls.' Undoubtedly in Asia, civil society organizations frequently restrict media freedom, but mostly when co-opted by the state. In Indonesia and Pakistan, for example, strict blasphemy laws demanded by religious conservatives limit freedom of expression (Harsono 2018; Human Rights Watch 2017; see Evans, Chapter 10).

Dennis McQuail (2003: 170–171) describes media freedom as the right of individuals or organizations to own, produce, publish and distribute information without legal penalties or censorship. From this perspective, media freedom is 'a property right, exercised by publishers on behalf of society, their free market-regulated actions considered consistent with public opinion and the public interest' (Dawes 2014: 21). The freedom to publish within a free market, however, does not guarantee a free media representing the will of the people (Curran 1979: 59). Liberal theory assumes that private ownership will defend against government interference, but commercialization and concentration equally threaten the critical functions performed by a free media (Habermas 1992: 185). Unregulated market competition creates incentives to cut costs and boost profits, in many cases leading to a decline in media standards and the blurring of the boundaries between information, entertainment and advertising (Keane 1991; Curran and Seaton 2003; Barnett 1998). Furthermore, the distorting effects of market capitalism can produce a partisan rather than neutral press, as in the case of South Korea, Malaysia and Indonesia, which have strongly partisan market-based media systems (Ki-Sung 2016: 219; Evans, Chapter 10; Seo, Chapter 8; Venkiteswaran, Chapter 11).

A lack of regulation of the commercial press also allows media owners to pursue their private interests, using their power over public opinion to influence government policies that in turn further deregulate the media or other sectors in which they have an economic stake (Dawes 2014: 22). The view of the commercial media as an independent watchdog ignores the size of the multinational corporations that often own them. The Network 18 Group, India's largest news conglomerate, for example, is owned by Reliance Industries, whose business interests range from petroleum to telecoms, many of which are dependent on government policy (Bahree 2014). Furthermore, the media's influence over public opinion and election results means that not only can the government be a threat to media freedom, but the commercial media can also threaten government independence. It is the power of the media to sway public attitudes that leads many states in Asia to impose strict controls on the information environment.

The watchdog theory overlooks the shared interests between the press and political parties. In a clear case of mutual backscratching, for example, in 2018, Zee News owner and media baron Subhash Chandra won election to India's upper house with the backing of the ruling Bharatiya Janata Party (BJP) (*Hindustan Times* 2016). He was joined in the legislature in 2018 by Republic TV investor Rajeev Chandrasekhar, who stood on the BJP ticket (*The Telegraph* 2018). Even more incestuously, in Sri Lanka, the popular television channel TV Derana is run by Varuni Amunugama Fernando, whose father Sarath Amunugama is a government minister. Moreover, Sri Lankan Prime Minister Ranil Wickremesinghe's family owns the *Wijeya* newspaper group that accounts for almost 50 per cent of the country's print readership share (Reporters without Borders 2018; see Hoole and Hoole, Chapter 22).

A free media should enable people to communicate without interference. It should also ensure that a multiplicity of ideas and views are being communicated by a wide section of society. But as outlined previously, the market mechanisms by which modern democracies have sought to uphold non-interference principles often have negative consequences for diversity of expression (Lichtenberg 1990: 107).

What are the benefits of media freedom?

Defenders of a free press often begin from the principle that it is essential to individual autonomy and self-expression. An ability to think for oneself, and not to be subjugated to another's will, has been seen as of paramount importance to individual autonomy since at least Socrates (Lichtenberg 1990: 108). So understood, autonomy requires freedom of speech, because a person cannot think if they cannot speak, nor if they cannot hear the thoughts of others. It is by expressing one's own thoughts and hearing other's thoughts that we develop our ideas and understanding (Scanlon 1972). The media are seen as synonymous with an individual voice, or as the sum of individual voices composing the public sphere. Hence, defending media freedom is tantamount to defending free speech in general (Reiss 1991). The idea of the press as expressing the will of the people, however, ignores that fact that the modern mass media often inhibit rather than enhance the flow of opinions and information. Today's mass media are part of vast corporations that fundamentally differ from the early press around which the concept of freedom of the media as free expression originally grew (Lichtenberg 1990: 106).

Another group of arguments supporting a free media rest on its indispensability to democracy. The case for democracy, in turn, is predicated on the idea that individuals are equal in their *potential* to make a valuable contribution to society. As democracy is based on popular sovereignty, with the people as the ultimate decision-makers, unbiased – or at least a plurality of – information is needed for voters to make informed choices. A free press is therefore necessary to provide citizens with information and to keep political leaders abreast of public interests and opinions (Richter 2016: 130). By communicating citizens' concerns to public officials, a free media enables government institutions to respond more effectively to societal needs (Norris 2006). This function is especially important at times of emergency, when other channels of communication between citizens and government breakdown. Regional authorities in Indian states with high levels of newspaper circulation, for example, are more effective in responding to food shortages than other states, with officials gaining timely information on grassroots conditions from the local press (Besley and Burgess 2001). By improving government accountability and responsiveness, a free media also improves health and longevity. A study of 170 countries by the Lancet found that life expectancy grew the fastest in countries that had switched to democracy since 1970 (Epstein 2019).

From a democracy standpoint, the media also act as a watchdog of government, ensuring that it does not overstep its electoral mandate or legal powers. Media freedom and free speech are also conceived as essential to the attainment of 'truth,' or more practically, to achieving the best policy outcomes (Mill 1989). Only when everyone is free to contribute to the 'marketplace of ideas' and to defend and repudiate arguments made in public debates, will vested interests be exposed and the best ideas become clear. An obvious qualification to this defence of media freedom is the unequal access to the press for marginalized groups and opinions. Not all voices are heard equally in public debates framed and presented by the mass media.

Democratic aspirations have spread across the globe, not only because of a belief in the morality of equality and of free expression, but also because things turn out better in democracies. Democracy and a free press strengthen good governance, political rights and human development, while deterring corruption and political instability (Lipset 1959; Pye 1963; Norris 2006; Siegle, Weinstein and Halper 2004). Amartya Sen argues that a free media enhances the voice of the poor, generating more informed government decisions addressing economic needs (Sen 2001). A free media also shines a spotlight on corruption, helping society to minimize the economic costs of maladministration by public officials or scandals in the corporate sector. In Taiwan, for example, as the media liberalized in the 1990s, it exposed cases of corruption by the Kuomintang (KMT) government, contributing to the establishment of new norms of clean governance (Fell 2005: 875). But although there is a correlation between a free press and economic development, there are important exceptions. Singapore and Malaysia, for example, are relatively affluent societies, despite placing strong restrictions on media freedom (see Venkiteswaran, Chapter 11).

Public access to the media in itself is insufficient to promote good governance and human development. The media can be as easily used to maintain autocracies and reinforce crony capitalism as to provide a channel for democratization and equitable economic development. In Singapore, the People's Action Party (PAP) has maintained unbroken rule since 1959 in part by controlling the press. The country's leading newspaper, the *Straits Times*, is often perceived as a propaganda tool for the state, as it rarely criticizes government policy or covers much about the opposition. The main press holdings corporation has close links to the ruling party and censorship is common, with editors facing the threat of heavy fines or distribution bans (Freedom House 2018).

Singapore's PAP government has perhaps learned from observing other states that granting the media greater freedom can quickly lead to the unravelling of authoritarian power. The media play an integral role in the process of democratization. The specific functions they perform depend on the impetus for democratization – whether the process is initiated by reformers within the ruling regime from above, or by opposition activists from below (Voltmer 2013). When democratization is begun from above, independent journalists can increase the pace of change and chances of successful consolidation by aligning with regime reformists against hardliners. When the process is bottom-up, the underground or exiled media can be tools for building alliances across diverse opposition groups, divided by race and class. By building narratives that contradict information available from state media sources, they can contribute to destabilizing the regime and rallying popular resistance, as in the case of Myanmar's dissident media prior to 2012 (Burrett 2017).

Equally, the media can function to undermine democratization. Developing professional practices and ethics can prove difficult for journalists in democratizing states, where for decades state censors have externally imposed standards on the media. In many transitional societies, media organizations are young and inexperienced. A lack of training and experience can lead unseasoned journalists to abdicate their professional responsibilities in the pursuit of financial gain or celebrity. In ethnically fractured states like Sri Lanka and Myanmar, journalists have used their hard-won freedoms to engage in hate speech that has exacerbated sectarian violence, creating a pretext for the reestablishment of authoritarian rule (see Hoole and Hoole, Chapter 22; Burrett, Chapter 12; Kingston, Chapter 13). The privatization of the media that often accompanies democratization can foster tabloidization, undermining the media's ability to perform its civic functions that are especially important in emergent democracies, a phenomenon witnessed in the Philippines and Indonesia (see Evans, Chapter 10; Coronel, Chapter 14).

Only when the media promotes accountability, facilitates informed electoral choices and strengthens government responsiveness to social problems can it contribute to positive social change (Norris 2000; Kaul 2012). The ability of the media to fulfil these essential functions varies substantially between Asian states (Freedom House 2017).

What are the major impediments to media freedom in Asia?

Nowhere are the media total free of constraints. The media always work within economic, legal and political limits. Audiences' expectations, journalists' professional practices and the characteristics of technology are also continual constrains. The sections that follow analyze some of the common factors constraining media freedom across multiple Asian states. Analysis is presented under four headings: the state and politics, economics and ownership, journalistic norms and practices, and technology and social media.

The state and politics

In traditional theories of press freedom, the state is perceived as the main impediment to media independence. To be sure, in many Asian countries today, the state remains a major constraint on media freedom. In general, across the region, even in established democracies such as Japan, the state has greater influence over the media than in most Western countries (Kingston 2017). But the presence of the state in the media sector is not always detrimental. In developing countries such as Pakistan and India, state-funded public broadcasters are instrumental in bringing news and information in local dialects to impoverished, remote communities. More often, however, the influence of the state over the media is negative.

Today's Asia is home to the world's last remaining communist countries. In China, Vietnam, Laos and North Korea, the state retains ownership of the news mass media. In all four, the state-owned media adhere to the Soviet press model, acting as propagandists for the regime (Siebert, Peterson and Schramm 1956). But in China and Vietnam, media commercialization has been part of the state's development of a market economy. Private media have proliferated in both states, creating competition for audiences and advertising revenues. In the early 2000s, compelled by competition and encouraged by their government's liberalizing reforms, journalists in both countries began to experiment with investigative reporting. Unlike under the traditional rigid Soviet press model, the Chinese and Vietnamese commercial media exposed corruption by state officials, supported by some figures in the government as a means of rooting out mismanagement and of venting societal anger against malfeasance (Cain 2014). This limited watchdog role was tolerated only up to a point. Exposés of high-ranking officials required government approval and journalists who failed to play by the states' rules found themselves in detention or worse (Jiafei 2008; see Moser, Chapter 5; Nguyen-Thu, Chapter 16). More recently, in part as a response to the growing reach and anonymity afforded to the government's critics by the internet, leaders in China, and to a lesser extent Vietnam, have curtailed the media's limited freedom to dissent (see Anonymous, Chapter 3). Under the leadership of President Xi Jinping since 2012, the Chinese state has taken strong measures to control its image at home and abroad (see Moser, Chapter 5; Lim, Chapter 4). In 2018, Vietnam passed a new Cyber Security Act that will force tech giants like Google and Facebook to remove content and accounts criticizing the government (Thoi 2019). The use of legislation to harass and restrict journalists is also common practice in Sri Lanka, Thailand and Malaysia, among other states in the region (see Hoole and Hoole, Chapter 22; Chachavalpongpun, Chapter 15; Venkiteswaran, Chapter 11).

Asia is also home to some of the world's newest and most volatile democracies. After ousting its repressive dictator, the Philippines embarked on the difficult road to democracy in 1986, with Indonesia setting out on a similar path in 1998. In both states, the media played an integral role in challenging authoritarian rule, becoming strong defenders of their own freedoms in the process (see Coronel, Chapter 14; Evans, Chapter 10). But after successfully struggling against dictatorship, journalists have found political activism difficult to leave behind, with newspapers in both states hitching their wagons to popular politicians, only to switch horses when the path gets bumpy. Partisanship is also strong, and more consistent, in the Malaysian and Thai press (see Chachavalpongpun, Chapter 15; Venkiteswaran, Chapter 11). Cross-country analysis finds that where the press are politically polarized, public trust in the mainstream media and other political institutions is low, providing an opening for populist politicians claiming to challenge the establishment (Reuters Institute 2018).

Autocratic-leaning populists have already won power, or are attempting to gain office, in several Asian states. Where populists have won in India, Thailand and the Philippines, press freedom has been eroded and violence against journalists has increased (see Deb, Chapter 18; Chachavalpongpun, Chapter 15; Coronel, Chapter 14). Asia's populists differ in many ways from counterparts in the West, focusing less on immigration, economic decline and trade. In Asian states that have elected populists, trade-based economic growth remains relatively strong and immigration is not a prominent issue. Instead, Asia's populists focus on stoking religious and ethnic divides, and resentments against the clientelism and neopatrimonialism of established political parties, that themselves are far from paragons of democracy (Kurlantzick 2018). Populists appeal to the working and aspirational middle classes, who are frustrated with the political establishment, including the media, for failing to adequately address inequality, crime, social mobility and poor public services. The relatively free media environment in India and the Philippines, in particular, has exposed inter-religious and political fault lines. These tensions are inflamed by social media, with populists proving skillful at using digital media to communicate directly with disaffected voters. In the Philippines, for example, President Rodrigo Duterte has an army of die-hard Facebook followers who engage in 'patriotic trolling' against his critics, including the prominent journalist Maria Ressa (Etter 2017).

Elsewhere in Asia, political leaders have used nationalism and national security as mechanisms to curtail journalists' freedom and independence. In Japan, Prime Minister Shinzo Abe and his nationalist supporters have pressured media owners and executives to purge reporters who question their interpretation of Japan's actions in World War II or government plans to water down constitutional commitments to pacifism (Kingston 2017). In South Korea, conservative administrations have used national security laws prohibiting the expression of sympathy for North Korea to censor their critics in the media (see Seo, Chapter 8). Draconian security statutes carrying heavy custodial sentences also limit what journalists can report on a range of topics beyond genuine security concerns in Myanmar, China, Sri Lanka, Thailand and Pakistan (Freedom House 2017). Strict defamation laws are another favourite tool of Asian governments for undermining free expression and encouraging journalistic self-censorship. In many cases, however, the state does not need to invoke the law to cow the media. Instead, governments exploit their cozy relations with the media's corporate and oligarchic owners to secure favourable coverage.

Economics and ownership

Many of the economic challenges confronting the media in Asia are global – rather than regional – trends. These include high degrees of concentration and cross ownership, and the subordination of public service and professionalism to the pursuit of profits. The consequences of these trends for news reporting are limited diversity, highly selective information and systematically biased opinion (Baker 2000). The media's concentration opens them up to greater penetration by actors with economic or political power. Close ties between political and media-owning elites tends to be even more acute in newly democratizing states, where privatization often results in the replacement of state ownership by crony capitalism (Norris 2006). Ownership of the media in Myanmar and Indonesia, for example, remain in the hands of friends and family of their former authoritarian regimes (Burrett 2017; Sen and Hill 2010).

The media's ownership by corporations with wider economic interests still further reduces their independence. As cogs in the capitalist wheel, it becomes difficult for journalists to critique the market and monopolistic systems that generate profits for their parent company's shareholders (Chomsky and Herman 1988). The mainstream media in India, for example, have been criticized for focusing on elite institutions and prominent figures rather than the needs of the poor, the deprived and the marginalized (Namra 2004).

The rise of online media is deepening the financial woes of newspapers and broadcasters everywhere (see Anonymous, Chapter 3). Across Asia, the use of online news sources is growing. In Malaysia, online sources have outstripped the traditional media, with 89 per cent getting their news from the web, compared to 57 per cent from TV and 41 per cent from the print media (Reuters Institute 2018). This rejection may reflect the mainstream media's close association with the authoritarian Barisan Nasional coalition government that dominated Malaysia from independence in 1957 until the opposition's surprise victory in May 2018 (see Venkiteswaran, Chapter 11). Online news is also the preference of South Koreans, 84 per cent of whom consult digital news sources compared to 74 per cent who get their news from TV (Reuters Institute 2018). In Japan, newspapers still sell over 39 million copies a day, the largest number in the world. But for the past decade, circulation rates have dropped by 1 million a year (*Nihon Shimbun Kyokai* 2018). In Japan and elsewhere, as the newspaper market has declined, partisan biases have increased as publishers seek to retain readers by catering to niche audiences at either end of the ideological spectrum (Sato 2016).

Falling sales are also increasing newspapers' dependence on the state. In Thailand, some broadcasters and newspapers have become beholden to the military government to stay afloat (Macan-Markar 2018). Despite an overall increase in the Thai advertising market in 2019, advertising revenues dropped by 19 per cent for newspapers and by 17 per cent for television, with advertisers switching to online platforms (Morris and Son 2019). When the opposition Pakatan Harapan coalition took power in Malaysia in May 2018, the new government quickly reduced state subsidies for newspapers that had supported the previous regime. In September 2018, without government assistance, the right-leaning *Utusan Malaysia* was forced to declare bankruptcy (*Nikkei Asian Review* 2018).

Competition from the steady stream of sensationalism and conspiracy theories available on the internet is driving down standards all around, drawing resources and attention away from unprofitable content that typically includes a strong component of political background information and international news. Political journalism does not usually attract large audiences, but is essential to the health of democracy. Politics is increasingly treated less seriously than in the past, with the media focusing on human interest stories, scandals and the sensational (Entman 1989; Postman 1986). The political news coverage that does exist tends to frame politics in terms of games or personal conflicts, neglecting the substance of debates. In general, the media globally are becoming more devoted to promoting individual consumerism and increasingly neglecting societal concerns.

Journalistic norms and practices

In societies where reporting on politics can be dangerous, journalists often focus on entertainment and human interest news as a way of avoiding trouble with powerful political and economic forces. Media self-censorship is a widespread problem in Asia, where the legacy of authoritarianism weighs heavy in many states. The causes and mechanisms though which self-censorship operates, however, varies substantially between countries.

In Japan, self-censorship is informally institutionalized in the press club system that embeds journalists at the ministries and government agencies they are assigned to cover. This system enables journalists to develop close ties to official sources, but inhibits critical reporting that could endanger their privileged access. Hence, press club journalists have a tendency to pull their punches and repeat official narratives (Nakano 2017). South Korea formerly had a similar system, but it was dissolved in 2003 (Ki-Sung 2012).

In most Asian countries where it is a problem, self-censorship is motivated by self-preservation. Journalists who offend the authorities can lose their livelihoods, liberties or even their lives. Globally, China has the largest number of journalists behind bars, 47 as of December 2018 (Beiser 2018). In 2018, India was the most deadly place to be a journalist outside of war zones (McCarthy 2018). Five Indian journalists were killed, including Sandeep Sharma, who was murdered after reporting on police corruption and illegal sand mining (Committee to Protect Journalists 2018). The threat of violence stifles reporting of critical issues, creating a dangerous information void.

In many cases, governing authorities do not need to resort to violence, as media owners and their employees internalize unwritten government rules about what it is permissible to print. In Thailand, for example, reporters censor themselves, mindful of the invisible rules about coverage of the monarchy, security matters and other sensitive topics (see Chachavalpongpun, Chapter 15). In Myanmar, journalists are careful not to threaten the interests of their proprietors or those of their factional allies in the military (see Burrett, Chapter 12). Fear of offending public opinion or civil society groups can also lead journalists to self-censor. In Indonesia, journalists are wary of reporting on issues relating to Islam, since the Christian governor of Jakarta was driven from office and later jailed for blasphemy after a doctored video mischaracterizing his comments about the Quran went viral, instigating massive protests in 2016. Indonesian journalists and others who question the tenets of Islam or the teachings of conservative Muslim scholars are targeted by religious activists and forced to apologize, and are sometimes subject to violence (Lamb 2019).

Media freedom is a double-edged sword that can expose injustice and wrong-doing, but can equally pollute the public sphere with false or misleading information when freedom is abused. The media hold a mirror up to society, and when that society is characterized by corruption, this is reflected in reporting. Corruption is pervasive in many Asian states, giving rise to a culture of 'envelop journalism,' whereby reporters receive cash from news sources in exchange for positive coverage or the suppression of bad news (*Transparency International* 2018; see Evans, Chapter 10; Burrett, Chapter 12; Coronel, Chapter 14). The phenomenon of 'journalists for sale' is not restricted to countries where media salaries are low. It is also a common problem in South Korea, where government officials and corporate executives frequently wine and dine or bestow gifts on journalists in exchange for favourable articles, prompting the government to introduce a new anti-graft law in 2016 (Ramirez 2016; see Seo, Chapter 8).

Commercial pressures, along with journalists' desire to make money, win ratings or to break an exclusive, are fuelling the growth of fake news and misinformation in many Asian states. In some cases, reporters spread false information through sloppy standards rather than with malicious intent. In Myanmar and the Philippines, a lack of professional training and maturity frequently leads journalists to present stories without checking the credibility of their sources (see Burrett, Chapter 12; Coronel, Chapter 14). In Taiwan's more professional but highly competitive media industry, journalists to get ahead often take sensationalist content from social media with little regard for authenticity or reliability (Reuters Institute 2018). The proliferation of fake news is just one way in which digital technologies are creating new challenges to media freedom.

Technology and social media

The advent of the internet as a mass communication tool in the mid-1990s was initially met with great optimism for the revival of democratic governance. Scholars argued that the internet would benefit democratic processes by removing some of the barriers to publication, increasing the volume and diversity of political information – and in so doing, reduce the mainstream media's role as gatekeeper (Blumler and Gurevitch 2001). In the new millennium, a fresh wave of optimism accompanied the arrival of social media platforms like Twitter, Facebook, YouTube, wikis and blogs. This second generation of digital technologies was seen as further enabling democratic renewal by facilitating greater voter participation and collective action through the creation of virtual public spheres (Loader and Mercea 2011). Equipped with social media, citizens would no longer be passive consumers of political party propaganda, government spin or mass media news, but instead could challenge these discourses by sharing alternative perspectives and authoring their own content. These utopian visions, however, quickly waned when instead of transforming democracy, 'new' technologies were found to be just as likely to entrench existing social and economic interests.

In some Asian countries, new communication technologies have successfully enabled social groups to challenge dominant political powers, but more often, they have allowed governments to extend their control over society. The case of South Korea shows both phenomena at work. In the late 1990s, weak political parties and a polarized mainstream media that had lost public trust allowed Korean civil society organizations to form a nationwide online network that was instrumental in electing underdog candidate and progressive Roh Mu-Hyun president in 2002. After witnessing the power of the internet in 2002, mainstream parties and newspapers deployed their considerable resources to maximize their online presence before the 2007 presidential election, which resulted in victory for conservative Lee Myung-Bak (Ki-Sung 2011). Social media also played a key role in putting across the messages of Malaysia's opposition that unexpectedly won the May 2018 general election, ending decades of authoritarian rule. Smartphones were the most popular way to view digital news, with Malaysians trusting independent online portals like Malaysiakini and international media like Yahoo! News over mainstream newspapers and broadcasters aligned with the government (Reuters Institute 2018; see Venkiteswaran, Chapter 11).

In contrast to traditional media, online platforms potentially allow citizens to challenge the monopoly control of information production and dissemination by state and commercial institutions. But rather than the internet encouraging diversity of content, in most Asian states, sites operated by giant corporations attract the majority of users. Yahoo! News is the most popular online information source in Japan and Taiwan, while South Koreans prefer Naver, the domestic equivalent of Google (Reuters Institute 2018). The internet's potential to encourage competition between varied political discourses is also undermined by mechanisms such as search engine ranking algorithms. Access to iPhones and Facebook does not automatically equate to more politically engaged citizens. In many countries, virtual public spheres fail to develop not because of state restrictions or commercial algorithms, but because citizens prefer to use online platforms for gossiping, shopping and socializing with existing friends rather than for political communication. Moreover, the 'networked individualism' that characterizes social media can exacerbate social fragmentation and corrode collective action (Loader and Mercea 2011: 762). This is not to argue that citizen journalism and online activism are not influential, but rather to caution that the transformative power of the internet is often limited by contemporary consumer culture.

In Hong Kong, citizen journalists have been essential in covering issues ignored by a mainstream media that faces growing pressure from Beijing. Citizen journalists reported extensively on the 2014 'umbrella movement' protests against China's plans to vet candidates for the Hong Kong assembly. The city's traditional media, owned by local tycoons with mainland business ties, were wary of offending Beijing by covering the protesters' demands (Kaiman 2014).

Citizen journalism can disrupt dominant power practices and enable a more inclusive democracy. But user-generated content can also undermine rational deliberation by fostering celebrity politics and encouraging populism or even extremism. Posts on social media have contributed to sectarian violence in Myanmar and Sri Lanka (Waters 2018). Governments seeking to repress internet freedom use online hate speech and incitement of violence to justify crackdowns on free speech. In recent years, both China and Malaysia have introduced fake news laws that criminalize speech on a wide array of topics while claiming to protect the public information space (Repnikova 2018; Reuters Institute 2018).

Online communication technologies are allowing Asian governments to develop new systems of information control. The same technologies that spawned the global information explosion are co-opted by governments to stifle free expression, monitor critics, block websites and to troll and shout down opposition voices (Simon 2019). Most insidiously of all, governments use social media to confuse through propaganda and fake news both at home and abroad. The Chinese government is particularly adept at exploiting the incursive capabilities of the internet (See Lim Chapter 4). China's People's Liberation Army (PLA) uses fake news posted on social media to manipulate Taiwanese public opinion (Ying 2018). Taiwan's competitive news industry, which is heavily influenced by social media, helps Chinese propaganda to spread. China is also innovating its online control techniques at home. The government is developing a social credit system that could see journalists who post critical content on social media receiving poor scores, resulting in a ban on travelling, buying property or taking out a loan (Yaqiu 2017). China's innovations are being watched with interest and envy by other repressive governments around the world.

Conclusion

The research presented in this volume demonstrates that perceptions and practices of media freedom vary significantly between Asian countries. The media system in each state is the product of its own history, politics and culture. Yet, many states face common challenges in establishing or maintaining a free media environment. Trust in the news media is worryingly low in many countries, and is often linked to high levels of polarization or concerns about undue political interference in the press. On the economic side, growing commercial competition exacerbates the trend towards tabloidization and in some cases, is increasing financial dependence on the state. Overall, the outlook is gloomy. The enemies of free expression are attacking the information system from multiple angles, in many places using intimidation and violence against journalists, feeding an existing culture of self-censorship. States and other agents of repression have co-opted the technologies that journalists use to deliver the news to disorientate, demoralize and sow disinformation. But the battle is not lost. The upsurge in repression against the media in many Asian states is a response to the democratizing power of independent information. Advocates of media freedom across Asia have shown they will not be silenced.

Works cited

Albaek, E., van Dalen, A., Jebril, N., and de Vreese, C. (2014) *Political Journalism in Comparative Perspective*, Cambridge: Cambridge University Press.

Bahree, M. (2014) 'Reliance takes over Network18: Is this the death of media independence?', *Forbes*. Online. Available HTTP: <www.forbes.com/sites/meghabahree/2014/05/30/reliance-takes-over-network18-is-this-the-death-of-media-independence/#1c9c240465c1> (accessed 19 March 2019).

Baker, E. (2000) *Media, Markets and Democracy*, Cambridge: Cambridge University Press.

Barnett, S. (1998) 'Dumbing down or reaching out: Is it tabloidisation wot done it', in J. Seaton (ed.) *Politics and the Media: Harlots and Prerogatives at the Turn of the Millennium*, Oxford: Blackwell.

Beiser, E. (2018) 'Hundreds of journalists jailed globally becomes the new normal', *Committee to Protect Journalists*. Online. Available HTTP: <https://cpj.org/reports/2018/12/journalists-jailed-imprisoned-turkey-china-egypt-saudi-arabia.php> (accessed 16 August 2019).

Benson, R. (2004) 'Bringing the sociology of media back in', *Political Communication*, 2: 275–292.

Besley, T. and Burgess, R. (2001) 'Political agency, government responsiveness and the role of the media', *European Economic Review*, 45: 629–640.

Blumler, J. and Gurevitch, M. (2001) 'The new media and our political communication discontents: Democratizing cyberspace', *International Journal of Communication*, 4: 1–13.

Braizat, F. (2010) 'What Arabs think', *Journal of Democracy*, 21: 131–138.

Bratton, M. (2010) 'Anchoring the "D-word" in Africa', *Journal of Democracy*, 21: 106–113.

Burrett, T. (2017) 'Mixed signals: Democratization and the Myanmar media', *Politics and Governance*, 5.

Cain, G. (2014) 'Kill one to warn one hundred: The politics of press censorship in Vietnam', *The International Journal of Press/Politics*, 19: 85–107.

Carnaghan, E. (2011) 'The difficulty of measuring support for democracy in a changing society: Evidence from Russia', *Democratization*, 18: 682–706.

Castells, M. (2010) *The Rise of the Network Society* (1 of 3 vols.), Oxford: Blackwell.

Chomsky, N. and Herman, E.S. (1988) *Manufacturing Consent: The Political Economy of the Mass Media*, New York: Pantheon Books.

Committee to Protect Journalists. (2018) 'Sandeep Sharma'. Online. Available HTTP: <https://cpj.org/data/people/sandeep-sharma/index.php> (accessed 19 March 2019).

Curran, J. (1979) 'Press freedom as a property right: The crisis of press legitimacy', *Media, Culture & Society*, 1: 59–82.

Curran, J. and Seaton, J. (2003) *Power without Responsibility: The Press, Broadcasting and New Media in Britain*, 6th ed., London: Routledge.

Dawes, S. (2014) 'Press freedom, privacy and the public sphere', *Journalism Studies*, 15: 17–32.

Diamond, L. and Plattner, M. (2001) *The Global Divergence of Democracy*, Baltimore, MD: John Hopkins University Press.

Donohue, G., Tichenor, P. and Olien, C. (1995) 'A guard dog perspective on the role of media', *Journal of Communication*, 45: 115–132.

Entman, R. (1989) *Democracy without Citizens: Media and the Decay of American Politics*, New York: Oxford University Press.

Epstein, H. (2019) 'Good news for democracy', *The Lancet*. Online. Available HTTP: <www.thelancet.com/journals/lancet/article/PIIS0140-6736(19)30431-3/fulltext> (accessed 19 March 2019).

Esser, F. and Umbricht, A. (2013) 'Competing models of journalism? Political affairs coverage in US, British, German, Swiss, French, and Italian newspapers', *Journalism*, 14: 89–107.

Etter, L. (2017) 'What happens when the government uses Facebook as a weapon?', *Bloomberg*. Online. Available HTTP: <https://www.bloomberg.com/news/features/2017-12-07/how-rodrigo-duterte-turned-facebook-into-a-weapon-with-a-little-help-from-facebook> (accessed 16 August 2019).

Fell, D. (2005) 'Political and media liberalization and political corruption in Taiwan', *The China Quarterly*, 184: 875–893.

Freedom House. (2017) 'Freedom of the press 2017'. Online. Available HTTP: <https://freedomhouse.org/report/freedom-press/freedom-press-2017> (accessed 19 March 2019).

Freedom House. (2018) 'Freedom in the world 2018: Singapore profile'. Online. Available HTTP: <https://freedomhouse.org/report/freedom-world/2018/singapore> (accessed 19 March 2019).

Graber, D. (1986) 'Press freedom and the general welfare', *Political Science Quarterly*, 101: 257–275.

Habermas, J. (1992) *The Structural Transformation of the Public Sphere*, Cambridge: Policy Press.

Hallin, D. and Mancini, P. (2004) *Comparing Media Systems: Three Models of Media and Politics*, New York: Cambridge University Press.

Hallin, D. and Mancini, P. (2012) *Comparing Media Systems Beyond the West*, Cambridge: Cambridge University Press.

Harsono, A. (2018) 'The human cost of Indonesia's Blasphemy Law', *Human Rights Watch*. Online. Available HTTP: <www.hrw.org/news/2018/10/25/human-cost-indonesias-blasphemy-law> (accessed 10 March 2019).

Hindustan Times. (2016) 'Subhash Chandra wins RS seat as 12 Cong votes were rejected due to "Wrong Pen"'. Online. Available HTTP: <www.hindustantimes.com/india-news/subhash-chandra-wins-rs-poll-as-12-cong-votes-were-rejected-due-to-wrong-pen/story-pVv4dssn0Zz2hWsWpAd8wO.html> (accessed 14 March 2019).

Human Rights Watch. (2017) 'Pakistan: Escalating crackdown on internet dissent'. Online. Available HTTP: <www.hrw.org/news/2017/05/16/pakistan-escalating-crackdown-internet-dissent> (accessed 10 March 2019).

Jiafei, Y. (2008) 'Beyond four theories of the press: A new model for the Asian & the world press', *Journalism and Communication Monographs*, 10: 3–62.

Kaiman, J. (2014) 'Hong Kong protests bring crisis of confidence for traditional media', *The Guardian*. Online. Available HTTP: <www.theguardian.com/world/2014/oct/29/hong-kong-protests-confidence-media> (accessed 19 March 2019).

Kaul, V. (2012) 'Interface between media, democracy and development', *China Media Research*, 8: 52–64.

Keane, J. (1991) *The Media and Democracy*, Cambridge: Policy Press.

Kingston, J. (2017) *Freedom of the Press in Contemporary Japan*, London: Routledge.

Ki-Sung, K. (2011) 'From "revolutionary changes" to "things as usual": The political role of online media in South Korea', *Media International Australia*, 141: 87–97.

Ki-Sung, K. (2012) *Media and Democratic Transition in South Korea*, New York: Routledge.

Ki-Sung, K. (2016) 'Digital media and democratic transition in Korea', in Y. Kim (ed.) *Routledge Handbook of Korean Culture and Society*, London: Routledge.

Kumar, K. (2006) *Promoting Independent Media: Strategies for Democracy Assistance*, Boulder, CO: Lynne Rienner.

Kurlantzick, J. (2018) 'Southeast Asia's populism is different but also dangerous', *Council on Foreign Relations*. Online. Available HTTP: <www.cfr.org/article/southeast-asias-populism-different-also-dangerous> (accessed 19 March 2019).

Lamb, K. (2019) 'Ahok, Jakarta's former governor, released after jail term for blasphemy', *The Guardian*. Online. Available HTTP: <www.theguardian.com/world/2019/jan/24/ahok-jakartas-former-governor-released-after-jail-term-for-blasphemy> (accessed 3 March 2019).

Lichtenberg, J. (1990) 'Foundations and limits of freedom of the press', in J. Lichtenberg (ed.) *Democracy and the Mass Media*, Cambridge: Cambridge University Press.

Lipset, M.S. (1959) 'Some social prerequisites of democracy: Economic development and political legitimacy', *American Political Science Review*, 53: 69–105.

Loader, B. and Mercea, D. (2011) 'Introduction networking democracy? Social media innovations and participatory politics', *Information, Communication & Society*, 14: 757–769.

Macan-Markar, M. (2018) 'Ailing Thai media grow dependent on Junta's financial support', *Nikkei Asian Review*. Online. Available HTTP: <https://asia.nikkei.com/Business/Companies/Ailing-Thai-media-grow-dependent-on-junta-s-financial-support> (accessed 10 March 2019).

McCarthy, N. (2018) 'The deadliest countries for journalists in 2018', *Forbes*. Online. Available HTTP: <www.forbes.com/sites/niallmccarthy/2018/12/19/the-deadliest-countries-for-journalists-in-2018-infographic/> (accessed 3 March 2019).

McQuail, D. (2003) *Media Accountability and Freedom of Publication*, Oxford: Oxford University Press.

Mill, J.S. (1989) *On Liberty*, Cambridge: Cambridge University Press.

Milton, J. (2014) *Areopagitica and Other Writings*, London: Penguin.

Morris, J. and Son, N. (2019) 'Thailand's advertisers power the shift to online media in 2019 as print loses out to the internet', *Thai Examiner*. Online. Available HTTP: <www.thaiexaminer.com/thai-news-foreigners/2019/02/18/advertising-thailand-media-thai-social-media-online-broadcast-tv-brands/> (accessed 1 March 2019).

Nakano, K. (2017) 'The right-wing media and the rise of illiberal politics in Japan', in J. Kingston (ed.) *Press Freedom in Contemporary Japan*, New York: Routledge.

Namra, A. (2004) 'Development journalism vs. "envelopment" journalism', *Counter Currents*. Online. Available HTTP: <www.countercurrents.org/hr-namra190404.htm> (accessed 10 March 2019).

Nihon Shimbun Kyokai. (2018) 'Facts and figures about Japanese newspapers'. Online. Available HTTP: <www.pressnet.or.jp/english/data/circulation/circulation01.php> (accessed 10 March 2019).

Nikkei Asian Review. (2018) 'Mahathir moves to free Malaysian media from political parties'. Online. Available HTTP: <https://asia.nikkei.com/Politics/Malaysia-in-transition/Mahathir-moves-to-free-Malaysian-media-from-political-parties> (accessed 5 March 2019).

Norris, P. (2000) *A Virtuous Circle: Political Communications in Post-Industrial Societies*, Cambridge: Cambridge University Press.

Norris, P. (2006) 'The role of the free press in promoting democratization, good governance, and human development', Cambridge, MA: John F. Kennedy School of Government, Harvard University. Online. Available HTTP: <https://pdfs.semanticscholar.org/3f2d/b28b21bba6d0958944b836d4e6578f832886.pdf> (accessed 16 August 2019).

Nuribaiti, A. (2005) 'A balance between profit, readers' needs and idealism', *Jakata Post*. 30 December.

Postman, N. (1986) *Amusing Ourselves to Death: Public Discourse in the Age of Show Business*, London: Heinemann.

Pye, L. (1963) *Communications and Political Development*, Princeton, NJ: Princeton University Press.

Ramirez, E. (2016) 'No more free lunch for South Korean journalists', *The Diplomat*. Online. Available HTTP: <https://thediplomat.com/2016/09/no-more-free-lunch-for-south-korean-journalists/> (accessed 10 March 2019).

Rawnsley, G. (2004) 'Treading a fine line: Democratisation and the media in Taiwan', *Parliamentary Affairs*, 57: 209–222.

Reiss H. B. (1991) *Kant: Political Writings*, Second Edition, Cambrige: Cambridge University Press.

Repnikova, M. (2018) 'China's lessons for fighting fake news', *Foreign Policy*. Online. Available HTTP: <https://foreignpolicy.com/2018/09/06/chinas-lessons-for-fighting-fake-news/> (accessed 5 March 2019).

Reporters without Borders. (2018) 'Media ownership monitor Sri Lanka'. Online. Available HTTP: <http://sri-lanka.mom-rsf.org/en/findings/findings/#c15870> (accessed 20 March 2019).

Reuters Institute. (2018) 'Digital news report', Oxford University. Online. Available HTTP: <http://media.digitalnewsreport.org/wp-content/uploads/2018/06/digital-news-report-2018.pdf?x89475> (accessed 2 March 2019).

Richter, A. (2016) 'Defining media freedom in international policy debates', *Global Media and Communication*, 12: 127–142.

Sato, T. (2016) 'The polarization of the Japanese media and the need for middle ground', *Nippon.com*. Online. Available HTTP: <http://nippon.com/en/in-depth/a05002> (accessed 9 March 2019).

Scanlon, T. (1972) 'A theory of freedom of expression', *Philosophy and Public Affairs*, 1: 204–226.

Searle, J. (1995) *The Construction of Social Reality*, New York: The Free Press.

Sen, A. (2001) *Development as Freedom*, Oxford: Oxford University Press.

Sen, K. and Hill, D. (2010) *Politics and the Media in Twenty-First Century Indonesia*, London: Routledge.

Shi, T. and Lu, J. (2010) 'The shadow of confucianism', *Journal of Democracy*, 21: 123–130.

Siebert, F., Peterson, T., and Schramm, W. (1956) *Four Theories of the Press*, Champaign: University of Illinois Press.

Siegle, J., Weinstein, M., and Halper, M. (2004) 'Why democracies excel', *Foreign Affairs* 83(5): 57–71.

Simon, J. (2019) *The New Censorship: Inside the Global Battle for Media Freedom*, New York: Columbia University Press.

Street, J. (2001) *Mass Media, Politics and Democracy*, London: Macmillan.

Taylor, R.H. (2002) *The Idea of Freedom in Asia and Africa*, Stanford: Stanford University Press.

The Telegraph. (2018) 'BJP picks republic TV investor', *The Telegraph*. Online. Available HTTP: <www.telegraphindia.com/india/bjp-picks-republic-tv-investor/cid/1338355> (accessed 5 March 2019).

Thoi, N. (2019) 'Vietnam's controversial cybersecurity law spells tough times for activists', *The Diplomat*. Online. Available HTTP: <https://thediplomat.com/2019/01/vietnams-controversial-cybersecurity-law-spells-tough-times-for-activists/> (accessed 19 March 2019).

Transparency International. (2018) 'Corruption perceptions index 2018'. Online. Available HTTP: <www.transparency.org/cpi2018?gclid=CjwKCAjwmq3kBRB_EiwAJkNDp5v2p9xbCg4pdK1tk6VRY6uaJ_L7tDnin2pw_txoPyyxjCXiHd_31hoCeIkQAvD_BwE> (accessed 10 March 2019).

Voltmer, K. (2013) *The Media in Transitional Democracies*, Cambridge: Policy Press.

Voltmer, K. and Wasserman, H. (2014) 'Journalistic norms between universality and domestication: Journalists' interpretations of press freedom in six new democracies', *Global Media and Communication*, 10: 177–192.

Walton, M. (2016) *Buddhism, Politics and Political Thought in Myanmar*, Cambridge: Cambridge University Press.

Waters, R. (2018) 'Facebook starts to block content that incites violence', *The Financial Times*. Online. Available HTTP: <www.ft.com/content/8ec3cadc-8afa-11e8-bf9e-8771d5404543> (accessed 19 March 2019).

Wells, T. (2018) 'Democratic "freedom" in Myanmar', *Asian Journal of Political Science*, 26: 1–15.

Yaqiu, W. (2017) 'Discredited', *Committee to Protect Journalists*. Online. Available HTTP: <https://cpj.org/2017/04/discredited.php> (accessed 5 March 2019).

Ying, Y.L. (2018) 'China's hybrid warfare and Taiwan', *The Diplomat*. Online. Available HTTP: <https://thediplomat.com/2018/01/chinas-hybrid-warfare-and-taiwan/> (accessed 10 March 2019).

Zassoursky, I. (2004) *Media and Power in Post-Soviet Russia*, London: M.E Sharpe.

PART 1
East Asia

3

SOCIAL MEDIA WITH CHINESE CHARACTERISTICS

Implications for press freedom

Anonymous

Social media, which created a platform for citizen journalism in China during the late 2000s, is now a tightly controlled space for sharing news and expressing opinions. Weibo, WeChat and almost all new forms of social media that initially subverted the state's press controls have been co-opted into the system. These developments in social media emerged against the backdrop of severe problems in the mainstream Chinese media. In 2018 alone, at least 42 local newspapers ceased publication due to the recession in the media industry and the rise of social media. Since 2017, advertising revenue in China's television sector have experienced an ongoing decline (Cui 2018). In comparison, the mobile internet market reached 254.96 billion yuan, nearly 70 per cent of total revenue for internet advertising, far eclipsing that for traditional media (iResearch 2018). Due to growing financial constraints, many capable media professionals are leaving the traditional news media industry and joining internet companies or public relations firms. Though their individual lives may be improved by bigger paychecks, China's media environment pays the cost.

The unprecedented freedom brought by Weibo and its downfall

China has developed its own alternatives to social media platforms popular in the West: WeChat is the Chinese equivalent of Facebook, Weibo is the Chinese Twitter and Youku is China's YouTube. Social media, by connecting people instantly, expands the boundary of free speech, although the government is quite vigilant and adept at cracking down on these newfound freedoms. The great danger of social media from the state's perspective is that it provides unprecedented opportunities for Chinese people to enjoy potentially unlimited access to information that may facilitate the rise of anti-state social movements. The relationship between social media platforms and the state cannot be reduced, however, to a simple dichotomy of freedom versus control; rather, this relationship is changing China in complex ways. Social media challenges the authorities, and shapes norms and beliefs, but also remains constrained by the authorities who seek to co-opt these platforms to promote officially sanctioned narratives.

Weibo and WeChat are important channels through which Chinese citizens weigh in on public issues, a recent phenomenon that was previously unseen in China's almost non-existent public sphere. Based on my observations, when Weibo was first created in 2009, it was an important public opinion battleground for government institutions, civil society organizations, corporations and individuals selling their own narratives. One typical example is the Wenzhou train crash in 2011. Four minutes after the incident, a Weibo post asking for help went viral. After two hours, a message appealing for blood donations was posted on Weibo. A week after the incident, when reports appeared claiming that the wreckage of the train was buried, posts demanding government accountability went viral on Weibo, with many ridiculing the Railway Ministry spokesperson's explanation that the wreckage was moved to facilitate rescue efforts (Chen 2011).

With the rise of Weibo came the emergence of Big Vs, signifying 'verified account holder' – a status symbol on Weibo. Anyone deemed an opinion leader in a certain field can apply for Big V verification from Weibo by submitting a copy of their name card and employment contract. Examples of influential Big Vs in the early 2010s include Chinese actress Yao Chen, technology executive Kai-Fu Lee and angel investor Charles Xue, each of whom expressed their opinions about social issues on Weibo. Most Big Vs are celebrities, CEOs or cultural icons, and thus enjoy a degree of government leeway – except when they challenge state narratives and prerogatives. Even the Big Vs have to be careful not to threaten the fundamental interests of the state, or face potentially harsh consequences.

Chinese actress Yao Chen, once dubbed as 'Queen of Weibo' for her large number of followers, was once extremely vocal on social issues. Her Weibo posts covered issues such as forced demolition, environmental pollution and government corruption, to name a few. When state media suggested that environmental pollution in Beijing was a result of car emissions, Yao ridiculed the claim, posting a photo of heavy smog in Beijing on a national holiday when the number of cars on the street was low, with the caption, 'the theory that cars are the main polluters is now debunked' (China News 2013). The editor-in-chief of the *People's Daily*, in a meeting with university students, admitted that Yao's large influence on Weibo represented stiff competition for his newspaper. Yao had more than 19 million fans in 2012, while the circulation of the *People's Daily* was just 2.8 million (Wang, 2012).

Before the rise of Weibo, the media system in China was almost entirely state-dominated. All traditional news outlets, state-owned or private, were under the supervision of either the Ministry of Propaganda or the Central Cyber Administration. The state viewed Big Vs as an unprecedented challenge to their monopoly on shaping public opinion and were alarmed that they did not follow directives issued by the Ministry of Propaganda. The state came to understand that social media can subject the government to withering scrutiny, satire and mockery, diminishing its aura of unassailable power and shifting the terms of debate that it was accustomed to dictating. It therefore stepped up social media monitoring and has tightly circumscribed what is permissible on these platforms. Since 2012, there has been a gradual tightening of control over Weibo. Real-name registration became compulsory, and in 2013 a law was passed specifying that any 'slanderous' online post seen by 5,000 viewers or reposted more than 500 times would be subject to prosecution for defamation. After the law was passed, a few opinion leaders who had not reached the status of Big Vs on Weibo were detained. One was the Weibo user nicknamed Qin Huohuo. Police said Qin was profiting from spreading rumours online (*Xinhua News* 2013a and 2013b). For example, Qin accused the government of paying hefty compensation to Italian victims in the Wenzhou train crash but not to Chinese victims (An 2016).

A 2013 public confession of immoral behaviour by Charles Xue, an influential Big V on Weibo, was a watershed moment. He was briefly detained for soliciting prostitutes, though rumours abound that his vocal style on Weibo was the real cause for his downfall; in common parlance, he was 'johned' – one of many euphemisms that refers to the methods of state repression. Though a direct connection between Charles Xue's case and the detention of Qin is unproved, the fact that many influential figures on Weibo face trouble exerts a chilling effect, intimidating others into silence or into softening their criticisms. Following a meeting with then State Internet Information Director Lu Wei, several Big Vs joined Lu in saying there are 'seven bottom lines' for postings on social media: to protect the law, socialist ideals, morals and national interests; to help maintain order, be truthful and look out for people's legal rights (*People.cn* 2013). And the state gets to decide if postings transgress these principles, granting it sweeping discretionary authority that makes all posters hesitant.

Following the crackdown on Big Vs, Weibo started to embrace an entertainment-oriented approach, cashing in on the huge number of pop culture fans in China as a way to enliven and expand the online community within the bounds of what is acceptable to the authorities. Weibo was transformed from a vibrant online meeting place for intellectual and political engagement into a place for commerce or for fans to interact with their celebrity crushes. The pop culture approach worked well for Weibo, expanding its market and keeping its executives out of trouble with the authorities. In October 2017, a Weibo post by Chinese pop star Lu Han, announcing that he was in a relationship, crashed the Weibo server (*Zaobao* 2017) In 2018, another post announcing that two famous Chinese celebrities were getting married paralyzed Weibo's server. Today, search the top ten trending topics on Weibo, and eight will be related to celebrities, indicating the degree of online lobotomization.

Though Weibo has lost much of its function as an online public opinion forum, important discussions still happen there, though the scale is more limited than before 2012.

In 2018, two significant social media movements broke out in China; one was the #MeToo movement, the other the outcry over a major vaccine scandal. From January to September 2018, more than 20 Chinese women, through WeChat and Weibo, made sexual misconduct allegations against well-known men, including many prominent figures in the media, non-governmental organization (NGO) and academic fields.

While a few allegations prompted serious action – Beihang University quickly suspended a male professor accused of sexual harassment by a female doctoral student – some still await a response, with few signs of resolution (Mistreanu 2019). A Weibo post accusing Chinese state media newscaster Zhu Jun of sexual misconduct was taken down a few hours after it was posted, and all subsequent pieces on the story disappeared quickly. Rather than Zhu being subject to investigation, instead he vowed to sue the young female intern behind the allegation for defamation.

The #MeToo movement, which was originally lauded by state media as fighting for women's rights, was gradually suppressed as more prominent figures in institutions close to the state became entangled in the unsavoury revelations and allegations. Though the professor accused of sexual misconduct in Beihang University was stripped of his title, a professor facing a similar allegation in Peking University was not, purportedly because Peking University was the alma mater of many Chinese politicians and thus enjoyed a degree of protection due to such powerful connections (Lu 2018). One year after the initial spark, the movement died down. But there were at least 56 allegations of sexual misconduct against male figures when the movement still had momentum (Matters 2018). A few prominent figures in the NGO circle, after being accused of sexual misconduct, stepped down from their positions, but many others enjoy impunity.

As veteran observer of Chinese media Ma Tianjie wrote, 'from the outset, observers realized that the #MeToo outburst in charity groups and media organizations was not an indication of the relative terribleness of gender situations in those sectors. It was rather a sign that they were not covered by the protective shield of the "system"' (Ma 2018). For those who are close to the 'system' – for example, Zhu Jun – the movement did not have much damaging effect, except for the fact that he did not appear on the national television anymore. This is probably why there were no allegations against any Chinese politicians during the #MeToo movement, insulated as they are from accountability.

But at least there has been a positive outcome. In August 2018, a draft version of China's first Civil Code showed that legal protection against sexual harassment will be incorporated. The draft read, 'Employers should take reasonable precautions, hear complaints, and implement management measures' (Sixth tone 2018). Even if some are still not held accountable for their misconduct, there has been some improvement at the institutional level and regulatory environment due to the #Me Too movement. For example, a new Civil Code draft imposed stronger obligations on employers to prevent sexual harassment, and for the first time, set out a clear definition of what constitutes 'sexual assault' (Yu 2018). This may not seem to be much, but in the Chinese political context, it is quite encouraging. Given that there is no law that clearly defines what sexual harassment entails, Chinese lawyers have found it impossible to take cases of sexual harassment to court and sexual harassment allegations were often presented as labour disputes (Zuo 2018). Reports show that most cases that involved sexual harassment allegations were brought by alleged harassers claiming breach of contract after they were dismissed from their jobs (Richardson 2018). Given that the law had virtually stayed silent on the issue of sexual harassment, the draft legislation of Civil Code is certainly a sign in the right direction. But holding influential perpetrators accountable may still be difficult in the current political context.

WeChat and private opinion space

In 2011, when discussion on Weibo was still heated, a silent revolution was brewing with the creation of WeChat. Tencent, the parent company of WeChat, initially conceived it as a messaging service, but it quickly became a combination of Facebook, Instagram and Messenger. After Tencent rolled out its WeChat official account platform, allowing users to access information from more than 3.5 million accounts for free, it gradually replaced Weibo as the dominant force in the Chinese social media space. By the end of 2017, there were already 30 million active users on WeChat, and 58.8 per cent of them cited it as their primary source of information (Penguin Intelligence 2016).

In this initial stage, WeChat was a bonanza for news sharing, just as with early Weibo, but its impact also ebbed due to official pressure. The first sign of the state reining in WeChat came in August 2014, when the State Internet Information Office published new guidelines stating that instant messaging service providers who engage in 'public information service activities' must obtain an internet news service permit. This was a huge blow to thousands of WeChat official accounts that repackaged news information to attract clicks. Since these accounts were operated by individual entrepreneurs, not establishment media organizations, they couldn't get internet news service permits (Kan 2019).

In 2017, official ire was extended to entertainment news. In June 2017, 25 entertainment-focused WeChat accounts were closed down, including the official WeChat account of *Nanfang Metropolitan Entertainment Magazine*, the Chinese *For Him Magazine* and the personal account of the most notorious paparazzi in China, Zhuo Wei (iResearch 2017). The Beijing Internet Information Office, around the same time, met with executives from some social media platforms, asking for their 'greater assistance in spreading socialist core values and in creating a positive and healthy public opinion space' (Shui 2017).

The most recent government attempt to regulate WeChat came in 2018 when the Central Cyber Administration announced that it would establish a classification system to regulate WeChat official accounts and Weibo accounts. Responsibility was delegated to the local cyber administration authorities to manage self-media accounts registered in their region. This led to the 2018 closure of 9,800 accounts in Weibo and WeChat (*Xinhua News* 2018).

It is important to note that the state's attempt to clamp down on social media does not all come from an incentive to limit free speech. There are times when clickbait self-media accounts go too far. For example, in May 2018, after reports came out that a young female passenger was murdered by a driver working for the hailing service Didi, a citizen journalist published a story vividly depicting her death, even describing her rape in horrible detail (People's Daily 2018). The story provoked outrage among Chinese netizens and the provincial Internet Information office later required the account holder to clear all 'negative information' related to the story – a move welcomed by netizens (Unicorn entertainment 2018).

When the *People's Daily* weighs in on a certain issue, it is a sign that the state will soon take action on behalf of the public's interests. Yet even if the state meddles for good reasons in some cases, mostly it aims to cover up government institutions' mistakes, as seen in the 2018 vaccination scandal. In July, a former veteran investigative journalist published a story titled 'King of Vaccines' on his personal WeChat account, detailing how three individuals, through mergers and acquisitions, came to dominate China's vaccine market and, eventually, to produce hundreds of thousands of faulty vaccines (Shou 2018) The post, which touched on the deepest nerve in China, children's health, quickly went viral. WeChat Index shows the keyword 'vaccine' appeared in more than 300 million WeChat posts after the story was published. Though the story prompted President Xi to issue a direct order for a thorough investigation and severe punishment, the hashtag 'Changsheng bio-tech vaccine incident' was quickly deleted on Weibo and relevant stories on WeChat official accounts became unavailable. One month after the scandal broke, public discussion surrounding the issue went silent. This is a result of the heavy censorship on the topic – since little public information was available, discussion was toned down. But it is also because another scandal, the #MeToo movement emerged, and the public's limited short-attention span was diverted.

In contrast, the print media, because of heavy-handed government censorship, has lost much of its ability to report stories that may strike a nerve. This is why the print media was virtually non-existent in the public discourse about the two biggest scandals in 2018, the vaccine scandal and the Me Too movement.

Social media as the greatest equalizer? The rise of ByteDance and Kuaishou

In the past few years, China's social media users have witnessed several important changes. First, the market for social media use in first- and second-tier cities reached a saturation point. Companies began to target third-tier cities and below as the main growth markets. Second, users of social media in China became younger, with an average age of 28 years old (*Beijing Morning News* 2017). The third important trend is that users generally came to prefer mobile devices over laptops, and short videos over text (*China News* 2019).

The most rapid growth in social media use is in third-tier cities, where users are extremely young, predominantly male and politically less engaged than the average Chinese citizen. Tech start-ups saw the market potential in this growing population, and two new media platforms were born: video-sharing apps Douyin and Kuaishou. At first glance, one might be horrified to find out what is trending on these two apps. On Kuaishou, the top buzz in 2018 was generated by a 13-year-old mother showing off her swollen belly; on Douyin, it was young men setting off firecrackers in their underwear. Yet both apps are hugely popular in China. Kuaishou now boasts more than 234 million monthly active users, whereas for Douyin that figure is around 300 million (Chen 2018).

One central reason behind the popularity of Douyin and Kuaishou is their ability to fill a void in the market – the desires and demands of ordinary third- and fourth-tier city people to see their own lives reflected. On Kuaishou, farmers have become celebrities, a phenomenon that is unheard of on Big V-dominated Weibo. But the popularity of the two apps drew unwelcome government attention. Douyin was required to take down all its advertisements indefinitely following a promotional spot for the app that involved jokes about a war hero. It was criticized for 'not showing responsibility for content moderation and for spreading negative information denigrating a war hero on the internet' (*Beijing Youth Daily* 2018).

Kuaishou, on the other hand, was ordered to clean up its site after the state central television criticized the rampant livestreaming of teenage moms on the platform. The State Internet Information Office said in a statement, 'Kuaishou failed to regulate accounts and let teenage live streamers publish vulgar and unhealthy content, damaging the online environment and exerting a negative impact on the healthy growth of teenagers' (*The Beijing News* 2018).

These short-video platforms, though in no way challenging the state, still run the risk of arousing official ire by broaching taboo topics. China passed a law in 2018 banning the slander of heroes and martyrs – those central to the Communist Party's version of history. Moreover, these platforms are also seen as promoting internet addiction among teens, long identified as a social evil by the authorities.

Social media companies have attempted to dodge accusations of politicizing the news by replacing editors with algorithms. ByteDance, the parent company of Douyin, which also owns the most popular news-aggregating app Jinri Toutiao, prides itself over its algorithms-driven mechanism. 'We are a technology company, not a news company,' says Yiming Zhang, the founder of ByteDance (Wu 2015). Other news portals such as Sina, Sohu and Netease all began to embrace algorithm-driven news content rather than letting editors select the news, bypassing the traditional gatekeepers.

But the problem of this mechanism is that it bypasses government regulations and traditional means to censor unwanted news; there is no editor to intimidate or issue instructions to. News apps use artificial intelligence to deliver content to users based on their browsing history, and thus, users get what they are interested in. But this approach subverts government control over the news and what is consumed. In contrast, on Tencent News or Baidu News, the first few news items are always about President Xi, as mandated by authorities.

The danger to the state is amplified by the fact that ByteDance's news app, Jinri Toutiao, is not powered by traditional news, but by content from self-media accounts. ByteDance revealed that 90 per cent of the app's content comes from bloggers rather than traditional news media (Zhong 2018). Since bloggers do not receive similar levels of government scrutiny as do the accounts of professional journalist at news media like the *People's Daily* or the *Beijing News*, sometimes the content may cross the line of government censorship. In response to government criticism, ByteDance started to recruit 2,000 content reviewers in 2018, with preference given to Communist Party members, saying that it hoped to achieve the target of recruiting 10,000 content reviewers in the near future (Yang 2018). The reviewers' job responsibilities includes scrutinizing around 1,000 posts every day to see if there is any violation of the rules and to report any such cases to the government.

Despite this attempt to appear loyal to the state, ByteDance went beyond the government's boundaries when its popular parody and meme app, Neihan Duanzi, went mainstream. On Neihan Duanzi, users created a secret code to identify each other offline, a car honk, followed by a pause and two more car honks. Users took pride in belonging to the Duanzi Community, with many posting stickers of Duanzi on the back of their cars to identify themselves as part of the community. When online connections go offline, they become even more potentially dangerous to the state. Not surprisingly, the app was ordered to shut down. In April 2018, the State Administration of Press, Publication, Radio, Film and Television published a notice on its website which stating that, 'the vulgar and improper content hosted on Neihan Duanzi triggered strong resentment among other internet users' (State Administration of Press, Publication, Radio, Film and Television 2018). It added that in order to create a better online environment, the company must close the app and clean up its other audiovisual programmes. The notice did not specify what the 'vulgar and improper content' was exactly. But Neihuan Duanzi, which originally was a hub for funny GIFs and jokes, did suffer a deterioration in the quality of its content with many sexual innuendos, curse words and racist and sexist comments appearing. As the app became more popular, videos with semi-pornographic content were also displayed. By way of an apology, Yiming Zhang, the founder of ByteDance, which owns Neihan Duanzi, acknowledged that, 'The content that appears on Neihan Duanzi goes against core socialist values and we did not do a thorough job in guiding public opinion.' Zhang specifically cited his 'weak understanding and implementation of the four consciousness of Xi Jinping' as one reason ByteDance made this mistake (Sina Technology 2018).

To make up for this mistake, Jinri Toutiao, the news aggregator ByteDance owns, launched the New Era channel on the opening page of the app to highlight

'China's accomplishments and efforts of socialism with Chinese characteristics' (*Beijing Business News* 2018).

The clampdown on short-video apps and Toutiao shows that taboo topics in China are not just political as anything deemed contrary to 'socialist core values' may invite trouble, ranging from vulgar pornographic materials to innocent jokes. Because of the all-encompassing category of 'against socialist values,' social media platforms and technology companies are treading a fine line between appealing to users' interests and appearing to be loyal to the state. Giving a new meaning to self-censorship, by 2019 one-fourth of ByteDance's 40,000 employees were engaged in 'content-monitoring,' twice the number of the firm's software engineers (Zhang 2019).

State media getting trendy on social media

Understanding that social media is an important battlefield for public opinion, Chinese state media has been adept at leveraging the digital transformation of the media space to consolidate the state's power. In a visit to the *People's Daily* headquarters in early 2019, President Xi stressed at length the importance of digital media platforms, citing Weibo, WeChat, websites, electronic newspaper bulletins, mobile newspapers, IPTV and other forms of new media as the state's priority for disseminating its agenda (Zheng 2019).

Almost all state-owned media outlets now each have their own digital arm. An official media account operated by the *People's Daily, Xia Ke Dao* – or 'Swordsman of the Island' – has more than 1 million active followers and regularly posts stories hailing the success of China in the great power competition of world politics (GSdata 2019). A newly created production center called the Central Kitchen is specifically designated to create multimedia content for the *People's Daily*, and its output can be seen on almost all social media platforms.

The success of state-owned media outlets squeezes out non-state media, since they have exclusive access to headline news and enjoy greater promotion on social media platforms, a tactic that technology companies employ to curry favour and show that they are toeing the Party line. As of early 2019, the *People's Daily* Weibo account boasted more than 80 million followers and regularly topped the viewership rankings. The campaign to win the hearts and minds of internet-savvy Chinese millennials is also supported by Party organs. The Central Communist Youth League of China launched an aggressive promotion campaign on the video-sharing platform Bilibili, which is known as the headquarters of online alternative youth culture. Calling itself 'tuan tuan,' the Party's youth league creates catchy animations and short videos about contemporary Chinese history to cultivate patriotic feelings among youth (Bandurski 2019) It even created an animation franchise where the central character is an innocent-looking bunny with a Maoist hat. In the series, the bunny fights against an American bald eagle and a white Japanese crane – a reference to Chinese contemporary history as told by the Party (Yang 2017). Some of the other most popular short videos include a collection of comments by the spokesperson of the Chinese Ministry of Defense lambasting accusations of Chinese expansionism, and an ensemble of video clips showcasing advanced weapons of the People's Liberation Army. Though the method of delivery changes, the core message of state media stays the same – loyalty to the Party is paramount.

It is undeniable that social media platforms and self-media accounts provide Chinese netizens with greater access to information – not only are they under less government scrutiny than the traditional media, it is easier for them to use various means to evade censors. But self-media accounts, once they are identified by the state as 'trouble-makers,' can be shut down easily. With state-owned media's aggressive expansion on social media, online platforms are now increasingly dominated by slick nationalistic posts and short videos, such as the Communist Youth League's bunny anime. Social media, after its initial stage as a bonanza for citizen journalism, has now been co-opted by the system.

China faces its own 'fake news' problem

The rise of social media in China brought one unintended consequence – the proliferation of misinformation, especially with the growing popularity of WeChat subscription accounts.

WeChat accounts operate similarly to a newsfeed whereby users get news updates from accounts they follow. Many Chinese now rely on WeChat as their primary source of news.

Unlike Weibo, WeChat is a private platform on which users can only interact with others through individual chats, group chats or WeChat moments, not unlike WhatsApp but with powerful additional e-commerce features. Rumours are mostly spread within WeChat groups and WeChat moments. Any attempt to debunk the rumour rarely penetrates these private groups. Moreover, since most users simply copy and paste rumours, or share articles that contain rumours without citing the origins, tracing the source of a rumour is virtually impossible. The low cost of spreading rumours also contributes to WeChat being a hotbed for misinformation.

Research shows that more than 40 per cent of rumours on WeChat are health hoaxes, one-third of which are about so-called cancer-inducing food or lifestyles (*Beijing Morning News* 2017). They appeal strongly to middle-aged and elderly WeChat users, tapping into their anxieties. The health hoaxes are mostly shared in private groups among friends and family members. The unwavering trust in close relatives creates a breeding ground for rumours ranging from conspiracy theories to human interest 'news.'

Political and economics-related news also occasionally become the source of misinformation. During the standoff between China and the United States over trade talks, false news stories that claimed either the Chinese or US side had made concessions were rife on social media. Paradoxically, rumours proliferated due to censorship. In 2018, the US-China trade war was the most-censored topic on WeChat, thus generating a heightened demand for 'news' and creating an atmosphere where people were inclined to believe rumours precisely because the state was suppressing news reporting on the issue (Gan 2019).

Even conspiracy theories originating in the West are 'imported' to China's social media platforms – though rarely do they touch upon Chinese politics, given how closely the state monitors the media scene in China. During the 2016 US presidential election, misinformation on WeChat reached an unprecedented level. Fake news stories abounded like the New York Police Department accusing Democratic Party nominee Hillary Clinton of being a pedophile or the killer of Supreme Court Justice Antonin Scalia. In July 2017, a news story circulated on Chinese social media that linked the death of so-called 'former Democrat data director' Seth Rich to Clinton's email scandal. It claimed Rich may have been the one leaking Clinton's emails and his death might have been related to attempts to cover up the leak. (*College Daily* 2016) His death sparked conspiracy theories in the US right-wing media, including on Fox News and on a few smaller websites (Coaston 2018). Yet no mainstream American news outlet, when reporting the story, drew a specific connection between Rich's death and Clinton's email leak. Moreover, Rich's position in Clinton's campaign was voter expansion data director rather than a high-level director as described in the Chinese-language news. The conspiracy theory that linked Rick's death with Clinton's email scandal plays well into the deep antagonism many Chinese internet users have against Clinton – she is considered to be too manly and too ambitious by Chinese netizens. Moreover, she is believed to be the principal designer of former US President Barack Obama's Pivot to Asia policy, seen as an effort to 'contain' a rising China (Tatlow 2016).

One reason that these for-profit self-media companies tend to spread misinformation is that, unlike traditional news outlets, these companies rarely follow a rigorous editorial process, performing no fact-checking on the stories they translate. Moreover, they tend to include an even more shocking, clickbaiting headline with the already very sensational story they import and translate. But mostly, WeChat trades in misinformation deliberately for profit rather than because of an unintended lack of professional standards. Sensationalist stories with titles like 'the health hazard of drinking milk' can quickly reach 100,000 views and with growing traffic comes advertising revenues. The *Beijing News* reports that some subscription accounts charge between 150 yuan (US$20) and 200 yuan (US$29) to reach 10,000 followers. For subscription accounts with more than 100,000 followers, therefore, the price of posting an advertisement would be anything from 1,500 yuan (US$223) to 3,000 yuan (US$446) (*The Beijing News* 2015).

Seeing the market potential, subscription accounts are now increasingly managed by for-profit self-media companies instead of by individual bloggers sharing their opinions. An entire marketplace has sprung up as PR companies have started to offer services to help increase views or to add followers. Multiple Weibo or WeChat accounts, owned by the same company, repost content, thus multiplying views. On Taobao, the Chinese equivalent of eBay, one can buy services that add 1,000 fans for only 1 yuan. 'Article-laundering' – plagiarizing others' content with slight modifications – is also now a popular commercial service (CCTV.com 2018).

Many of the rumours that go viral tap into some of the Chinese users' deepest ethno-nationalistic beliefs. According to research by the Tow Center for Digital Journalism, among the right-leaning WeChat accounts popular with Chinese-American Trump voters, the most common topics of fake new stories were about Islam and affirmative action/census disaggregation (Zhang 2018). This phenomenon coincides with the situation inside China. Stories claiming that Islam is rapidly expanding in China often go viral since they tap into the existing rampant Islamophobia on the Chinese internet. A Weibo account called 'In-depth News' regularly posts stories of rape cases allegedly perpetrated by Muslim men. The account now boasts more than 270,000 followers and often receives more than 1 million views for its posts ('In-depth News' Weibo 2019).

Unusually, the state refrains from meddling with Islamophobic postings, not sowing further antagonism nor promoting greater tolerance. Hate speech against Muslims or Uighurs does not pose a threat to the Han-majority Chinese society, and there is little danger of a backlash from ethnic minorities.

As well as appealing to readers' prejudices, exploiting nationalism is another common tactic on self-media. Anti-Japanese sentiments and anti-imperialism, coupled with clickbait titles, sell well. In 2017, one of the top ten stories that went viral on WeChat was titled 'Chinese should boycott Christmas because it is the day when the imperialist forces invaded China.' The story claimed that people in the West celebrate Christmas because on 25 December 1898, the eight-nation alliance invaded China, raping Chinese women and murdering hundreds of innocent civilians (Sohu 2017). The story of course, is factually wrong.

Because of language barriers and the existence of the Great Firewall, it is very hard for Chinese internet users to trace a story to its original source in the foreign media. Moreover, the way that Chinese self-media accounts report 'imported news,' using the umbrella term 'foreign media' to describe all international news outlets, makes it harder for Chinese internet users to do fact-checking. The term 'foreign media' is used to lend a factual tone and credibility to the story, and thus out of convenience, the umbrella term – rather than the specific name of the foreign media outlet – is used in the story. Even when the origin of the story is reported, many Chinese internet users lack sufficient understanding of foreign media institutions to make their own judgement call about its reliability. For example, the British tabloid *Daily Mail*, serving up a diet of right-wing, anti-immigration and celebrity-focused sensationalism, is one of the most frequently cited news sources among Chinese self-media accounts. Right-wing news outlets like Breitbart News and the Drudge Report, which are viewed as partisan by American readers, are taken as authoritative voices by Chinese readers. This points to a systematic problem in the Chinese media environment – readers' lack of media literacy. This is a consequence of extensive censorship, as readers expect Chinese sources to feed them propaganda, but imagine that foreign sources are more objective and reliable. Restrictions on access to alternative sources makes Chinese readers less able to distinguish the truth from rumours, because their critical reading skills are stifled by design. Moreover, the entire concept of truth has been heavily blurred in China, due to government control over the press. Even for establishment media, sometimes a touch-up of the truth is essential in order to get stories published. Whenever international news portrays China in a negative light, the Chinese news media, in order to get the stories out, have to twist the original story in a direction that is favourable to China. And some do this as a matter of national pride.

For example, the *Global Times*, when reporting on Bloomberg's bombshell story that the Chinese government had used tiny microchips to infiltrate the data centres of Apple and Amazon, claimed it was a 'set-up.' The *Global Times* editorial lambasted the Bloomberg reporter, accusing him of denigrating China (*Global Times* 2018). Similarly, most critical stories against China have to be reported in the same manner, using phrases to spin the story such as 'a set-up,' 'wildly claim,' 'baseless allegation,' etc. The line between misinformation and inconvenient truth is blurry in China.

Hong Kong University Journalism School professor Dr. Fu King-Wa states that, 'fake news in China must be understood in the context of media control . . . fake news is defined by the authorities, but it's really hard to identify if it is really fake or if it is just inconvenient' (Guo 2017). The proliferation of misinformation on social media is compounded by the fact that the old gatekeepers of news have lost their power, especially local newspapers. Due to increased financial pressure and pressure from the government on what to report and what not to report, all forms of media are increasingly hesitant to report about political scandals, corruption and abuses of power that might provoke a negative state reaction.

In early 2018, the Shanghai-based online news outlet, the Paper, published an investigative story called 'Finding Tang Lanlan' in which it details the horrifying sexual abuse of 14-year-old Tang Lanlan by her family members, including her own father, grandfather and uncles, with permission from her mother (The Paper 2018). The reporter followed the girl's mother, who was just released from prison as she embarked on a journey to try to locate her daughter and seek justice for the family members who she said were wrongfully convicted. The story caused an uproar on the Chinese internet; the reporter was criticized for revealing the personal information of the underage girl and for only quoting one side of the story, since she did not manage to reach Tang herself and failed to get comments from people at the court who handled the case. The public was mostly outraged because the reporter suggested Tang may have lied to the police, leading to the wrongful conviction of family members. Many criticized her for 'victim-shaming' and attacked her for questioning the ruling of the criminal justice system. Netizens even threatened to dig out the personal information of the journalist so as to let her bear the consequence of 'doing biased reporting' (Douban 2018).

It was later reported that another story on the same sexual abuse case in the Chinese newspaper *Southern Weekly*, one that provided a more balanced coverage by interviewing both sides of the story – people at the court who handled the case and Tang's mother who claimed to be wrongfully imprisoned – was suppressed before the newspaper went to print (Fang 2018). The story cast doubt on the local law enforcement agencies, presenting evidence that suggested the local prosecutors relied on dubious evidence at the trial. The *Southern Weekly* reporter who penned the piece published it on his own WeChat personal account, but the piece was censored soon after publication (Fang 2018).

As Fang Kecheng, a former *Southern Weekly* journalist wrote, 'it is easy to ask for the whereabouts of the teenage girl Tang, but it is hard to ask for accountability from the law enforcement agency' (Fang 2018). The veteran Chinese media observer Ma Tianjie observed that the 'flawed' Paper article got the green light because of its 'personal story' angle, whereas the *Southern Weekly* piece, which shed an unfavourable light on the local prosecution, was suppressed (Ma 2018). The debate surrounding the story revealed one distinct feature of the Chinese media system – if a story might damage the interests of the state, and any institution affiliated with the state, it is spiked. Silence or a partial truth is all that is allowed. The rights and reputations of private individuals, however, are up for grabs.

This points to the biggest difficulty both establishment and social media platforms encounter in combatting fake news – no one is allowed to report the real truth in China – a fact widely acknowledged by the public. If the truth can't be reported, how can anyone know what is fake or what is true? Any media institution publishing a critical story about the state may be attacked as 'fake media' by nationalists; any reporter trying to fact-check a rumour that has gone viral may be faulted for engaging in a 'cover-up' for the state, or for business interests. Media outlets in China lack credibility because they are seen as either too close to the state, or too close to business interests. To some extent, this is true. No establishment media outlet in China is free from government supervision; no self-media can survive without funding from advertisers and VC investors. Frequent intervention by either the state or business interests tarnishes the reputation of the industry, so that even when the media genuinely wants to do serious reporting, it faces a massive trust deficit.

It is hard to imagine how the Chinese media can gain credibility, given the state's continued reliance on extensive censorship to deprive people of information and to avoid accountability. The state understands that the truth is a powerful enemy that must be thwarted and manipulated at all costs. As a result, social media has been tamed and mainstream media co-opted. Public expectations of the media have been managed downward, and few readers expect anything from the media other than entertainment and basic information. Nationalistic hubris is common in the Chinese media, further casting doubts on prospects for meaningful reform because nothing can be reported that subverts that narrative. The climate of fear and intimidation ensures that the news remains beholden to the state, and vulnerable to market forces that privilege the sensational over thoughtful analysis. There is no basis to imagine that this will change soon, or that social media can become a panacea for an authoritarian polity.

Bibliography

Bandurski, D. (2019) 'Blockbuster nationalism and viral propaganda', *China Media Project.* Online. Available HTTP: <http://chinamediaproject.org/2019/02/10/blockbuster-nationalism-and-viral-propaganda/> (accessed 28 April 2019).

Beijing Business News. (2018) 'Jinti Toutiao closes down society channel', *Sina Technology.* Online. Available HTTP: <http://tech.sina.com.cn/i/2018-01-02/doc-ifyqc-sft9089323.shtml> (accessed 28 April 2019).

Beijing Morning News. (2017) 'After thirty years of development, what is the key feature of Chinese Internet?', *Xinhua Net.* Online. Available HTTP: <www.xinhuanet.com//tech/2017-09/22/c_1121705447.htm> (accessed 28 April 2019).

The Beijing Morning News. (2017) 'Health hoax constitutes majority of rumors on WeChat', *Xinhua News.* Online. Available HTTP: <www.xinhuanet.com/food/2017-12/21/c_1122144282.htm> (accessed 28 April 2019).

The Beijing News. (2015) 'Interest behind the spread of the six-winged chicken rumor: Spreading one rumor earns 800 yuan', *Sina Tech News.* Online. Available HTTP: <http://tech.sina.com.cn/i/2015-06-09/doc-icrvvsuv9077426.shtml> (accessed 28 April 2019).

The Beijing News. (2018) 'Kuaishou and Huoshan videos summed for a meeting for propagating vulgar content'. Online. Available HTTP: <www.xinhuanet.com/fortune/2018-04/08/c_1122646522.htm> (accessed 28 April 2019).

Beijing Youth Daily. (2018) 'Douyin and Sougou asked for rectification for "denigrating martyrs"'. Online. Available HTTP: <www.xinhuanet.com/2018-06/07/c_112294 8438.htm> (accessed 28 April 2019).

CCTV.com. (2018) '"Article-laundering" became an industry: Writing a viral post in minutes and earn more than 10,000 a month', *Xinhuanet.com.* Online. Available HTTP: <www.xinhuanet.com/legal/2018-08/29/c_1123347400.htm> (accessed 28 April 2019).

Chen, L. (2011) 'Spokesman for Ministry of Railway stepped down: Expert says he had made "stupid mistake"', *People.com.cn.* Online. Available HTTP: <http://media.people.com.cn/GB/40606/15434058.html> (accessed 28 April 2019).

Chen, Q. (2018) 'The biggest trend in Chinese social media is dying, and another has already taken its place', *CNBC.* Online. Available HTTP: <www.cnbc.com/2018/09/19/short-video-apps-like-douyin-tiktok-are-dominating-chinese-screens.html> (accessed 28 April 2019).

China News. (2013) 'Actress Yao Chen debunked the rumor that pollution from automobile is the biggest source for smog in Beijing', *ifeng.com.* October 9. Online. Available HTTP: <http://news.ifeng.com/mainland/special/kongqizhiliang/content-3/detail_2013_10/09/30141737_0.shtml> (accessed 28 April 2019).

China News. (2019) 'Chinese netizens use mobile much more frequently than PC', *China News.* Online. Available HTTP: <www.chinanews.com/cj/2019/02-20/8760062.shtml> (accessed 28 April 2019).

Coaston, J. (2018) 'A right-leaning newspaper is finally retracting the conspiracy theories it published about Seth Rich', *Vox.* Online. Available HTTP: <www.vox.com/policy-and-politics/2018/10/1/17923178/washington-times-seth-rich-aaron-rich-trump-fox-news> (accessed 28 April 2019).

College Daily. (2016) 'The man behind Clinton email scandal was murdered: What is the reason?'. Online. Available HTTP: <www.sohu.com/a/110220292_170104> (accessed 28 April 2019).

Cui, B. (2018) 'Report on development of china's media industry', *Social Sciences Academic Press.* Online. Available HTTP: <www.sohu.com/a/237156451_654813> (accessed 28 April 2019).

Douban. (2018) 'Have the paper and the Beijing News apologized the reporter for the case of Tang Lanlan?'. Online. Available HTTP: <www.douban.com/group/topic/121062060/> (accessed 28 April 2019).

Fang, K. (2018) 'The easy and hard things to do when reporting the Tang Lanlan case', *The Initium*. Online. Available HTTP: <https://theinitium.com/article/20180202-opinion-fangkecheng-sexual-assault/> (accessed 28 April 2019).

Gan, N. (2019) 'US-China trade war among most censored topics of 2018 on WeChat', *South China Morning Post*. Online. Available HTTP: <www.scmp.com/news/china/politics/article/2185885/us-china-trade-war-among-most-censored-topics-2018-wechat> (accessed 28 April 2019).

Global Times. (2018) 'Bloomberg's sinister motive to denigrate China is very obvious'. Online. Available HTTP: <http://world.huanqiu.com/exclusive/2018-10/13188923.html?agt=15422> (accessed 28 April 2019).

Guo, E. (2017) 'How WeChat spreads rumors, reaffirms bias, and helped elect Trump', *Wired*. Online. Available HTTP: <www.wired.com/2017/04/how-wechat-spreads-rumors-reaffirms-bias-and-helped-elect-tru mp/> (accessed 28 April 2019).

GSData. (2019) 'Ranking of WeChat official accounts'. Online. Available HTTP: <http://www.gsdata.cn/rank/wxrank> (accessed 18 August 2019).

iResearch. (2017) 'Twenty WeChat officials accounts closed down'. Online. Available HTTP: <http://news.iresearch.cn/content/2017/06/268645.shtml> (accessed 28 April 2019).

iResearch. (2018) 'Report on China's internet advertisement market'. Available HTTP: <http://report.iresearch.cn/wx/report.aspx?id=3264> (accessed 28 April 2019).

'In-depth News' Weibo. (2019) Available HTTP: <https://weibo.com/sdonews?is_hot=1> (accessed 18 August 2019).

Kan, K. (2019) 'Dearth of news', *Index on Censorship*, 48. Online. Available HTTP: <https://reader.exacteditions.com/issues/80636/spread/3> (accessed 28 April 2019).

Lu, Q. (2018) 'Me too in China', *New York Shalong*. Available HTTP: <www.youtube.com/watch?v=J_PVH90BzQA> (accessed 28 April 2019).

Ma, T. (2018) 'In search of Tang Lanlan', *Chublicopinion*. Online. Available HTTP: <https://chublicopinion.com/2018/03/11/in-search-of-tang-lanlan/> (accessed 28 April 2019).

Matters. (2018) 'An overview of Me Too movement in China', *Matters*. Online. Available HTTP: <https://matters.news/@jidongjie/%E4%B8%AD%E5%9B%BDme-too%E8%BF%90%E5%8A%A8%E8%B5%84%E6%96%99%E6%95%B4%E7%90%86-%E6%8C%81%E7%BB%AD%E6%9B%B4%E6%96%B0-zdpuAx7pyxGTuLAjanKJDtzgJ2i671xvNXuESx6H52yn21XN7> (accessed 18 August 2019).

Mistreanu, S. (2019) 'China's #MeToo activists have transformed a generation', *Foreign Policy*. Online. Available HTTP: <https://foreignpolicy.com/2019/01/10/chinas-metoo-activists-have-transformed-a-generation/> (accessed 28 April 2019).

The Paper. (2018) 'In search of Tang Lanlan: Teenage girl sexually assaulted, imprisoned for 11 years and lost contact'. Online. Available HTTP: <http://news.163.com/18/0130/22/D9ECLIRA00018AOR.html> (accessed 28 April 2019).

Penguin Intelligence. (2016) 'A guide to content-monetization: Self-media readers' consumption habit', *Penguin Intelligence*. Online. Available HTTP: <https://wj.qq.com/article/single-82.html> (accessed 28 April 2019).

People.cn. (2013) 'China internet conference calls for adhering to seven principles'. Online. Available HTTP: <http://opinion.people.com.cn/n/2013/0816/c368024-22589378.html> (accessed 28 April 2019).

People's Daily. (2018) 'Founder of WeChat official account Ergeng apologized and announced to close down the account'. Online. Available HTTP: <http://bj.people.com.cn/n2/2018/0515/c233086-31577671.html> (accessed 28 April 2019).

Richardson, S. (2018) 'China's victims of sexual harassment denied justice', *Human Rights Watch*. Online. Available HTTP: <www.hrw.org/news/2018/07/31/chinas-victims-sexual-harassment-denied-justice> (accessed 28 April 2019).

Sixth Tone. (2018) 'Sexual Harassment Protections Included in China's Civil Code'. Online. Available HTTP: <https://www.sixthtone.com/ht_news/1002835/sexual-harassment-protections-included-in-chinas-civil-code> (accessed 18 August 2019).

Shou, Y. (2018) 'King of vaccines', *The Initium*. Online. Available HTTP: <https://theinitium.com/article/20180722-mainland-king-of-the-vaccine/> (accessed 20 April 2019).

Shui, Y. (2017) '25 WeChat official accounts including serious gossiping, mean gossiping and we love gossip are closed down', *Huxiu.com*. Online. Available HTTP: <www.huxiu.com/article/198971.html> (accessed 28 April 2019).

Sina Technology. (2018) 'Zhang Yiming apologized for app Neihan Duanzi: The product goes to the wrong direction'. Online. Available HTTP: <http://tech.sina.com.cn/i/2018-04-11/doc-ifyuwqez8677545.shtml> (accessed 28 April 2019).

Sohu. (2017) 'If you hear people say "Christmas is celebrated because of invasion of the eight-allied nations" please share this piece'. Available HTTP: <www.sohu.com/a/206642112_406833> (accessed 28 April 2019).

State Administration of Press, Publication, Radio, Film and Television. (2018) 'State administration of press, publication, radio, film and television asks Jinri Toutiao to close down Neihan Duanzi'. Online. Available HTTP: <www.sapprft.gov.cn/sapprft/contents/6582/365922.shtml> (accessed 28 April 2019).

Tatlow, D. (2016) 'Hillary Clinton, as seen through a Chinese prism', *The New York Times*. Online. Available HTTP: <www.nytimes.com/2016/07/11/world/asia/hillary-clinton-as-seen-through-a-chinese-prism.html> (accessed 28 April 2019).

Unicorn Entertainment. (2018) 'The heaviest punishment ever: A self-media account with millions of fans were closed', *Sohu.com*. Online. Available HTTP: <www.sohu.com/a/231730484_549401> (accessed 28 April 2019).

Wang, L. (2012) 'People's daily president: "Weibo queen" Yao Chen is our competitor', *ifeng.com*. Online. Available HTTP: <http://culture.ifeng.com/1/detail_2012_04/29/14235106_0.shtml> (accessed 28 April 2019).

Wu, L. (2015) 'Founder Zhang Yiming said Jinri Toutiao is not a media company but a technology company', *QDaily*. Online. Available HTTP: <www.qdaily.com/articles/9019.html> (accessed 28 April 2019).

Xinhua News. (2013a) 'Hypocrisy of Charles Xue exposed', *Sina Finance*. Online. Available HTTP: <http://finance.sina.com.cn/review/sbzt/20130829/005316594547.shtml> (accessed 28 April 2019).

Xinhua News. (2013b) 'Internet celebrity Qin Huohuo who once claimed a national hero was fabricated was caught by police', *163.com*. Online. Available HTTP: <http://news.163.com/13/0821/00/96OSLPCN00014JB5.html> (accessed 28 April 2019).

Xinhua News. (2018). 'Office of the Central Cyberspace Affairs Commission closes down tens of thousands of WeChat accounts'. *Xinhuanet*. Online. Available HTTP: <http://www.xinhuanet.com/2018-11/13/c_1123706812.htm> (accessed 18 August 2019).

Yang, X. (2018) 'Today's headline app recruits 2000 content monitors and party members are the most favored', *The Paper*. Online. Available HTTP: <www.thepaper.cn/newsDetail_forward_1932733> (accessed 28 April 2019).

Yang, Y. (2017) 'China: The soft power', *Financial Times*. Online. Available HTTP: <www.ft.com/content/9ef9f592-e2bd-11e7-97e2-916d4fbac0da> (accessed 28 April 2019).

Yu, K. (2018) 'When will China implement laws to combat sexual harassment?', *Aljazeera*. Online. Available HTTP: <www.aljazeera.com/news/2017/12/ireland-brexit-171213121309274.html> (accessed 28 April 2019).

Zaobao. (2017) 'Luhan's Weibo post announcing that he is in a relationship crashed the Weibo server'. Online. Available HTTP: <www.zaobao.com.sg/realtime/china/story20171008-801389> (accessed 28 April 2019).

Zhang, C. (2018) 'Wechatting American politics: Misinformation, polarization, and immigrant Chinese media', *Tow Center for Digital Journalism*. Online. Available HTTP: <www.cjr.org/tow_center_reports/wechatting-american-politics-misinformation-polarization-and-immigrant-chinese-media.php#citations> (accessed 28 April 2019).

Zhang, Y. (2019) 'The people behind byte dance's app factory', *The Information*. Online. Available HTTP: <www.theinformation.com/articles/the-people-behind-bytedances-app-factory> (accessed 28 April 2019).

Zheng, W. (2019) 'How official Chinese propaganda is adapting to the social media age as disaffection spreads among millennials', *South China Morning Post*. Online. Available HTTP: <www.scmp.com/news/china/politics/article/2185300/how-official-chinese-propaganda-adapting-social-media-age> (accessed 28 April 2019).

Zhong, A. (2016) 'Qin Huohuo: I don't want to be an Internet celebrity, I want to be a commentator', *The Beijing News*. Online. Available HTTP: <www.bjnews.com.cn/inside/2016/07/23/410980.html> (accessed 28 April 2019).

Zhong, R. (2018) 'A saucy app knows China's taste in news: The censors are worried', *The New York Times*. Online. Available HTTP: <www.nytimes.com/2018/01/02/business/china-toutiao-censorship.html> (accessed 28 April 2019).

Zuo, M. (2018) 'Why Chinese women don't speak out about sexual harassment in the workplace', *South China Morning Post*. Online. Available HTPP: <www.scmp.com/news/china/society/article/2142703/why-chinese-women-dont-speak-out-about-sexual-harassment> (accessed 28 April 2019).

4

BORROWING, BUYING AND BUILDING BOATS

How China exerts its influence over the press in Asia

Louisa Lim

China is increasingly asserting its influence throughout the Asia-Pacific media in ways which are ultimately deleterious to press freedom. Beijing's ultimate aim is to build its 'discourse power' overseas, and to this end it is buying advertorial coverage in regional papers, overtly and covertly injecting state-approved propaganda into the Asian news ecosystem and setting up journalistic joint ventures across the region, sometimes through proxies. China is also investing in training individual Asian journalists as part of its public diplomacy programme with the aim of building a young cadre of supporters sympathetic to its policy positions. Thus, China is slowly and steadily reshaping the Asian media ecosystem through its long-term investments in media producers, media outlets and media communication technologies. This strategy has the effect of narrowing media diversity by choking off venues that once might have carried independent voices critical of Beijing. At the same time, state-run newspapers are beginning to play a more aggressive role targeting vocal critics of Beijing.

Telling China's story well: China's state-run press overseas and its proxies

Four words sum up the media strategy of China's President Xi Jinping: 'Telling China's story well.' The Chairman of Everything has even furnished a handy list of bullet points to help locate the right emphasis: the world should see China as multidimensional and colourful, a builder of world peace, a contributor to global development and an upholder of international order (Stone 2018). This narrative campaign is driven by the need to correct what Beijing sees as its 'discourse power deficiency,' a sentiment articulated by China Global Television Network (CGTN) journalist Pan Deng, who wrote in the *Global Times*, 'As the world's second largest economy, China needs a discourse that fits its reality and global stature' (Pan 2018). Beijing's concern is countering the 'Western media imperial-ism' it sees as dominating press discourse and propagating biased narratives about China's rise (Thussu et al. 2018; Xiao 2018).

President Xi himself has advocated 'enhancing our international discourse power, telling China's story properly in a centralised manner' (Bandurski 2016). In recent years, Beijing has adopted a more assertive strategy to offset nega-tive messages with positive depictions of its achievements through the expansion of China's state-run media overseas and the use of non-Chinese journalists to spread its message by leveraging their credibility in foreign news markets. To this end, Beijing has exploited the vulnerabilities of the Western press – especially the financial difficulties suffered in the age of digital disruption – to sponsor exchange and training schemes for individual journalists, setting up institutional mechanisms that locate such work as part of its public diplomacy programme.

China's latest big push to strengthen its global media presence began in 2009 with a spending pledge of US$6.6 billion (Wu and Chen 2009). The state-run CGTN television network, the international arm of CCTV, has been the poster child of this expansion, establishing three overseas regional hubs in Washington, London and Nairobi since 2012. The primary role of Chinese state-run media overseas, as characterized by Vivien Marsh, is 'a product of the very core of the Chinese state – a potential emissary of soft power, spreading the notion of a reimagined world order with China at its centre' (2018: 103). But in 2019, there are signs that state-run media are beginning to play a more aggressive role, with evidence that they are being used to interfere in local politics, in particular in Hong Kong.

China puts a local face on its global media push by employing non-Chinese journalists on generous salaries. In interviews, current and former non-Chinese state media workers clearly understood their role. One former state media worker, who – like many others – asked for anonymity due to fear of retribution, said, 'You've got to be the 'mouth and throat' of the party.'[1] Christian Edwards, an Australian journalist who worked for Xinhua News agency in Sydney for four years, told the *Guardian* that the job's aims were explicit, 'At whatever cost, their objectives were loud and clear, to push a distinctly Chinese agenda' (Lim and Bergin 2018). He described his role as 'combining journalism with a kind of cre-ative writing to find cracks in the system of liberal democracy and exploit them' (Lim and Bergin 2018). A third former employee described ripping out news and massaging language to pursue a particular political line in their work, often resulting in what they described as 'context-free news stories.'

For non-Chinese journalists, the incentives to work for Chinese state media are both financial and professional. Their work can reach massive audiences, and generous funding provides opportunities that may not be available at cash-strapped Western news outlets. One former state media worker describes 'extraordinary' travel allowances for reporters, unlike at Western media outlets where employees often scrape by on trips, staying at budget hotels and deliver-ing multiple commissions. At Chinese state-run media, the former employee described getting what was effectively a blank check, saying, 'Any time you want to travel, you can. As long as you produce the work they want.'

However, the work sometimes crosses journalistic red lines. Three separate former state media workers, none of whom are Chinese citizens, said that they had written confidential *neibu* reports, which were not for publication, but instead were research reports written solely for senior Chinese officials. Edwards wrote a report on Adelaide's urban planning, including the Australian city's experience at dealing with scarce water supplies. He later admitted he saw the report as part of 'panda diplomacy' rather than anything more malevolent (Lim and Bergin 2018; Shepherd 2018).

In Hong Kong and Taiwan, the Chinese state-run media is beginning to perform more of an attack dog function, smearing vocal government critics with inaccurate stories or collecting intelligence on them. In December 2018, outspoken American academic Kevin Carrico, based at Australia's Macquarie University, tweeted that he was being followed in Hong Kong, writing, 'TFW the people following you in Hong Kong do a really bad job of hiding the fact that they are following you.' Ten days later, the identity of his stalkers became clear when the state-run *Wenweipo* ran a front-page story about Carrico. The article, titled 'Australian independence advocate spreading independence in Hong Kong' (Zhang 2018), included a surreptitiously taken photograph of him dining with a local publisher, and such minor details as the fact that he returned to his hotel to change his shirt. In response, Carrico characterized the newspaper as 'essentially an intelligence service masquerading as a paper' (AFP 2018).

A 2019 investigation by Reuters found that over the previous three years, at least 25 people linked to anti-China or independence causes had been covered intensively by the two papers in Taiwan, including the use of covert photography (Pomfret and Lee 2019). In recent years, reporters for the state-run *Takungpao* newspaper have variously infiltrated the campaign team of pro-democracy politician Lee Cheuk-yan (Cheng 2018a), followed and physically attacked localist politician Edward Leung (Ng 2016) and accused Malaysian politician Lee Khai Loon of plotting to move a 'separatist training camp' to Malaysia (Malaysiakini 2019). In 2018, the *Takungpao* was also accused of 'factually inaccurate and misleading reporting' by the British consulate, which demanded an apology after the paper incorrectly said it had funded a pro-democracy project (Cheng 2018b).

Another example of the paper's interference in local politics was during Hong Kong's 2018 legislative council by-election when it ran a full-page advertisement for a pro-Beijing candidate, Chan Hoi-yan, on election day in a move that many saw as contravening laws regarding electoral advertising (Chung 2018). The paper had already carried many articles accusing the democratic candidate of politically sensitive acts such as meeting Taiwan independence activists (Pepper 2018). The seat in question was won by Chan Hoi-yan by a sizeable margin.

These recent examples show an increasingly brazen use of state-run media for political ends outside mainland China, including the harassment and intimidation of critics, as well as propagating and amplifying 'fake news' stories. Such incidents should fuel concern about the increasingly blurred line between journalism, propaganda work, influence projection and intelligence gathering trod by China's state-run outlets. In September 2018, the US government ordered CGTN and the Xinhua news agency to register under the Foreign Agents Registration Act (FARA), which was set up in 1938 to curb Nazi propaganda in the United States. The US-China Economic and Security Commission has taken that a step further by recommending that all staff of Chinese state-run media entities register as foreign agents (Smith 2018).

Borrowing and buying boats to reach the ocean

Beijing's strategy to infuse CCP-approved messages into the existing media ecosystem is known as *jiechuanchuhai* or 'borrowing a boat to reach the ocean.' This 'borrowed boat' approach, underwritten by Beijing's deep pockets, has effectively been rolled out across global television, radio and print media, with one key target being overseas Chinese-language media (Brady 2018). Strategies used include placing paid supplements in existing newspapers, striking content partnership deals providing free Xinhua copy to Chinese-language newspapers and acquisitions of previously independent news outlets. Although this steady encroachment on foreign media markets has serious consequences for press freedom, it has not raised significant alarms yet, perhaps as few observers believe the turgid content holds much attraction for global audiences.

Yet in print media, the world's most prestigious mastheads have become 'borrowed boats' ferrying Chinese propaganda in the form of the *China Daily*'s China Watch supplement to its readers. This insert of propaganda material is now carried by at least 30 newspapers, including the *New York Times* and the *Washington Post*, to combined audiences of more than 16 million. 'That's the more effective tactic in general in reaching foreign audiences,' says Freedom House's Sarah Cook, who believes the inserts allow Chinese propaganda to reach non-Chinese consumers, often without their knowledge.[2] Some of Asia's most influential papers, such as Indonesia's *Jakarta Post*, Thailand's *Nation* newspaper and Japan's *Mainichi Shimbun* – that boasts of a readership of 6.6 million – have signed agreements to carry the China Watch supplement.[3]

The *Wall Street Journal* and the *Telegraph* also carry China Messenger advertising supplements online and in their print editions, which is a joint venture with Xinhua news agency rather than *China Daily*. For Beijing, this could also serve as an exercise in signalling: the ultimate aim may not be attracting foreign readers so much as using these authoritative outlets as media Trojan horses to provide validation and legitimation to Chinese state-run messages.

The cost of these inserts is still unclear, with estimates spanning US$250,000 per year per insert for a major US daily (Diamond 2018) to US$940,000 for the United Kingdom's *Daily Telegraph* (Hazlewood 2016). The magnitude of these outlays helps explain why the *China Daily* is the highest registered non-governmental spender on US lobbying; regulatory filings under the Foreign Agents

Registration Act show that it spent US\$23.86 million on US lobbying in 2017 and 2018 (CRP 2019). Beijing's willingness to invest such eye-popping amounts of money on its media operations overseas underlines the importance it accords to information warfare.

At the same time, Beijing is waging an even more intense campaign to woo overseas Chinese-language media, especially in Asia, where it has struck many more deals with Chinese-language media than with outlets in other languages. An investigation by Emily Feng for the *Financial Times* found 221 content partnerships with nominally independent Chinese-language publications round the world, with more such deals in Asia – 85 – than in any other part of the world (Personal communication). Of those, 51 were in Japan, eight were in Thailand, seven in South Korea and six in Indonesia (Feng 2018). These agreements allowing publications to use state-run propaganda for free are part of a global campaign to turn Chinese-language titles into what Brady (2018) describes as outlets of official Chinese messaging.

In Australia, which is often viewed as a petri dish for Chinese influence operations overseas, all but a tiny handful of more than 50 Chinese-language newspapers and magazines are now controlled by businessmen sympathetic to Beijing.[4] The last remaining independent standouts are struggling to survive amid Beijing's hardline tactics, which are designed to cut off their advertising revenues (Chan 2018; Lim & Smith 2016). Chinese state security officers even camped for a fortnight in the Beijing offices of one advertiser at the independent Vision Times Media to try to intimidate it into withdrawing its business from the publication, according to Vision Times staff; another advertiser was questioned for three hours by Chinese consular officials on Australian soil (Chan 2018; Lim and Smith 2016). Such moves have a major impact on press freedom since their aim is to systematically choke off platforms that might host critical views. Over time, such moves create a rigid uniformity in Chinese-language media, ensuring that Chinese-speaking audiences are only exposed to newspaper content that echoes CCP messaging.

The 'borrowed boat' strategy is also used in television, whereby CCTV news stories and footage are distributed through its video news agency CCTV Plus. By 2015, CCTV Plus was used by 1,700 TV channels in 92 countries and regions (Hu, Ji & Gong 2018) partly through cooperation agreements with Reuters and Associated Press Television News. The stories that gain traction are often softer features – for example, about exciting young Chinese fashion designers or cute baby pandas – but their widespread usage also serves CCP aims by boosting global perceptions of China as multidimensional and colourful.

Co-productions are also becoming more popular, with joint control by Chinese and non-Chinese partners ensuring that the content remains on-message. One recent example is a 2018 partnership to co-produce television programmes between the Voice of Vietnam and Guangxi People's Radio Broadcasting. Under the agreement, the Voice of Vietnam has sent reporters to China to produce pieces about the two countries' relations, while the Chinese station has sent staff to Vietnam to cooperate on television programmes (VOV.VN 2018). This can be seen as an extension of state-run China Radio International (CRI) strategy of establishing radio stations in border provinces to target countries bordering China (Kuo 2018).

In radio, Reuters drew attention to the 'borrowed boats,' describing a network of nominally independent radio stations carrying material from CRI using seemingly independent 'front companies' to mask the origin of the content (Koh and Shiffman 2015). It also reported on the existence of 33 radio stations in 14 countries running CRI content through three companies: Global CAMG, GT Times in Europe and G&E Radio Network in the United States. Three years on, those companies now operate 58 stations in 35 countries, according to information from their websites. These networks likely represent only a small percentage of global radio outlets that run material from Chinese state-run media, since CRI boasted of having cooperation agreements with 160 global radio channels globally in its 2016 annual report (Kuo 2018).

The Melbourne-headquartered Global CAMG serves as an Asian hub, managing radio frequencies in 21 different countries, including 11 in Asia – South Korea, Mongolia, Indonesia, Philippines, Sri Lanka, Thailand, Afghanistan, Nepal, Laos, Cambodia and Myanmar – as well as a number of stations in Australia and New Zealand. Global CAMG produces its own content for these stations – which are sometimes run as joint ventures with local entrepreneurs – as well as broadcasting CRI content through them. The complicated ownership structures of these companies mask the fact that they are majority-owned by state-run Chinese bodies. One example is the parent company, Global CAMG, which was set up by a Chinese-Australian businessman, Tommy Jiang, though corporate filings show that the company is 60 per cent owned by Beijing Guoguang Century media, which in turn is fully owned by CRI (Koh and Shiffman 2015).

Many of the local stations have been structured in this way, bringing in local entrepreneurs as part-owners, which allows them to adapt to local conditions and needs. One example is Global CAMG's Thai subsidiary, 103 Like FM, which is operated through a local affiliate called CAMG (Thailand), formed in 2011 with a Thai golf-course operator and fibre-optics executive, Kobsak Chinawongwattana. This is a youth-focused music channel with at least six frequencies around Thailand and 1 million listeners (Kuo 2018; Suchiva 2016). To engage its young audience, the station uses social media extensively and runs celebrity-themed promotional activities including cooking competitions and concerts (Kuo 2018).

When CAMG (Thailand) was founded, its CEO told the *Nation* newspaper that 'CRI was focusing on expansion in Southeast Asia and using Thailand as a strategic media hub for China to export entertainment and news content as well as other kinds of media platforms to the region' (Thongtep 2011). This type of localization – and the need to turn a profit – means that each subsidiary must be responsive to its own specific media market. Some have developed strategic partnerships – for example, 103 Like FM's hook-up with an e-commerce platform called Lazada – to drive up audience numbers, which ultimately allows China-friendly messages to reach more listeners.

In this way, Chinese propaganda is being exported and monetized in the Xi Jinping era.

In 2014, propaganda czar Liu Qibao endorsed such strategies, writing,

> We should strengthen the construction of platforms and channels for cultural exports, through the methods of 'buying the boat to reach the ocean' and 'borrowing the boat to reach the ocean' in order to expand international markets, perfect the distribution of overseas networks, and push our cultural products into more international markets.
>
> *(Liu 2014)*

In practice, this means encouraging Chinese entrepreneurs to serve as state proxies by acquiring overseas media companies or setting up joint ventures.

In Asia, the highest-profile example of this was the 2015 acquisition of Hong Kong's 114-year-old *South China Morning Post* by China's richest man, Alibaba's Jack Ma, for US$266 million. When asked outright whether he was told to buy the paper, Ma did not give a straight answer, saying, 'I have always encountered speculation from other people. If I had to bother about what other people speculated about, how would I get anything done?' (*South China Morning Post* 2015).

Senior Alibaba executives have repeatedly stated that the aim of the purchase was to provide a more positive view of China. For those working at the *Post*, the largest change has been in resourcing. The paper's new cash-rich owners have shown a willingness to bankroll its reinvention, lifting its paywall and publicly talking about a ten-year 'gestation period' before it returns to profitability. Staffers talk about 'staggering' expenditures, with a small army of new hires and a swanky new headquarters sprawling over six stories in pricy Causeway Bay, complete with two game rooms, a yoga studio and an in-house pub with its own IPA brew, memorably named the Post Hop.

The *SCMP* does still run critical reporting on China, yet within certain limits. 'There's a veneer of press freedom,' says one current employee, who complains that the digital revolution has made it easy to bury pieces that are critical of China. According to the employee, politically sensitive pieces are written and sometimes posted on the website, but often sink without a trace, 'They can splash on it for just ten minutes, and then they drop it. It nods to press freedom but there's no deep or meaningful commitment.' Another former contributor, Stephen Vines, described the paper's coverage as 'all smoke and mirrors.' In strongly worded public repudiation of the paper, Vines declared he would no longer write for an outlet he described as a 'willing participant in a grotesque propaganda ploy' (Vines 2018) serving the Chinese state.

This was a reference to the *SCMP*'s decision to publish a 'government-organized interview' with Gui Minhai while the bookseller was in a mainland Chinese detention facility flanked by security guards. 'This was an editorial decision that you might disagree with but we stand on our conviction that this was a story that needed to be reported,' said CEO Gary Liu, defending the decision to take part in what many saw as a coerced interview.[5] Although the paper was heavily criticized, Liu said the new details reported by the paper – including the presence of the guards – justified the article:

> I think that what we expect to see on state propaganda is statements presented as true-to-the-heart confessions. And that's not how the story was presented in the South China Morning Post. The story was just as much about the arrangement and the situation in which Gui Minhai made his first public statement in years.[6]

Under Chinese ownership, the *SCMP* has trodden a delicate line, running some critical coverage and original reporting on some sensitive subjects such as censorship and human rights lawyers, but increasingly amplifying Beijing's line on hot-button issues touching on China's territorial integrity, such as Hong Kong independence. Over the years, the paper's op-eds on such issues have increasingly echoed the CCP line, while it has slowly shed editorial writers and columnists with critical views of Beijing.

In recent years, the strategy of 'borrowing boats' has expanded into 'buying boats' outright or 'building boats' in partnership with local businessmen or governments. The variety of strategies taken across legacy media outlets, including using softer means – such as 103 Like FM's music channel – ultimately allow Chinese propaganda to hit new demographics, furthering their reach. Thus, the necessity of turning a profit is a driving imperative in finding and engaging new audiences, yet these money-making moves ultimately serve the Chinese state's aim of increasing its discourse power.

Technological innovation

China's growing flotilla of 'bought boats' and 'borrowed boats' must innovate to survive and thrive in the new media environment, and China-affiliated media outlets in the Asia-Pacific have shown a willingness to experiment with new digital products and delivery methods.

These include 'verticals,' or spin-off digital-only channels that supplement existing outlets, as well as apps that provide new functionality and brand new digital-only outlets. In some markets, China-affiliated outlets are at the leading edge of technological change. In 2018, there were also reports that Beijing was behind Russian-style disinformation campaigns in Taiwan, potentially signalling a new stage in its information warfare campaign.

In Hong Kong, the *South China Morning Post* has adopted slick Silicon-Valley-style digital-only products, including three separate 'verticals' or spin-off digital channels: Inkstone on China, Abacus on tech in China and a video-led pop culture channel called Goldthread. The aim is to reach young, new,

China-curious audiences, and the teams often use a data-driven approach, looking at analytics to decide whether stories will appeal to this readership. 'We're trying to reach global millennial readers,' says Inkstone's Chief Editor Juliana Liu, 'The way I think about whether we do a story, if somebody's on a Tinder date, does our reader want to impress their date by talking about a story they've read?' (Interview October 2018). The *SCMP* does not release numbers on its new products.

In Cambodia, a China-based group, NICE Culture Investment from Guangxi province, set up a joint venture with the Ministry of Internal Security in 2017, to run a television station – which cooperates with Chinese state media outlets – headquartered in the ministry itself (Freeman & Se 2018) (Vanderklippe 2017). The company has developed an app called Tutu Live, which allows viewers to Skype into programmes and broadcast themselves, a concept that a company official called 'social news' using the Ministry of Internal Security's police network (Boyle & Sun 2017).

Company executives have trumpeted the fact that NICE TV is on a modernization mission, with one executive telling the *Globe and Mail*, 'NICE can help Cambodian media by importing Chinese expertise in technology and live online streaming' (Vanderklippe 2017). Such comments have sparked fears that the Chinese company might leverage its partnership with the Ministry of Internal Security to help upgrade the country's surveillance and tracking technologies. But the television station has a clear geopolitical aim, according to the executive director of the Cambodia Centre for Independent Media, Pa Nguon Teang, who said, 'This television station aims to promote the good relationship between Cambodia and China' (Interview December 2018).

As Cambodia moves further into China's orbit, other recent entrants to the media market have shown similar pro-China sympathies. In 2016, Cambodian businessman Lim Chea Vutha set up an online news outlet called Fresh news, which uses China's state-run Xinhua for foreign news and sends its journalists on educational trips to China. Lim has been vocal in his support for Beijing, telling AFP, 'As a Cambodian citizen, I declare that I support China, I support Chinese investment in Cambodia' (Freeman & Se 2018). In 2018, he began a Mandarin language site. Pa Nguon Teang says the messaging is overt, as 'They try to show that the Chinese government is the best friend of Cambodia, and any news is directed to promoting this image.'

In recent years, Chinese state media outside China has also shown technological innovation by embracing Western social media outlets banned inside China. At the end of 2018, CGTN's English Facebook account counted 71 million followers – more than any other news outlet on Facebook, while four out of five of the fastest-growing Facebook media pages belong to Chinese state-run outlets including Xinhua, *Global Times*, CGTN and *People's Daily* (Cook 2018).

Another recent technological innovation was seen in Taiwan at the end of 2018, when Taiwanese officials blamed China for an aggressive social media disinformation campaign.

In the run-up to Taiwan's local elections, voters noticed an uptick in fake news stories on social media denigrating the independence-leaning Democratic Progressive Party (DPP) for trying to push Taiwan away from its Chinese roots, and praising the China-friendly Kuomintang (KMT) (Horton 2018a). The results were a rout for the DPP, while the KMT did better than expected (Horton 2018b).

'They are doing the kind of disinformation that the Russians are known for doing,' said Peter Mattis, a former CIA analyst, now at the Jamestown Foundation.[7] '[They] are not only sort of recruiting sources to push messages into the Taiwan information space but also creating sort of automatic content farms that are rebroadcasting and flooding Taiwanese social media with exaggerated stories.' Since 2003, 'media warfare' has been part of Beijing's military strategy, aimed at influencing public opinion – and foreign governments – into shaping the global conversation around China's strategic interests (Mattis 2018).

Building a Digital Silk Road

In the interests of shaping global conversations, Beijing is also reaching out to Asian journalists with the lure of generous fellowship and training schemes. Its active courtship of journalists has been centralised under the auspices of the China Public Diplomacy Association, which was set up under the Ministry of Foreign Affairs in 2012. It established three regional bodies, including the China Asia Pacific Press Centre, to conduct exchanges, symposiums and study tours to China, starting in 2014 (Yafoi 2018). Their targets are extraordinarily ambitious including the training of 1,000 African journalists a year by 2020 (Ministry of Foregin Affairs of the People's Republic of China 2015).

These schemes administer generous all-expenses-paid media fellowships, some of which are earmarked for recipients from countries participating in China's grand global infrastructure push, the Belt and Road Initiative. In 2018, it brought 44 journalists from Asia and Africa to China for ten months, 17 of whom were also studying for Masters' degrees at Renmin University of China. For ten months, these journalists study in China, travelling all over the country and doing internships at state-run news outlets. They also attend the annual parliamentary sessions, interview senior officials and have the option of studying classes on language, culture, politics and new media towards a Masters' degree in Communication at Renmin, one of the country's best universities.

One prize for those taking part in the scheme: top-level access to government officials, of the kind that is extremely rare for correspondents based in China. Journalists on this scheme – from India, Bangladesh, Pakistan and the Philippines, among others – have penned dispatches from China, although all have been written under controlled conditions, travelling with Chinese government minders, a fact which was not often mentioned as part of the story (Krishnan 2018). 'We were told that if we wanted to complete the fellowship,' one journalist is reported as saying, 'we should write positive stories' (Krishnan 2018).

One recipient was Filipino journalist Greggy Eugenio, who in a 2018 email described the programme as having opened 'my mind and heart on a lot of misconceptions I've known about China.' When asked what he had learned, he wrote, 'I've learned that a state-owned government media is one of the most effective means of journalism. The media in China is still working well and people here appreciate their work.'[8]

Similar schemes have been put in place to allow American and Australian journalists to visit China on sponsored schemes. The US programme is administered by the China US Exchange Foundation (CUSEF), an outlet funded by Hong Kong's former Chief Executive, Tung Chee-hwa, who is a vice-chairman of an advisory body called the Chinese People's Political Consultative Conference. It has taken 127 US journalists from 40 different outlets on all-expenses paid tours of China, while the Australia-China Relations Institute (ACRI) – run out of the University of Technology Sydney – has brought at least 28 Australian journalists to China (Lim & Bergin 2018).

Regulatory filings by a lobbyist, BLJ Worldwide, working for CUSEF show how it has tried to sway coverage of China inside the United States.[9] The lobbyist was paid US$20,000 a month to place an average of three articles per week in the US media, and it also cultivated what it called 'third-party supporters' who it helped research, write and place op-eds inside US media. Interestingly, BLJ's memo underlines that it cannot guarantee that the supporters will always speak positively about China, writing, 'Third-party supporters will more often than not speak constructively and with a strong understanding of China's perspective on the issues.' Such findings underline a nuanced understanding of how seemingly authentic voices – even if they are sometimes critical – can lend more currency than outright shills.[10]

In 2010, BLJ discussed introducing a 'strong counter-factual narrative' to counter criticism of Chinese actions in Tibet, after a study of US school textbooks. The lobbyist also helped organize journalist tours to China, and in mooting a tour to Tibet, it specifically suggested selecting 'participants chosen for effectiveness and opportunities for favourable coverage.[11]'

The effect of such sponsored tours on news coverage is hard to quantify. In the Australian context, many of the stories resulting from ACRI tours parrot Beijing's talking points, warning Canberra not to criticize Beijing's claims in the South China Sea and cautioning that Australian businesses will be left behind if Canberra does not take part in China's Belt and Road Initiative. One close observer, economist Stephen Joske, who met and briefed one of the tours, has described their reports as containing 'very, very one-sided information' which seeks to fill a vacuum in China coverage (Lim & Bergin 2018).

For news outlets struggling with diminishing advertising revenues, these schemes effectively offer free China coverage delivered by their own correspondents, who gain valuable Chinese-language training, cultural knowhow and high-level contacts. Such opportunities may seem like a no-brainer to cash-strapped news outlets, but participating in these programmes compromises press freedom since it allows Beijing to use economic sweeteners to effectively buy coverage in foreign newspapers, again turning them into 'borrowed boats.' In the long term, such schemes undermine the independence and neutrality of the media by allowing Beijing to groom a cadre of young journalists sympathetic to its policy positions and its views on how journalism should be conducted.

Another side benefit for Beijing is the capacity for this scheme to generate domestic propaganda. One prime example is a *China Daily* story entitled 'Visiting Journalists Give Glowing Report' (Daffae Senkpeni 2017) which marked the end of the 2017 media fellowship for 42 African and Asian journalists. The report outlines the programmes aims, with one Cameroonian journalist quoted as saying it was intended to 'counteract prejudice fuelled by persistent negative reporting' (Daffae 2017) on China. Another incentive, as spelled out by a senior Chinese official, is to familiarize the reporters with China's Belt and Road Initiative, and this aim is underlined by a Filipino journalist, Jelly Musico, who proclaims, 'Let this Belt and Road Initiative serve as a platform that will bind us together as we take off for a new era of media collaboration' (Daffae 2017). Another story, written by Musico himself for the *People's Daily Online*, aptly encapsulates the scheme's raison d'etre in its title, 'Foreign journalists lauded for promoting China's diplomatic achievements' (Musico 2017).

The formation of the Belt and Road News Alliance in 2017 formalizes this foreign policy goal by bringing together media from China, Hong Kong, Macau and around 20 other countries, including the Philippines, Mongolia, Romania and Ukraine. Its own publicity underlines that it should not just glorify the Belt and Road, but show its reality 'in order to appear trustable (sic) to the general audience and decision-makers' (OBOR Europe 2017). This again underlines a more nuanced approach towards influence projection, relying on authentic voices.

A further element of the Belt and Road project is the Digital Silk Road, under which private Chinese companies are working to upgrade digital telecommunications infrastructure around the world. This includes installing fibre-optic cables and data centres to carry information around the world, as well as launching television satellites and helping drive the switchover from analogue to digital television. Information from RWR Advisory Group, which is tracking Chinese activity overseas, shows that many of the 71 countries where China is installing fibre-optic internet cables are in Asia (Prasso 2019). Freedom House's Sarah Cook points out that building control over the nodes of information may be a bigger long-term threat than current attempts to limit content, saying 'It might not be necessarily clear as a threat now. But once you have got control over the nodes of information, you can use them as you want' (Interview August 2018).

Conclusion

Beijing is rolling out an audacious strategy to shape the global information environment in a way that serves Xi Jinping's dictates to 'tell China's story well.' This broad survey underlines how Beijing has taken advantage of its own deep pockets – and the vulnerability of cash-strapped international news outlets – to throw money at the problem variously through funding advertorial coverage, providing free state-sponsored content, sponsoring journalistic exchanges, embarking on joint co-productions and even acquiring foreign news outlets. Through such schemes, the scope and long-range ambition of Beijing's campaign – and its ability to exploit the vulnerabilities of the market-driven free press – can be clearly seen.

Though Beijing has shown its impatience in building its discourse power, in terms of content it is still falling short. Chinese authors, writing in the state-run media, have admitted that Beijing's turgid propaganda holds little attraction for Western audiences, and the restrictions imposed by censorship act as a drag on its media output. While the construction of discourse power is key for a rising power, Beijing's aggressive attempts to impose narrative discipline – and choke off critical voices – are a cause for concern.

In the Asia-Pacific region, China has paid more attention to co-opting Chinese-language media than providing material in local languages. This is illustrated by the fact that only a small handful of Asian newspapers – three at the last count – have struck deals to carry the China Watch supplement, yet there are 51 agreements providing Xinhua copy to local Chinese-language newspapers. The rapid expansion of Global CAMG's outlets also speaks to the importance placed on messaging to Chinese-language audiences in Asia and beyond.[12]

Such deals have a substantial impact on press freedom, since they ensure that Chinese-language media toe the party line and do not carry content that is critical of Beijing. In this way, Beijing is effectively neutering the Chinese-language media. Through aggressive intimidation campaigns, it is also actively targeting the financial resources of those Chinese-language outlets that still carry critical coverage with the aim of ensuring the uniformity of Chinese-language coverage across Asia.

In Asia as a whole, Chinese interests are increasingly playing a bigger role in the media industry, namely through an increasing number of acquisitions, joint ventures and co-production deals which allow Chinese state-run companies – or businessmen acting as their proxies – to exert more control over content. Such moves underline the sophistication of Beijing's approach. Its strategy is to harness the credibility of existing press outlets in countries with well-established authoritative media, while actively helping build new digital outlets in countries where press freedom – and democracy – are still marginal. The fact that Chinese media companies are helping to build new digital outlets in countries with young populations such as Vietnam and Cambodia – where the median age is respectively 30.5 and 25.3, according to Index Mundi (Mundi 2018a, 2018b) – shows the long-term nature of their ambitions.

Yet Beijing is not just investing in technological innovation in the region; it is also spending on media technologies that are widely viewed as outdated. In the Pacific, as many as ten shortwave frequencies abandoned by ABC Australia are now being used to broadcast CRI programmes. In this way, Beijing is adopting a full-court-press strategy, using whatever type of media is likely to reach audiences, no matter where they are. As Xi Jinping said, 'Wherever the readers are, wherever the viewers are, that is where propaganda reports must extend their tentacles, and that is where we find the focal point and end point of propaganda and ideology work' (Bandurski 2016).

One darker side of Beijing's strategy, seen in particular in Hong Kong and Taiwan, is the nascent use of Chinese state-run media and information warfare to interfere with local politics. The use of a social media disinformation campaign in Taiwan – and the increasing role of the state-run media as a channel disseminating fake news stories and targeting those perceived to be critics of Beijing – signals an increasing brazenness towards the use of media warfare tools. The lack of international condemnation may embolden Beijing to ramp up such tactics in the future.

Notes

1 The interview material comes from the author's own interviews and communications, carried out in 2018 and 2019. Some material was also used in a *Guardian* piece, written by the author and Julia Bergin, and entitled 'Inside China's Audacious Global Propaganda Campaign,' published 7 December 2018.
2 Phone interview conducted in August 2018.
3 Information from database of material compiled by author and Julia Bergin.
4 Information from database of material compiled by author and Julia Bergin.
5 Skype interview conducted in October 2018.
6 Skype interview as above, conducted in October 2018.
7 Interview conducted in November 2018.
8 Facebook messenger interview conducted in October 2018.
9 Regulatory filings are available by searching the Foreign Agents Registration Act website at https://www.fara.gov/efile.html
10 Internal memos acquired during the course of author's research into BLJ.
11 Information from FARA filing available here. Available HTTP: <https://efile.fara.gov/docs/5875-Exhibit-AB-20100803-10.pdf>
12 Information from databases of material compiled by author and Julia Bergin, as well as Emily Feng at the Financial Times.

Works cited

AFP. (2018) 'Beijing linked to tailing in HK, fears academic', *RTHK*. Online. Available HTTP: <https://news.rthk.hk/rthk/en/component/k2/1434259-20181220.htm?spTab Changeable=0> (accessed 5 March 2019).

Bandurski, D. (2016) 'How Xi Jinping views the news', *China Media Project*. Online. Available HTTP: <https://medium.com/china-media-project/how-the-president-views-the-news-2bee482e1d48> (accessed 10 March 2019).

Boyle, D & Sun, N (2017), *Cambodia's Nice New Tv Channel from China*, Voice of America, 13 January 2019. Available HTTP: <https://www.voanews.com/a/cambodia-nice-new-tv-channel-from-china/4354124.html>.

Brady, A.M. (2018) 'New Zealand and the CCP'S "magic weapons"', *Journal of Democracy*, 29: 68–75.

Chan, T.F. (2018) *A Chilling Story about Chinese Pressure in Australia shows How Far Beijing Will Reach to Silence Critics*. Online. Available HTTP: <www.businessinsider.com.au/chinese-influence-in-australia-media-2018-5> (accessed 10 March 2019).

Cheng, K. (2018a) 'Pro-Beijing newspaper reporter accused of infiltrating election team of democrat Lee Cheuk-yan', *Hong Kong Free Press*. Online. Available HTTP: <www.hongkongfp.com/2018/11/22/pro-beijing-newspaper-reporter-accused-infiltrating-election-team-democrat-lee-cheuk-yan/> (accessed 10 March 2019).

Cheng, K. (2018b) 'UK consulate demands local pro-Beijing newspaper retract 'factually inaccurate and misleading' report', *Hong Kong Free Press*. Online. Available HTTP: <www.hongkongfp.com/2018/10/16/uk-consulate-demands-local-pro-beijing-newspaper-retract-factually-inaccurate-misleading-report/> (accessed 10 March 2019).

Chung, K. (2018) 'Pro-Beijing newspaper accused of running illegal election ad', *South China Morning Post*. Online. Available HTTP: <www.scmp.com/news/hong-kong/politics/article/2175295/pro-beijing-newspaper-accused-running-illegal-election-ad> (accessed 16 March 2019).

Cook, S. (2018) *The Globalisation of China's Media Controls: Key Trends from 2018*. Online. Available HTTP: <https://thediplomat.com/2018/12/the-globalization-of-chinas-media-controls-key-trends-from-2018/> (accessed 5 March 2019).

CRP (2019), *China Daily of Beijing*, Center for Responsive Politics, viewed 25 August 2019. Available HTTP: <https://www.opensecrets.org/fara/foreign-principals/G2435>.

Daffae, S.A. (2017) 'Visiting journalists give glowing report', *China Daily Africa*. Online. Available HTTP: <http://africa.chinadaily.com.cn/weekly/2017-12/08/content_35257660.htm> (accessed 5 March 2019).

Diamond, L.O. (ed.). (2018) 'Chinese influence and American interests: Promoting constructive vigilance', *Hoover Institution*. Online. Available HTTP: <www.hoover.org/research/chinese-influence-american-interests-promoting-constructive-vigilance> (accessed 10 March 2019).

Feng, E. (2018) 'China and the world: How Beijing spreads its message', *The Financial Times*. Online. Available HTTP: <www.ft.com/content/f5d00a86-3296-11e8-b5bf-23cb17fd1498> (accessed 10 March 2019).

Freeman, J. and Se, S. (2018) 'With Cambodia's Once-Robust Free Press Under Fire, the "China Model" Makes Inroads', 3 June 2018. Available HTTP: <https://www.hongkongfp.com/2018/06/03/cambodias-robust-press-freedom-fire-china-model-makes-inroads/>.

Hazlewood, J. (2016) 'China spends big on propaganda in UK, but returns are low', *Hong Kong Free Press*. Online. Available HTTP: <www.hongkongfp.com/2016/04/03/china-spends-big-on-propaganda-in-britain-but-returns-are-low/> (accessed 3 March 2019).

Hu, Z., Ji, D. and Gong, Y. (2018) 'From the Outside In; CCTV Going Global in A New World Communication Order', in Thussu, D., Burgh, H., Shi, A. and ProQuest (eds.), *China's Media Go Global*, New York: Routledge, 1st edn, pp. 67–78.

Mundi, I. (2018a) *Cambodia Median Age*, viewed 25 August 2019. Available HTTP: <https://www.indexmundi.com/cambodia/median_age.html>.

———. (2018b) *Vietnam Median Age*, viewed 25 August 2019. Available HTTP: <https://www.indexmundi.com/vietnam/median_age.html>.

Koh, G. and Shiffman, J. (2015) 'Beijing's covert network airs China-friendly news across Washington, and the world', *Reuters*. Online. Available HTTP: <www.reuters.com/investigates/special-report/china-radio/> (accessed 3 March 2019).

Krishnan, A. (2018) 'China is buying good press across the world, one paid journalist at a time', *The Print*. Online. Available HTTP: <https://theprint.in/opinion/china-is-

paying-foreign-journalists-including-from-india-to-report-from-beijing/154013/> (accessed 3 March 2019).

Kuo, H. (2018) 'The "going out" of China Radio International', in D. Thussu, H. Burgh and A. Shi (eds.) *China's Media Go Global*, London and New York: Routledge.

Lim, L. and Bergin, J. (2018) 'Inside China's audacious global propaganda campaign', *The Guardian*. Online. Available HTTP: <www.theguardian.com/news/2018/dec/07/china-plan-for-global-media-dominance-propaganda-xi-jinping> (accessed 10 March 2019).

Lim, L. and Smith, G. (2016) *The Little Red Podcast*, Australia. Online. Available HTTP: <https://omny.fm/shows/the-little-red-podcast/control-and-capture-taming-overseas-chinese-media?in_playlist=the-little-red-podcast!podcast> (accessed 10 March 2019).

Liu, Q. (2014) 'Big push for Chinese culture to go out into the world (Dali tuidong zhonghua wenhua zouxiang shijie)', *Guangming Ribao*. Online. Available HTTP: <http://epaper.gmw.cn/gmrb/html/2014-05/22/nw.D110000gmrb_20140522_1-03.htm> (accessed 10 March 2019).

Malaysiakini (2019), 'PKR rep slams pro-Beijing Daily for its "imaginative" reporting', *Malaysiakini*, viewed 25 August 2019. Available HTTP: <https://www.malaysiakini.com/news/460385>.

Marsh, V. (2018) 'Tiangao or Tianxia? The ambiguities of CCTV's English language news for Africa', in D. Thussu, H. Burgh, A. Shi, and ProQuest (eds.) *China's Media Go Global*, New York: Routledge.

Mattis, P. (2018) 'China's "three warfares" in perspective', *War on the Rocks*. Online. Available HTTP: <https://warontherocks.com/2018/01/chinas-three-warfares-perspective/> (accessed 16 March 2019).

Ministry of Foreign Affairs of the People's Republic of China. (2015) *The Forum on China-Africa Cooperation Johannesburg Action Plan (2016–2018)*. Online. Available HTTP: <www.fmprc.gov.cn/mfa_eng/zxxx_662805/t1323159.shtml> (accessed 10 March 2019).

Musico, J. (2017) 'Foreign journalists lauded for promoting China's diplomatic achievements', *People's Daily Online*. Online. Available HTTP: <http://en.people.cn/n3/2017/1211/c90000-9302897.html> (accessed 16 March 2019).

Ng, E. (2016) 'Ta Kung Pao reporter arrested for fighting with localist Edward Leung in MTR station', *Hong Kong Free Press*. Online. Available HTTP: <www.hongkongfp.com/2016/12/21/ta-kung-pao-reporter-arrested-fighting-localist-edward-leung-mtr-station/> (accessed 1 March 2019).

OBOR Europe. (2017) 'The belt and road news alliance'. Online. Available HTTP: <www.oboreurope.com/en/belt-road-news-alliance/> (accessed 6 March 2019).

Pan, D. (2018) 'China needs to catch up in discourse power', *Global Times*. Online. Available HTTP: <www.globaltimes.cn/content/1115274.shtml> (accessed 6 March 2019).

Pepper, S. (2018) 'One more blow tips the balance: How Hong Kong's democrats were defeated again in Kowloon West', *Hong Kong Free Press*. Online. Available HTTP: <www.hongkongfp.com/2018/12/01/one-blow-tips-balance-hong-kongs-democrats-defeated-kowloon-west/> (accessed 16 March 2019).

Pomfret, J. and Lee, Y. (2019) 'Activists in Hong Kong and Taiwan feel heat as China fears "separatist" collusion'. Online. Available HTTP: <www.reuters.com/article/taiwan-china-hongkong/feature-activists-in-hong-kong-and-taiwan-feel-heat-as-china-fears-separatist-collusion-idUSL3N2122W5> (accessed 13 March 2019).

Prasso, S. (2019) 'China's digital silk road is looking more like an iron curtain', *Bloomberg Businessweek*. Online. Available HTTP: <www.bloomberg.com/news/features/2019-01-10/china-s-digital-silk-road-is-looking-more-like-an-iron-curtain> (accessed 10 March 2019).

Shepherd, T. (2018) 'Chinese spies likely to target Adelaide as it becomes defence and space centre', *The Adelaide Advertiser,* 16.12.18.

Smith, G. (2018) 'See the difference; CGTN's Australian gambit', *The Interpreter.* Online. Available HTTP: <www.lowyinstitute.org/the-interpreter/see-difference-cgtn-aus tralian-gambit> (accessed 10 March 2019).

South China Morning Post. (2015) 'Trust us, says Jack Ma, when asked about editorial independence'. Online. Available HTTP: <www.scmp.com/news/hong-kong/article/1892251/trust-us-says-jack-ma-when-asked-about-scmp-editorial-independence> (accessed 10 March 2019).

Stone, C. (2018) 'World needs a better understanding of China, "Voice of China" can help', *People's Daily Online.* Online. Available HTTP: <http://en.people.cn/n3/2018/0322/c90000-9440715.html> (accessed 10 March 2019).

Suchiva, N. (2016) 'One channel taps Lazada, like 103 fm', *Bangkok Post.* Online. Available HTTP: <www.bangkokpost.com/business/news/1148605/one-channel-taps-lazada-like-103-fm> (accessed 5 March 2019).

Thongtep, W. (2011) 'Media JV gears up for expansion', *The Nation.* Online. Available HTTP: <www.nationmultimedia.com/home/Media-JV-gears-up-for-expansion-30164673.html> (accessed 10 March 2019).

Thussu, D., Burgh, H., Shi, A., and ProQuest. (2018) *China's Media Go Global,* London and New York: Routledge.

Vanderklippe, N. (2017) 'In Cambodia, independent media close as Chinese content moves in', *The Globe and Mail.* Online. Available HTTP: <www.theglobeandmail.com/news/world/in-cambodia-independent-media-have-closed-as-chinese-content-moves-in/article37464168/> (accessed 10 March 2019).

Vines, S. (2018) 'Why I will no longer write for the South China Morning Post', *Hong Kong Free Press.* Online. Available HTTP: <www.hongkongfp.com/2018/11/13/i-will-no-longer-write-south-china-morning-post/> (accessed 10 March 2019).

VOV.VN. (2018) 'Guangxi radio station partner for TV programmes', *Voice of Vietnam.* Online. Available HTTP: <https://english.vov.vn/society/vov-guangxi-radio-station-partner-for-tv-programmes-371017.vov> (accessed 10 March 2019)(Wu & Chen 2009)

Xiao, Y.S. (2018) 'Soft power and the strategic context for China's "Media going global" policy', in Thussu, D., Burgh, H. and Shi, A. (eds.), *China's Media Go Global,* London: Routledge.

Yafoi, M. (2018) 'Journos in China for media exchange program', *The Post-Courier.* Online. Available HTTP: <https://postcourier.com.pg/journos-china-media-exchange-program/> (accessed 6 March 2019).

Zhang, Y. (2018) 'Australian independence advocate spreading independence in Hong Kong', *Wenweipo.* Online. Available HTTP: <http://news.wenweipo.com/2018/12/17/IN1812170001.htm?fbclid=IwAR3f6-74f_bjY72Q8pfr18EsdS0YNTI6mDIvc-yhiqaWcyNYVMYxmHDle20> (accessed 10 March 2019).

5

PRESS FREEDOM IN CHINA UNDER XI JINPING

David Moser

Introduction

In the decades of social and economic change during the post-Deng era, the Chinese Communist Party's view of the press and its role has been a conflicted one. Years of relative openness have alternated with periods of renewed restrictions and crackdowns, especially at times of leadership transition or political struggles within the Party. This cycle of contraction (*shou* 收) and relaxation (*fang* 放) came to be regarded as a normal dynamic between the press and the Party, though the rise of the internet in the first years of the twenty-first century brought fundamental changes that seemed to hold the promise of an era of greater liberalization. (For a summary of this history, see Kalathil 2003). However, there is now a general agreement among China media observers that the current state of press freedom in China is the worst it has been in decades, and in particular that it has seen an unprecedented erosion in the years since Xi Jinping's rise to power in 2012.

In 2018, for the fourth year in a row, China was ranked near the bottom of the World Press Freedom Index at number 176, followed only by Syria, Turkmenistan, Eritrea and North Korea (Reporters without Borders 2018a). China is also now the country with the highest incarceration rate for journalists, with 47 reporters behind bars as of 2018 (Beiser 2018). It is also reported that the Chinese government maintains a blacklist of journalists who have conducted 'illegal reporting,' the penalties for which include revoking press credentials and restrictions on future employment (PEN America 2018).

Since Xi Jinping took office, the government has coordinated a wave of new and disturbing assaults on free expression in academia, the mass media, social media and on other news outlets. Some of these attacks have extended beyond the measures taken by Xi's predecessors, Jiang Zemin and Hu Jintao, and to many observers seem to harken back to the kind of totalistic information control system of the Mao era. Some of these developments include:

- An intensification and expansion of ideological requirements for news reportage, including an increasing number of bans on certain topics, strict adherence to Party propaganda and messaging, and increasing demands for a full-throated championing and support for the Party leadership in thought and action (Brady 2017).
- New mandatory requirements for reporters to be trained in 'Marxist journalism,' indoctrination in journalistic standards for guiding public opinion on Party leadership and policies, and strictly enforced limits and harsh punishments for un-sanctioned investigative reporting (Brady 2017).
- A rapid shutting down of independent online journalism and non-state news outlets through regulatory pressure and restrictive and burdensome regulatory requirements that render the business model for independent news outlets unsustainable (Dasgupta 2016a, 2016b).
- A long-term plan to centralize the dissemination of all news content into a single comprehensive information 'hub,' conceptualized as a 'Central Kitchen' that will 'serve' news content for distribution among all the various internet, social media and traditional media outlets (Bandurski 2019).
- An exodus of professional salaried journalists, as smaller outlets struggle to keep up in the regulatory environment, and serious reporters are increasingly subject to fines, harassment, demotion or detention when attempting to report on sensitive topics (*The Economist* 2019).

In order to better understand the extent of this radical overhaul of the Chinese press system under Xi, it is helpful to first retrace the trajectory of China's repression of press freedom over the past three decades.

Brief historical context

In the 1990s, as China's news outlets began to diversify amid new market forces, a form of investigative reporting began to gain a foothold, referred to as *yulun jiandu* 舆论监督, literally 'public opinion supervision,' a kind of 'watchdog journalism' that was often tolerated by the Party as a check on rampant official corruption. Such journalism tended to attract a large readership, and during this era commercial newspapers saw massive growth, while readership of official Party and state news outlets declined sharply (Qian and Bandurski 2011).

As this trend continued in the 1990s, the government cut spending for official state news outlets, closed down unprofitable newspapers and reduced subsidies. Though important Party newspapers like *People's Daily* and Xinhua news agency continued to be funded, a large number of smaller official media outlets found themselves increasingly without state subsidies and were forced to look elsewhere for revenue. There emerged commercially oriented publications like

Caijing, under iconoclastic chief editor Hu Shuli, and muckraking newspapers such as *Southern Weekend,* which tended to push the limits of safe reporting, resulting in a viable (if intermittently cracked down on) 'Fourth Estate.' Due to the complicated and often ambiguous regulatory environment, professional state journalists were able to push back against the usual press controls, providing in-depth coverage of sensitive issues such as the illegal blood selling that led to an AIDS epidemic in China's Henan province (Bandurski and Hala 2010).

Broadcast media also saw a modest golden age of investigative journalism programming in the 1990s. CCTV offered weekly shows such as Oriental Horizons (*Dongfang shikong* 东方时空) and Focus (*Jiaodian fangtan* 焦点访谈), which featured hard-hitting (if highly selective) exposés of official corruption, shoddy consumer products and police overreach, garnering high ratings and popularity with the public. The overt intent of many of these shows was to reassure audiences that the Party was effectively doing its job in exposing corruption.

The rise of the internet in the late 1990s and early 2000s was a very consequential period in the battle for press freedom. In recent decades, China – unlike many authoritarian countries, such as North Korea – has actually accepted and promoted the digital revolution and internet media, understanding these to be essential components of a modern knowledge economy. Yet, the advent of the internet has posed an ongoing series of challenges to the Party's information control project, resulting in a cat-and-mouse game such that the ingenuity and dedication of internet-savvy citizens has forced the Party to continually upgrade and expand its censorship system. The rise of social media, in particular Sina's microblogging site Weibo, produced a tsunami of raw, unchecked information, as a new wave of independent bloggers began posting leaked information and rumours about instances of official corruption, as well as unvarnished political commentary. Many veteran mainstream Chinese journalists began to contribute content to the new medium, freed from the restraints of state supervision.

The relative anonymity of blogging gave rise to the online phenomenon of *renrou sousuo* 人肉搜索, 'human flesh search engines,' the term for informal bands of muckraking netizens who scour the internet for evidence of misbehaviour on the part of the rich and powerful, and then pool the information among fellow bloggers, posting scandalous videos of corrupt officials or obnoxious celebrities, all of which would go viral before the Party censors could react to them. Under President Xi, 'Great Firewall' internet surveillance is now carried out on an industrial scale, with at least 2 million government censors kept busy scrubbing offensive content, or one censor for every 375 internet users, not counting the tens of thousands of in-house censors employed by social media companies such as Tencent (Reporters without Borders 2018b).

During the two decades after Reform and Opening Up, the Party adhered to its Leninist ideology and continued to supervise the press in order to guide public opinion, but for much of that time, the top priority of the leaders was economic development. This conflict between control and commercialization resulted in a conflicted information environment that was tightly controlled, yet also allowed a relatively open space for principled journalists to work.

Despite uneven development, it is fair to say that during the last 20 years, the overall trajectory of the Chinese media sector has been toward expansion, commercialization and occasional periods of liberalization. China's alternating cycles of tension and relaxation have been the norm in the Party's approach to the media, and when Xi Jinping took power in 2012, it's fair to say that most China media watchers cautiously predicted that this trend would continue.

Deterioration of press freedoms under Xi Jinping

In the seven years Xi has been in power, all print, broadcast and online forms of news media have been besieged with unprecedented regulatory and content restrictions. The government has systematically identified and rooted out media sources that had survived years of tightening and crackdowns, and Xi has moved with astonishing speed to gain control over China's internet of 800 million users (McCarthy 2018). In my opinion, no Chinese president has been so successful in moulding all news outlets into a unified and rigidly scripted mouthpiece for Party propaganda. Here I will present a brief overview of some of the strategies Xi has applied to achieve this goal.

Intensification of the propaganda function of state media

Defying market forces and trends of internet diversification, Xi began his administration with a series of bold measures to compel strict ideological compliance from the news media. From the outset, Xi struck a very different tone than his predecessors, unambiguously sending out a chilling signal that dissent, independent reporting, and even the slightest deviation from Party orthodoxy would not be tolerated. In a speech on 19 August 2013, Xi put forth his standards for a more ideologically assertive media. Domestic media outlets were told to avoid negative reporting, to promote 'positive energy' (*zheng nengliang* 正能量), to emphasize 'the great struggle and the exciting life of the people,' and to feature stories of 'exemplary people and deeds' (Teon 2019).

Xi brought back with a vengeance the rhetoric of steadfast Party loyalty that had been somewhat deemphasized under his predecessors Jiang Zemin and Hu Jintao:

> We must unwaveringly persist in the principle that the Party manages the media, persist in politicians running newspapers, periodicals, stations and news websites, and strengthen education on the Marxist view of news. Propaganda and ideology workers must strengthen their Party mentality, and do their duty in serving the undertaking of the Party and the people. They must conform to the demands of the Party in what they persist in, what they oppose, what they say and what they do
>
> *(Xi, quoted in Creemers 2014).*

The broad outlines provided in the speech were soon fleshed out with specific targets. In April 2013 there surfaced an internal Party directive, later referred to as 'Document 9,' in which the Party was urged to guard against seven political taboo topics – the 'Seven Don't Mentions' (*qi bu jiang* 七不讲) – which included constitutionalism, civil society, historical 'nihilism,' 'universal values' and the promotion of 'the West's view of media.' The text also exhorted Party members to strengthen resistance against the 'infiltration of outside ideas,' and to increase commitment to 'work in the ideological sphere' (ChinaFile 2013).

All mentions of the document on Weibo were censored, and in April 2015, investigative journalist Gao Yu was sentenced to seven years in prison for 'leaking state secrets,' allegedly having sent the text of Document 9 to a Chinese news outlet. The arrest was a harbinger of a subsequent harsh crackdown against news outlets, outspoken academics, and well-known social critics (Moore 2014).

In late 2015, one year before he was anointed as 'the core of the Party,' Xi Jinping warned newsmakers to strictly guard against news analysis that involved 'improper criticism of the central Party' (*wangyi zhongyang* 妄议中央), a phrase that was quickly added to the Party's updated Disciplinary Regulations. The declaration effectively put a permanent damper on any objective political news analysis of Party policies and methods. All reporting on Party actions were henceforth to be described and reported strictly according to the official Party framing and phraseology (*The Guardian* 2016).

The ideological push culminated in February 2016, as Xi made a high-profile inspection tour of China Central Television (CCTV) and other state-run media outlets. Photos showed Xi sitting at an anchor's desk, amid fawning reporters and editors, as he announced that all state media must pledge absolute loyalty to the Party, must continue to obey the leadership in thought, politics and action, and 'must take the Party as their surname,' (*bixu xing dang* 必须姓党), i.e., 'maintain a familial devotion to the Party' (*The Guardian* 2016). 'All the work by the party's media must reflect the party's will, safeguard the party's authority, and safeguard the party's unity,' Xi said. 'They must love the party, protect the party, and closely align themselves with the party leadership in thought, politics and action' (*The Guardian* 2016).

It should be noted that Xi's sharp ideological rhetoric did not, strictly speaking, represent a redefining of the state news media's role. State orthodoxy has always characterized the media as the 'throat and tongue of the Party' (*dang de houshe* 党的喉舌). However, Xi's highly ritualistic appearance and pronouncements, made in classic Chairman Mao style, signalled to the world that the CCP was finally going to get serious about realizing the unfinished task of expunging any vestiges of media objectivity or independence, reversing the decades-long trend of gradual (if uneven) liberalization.

The push for total unity and focus on Xi as the 'core of the Party' had immediate effects. Chinese news organizations, including formerly adventurous commercially outlets, acquiesced to the new marching orders. The *People's Daily*, already the official Party mouthpiece, quickly became a sycophantic advertisement for Xi's new cult of personality. On one day in December, Xi's name appeared in 11 of the 12 headlines on the front page, a glorification of a leader not seen since the Mao era (Sonmez 2015).

Reporters required to practice 'Marxist journalism'

The journalistic new normal involves total political indoctrination of China's media professionals. As of 2013, all Chinese journalists are required to undergo extensive ideological training, and must take an examination on 'socialism with Chinese characteristics' and 'Marxist journalism theory' in order to have their press credentials renewed (Brady 2017).

In that year, state media began to promulgate this notion of Marxist journalism at all levels and formats. The message was aimed at the foreign press and a foreign media audience, as Xi's propaganda strove to present to the world an alternate view of the role of journalism. Press outlets were schooled in alternative narratives to challenge perceived negative bias in Western reportage on China. Press outlets were exhorted to 'tell the China story' to 'take back the international discourse,' and to vigorously challenge the supposedly Western notion of 'universal values' (*pushi jiazhi* 普世价值), insisting that the notion of 'human rights' was a relativistic standard that each nation defined according to its own national conditions.

In a series entitled 'My Life in China' (*Wode shenghuo, wode Zhongguo* 我的生活, 我的中国), several segments under the subheading 'I am a reporter' featured interviews with professional journalists from outlets such as the *Global Times*. In episode 5, entitled 'I don't want that free media,' one of the reporters waxes philosophically about the news media's role in supporting the Party:

> A kite is only beautiful when it is attached to a string. It flies freely in the sky. But once you cut the string, the kite will fall to the ground. The same applies to journalism. Journalism is attached to its share of social responsibilities; that is, to guide public discourse towards a positive and constructive outlook. It has to be in line with the fundamental interests of the nation and its people. Western media is not free.
>
> *(Guan Video 2017)*

In a reversal of the previous practice of avoiding the topics of free speech and an independent press altogether, Xi is now engaged in an unapologetic, full-throated defence of the China model of a news media tightly tethered to the Party and its goals.

The suppression of independent journalism

The advent of social media gave rise to an explosion of independent news outlets and citizen journalism that became a supervisory nightmare for the Party. After a deadly train crash in Wenzhou in 2011, raw news about the crash appeared minutes after the event, followed by intense speculation about the quality of the hastily constructed infrastructure and the possibility of official corruption as the cause. All this information was posted and reposted millions of times in the space of few hours before the government had time to react (Makinen 2016).

A particularly threatening social media phenomenon was the appearance of so-called 'Big V's,' celebrity bloggers who attracted tens of millions of loyal readers. Protected by their status and visibility, such bloggers could post breaking news from both domestic and foreign sources with relative impunity. One such Big V was property mogul Pan Shiyi, who had amassed more than 1.6 million followers on his blog. Responding to the worsening air pollution in China at the time, Pan began to publish information available from the US Embassy about the pollution index readings for major Chinese cities, specifically the daily levels for dangerous atmospheric particulate matter (PM2.5), information which at the time was considered a state secret. The facts about this health threat, spread by Pan's followers, soon consumed public discourse, and the revelation had the positive effect one would expect from a healthy free press: in January 2012 the Beijing government began to regularly publish the PM2.5 levels, and Chinese citizens now receive air quality reports as part of the daily weather forecasts (Cheung 2013).

In order to discourage the activity of these celebrity bloggers, the government first employed a crude intimidation technique, referred to in Chinese as 'Killing a chicken to scare the monkeys.' The 'chicken' in this case was Charles Xue, a popular Chinese-American businessman whose posts criticizing the government had attracted 12 million followers to his Weibo account. In August 2015, Xue was arrested for supposedly soliciting prostitutes, the arrest being broadcast widely on state television. Later in September, he appeared again on CCTV, sitting in his detention cell dressed in orange prison garb and confessing on camera that his enormous number of followers had inflated his ego and made him feel 'like an emperor.' In the space of the next few months, the Big V phenomenon disappeared as most of the high-profile bloggers went silent and sold off their accounts (Freedom House 2013).

The rogue reporting of the Big Vs was thus a thing of the past, but the Weibo platform itself continued to produce a stupendous amount of citizen journalism and netizen gossip. Government internet supervisors realized that this form of citizen watchdog journalism was the result of the hair-trigger 'viral' potential of social media. To address the problem, in September 2013, China's Supreme People's Court issued a legal interpretation on prosecution of internet-speech-related crimes. The ruling stipulated that bloggers would be subject to arrest and detention if any rumour posted online was forwarded more than 500 times or viewed more than 5,000 times. This intimidating warning had the inevitable effect of massively discouraging viral repostings on social media altogether. Dozens of high-profile blogger-journalists were arrested after the edict was issued (Brady 2017).

Another reason for the directives mandating that news outlets use only 'official sources' in their reporting was that at the time, even state-owned media were citing social media accounts for breaking stories (Dasgupta 2016a). In 2016, the Cyberspace Administration of China had responded to this by issuing the 'Circular on Further Strengthening Management and Suppression of False News,' a new regulation making it illegal for journalists to publish unverified reports from social media (Dasgupta 2016b). The regulation blocked a once-promising path for social media and mainstream journalism to share news resources. The ruling also meant that independent journalists that cite news stories from social media now risked fines or detention.

In May 2017, the CAC released an updated and expanded set of 'Chinese Internet News Information Service Management Regulations,' which extended the ban on unofficial news to cover all forms of internet information, including online media, blogs, and even instant messaging (Cyberspace Administration of China 2017). This expansion constituted a de facto prohibition against using social media to report on natural disasters, protests, scandals or any current event that the Party might consider sensitive (PEN America 2017). The effect on social media sites was chilling. Companies were hit with penalties, or were shut down. Social media platforms such as Weibo cancelled dozens of unofficial news accounts, and in 2018, over 3,000 websites were shut down or had their licences revoked (Freedom House 2018).

To continue to operate legally, many social media platforms had to employ more in-house censors, and were forced to devote company resources to cooperate with state internet supervisors. This represented another blow to the survival of independent media, since the new regulations effectively increased the actual operational costs of running an internet company in China (Freedom House 2017). Using this and other legal strategies, the media regulatory system has succeeded in largely clearing the internet of independent online news and of citizen journalism, for the ultimate goal of rendering their control over social media as complete as their control over print media. In addition, with the decline of print publications, journalism has largely migrated to cyberspace, and thus now falls under the jurisdiction of the Cyberspace Administration of China. The Party rationale for internet censorship is now conceptually merged with the interests of cybersecurity, and as such is also conflated with the concept of national security, making internet speech violations subject to much stricter penalties.

Centralization of the online news information system

The fading of traditional print media has provided the Party the opportunity to recreate the state media apparatus in digital form, restructuring the network of various propaganda outlets to maximize content production, monitoring and supervision. In 2016, the government announced a radical new media convergence plan to unify the fragmented set of media propaganda sources. Referred to in Chinese as the 'Central Kitchen' (*zhongyang chufang* 中央厨房), the plan is for the centralized production resource to 'cook up' the news to be served to the various media branches for consumption – with no other 'kitchens' or independent 'cooks' allowed (Bandurski 2019).

After three years of development, the central hub, located at the headquarters of the *People's Daily*, had its official launch in February 2019. The importance of the occasion could be gauged from the fact that all seven members of the politburo standing committee, including Premier Li Keqiang, visited the *People's Daily* office on that day.

The various Party outlets currently promulgated in digital form – online versions of newspapers and magazines, and website video/audio versions of state television and radio programmes – are now able to receive ready-made digital videos, photos and texts that can be shared across all internet distribution channels.

As the Party's 19th National Congress convened in Beijing in February 2019, the media hub's first product, a slickly produced propaganda video, went viral on social media. The animation presents a thumbnail history of the Communist Party, and the economic miracle of China's rise to the world's second largest economy, all accompanied by a techno-beat soundtrack (Liao 2017). This video attracted considerable ridicule overseas as a particularly cringeworthy example of propaganda.

Xi has also moved to consolidate China's broadcast media in similar fashion. In March 2018, the state media announced the merger of China Central Television (CCTV), China Radio International and China National Radio under a single network to be called Voice of China (Kuo 2018). This move not only enables the sharing of resources, but also allows the totality of broadcast media to speak with one voice during critical news junctures. The Xinhua news agency reported that the goal of the merger was to 'guide hot social issues, strengthen and improve public opinion, push multimedia integration, strengthen international communication and tell good China stories' (The Paper 2018).

Fake news with Chinese characteristics

In the Chinese context, the term 'rumours' has some semantic overlap with the relatively new Western concept of fake news, and many press crackdowns and arrests are justified on charges of spreading rumours. False or misleading news appears all the time, of course, but ironically, it turns out the Party itself might be the biggest purveyor of fake news.

Struggling to control the sheer amount of social media, the Party censorship apparatus seems to have arrived at a solution that, after the 2016 election of US President Donald Trump, is now familiar to us; namely, injecting torrents of bogus social media opinion into the system to cloud or obscure damaging genuine news. For many years, the censorship apparatus has made use of what has been called the 'Fifty-Cent Party,' a group of youth netizens recruited by the government to insert fake postings that praise the Party, or cast doubt on news reports damaging to the leadership. The name comes from the fact that such internet commentators are rumoured to be paid 50 cents (5 *mao*, or about US$0.08) for each comment they are able to successfully post. Though it is very difficult to assess the actual number of 50-cent party commentators active at any time, scholars King, Pan, and Roberts (2017), who have undertaken an exhaustive study of this phenomenon, estimate that every year there are on the order of 448 million fake posts planted on the Chinese internet.

Commercial pressures on journalists

The Chinese traditional media are under the same economic pressures as the news media elsewhere in the world, as advertising revenue has dried up due to the impact of information-communication technology. The accelerated commercialization of the media since the end of the last century has put a double burden on media companies, which have had to both tow the Party line and satisfy the bottom line.

The result has been an exodus of full-time professional journalists. Many have given up on journalism as a full-time vocation, and now approach it as a hobby. Parents are discouraging children from going into journalism not only because of low income, but out of fear for their safety. Despite the enormous profitability of many media outlets, journalist salaries have fallen dramatically in recent years. A 2016 national survey of Chinese journalists revealed that 80 per cent earned below 10,000 *yuan* a year, which is less than twice the average monthly wage in Chinese cities – a dismally small amount for the university-educated, urban professionals who tend to apply for journalist positions (Announcer and Anchor Arts Network 2016).

Newspaper advertising revenues have also suffered, dropping by 75 per cent between 2012 and 2016. Part of the problem is that the Party's increasing restrictions on investigative reporting into official corruption have negatively impacted the bottom line of many newspapers. Commercial papers such as *Southern Daily* in Guangdong province were at their most profitable and prestigious when they could attack lowly officials, if not the 'tigers' at the top level. Investigative journalism sells newspapers – fawning praise of the Party does not. Meanwhile, staid outlets such as *People's Daily* have upgraded and gone digital with high-tech apps, making the product at least superficially more attractive (*The Economist* 2019).

Another downside is that, with the maverick social media news taken down, the salaried journalists from official state media can be controlled by other means, including suspension, sacking, withdrawing press accreditation and preventing reporters from travelling to sensitive areas.

News stories are micromanaged through directives from the Central Propaganda Department

One of the most important aspects of information control in China is properly framing the message, a requirement referred to in Chinese as *tifa* 提法 (literally, 'the way of mentioning'). This means that very often a news story is not censored outright, but the information is massaged in such a way as to minimize its impact (Brady 2017). The Central Propaganda Department and other government offices issue regular detailed instructions to media outlets to set the *tifa* for news stories in China. These guidelines restrict the range of information available to the public, establish the correct phraseology to be used and set the tone of discourse.

The organization tasked with this function is the State Council Information Office (SCIO), which is the primary government office that oversees news media and ensures that media and cultural content follow the official line. The SCIO in turn manages the Internet Affairs Bureau, responsible for overseeing all websites that publish news. These Party organs send out specific instructions daily to all the major news outlets, often multiple times per day. The instructions range from interdictions against coverage of certain events, to restrictions on sources and requirements to guide public opinion,

For many years, the China Digital Times, thanks to anonymous inside sources, has leaked examples of such propaganda directives as part of the series 'Directives from the Ministry of Truth' (China Digital Times 2019). This technique of micromanaging the news by edicts has been used for decades, but its use has been ratcheted up since the 2008 Olympics, and particularly during the Xi era.

The following are just a few examples of such directives, these being issued between October and November 2018:

- As tensions between the China and US mounted, directives were sent out concerning how to handle press reports about the meeting between Xi and Trump at the G20 summit in Argentina. Media were instructed to 'strengthen inspection of relevant video information. Only publish standard source content, and do not modify the title. Without exception, do not promote content related to coverage by social media.'

  (China Digital Times 2018a)

- Following Japanese Prime Minister Shinzo Abe's visit to China, the various Party offices sent out directives to the media requesting 'please quietly handle sensitive topics to avoid disturbing the overall positive mood of the bilateral relationship.' Websites received the request, 'Please do not draw direct links between Sino-US and Sino-Japanese relations, and prevent the appearance of clickbait and hot takes about 'embracing Japan to resist America.'

  (China Digital Times 2018b)

- The 2018 World Internet Conference prompted an order issued on 2 November, instructing the media to 'uniformly refrain from reporting, reposting, and commenting on the special Great Firewall-circumventing Internet connections set up for the event.'

  (China Digital Times 2018c)

- Another directive on 6 November prohibited live broadcasts of the conference, along with hype, interviews, or reports about banquets at the event, or attendees' clothing.

(China Digital Times 2018d)

With this tool, the state censors can micromanage the message on a daily basis, dictating what aspects of the story to emphasize, what to downplay, and what to expunge completely from the news feed. This tweaking of the message can be used flexibly to manage a news story in real time as it develops.

Conclusions

As discussed in this chapter, heretofore the extent of government control over the news media tended to wax and wane, alternating in periods of relative openness and restriction. While it may be too early to evaluate the arc of control under Xi, there is a general feeling that under the current regime, press restrictions have encountered a kind of 'ratcheting' effect. That is to say, Xi has made structural changes to the system such that the more tightly controlled environment constitutes a self-perpetuating new normal, one that is less likely to return to a relaxed state at some point in the future.

Xi has arguably entrenched his personal power more firmly than any leader since Mao. In current political ontology, the Party is the 'core' of the nation, and Xi himself is 'the core of the Party.' Since the Party's 19th National Congress in 2018, his governance theory 'Socialism with Chinese characteristics in the new era' has been incorporated into the Constitution as 'Xi Jinping Thought,' an honour no one since Mao has enjoyed. And with the abolishing of the ten-year term limit on presidents, Xi is now potentially China's leader for life. Given Xi's level of absolute authority, the media control system he is establishing is unlikely to be challenged by the Party apparatus, or his successor, when he eventually has one.

Some observers also warn that Xi may be risking an information crisis, a situation in which he may inadvertently lose access to the kinds of information an authoritarian state needs in order to make effective decisions (Bandurski 2018). If all this is so, it may be that Xi is walking a perilous path. Clearly Xi's clampdown is part of an attempt to permanently stabilize Chinese society, but in the process, it has perhaps swept away many of the societal pressure valves tolerated by his predecessors. If one can compare the body politic in China with a biological system, Xi's changes may be depriving the system of its rebalancing and recalibration functions that would usually take effect during periods of relaxation. Xi's administration has systematically cracked down not only on the news media, but also on corrupt officials, university professors, public intellectuals, human rights lawyers, NGOs and, recently, Winnie the Pooh (Xi's perceived resemblance to the cartoon bear having been lampooned by netizens) (McDonnell 2017). By attempting to seal off not only the news media, but all other forms of technologically mediated public discourse, one might ask whether Xi Jinping hasn't made the digital space so airtight that it is gasping for air.

Bibliography

Announcer and Anchor Arts Network [*Boyin zhuchi yishu wang* 波音主持艺术网]. (2016) '2016 survey reports more than 80% of reporter yearly salaries less than 10,000', [2016 *Zhongguo jizhe hangye_diaocha baogao chao 8 cheng shouru wanyuan yixia* 2016 中国记者行业调查报告 超8成收入万元以下]. Online. Available HTTP: <www.cnbyzc.com/article-1901-1.html> (accessed 6 March 2019).

Bandurski, D. (2018) 'China's crisis of self confidence', *The Diplomat*. Online. Available HTTP: <https://thediplomat.com/2018/12/chinas-crisis-of-overconfidence/> (Accessed 6 March 2019).

Bandurski, D. (2019) 'PSC converges for media convergence', *Media Project*. Online. Available HTTP: <http://chinamediaproject.org/2019/01/29/psc-converges-for-media-convergence/> (accessed 6 March 2019).

Bandurski, D. and Hala, M. (eds.). (2010) *Investigative Journalism in China: Eight Cases in Chinese Watchdog Journalism*, Hong Kong: Hong Kong University Press.

Beiser, E. (2018) 'Hundreds of journalists jailed globally becomes the new normal', *Committee to Protect Journalists (CPJ)*. Online. Available HTTP: <https://cpj.org/reports/2018/12/journalists-jailed-imprisoned-turkey-china-egypt-saudi-arabia.php> (accessed 6 March 2019).

Brady, A. (2017) 'Plus ça change?: Media control under Xi Jinping', *Problems of Post-Communism*, 64: 128–140.

Cheung, H. (2013) 'Who are China's Weibo super stars?', *BBC News*. Online. Available HTTP: <www.bbc.com/news/world-asia-china-23925364> (accessed 6 March 2019).

China Digital Times. (2018a) 'Minitrue: No hyping Xi-Trump meeting at G20'. Online. Available HTTP: <https://chinadigitaltimes.net/2018/12/minitrue-no-hyping-xi-trump-meeting-at-g20/> (accessed 29 March 2019).

China Digital Times. (2018b) 'Minitrue: Positive energy for Japanese PM's visit'. Online. Available HTTP: <https://chinadigitaltimes.net/2018/11/minitrue-positive-energy-for-japanese-pms-visit/> (accessed 29 March 2019).

China Digital Times. (2018c) 'Minitrue: Web access at world internet conference'. Online. Available HTTP: <https://chinadigitaltimes.net/2018/11/minitrue-open-web-access-at-world-internet-conference/> (accessed 29 March 2019).

China Digital Times. (2018d) 'Minitrue: No hyping banquets at Internet conference'. Online. Available HTTP: <https://chinadigitaltimes.net/2018/11/minitrue-no-hyping-banquets-live-streaming-world-internet-conference/> (accessed 29 March 2019).

China Digital Times. (2019) 'Directives from the Ministry of Truth'. Online. Available HTTP: <https://chinadigitaltimes.net/china/directives-from-the-ministry-of-truth/> (accessed 6 March 2019).

ChinaFile. (2013) 'Document 9: A ChinaFile translation: How much is a hardline party directive shaping China's current political climate?'. Online. Available HTTP: <www.chinafile.com/document-9-chinafile-translation> (accessed 6 March 2019).

Creemers, R. (ed.). (2014) 'Xi Jinping's 19 August speech revealed? (Translation)', *China Copyright and Media*. Online. Available HTTP: <https://chinacopyrightandmedia.wordpress.com/2013/11/12/xi-jinpings-19-august-speech-revealed-translation/> (accessed 6 March 2019).

Cyberspace Administration of China. (2017) 'Internet news information service, Internet Information Office order management regulations (2017)'. Online. Available HTTP: <www.cac.gov.cn/2017-05/02/c_1120902760.html> (accessed 6 March 2019).

Dasgupta, S. (2016a) 'Chinese journalists restricted in use of social media content', *VOA News*. Online. Available HTTP: <www.voanews.com/a/chinese-media-restricted-usage-social-media-content/3405826.html>(accessed 6 March 2019).

Dasgupta, S. (2016b) 'Chinese journalists restricted in use of Social media content', *VOA News*. Online. Available HTTP: <www.voanews.com/a/chinese-media-restricted-usage-social-media-content/3405826.html> (accessed 6 March 2019).

The Economist. (2019) 'Economic woes hurt Chinese journalists as much as censorship does', *Chaguan*. Online. Available HTTP: <www.economist.com/china/2019/02/23/economic-woes-hurt-chinese-journalists-as-much-as-censorship-does> (accessed 6 March 2019).

Freedom House. (2013) 'China's new leadership declares war on social media', *Freedom House Blog*. Online. Available HTTP: <https://freedomhouse.org/blog/china%E2%80%99s-new-leadership-declares-war-social-media> (accessed 6 March 2019).

Freedom House. (2017) 'Freedom on the Net 2017: Manipulating social media to undermine democracy'. Online. Available HTTP: <https://freedomhouse.org/report/freedom-net/freedom-net-2017> (accessed 6 March 2019).

Freedom House. (2018) 'Freedom on the Net 2018: China'. Online. Available HTTP: <https://freedomhouse.org/report/freedom-net/2018/china> (accessed 6 March 2019).

Guan Video *Guan shipin gongzuoshi* 观视频工作室. (2017) 'My life my China 5: I don't want that free media! *Wo buyao nayang de ziyou meiti* 我不要那样的自由 媒体! Online. Available HTTP: <www.youtube.com/watch?v=0Vwk6jbiF_g&list=PLr0J U8OOrK4gx_BvilDWprTT80LKy2f3p&index=6> (accessed 6 March 2019).

The Guardian. (2016) 'Xi Jinping asks for "absolute loyalty" from Chinese state media'. Online. Available HTTP: <www.theguardian.com/world/2016/feb/19/xi-jinping-tours-chinas-top-state-media-outlets-to-boost-loyalty> (accessed 6 March 2019).

Kalathil, S. (2003) 'Chinese media and the information revolution', *China Digital Times*. Online. Available HTTP: <https://chinadigitaltimes.net/2003/09/chinese-media-and-the-information-revolution/> (accessed 6 March 2019).

King, G., Pan, J., and Roberts, M.E. (2017) 'How the Chinese government fabricates social media posts for strategic distraction, not engaged argument', *American Political Science Review*, 111: 484–501.

Kuo, L. (2018) 'China state media merger to create propaganda giant', *The Guardian*. Online. Available HTTP: <www.theguardian.com/world/2018/mar/21/china-state-media-merger-to-create-propaganda-giant> (accessed 6 March 2019).

Liao, R. (2017) 'An HTML5 Animation made by China's official party paper went viral', *China Film Insider*. Online. Available HTTP: <http://chinafilminsider.com/an-html5-animation-made-by-chinas-official-party-paper-just-went-viral/> (accessed 6 March 2019).

Makinen, J. (2016) 'China's censors are cracking down on the online news industry', *The Los Angeles Times*. Online. Available HTTP: <www.latimes.com/world/asia/la-fg-china-censorship-20160726-snap-story.html> (accessed 6 March 2019).

McCarthy, N. (2018) 'China now boasts more than 800 million Internet users and 98% of them are mobile [infographic]', *Forbes*. Online. Available HTTP: <www.forbes.com/sites/niallmccarthy/2018/08/23/china-now-boasts-more-than-800-million-internet-users-and-98-of-them-are-mobile-infographic/#4097fd417092> (accessed 28 March 2019).

McDonnell, S. (2017) 'Why Chinese censors banned Winnie the Pooh', *BBC News*. Online. Available HTTP: <www.bbc.com/news/blogs-china-blog-40627855> (accessed 6 March 2019).

Moore, M. (2014) 'Chinese journalist Gao Yu faces life sentence for leaking state secrets', *The Telegraph*. Online. Available HTTP: <www.telegraph.co.uk/news/worldnews/asia/china/11244945/Chinese-journalist-Gao-Yu-faces-life-sentence-for-leaking-state-secrets.html> (accessed 6 March 2019).

The Paper (*Pengpai* 澎湃). (2018) 'Merger of state radio and TV, canceling CCTV and China National Radio' (*Zujian Zhongyang guangbo dianshi zongtai, chexiao Zhongshi, Yangguang deng jianzhi* 组建中央广播电视总台，撤销央视、央广 等建制). Online. Available HTTP: <www.thepaper.cn/newsDetail_forward_2036400> (accessed 6 March 2019).

PEN America. (2017) 'China: New regulations increase control over both internet and media'. Online. Available HTTP: <https://pen.org/press-release/china-new-regulations-increase-control-internet-media/> (accessed 6 March 2019).

PEN America. (2018) 'Forbidden feeds: Government controls on social media in China'. Online. Available HTTP: <https://pen.org/research-resources/forbidden-feeds/> (accessed 6 March 2019).

Qian, G. and Bandurski, D. (2011) 'China's emerging public sphere-the impact of media commercialization, professionalism, and the internet in an Era of Transition', in S. Shirk (ed.) *Changing media, changing China*, New York: Oxford University Press.

Reporters without Borders. (2018a) *2018 World Press Freedom Index*. Online. Available HTTP: <https://rsf.org/en/ranking/> (accessed 6 March 2019).

Reporters without Borders. (2018b) 'Chinese regime's true face: One of the worst free speech predators'. Online. Available HTTP: <https://rsf.org/en/news/chinese-regimes-true-face-one-worst-free-speech-predators> (accessed 6 March 2019).

Sonmez, F. (2015) 'China's People's Daily runs 11 Xi Jinping headlines on its front page', *The Wall Street Journal*. Online. Available HTTP: <https://blogs.wsj.com/chinarealtime/2015/12/04/chinas-peoples-daily-runs-11-xi-jinping-headlines-on-its-front-page/> (accessed 6 March 2019).

Teon, A. (2019) 'The deterioration of China's media freedom in the Xi Jinping era', *The Greater China Journal*. Online. Available HTTP: <https://china-journal.org/2019/02/20/the-deterioration-of-chinas-media-freedom-in-the-xi-jinping-era/> (accessed 6 March 2019).

6

JAPAN'S ACTIVIST NEWS MEDIA

How and why reporters and news organizations became a positive force in confronting a negative past

Andrew Horvat

Introduction

It is difficult to pinpoint just when after World War II it was that Japan's news media became a force advocating reconciliation with neighbouring nations, victims of Japanese expansionism and harsh colonial rule during the first half of the last century. Also hard to understand is why the advocacy activities of the Japanese news media with regard to East Asia's long festering history problem have garnered so little attention outside Japan in spite of the massive output of articles, editorials, documentaries and media-sponsored conferences, a good number of which have triggered changes in official policy on how to deal positively with war and war memory issues.

For example, a 1971 series of articles by *Asahi* correspondent Honda Katsuichi, retracing the route Japanese forces took from Shanghai to Nanking in the autumn of 1937, challenged postwar silence on the Nanking Massacre in which tens of thousands of Chinese, including many non-combatants, were murdered by troops of the Japanese Imperial Army (Honda 1972). In 1982, disclosures in Japanese newspapers that the Ministry of Education was preparing to authorize textbooks that whitewashed Japanese military expansion by replacing the word 'aggression' with 'expansion' resulted in the introduction of the so-called 'neighboring country clause' that functioned for decades as a guideline for history textbook writers to keep the sensitivities of former victim nations in mind (Minamizuka 2006). In 1995, the publication of an editorial in the *Asahi* advocating joint hosting by South Korea and Japan of the FIFA World Cup football tournament resulted in its realization in 2002. An unprecedented open discussion in 2006 by senior media personalities of two mass-circulation national dailies, the liberal *Asahi* and the conservative *Yomiuri*, to express their shared opposition to visits by Japanese prime ministers to Yasukuni Shrine, where the spirits of

14 Japanese wartime leaders, all convicted of war crimes, had been consecrated and which regularly triggered protests from Beijing and Seoul, would lead to the elimination of all but one such visit until the present day.

These examples barely scratch the surface of a huge archive of history-related news articles and television documentaries that have not only led to policy initiatives, but also to changes in how people thought about their country's past and their views regarding the responsibility of their elected officials to deal with it both domestically and in relations with neighbouring countries (Saaler 2005). Evidence for the effectiveness of the Japanese news media's advocacy activities in promoting a nuanced vision of a difficult past can also be had from attempts by conservative politicians and affiliated nationalist groups to discredit those media practitioners who have through their work advocated reconciliation and to punish them as well as their employing organizations (Yamaguchi 2017; Mulligan 2017). This is especially clear in the case of reporting by the Japanese press in the early 1990s on the so-called comfort women, recruited to provide sexual services to troops before and during World War II mostly under inhumane conditions. There is no question that the massive coverage by the Japanese news media of the sufferings of these women led directly to a series of official apologies and subsequent attempts to provide compensation, including from official funds (Horvat 2007).

As can be seen from these examples, it is not only clear that news activism took place on such a huge scale, but also that the news media's efforts resulted in policy changes aimed at dealing with a negative past in a positive way.

Often the correlation between media attention and policy initiatives is not one to one. Nonetheless, a pattern of media focus on a history-related issue followed by official action is discernible in many cases. Perhaps the most salient of these is the contribution toward Sino-Japanese rapprochement by Honda's 1971 series on Japanese atrocities in China. While Japan never had to pay official reparations to China after World War II, leading Japanese industrialists were known to be keen to invest in China even during the Cold War, at a time when corporations and governments of no other industrialized nation were willing to take what was considered then to be a commercially unjustifiable risk. Honda's 1971 series in the *Asahi* came at a time when there was a practical need for Japan to be seen to be confronting its past. Without acknowledgement of the horrors perpetrated by Japanese troops during the so-called China Incident (1937–1945), normalization of relations with the People's Republic in 1972 would have been unthinkable. Historian John Boyle assessed the significance of Honda's work in a review of a book that brought together in 1999 for the first time in English Honda's series of articles on China:

> It is difficult to exaggerate the impact that Honda's reportage had on Japan. Until Honda's articles appeared, Japanese tended to think back on the war years with a strong sense of victimization. Everyone knew of the food shortages, evacuations, the war widows and orphans, the devastating

firebomb raids, as well as Hiroshima and Nagasaki. . . . Honda's revelations did not suddenly produce a wave of national revulsion by a contrite citizenry bravely confronting its past. More accurately, it stimulated a vigorous debate among popular critics, readers, academics, and political leaders. A wide spectrum of views was ventilated in the Japanese press and in academic journals. At one end were denialists, but at the other end appeared some of the most conscientious, balanced, and searching studies of the Sino-Japanese War.

(Boyle 2001)

One can argue, however, that Honda's months-long series of shocking reports in a mass-circulation national daily also had other more immediate results. The regular airing of atrocities committed by Japanese troops in China in 1937 made it not only possible but also imperative for Prime Minister Tanaka Kakuei to acknowledge in front of Chinese leaders that Japan had acted in a way that demanded atonement and that China could expect assistance from Japan – which though never clearly articulated as reparations, would in reality have the same effect. While Tanaka would later be criticized for using a Japanese expression in his speech in Beijing in 1972 that failed to convey the magnitude of the devastation inflicted by Japan's invasion of China, Japanese companies would go on to provide the equivalent of US$32 billion in aid through officially financed megaprojects, including a state-of-the-art steel mill at Baoshan, a subway in Beijing and a major part of the Chinese capital's airport (Takamine 2006; Ota 2019). Although Honda's series, later published in book form as *The Road to Nanking*, triggered a domestic tug of war between progressives and nationalists on historical issues that has lasted to the present day, it broke new ground by forcing millions of Japanese to accept that their country had been an aggressor nation in World War II (Honda 1972). Honda's series of articles on Japanese atrocities in China did for Japanese what the 1978 American TV miniseries *Holocaust* when it was shown on German television did for Germans: it brought war crimes into living rooms.

Japanese news media as advocacy NGOs

At risk of gilding the lily, I should add that in 2015, of ten finalists in the prestigious Ishibashi Tanzan journalism prizes awarded by Waseda University, which has sent more graduates to Japan's major news organizations than any other Japanese institute of higher learning, five entries dealt with subjects related to war and war memory. In other words, despite the present tensions in Japan-China relations and the continuing difficulties on history-related issues between Japan and Korea, more than seven decades after the last Japanese soldier left the Asian mainland, Japanese continue to discuss and debate their country's past as an imperialist aggressor. Moreover, the Japanese news media continues – despite attempts of nationalists to suppress its activities – to play a leading role in this process.

Historian Philip Seaton, taking issue with the widely held perception outside Japan that the Japanese public suffers from historical amnesia, wrote in his *Japan's Contested War Memories* that Japanese have stood up to the official war narrative pushed by their country's entrenched conservative political elite, 'through public expression in the forms at their disposal' (Seaton 2007: 36). In order to illustrate the active debate on war memory, Seaton provides a lengthy list of films, books, news articles and documentaries, some of which perpetuate a narrative of victimhood but a large portion of which keep alive memories of the brutality of a war of aggression perpetrated by one's co-nationals. But whereas Seaton's work, probably the most detailed so far on the link between media production and war memory, focuses on the news media's massive output, the aim of the present chapter is to provide both historical and contemporary context to the activities of Japan's news media actors in connection with war memory.

In this regard, it can be argued that the Japanese news media has functioned very much like the transnational non-state actors (TNAs), referred to by Lily Gardner Feldman in her work chronicling the generally successful record of TNA-state engagement aimed at achieving reconciliation between Germany and the victims of Nazi crimes (Gardner Feldman 2012). Gardner Feldman's work has triggered a steady flow of discussion – both popular and academic – comparing the remarkable success of postwar reconciliation in Western Europe with the virtual absence of concerted and sustained work at the grassroots level by civil society in the nations of Northeast Asia toward forging a shared understanding of negative aspects of the region's recent past.

Among reasons that have been put forward to explain this contrast is the difference in Cold War geopolitics (Horvat 2014), legal and financial constraints preventing the growth of vibrant advocacy NGOs in Japan (Schwartz 2002) – and, until recently, in South Korea (Kim and Hwang 2002) – and the rise of nationalism in all three nations in Northeast Asia. More recently, attention is being paid to the role of an entrenched conservative political elite centred largely on Japan's long-ruling Liberal Democratic Party (in power for all but three years since 1955) which seeks to stifle discussion on Japanese war crimes and promote a sanitized version of negative aspects of Japan's past (Kingston 2017).

It is the view of this author that the Japanese news media have played the role of an advocacy NGO in Japan's historical debates because: a) the news media in Japan is guided by moral principles that encourage its members to take active roles in the politics of their country; (Hayashi 2015) b) leading members of major news organizations share social origins and educational backgrounds with those in power and are able to exert influence (Kim 1981); and c) unlike civil society organizations, which in Japan have suffered from legal and financial constraints, Japanese news organizations, at least until recently, were in good financial health and therefore were in a position to take actions with lasting effects.

The structural similarities between Japanese newspapers and US-based non-profit organizations should also be noted, since these provide a clue as to why Japan's mass-circulation national dailies have been able to challenge political authority and, in many cases, to influence public policy. Unlike in other capitalist countries, the shares of Japanese newspapers are not openly traded. When newspapers earn a profit, the funds are reinvested in the work of the organization and are not distributed to shareholders. It is this last point which should cause concern for those interested in the outcome of Japan's domestic debate on war and war memory. Although Japan still boasts national dailies with huge circulation figures, as in other countries, readership is declining both for demographic and technological reasons (Kawachi 2007). Television, though facing challenges from the internet and from computer games, still makes money, and it is profits from the affiliated networks of newspapers that permit Japanese newspapers to survive. However, as the television stations are licensed by the government, their independence is not at all secure (Kingston 2017). In spite of such pressures, however, television documentaries continue to challenge conservative views of World War II.

Patterns of engagement in the news media's policy advocacy in Japan

It is possible to categorize the manner in which Japanese news practitioners and their organizations have sought to influence policy with regard to the history issues in the following five ways: a) using high market penetration to set the agenda; b) launching lengthy and detailed series of team-written articles known collectively as 'campaigns'; c) utilizing the convening power of news organizations to hold symposiums on policy-relevant issues; d) cultivating close relationships and collaborating with political leaders to introduce new ideas; and e) as individual media personalities drawing attention to issues both as media and as civil society actors.

Using high market penetration to set the agenda

The market penetration of Japanese newspapers and their affiliated terrestrial television networks has virtually no parallel outside Japan. Although their print runs have declined, left-of-center dailies *Asahi* and *Mainichi* still have a combined daily circulation of about 10 million, roughly the same as the right-of-centre *Yomiuri*, which, though pro-government in many respects, has taken a progressive position on historical issues. *Yomiuri* CEO Watanabe Tsuneo was a private in the Imperial Army in the closing days of World War II, an experience that has left him with lasting unpleasant memories. (By way of comparison, the *Wall Street Journal*, which boasts the largest circulation of any American newspaper, has a daily print run of less than 2.4 million, or about a third of *Asahi's*).

The *Yomiuri* media personality who collaborated with rival *Asahi* to form a joint front opposing visits to Yasukuni Shrine mentioned earlier is none other than Watanabe. His *Asahi* counterpart was the indefatigable Wakamiya Hirobumi. Using the combined daily circulations of their two papers, nearly 20 million at the time, the *Asahi* and the *Yomiuri* both launched year-long series of articles delving into war responsibility. Both newspapers published two-volume sets containing the collected articles (*Asahi Shimbun* 2006, 2007; *Yomiuri Shimbun* 2006). The *Yomiuri*'s version, which took upon itself to finish the job started by the Tokyo War Crimes Trials and to look for war criminals who had not been prosecuted, is still available online in both Japanese and English.

The effectiveness of these newspapers and TV networks in triggering debate can be witnessed when the Japanese Diet (Parliament) is in session. There is hardly a committee in which opposition representatives do not rely on material gathered by news reporters to grill government officials. The influence of the *Asahi* and the public television network NHK, both of which have placed war and war memory issues high on their editorial agendas, has long been a thorn in the side of conservative politicians. Proof of this fact can be had from the manner in which the administration of Prime Minister Abe has moved to suppress their influence. In the case of the *Asahi*, in the summer of 2014, ruling party politicians, including the Prime Minister, publicly called on that paper to retract a series of articles – published some 22 years earlier – that had been based on the fabricated testimony of a confidence trickster who claimed to have led a detachment of Japanese soldiers to Cheju Island in Korea in order to kidnap 200 women whom he sent to the front to military brothels during World War II (Yamaguchi 2017). For reasons that shall be made clear ahead, the *Asahi* suffered seriously from this campaign, even though other papers which participated in the government-instigated pillorying the *Asahi* had themselves reported the same fabricated story (Fackler 2017).

In a similar vein, in 2014, the ruling party appointed to the governing board of public broadcaster NHK a nationalist scholar together with a writer of well-known extreme right-wing political views, enabling the selection of an openly pro-government chairman under whose leadership programming related to war and war memory, at least from the news section, was virtually eliminated (Seaton 2017). Such open interference in news coverage by the government is one reason for Japan being downgraded in 2016 in the Reporters without Borders' Press Freedom Index from 62 to 71, well below the standings of former communist countries such as Mongolia (60) and Slovakia (12) (Mulligan 2017). Government suppression can also be taken as proof that the liberal Japanese media's concern with war and war memory has had a positive impact and continues to do so, despite the efforts of conservative politicians.

Launching lengthy and detailed series of team-written articles known as 'campaigns'

A unique aspect of the Japanese mass-circulation newspaper is the so-called 'kyanpeen' (campaign), a series of often team-written articles on a single theme published regularly every day for several months. Honda's articles on Japanese atrocities in China are one example of a history-related campaign. *Yomiuri*'s and

Asahi's parallel series asking who led Japan into a war that it could not win belongs to the same genre. At this juncture, the special relationship between the *Nishinihon Shimbun* of Fukuoka and the *Pusan Ilbo* of South Korea cannot be overlooked. For more than 20 years, the two papers have exchanged news reporters for six-month periods, during which time the reporters move with their families to their host city, learn the language of their host country and write regular columns in their host paper of their impressions of their life in the sister city. Though not necessarily about history, the exchange is clearly intended to deal with problems stemming from an unresolved past.

Though, strictly speaking, not the same as the lengthy series of 'campaign' articles, television documentaries should be classified into the same category – if for no other reason than that they require mobilizing human and financial resources on a large scale. Moreover, in a survey of university students that asked which medium has been most effective in promoting awareness of historical issues, television documentaries were rated the highest by the largest number of respondents (Seaton 2007).

In this regard, the work of regional television stations needs to be noted. One of two documentaries on the fate of farmers sent to the Japanese puppet state of Manchuria in the late 1930s – ostensibly as pioneers but in fact to till land seized from their original Chinese owners – produced by Shin'etsu Broadcasting, a local television station in Nagano Prefecture, was a finalist to the 2014 Ishibashi awards. In this documentary, an elderly farmer who barely escaped from Manchuria after Japan's defeat recalled, 'If we had learned to live together with Chinese farmers, they might have asked us to stay' (Kokuin 2013). A 90-year-old former junior high school teacher whose student was killed when the Soviet Army overran the undefended Japanese pioneer villages broke down in tears, blaming himself for having sent his pupil to his death.

Making use of the capacity to convene

A third way in which the Japanese news media seeks to influence policy – and at times set the agenda – is to harness its convening capabilities. For this purpose, all major national dailies have their own facilities, including large public halls centrally located in major cities. They all convene symposiums on timely topics, and all use the material gained through the support of such events to fill their pages with policy-relevant comments from leading luminaries on a broad range of issues. In 2008, the *Asahi* held a full-day public seminar titled 'For the Sake of Historical Reconciliation' at one of its halls located in central Tokyo. Among invited speakers were Simone Lassig, director of the Georg Eckert Institute for school textbook research in Germany, and Park Yuha, a Korean author whose works promoting reconciliation would win her prizes in Japan and land her in court in Korea, as well as a long list of distinguished Japanese, Korean and Chinese historians of various political persuasions. A precis of the proceedings appeared in the *Asahi* and a faithful transcript of the entire symposium can still be accessed on the *Asahi* website, all 60 pages of it (*Asahi Shimbun* 2008).

Advising political leaders

In Japan, unlike in North America, close personal and professional ties between journalists and politicians are relatively common at all levels. The tradition of news reporters as experts goes back to the prewar period, when Prime Minister Konoe Fumimaro had no fewer than six *Asahi* journalists as advisers, including economist Ryu Shintaro, who went on to become editor-in-chief of the paper after World War II.

A more recent example of reporter-politician collaboration on the policy level, specifically in the history field, is that of the late Prime Minister Obuchi Keizo and the former editor-in-chief of the *Asahi*, Funabashi Yoichi, who became a leading member of the former's brain trust. It was Funabashi, author of books such as *Travels through the History Problem* and *How Should We Tackle the History Problem Now?*, who advised Obuchi to sign a declaration with Korean President Kim Dae-jung containing a de facto apology for 35 years of colonial rule (Funabashi 2001, 2004). The document, signed by both leaders in 1998 envisioning a new, 'future oriented relationship' between the two countries, was immediately followed by relaxation on restrictions against the importation of Japanese cultural products to South Korea.

The *Asahi*'s Wakamiya, speaking at a conference in Washington, DC in 2011 comparing Japanese and German efforts to deal with difficult aspects of the past, provided another example of how close ties between reporters and their sources had a positive impact on the history issue in Japan-Korea relations:

> During the difficult days leading up to the signing of the Treaty of Normalization between South Korea and Japan, it was members of the Japanese Foreign Ministry's press club, the reporters covering the negotiations, who came up with the key phrases to be used in the apology that Japanese Foreign Minister Shiina Etsusaburo would deliver on his arrival in Seoul.
>
> *(Wakamiya 2011)*

Other reporter-politician relationships are former Prime Minister Nakasone Yasuhiro's (1982–1987) very public friendship with *Yomiuri* CEO Watanabe and the far more discreet good relations between the *Asahi*'s former chief editorial writer Wakamiya and Prime Minister Fukuda Yasuo (2007–2008). Given Wakamiya's active promotion of reconciliation with Korea, had Fukuda remained in office, Korea-Japan relations today might be on a far firmer foundation.

Individual media personalities drawing attention to issues through influence achieved as journalists

The activities of media personalities such as the *Asahi*'s Wakamiya and Funabashi and the *Yomiuri*'s Watanabe have already been mentioned. But there is no shortage of individual journalists who have worked hard both in their professional capacity and privately to overcome the legacy of military conflict and colonial rule.

In this regard, the work of one particular freelance journalist, Kumagai Toru – who gave up a career as a foreign correspondent working for NHK to devote himself to reporting on Germany for Japanese readers – must be mentioned, if for no other reason than the enormous impact of his short essay, republished many times, titled 'How Germany Confronted its Past' (Kumagai 2006). Originally delivered as a speech directed at business executives in 2006, the work has appeared as a pamphlet, a book and as a downloadable file. It has been used as an educational supplement and has established Kumagai as an authority on 'how Germany got it right.' Kumagai, who works out of Munich, has published some 15 books in the past ten years, a good number of them on the history issue. In 2015, he repeated the content of his lecture on the pages of the Japanese edition of *The Huffington Post*, explaining in great detail and in simple language the popular support that reconciliation has had in Germany and how the country has benefitted from a foreign policy based on expressions of regret combined with compensation for past wrongs.

Another example is the work of Kondo Motohiro, former editor of the once influential *Chuo Koron* magazine who, after early retirement in 1990, went on to promote and to help organize the first reunion of American and Japanese veterans of Pearl Harbor. Kondo, who spent time as a guest journalist at an Atlanta newspaper, was inspired by the meeting of Union and Confederate veterans to mark the 50th anniversary of the end of the American Civil War. Kondo, who was born in Beijing to Japanese parents, collaborated with a senior writer of the *Mainichi*, who spent the first ten years of his life in China during and after World War II, to set up a joint Japan–China graduate school at a university in Tientsin, which unfortunately failed to obtain sufficient financial backing.

And yet another former journalist who has worked tirelessly to promote public discussion of unresolved history is Kudo Yasushi, who retired from the Kyodo News Agency to found 'Genron NPO,' (Media NPO), one of very few Japanese non-profits that can be classified as a transnational non-state actor. For well more than a decade, Kudo's staff have collaborated with counterparts in China to produce an annual survey of popularly held mutual images citizens of the two countries have of each other. Genron NPO also works with the German foundation Friedrich Ebert Stiftung to hold symposiums comparing the efforts of Germany and Japan in coming to terms with negative aspects of their histories. Also worthy of mention is the work of the late Matsuo Fumio, who, like Kudo, after leaving Kyodo threw himself into reconciliation work. Matsuo is credited with successfully campaigning to have then US President Barack Obama visit Hiroshima in 2016.

But perhaps the most visible impact on the history question achieved by a Japanese journalist-turned-activist has been that of the late Matsui Yayori, who in 1976 while still employed by her paper founded an NGO to protest 'sex tourism,' then rampant on the Asian mainland. She would go on to establish the Violence Against Women in War Network (VAWW), and through it convene the Women's International War Crimes Trial held in Tokyo in 2000, which found World War II-era Emperor Hirohito responsible for the policies by which women throughout Asia were coerced into becoming 'sex slaves' for the Japanese military (Seaton 2007). Matsui and her supporters sued public broadcaster NHK for making changes to a documentary on the Women's War Crimes Trials. Although VAWW lost the suit in which it accused conservative politicians, including Abe Shinzo, with interfering in the editing process, they succeeded in bringing worldwide attention to the cause of the comfort women. After Matsui's untimely death in 2002 at the age of 68, her supporters founded a museum in Tokyo devoted to keeping alive the memory of comfort women specifically from countries overrun by the Japanese military.

And finally, although already mentioned many times, the name that is possibly the most synonymous with the Japanese media's effort to encourage an official action on unresolved matters of history is that of Wakamiya Yoshibumi, prime mover of the 2002 joint Japan-Korea World Cup effort, organizer of the successful *Yomiuri-Asahi* joint effort to stop prime ministerial visits to Yasukuni Shrine and convener of the 2008 *Asahi*-sponsored international conference on unresolved historical issues. Wakamiya's contribution to improved relations with Korea cannot be overstated. Unlike his colleagues, many of whom studied English to be able to report from abroad, Wakamiya spent a year at a university in Seoul where he learned Korean. Under his leadership, the *Asahi* and its Korean partner, the *Dong-A Ilbo*, regularly published jointly researched articles on historical issues. Wakamiya was responsible for introducing Korean public intellectual Park Yuha's works into Japan, including one aptly titled *For the Sake of Reconciliation*, which garnered a Japanese literary award (Park 2006). After retiring from the *Asahi*, Wakamiya moved to Seoul, where he wrote a regular column in Korean for the *Dong-A*.

A media with a different heritage

At this point, one needs to ask why have Japan's news reporters and their organizations chosen to act as the conscience of their nation, and simultaneously, what characteristics of the individual reporters and their employers have contributed to their success. Finally, given the negative impact of digitalization on the business model of the traditional news media, as well as resurgent nationalistic feelings in many parts of the world, including East Asia, will the Japanese news media be able to continue to fulfil their longstanding positive role on history-related matters?

To find clues that might help answer these questions, we need to look at the modern-day self-perception of Japanese news media practitioners, as well as the historical origins of the Japanese press. We should be prepared to discover a vision of the press and its role in politics and society that is at odds with the Fourth Estate role news reporters in Anglo-American and Western European countries have assigned themselves. As for the significance of the historical origins of the Japanese press, it should be noted that the first newspapers were created by a government founded by the victors of a civil war, and that the first news reporters were samurai who had been on the losing side of that conflict. In other words, though these two groups of samurai may have had different past loyalties, they shared social origins, ethical beliefs and a self-perception as leaders of their country. With respect to how reporters see themselves and are seen by others in Japan, not much has changed in the past century and a half; cooperation between journalists and their sources has made it possible for Japanese news reporters to cross the proscenium arch and appear simultaneously as observers and actors in the same play. In countries where the news media is seen as a Fourth Estate, the line between reporters and sources is far more distinct.

Elitism remains a defining quality of Japan's national dailies, which recruit new employees from no more than a handful of top universities, drawing from the same talent pool as government ministries and leading industrial conglomerates. As reporters and their sources share social and educational backgrounds, there is little wonder that an atmosphere of cooperation exists between them that enables Japanese reporters to influence policy. Yet these relations are not solely cooperative, as on many occasions, specifically in connection with historical reconciliation, Japan's news media activists resort to confrontation.

Another characteristic of the Japanese press is that participating in the politics of one's country while being a news reporter is not merely permitted; it is a tradition that goes back to the earliest days of the news industry. As James Huffman, historian of the nineteenth century Japanese press, has written:

> Neither was it only the government to which the press maintained ties. . . . It was the entire establishment, the entire power structure of the nation, whether economic, political, or intellectual. Nearly every leading newspaper editor and writer eschewed reportorial independence whenever it threatened to deprive him of the influence that came from deep involvement in other areas of life. The early journalists ran for public office, moved back and forth between the bureaucracy and the press, helped establish and run the stock exchange, formed their own political parties and founded educational institutions.
>
> *(Huffman 1977: 460)*

It can be argued that the blurred line between journalism and activism has contributed to the effectiveness of Japanese news practitioners in promoting historical reconciliation. At the same time, however, it should be noted that the crusading reporter, whose mandate includes the improvement of society through work beyond the strict parameters of his or her profession, is vulnerable to what from a Western perspective would appear to be unreasonable expectations of impeccable moral rectitude.

Unlike in the West, where reporters justified the existence of their profession by appealing to 'inalienable rights' based on ideas stemming from the European Enlightenment, fought for in the American and French revolutions and defended in courts of law, in Japan, the early samurai news reporters relied on the Confucian concept of the 'superior man,' who having acquired a high level of education, could claim to criticize government actions from a position of moral authority. It is this aspect of Japanese journalism, the requirement of unassailable moral purity, that has proven to be the Achilles' heel of pro-reconciliation liberal critics of Japan's present conservative government. The Abe administration and its neonationalist supporters have chosen to apply the moral litmus test in a selective manner, to discredit liberal elements in the press.

On several occasions, conservative nationalist elements have succeeded in discrediting liberal news professionals through attacks on their 'moral conduct.' For example, the removal of NHK commentator Kuniya Hiroko and the ultimate cancellation of her programme was preceded by allegations of a 'faked' interview (Ishido 2017). The strategy was clearly designed to give the impression that such a programme is unworthy to be presented, as it is the work of people who do not maintain the moral standards required of news professionals. Again, in a Western democracy, such accusations would have been met with disciplinary action against those who had willfully or otherwise permitted the interview to be aired.

But the most recent case of the use by the advocates of an unrepentant Japan against advocates of reconciliation was that of the 2014 orchestrated attack on the *Asahi* for articles it had published 22 years earlier. The first salvo was launched by none other than the prime minister at a hearing of the Diet. Again, one might ask why hundreds of thousands of readers would cancel their subscriptions to a paper that had made errors 22 years earlier, and like all other Japanese newspapers had been reluctant to issue corrections.

The media's moral conundrum

However, to understand the vulnerability of the activist liberal press to accusations of 'immoral conduct,' one needs to keep in mind that no Japanese newspaper prints letters to the editor that disagree with any article that the paper has published. Opinion pieces from different perspectives may occasionally be published, but none that take issue with the editorial position of the newspaper. Retractions or corrections are virtually unheard of, and not a single major daily maintains a humour column. There are no Japanese Maureen Dowds and certainly no one remotely like the late Art Buchwald. The lack of humour and the absence of a dividing line between news and editorial copy are consistent with the requirements of the 'morally superior' samurai turned news reporter. Frivolousness, of the kind that one might encounter on the pages of the *New York Times* or the hilarious puns in the *Financial Times* cannot be found in a Japanese newspaper, since the lack of seriousness would be seen to be detracting from the morally correct behaviour justifying the paper's right to speak truth to power. Incidentally, both Dowd and Buchwald are Pulitzer Prize recipients, something also unthinkable in Japan where usually massive, lengthy and serious news reports – some published daily over a six-month period, or similarly impressive documentaries – garner most journalism honours.

Walter Lippmann, founder of *New Republic* magazine, syndicated political columnist and a much-respected early observer of media-state relations in the United States, wrote:

> The press is no substitute for institutions. It is like the beam of a searchlight that moves restlessly about, bringing one episode and then another out of darkness into vision. Men cannot do the work of the world by this light alone. They cannot govern society by episodes, incidents, and eruptions. It is only when they work by a steady light of their own, that the press, when it is turned upon them, reveals a situation intelligible enough for a popular decision.
>
> *(Lippmann 1982: 401)*

It may not be fair or accurate to suggest that Lippman's writings represent a majority view of the press in America, either at the time of his writing or today, but his caution against demanding that the news media go so far as to provide a useful vision of reality does lead one to conclude that Japanese expectations of the news media, and its practitioners – for example, 'to contribute to world peace' – are far greater than those one might find in America, or for that matter, in many other countries. But this is a mission that Japanese news reporters, especially on the left, take very seriously.

Documentary evidence

With the passing of Matsui in 2002 and Wakamiya in 2016, and the ageing of many other of the other activist journalists of the postwar era, combined with the resurgence of an unrepentant rightist nationalist political elite, many of whose members are to be found in government, one might be tempted to conclude that the cause of historical reconciliation in the Japanese news media has been lost. But the evidence would seem to indicate that work of a very high quality continues to be produced. Moreover, the output has come from a most unlikely quarter: television. Both public and, to a lesser degree, private networks have released in recent years a number of hard-hitting documentaries, most of which have gone on to garner prestigious awards. For example, the Nippon Television Network's 'Nanking, the Testament of the Soldiers' contains an eyewitness interview with a 92-year-old veteran of the Japanese Imperial Navy, who watched from the deck of his battleship moored in the Yangtze River within a few hundred yards of the shoreline, as Chinese prisoners were marched in large groups to the riverbank and machinegunned by Japanese soldiers (*Nankin* 2015). The documentary also interviews an amateur historian who as a hobby collected the war diaries of some 200 Japanese soldiers, several of whom had taken part in the capture of Nanking and had written about their participation in the massacres.

Not to be outdone, NHK has produced so far three works on war responsibility from several different perspectives. Thanks to the end of the Cold War, NHK was able to obtain material from Russia on the trials in Khabarovsk of members of Unit 731, which had carried out bacteriological and chemical weapons experiments on Chinese prisoners of war (*731 butai no shinjitsu* 2017). The testimony of the accused is nothing short of riveting, with one doctor promising to devote the rest of his life to curing the sick. We are told later that he committed suicide.

Two additional NHK documentaries, both on Japanese military disasters, one on the defeat at Nomonhan in the summer of 1939 and the other on the failed campaign to capture Imphal on the India-Burma border in 1944, use both historical evidence and interviews with survivors to take to task military planners for their disregard for human life, but not of the enemy, but soldiers under their command (*NHK* 2017; *Nomonhan* 2018). *Imphal*, aired in 2017 on the anniversary of Japan's defeat, has already received four prestigious journalism prizes, including the Ishibashi Tanzan from Waseda. *Nomonhan*, broadcast in 2018, is destined to receive a similar reception.

As is often said, history lives in the present, and that is certainly the case with the choice of subject matter by both NHK and Nippon Television, as well as the Shin'etsu Broadcasting Company in its focus on the tragedies that befell Japanese 'pioneers' in Manchuria. At first glance, one might think that these recent documentaries dwell only on the sufferings of Japanese soldiers and civilians, but they are also an indictment of wartime leaders who treated them as cannon fodder. It is not a coincidence that these indictments impugn the contemporary efforts of conservative political leaders to bolster Japan's military and to revise Japan's postwar Peace Constitution. The Japanese news media have not stopped engaging in political activism; they just do so more subtly.

Works cited

731 butai no shinjitsu: eriito igakusha to jintai jikken (*The Truth about Unit 731: Medical Scientists and Vivisection*). (2017). [TV programme] NHK, 13 August.

Asahi Shimbun. (2006) *Sensosekinin to tsuito: rekishi to mukiau 1* (*War Responsibility and Memory: Confronting History 1*), Tokyo: Asahi Shimbunsha.

Asahi Shimbun. (2007) '*Kako no kokufuku' to aikokushin: rekishi to mukiau 2* ('*Overcoming the Past' and Patriotism: Confronting History 2*), Tokyo: Asahi Shimbunsha.

Asahi Shimbun. (2008) *Shinpojumu: rekishi wakai no tame ni* (*Symposium: Toward Historical Reconciliation*). Online. Available HTTP: <www.asahi.com/sympo/080505/01.html> (accessed 18 April 2019).

Boyle, J.H. (2001) 'The Nanjing Massacre: A Japanese journalist confronts Japan's national shame by Honda Katsuichi, Frank Gibney and Karen Sandness', *The American Historical Review*, 106: 148–149.

Fackler, M. (2017) 'A pooch after all? The Asahi Shimbun's foiled foray into watchdog journalism', in J.B. Kingston (ed.) *Press Freedom in Contemporary Japan*, Abingdon, UK: Routledge.

Funabashi, Y. (ed.). (2001) *Ima rekishi mondai ni do torikumu ka* (*How Should We Tackle the History Problem Now?*), Tokyo: Iwanami.

Funabashi, Y. (2004) *Rekishi mondai no tabi: tairitsu no kako kara kyosei no mirai e* (*Travels through the History Problem: From a Conflicted Past to a Harmonious Future*), Tokyo: Asahi shimbunsha.

Gardner Feldman, L. (2012) *Germany's Foreign Policy of Reconciliation: From Enmity to Amity*, Lanham, MD: Rowman & Littlefield.

Hayashi, K. (2015) 'Japanese media, their problems and challenges', *YouTube Video*, added by 日本外国特派員協会 会見映像 オフィシャルサイトFCCJchannel. Online. Available HTTP: <www.youtube.com/watch?v=DdaAsilg1qo> (accessed 18 April 2019).

Honda, K. (1972) *Chugoku no tabi* (*Journey to China*), Tokyo: Asahi Shimbunsha.

Horvat, A. (2007) 'A strong state, weak civil society, and Cold War geopolitics: Why Japan lags behind Europe in confronting a negative past', in G.W Shin, S.W. Park, and D. Yang (eds.) *Rethinking Historical Injustice and Reconciliation in Northeast Asia: The Korean Experience*, Abingdon, UK: Routledge.

Horvat, A. (2014) 'Why telling Japan's prime minister to stop going to Yasukuni Shrine is not enough', *AICGS*. Online. Available HTTP: www.aicgs.org/2014/04/why-telling-japans-prime-minister-to-stop-going-to-the-yasukuni-shrine-is-not-enough/ (accessed 18 April 2017).

Huffman, J. (1977) 'The Meiji roots and contemporary practices of the Japanese press', *The Japan Interpreter*, 11: 448–466.

Ishido, S. (2017) 'Kurogen moto kyasuta Kuniya Hiroko-san ga akasu, NHK de toriagerarenakatta ano "mondai" (Ex-host of Closeup Gendai, Kuniya Hiroko talks about "the problem" NHK did want brought up)', *Buzzfeed Japan*. Online. Available HTTP: <www.buzzfeed.com/jp/satoruishido/kuniya-hiroko> (accessed 19 April 2019).

Kawachi, T. (2007) *Shimbunsha: hatan shita bijinesu moderu* (*The Newspaper Company: The Collapse of the Business Model*), Tokyo: Shinchosha.

Kim, I.C. and Hwang, C.S. (2002) 'Defining the non-profit sector: South Korea', in L. Salamon (ed.) *Working Papers of the Johns Hopkins Nonprofit Sector Project*. Online. Available HTTP: <http://ccss.jhu.edu/wp-content/uploads/downloads/2011/09/Korea_CNP_WP41_2002.pdf> (accessed 18 April 2019).

Kim, Y.C. (1981) *Japanese Journalists and Their World*, Charolotteseville: University of Virginia Press.

Kingston, J. (2017) 'Introduction', in *Press Freedom in Contemporary Japan*, Abingdon, UK: Routledge.

Kokuin: futsugo na shijitu wo kataritsugu (*Passing on an Inconvenient History Engraved in Memory*), (2013). [TV programme] SBC, 31 July.

Kumagai, T. (2006) *Doitsu wa kako to do mukiatte kita ka* (*How Germany Confronted its Past*), Tokyo: Keizai koho senta.

Lippman, W. (1982) 'Some notes on the press', in C. Rossiter and J. Lare (eds.) *The Essential Lippmann*, Cambridge, MA: Harvard University Press.

Minamizuka, S. (2006) 'The history textbook problem in Japan'. Online. Available HTTP: <www.npo-if.jp/worldhistory/wp-content/uploads/2015/11/The-History-Textbook-Problem-in-Japan.pdf> (accessed 16 April 2019).

Mulligan, G.A. (2017) 'Media muzzling under the Abe Administration', in J.B. Kingston (ed.) *Press Freedom in Contemporary Japan*, Abingdon, UK: Routledge.

Nomonhan: sekinin naki tatakai (*Nomonhan: The Irresponsible Battle*). (2018) [TV programme] NHK, 15 August.

Nankin jiken heishitachi no yuigon (*The Nanking Incident: The Testimony of the Soldiers*), (2015) [TV programme] NNN, 4 October.

Ota, T. (2019) 'Chugoku kaikaku kaiho 40-nen to nihon no yakuwari (Japan's Role in China's 40 Year Period of Economic Reforms)', *Sekai Keizai hyoron*. Online. Available HTTP: <www.world-economic-review.jp/impact/article1318.html> (accessed 17 April 2019).

Park, Y.H. (2006) *Wakai no tame ni: kyokasho, yasukuni, ianfu, dokuto* (*For the Sake of Reconciliaiton: Textbooks, Yasukuni, Comfort Women, Takeshima*), Tokyo: Heibonsha.

Saaler, S. (2005) *Politics Memory and Public Opinion*, Munich: Iudicium Verlag.

Schwartz, F. (2002) 'Civil society in Japan reconsidered', *Japanese Journal of Political Science*, 3: 195–215.

Seaton, P. (2007) *Japan's Contested War Memories*, Abingdon, UK: Routledge.

Seaton, P. (2017) 'NHK, war-related television and the politics of fairness', in J.B. Kingston (ed.) *Press Freedom in Contemporary Japan*, Abingdon, UK: Routledge.

Senritsu no kiroku: Inpaaru (Imphal: Horror Recorded). (2017) [TV programme] NHK, 15 August.

Takamine, T. (2006) 'The political economy of Japanese foreign aid: The role of yen loans in China's economic growth and openness', *Pacific Affairs*, 79: 29–48.

Wakamiya, Y. (2011) *Keynote Address at Making Friends While No One Is Looking: The Role of Sub-National Actors in Reconciliation in East Asia and Europe*. 14 February, American Institute of Contemporary German Studies, Johns Hopkins University, Washington, DC. (translated by A. Horvat).

Yamaguchi, T. (2017) 'Press freedom under fire: Comfort women, the *Asahi* affair and Uemura Takashi', in J.B. Kingston (ed.) *Press Freedom in Contemporary Japan*, Abingdon, UK: Routledge.

Yomiuri Shinbun. (2006) *Kensho: sensosekinin I and II (War Responsibility: An Investigation I and II)*, Tokyo: Chuo koron shinsha.

7

FORTRESS OKINAWA

Japan's media and the US military footprint

Justin McCurry

The sports field below had been temporarily transformed into a gladiatorial arena. I watched from a safe distance as dozens of men did their best to inflict as much pain on their comrades as possible, first with pepper spray and then during bouts of unarmed combat. This was my introduction to Camp Schwab on a blustery February morning on Okinawa, a subtropical island most Japanese associate with sun-kissed beaches and US military bases.

In many respects, it is the former that shapes the popular image of Okinawa, located roughly 1,000 miles south of Tokyo – a speck in the ocean that comprises just 0.6 per cent of Japan's total land area but hosts around 75 per cent of its US military bases. It is a venue for preseason baseball training camps and a trusty retreat for celebrities who, assailed by eager 'wide show' reporters on their return to Tokyo, dispense pleasantries about their sojourn in paradise. Every summer, TV shows gush about Okinawa's food, music, climate, crystal clear seas and its 'otherness' – the sense that as soon as you disembark at Naha airport, you have left Japan behind. The closest millions of holidaymakers will ever come to experiencing Okinawa's role as host to tens of thousands of US and Japanese military personnel are catching sight of Japanese Self Defense-Force fighter jets sharing tarmac with commercial airliners, or rubbing shoulders with off-duty US personnel. They may be taken aback by their hotel's proximity to Fortress Okinawa – mile after mile of high security fences, reminding them that what lies on the other side is the property of the US military. But as they dip a toe into the warm waters of the East China Sea, the Okinawa of jet sorties, low-flying helicopters, soldiers, sailors and airmen occupy a parallel universe. Few will be aware that Okinawa for years hosted nuclear weapons, that a hydrogen bomb was once 'lost' 130 kilometres off its coast, or that Agent Orange, the deadly toxin used in the Vietnam War to destroy jungle cover for the enemy, was sprayed across the island and 'routinely' buried underneath the bases or dumped into the sea (Mitchell 2017).

As a British correspondent covering Japan for a global audience, including a large and growing number of readers in the United States, I have followed events on Okinawa for more than 15 years. That period has been dominated by one issue: the planned relocation of Futenma Marine Corps Air Station to the village of Henoko – officially part of the city of Nago – which stretches across a narrow strip of land on the northern half of the main Okinawan island. The move was supposed to be the centrepiece of a planned realignment of US forces in Okinawa, where public opposition to their presence hardened after the 1995 rape and abduction of a 14-year-old girl by two Marines and a Navy corpsman. In 2006, Japan and the United States signed the Futenma agreement, which included plans to move about 8,000 Marines and their dependents to Guam, Hawaii and parts of Australia. By reducing the US military footprint – or so the reasoning went – Okinawans would be at least partially freed from the burden they have endured since the end of World War II.

Almost 15 years on, not a single Marine or piece of military hardware has left Futenma. When they drew up a blueprint for the base's future, Japanese and US officials seem to have overlooked what has become the relocation plan's single biggest obstacle: the Okinawan people themselves. Construction on the alternative to Futenma – an ambitious expansion of Camp Schwab, complete with two 1,800-metre V-shaped runways jutting out into Oura Bay – has been delayed by political, legal and environmental challenges. In March 2019, the Japanese defence ministry conceded that the land now occupied by Futenma was unlikely to be returned by the fiscal year 2022 deadline. An Okinawa prefectural government study claimed the cost of building the new base could reach 2.65 trillion yen, with the facility unable to start operations for another 13 years (*Mainichi Shimbun* 2019).

No pro-relocation candidate for Okinawa governor has won an election since 2006, although it should be noted that pro-relocation Taketoyo Toguchi won the election for Nago mayor in February 2018, and in late 2013, the then governor Hirokazu Nakaima reversed course and approved landfill at Henoko in exchange for government investment in Okinawa's creaking infrastructure. Denny Tamaki, who was elected as the island's governor in late 2018, like his predecessor Takeshi Onaga, who died in August that year, has vowed to fight the Henoko move – a stance backed by a majority of local voters in opinion polls (*Asahi Shimbun* 2018) and in a 24 February 2019 prefecture-wide referendum that saw a turnout of 52 per cent of eligible voters.

National newspapers toe the government line

For the majority of the Japanese media, the dispute now being played out in courtrooms and along the remote coastline of northern Okinawa hinges on a single premise: that one day, the people of Okinawa will bow to the inevitable and the Henoko base will be built. That much was discernible from some of their coverage of the referendum result. While Kyodo newswire went with the simple, and accurate, headline: 'Over 70 per cent of voters reject US base transfer in Okinawa referendum,' the conservative *Yomiuri Shimbun* relegated the Henoko result to the lower half of the front page, giving prominence instead to Emperor Akihito's address to mark the 30th anniversary of his reign. NHK's English-language website announced: 'Okinawa "no" vote exceeds 25 per cent benchmark' – a reference to the minimum level of support among those who cast their votes required for the result to be formally accepted by Tamaki. Readers will not have learned from the NHK online report that 70 per cent of those who voted opposed the relocation; only that 38 per cent of *all* eligible voters felt that way. Japan's public broadcaster has never performed similar psychological cartwheels in its coverage of general elections that return the conservative Liberal Democratic Party (LDP), which has governed Japan for most of its postwar history, to power on comparatively low turnouts. The relatively liberal *Tokyo Shimbun* and the *Asahi Shimbun* played up the challenges the vote posed to LDP Prime Minister Abe Shinzo, while the *Yomiuri* urged continued efforts to lessen the impact of US bases on local communities. The more conservative *Sankei* mirrored the government's position: the Okinawan people have spoken . . . and they shall be ignored. Henoko's construction, the paper said in a commentary, still represents the only chance of seeing through Futenma's permanent closure (*Sankei Shimbun* 2019).

The message had been the same in 2016 when I talked to members of the Tokyo media at an anti-relocation protesters' tent village on Henoko beach. 'I understand the feelings of Okinawans,' one journalist for a liberal Japanese newspaper told me. 'But when we think about the threat from China, it's a case of, well, it can't be helped.' The *shikata ga nai* ('can't be helped') mindset that accepts the inevitability of the relocation plan, however unpalatable it may be to local people, is a staple of the Tokyo-centric coverage of the 'Okinawa problem' – that Japan's security interests, and by extension the future of its alliance with the United States, hinge on the relocation plan.

Ever since the Futenma deal was formally agreed, the majority of Japan's media has toed the official line: that in these uncertain days of Chinese maritime aggression in the East China Sea and the South China Sea, and a North Korea armed with nuclear weapons, no realistic alternative exists to the Futenma relocation plan. No reasonable person would dispute that Futenma, an ageing airfield built by US occupation forces in 1945, has outgrown its surroundings. In 2008, during one of half a dozen reporting trips I have made to Okinawa, I stood in the grounds of Futenma No. 2 Elementary School, watching children play soccer next to the base's perimeter fence as aircraft roared overhead with alarming regularity. Would I happily send my own son and daughter here? The answer was, unequivocally, no. I had an unlikely ally in the former US Secretary of Defense Donald Rumsfeld, who described Futenma as the 'most dangerous base in the world' during a flyover in 2003 (Lummis 2018). But it wasn't until I looked down on Ginowan, Futenma's reluctant host city, from the top of a nearby hill that I realized just how closely intertwined the lives of US Marines and Japanese civilians had become in the decades since the end of the war. Either end of the two runways – which were separated by a strip of grass – was a cluttered skyline of apartment blocks, offices, schools, hospitals and other public buildings. On the base's southeastern corner, I could make out the campus of Okinawa International University, the scene of a crash involving a CH-53D Sea Stallion helicopter on 13 August 2004. The accident did not kill or injure anyone, but it was a reminder of the ever-present danger posed by the proximity of low-flying aircraft to a populous urban centre. For older people, it also evoked painful memories of a US military aircraft crash in 1959 at Miyamori Elementary School in which 18 children died.

Japanese mainland newspapers treated the 2004 crash like a minor mishap. Local people recall the US military officials taking over the crash site for hours, supplanting the island's police in another reminder of what some see as their quasi-colonial status, almost half a century since the island, occupied by US forces after the war, reverted to Japanese civilian control. Had the crash happened on the campus of Tokyo University, it would have been the lead story on the front page of every major newspaper in Japan, with all the attendant public debate on the US–Japan security treaty and the need to spread the hosting burden more evenly across the country. The exceptions were Okinawa's two main newspapers – the *Okinawa Times* and the *Ryukyu Shimpo*. While they issued special editions on the day of the crash, the lead story in the national *Asahi* and *Mainichi* newspapers was Watanabe Tsuneo's resignation as president of the Yomiuri Giants baseball club, following revelations that it had broken player scouting rules (Watanabe, incidentally, returned to the Giants' fold, this time as chairman, just ten months later). The *Yomiuri* understandably ignored Watanabe's travails and led with the opening ceremony of the Athens Summer Olympics.

There are other examples of how the major newspapers, along with NHK and the private TV networks, skew coverage to support the status quo: that Okinawa must continue to shoulder the burden of hosting US bases for the sake of the US–Japan alliance and, ergo, Japan's national security. They emphasize the importance of Okinawa's 'strategic location,' while avoiding discussion of alternatives to the idea that basing large number of troops on Okinawa is the only way to counter the perceived threat to national security posed by North Korea and China.

This approach has brought Okinawa's media into direct conflict with conservative politicians on the mainland. In 2000 – the year Okinawa hosted the Group of Eight summit – Mori Yoshiro, the then secretary general of the LDP who would become prime minister by the time the summit opened, accused the island's daily newspapers of indiscriminately 'opposing the government.' He likened them to the left-wing Japan Teachers' Union and accused them of being dominated by the Japan Communist Party (McCormack 2014). In 2006, the current governor of Tokyo, Koike Yuriko, who was then Minister of State for Okinawa and Northern Territories Affairs, labelled the Okinawa media 'anti-American' (*The Okinawa Times* 2017).

Hyakuta Naoki, a right-wing author and former board member of NHK during the much-maligned reign of its conservative chairman, Momii Katsuto, went further. As a guest speaker at a meeting of the LDP's youth wing in June 2014, Hyakuta called for the 'destruction' of the *Ryukyu Shimpo* and the *Okinawa Times*. Rather than criticize government policy on Futenma, the newspapers, he said, should consider how much more difficult life would be if some of the Okinawan islands were invaded by China (Aoki 2015). The remarks drew a furious response from the newspapers' editors, who warned that the threat could be extended to other 'troublesome' publications in the future (Aoki 2015).

Robert Eldridge, a former academic at Osaka University who has written extensively about Okinawa, defended Hyakuta's call for the destruction of Okinawa's two biggest newspapers, and accused their editors of seeking to trample on the novelist's freedom of speech. 'What was most surprising, however, about the Hyakuta Incident was not his comments,' Eldridge wrote in a commentary for Nippon.com in July 2015 (Eldridge 2015). He continued:

> Nor was it the strongly negative reaction of the two Okinawan newspapers — issuing a protest statement, partnering with their business allies such as the *Asahi Shimbun* to condemn Hyakuta in their editorials, and speaking before gatherings of their recent allies in the Foreign Correspondents Club of Japan. Rather, it was the slowness of people to realize that the media itself was crudely violating a private citizen's freedom of speech, all in the name of protecting free speech and a free press.

It takes quite a leap of imagination to equate criticism of Hyakuta with an attempt to muzzle him. He wasn't a private citizen by any reasonable definition, but a bestselling novelist, an ally of the prime minister Abe, and a former NHK governor who was addressing a group of ruling party politicians. Is it any wonder that his enthusiasm for the destruction of Okinawan newspapers triggered such an angry response?

The stances adopted by the mainland and Okinawan media appear irreconcilable, as Philip Brasor noted in a 2015 *Japan Times* column about coverage of anti-base demonstrations (Brasor 2015). With few exceptions, Brasor wrote, 'the national networks and dailies always give the impression that the protests constitute an impassioned movement pushing against an unmovable object. The Okinawan press, however, views the US military as an occupying force assured of its own entitlement by the Japanese government.'

The decade-long protests over the construction of helipads in Takae in the northernmost reaches of the main Okinawan island, Jinshiro Motoyama's hunger strike over the organization of the 2019 referendum, and the detention and suspended prison sentence given to Hiroji Yamashiro, a prominent anti-base protester arrested in 2016 for obstruction and damaging the construction site, received almost no coverage in the mainstream media (with the *Asahi* being the exception). To that could be added the decision to nominate as a World

Heritage Site an area of northern Okinawa that includes a US military training site, and the detection of high levels of carcinogens in rivers and water treatment plants around Futenma and Kadena – the biggest US military base in the Asia-Pacific (Narisawa 2018).

Opposition in the Okinawa media

Okinawa's media do not emerge from the base debate unblemished, however. Some of the people I contacted for comment for this chapter noted their tendency to avoid any criticism of the anti-base movement, including local politicians elected on a 'stop Futenma' platform. If sections of the Tokyo media were guilty of downplaying the strength of opposition to Henoko, their local counterparts overlooked the relative low turnout of 52 per cent in the 2019 referendum. In their unshakeable opposition to the Futenma relocation and support for the previous governor, Onaga Takeshi, who was elected in late 2014 on an anti-relocation ticket, were the Okinawa media, too, guilty of placing politics before objectivity? In a January 2016 report for the Congressional Research Service, Emma Chanlett-Avery, a specialist in Asian affairs, and Ian E. Rinehart, an analyst in Asian affairs, noted that Okinawa's two major newspapers viewed 'many developments in the base negotiations as further evidence of mainland discrimination' (Chanlett-Avery and Rinehart 2016). The publications, they wrote, 'are generally seen as left-leaning and deeply unsympathetic to Tokyo's security concerns.' They cited the 'scant' local coverage of the US military's humanitarian response to the March 2011 tsunami and earthquake along Japan's northeast coast, contrasting it with the mainland media's more positive reporting on 'Operation Tomodachi.' Chanlett-Avery and Rinehart added:

> In its reporting on the 2014 summit between Prime Minister Abe and President Obama, rather than applaud their intention to reduce the 'burden' of US bases on Okinawans, the *Ryukyu Shimpo* drew attention to the phrase 'long-term sustainable presence for US forces' and criticized its implication of a permanent military presence on Okinawa.

To my surprise, anti-base campaigners I spoke to in 2016 were not unflinching in their support for the *Ryukyu Shimpo* and the *Okinawa Times*, although they recognized the newspapers' campaigning journalism. Some sensed a reluctance to be overtly critical of Onaga, despite his fruitless legal bid to block construction work at Henoko and a much-vaunted trip to the United States in 2015, during which he failed to win much sympathy from lawmakers on the other side of the Pacific. Tamaki also failed to make any diplomatic headway when he made a similar trip in November 2018.

Faced with largely negative coverage on the mainland, the Okinawan media risk developing a siege mentality that compels them to defend anti-base political leaders under any circumstances. And by becoming less critical of the representatives on their own doorstep, both the main Okinawan newspapers expose themselves to claims of bias.

Yoshikawa Hideki, who teaches international communications at Meio University in Nago, said his Japanese students complain that the local newspapers ignore 'feel-good' stories involving US military personnel in Okinawa: volunteering to clean up local beaches, rescuing people from drowning or hosting on-base public events. Instead, they turn to the internet and *Big Circle*, the US Marine Corps' bilingual magazine. And in the same July 2015 Nippon.com article, Eldridge (2015) accused the island's newspapers of deliberately ignoring positive stories involving US military personnel, since they do nothing to promote their political agenda. Eldridge noted that the papers had failed to report acts of heroism and other good deeds performed by Okinawa-based US personnel:

> These stories include those about friendships, acts of humanity, good deeds, community relations, and many other aspects of the US military presence or the Japan-US relationship. By not reporting the positive things, the media misrepresents the actual relationship that does exist, instead focusing on the negative and sensational.

Yet these are minor quibbles. On the whole, Yoshikawa said, the Okinawan newspapers were performing the traditional media role of holding the government of the day to account. 'They are the most effective way of communicating the voice of Okinawan people to the Japanese and US governments,' he told me in an email interview. 'Most journalists I know at the newspapers believe that is their role. And many Okinawans agree with them' (Interview 26 February 2019). As a result, the Okinawan and mainland media occupy parallel universes. In the former, coverage is framed in the emotive language of foreign occupation and the wilful violation of human, legal and democratic rights; in the latter, the aim is to perpetuate what anti-base campaigners refer to as the 'three myths' of Okinawa: that the bases must remain due to the island's geopolitical significance, that US Marines on Okinawa are a deterrent against Chinese aggression and that Okinawans are economically dependent on the bases. Skilfully posited, those myths enable Abe's LDP to push the official narrative that there is no alternative to Henoko.

Alternatives to relocation

In fact, alternatives do exist, including those proposed by supporters of the Japan-US security treaty – people who would no sooner see Okinawa bid farewell to Uncle Sam than invite China to build a naval base off the coast of California. They include the late Republican Senator John McCain, a respected veteran and former POW of the Vietnam War. In May 2011, McCain, who died in 2018, put his name on a statement calling for Washington to consider abandoning the original plan to build an 'expensive replacement facility' for Futenma in Henoko

(BBC News 2011). McCain, along with fellow senators Carl Levin, then chairman of the Senate Armed Services Committee, and Jim Webb, then chairman of the Foreign Relations Subcommittee on East Asian and Pacific Affairs, released a statement describing the existing plans for US military realignment around the Futenma move as 'unworkable and unaffordable.' They proposed stationing some of the Marines currently at Futenma at nearby Kadena, the largest US military installation in the Asia-Pacific. The suggestion barely generated a flicker of interest in Japan, where it was all but ignored by the media. The White House, meanwhile, continued to insist that Henoko was the only location that made sense politically, economically and militarily. To retain their ability to respond quickly to, say, an emergency in the East China Sea, their logistical, air and ground forces must be close together, according to the Marines, who have warned that the removal of one or more of those groups would compromise their ability to safeguard the region's security (McCurry 2014). It is an assertion that goes largely unchallenged in the Japanese domestic media.

Even if we accept that US bases are necessary, is it really the case that Japan's defence would be compromised if Futenma were closed and the Henoko project cancelled? Mike Mochizuki, a widely respected expert on Japan-US relations at George Washington University, disagrees with the US administration's insistence that the Henoko landfill project is the only way in which Washington can maintain its deterrence capability in the Asia-Pacific. Mochizuki and Hashimoto Akikazu, project professor at J.F. Oberlin University in Tokyo, called on both countries to rehabilitate an earlier plan to build a heliport inside Camp Schwab and ditch the offshore runway (Hashimoto and Mochizuki 2015). The heliport option, they argued, would be more in keeping with the Marine Corps' expeditionary role, especially since the recent arrival in Okinawa and in other parts of Japan of more than two dozen MV-22 tilt-rotor aircraft, commonly known as Ospreys. The Ospreys' range of more than 1,000 miles means the Marines now have less need to be stationed near ground units in Okinawa, Mochizuki and Hashimoto have argued. They could just as easily be based in, say, Kyushu, and fly to collect ground forces on Okinawa when necessary.

The heliport option would be much cheaper than the offshore runway, particularly at a time when the United States is committing fewer resources to its military capability in the Asia-Pacific, and while Japan, with an eye on Chinese naval activity, is taking its own steps to bolster defences along its outlying island territories. And, as Mochizuki and Hashimoto point out, their option has the bonus of avoiding the environmental damage inflicted by land reclamation work in Oura Bay. 'By avoiding the economically and politically costly landfill base project at Henoko, this alternative proposal should be a win for Okinawa, a win for Japan, and a win for the United States,' they wrote in *The Diplomat* magazine in September 2015 (Hashimoto and Mochizuki 2015).

Here were two potential solutions that, on the surface, appeared far more palatable than the current – and apparently only – relocation plan. Yet Japan's mainstream media have deemed them undeserving of serious debate. Sandi Aritza, an American who translates articles from the *Ryukyu Shimpo* into English, is familiar with what she calls 'the lack of analysis or alternative opinions, and lack of depth' in mainstream Japanese media coverage of the base controversy. 'An article may lay out the facts and then give a quote from a central government representative and an Okinawan prefectural government representative, and that might be called "fair" because it presents the opinions of both sides, but I disagree,' Aritza told me in an email interview. 'I think the media fail to give sufficient analysis to provide readers with the means to form informed opinions, and fail to highlight the importance of the issue for all of Japan. They perpetuate the idea that it is just an Okinawa issue with no broader repercussions' (Interview September 2016).

A necessary defence against China?

Does Okinawa's apparently non-negotiable status as a frontline defence against potential Chinese aggression stand up to scrutiny? In April 2019, as the media quickly moved on from the Henoko referendum result, the *Asahi* ran a story, based on US military archives, suggesting that a Marine Corps unit based on Okinawa had spent long periods off the island. The 31st Marine Expeditionary Unit, comprising about 2,000 troops, had visited or deployed to at least 15 countries between 1992 and 2017, with annual absences amounting to more than 100 days most years, including around 160 in 2009 (Aibara 2019). The newspaper quoted Gabe Masaaki, a professor of political science at the University of the Ryukyus, as saying:

> The Japanese government says that the US Marine Corps stationed in Okinawa is a deterrent force and that the corps are stationed for the benefit of Japan. But this is only rhetoric to put Japanese people at ease. Why doesn't discussion on the US Marine Corps in Okinawa deepen? For many Japanese, there is only the abstract view that the US forces are necessary.
>
> *(Aibara 2019)*

Sato Manabu, a law professor at Okinawa International University, shares Gabe's concern that the media have failed in their duty to generate public discussion on Okinawa's deterrent effect. 'The media portray the US Marine Corps as an assault unit that would go to battle in the event of a confrontation over the Senkaku islands,' Sato said at a symposium on the Japanese media at Sophia University in Tokyo in May 2016. 'But the Marines cannot, and will not, do that. Even so, the Japanese public has been made to believe that Marines will be the first responders to any potential Chinese aggression. The security element of the issue has been overwhelmed by the Chinese threat. The Japanese media have lost their ability to think properly.'

Why, then, have the media shied away from analysis of potential solutions to the Futenma mess, even if only to decide that those alternatives are unworkable, or, at the very least, need revising? Much of the blame lies with a Japanese prime minister whom history has largely forgotten: Hatoyama Yukio. The Democratic Party of Japan's election victory in 2009 brought hope to some Okinawans that in Hatoyama they had a prime minister who was sensitive to their concerns and willing to take the bold political action necessary to reduce the island's military burden. Yet within months of his party's historic election victory, Hatoyama was forced into an ignominious retreat, conceding that it would be 'impossible' to relocate Futenma off Okinawa. His Futenma volte-face was not only sobering for Hatoyama and his party; it effectively buried any prospect for serious discussion in the media of any of the alternatives. What editor in his right mind, having seen how Hatoyama was pilloried for thinking he could confront the military establishment, would want to reopen the Pandora's box of potential alternatives to the Futenma plan?

Shooting the messenger

The mainstream media, frozen in the headlights of the Futenma juggernaut, also remember the unenviable fate that befell one of the few mainstream journalists to have scratched beneath the surface of the official version of Okinawa's modern history. Nishiyama Takichi was a reporter for the *Mainichi Shimbun* in 1971 when he produced a career-defining scoop. During negotiations over Okinawa's return to Japanese control, he discovered, Tokyo had secretly agreed to cover the cost of restoring farmland requisitioned for military use to its former state – payments to landowners estimated at US$4 million. The reversion agreement stated, however, that the United States would foot the bill. Cue a concerted attempt to first humiliate and then punish Nishiyama, who was found guilty of leaking state secrets, but did not serve time in prison. His fall from grace was dramatic, hastened by the revelation that he had acquired documents for his exclusive from a married foreign ministry clerk with whom he was having an affair. He was hounded out of his job in journalism and went into self-imposed exile for 30 years, helping his father run his fruit business. His former mistress was forced to leave her job at the foreign ministry, and her marriage ended in divorce (Jacobson 2005).

Journalists everywhere are not above indulging in *schadenfreude* when colleagues on a rival newspaper find themselves in trouble. Nishiyama, while reckless in his personal conduct, had been caught in the crosshairs of two governments desperate to conceal what amounted to a financial arrangement governing the future of a group of islands with a population of 1.4 million. Whatever *esprit de corps* existed among journalists keen to protect the public's right to know quickly vanished beneath the weight of the media's obsession with the salacious details of Nishiyama's private life, while the officials who allegedly drew up the pact and then kept it secret escaped scrutiny. To this day, the Japanese government refuses to admit the existence of the secret pact. It wasn't until 2000 that declassified US documents proved that every word Nishiyama had written was true. In 2011, the

Tokyo High Court concluded that the government had probably destroyed all documentary evidence of the secret pact. Nishiyama, now in his late 80s, could be forgiven for harbouring a grudge against the people who destroyed his career and reputation. In fact, he reserves most of his disdain for his fellow journalists. 'The Japanese media is sucking the life out of democracy and keeping the public in the dark,' he said in 2012 (McNeill 2012). 'They protect the powerful instead of reporting on them.'

Reporting environmental concerns

If Okinawa's 'strategic value' dictates much of the Japanese mainstream media coverage, the widening environmental crisis facing the relocation is finally beginning to resonate. Initial concerns about the environment centred on the degradation of the biodiversity-rich marine ecosystem of Oura Bay, one of the world's last remaining habitats of the dugong, an endangered species of marine mammal. Building Henoko's two runways off the coast will require the destruction of coral reefs. An environmental impact study conducted by the Japanese government concluded that construction would not cause significant harm to the dugong's habitat, but those findings were disputed by academics in Okinawa (Yoshikawa 2019). In February 2015, a US federal judge dismissed a lawsuit against the US Department of Defense that sought to prevent Henoko's construction on the grounds that it would harm the dugong.

Government officials who thought the environmental argument had been won had not reckoned with Mochizuki Isoko, whose reporting on landfill work at Henoko drew an official reaction that should horrify journalists. When Mochizuki, a reporter at the *Tokyo Shimbun* – a bastion of centre-left opposition to the Abe administration – started asking uncomfortable questions about the environmental impact of the Henoko base, the government responded by attempting to silence her. In a letter to the Cabinet Office press club, it called for 'restrictions' on questions by a certain reporter, whom it accused of spreading 'misinformation' about the potential damage the Henoko landfill work could inflict on the marine environment (Thompson 2019). Although the letter did not refer to Mochizuki by name, few were in any doubt as to the identity of the 'troublesome' reporter. Mochizuki had challenged official explanations of construction work, asking the chief cabinet secretary, Suga Yoshihide, during a briefing in late 2018 to comment on claims that 'red soil' – which can harm marine life and whose use in landfill in Okinawa is illegal – was being used in Henoko Bay and not ordinary gravel, as the government had claimed. Mochizuki pressed Suga, but was reportedly cut off in mid-flow, with Suga simply asserting that he was 'not required' to answer her questions. The Cabinet Office directive drew a written protest from the Japan Federation of Newspaper Workers' Unions after it came to light in the February 2019 edition of *Sentaku* magazine, while Mochizuki described it as 'a form of psychological pressure on me and my company' (*Asahi Shimbun* 2019). During questions a week later, the deputy chief cabinet secretary, Nishimura Yasutoshi, insisted there was 'absolutely no intention to restrict the asking of questions or to limit the (public's) right to know' (*Asahi Shimbun* 2019).

The episode exposed the absence in Japan of the professional solidarity that journalists in other liberal democracies take for granted. Having been unfairly treated by the people she is supposed to hold to account, Mochizuki received lukewarm support from her press club colleagues. By refusing to allow Suga to wriggle off the hook, according to a blog post by journalist Tanaka Ryusaku, Mochizuki had made life more difficult for other press club members who prefer a less adversarial approach (Tanaka 2019). Her 'crime' had been to ignore the conventions that ensure the smooth functioning of the press club system – a quid pro quo in which journalists are granted access to official sources in return for avoiding controversy. The furore caught the attention of Reporters without Borders, which called on Abe 'to respect the Japanese public's right to information by requiring his team to respond to all journalists' questions, without exception' (Reporters without Borders 2019). It added: 'This incident is the latest in a series of clashes between the Abe administration and Tokyo Shimbun journalists. Mochizuki, who has built a reputation for asking tough questions, almost always sees her questions ignored or rejected.'

The second battle of Okinawa

In so enthusiastically pushing the Henoko solution and paying only lip service to the concerns of local people, the central government and its allies in the Tokyo-based media may yet get their way on Henoko. In doing so, they risk further alienating large sections of the population of Okinawa and others who have their doubts about Henoko but support some form of US military presence on Okinawa. For their part, the Okinawa media have come to see themselves as defenders of a noble cause, their coverage dictated by a belief that any concession in the campaign would constitute a betrayal of their readership. They are now so tightly locked into a battle of wills with their mainland counterparts that the very idea of reporting anything but negatively on American military presence has become ideological anathema.

The 40th anniversary of Okinawa's 1972 reversion to Japanese control was an opportunity for the media to take stock of the island's unenviable position in the contemporary security landscape. As it turned out, it was an opportunity missed. As Brasor noted in his *Japan Times* 'Media Mix' column in May 2012, the tone of newspaper editorials marking the milestone made Okinawa 'seem like a dependency rather than an integral part of the nation' (Brasor 2012). Most national networks and daily newspapers, he added, give the impression that the protests 'constitute an impassioned movement pushing against an unmovable object. The Okinawan press, however, views the US military as an occupying force assured of its own entitlement by the Japanese government.' Brasor poked fun at the mainland media's own ridiculing of Hatoyama and his doomed plans to move Futenma's functions to another part of Japan. Noting that Hatoyama had explained in an interview with the *Ryukyu Shimpo* that his policy failed when it struck two immovable objects in the form of the Japanese defence and foreign ministries, he wrote: 'Hatoyama wanted to ditch the plan and start from scratch by negotiating directly with the US. The mainland media laughed at him for being naive. Who did he think he was, the prime minister? Oh . . .' (Reporters without Borders 2019).

The fast-moving media narrative surrounding the Futenma relocation, however, camouflages historical factors whose complexities do not lend themselves to media-friendly sound bites. The media consensus that has emerged from the Futenma debacle is that the 'Okinawa problem' is one of perception, not of grievance rooted in decades of injustice at the hands of policy makers in Tokyo and Washington. How many times have we heard national politicians talk of the need for the government to 'win the understanding' of the Okinawan people, while ignoring the uncomfortable reality that, in all likelihood, a consensus may never be reached?

And so Okinawa rumbles on in a state of limbo, trapped inside a historical legacy that its people had no part in creating. I left Camp Schwab that day in 2016 blinking furiously with pain from a droplet of errant pepper spray that had lodged itself in the corner of my eye – a reminder of my many shortcomings when set against those of the battle-ready men of the US Marine Corps. My military hosts had been unfailingly polite and as helpful as they could have been when confronted with questions about Okinawa's geopolitical role. But a slick public relations operation and the undeniable capacity for lasting friendship between guest military personnel and members of the host community pale when set against popular sentiment evoked by US bases and their unbreakable link to Okinawa's tragic history.

Between April and mid-June 1945, the first Battle of Okinawa claimed the lives of as many as 100,000 Japanese and 12,281 American soldiers during the 'typhoon of steel.' Estimates of civilian deaths vary from 40,000 to well over 100,000, including a large number of women and children who were forced to commit suicide by the Japanese Imperial Army (Brasor 2019). In the eyes of many Okinawans, militarist leaders in Tokyo regarded the island and its people as sacrifices worth making if it meant sparing the mainland from a US invasion.

Today, Okinawa's status as a vassal territory continues, abetted by large sections of the national Japanese media. It is worth noting that barely a month after the island's voters issued a resounding no to Henoko in the February 2019 referendum, the Japanese land ministry, at the behest of the defence ministry, nullified the prefecture's latest legal challenge to landfill work, which had been likened to 'digging holes in mayonnaise' (Dias and Murayama 2019).

The second Battle of Okinawa is, mercifully, largely peaceful. But it is not without victims: local voters whose democratic voice has been summarily silenced, and their fellow Japanese citizens, bombarded by the official mantra of 'Henoko or nothing,' repeated, with few exceptions, by the country's media.

And now, as at the height of hostilities more than seven decades ago, the prospects for a truce appear agonizingly remote.

Works cited

Aibara, R. (2019) 'U.S. Marines unit in Okinawa leaves Japan more than 100 days a year', *Asahi Shimbun*. Online. Available HTTP: <www.asahi.com/ajw/articles/AJ2019040 10054.html> (accessed 6 May 2019).

Aoki, M. (2015) 'Kameda Masaaki, Osumi, Magdalena, Media fire back at LDP for targeting revenue of newspapers critical of security bills', *The Japan Times*. Online. Available HTTP: <www.japantimes.co.jp/news/2015/06/26/national/politics-diplo macy/media-fire-back-ldp-targeting-newspaper-funding/#.XMaP3hMzZ-V> (accessed 6 May 2019).

Asahi Shimbun. (2018) 'Asahi poll: 63% of Okinawans oppose Abe's U.S. military policy'. Online. Available HTTP: <www.asahi.com/ajw/articles/AJ201809250041.html> (accessed 6 May 2019).

Asahi Shimbun. (2019) 'High-ranking official denies attempt to curb press freedom'. Online. Available HTTP: <www.asahi.com/ajw/articles/AJ201902080034.html> (accessed 6 May 2019).

BBC News. (2011) 'US senators urge rethink on Okinawa base plan'. Online. Available HTTP: <www.bbc.com/news/world-asia-pacific-13372194> (accessed 6 May 2019).

Brasor, P. (2015) 'Okinawa's story told differently in Tokyo', *The Japan Times*. Online. Available HTTP: <www.japantimes.co.jp/news/2015/03/07/national/media-national/ okinawas-story-told-differently-tokyo/> (accessed 6 May 2019).

Brasor, P. (2012) 'Anniversary of Okinawa's reversion highlights opposing press views', *The Japan Times*. Online. Available HTTP: <www.japantimes.co.jp/news/2012/05/27/ national/media-national/anniversary-of-okinawas-reversion-highlights-opposing-press-views/#.XYxH2pMzZ-U> (accessed 6 May 2019).

Chanlett-Avery, E. and Rinehart, I. (2016) 'The US military presence in Okinawa and the futenma base controversy', *Congressional Research Service*. Online. Available HTTP: <https://fas.org/sgp/crs/row/R42645.pdf> (accessed 6 May 2019).

Dias, T. and Murayama, H. (2019) 'A rocky way forward for Henoko base', *The Japan Times*. Online. Available HTTP: <www.japantimes.co.jp/opinion/2019/02/27/commentary/ japan-c ommentary/rocky-way-forward-henoko-base/#.XMaf1hMzZ-U> (accessed 6 May 2019).

Eldridge, R. (2015) 'Words to worry about: The danger of media bias in Okinawa', *Nippon.com*. Online. Available HTTP: <www.nippon.com/en/column/g00298/words-to-worry-about-the-danger-of-media-bias-in-okinawa.html> (accessed 6 May 2019).

Hashimoto, A. and Mochizuki, M. (2015) 'Revise the plan to build the U.S. Marine air base in Henoko, Okinawa', *The Diplomat*. Online. Available HTTP: <https://the diplomat.com/2015/09/revise-the-plan-to-build-the-u-s-mari ne-air-base-in-henoko-okinawa/> (accessed 6 May 2019).

Jacobson, D. (2005) 'Disgraced Mainichi journalist reopens 30-year-old scandal over Okinawa reversion', *The Asia-Pacific Journal*. Online. Available HTTP: <https://apjjf. org/-David-Jacobson/1983/article.html> (accessed 6 May 2019).

Lummis, D. (2018) 'Futenma: The most dangerous base in the world', *The Diplomat*. Online. Available HTTP: <https://thediplomat.com/2018/03/futenma-the-most-dangerous-base-i n-the-world/> (accessed 6 May 2019).

Mainichi Shimbun. (2019) 'Further delay eyed for Futenma return due to seabed reinforcement'. Online. Available HTTP: <https://mainichi.jp/english/articles/20190313/p2g/00m/0fp/090000c> (accessed 6 May 2019).

McCormack, G. (2014) 'The end of the postwar? The Abe government, Okinawa, and Yonaguni Island', *The Asia-Pacific Journal*, 12. Online. Available HTTP: <https://apjjf.org/2014/12/49/Gavan-McCormack/4233.html> (accessed 6 May 2019).

McCurry, J. (2014) 'US envoy visits Okinawa amid long-running row over military bases', *The Guardian*. Online. Available HTTP: <www.theguardian.com/world/2014/feb/11/us-envoy-okinawa-di spute-caroline-kennedy> (accessed 6 May 2019).

McNeill, D. (2012) 'Stories spiked despite journalism's mission to inform', *The Japan Times*. Online. Available HTTP: <www.japantimes.co.jp/life/2012/01/08/general/stories-spiked-d espite-journalisms-mission-to-inform/#.XMabTxMzZ-U> (accessed 6 May 2019).

Mitchell, J. (2017) 'Agent orange on Okinawa: Six years on', *The Asia-Pacific Journal*, 15: 1–7. Online. Available HTTP: <https://apjjf.org/2017/21/Mitchell.html> (accessed 6 May 2019).

Narisawa, K. (2018) 'Okinawa denied access to U.S. bases to trace source of toxins', *The Asahi Shimbun*. Online. Available HTTP: <www.asahi.com/ajw/articles/AJ201811250030.html> (accessed 6 May 2019).

The Okinawa Times. (2017) 'Koike Yuriko-shi, Bōei-shō jidai ni henoko suishin "Okinawa masukomi wa hanbei" tatakau aite (While promoting the Henoko project as defense minister, Koike Yuriko labelled the Okinawa media "Anti-American" and "our opponents")'. Online. Available HTTP: <www.okinawatimes.co.jp/articles/-/149371> (accessed 6 May 2019).

Reporters without Borders. (2019) 'Japan government must not judge the relevance of press questions'. Online. Available HTTP: <https://rsf.org/en/news/japan-government-must-not-judge-relevance-press-questions> (accessed 6 May 2019).

Sankei Shimbun. (2019) 'Okinawa kenmin tōhyō-koku wa isetsu o nebaritzuyoku toke (The Okinawa prefectural referendum: The country's forceful case for relocation)'. Online. Available HTTP: <www.sankei.com/column/news/190225/clm1902250001-n1.html> (accessed 6 May 2019).

Tanaka, R. (2019) 'Eiten o keikai seyo (Beware the rise of Mochizuki the journalist)'. Online. Available HTTP: <https://blogos.com/article/355515/> (accessed 6 May 2019).

Thompson, N. (2019) 'Japanese PM staff "restrict" reporter from pressers for "spreading misinformation" about environmental harm', *Global Voices*. Online. Available HTTP: <https://globalvoices.org/2019/02/09/japanese-pm-staff-restrict-reporte r-from-pressers-for-spreading-misinformation-about-environmental-har m/> (accessed 6 May 2019).

Yoshikawa, H. (2019) 'Abe's military base plan for Okinawa sinking in mayonnaise: Implications for the U.S. court and IUCN', *The Asia-Pacific Journal*, 17. Online. Available HTTP: <https://apjjf.org/2018/04/Yoshikawa.html> (accessed 6 May 2019).

8

PRESS FREEDOM IN SOUTH KOREA

Hyunjin Seo

Introduction

South Korea, officially the Republic of Korea, is widely considered to be a consolidated democracy that has a diverse and vibrant media environment with freedom of the press guaranteed by the Constitution (Freedom House 2017; Haggard and You 2015; Korea Press Foundation 2017a; Reporters without Borders 2017, 2018a; Youm 2003). According to the latest Korea Press Foundation report (Korea Press Foundation 2017a), there were 4,459 domestic newspapers comprising of 1,528 print or paper newspapers and 2,931 internet newspapers as of the end of 2016. There are also about 100 broadcasting companies that include public broadcasters, private broadcasting companies, special broadcasting companies, cable channels and terrestrial digital multimedia broadcasting companies. The top three newspapers in terms of media revenue are *Chosun Ilbo*, *Joongang Ilbo* and *Dong-a Ilbo* while KBS, MBC and SBS lead the broadcasting sector in terms of revenue.

South Korea's press freedom improved significantly following the country's first democratic and direct presidential election in 1987, earning the status 'free' from leading press freedom rating agencies, such as Freedom House, in the early 2000s (Freedom House 2012, 2017). However, its rating was downgraded to 'partly free' in 2011 and remained so until 2017. Deterioration in press freedom occurred under the conservative governments led by President Lee Myung-bak (2008–2013) and President Park Geun-hye (2013–2017), who both often attempted to censor media content unfavourable to their administrations. Reporters without Borders described the period as 'a dark decade for press freedom' in South Korea (Reporters without Borders 2018b). The situation improved following the election of progressive human rights lawyer Moon Jae-in as president in 2017. South Korea's World Press Freedom Index ranking moved from 63 in 2017 to 43 in 2018 (Reporters without Borders 2018a).

Political meddling, national security limitations on free speech and abuse of criminal defamation are considered some of the major problems that challenge press freedom in South Korea (Haggard and You 2015; Reporters without Borders 2017, 2018b). There have been concerns that government and business conglomerates attempt to influence media content through allocation of public subsidies or advertising. According to a Korea Press Foundation survey of 1,677 South Korean reporters in 2017, advertisers, their management and media owners, and government/political actors were seen as the most significant factors in restricting press freedom (Korea Press Foundation 2017b). Some administrations, including that of former President Park Geun-hye, attempted to penalize media organizations critical of the government (Fifield 2014). Censorship of online content and defamation lawsuits against the media also increased significantly during the Park administration, inviting concerns and criticism from national and international organizations working to enhance press freedom.

The National Security Law in South Korea is a source of contention regarding press freedom and freedom of expression, as conservative administrations sometimes used the law, which prescribes imprisonment for praising or expressing sympathy for North Korea, to selectively censor editorial content (Choe 2012). The Korean Peninsula, which is divided into North Korea and South Korea along the heavily fortified 38th parallel, is the last vestige of the Cold War. The issue of reconciliation with or threats from North Korea has often been covered in a partisan manner in South Korean media, with conservative media calling for hardline policies toward the North, while liberal and progressive media favour rapprochement (Lim and Seo 2009; Seo 2009). In this highly charged debate, the liberal media has to exercise self-censorship so as not to risk being charged with pro-North Korean sympathies under the National Security Law.

Despite these problems, South Korean media organizations and journalists largely enjoy freedom to practice journalism. The country also has strong civic organizations, such as the People's Coalition for Media Reform, which work to enhance the freedom and transparency of media organizations in South Korea.

Legal/regulatory environment

The Constitution of South Korea guarantees freedom of the press, and this is largely respected in practice. Specifically, Article 21 of the Constitution concerning 'speech, press, assembly, honor, and public morals' states that:

1   All citizens shall enjoy freedom of speech and the press, and of assembly and association.
2   Licensing or censorship of speech and the press, and licensing of assembly and association may not be recognized.
3   The standard of news service and broadcast facilities and matters necessary to ensure the functions of newspapers is determined by law.
4   Neither speech nor the press shall violate the honor or rights of other persons nor undermine public morals or social ethics. Should speech or the press

> violate the honor or rights of other persons, claims may be made for the damage resulting therefrom.
>
> *(Republic of Korea 1987)*

Under South Korean law, both individuals and business entities can establish and operate private media outlets. By the end of 2016, there were about 5,000 private media organizations operating in South Korea (Korea Press Foundation 2017a, 2017b). Internet organizations accounted for a large portion, with about 3,000 internet newspapers in operation. In a move seen as restricting the dynamic internet newspaper environment in South Korea, in 2015 the Park Geun-hye administration approved an amendment to the enforcement decree of the Newspaper Act that applied stricter rules for registering an online newspaper. This amendment revised the requirement for registering an online newspaper from three or more reporting and editorial staff to five or more (Choi 2015; Yoo 2015). The amendment was widely seen as the Park government's attempt to reduce press freedom among internet news publications. The Constitutional Court of Korea ruled the amendment unconstitutional in 2016 citing the importance of minimizing regulation of internet media outlets to ensure their autonomy (Jung 2016a).

In 2011, the South Korean government revised a set of media laws to allow investment by conglomerates and newspaper companies in the broadcasting sector. After this change, five new cable television channels, including four general-programming stations and one all-news channel, were launched, challenging the market dominance of the three major networks – two public service broadcasters (Korean Broadcasting System, or KBS, and Munhwa Broadcasting Corporation, or MBC), and one private broadcaster (Seoul Broadcasting System, or SBS). These three networks previously held exclusive rights to provide general programming, including news (Freedom House 2012). This change permitted leading conservative newspapers – *Chosun Ilbo*, *JoongAng Ilbo* and *Dong-a Ilbo* – to open broadcasting channels with the potential to serve as supporters of the conservative Lee administration.

In the wake of corruption scandals surrounding former President Park Geun-hye in 2016 and the subsequent candlelight vigils by South Korean citizens calling for Park's impeachment, a *JoongAng Ilbo*-affiliated broadcasting channel, JTBC, emerged as 'the frontrunner in South Korean broadcast journalism' with its investigative journalism (Korea Press Foundation 2017a). Despite the conservative leanings of *JoongAng Ilbo*, JTBC early on demonstrated its editorial independence and investigative integrity, holding conservative governments accountable. A major turning point in media coverage of the political corruption scandal involving Park and her close friend Choi Soon-sil took place on 24 October 2016, when JTBC reported that it had obtained one of Choi's computers which showed she had inappropriate access to confidential government documents and had been closely involved in Park's national security decision-making (Emergency Citizen Action 2018, Jung 2016b). News that someone with no official government position not only had access to such significant information, but that she had used that information to influence major corporations for her personal gain, angered many South Koreans. The JTBC story received wide attention among South Korean citizens, increasing the numbers participating in the candlelight vigils that provided crucial momentum for the impeachment of President Park in 2017.

In South Korea, there is freedom to both become a journalist and practice journalism. In addition, various media advocacy groups and journalist associations work freely to support journalists' rights and interests. However, under the conservative Lee Myong-bak and Park Geun-hye administrations, some journalists were dismissed for alleging political bias on the part of their management or media owners (Choe 2016; Freedom House 2016). During President Lee's administration, his advisers were appointed to key positions at public service broadcasting companies over the objections of journalists who sought to maintain those broadcasters' editorial independence. More than 500 union members of the public broadcaster MBC went on strike in January 2012, demanding the resignation of MBC President Kim Jae-chul, who was close to President Lee, over interference in coverage at the station. The union accused MBC of intentionally reducing coverage of politically sensitive issues, such as corruption allegations against President Lee and anti-government rallies (Lee 2017). During Lee's tenure, more than 180 South Korean journalists were penalized for their roles in advocating for press freedom or for filing reports critical about government policies. Among these 180 journalists, 20 reporters, including six at the Yonhap Television News (YTN), were dismissed from their newsroom positions. Most of these reporters were later reinstated based on court rulings or changes in the administration (Park 2017b).

One of the most controversial issues related to freedom of the press and expression in South Korea concerns North Korea. Since the conclusion of the Korean War in 1953, the two sides have had several military skirmishes and continue to consider each other as enemies. Specifically, Article 7 of South Korea's National Security Law prescribes imprisonment for praising or expressing sympathy for North Korea, and selective enforcement of the law has been a major issue for working journalists (Haggard and You 2015). The conservative administrations of Lee Myung-bak and Park Geun-hye were particularly aggressive in using the National Security Law to regulate news content with reference to North Korea. In January 2012, Park Jung-geun, a 24-year-old photographer and blogger, was arrested on charges of violating the National Security Law for reposting content from the North Korean government's Twitter account (Choe 2012). Despite Park's contention that his Twitter posts were meant to ridicule North Korea's leadership, the South Korean prosecution charged that his actions served as a vehicle to spread North Korean propaganda, regardless of his intention. Park was given a ten-month suspended sentence in November 2012. In March 2016, the Korea Communications Standards Commission (KCSC), an official body responsible for monitoring online content, blocked a British journalist's website dealing with North Korean technology issues, alleging that it violated the

National Security Law (Lee 2017). The Lee and Park administrations received substantial criticism from national and international freedom of expression organizations for their censorship of online content. According to the KCSC, the number of South Korean websites or social media accounts shut down for pro-North Korean content rose from ten in 2009 to 304 in 2011. Approximately 14,430 web posts were deleted by the police in 2009 for 'threatening national security by praising North Korea' and/or for 'denouncing the U.S. and the (South Korean) governments,' and the number increased to over 67,000 in 2011 (Freedom House 2012; Haggard and You 2015). In 2017, press freedom advocacy groups criticized the Moon Jae-in administration for banning a journalist, a former North Korean defector currently working for the conservative daily *Chosun Ilbo*, from covering inter-Korean government talks (Reporters without Borders 2017). The South Korean government cited 'special circumstances' in banning the journalist, who has published reports critical of North Korea, thus illustrating how the politics of a divided peninsula affect press freedom regardless of who is in power.

While defamation of public figures is rarely criminalized in most established democracies, defamation remains a criminal offence in South Korea that carries a sentence of up to seven years in prison (Haggard and You 2015). Incumbent governments and politicians in South Korea are often accused of using criminal defamation to silence their critics and opponents. In particular, during the Park Geun-hye administration, international media advocacy organizations expressed concerns that the government abused defamation laws to silence the media (Choe 2016; Haggard and You 2015; Human Rights Watch 2014). Journalists or commentators who criticized the Park government were often threatened with or prosecuted on defamation charges. For example, in October 2014, prosecutors indicted Tatsuya Kato, then the Seoul bureau chief of the Japanese newspaper *Sankei Shimbun*, for defaming President Park by citing rumours about the president's activities on the day of the Sewol ferry disaster, which killed more than 200 South Korean teenagers (Choi 2015). In an online article published in August 2014, Kato mentioned rumours in the financial industry that President Park may have been having a romantic encounter with a former aide as the ferry was sinking (KBS 2016). The government's delayed response at that time was widely viewed as one reason why the number of deaths was so high. In December 2015, the Seoul Central District Court acquitted Kato, ruling that he had engaged in a protected form of speech. In November 2014, eight aides of President Park filed a criminal defamation complaint against *Segye Ilbo* newspaper's reporters and staff members for reporting on a leaked document from President Park's office (Human Rights Watch 2014). The document contained a summary of rumours that Park's former aide, with no official government role at that time, was involved in important government decision-making. In July 2015, the KCSC announced a regulation change allowing third parties to request defamation reviews, in addition to the affected individuals and their representatives.

This change allowed the commission to remove content, even if the purported victim did not consider it defamatory (Freedom House 2016).

Political environment

Following liberation from Japanese colonial rule (1910–1945) until the late 1980s, South Korea was ruled by a series of authoritarian or military regimes that restricted the news media's access to information and freedom to report on different issues (Freedom House 2017; Youm 2003). After the country's first democratic and direct presidential election in 1987, South Korea quickly emerged as a vibrant democracy. As of 2019, South Korea has a multiparty system, and its National Assembly is composed of 300 elected members. The Democratic Party of Korea became the ruling party in 2017 with the election of its leader Moon Jae-in as president following the impeachment of President Park Geun-hye. The Moon administration has made efforts to fight against corruption in different sectors, and there were early signs of improvement in press freedom as well. For example, journalists and artists who had been blacklisted by the Lee and Park administrations for being critical of the government were reinstated, and there have been wide national discussions about how to reduce political influence on public broadcasters (Park 2017b).

The democratic changes in the political environment from the late 1980s allowed the Korean news media to enjoy more freedom in reporting on and criticizing the government. Today, news reports by about 5,000 media organizations offer diverse views on political, social, and economic issues (Korea Press Foundation 2017a). Journalists enjoy access to a wide range of information on different topics, and cases of physical violence against or harassment of journalists are almost non-existent. Passed by the National Assembly in 1996, the Act on Disclosure of Information by Public Agencies allows journalists and citizens to request information held by public agencies.

However, press freedom in South Korea is often challenged by government or political entities' attempts to influence news content. For example, the administrations of former Presidents Lee and Park attempted to clamp down on media outlets that were critical of the government (Fifield 2014). Government-funded national public broadcasters such as KBS and MBC have been particularly vulnerable to political influence, as the government and ruling party often determine the appointment of top-level management personnel in the broadcasting companies. For example, during the tenure of conservative presidents Lee and Park (2008–2017), programming at these stations was largely determined by the management team handpicked by the government (Freedom House 2016, 2017). This resulted in news coverage by KBS and MBC being tilted in favour of these governments. One recent example is their coverage of the corruption scandal involving President Park and her confident Choi Soon-sil in 2016 and 2017. At that time, these broadcasting stations often simply followed the Park government's narratives and failed to independently investigate the case. South Korean citizens called reporters from these stations *Giregi*, translated as 'garbage reporters,' expressing dismay at their lack of independent reporting on the corruption scandal that eventually led to Park's impeachment. In contrast, the public credibility and popularity of JTBC, a relatively new player in broadcast journalism, increased significantly through its strong investigative journalism about the Park-Choi scandal (Korea Press Foundation 2017a).

Similarly, during the progressive governments under President Kim Dae-jung (1998–2003) and Roh Moo-hyun (2003–2008), progressive or liberal individuals were picked by those governments to lead public broadcasting companies. And, since President Moon took office in 2017, progressives have begun to replace conservatives in managerial positions at the public broadcasting companies. Consequently, media outlets and journalists sometimes engaged in self-censorship to avoid professional repercussions when the government changes. Given the lack of transparency in selecting board members of KBS and MBC, it remains a major concern that government-funded broadcast media companies may be influenced by the political orientation of the incumbent government.

The National Security Law, which was discussed in the previous section, is often used for political purposes. The application of the National Security Law to journalists and citizens tends to be rigid and strict under conservative governments, but more relaxed under liberal governments. For example, the number of people charged under the law fell sharply under the liberal governments of Kim Dae-jung and Roh Moo-hyun (Haggard and You 2015), while the number increased under the conservative governments of Lee Myung-bak and Park Geun-hye, with journalists, bloggers and scholars indicted for violating the law. Specifically, the number of people indicted for violations of the National Security Law grew from 34 in 2006 and 2007 to 91 in 2011 and 74 in 2012 (Haggard and You 2015).

In 2015, the conservative Park Geun-hye administration accused Shim Eun-mi, a Korean-American talk show host and author who was on a speaking tour in South Korea, of making comments sympathetic toward North Korea and eventually deported her (Choe 2015). Soon after Shim's deportation, Hwang Sun, an activist and former opposition party member who had organized her lectures, was arrested on charges of violating the National Security Law. In particular, conservative governments have censored online content. The number of people prosecuted for online activities deemed favourable to North Korea rose from five in 2008 to 51 in 2011. In addition, the number of Korean websites closed for pro-North Korean posts increased from 18 in 2009 to 178 in 2011 (Freedom House 2012; Haggard and You 2015). Media advocacy groups in and outside of South Korea condemned the government's censorship.

Not only editorial content but also news content of leading newspapers in South Korea tends to follow the newspaper's partisan lines (Lee and Paik 2017). For example, *Chosun Ilbo* and *Dong-a Ilbo*, two of the top three newspapers in South Korea, have a record of backing conservative governments or agendas. In contrast, *Hankyoreh* and *Kyunghyang Shinmun* have consistently supported progressive or liberal agendas. While these newspapers work largely within ethical boundaries, they are sometimes accused of engaging in character assassination of opposition politicians. For example, conservative *Dong-a Ilbo* ran opinion pieces and news stories on the lack of discipline and cultural sophistication of liberal President Roh, who didn't attend college (KBS 2019).

Commercial/economic environment

One of the major economic power houses in Asia, South Korea is the world's 11th largest economy and home to several leading global brands, including Samsung (OECD 2017). According to the 2018 Index of Economic Freedom (Heritage Foundation 2018), South Korea's economic freedom score was 73.8, ranking 27th out of 170 countries in the 2018 Index. The country's gross domestic product is US$1.9 trillion, with a 2.8 per cent five-year compound annual rate of growth.

Many newspapers are controlled by large industrial conglomerates and depend on major corporations for their advertising revenue. The television and radio sectors include both public and private outlets. According to the Korea Press Foundation's survey of 4,100 media organizations in South Korea in 2016, the average revenue per media organization was about US$2.2 million (Korea Press Foundation 2017a). The organizations include 1,423 print newspapers, 2,604 internet newspapers and 52 broadcasting stations. The average revenue for broadcasting companies was significantly higher (about US$102.7 million) than that for print newspapers (about US$2.2 million) or internet newspapers (US$74,000). Specifically, public broadcasting companies such as KBS, MBC and SBS earned the largest revenue, followed by cable channels. In a competitive commercial environment, news organizations have made efforts to enhance their audience reach and engagement through infotainment and human interest stories.

There are no significant operational restrictions on news production and distribution (Freedom House 2017). South Korea boasts one of the world's highest internet penetration rates, at about 92.6 per cent (Internet World Stats 2018), and most users have access to affordable high-speed connections. An increasing number of residents obtain news exclusively from online sources. Foreign media sources are widely accessible, with the exception of news from North Korea, which remains severely restricted.

As discussed earlier, political or business entities' attempts to influence media coverage through allocation of advertising or subsidies remains a concern in the country. For example, big corporations reduce their advertisement budget allocation to media outlets that are critical of their company. South Korean journalists indicated that advertisers, their managers and media owners, and government or political actors are the most significant factors in restricting press freedom (Korea Press Foundation 2017b).

Journalistic training/citizen journalism

Newsroom editorial structures and journalist training in South Korea are largely similar to those in Western journalism, as a significant proportion of media scholars/educators and journalists receive their education in the West, especially in the United States (Erni and Chua 2008). Some become media professionals after earning a degree in journalism, while another significant proportion of journalists have different academic backgrounds, ranging from political science to business administration.

Becoming a journalist in South Korea in a major media organization generally involves resume screening, passing an exam unique to each outlet and also interviews. The overwhelming majority of journalists (85.5 per cent) in 2016 held four-year college or graduate school degrees (Korea Press Foundation 2017a). Journalism is considered a prestigious profession that comes with access to important sectors of society and a stable income (Erni and Chua 2008). However, a recent report shows that journalists' job satisfaction levels have remained relatively low and have continued to decline: 6.38 in 2007 (out of 11) and 5.99 in 2017 (Korea Press Foundation 2017b). Also, a significantly higher proportion of journalists (76.8 per cent) in 2017 perceived that morale within their newsroom had declined compared with in the past, whereas about 52 per cent said so a decade ago. This may reflect increasing competition and demands within the news industry, with a variety of news providers and user-generated content influencing the rapidly evolving media ecosystem. Indeed, the average number of stories that journalists submitted every week increased from 15.3 in 2007 to 22.4 in 2017. At the same time, the average annual salary has remained almost the same for a decade (Korea Press Foundation 2017b).

As indicated earlier, a significant proportion of South Korean journalists have fought against meddling by politicians and business entities, even at the risk of losing their job (Kim 2014). However, journalists receiving bribes from business or political entities was a concern until recently. A 2000 Korea Press Foundation survey showed that only about 30 per cent of journalists surveyed responded that bribes should never be accepted. About 34 per cent indicated that bribes are acceptable, so long as they don't influence news contents (Erni and Chua 2008). South Korea passed a new anti-graft law in 2016 aimed at rooting out corruption and bribery. Under the law, journalists could face up to three years in prison for accepting a meal worth more than US$27 and gifts worth more than US$45 if there is a potential conflict of interest (Kwon and Hancocks 2016).

Citizen journalism has played an important role in South Korea (Erni and Chua 2008; Kern and Nam 2009). The national leader in citizen journalism is OhMyNews, a comprehensive internet newspaper based on the contributions of thousands of citizens. Established in 2000 with the motto of 'Every citizen is a reporter,' OhMyNews is considered the most successful internet newspaper in South Korea, receiving 2 million visitors to the site a day in 2004 (Kang 2016; Kern and Nam 2009). As of 2016, OhMyNews had 100 professional staff including beat reporters and editorial staff, along with roughly 70,000 citizen journalists registered with the site (Nah and Chung 2016). While only a small number of registered citizens contribute actively to the site, reporting by citizen journalists accounted for almost half of news items featured on the site as of 2016.

Role of technology in journalism

A world technology leader, South Korea boasts about 92.7 per cent internet penetration as of early 2018 (Internet World Stats 2018). There is high-speed internet access in most areas of the country, and South Korea shares direct internet bandwidth with many different countries (Seo and Thorson 2012, 2016). Social media sites are widely used in South Korea, with 84 per cent of the population active on social media as of 2017 (Statista 2017). While statistics slightly vary in terms of popular social media sites, YouTube is considered the most popular social media site in South Korea with a penetration rate of 74 per cent, followed by Facebook (62 per cent), KakaoTalk (58 per cent), Instagram (39 per cent), Twitter (28 per cent), and Messenger (24 per cent) (Statista 2017). As of 2018, YouTube is also the No. 1 social media site in terms of time spent on the platform, with users having spent an average of 882 minutes watching video clips on the site in April 2018 (Jun 2018). Korean users in total spent 25.8 billion minutes on YouTube that month. Those in their teens to their 40s spent the most time on YouTube. Specifically, Korean teens spent a cumulative 7.6 billion minutes, and those in their 20s spent 5.3 billion minutes on YouTube in April 2018. KakaoTalk, South Korea's most popular messaging app, was the second most popular social media site in terms of time spent on the platform. Teenagers spent 2.4 billion minutes using KakaoTalk and 1.6 billion minutes on Facebook in April 2018.

These social media sites have become important platforms for collective action. For example, in the wake of the Sewol ferry disaster in 2014, South Koreans used social media such as KakaoTalk to mobilize protests against the South Korean government for its perceived 'mishandling of the situation' (BBC 2014). In addition, popular social media sites (e.g., KakaoTalk, Facebook, Twitter and YouTube) were key platforms for citizens mobilizing candlelight vigils calling for the impeachment of President Park. Participants in the vigils used Facebook Live and KakaoTalk to broadcast their participation in them and to encourage others to become involved. Moreover, some social influencers – citizens with a lot of social media followers and clout – served as important sources of information related to the vigils. Leading civic groups used Facebook, Twitter and KakaoTalk as primary channels for sharing information related to the candlelight vigils. Since the candlelight vigils ended and the Moon Jae-in government was inaugurated, activists and citizens have nonetheless continued attempting to promote substantive changes in society utilizing social media platforms.

These technological advances in the country have also influenced journalistic practices in South Korea. Leading media organizations monitor citizen conversations around different topics and actively share news stories via popular social media sites. In addition, individual journalists are encouraged to use the medium to promote their stories and engage with readers. Virtual reality (VR) and augmented reality (AR) applications are also gaining attention from South Korean media organizations (Renner 2017). Citizen journalism is also amplified, as more and more citizens use social media platforms to share information and commentaries (Kang 2016).

As more and more people produce and share content online, misinformation and disinformation has emerged as a serious problem. For example, in 2019, some right-wing politicians and activists spread falsified documents claiming that the Gwangju Uprising, a pro-democracy protest on 18 May 1980, included the participation of North Korean military personnel (Lee 2019). In response, the May 18 Gwangju Uprising Foundation announced the launching of a YouTube channel to combat misinformation and disinformation related to the pro-democracy movement (Lee 2019). This is in line with increasing efforts by organizations to employ YouTube in efforts to fight against misinformation. In 2018, the Roh Moo-hyun Foundation started a YouTube series aimed at informing citizens about complicated political, social, and economic issues in an easy-to-understand manner and to combat misinformation and disinformation online. The Moon Jae-in administration also announced a series of legal and education measures to address the issue (Moon 2018).

Conclusion

In the wake of the corruption scandal surrounding President Park Geun-hye, which led to her impeachment in 2017, there were calls for increased media freedom and reform, as the case highlighted some major media outlets' failure to function as watchdogs in monitoring the government (Kim 2016). With the election of progressive Moon Jae-in as president in 2017, press freedom in the country, which had deteriorated under conservative former Presidents Lee and Park, has shown signs of improvement (Reporters without Borders 2018a, 2018b). For example, broadcast journalists, who were dismissed during the Lee and Park administrations, were reinstated soon after Moon took office (Park 2017a). The country has seen other positive signs in this area, including formal reviews of policies and regulations directly or indirectly restricting press freedom, including government involvement in appointments of managerial positions in public broadcasting companies. However, there are several sources of concern with regard to the Moon administration's approach to press freedom or freedom of expression. In 2018, South Korea's Unification Ministry decided to exclude a North Korean defector-turned-journalist from covering high-level talks between North and South Korea, citing 'special circumstances' (Kang 2018). In response, the press corps of the Unification Ministry issued a statement criticizing the move as a 'serious violation' of press freedom. In addition, South Korea's Ministry of Justice's implementation of a series of measures to crack down on the circulation of false and fabricated information raised concerns regarding freedom of expression (Moon 2018). The measures include imposing fines on those spreading false information online.

Balancing the National Security Law and defamation laws with freedom of the press and expression continues to be a significant challenge in South Korea. In addition, journalists remain concerned about the negative impact of advertisers, media owners and political actors using their influence to infringe on press freedom (Korea Press Foundation 2017b). As is the case in other countries, media outlets in South Korea are also dealing with the issue of misinformation and disinformation being quickly spread via social media sites (Park 2018). Effectively navigating rapid innovations in communication technologies and the consequent changes in information generation and sharing will remain a significant issue for South Korea's vibrant media sector. The division with North Korea and subsequent security concerns, as well as ideological divides within South Korean society, pose unique challenges to press freedom in South Korea.

References

BBC. (2014) '#BBCtrending: Why South Koreans are fleeing the country's biggest social network'. Online. Available HTTP: <www.bbc.com/news/blogs-trending-29555331> (accessed 22 March 2018).

Choe, S.H. (2012) 'South Korean man given suspended sentence for twitter posts', *The New York Times*. Online. Available HTTP: <https://cn.nytimes.com/world/20121123/c23korea/en-us/> (accessed 22 March 2018).

Choe, S.H. (2015) 'South Korea deports American over warm words for trips to north', *The New York Times*. Online. Available HTTP: <www.nytimes.com/2015/01/11/world/asia/south-korea-to-deport-american-over-warm-words-about-north-korea.html> (accessed 22 March 2018).

Choe, S.H. (2016) 'South Korea government accused of using defamation laws to silence critics', The New York Times. Online. Available HTTP: <www.nytimes.com/2016/03/06/world/asia/defamation-laws-south-korea-critics-press-freedom.html> (accessed 22 March 2018).

Choi, S.H. (2015) 'Sankei Shinbun innocent (산케이 무죄 . . . "언론 자유 중요" 부각)', *Journalism Association of Korea*. Online. Available HTTP: <http://www.journalist.or.kr/news/article.html?no=38117> (accessed 7 March 2018).

Choi, W. (2015) 'Requiring 5 or more staff for registering for an online newspaper is against the Constitution ('5인 이상 돼야 인터넷신문'은 허가제 금지한 헌법에 위반')', *The Hankyoreh*. Online. Available HTTP: <www.hani.co.kr/arti/society/media/723849.html> (accessed 28 March 2018).

Emergency Citizen Action. (2018) *Record of Candlelight Vigils for Impeaching President Park Geun-hye*, Seoul: Emergency Citizen Action for the Park Geun-hye Administration's Resignation.

Erni, J.N. and Chua, S.K. (2008) *Asian Media Studies: Politics of Subjectivities*, Hoboken, NJ: Wiley-Blackwell.

Fifield, A. (2014) 'In South Korea, journalists fear a government clampdown on the press', *The Washington Post*. Online. Available HTTP: <www.washingtonpost.com/world/asia_pacific/in-south-korea-journalists-fear-a-government-clampdown-

on-the-press/2014/12/09/ff13603e-7a2f-11e4–8241-8cc0a3670239_story.html>
(accessed 28 March 2018).

Freedom House. (2012) 'Freedom of the press: South Korea'. Online. Available HTTP: <https://freedomhouse.org/report/freedom-press/2012/south-korea> (accessed 22 March 2018).

Freedom House. (2016) 'Freedom of the Press: South Korea'. Online Available HTTP: <https://freedomhouse.org/report/freedom-press/2016/south-korea> (accessed 18 March 2018).

Freedom House. (2017) 'South Korea: Freedom of the press 2016'. Online. Available HTTP: <https://freedomhouse.org/report/freedom-press/2017/south-korea> (accessed 7 April 2018).

Haggard, S. and You, J.S. (2015) 'Freedom of expression in South Korea', *Journal of Contemporary Asia*, 45: 167–179.

Heritage Foundation. (2018) 'South Korea economy: Population, GDP, inflation, business, trade, FDI, corruption'. Online. Available HTTP: <https://www.heritage.org/index/country/southkorea> (accessed 7 March 2018).

Human Rights Watch. (2014) 'South Korea: Stop using criminal defamation laws'. Online. Available HTTP: <https://www.hrw.org/news/2014/12/14/south-korea-stop-using-criminal-defamation-laws> (accessed 10 March 2018).

Internet World Stats. (2018) 'Asia internet stats by country and 2018 population statistics'. Online. Available HTTP: <www.internetworldstats.com/stats3.htm> (accessed 7 March 2018).

Jun, J. (2018) 'YouTube most used app in Korea', *The Korea Times*. Online. Available HTTP: <www.koreatimes.co.kr/www/news/tech/2018/05/133_249017.html> (accessed 7 March 2019).

Jung, C. (2016a) 'Constitutional court, "A news media outlet with 5 or fewer reporting and editorial staff members is still a news media outlet"' (헌법재판소 "5인 미만 언론사도 언론이다)', *Media Today*. Online. Available HTTP: <www.mediatoday.co.kr/?mod=news&act=articleView&idxno=132917> (accessed 22 March 2019).

Jung, C. (2016b) *Park Geun-hye collapses*, Seoul: Medichi Press.

Kang, I. (2016) 'Web 2.0, UGC, and citizen journalism: Revisiting South Korea's OhmyNews model in the age of social media', *Telematics and Informatics*, 33: 546–556.

Kang, J. (2018) 'Unification Minister says the exclusion of a North Korean defector turned reporter is for smooth talks between North Korea and South Korea' (통일부 탈북기자 배제.조명균 "원만한 회담 진행 위한것"'). Online. Available HTTP: <www.http://www.fnnews.com/news/201810151828188021> (accessed 7 March 2017).

KBS. (2016) 'How did the Blue House tame the news media? (청와대는 언론을 어떻게 길들였나?)'. Online. Available HTTP: <http://news.kbs.co.kr/news/view.do?ncd=3377967&ref=A> (accessed 3 April 2019).

KBS. (2019) 'Inconsistent media framing of diplomacy (그때는 틀리고 지금은 맞는 '외교 무능' 프레임)'. Online. Available HTTP: <http://news.kbs.co.kr/news/view.do?ncd=4169442&ref=A> (accessed 3 April 2018).

Kern, T. and Nam, S. (2009) 'The making of a social movement: Citizen journalism in South Korea', *International Sociological Association*, 57: 637–660.

Kim, H. (2014) 'Supreme Court to exonerate government on influence peddling (대법, 언론사에 기업 잣대 . . . 정권의 방송장악에 "면죄부)', *The Hankyoreh*. Online. Available HTTP: <www.hani.co.kr/arti/society/media/666593.html> (accessed 28 March 2018).

Kim, S. (2016) 'A joint statement by three journalism associations (3대 언론학회 첫 공동성명 "공영방송이 권력 호위병 노릇")', *OhmyNews*. Online. Available HTTP: <http://m.ohmynews.com/NWS_Web/Mobile/at_pg.aspx?CNTN_CD=A0002261870#cb> (accessed 7 March 2018).

Korea Press Foundation. (2017a) *2017 the Korea Press*, Seoul: Korea Press Foundation.

Korea Press Foundation. (2017b) *A survey of Korean journalists*, Seoul: Korea Press Foundation.

Kwon, K.J. and Hancocks, P. (2016) 'South Korea: New law could jail people for $50 gift', *CNN*. Online. Available HTTP: <www.cnn.com/2016/09/27/asia/korea-corruption-law-begins/index.html> (accessed 7 February 2018).

Lee, J. (2019) 'May 18 Gwangju Uprising Foundation launches a YouTube channel to combat fake news (5.18 재단 "유튜브 TV 개설" . . . "가짜뉴스" 철퇴)'. Online. Available HTTP: <http://news1.kr/articles/?3576454> (accessed 23 March 2019).

Lee, S. (2017) 'MBC President Kim dismissed: Labor union to resume work 김장겸 사장 해임 . . . 노조, 이르면 15일 업무 복귀'. Online. Available HTTP: <www.hankookilbo.com/News/Read/201711311876677589> (accessed 3 April 2019).

Lee, S. and Paik, J.E. (2017) 'How partisan newspapers represented a pandemic: The case of the Middle East respiratory syndrome in South Korea', *Asian Journal of Communication*, 27: 82–96.

Lim, J. and Seo, H. (2009) 'Frame flow between government and the news media and its effects on the public: Framing of North Korea', *International Journal of Public Opinion Research*, 21: 204–223.

Moon, J. (2018) 'Ministry of justice introducing measures to combat "fake news" ("가짜뉴스"에 칼 빼든 법무부 . . . 검찰에 엄정 대응 지시)', *Asia Economy*. Online. Available HTTP: <http://view.asiae.co.kr/news/view.htm?idxno=2018101610532535321> (accessed 21 March 2019).

Nah, S. and Chung, D.S. (2016) 'Communicative action and citizen journalism: A case study of OhmyNews in South Korea', *International Journal of Communication*, 10: 2297–2317.

OECD. (2017) 'Data on Korea. Organisation for Economic Cooperation and Development', Online. Available HTTP: <https://www.oecd.org/korea/> (accessed 7 March 2018).

Park, H. (2018) 'Fake news on President Moon ("文" 가짜뉴스 제천시의장 항소심도 직위상실형)', *No Cut News*. Online. Available HTTP: <https://www.nocutnews.co.kr/news/4928143> (accessed 10 April 2018).

Park, J. (2017a) 'Journalists' determination to stop journalist layoffs (해직 사슬 끊어낸 언론인들의 다짐)', *No Cut News*. Online. Available HTTP: <https://www.nocutnews.co.kr/news/4890794> (accessed 17 February 2018).

Park, J. (2017b) '"Blacklisted" journalists, celebrities return to small screen', *The Korea Times*. Online. Available HTTP: <www.koreatimes.co.kr/www/art/2018/09/688_241053.html> (accessed 7 March 2018).

Renner, N. (2017) 'The media today: The rise of virtual reality journalism', *Columbia Journalism Review*. Online. Available HTTP: <https://www.cjr.org/tow_center/virtual-reality-journalism-media-today.php> (accessed 7 March 2018).

Reporters without Borders. (2017) 'South Korea: Polarization and self-censorship'. Online. Available HTTP: <https://rsf.org/en/2017-world-press-freedom-index-tipping-point> (accessed 17 March 2018).

Reporters without Borders (2018a) '2018 World Press Freedom Index'. Online. Available HTTP: https://rsf.org/en/ranking (accessed 7 March 2018).

Reporters without Borders. (2018b) 'Press freedom admits no exceptions, RSF tells South Korea'. Online. Available HTTP: <https://rsf.org/en/news/press-freedom-admits-no-exceptions-rsf-tells-south-korea> (accessed 7 March 2018).

Republic of Korea. (1987) *Constitution of Korea*. Online. Available HTTP: <http://www.law.go.kr/lsInfoP.do?lsiSeq=61603&efYd=19880225#0000> (accessed 17 March 2018).

Seo, H. (2009) 'International media coverage of North Korea: Study of journalists and news reports on the six-party nuclear talks', *Asian Journal of Communication*, 19: 1–17.

Seo, H. and Thorson, S. (2012) 'Networks of networks: Changing patterns in country bandwidth and centrality in global information infrastructure 2002–2010', *Journal of Communication*, 62: 345–358.

Seo, H. and Thorson, S. (2016) 'A mixture model of global internet capacity distributions', *Journal of the Association of Information Science and Technology*, 67: 2032–2044.

Statista. (2017) 'South Korea: Social network penetration 2017 | Statistic'. Online. Available HTTP: <www.statista.com/statistics/284473/south-korea-social-network-penetration/> (accessed 7 March 2018).

Yoo, S. (2015) 'Online newspaper registration requirement from 3 to 5 staff (인터넷 신문 등록요건 "기자 3명→ 5명" 강화)', *The Chosun Ilbo*. Online. Available HTTP: <http://news.chosun.com/site/data/html_dir/2015/11/17/2015111700312.html> (accessed 8 March 2018).

Youm, K.H. (2003) *Political Libels and Democracy: Are They Compatible?*, International Communication Association, San Diego, CA, May 23–27.

9

EXTERNAL THREAT AND INTERNAL DEFENCE

Freedom of the press in Taiwan, 2008–2018[1]

Jaw-Nian Huang[2]

Growing concerns have arisen regarding China's ambition to pursue a 'new world media order' and its potential impact on freedom of the press throughout the world (Reporters without Borders 2019). Taiwan stands right at the forefront of the struggle to counter China's authoritarian influence and to sustain the liberal way of life of a democracy. The recent developments of Taiwan's press freedom deserve attention from the international community.

This chapter aims to explore the internal and external threats facing freedom of the press in Taiwan in the last decade, as well as the efforts that Taiwan has made to combat these threats and defend its press freedom. After remaining underdeveloped for more than 40 years under the Kuomintang's (KMT) authoritarian rule during the Cold War, Taiwan's media freedom progressed significantly alongside liberalization and democratization from the late 1980s. According to Freedom House, the level of Taiwan's press freedom increased incrementally from the 1990s to the mid-2000s, peaking in 2006–2008 (Figure 9.1).

China's influence was the main threat to Taiwan's press freedom over the past ten years. Beijing not only exerted its influence, but it also interacted with Taiwan's state and corporate powers to affect media activities, public opinion and press freedom in Taiwan. Efforts by the Taiwanese government and civil society to counter China's influence and nurture democratic defence mechanisms played a key role in reviving Taiwan's press freedom from 2015.

External threat: China's influence

China's influence has been the main threat to freedom of the press in Taiwan over the last ten years. As well as narrowing down the Taiwanese media's access to international institutions/events and carrying out cyberattacks on the websites of Taiwanese media, political parties and government organizations, Chinese authorities are also attempting to manipulate the Taiwanese media by various other means.

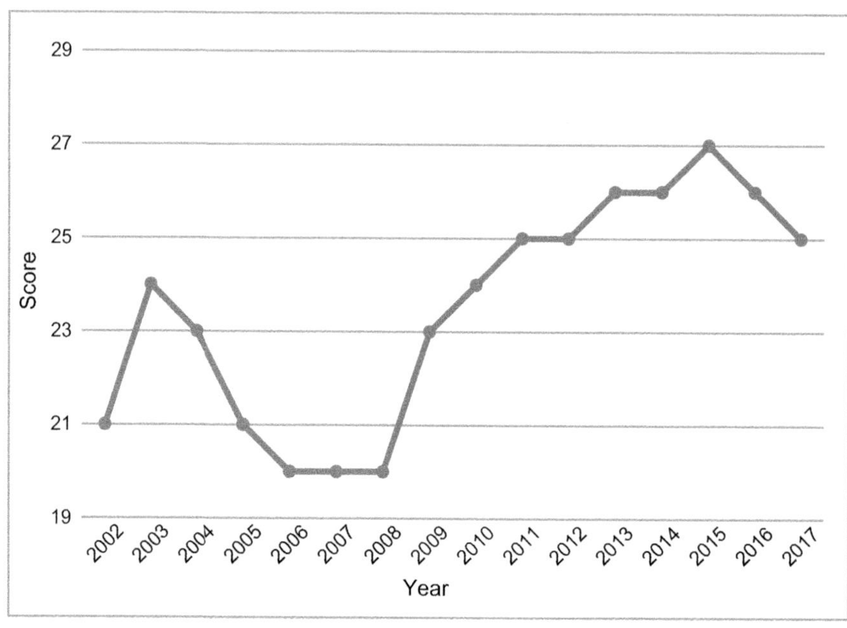

FIGURE 9.1   Taiwan Press Freedom Index by Freedom House (2017a)

Source: Freedom House 2017a

Note: The higher the score, the lower the level of press freedom

Beijing's financial permeation

For a long time, the Chinese government has used 'promoting unification by economic means' as part of its 'united front' strategy towards Taiwan. Alongside Taiwan's increasing economic connections with China, Taiwanese media companies have become increasingly commercially tied with the Chinese market since 2000 (Chen 2006). Taiwan's media sought economic resources from China to improve their finances when advertising revenues from Taiwanese private enterprises declined due to the 2008 financial crisis. This need for funding was compounded by lost revenues following the prohibition of government-sponsored embedded marketing in 2011 (Chung 2012: 67–70). Under these circumstances, from the late 2000s, many Taiwanese media companies, regardless of their position on the unification–independence issue, started to conduct self-censorship to curry favour with Beijing for fear of losing access to the Chinese market (Cook 2013; Hsu 2014; Kawakami 2015; Huang 2017).

The Chinese government pressures Taiwanese media companies by threatening not to approve their entry into the Chinese market.[3] For example, from 2006–2009, Taiwan's Formosa Television (FTV), a pro-independence outlet, sought to have some of its Taiwanese-language soap operas dubbed into Mandarin Chinese and broadcast in China by cooperating with China Central Television (CCTV).

In order to smooth cooperation with China, FTV's founder, Chai Trong-rong, declined a 2009 proposal from the Democratic Progressive Party's (DPP) Central Standing Committee for FTV to purchase and broadcast *The Ten Conditions of Love*, a documentary film about Rebiya Kadeer, the spiritual leader of the Xinjiang independence movement (Hsu 2014: 525–526).

Similarly, since 2008, Sanlih E-Television (SET), another pro-Taiwanese-independence outlet, has striven to sell its TV dramas to China. Following Beijing's warning that they planned to reject the sale, SET's management asked the company's news department to reduce their reports about the Tiananmen incident, Tibetan independence and Falun Gong, all issues that vex China's leaders.[4] Since this request, SET has reduced its news coverage of Tiananmen each year from 2010 (Hung, Yang, and Chen 2014). To smooth business interests in China, in December 2011, SET General Manager Chang Jung-hua coined the politically controversial term 'Chinese drama' to describe the company's productions, previously referred to as 'Taiwanese drama.' Moreover, in May 2012, SET stopped broadcasting 'Big Talk News,' a popular pro-Taiwan, anti-Beijing political talk show, following an implicit request from China's National Broadcasting Headquarters, the institution charged with approving content imported from abroad (Ji 2012; Sun 2012; Chung 2012; Huang 2017: 31–32, 34–35).

Chinese authorities also influence Taiwanese media by incentivizing them with advertising revenues.[5] In particular, some pro-unification newspapers in Taiwan, such as the *China Times* and *United Daily News* (*UDN*), frequently accepted embedded advertisements for Chinese investment and for tourism promotion from China's State Council Taiwan Affairs Office or from Chinese provincial/municipal governments at least since 2010. These advertisements still appear, even though they have been forbidden by Taiwanese law (The Taiwan Control Yuan 2010). The Taiwanese mega-corporation, the Want Want Group, established the Want Want-China Times Cultural Media advertising agency in Beijing to subcontract advertising packages from the Chinese authorities to other media firms in Taiwan. For instance, the Want Want-China Times Media Group received money from the Fujian provincial government and the Amoy municipal authorities to embed a series of propaganda news stories in the *China Times* and its affiliates during the Fujian governor's visit in Taiwan in March 2012 (Lin 2012; Lee 2014: 118–127).

Research by Chang Chin-Hwa (2011) found that the *China Times* and *United Daily News* tend to report visits to Taiwan by Chinese leaders more favourably than other major Taiwanese newspapers that do no accept embedded advertising contracts from China. Also, compared to their competitors, the *China Times* and *UDN* tend to conform to 'China's official frame' when covering the conflict between the Uighur people and the Chinese state in Xinjiang in North West China. The *China Times* even relies exclusively on the Chinese official news sources when reporting on Xinjiang (Chang 2015; Huang 2017: 32–35).

Beijing's disinformation operations

Disinformation campaigns are another primary strategy that Beijing adopts to influence the mass media and public opinion in Taiwan (US–China Economic and Security Review Commission 2018: 343, 362–364; Reporters without Borders 2019: 18; see Lim, Chapter 4). In 2014, the Chinese Communist Party (CCP) founded a 'Central Leading Group for Cybersecurity and Informatization' with President Xi Jinping himself serving as the leader, formulating and implementing internet-related policies. In 2015, China's People's Liberation Army (PLA) also established a 'Strategic Support Force' to conduct space, cyberspace and electronic warfare. In recent years, it has been reported that the CCP's Central Leading Group for Cybersecurity and Informatization and its publicity department have jointly formed a 'Taiwan Affairs Task Force' to develop guidelines for creating and conducting disinformation campaigns against Taiwan (Central News Agency 2018a). Meanwhile, it is believed that the PLA's Strategic Support Force has started to serve as the managers of 'content farms' that systematically engage in disinformation campaigns towards Taiwan (Lin 2018; Central News Agency 2018b). False information produced either by official media outlets or by content farms is disseminated from China to Taiwan by journalists, cyber armies or common citizens for commercial, political or emotional reasons. This fake news reaches Taiwanese audiences via traditional media outlets or through social media. Problematically, the prevalence of fake news weakens the credibility of Taiwan's media and the ability of Taiwanese people to make informed judgements.

In some cases, fake news originates from official media in China. For example, the CCP-owned *Global Times* released several news reports and editorials starting on 12 April 2018 which indicated that a non-routine large-scale live-fire military exercise was about to be held in the Taiwan Strait on 18 April in response to the claim of Taiwan's Prime Minister Lai Ching-te to be a 'Taiwan independence activist' (*Global Times* 2018a, 2018b). Mainstream media in Taiwan then followed up with a series of related news reports, with some of them even sending reporters to the ostensible scene of the exercise (Quanzhou, China) for on-the-spot interviews (United Daily News 2018; TVBS News 2018). The response of the Taiwanese media increased public concern about cross-strait instability, leading to a decline in Taiwanese stock prices on 17 April. However, it was later confirmed that the so-called exercise was just routine small-scale artillery training, geographically limited to the offshore area of Quanzhou, China (Central News Agency 2018c; BBC News 2018). This example demonstrates how fake news can have real-world consequences and how vulnerable Taiwan is to China's meddling.

In other cases, false information came initially from content farms in China. For instance, Guancha.cn, a content farm considered part of China's foreign propaganda machine, posted an article on 5 September 2018, claiming that China's embassy in Japan had rescued Taiwanese tourists, declaring themselves to be Chinese, who had become trapped by flooding at Japan's Kansai International Airport on 4 September 2018 following Typhoon Jebi (Guancha.cn 2018). On the next day, a netizen, whose internet protocol (IP) address was located in Beijing, then shared the Guancha.cn story on the Taiwanese social media site PTT (TigerLily 2018). The *Global Times* also covered the same story on its website (*Global Times* 2018c). Following this report, mainstream media outlets in Taiwan, regardless of their positions on unification-independence, started to circulate related reports and commentaries, many of which blamed Taiwan's Representative Office in Osaka for neglecting its duties (Sanlih E-Television 2018; *China Times* 2018). Under pressure from public opinion, Su Chii-cherng, who served as director of Taiwan's Representative Office in Osaka, committed suicide on 14 September 2018, before the reports of his failures were proven false. In fact, the Taiwanese tourists trapped at the airport were evacuated by Japanese authorities, not by China's embassy (Reporters without Borders 2019: 17).

In some cases, fake news is produced and broadcast by pro-Beijing Taiwanese media. For example, The *China Times* and CtiTV released a news report on 28 February 2019 which indicated that Taiwan's representative to Singapore, Francis Liang, was monitoring KMT's Kaohsiung Mayor Han Kuo-yu's movements during his visit to Singapore, and then reporting them to the DPP-led government with mobile instant messaging. This news was immediately distributed on PTT and other Taiwanese social media sites, triggering a heated debate among Taiwanese netizens and undermining the credibility and approval rating of the DPP administration (Sincsnow 2019). Later on the same day, the Ministry of Foreign Affairs issued a statement denouncing The *China Times* and CtiTV for their failure to verify the facts before making their report. The ministry explained that Liang was not reporting to the government, but seeking help from colleagues at the representative office regarding the questions raised by journalists at the scene (The Taiwan Ministry of Foreign Affairs 2019). Eventually, CtiTV was fined by the National Communications Commission (NCC) for its violation of fact-verification mechanisms stipulated in the Satellite Broadcasting Act.

In any case, China's disinformation operations have a substantial influence on the functioning of the mass media and public opinion in Taiwan. According to a national poll conducted by Wang Tai-Li (2018) after Taiwan's local elections in November 2018, 85 per cent of respondents had heard fake news claiming that President Tsai Ing-wen had ridden in an armoured vehicle, as she was reluctant to get wet, when she visited disaster sites in Central and Southern Taiwan in August 2018. The fake news about the Chinese embassy rescuing Taiwanese tourists trapped at Japan's Kansai Airport was seen by 78 per cent. In both cases, only around half of those who saw the fake news reports knew that the information was false on or before election day; in other words, the other half voted without knowing the truth. China's disinformation campaign undermined both freedom of the press and democracy in Taiwan.

Internal threat: state and commercial pressures

While China's influence is the main threat, state and corporate powers at home still play a role in shaping freedom of the press in Taiwan. China's influence provides more opportunities for internal state and corporate powers to affect media activities and press freedom.

State pressures

The government exerts its influence primarily through three channels. First, it intervenes in the publicly owned media via its control of their personnel and budget arrangements. Take the Taiwan Public Television Service (PTS) for example. According to the Public Television Act, the PTS is a non-profit television station that is supported by a government-oriented foundation, but independent from government intervention. However, no matter which party has been in power, the government frequently uses its discretion on personnel assignments and budget allocations to slant 'publicly owned' media's news and programme content in favour of the ruling party, especially during elections and times of social protest (Chen 2009: 58). For instance, the KMT-led government froze the PTS budget from 2008–2009 by relying on its majority-party advantage in Parliament, in order to urge the PTS to close down 'Have Something to Say,' a talk show which frequently criticized government policies. The government also manipulated personnel changes on the PTS board of directors from 2009–2010 to enhance its influence on the station's operations.[6] Moreover, the government had a hand in PTS's decision during the 2014 Sunflower Movement to turn down the programming department's request to rebroadcast an interview with the movement's student leader, Lin Fei Fan (Alliance for Civil Society Oversight of Public Television Service 2014).

Second, the government co-opted privately owned media outlets by providing them with advertisements until state-sponsored embedded advertisements were forbidden in 2011. Government agencies regularly solicited bids from media companies to submit advertising proposals for public relations campaigns.[7] From 2003–2005, the Government Information Office even combined all the propaganda budgets from all government departments, a total of 2 billion NTD, to better leverage its resources (Association of Taiwan Journalists 2008). Under these circumstances, some media corporations, such as FTV, established public relations companies which specialized in bidding for and implementing official advertising projects to solicit government accounts.[8] Facing financial pressure, FTV's editorial department was forced to cooperate with the business department, sacrificing its editorial independence by slanting news content in favour of the government (Chen 2005; Lin 2005; Huang 2010b). Since advertisements were in the form of embedded marketing (i.e. propaganda presented as news content), audiences were unlikely to discern that this was actually political advertising. As Huang Jhe-Bin notes:

> Paid news is almost another kind of government subsidy. That is, the Government of the Republic of China, which is encumbered with significant

debts, is using taxpayers money to buy the media, using them to advertise its own performance, in exchange for popular support and citizens' votes.

(Huang 2010b)

Third, the government has taken measures to restrict journalists' right to gather news, in some cases using the police to keep a lid on incidents that are inconvenient for the authorities, such as protests and demonstrations.[9] News reporters, along with protesters, have been expelled or in some cases arrested by the police during protests against the visit of Chen Yunlin (chairman of China's Association for Relations Across the Taiwan Straits [ARATS]) to Taiwan in November 2008 and during the Sunflower Movement in March 2014 (Freedom House 2009; Association of Taiwan Journalists 2014). Arrests also occurred during the protests against the visit of Zhang Zhi-jun (chairman of ARATS) to Taiwan in June 2014, as well as during the Anti-Black Box Curriculum Movement in July 2015 (Freedom House 2015; Association of Taiwan Journalists 2015). In addition, politicians such as Taiwan's former President Ma Ying-Jeou (Freedom House 2016, 2017b) have sued individual journalists for defamation, ensnaring journalists in expensive and time-consuming lawsuits and thus threatening their freedom to report and comment on the news.[10]

Commercial pressures

Corporate power shapes media operations and press freedom through control over circulation, advertising and influence peddling. In the circulation market, businesses which control newspaper distribution channels or cable television broadcasting networks have gained considerable influence.[11] For instance, the Uni-President Enterprises Corporation, the largest food production company and one of the most crucial newspaper distribution channels in Taiwan, postponed distributing *Business Weekly* magazine on 17 January 2013 in response to a half-page news report on the firm's high-level personnel arrangements, until public wrath caused the company to reverse its decision (Kuo 2013). Another example involved China Network Systems, a large cable system operator controlling 16.13 per cent of broadcasting networks and 21.81 per cent of the total broadcasting subscriptions in Taiwan (The Taiwan National Communications Commission 2013). When the Want Want-China Times Media Group's proposal to purchase China Network Systems triggered protests involving thousands of students on 31 July 2012, almost all of Taiwan's television stations – except TPS, Next TV and TVBS – ignored the demonstrations in order to not alienate the influential media group (Lee 2015).

In the advertising market, private businesses and the government, undermine editorial independence and news impartiality by generating crucial advertising revenues for cash-strapped media outlets. By including sales performance as a criterion in internal assessments for promotion and pay increases, some media groups treat journalists as advertising salespeople, a situation that steers them away from controversial investigative reporting about powerful people or firms. Given the competitive nature of Taiwan's media sector, advertising suppliers hold an advantage over media corporations, and thus business departments have the upper hand over editorial departments in internal wrangling (Chen 2005).[12] As Huang Jhe-Bin notes, 'news reporters have become advertising salespeople; public relations companies and advertisers have become news drafters; the government and big businesses are stretching their hands in to the editing console to decide media content' (Huang 2010a). As Lin Chao-chen notes, 'Businesses shaped their own images or influenced government policies with embedded marketing; the more money they had, the more news space they were able to buy, the more right they might hold to speak through the media' (Lin 2005). For instance, when Chao Teng-Hsiung, president of the Farglory Group, Taiwan's largest construction company with the largest advertising budget from 2006–2010, was detained in a bribery investigation in June 2014, most media outlets were reluctant initially to report the news in any depth, to avoid any possible reduction in advertising from the conglomerate.[13]

In the ownership market, some Taiwanese capitalists, who base their business interests in China, leverage media investments in Taiwan as political assets to woo business favours from Chinese authorities (Cook 2013: 9; Hsu 2014: 534; Lin and Lee 2017; Huang 2017).[14] This development has reinforced media concentration, and consequently reduced news diversity, in Taiwan. For example, the Want Want Group, the largest rice cracker maker in China, successfully purchased the *China Times* in 2008, as well as China Television (CTV) and CtiTV in 2009. However, sometimes there are reminders of who is boss. Want Want proposed acquiring the China Network Systems in 2011, a move that was turned down by the NCC in 2013. In 2012–2013, the Group's president, Tsai Eng-meng, also attempted to cooperate with two other Taiwanese capitalists to purchase Next TV, but the move failed mainly owing to concerns expressed by civic organizations about the potential monopoly this would give Tsai and about his tendency cleave to Beijing. The Ting Hsin Group, the largest instant noodle producer in China, similarly intended to acquire the China Network Systems in August 2014, but the bid failed due to a food security scandal involving the company in October 2014.

In contrast, Wang Cher, president of the High-Tech Computer Corporation (HTC), a mobile phone company mostly basing its manufacturing and sales in China, purchased a considerable percentage of the stocks of the TVBS Media Group in June 2011 and then gained full control over the Group in January 2015. Some foreign entrepreneurs, in addition to Taiwanese capitalists, are suspected of serving as proxies for Chinese capital to permeate Taiwan's media sector. For example, in 2015, Dan Mintz – the head of US-based DMG Entertainment and DMG Yinji, which he founded with two Chinese nationals in China – proposed acquiring the Eastern Broadcasting Company (EBC), the largest privately owned Mandarin-language TV network in Taiwan. The bid finally collapsed in October 2016, however, due to concerns from civil society groups and regulators over the potentially negative impact of allowing mainland control. The EBC was also concerned about the difficulty that Mintz's deep ties to China would cause to gaining regulatory approval (Freedom House 2016, 2017b). Even though many merger proposals are not successful, some media groups, such as the Want Want-China Times Media Group, have grown into cross-media conglomerates, threating the diversity of news and opinions offered to the Taiwanese public by concentrating ownership in a few well-connected hands (The Taiwan Legislative Yuan 2011: 252; Lin et al. 2012: 81–84; Huang 2017: 33–35).

Taiwan's efforts to build up a democratic defence mechanism

In the past decade, both the government and civil society have taken action to counter the internal and external threats to freedom of the press in Taiwan. Civil society has played a more influential role since 2014, as evident in the Sunflower Movement's tacit cooperation with the opposition DPP to press the ruling KMT to change its policies regarding China's influence. Moreover, the government and political parties are now playing a more active role to thwart Chinese control over Taiwan's media spaces by raising anti-monopoly legislation and subjecting takeover bids to greater scrutiny. Since the DPP's return to power in 2016, this trend has gained momentum, drawing on public support for such reforms.

There have also been significant efforts to moderate state and commercial pressures at home. For instance, Huang Jhe-Bin, a veteran *China Times* journalist, resigned in December 2010 to protest the proliferation of embedded advertisements purchased by both government agencies and private businesses, drawing public attention to the issue that led to a public campaign to end the practice (Freedom House 2011). In response, the government quickly revised the Budget Act in January 2011 to forbid embedded marketing by the national government, resulting in fewer cases of embedded advertising by the central government, but not eliminating the problem as far as local authorities are concerned.[15] Similarly, the government also amended Taiwan's three broadcasting laws (the Radio and Television Act, the Cable Radio and Television Act, and the Satellite Broadcasting Act) in December 2015 to forbid business-sponsored embedded advertisements in news and children's programmes. In addition, responding to longstanding demands by media reform groups to reinforce PTS's independence from the government, the Ministry of Culture proposed a draft Public Media Act in September 2018 to strengthen the public broadcasting system's financial autonomy by forming a cultural development fund. PTS's decision-making autonomy was also reinforced by modifying the rules governing appointment to its board and by establishing a public monitoring system (The Taiwan Ministry of Culture 2018).

There have also been efforts to counter China's financial penetration of Taiwan's business and media sectors. Scholars and columnists in Taiwan collaborated in founding an Anti-*China Times* Movement in February 2012 compelled by anger at the newspaper's parent company chairman Tsai Eng-meng's pro-Beijing false statement on the Tiananmen massacre in an interview with the *Washington Post* (Higgins 2012). The movement called on journalists not to write for the *China Times* and urged readers not to buy it (Taipei Society & Taiwan Democracy Watch Association 2012). Following the success of this movement, academics, civic groups, student organizations and the Association of Taiwan Journalists organized an Anti-Media Monopoly Movement that coordinated protests from July 2012 through January 2013 to oppose the proposed merger of Want Want-China Times Media Group with China Network Systems (Lin et al. 2012). Following these protests, the NCC rejected the merger in February 2013. While these two movements were active, more and more senior journalists left the *China Times*, while others were laid off for vocalizing their discontent with the newspaper's self-censorship on topics deemed sensitive for Chinese authorities. Many of those who left joined other media firms, while some devoted themselves to creating new online media outlets – such as Storm Media, the Reporter and Initium Media – to offer alternatives to the self-censoring press.[16] Born in part from the Anti-Media Monopoly Movement, a coalition of student and civic groups organized the Sunflower Movement in March 2014 to protest the ruling KMT's ramming of the Cross-Strait Service Trade Agreement (CSSTA) through the legislature without adequate review. Critics were concerned that the agreement exposed Taiwan's freedom of speech and expression to Chinese intervention by opening the country's printing, distribution, retail and advertising sectors to investment from China (Lin et al. 2014). Facing a backlash, the government postponed legislative review of the trade agreement in April 2014. The Sunflower Movement, therefore, successfully protected Taiwan's press freedom from Beijing's further interference.

Reacting to concerned voices within civil society, Taiwan's government has started to examine media investments and mergers more carefully. It has also established new institutions to manage investments in the media sector, prevent monopolies and promote media independence and diversity. In particular, the NCC proposed two drafts of the Media Monopoly Prevention and Diversity Protection Act respectively in April 2013 and July 2017. Several measures in the 2017 version are designed to prevent financial investors from having too much influence over the media they own. These measures include a) preventing financial and insurance enterprises from excessive investments in media businesses; b) imposing restrictions on concentration of media ownership and cross-media convergence; and c) requiring the NCC to consult related agencies when investors or their financial sources are suspected of links with China, Hong Kong or Macau in a manner that threatens financial order or national security. Other measures have been implemented to mitigate self-censorship, including promoting financial and editorial autonomy. Upon the passage of the bill, the NCC will administer a special fund, provided by the government, to reward media organizations for cultural diversity and journalistic professionalism. The establishment of this fund may improve media independence by providing alternative sources of finance to political and commercial forces at home or abroad. Also, each media organization will be required to create an independent editorial system, an editorial statute, a journalistic ethics committee and guidelines for reporting news about the media company itself. All of these new measures may help enhance the media's editorial autonomy by protecting journalists' activities and decisions from inappropriate intervention from their company's business departments or owners (The Taiwan National Communications Commission 2017). Even so, the anti-media monopoly legislation remains a work in progress, due mainly to the controversy between the reformist camp (i.e., DPP, the New Power Party and media reform groups) and the conservative camp (i.e., KMT and the Want Want-China Times Media Group) about what criteria should be used to separate the financial and media industries.

Newsrooms and the Taiwanese government are also fighting Beijing's disinformation operations. Two civic organizations, Taiwan Media Watch and the Association for Quality Journalism, jointly founded the non-profit Taiwan Fact Checking Center in July 2018, the first fact-checking organization in Taiwan. The NCC has also started to play a more active role since late 2018, warning TV stations such as TVBS, EBC, CTV and CtiTV to adhere to the fact-verification mechanism stipulated in the Satellite Broadcasting Act. It even fined CtiTV 1 million NTD in March 2019 for embedded marketing, for example, a report claiming that an 'auspicious cloud' had appeared in the sky when Taichung Mayor Lu Shiow-yen and New Taipei City Mayor Hou You-yi campaigned together (Central News Agency 2019). Moreover, the authorities proposed to revise the Digital Communication Act and other laws/acts in December 2018 with the aim of endowing social media companies with the responsibility to create mechanisms for reporting and managing fake news on their platforms (Chinese Television Service 2019).

After Taiwan's press freedom started to deteriorate in 2008, due mainly to China's financial penetration and disinformation operations, joint efforts by the Taiwanese government and civil society to build up the nation's democratic defences appear to have worked. Press freedom has rebounded, despite daunting challenges because of widespread public support for democracy and a vigorous media, but this positive trajectory is fragile and requires constant vigilance, given China's ongoing efforts to assert domination. Beijing does not want to acknowledge that identity politics in Taiwan draw on a commitment to freedoms it denies to its own people, and thus, its machinations stoke a backlash among Taiwanese who cannot imagine regressing to an authoritarian system similar to what they overcame in the 1980s. This mindset, and national pride in what Taiwan has achieved against the odds, provides a basis for cautious optimism concerning prospects for press freedom in Taiwan.

Notes

1 This article revises and summarizes portions of the author's book *The Political Economy of Press Freedom: The Paradox of Taiwan versus China*, by Jaw-Nian Huang, published in August 2019 by Routledge, Oxford, UK. Meanwhile, this article's discussion on China's disinformation operations is completely new.

2 Jaw-Nian Huang is an Assistant Professor of Development Studies at National Chengchi University in Taiwan. He holds a PhD in political science from the University of California, Riverside, and serves as an inaugural Hou Family Fellow at the Fairbank Center for Chinese Studies at Harvard University, as well as a research team member for China Impact Studies at the Institute of Sociology at the Academia Sinica in Taiwan.

3 Interview Lu Dong-Shi, former president of the Association of Taiwan Journalists, 24 June 2014; Interview with Chen Hsiao-yi, senior news reporter of *Liberty Times* and president of the Association of Taiwan Journalists, 27 June 2014; Interview with Ho Jung-hsing, founder and former president of the Association of Taiwan Journalists, 14 July 2014; Interview with Hu Yuan-Hui, former general manager of the Taiwan Television Enterprise and former president of the Central News Agency, 25 July 2014; Interview with Su Tzen-ping, former director of the Government Information Office and former chairman of the Central News Agency, 28 July 2014; Interview with Lee Chih-Te, senior news reporter of *Radio Free Asia*, 19 August 2014.

4 Interview with anonymous interviewee, senior editor of the Sanlih E-Television, 30 July 2014.

5 Interview with Chen Hsiao-yi, 27 June 2014; Interview with Ni Yen-Yuan, former chief editorial writer of *China Times*, 16 July 2014; Interview with Ho Jung-hsing, 14 July 2014; Interview with Su Tzen-ping, 28 July 2014; Interview with Lee Chih-Te, 19 August 2014.

6 Interview with Feng Sylvia, founder of the Alliance for the Birth of Public Media and former general manager of the Taiwan Public Television Service, 13 August 2014.

7 Interview with Hu Yuan-Hui, 25 July 2014; Interview with Hung Chien-Lung, chief secretary of the Information Bureau of Kaohsiung city government, 24 August 2014.

8 Interview with Tsai Paul, deputy manager of the Formosa Television News Department, 10 July 2014.

9 Interview with Chen Hsiao-yi, 27 June 2014.

10 Interview with Lu Dong-Shi, 24 June 2014; Interview with Wang Chien-chuang, former chief editor and president of *China Times* Taipei, 24 July 2014.

11 Interview with Ho Jung-hsing, 14 July 2014.

12 Interview with Ho Jung-hsing, 14 July 2014; Interview with Wang Chien-chuang, 24 July 2014; Interview with anonymous interviewee, senior editor of the Sanlih E-Television, 30 July 2014; Interview with Chen Chia-Dai, former director of United Evening News Editorial Center, 26 August 2014.

13 Interview with Feng Zichun, editor of United Evening News, 27 April 2014; Interview with anonymous interviewee, senior manager of the Want Want-China Times Media Group, 13 June 2014; Interview with Huang Jhe-Bin, former senior news reporter and editor of *China Times*, 16 June 2014; Interview with Chen Eric, former chief editor and president of *Apple Daily*, 2 July 2014; Interview with anonymous interviewee, senior manager of the United Daily News Television, 11 July 2014.

14 Interview with Chen Hsiao-yi, 27 June 2014; Interview with Su Tzen-ping, 28 July 2014.

15 Interview with Chiu Eve, chief executive officer of the Foundation for Excellent Journalism Award, 1 July 2014.

16 Interview with Chang Tieh-chih, former *China Times* columnist, 28 June 28 2014; Interview with Ho Jung-hsing, 14 July 2014; Interview with Huang Jhe-Bin, 16 June 2014; Interview with Tsai Chi-Ta, former senior opinion editor of *China Times*, 17 June 2014; Interview with Wang Chien-chuang, 24 July 2014; Interview with Yo Wan-chi, former *China Times* news reporter, 22 May 2014.

Bibliography

Alliance for Civil Society Oversight of Public Television Service. (2014) 'Public television service oversight report', Online. Available HTTP: <http://www.youthrights.org.tw/news/148> (accessed 27 August 2015).

Association of Taiwan Journalists. (2008) 'Petition statement about presidential candidates' opposition to news embedded marketing', *Taiwan Media Watch Educational Foundation, Campaign for Media Reform & Solidarity of Communication Student 2008*. Online. Available HTTP: <http://campaign.tw-npo.org/sign.php?id=200803622372700> (accessed 4 April 2019).

Association of Taiwan Journalists. (2014) 'The Taiwan Journalist Association 2014/4/28 Statement', Online. Available HTTP: <http://atj.twbbs.org/tai-wan-xin-wen-ji-zhe-xie-hui-da-shi-ji/ji-xie-gong-gao/20140428%E3%80%90jixieshengming%E3%80%91428jingfangquliqunzhongshijiantaiwanxinwenjizhexiehuiqianzejingfangbaoli%E3%80%81qinfanxinwenziyou> (accessed 19 August 2015).

Association of Taiwan Journalists. (2015) 'The Taiwan Journalist Association 2015/7/24 Statement', Online. Available HTTP: <http://atj.twbbs.org/tai-wan-xin-wen-ji-zhe-xie-hui-da-shi-ji/ji-xie-gong-gao2015/20150724jixieshengmingtaiwanxinwenjizhexiehuiqianze724jingchaweifadaibujizhexianzhiqinfanjizhexinwencaifangquan> (accessed 19 August 2015).

BBC News. (2018) 'China once again launched a live military exercise in the Taiwan Strait, Taiwan said the scale was exaggerated', *BBC News*. Online. Available HTTP: <www.bbc.com/zhongwen/trad/chinese-news-43805698> (accessed 4 April 2019).

Central News Agency. (2018a) 'Yomiuri reviews the Kansai Airport incident, Taiwan faces a false news crisis', Online. Available HTTP: <www.cna.com.tw/news/aopl/201810060004.aspx> (accessed 4 April 2019).

Central News Agency. (2018b) 'National security bureau: The intelligence data indicates that the fake news comes from the PLA', Online. Available HTTP: <www.cna.com.tw/news/aipl/201811010397.aspx> (accessed 4 April 2019).

Central News Agency. (2018c) 'Executive Yuan: The PLA exaggerated its routine military exercise in the Taiwan strait', Online. Available HTTP: <www.cna.com.tw/news/firstnews/201804180055.aspx> (accessed 4 April 2019).

Central News Agency. (2019) 'CtiTV is fined one million for reporting that the phoenix spreads wings in the sky when the three mayors campaigned together', <www.cna.com.tw/news/firstnews/201903275002.aspx> (accessed 20 April 2019).

Chang, C.H. (2011) 'Analysis of the news placement and coverage of three Chinese buying groups by Taiwan's four main newspapers from the perspective of van Dijk's discourse and manipulation theory', *Chinese Journal of Communication Research*, 20: 65–93.

Chang, C.H. (2015) 'How do different newspapers cover Xingjian conflicts from human right perspective? A frame analysis of 10 newspapers from Taiwan, Hong Kong, Mainland China, Britain and Unites States', *Mass Communication Research*, 125: 1–47.

Chen, P.H. (2005) 'Exploring advertorials in television news: Product placement vs. professionalism of news reporting', *Chinese Journal of Communication Research*, 8: 209–246.

Chen, P.H. (2006) 'Market entry modes and determinants of Taiwanese media firms into mainland China', *Mass Communication Research*, 89: 37–80.

Chen, P.H. (2009) 'The change of the television industry: The rise and fall of political and economic forces', in The Foundation for Distinguished Journalism Award (ed.) *The Reconstruction of Taiwan Media*, Chuliu, Taipei, Taiwan.

China Times. (2018) 'Those who identify themselves as Chinese can get on the bus? Taiwanese tourists clarified. Netzines shout: The representative office in Japan can be abolished', Online. Available HTTP: <www.chinatimes.com/hottopic/20180906002364-260803?chdtv> (accessed 4 April 2019).

Chinese Television Service. (2019) 'The Executive Yuan declares war on fake news by increasing the penalties', Available HTTP: <https://news.cts.com.tw/cts/politics/201904/201904031956782.html> (accessed 20 April 2019).

Chung, N. (2012) *My Life Experience in the Big Talk News*, Taipei: Avanguard.

Cook, S. (2013) 'The long shadow of Chinese censorship: How the Communist Party's media restrictions affect news outlets around the world', *The Center for International Media Assistance, National Endowment for Democracy, Washington, D.C.* Online. Available HTTP: <www.cima.ned.org/resource/the-long-shadow-of-chinese-censorship-how-the-communist-partys-media-restrictions-affect-news-outlets-around-the-world/> (accessed 10 November 2015).

Freedom House. (2009) *Taiwan: Freedom of the Press 2009.* Online. Available HTTP: <www.freedomhouse.org/report/freedom-press/2009/taiwan> (accessed 20 May 2013).

Freedom House. (2011) *Taiwan: Freedom of the Press 2011.* Online. Available HTTP: <www.freedomhouse.org/report/freedom-press/2011/taiwan> (accessed 20 May 2013).

Freedom House. (2015) *Taiwan: Freedom of the Press 2015.* Online. Available HTTP: <https://freedomhouse.org/report/freedom-press/2015/taiwan> (accessed 5 April 2019).

Freedom House. (2016) *Taiwan: Freedom of the Press 2016.* Online. Available HTTP: <https://freedomhouse.org/report/freedom-press/2016/taiwan> (accessed 16 March 2019).

Freedom House. (2017a) *Detailed Data and Sub-Scores 1980–2017.* Online. Available HTTP: <https://freedomhouse.org/report/freedom-press/freedom-press-2017> (accessed 16 March 2019).

Freedom House. (2017b) *Taiwan: Freedom of the Press 2017.* Online. Available HTTP: <https://freedomhouse.org/report/freedom-press/2017/taiwan>(accessed 16 March 2019).

Global Times. (2018a) 'The navy's military training in South China Sea ended earlier, the live-fire exercise in the Taiwan strait is about to start!', *Global Times.* Online. Available HTTP: <http://mil.huanqiu.com/world/2018-04/11839001.html> (accessed 4 April 2019).

Global Times. (2018b) 'Editorial: Yes, the military exercise is directed against "Taiwan independence" and Lai Ching-Te'. Online. Available HTTP: <http://opinion.huanqiu.com/editorial/2018-04/11845172.html> (accessed 4 April 2019).

Global Times. (2018c) 'What a great flood! It was unbelievable that China's embassy came to rescue: Taiwan compatriots asked . . .'. Online. Available HTTP: <http://world.huanqiu.com/article/2018-09/12941353.html?agt=15422> (accessed 4 April 2019).

Guancha.cn. (2018) 'What a great flood! It was unbelievable that China's embassy came to rescue. Taiwan compatriots asked . . .'. Online. Available HTTP: <www.guancha.cn/internation/2018_09_05_470949.shtml> (accessed 4 April 2019).

Higgins, A. (2012) 'Tycoon prods Taiwan closer to China', *The Washington Post.* Online. Available HTTP: <www.washingtonpost.com/world/asia_pacific/tycoon-prods-taiwan-closer-to-china/2012/01/20/gIQAhswmFQ_story.html> (accessed 13 April 2016).

Hsu, C.J. (2014) 'China's influence on Taiwan's media', *Asian Survey*, 54: 515–539.

Huang, J.B. (2010a) 'Leaving China Times on a jet plane', *China Times.* Online. Available HTTP: <http://blog.chinatimes.com/dander/archive/2010/12/13/579524.html> (accessed 4 April 2019).

Huang, J.B. (2010b) 'I made a dream about deciphering media crises'. Online. Available HTTP: <http://puppydad.blogspot.com/2010/12/blog-post_14.html> (accessed 4 April 2019).

Huang, J.N. (2017) 'The China factor in Taiwan's media: Outsourcing Chinese censorship abroad', *China Perspectives*, 3: 27–36.

Hung, Y., Yang, H.J., and Chen, C.W. (2014) *How Did China Factor Influence Taiwanese Media?*, Taipei, Taiwan: Graduate Institute of National Development, National Taiwan University.

Ji, S. (2012) 'Shutting off the big talk news for entering the Chinese market?', *Wealth Magazine*. Online. Available HTTP: <www.wealth.com.tw/article_in.aspx?nid=906> (accessed 4 April 2019).

Kawakami, M. (2015) 'Political permeation under the market mechanism: The mechanisms of China's influence in the Taiwanese media industry', *Taiwanese Sociological Association Communication*, 83: 17–20.

Kuo, Y.L. (2013) 'Sorry, the 1313th Business Weekly is absent at 7-ELEVEN', *Business Weekly*. Online. Available HTTP: <www.businessweekly.com.tw/KIndepArticle.aspx?id=18316> (accessed 4 April 2019).

Lee, C.T. (2014) *Journey Without Destination*, New Taipei: Gusa.

Lee, Kevin H.J. (2015) Taiwan Public Television Service Foundation. (2015) *The Taste of Apple*. Produced by Taiwan Public Television Service Foundation. Online. Available HTTP: <www.youtube.com/watch?v=gF3BvAMl2Z4&t=4s> (accessed 4 April 2019).

Lin, C. (2005) 'Who's purchasing the media?', *Common Wealth Magazine*. Online. Available HTTP: <https://sites.google.com/site/zhengzhixiaojiwan/project-updates/shuizaishou maimeitizuozhelinzhaozhen> (accessed 27 August 2019).

Lin, C. (2012) 'Fujian provincial government's embedded advertisements on China Times', *NewTalk*. Online. Available HTTP: <http://newtalk.tw/news/view/2012-03-30/23697> (accessed 4 April 2019).

Lin, H.L., Lin, L., Hung, C.L., Chang, C., Huang, K.C., and Jang, S.L. (2012) '12 reasons for rejecting media monster!', *Center for Public Policy and Law of National Taiwan University*, Taipei, Taiwan.

Lin, L. (2018) 'Taiwan', in N. Newman, R. Fletcher, A. Kalogeropoulos, D.A.L. Levy, and R.K. Nielsen (eds.) *Reuters Institute Digital News Report 2018*, Oxford: Reuters Institute for the Study of Journalism. Online. Available HTTP: <www.digitalnewsreport.org/survey/2018/taiwan-2018/> (accessed 4 April 2019).

Lin, L. and Lee, C.Y. (2017) 'When business met politics: The case of want want, a different type of media capital in Taiwan', *China Perspectives*, 2: 37–46.

Lin, Y.H., Chen, R.R., Hu, Y.H., and others. (2014) *Petition Statement for Opposing the CSSTA's Opening the Advertising and Printing Industries*. Online. Available HTTP: <http://tibimon.pixnet.net/blog/post/94028837-%E3%80%90%E9%80%A3%E7%BD%B2%E5%90%8D%E5%96%AE%E3%80%91%E5%82%B3%E6%92%AD%E5%AD%B8%E8%A1%93%E7%95%8C%E5%8F%8D%E5%B0%8D%E6%9C%8D%E8%B2%BF%E5%8D%94%E8%AD%B0%E9%96%8B%E6%94%BE%E5%BB%A3> (accessed 4 April 2019).

Reporters without Borders. (2019) *RSF Report: China's Pursuit of a New World Media Order*. Online. Available HTTP: <https://rsf.org/sites/default/files/en_rapport_chine_web_final.pdf> (accessed 4 April 2019).

Sanlih E-Television. (2018) 'Taiwanese were bullied even in a typhoon disaster: China's embassy: Those who identify themselves as Chinese can get on the bus'. Online. Available HTTP: <www.setn.com/News.aspx?NewsID=426132> (accessed 4 April 2019).

Sincsnow. (2019) '[NEWS]Secret Police got caught? It was witnessed that the ambassador in Singapore was monitoring and reporting Han Kuo-yu's movements', *PTT HatePolitics*. Online. Available HTTP: <https://disp.cc/b/1159-bcOI> (accessed 4 April 2019).

Sun, H.T. (2012) 'Cheng Hung-yi says goodbye to the big talk news', *The Journalist*. Online. Available HTTP: <www.new7.com.tw/NewsView.aspx?i=TXT20120523165353UMQ> (accessed 4 April 2019).

Taipei Society & Taiwan Democracy Watch Association. (2012) *Anti-China Times Movement Statement*. Online. Available HTTP: <http://rjcts2012.blogspot.tw/2012/02/blog-post.html> (accessed 4 April 2019).

The Taiwan Control Yuan. (2010) *The Correction # 099教正0022*. Online. Available HTTP: <www.cy.gov.tw/sp.asp?xdurl=./CyBsBox/CyBsR2.asp&ctNode=911> (accessed 18 August 2015).

The Taiwan Legislative Yuan. (2011) 'The market share rate of the want want-China Times Group and the China Network Systems', *The Legislative Yuan Gazette*, 100.

The Taiwan Ministry of Culture. (2018) *From the Public Television Act to the Public Media Act, the Ministry of Culture Plans Public Media with Forward Thinking*. Online. Available HTTP: <www.moc.gov.tw/information_250_89222.html> (accessed 4 April 2019).

The Taiwan Ministry of Foreign Affairs. (2019) *Statement for the False Report of China Times and CtiTV Titled "Secret Police Got Caught?"* 中華民國外交部 – 全球資訊網. Online. Available HTTP: <www.mofa.gov.tw/News_Content_M_2.aspx?n=D6D997396B64 7A7C&sms=9C41168DD8E4EB5C&s=991715B41BA29B22> (accessed 4 April 2019).

The Taiwan National Communications Commission. (2013) *NCC Performance Report 2012*. Online. Available HTTP: <www.ncc.gov.tw/chinese/files/13091/950_130916_1.pdf> (accessed 4 April 2019).

The Taiwan National Communications Commission. (2017) *Draft of the Media Monopoly Prevention and Diversity Protection Act*. Online. Available HTTP: <www.ncc.gov.tw/chinese/files/17071/3926_37605_170712_1.pdf> (accessed 4 April 2019).

TigerLily. (2018) 'RE: [NEWS] Director committed suicide: People are afraid that PTT became the source of fake news and public opinion', *PTT Gossiping*. Online. Available HTTP: <www.ptt.cc/bbs/Gossiping/M.1536983294.A.5E0.html?fbclid=IwAR1riE Upf8FJFXWP7hSOjL8OMb-cJub_If0JoYftVKrXqpbu_RE-0vWAUGo> (accessed 4 April 2019).

TVBS News. (2018) 'The PLA conducts a live-fire exercise in the Taiwan Strait from 8 to 24 today', *TVBS News*. Online. Available HTTP: <https://news.tvbs.com.tw/politics/903997> (accessed 4 April 2019).

United Daily News. (2018) 'Taiwan indicates mainland China's 18th military exercise in the Taiwan Strait as a disinformation campaign', *United Daily News*. Online. Available HTTP: <https://udn.com/news/story/11311/3084017> (accessed 4 April 2019).

US-China Economic and Security Review Commission. (2018) *2018 Annual Report*. Online. Available HTTP: <www.uscc.gov/Annual_Reports/2018-annual-report> (accessed 4 April 2019).

Wang, T.L. (2018) 'Fake news impacts the results of the county and city mayoral elections: Democracy is in danger', *Liberty Times*. Online. Available HTTP: <https://talk.ltn.com.tw/article/paper/1252877> (accessed 4 April 2019).

PART 2

Southeast Asia

10

THE INDONESIAN PRESS

Between the state, market, politics and society

Kevin Evans

Introduction/overview

Indonesia's political transformation liberated the media from government control and gave rise to an explosion of media outlets and platforms. A critical press soon makes enemies of the powerful, although attempts to bully the media through litigation have been rebuffed largely by structural support for hard-won press freedoms. The fast adoption by Indonesians of social media is transforming society, the economy and the press. Moral panics – promoted by the religiously reactionary and politically ambitious, then amplified through social media – have led to new media and public discourse controls, including the growing use of electronic transmissions and blasphemy laws. Overtly partisan media coverage in recent elections represents a threat to the authority and trustworthiness of the established media.

Indonesia's struggle for a free press has been a long and winding road. The last major series of press bans took place in June 1994, when two leading weekly magazines and one daily newspaper had their permit licences withdrawn. Those affected took the government to court to argue that these closures were illegal. In a stunning decision, certainly considering the authoritarian nature of the regime of the day, the Administrative Appeals Court (PTUN) declared the regulations that enabled the cancellation of the permits to be against the spirit of the then prevailing Press Law and thus unlawful. Even so, the declaration of the courts had little meaningful impact on government regulations, although no further press or media outlets were closed during the rest of the authoritarian era.

The closing of these publications sparked much energy by civil society and affected members of the press, including the establishment of a new journalist association, the Independent Journalists Association (AJI). In this pre-democratic era, this was an all-but-subversive act. Since that time, AJI has worked to uphold and advance the ethical standards of journralists, to advocate for decent wages for journalists and to struggle for freedom of the media to operate in an environment without state pressures.

The 1997–1998 Asian Financial Crisis, which presaged the sudden end to Indonesian authoritarianism, devastated the Indonesian economy more severely than elsewhere with assets valuations on the Jakarta Stock Exchange collapsing, in USD value, by over 90 per cent (Evans 1998: 5–36).

The media industry was certainly not immune to the economic impact of this meltdown. It was often stated at the time that, as the Rupiah lost almost 80 per cent of its pre-crisis value, the cost of the paper used in printing was worth more than the sales price of newspapers or magazines. The collapse in currency valuations created a significant increase in inflation from the single digit figures that has been standard for many years to over 80 per cent at its worst. For people on relatively fixed incomes, such as workers and other salaried people like journalists, the impact was very damaging to family incomes, especially for those with costs like mortgages to pay. For example, from personal experience at the time, mortgage repayments rose overnight from long-term rates at about 20 per cent to over 50 per cent.

Mr Bambang Harymurti, commissioner with the Tempo Media Group and former deputy chair of the national Press Council, observed that it was somewhat ironic that under the old authoritarian system, the press was more profitable. Due to the restrictions placed on the number of publications that were granted permission to operate by the government, there were significant commercial benefits to being one of those permitted agencies. Advertisers had few options – recalling too that this was also before the digital age. Mr Harymurti quipped, 'I believe that the seven pages of advertisements we could sell were valued at one BMW car. Today, you would need to sell about 100 pages of advertisement to create that much revenue' (Interview 3 February 2019).

Another key dynamic emerged with the massive deregulation of the press sector that commenced at the start of the democratization period, known in Indonesia as Reformasi. The first president of that era, President Bacharuddin Jusuf Habibie, oversaw the mass deconstruction of the old authoritarian control systems. His own term for this transformation was to 'open the democratic space.'

From the start of that era, and indeed even before there were any changes to the laws governing the media or press, the Habibie government, through its Minister of Information, Lt Gen (ret) Muhammad Yunus Yosfiah, discarded the application of permits and other restrictions on the establishment of new press outlets. In no time, the number of publications and new television stations surged.

At the same time, the old culture, whereby the Department of Information or other key government figures contacted press leaders after they published an article deemed 'unhelpful' to government sensibilities, with a none-too-subtle threat of permits cancellation should there be further unhelpful articles, etc., also ended (round table discussion with management and lead lecturers at the Dr Soetomo Press Institute, 6 February 2019). Mr Harymurti also observed that, 'there are more subtle approaches used in the modern era, such as not inviting certain journalists, who are critical, to interviews.' In a separate discussion, the executive director of the Press Legal Aid Institute (LBH Pers), Mr Ade Wahyudin, observed that, in terms of economic pressure on press outlets,

> it is not a tool much applied at the national or even provincial level. But at the local level there are cases where local political figures do try to discriminate against press outlets they deem to be critical of them. Even so, these are more specific cases rather than a common factor in the local regions.
>
> *(Interview 6 February 2019)*

Indeed, the dynamic identified here is that the press in Indonesia is very plural at the national level, and quite plural at the level of most provinces, but less so in many local districts.

The trajectory of the status of press freedom in Indonesia can be captured in a snapshot by reviewing Freedom House's annual *Freedom of the Press* reports on Indonesia over the past 20 years (Figure 10.1). The reports begin just as Indonesia enters its period of democratization (Reformasi), up to and including the latest data from 2017.

Prior to the start of democratization, the status of media freedom was quite poor. The euphoric changes at the start of Reformasi were quite dramatic, led by the sudden deregulation of the system and removal of state pressuring of the press. As the new political system began to consolidate, other forces began to play a role (discussed in more depth following), leading to some backsliding. Subsequent efforts to strengthen the legal and other regulatory protections for the press have led to some improvements.

The past few years have seen neither progress nor regression. Even so, there have been important developments within and around the sector that are changing

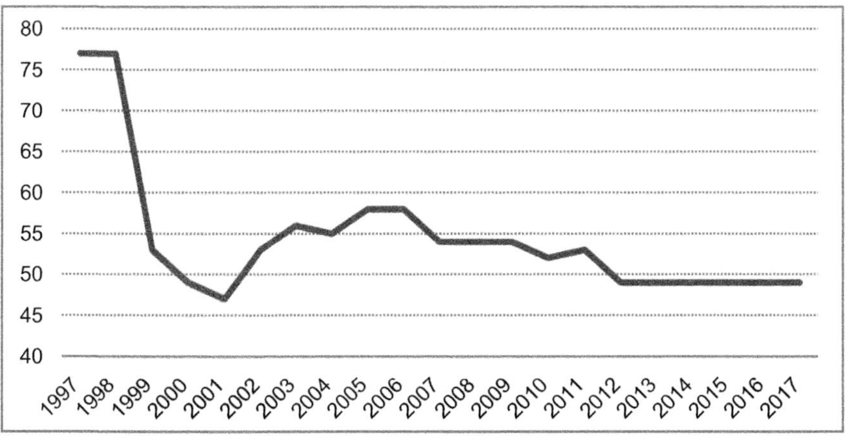

FIGURE 10.1 Press freedom in Indonesia, 1997–2017

Source: Freedom House (various years from 1973–2019)

the dynamics of the press. As is no doubt the case in other countries, wider developments in society, politics, the state and the economy are also having differential impacts on the status of the freedom of the press. The interplay of these factors will be discussed in the next section.

Key themes and issues

The legal/regulatory environment

The Indonesian Constitution provides vaguely worded guarantees for freedom of expression through Article 28: 'The independence to organise and gather, to express an opinion orally, in writing and so on is established through law.' Article 28E (2) states that 'Every person has the right of freedom to hold beliefs, to declare views and opinions in accord with his/her conscience.' Article 28E (3) states that 'Every person has the right of freedom to associate, to gather and to express an opinion.' Article 28 (F) states that 'Every person has the right to communicate and to obtain information to develop themselves and their social environment as well as the right to seek, obtain, own, store, manage and convey information by using any form of communication that is available.' Counterbalanced with rights are obligations outlined in Article 28J (2):

> In exercising their rights and freedoms, every person must submit to the limitations that are outlined in law that have the sole intention of guaranteeing the acknowledgement and respect of the rights and freedoms of other people and to fulfil just demands in accordance with considerations of morality, religious values, security and public order within a democratic society.
>
> *(translation by author)*

All of these articles were included in the Second Amendment to the Constitution agreed by the National Assembly (which has the power to amend the Constitution) in 2000 (see Press Freedom Legal Framework).

One of the prime laws governing Indonesia's media sector is the Press Law (most recently revised as Cabinet Secretariat of Indonesia: Law 40 of 1999). The first Law on the Press was passed in 1966 at the dawn of the Soeharto era. The application of the law was authoritarian (Cabinet Secretariat of Indonesia: Law 11 of 1966 on Principal Provisions on the Press). An important element of that law was the establishment of the Press Council. During the authoritarian period, this was led by the Minister of Information. Fortunately for press freedom, the revisions of this law at the dawn of the democratic era saw that situation change with the emergence of an autonomous, parastatal Press Council whose commissioners no longer include political/state officials. Its secretariat does, however, include officials from the civil service seconded to support the work of the Council.

Since the democratic era, Chairs of the Press Council have included a Magsaysay Awardee, a former rector of a respected university, the former Chief Justice of the Supreme Court and currently a former Commissioner for Human Rights. As observed by the founding chair of the Press Council in the democratic era, Mr Atmakusumah Astraatmadja, the 1999 Press Law was not intended to be restricted only to the print media. He notes that the law defines the press as:

> social institutions and vehicles of mass communication that conduct journalistic activities covering the seeking, obtaining, ownership, storage, processing and conveying of information both in the form of writing, voice and pictures together with data and graphics as well as in other forms used in print media, electronic media and all forms of channels that are available.
>
> *(Article 1 of Law 40 of 1999 on the Press author's translation)*

This inclusion of a wider sectoral mandate has importance in securing freedom of the press. Atmakusumah notes further that, 'The Indonesia Press Council, which is now independent, applies the traditions of similar institutions in other democratic countries, that is to protect the freedom of the press' (Atmakusumah 2018: 168, author's translation). This means that the Council sees itself as the defender of the press in all its forms, not just print journalists. Indeed, he observes that the democratization and deregulation of the press achieved in 1998 was truly historic and reached a level of that had never been achieved in the 254 years since the first newspaper was published in the Indonesian archipelago (Atmakusumah 2018: 227, author's translation).

A second law of importance is the Broadcast Law (Cabinet Secretariat of Indonesia: Law 32 of 2002). This law calls for the establishment of an Indonesian Broadcast Agency as a permanent institution consisting of non-partisan members of the community, although appointed by the Parliament.

Its core focus is on the broadcast media – specifically television and radio. Unlike the Press Council, which has sought to support wider issues related to freedom of expression as a means of supporting press freedom, the Indonesian Broadcast Commission has allowed itself to be used as a tool to promote the exorcism of sexual minorities from TV and radio as part of a wider moral panic driven by the ever-delicate sensibilities of religious reactionaries. Support by the Commission for these groups is also evident by the growing use on TV of 'blurring' the chest regions of women, including the wife of the US President, and even the blurring of traditional cultural statues, artefacts and performances.

A third law, and one that has been deployed with increasing frequency to threaten freedom of expression, is the Law on Electronic Information and Transactions Law (most recently revised as Law 19 of 2016). Prime authority for implementing this law is with the Ministry of Communications and Information. This law governs the management of internet and digital communication.

In 2008, a Law on Transparency in Public Information was established as part of efforts to promote more transparency in governance (Cabinet Secretariat of Indonesia: Law 14 of 2008 on Openness in Public Information). Supporting the implementation of this law is an Information Commission, an independent parastatal whose commissioners are appointed through public processes beginning with the identification of potential candidates by the Office of the President of twice the number people to be appointed and then submitting them to the Parliament for further public review and the selection of half of them. The Information Commission receives requests from people, including members of the press and wider media, seeking access to state documents that have not been given to them by officials. The Commission can propose mediation or, if that is unsuccessful, acts as arbiter in determining whether access is to be provided by officials.

There are other laws that affect the press, such as the Criminal Code, including Presidential Order 1 of 1965 on Preventing the Abuse and/or Besmirching of Religion. The last regulation has come to public prominence with its increased application creating considerable controversy in recent years. The most notable case involved the former Governor of Jakarta who was ultimately jailed for blasphemy in 2017. Other notable pieces of legislation relate to parts of the criminal code that deal with defamation (here insert suitable call out to the cab sec links to various laws listed in works cited) (Cabinet Secretariat of Indonesia: Presidential Order 1 of 1965). Attempts by powerful individuals to intimidate or shut down critical stories they believe defame them included the case in 2003 where a prominent business took offence at a story in the country's leading weekly, *Tempo*. The chief editor was soon before the court facing criminal charges of defamation. The case was finally dismissed by the Supreme Court.

State pressures

Overall, the state has not been able to exert the kind of pressure on the press that existed prior to democratization. There do, however, remain some areas where the press does remain meek and uncritical. The most notable is in relation to the performance and action of the armed forces. Veteran correspondent John McBeth, who has covered Asia for 48 years, about half of that time in Indonesia, observed that:

> major stories such as the recent attack by a mob of off-duty servicemen against a Jakarta suburban police did not receive the media coverage it deserved, including the reported use of hand grenades to blow up vehicles. The English-language Jakarta Post even relegated it to Page 5. There was no follow-up report on what disciplinary action was taken. The same treatment was given to a recent incident where the air force scrambled three jets out of Sumatra to force down an Ethiopian cargo plane. No reason was given for the interception and again there was no follow-up. In some cases, it is difficult to determine whether there is self-censorship in play, or whether journalists lack the commitment or the professionalism and news sense to pursue a story to its logical ending.
>
> (*Interview 1 February 2019*)

Equally and related to the preceding issue is the near national silence including from the press on the issues surrounding the profoundly traumatic transition in late 1965 from the Soekarno to Soeharto eras. Despite the deaths of many hundreds of thousands of people at the time, and the legal, political and physical extermination of the Indonesian Communist Party (PKI), public consideration of these issues remains effectively off limits. Now over 50 years later, this whole critical chapter of the nation's history remains all but closed to discussion. There appears to be no noted effort from the press and media to push the limits and break through to open a national conversation to begin to understand these events. Throughout this period, armed forces leaders, current and present, maintain the rage against the now ancient PKI. Even today, efforts by them to raise the 'spectre' of some or other communist threat is not met with any questions from the press about evidence of this 'spectre' or even to debate the sins and crimes of the old PKI, so that the public may at least know what it was. The PKI has been elevated to the status of the 'Boogey Man,' an undefined and unknowable threat used merely to scare and intimidate people.

Beyond these areas of restriction, either due to self-censorship or from aggressive ideologization of the issue from military figures, there have been indeed some important and positive developments in recent years that are creating a much more favourable basis for supporting freedom of the press with regards to state agencies.

Notably, the Press Council has worked with key agencies of law enforcement to develop a range of memoranda of understanding (MoU). In many ways, these memoranda of understanding build upon efforts by the Press Council to institutionalize standards of conduct within the journalist professions including the 2007 Council Guidance on the 'Right to Refuse.' This refers to the right of journalists to refuse to reveal sources in any law enforcement investigations.

Important also has been the issuance of a Circular from the Chief Justice of the Supreme Court at the end of 2008 in which courts at the district and provincial levels were urged when 'handling/investigating cases that involve press related charges, to listen to/request explanations from expert witnesses from the Press Council, because they are the ones who know best the ins and outs of the press in both theory and practice' (Supreme Court 2008). While circulars issued by officials are actually below legal precedence in Indonesia, Mr Bambang Harymurti observed that:

> since then the number of criminal cases against journalists has dropped to virtually zero. One exception was actually due to a poor effort by the defence team including witness. In an unfortunate way, the failure in this case actually demonstrated how effective the new processes have been operating.
>
> *(Interview 3 February 2019)*

Among arrangements signed was the 2013 MoU between the Press Council and the attorney general. This MoU, in essence, provides for the institutionalized access by the Council to any investigation involving journalists (from whatever branch of the media) including the provision of expert advice from the Press Council with regards to issues of investigation of press related issues involving journalists. The establishment of this process has reduced the propensity by aggrieved powerful people to harass journalists who report on them through criminal accusations. The MoU also covers the dissemination of information on the application of principles of freedom of the press under the law to prosecutors.

The Council has also established a MoU in 2012 with the police. The intent of this MoU is similar to the one with the office of the attorney general in terms of providing access by the Press Council to investigations involving journalists and also to disseminating information on the application of freedom of the press.

A separate MoU was signed in 2017 between the Press Council and the armed forces, specifically the press office of the armed forces. This provides for openness in terms of access for the press to Armed Forces information.

Mr Bambang Harymurti confirmed that these kind agreements were below legal precedence, observing that:

> despite their status as 'gentlemen's agreements,' since the endorsement of these agreements, many of the kinds of the problems that had impacted on the way journalists could operate, and also deal with these key state institutions, have been respected by officials in the field. They do seem to respect the decisions up their chains of command. Thus far changes in leadership in these institutions have had no impact on the willingness of people in these agencies to continue applying the principles outlined in the agreements.
>
> *(Interview 3 February 2019)*

Other notable MoU have been signed between the Press Council and agencies such as the Indonesian Broadcast Commission and the Witness and Victim Protection Institute.

In all references to the legal basis of each of these arrangements, several laws were mentioned. This reflects the basis upon which the state institution and parastatals believe they are bound by the terms of the MoU. Laws used to support their support for collaboration include the Press Law, the Broadcast Law and the law on openness to public information. Intriguingly, it does not include the Electronic Information and Transaction Law.

With regards to the MoU with the Indonesian Broadcast Commission, there was also the inclusion of the law on pornography (Cabinet Secretariat of Indonesia: Law 44 of 2008), a law that has been deemed in general as restricting freedom of expression. Mr Ade Wahyuddin observes that, 'the impact of this law has encouraged self-censorship and a reluctance by the press, and especially broadcast media, to discuss issues that might offend the sensibilities of religious conservatives lest this be seen as supporting pornography' (Interview 17 March 2019).

Society pressures and self-censorship

The previous subsection outlines the means by which various parts of the state have been developing, together with the Press Council, a *modus vivendi* that has provided a more secure operational basis for members of the press to work.

Despite these important advances, there remain other areas of society where the situation regarding the press has not been so encouraging. While pressure for the state has diminished, pressure from society has not. This is especially the case with regards to the issue of religion. In a multi-faith country where religiosity is all but universal, it should not perhaps be surprising that coverage of religious issues can give rise easily to community sensitivities.

There have been many cases when journalists have been threatened and attacked and media offices threatened and ransacked by mobs arguing that their religion has, in some or other way, been offended. This kind of mobilization on the basis of religious sensibilities is not, of course, restricted to the press. The startling downfall of the former governor of Jakarta, Basuki Tjahaja Purnama (who was a 'double minority' – race and religion) in the face of massive demonstrations against him claiming blasphemy reflects the fact that the issue of religion has massive appeal as a means of mobilizing public passions (Evans 2017: 33–35).

While it is an oversimplification to suggest that the issue of religious differences was the only issue that brought together these disparate groups to demand his removal, it was certainly the core mover of passions. Indeed, the key political cleavage throughout the electoral history of Indonesia (with the exception of the transitional democratic elections of 1999) has related to the role of majority religion and its adherents in the public domain of Indonesia (Evans 2012, 5:34–15:55).

Sensitivity to perceived slights on religion often manifest through accusations and ultimately prosecution for blasphemy. Blasphemy is a criminal offence in Indonesia under a special Presidential Order from 1965. Its definition is very vague and 'rubbery,' to use the Indonesian vernacular. Appeals by groups to the Constitutional Court to have blasphemy removed from the criminal code as they deem it infringes on freedom of expression have been rejected by the Court. Indeed, its application does appear to be quite rubbery. For example, a woman from a minority faith in North Sumatra was jailed recently for blasphemy after complaining to people at the local mosque about the high volume of its loudspeakers.

Indeed, too often the state – including law enforcement officials, rather than upholding the rights of the minorities – sides with the 'sensitivities' of the local majority. The incapacity or unwillingness of the state to protect the rights of minorities, especially marginalized minorities, perhaps reflects a tendency for people to see democracy as a matter of majority rule with insufficient respect for that other key element of democracy – namely, protection of minority rights. Evidence of this challenge with regards to protecting minority rights as part of the country's wider progress towards democracy can be seen through Freedom House's index *Freedom in the World*. The index is made up of two broad sets of indicators – the first focusing on political rights and a second focused on civil liberties. The results of each are brought to together to determine if the citizens of a country are deemed fully free, partly free or not free.

By late in the Soeharto era, Indonesia was categorized as not free. In the first five years after Soeharto's resignation, the country rose quickly to being partly free, and then in 2005, it reached a remarkable milestone, achieving the status of fully free. This status was retained until 2013, when it slipped back to partly free. What happened? Notably, the situation with regards to political rights has remained very solid and unchanged since 2005. What has changed is a weakening of civil liberties. This reflects a growing propensity for local (especially marginalized) minorities to not enjoy full rights. Security of the press, especially freedom of the press, is closely related to maters of civil liberties.

Attacks on freedom of expression cannot but have an impact on press freedom. The endorsement and application of a law on pornography (Cabinet Secretariat of Indonesia: Law 44 of 2008), which was, by any measure, the most contentious law to be deliberated and passed in the country in the past 20 years, has led to some censoring of coverage. The promotion by the Broadcast Commission of very conservative values is having an impact on press coverage certainly in the broadcast media. The passage of the Electronic Information and Transaction Law has also opened up new means of punishing people for what they upload and share on the internet. The Press Legal Aid Institute, LBH Pers, notes that people are using articles in the law dealing with defamation, spreading lies, immorality and hate mongering. 'In particular, politicians facing criminal investigation are using the defamation article to muzzle press coverage. Mind you thus far they have little success,' notes Mr Wahyudin (Interview 6 February 2019).

The Press Council has developed guidelines to help journalists in covering matters that touch on religion. Most of these guidelines are couched in terms of self-censorship, asserting easily aroused passions by communities of faith as the reason. Beyond that, it also suggests actual censorship in terms of noting that covering the issue of a caliphate should be avoided. It also argues that 'matters that contain secularism, atheism, communism and so on are in contravention of religion, can not be defended in the Pancasila nation which is religious and amid communities of faith that endorse Pancasila' (Priyambodo and Prawitasari 2014: 446–447). This kind of reticence to touch on or challenge these issues restricts greatly the capacity of the press to engage with and report on the use and abuse of religion. It also provides a cover for legitimizing timidity in coverage.

Mr Atmakusumah observes that:

> in [Soeharto's] New Order era, the press lost its hold on idealism because of pressure from political power which was sometimes mixed with economic power or, indeed, with military power. Now in the *Reformasi* era, the press can lose its hold on idealism and at the same time lose its sense of self-confidence because of pressure or acts of violence form the masses, or mobs, which can at times be mixed with political power. By caving in to acts of mass violence, it is as if the press is affirming the use of violence in society.
>
> *(Atmakusumah 2018: 223 author's translation)*

LBH Pers reports that over the past four years, there have been an annual average of 66 attacks against the press, including an average of 29 acts of violence (mob attacks on offices, physical injury to journalists, eradicating data, etc.) and an average of 37 non-violent attacks (criminalization, verbal abuse, banning from coverage, etc.) (based on the compilation of data released in several past annual reports from LBH Pers).

Mr John McBeth observes that:

> members of the press too often pull their punches and do not probe deeply enough to point out the significance of political events, such as former commander General Gatot Nurmantyo's unilateral decision to sever military ties with Australia without informing President Joko Widodo. This means politicians and other public figures often escape having to answer serious questions about their actions or more often inactions on important matters of public interest. Too often the voices of the victims do not get a fair hearing.
>
> *(Interview 1 February 2019)*

Mr Michael Vatikiotis, Regional Director for the Centre for Humanitarian Dialogue, Singapore observed that:

> the press, after 20 years of democratization, should be much less timid than it is now. Even by the standards of authoritarian regimes in Southeast Asia, the press during the Soeharto era enjoyed some advantages over their counterparts in say Malaysia and Singapore. The Indonesian state was never a major media investor. And those newspapers with close institutional links to state agencies had modest sales compared to the larger private ones.
>
> *(Interview 11 February 2019)*

He also noted that there is a lack of good investigative journalism, something else that he expected should have developed by now questioning: 'for example, where is Indonesia's version of [the news site] Rappler, which has been an important part of investigative journalism in the Philippines?'

One area, however, where the press has been quite relentless since democratization has been on prosecuting matters of corruption. This has certainly helped maintain public attention and pressure on these leaders. Even here in terms of probing, press attention has been focused on the 'catching the big fish' with minimal attempts at looking beyond the individual 'cases' to probe into 'institutionalized' problems that should also be redressed.

Commercial/economic pressures

This section explores pressure on the press by commercial and economic interests. At the turn of the century, the press was affected by a pair of massive changes (Asian financial crisis and democratization). Then, in 2008, the press was struck was a second pair of major changes: the global financial crisis and the arrival of digitalization of the local media. While Indonesia weathered the global financial crisis without coming close to a recession, it did see profits and revenue for many sectors – including the media – fall sharply. The rise of social media, including growth of mainstream media going online, has had a big impact on the environment of the press.

The impact of many of these changes has seen the media ownership landscape consolidate. While in principle, this may be creating a more commercially viable press and media sector, a major downside risk, under such circumstances, emerges should those media proprietors seek to mobilize their media outlets for overtly partisan interests. The Indonesian media during the first decade or so of democracy was notable for the plurality of views supported and the relatively moderated partisan perspectives presented. Since about 2012, this has begun to change, as was evidenced most starkly in the 2014 elections.

An era of hyper-partisan coverage by the media – print, broadcast and online – emerged. Fortunately, in the 2014 elections, there were plenty of media outlets supporting both presidential candidates thus providing some overall balance. In the 2019 elections, this appears to have weakened as most outlets are lining up behind the incumbent. Although 'mainstream' media groups may be more aligned to the same candidate, online and certainly social media remain as free flowing, multi-partisan, hyperventilated and hoax-infested, as in other societies.

Journalistic training, professionalism, collective action and norms

As noted in the introductory section, the impact of the Asian financial crisis created significant pressure on wages and salaries of people in the sector, while the subsequent deregulation of the media industries constricted profitability putting further pressure on salaries. Since it was established, AJI has sought to promote high ethical standards of journalists, most notably through rejecting long-established habits of newsmakers 'paying' journalists for coverage. This has formed part of the wider national effort to reject corrupt practices.

Audience/public support for media freedoms

It is not so easy to identify the extent to which the citizenry is supportive of media freedom. Questions like 'do you support freedom of the press?' is a rather one-sided question to which the answer will almost invariably be 'yes, of course.' More informative and substantive would be to know what people would compromise in order to secure press freedom. Or perhaps more tellingly, what they would be willing to sacrifice press freedom to secure.

The public has been very quick to adopt new forms of social media. Over the past 10 years, Jakarta has variously been termed the Facebook capital, then the Blackberry capital, and later the Twitter capital. While levels of penetration of the internet is finally passing 50 per cent of the population, the citizenry has certainly demonstrated an admirable capacity to mobilize online to fight against perceived injustices such as efforts a few years ago to criminalize members of the respected Anti-Corruption Commission and by efforts to support a woman being criminalized by a hospital for sharing online her views criticizing the quality of its services (Shubert 2009). This does suggest at least the potential for the public to support some or other press actor who may face unjust action by figures in authority.

Recent developments

The impact of the 'fake news' phenomenon

'This is a tragedy. Nobody knows how to deal with it,' says Ms Yuli Ismartono, senior Indonesian journalist, lamenting on the emergence of fake news through the media (Interview 5 February 2019). She explains further that 'there is a need to strike a balance between the right to know and be informed, but there is also a need to deal with the dissemination of obvious lies.' On this last problem, senior journalist and press figure Aristides Katoppo observed that, 'actually a bigger threat is not 'the death of the newspaper' but rather 'the death of journalism' (Interview 16 February 2019).

Mr Vatikiotis noted further that:

> political campaign teams have invested in abusing online platforms through the use of cyber-trolls in efforts to manufacture a base of support for their candidates or to discourage support for opponents. There has been a timidity by the mainstream media in investigating and exposing this behaviour, thus allowing it to continue.
>
> *(Interview 11 February 2019)*

The government has begun to make efforts to confront the threats of cybercrime through new cybercrime institutional arrangements, although this is still at an early stage of development.

The significance and role of social media

Ms Yuli Ismartono observes that, 'one of the key impacts of the emergence of social media has been to see the mainstream media 'dumb down' to try to retain audience attention' (Interview 5 February 2019). Separately, Mr Bambang Harymurti observed that today's journalists, especially due to the rise of online media services, are pressured 'to produce ten press items a day. They do not have the luxury of crafting probing interviews and reviews' (Interview 3 February 2019).

A more sinister development affecting the media and facilitated through cyber-connectivity is the emergence of doxing. Mr Wahyudin noted that his agency, LBH Pers, has begun to record and confront a new menace in the press over the past three years. He observed that:

> as the powerful have discovered it is essentially futile to seek to criminalize journalists and press outlets as a means of protecting their interests, they have focused attention on 'sources' that are used by the press. These people are bullied and harassed through doxing activities in the hope they relent on supporting any press investigations of their activities and thus to 'starve' the media of important sources of information.
>
> *(Interview 6 February 2019)*

He added that 'it is not yet very common, but we are tracking carefully with a view to seeing how to undermine this kind of indirect attack on the freedom of the press.'

Concluding remarks

Much of the progress achieved by the Indonesian press since democratization has been sustained since the initial burst of freedom. Old pressures by the government have been reduced as press representative agencies have worked with state agencies to build the control systems within the state. At the same time, limitations – often self-imposed – in the face of concerns about community backlash undermine the capacity of the press to cover those issues that have great impact on the social fabric and in learning from the nation's history.

As elsewhere, social media has been a mixed blessing. At one level, it has widened access by all citizens to reach vast audiences. Much of this is being used by people with no commitment to journalistic standards of conduct. It has allowed others to seek commercial and/or political benefit by abusing the cacophony of internet noise to mobilize public sentiment in their favour. Over the past decade, there has also been a growing concentration of media proprietorship. Not surprisingly, these proprietors are having a larger and more direct role in contemporary political decision-making.

Reduced pressure by the state are now being met by increased pressure by the market and (un)civil society that can be reflected in self-censorship. Amidst these competing pressures, senior press figure Aristides Katoppo states that 'members of the press need to retain not just a conscience and a sense of news, or an instinct to find it, but rather to remain brave and daring and go for it' (Interview 18 June 2018).

Bibliography

Atmakusumah. (2018) *Pers ideal untuk Masa Demokrasi (An Ideal Press for a Democratic Age)*, Jakarta: Lembaga Pers Dr Soetomo.

Cabinet Secretariat of Indonesia: Law 11 of 1966 on Principal Provisions on the Press (accessed 1 February 2019).

Cabinet Secretariat of Indonesia: Law 11 of 2008 on Electronic Information and Transaction (accessed 1 February 2019).

Cabinet Secretariat of Indonesia: Law 14 of 2008 on Openness in Public Information (accessed 1 February 2019).

Cabinet Secretariat of Indonesia: Law 19 of 2016 on Amendment of Law 11 of 2008 on Electronic Information and Transaction (accessed 1 February 2019).

Cabinet Secretariat of Indonesia: Law 32 of 2002 on Broadcasting (accessed 1 February 2019).

Cabinet Secretariat of Indonesia: Law 40 of 1999 on the Press (accessed 1 February 2019).

Cabinet Secretariat of Indonesia: Law 44 of 2008 on Pornography (accessed 1 February 2019).

Cabinet Secretariat of Indonesia: Presidential Order 1 of 1965 on Preventing the Abuse and/or Besmirching of Religion (accessed 1 February 2019).

Evans, K. (1998) 'Survey of recent developments', *Bulletin of Indonesian Economic Studies*, 34.

Evans, K. (2012) 'Ideological Divides and the Source of Indonesia's Political Stability', *TEDx JakSel*. Available HTTP: <www.youtube.com/watch?v=DXnI7P4XtV0> (accessed 31 January 2019).

Evans, K. (2017) 'Jakarta's gubernatorial election: A sign of the times', *Strategic Review*, 31–43.

Cabinet Secretariat of Indonesia: 1945 Constitution inclusive of 4th Amendment (accessed 1 February 2019).

Cabinet Secretariat of Indonesia: Law 4 of 1967 on Additions to the Law 11 of 1966 on Principals Provisions on the Press (accessed 1 February 2019).

Cabinet Secretariat of Indonesia: Law 11 of 1966 on Principal Provisions on the Press (accessed 1 February 2019).

The following resources were all accessed through the LBH Pers website. Available HTTP: http://lbhpers.org/

Freedom House. (various years from 1973–2019) *Freedom of the Press*. Available HTTP: <https://freedomhouse.org/report-types/freedom-world> (accessed 10 February 2019).

LBH Pers '20 Tahun Reformasi' [20 Years of Reform]. Available HTTP: <https://drive.google.com/file/d/1dQGqeCuCcZY0FuO50z_0LxPzhJLNExba/view> (accessed 7 February 2019).

Priyambodo, R.H. and Prawitasari, I. (2014) *Buku Saku Wartawan (Journalists Guide Book)*, Jarkarta: Lembaga Pers Dr Soetomo.

Shubert, A. (2009) 'Indonesian court case spans social movement', *CNN*. Available HTTP: <http://edition.cnn.com/2009/WORLD/asiapcf/12/22/indonesia.prita/index.html> (accessed 10 February 2019).

Supreme Court. (2008) 'Circular 133 of 2008, Supreme Court of Indonesia'. Available HTTP: <http://bawas.mahkamahagung.go.id/bawas_doc/doc/sema_2008_13.pdf>

11

PRESS FREEDOM IN MALAYSIA

An awakening for the media?

Gayathry Venkiteswaran

On 10 May 2018, Malaysians woke up to unexpected election results and with a sense of optimism that the new Pakatan Harapan (PH, loosely translated as Coalition of Hope)[1] government they voted in would introduce fundamental freedoms that had long been denied to them. Voters hoped that the 60-year political hegemony of the ousted Barisan Nasional (BN) would finally come to an end. *The Guardian* (2018) described the peaceful electoral win as a game changer in Southeast Asia, at a time when the region's democracies have been embattled by populist leaders and reversals in civil liberties. It was also seen as a second chance for the returning Prime Minister Mahathir Mohamad to undo the media controls he instituted during his first administration (1981–2003). Up to the very end of the campaign for the 14th general elections (GE14), the mainstream media provided no indication about the possible change or even whispers of shifting sentiments against the ruling government. On the contrary, they went into overdrive with their pro-BN propaganda to prop up the coalition government. Post-elections, Malaysian netizens and commentators shared anecdotes about renewed interest in the news because of perceptions that the media finally had the freedom to report freely and fearlessly. The PH leaders made themselves available to local and foreign journalists, and for the first time in many years, the media could directly put questions to the prime minister. They had been denied access to outgoing Prime Minister Najib Abdul Razak, who avoided the press, especially after the global financial scandal involving the state trust fund, 1Malaysia Development Berhad (1MDB), was tied to him.

Malaysia, a former British colony, is a parliamentary democracy with a federal constitutional monarch. Observers and experts describe the country post-independence as an illiberal democracy, a flawed democracy or an electoral-authoritarian regime, with the same government in control for decades (Economist Intelligence Unit 2018; Weiss 2015; Case 2009). Press freedom is one of the many fundamental liberties in which Malaysia always scores low in any global assessments. As Malaysiakini Editor in Chief Steven Gan said back in 2000, 'Malaysia is a democracy, but our system is full of contradictions. We have freedom of speech, but no freedom after speech. . . . We have a plethora of publications but no free press' (Committee to Protect Journalists 2000: para. 6). Reporters Sans Frontiers (RSF, Reporters without Borders), which assesses press freedom globally, has ranked Malaysia in the last quartile of the 170 countries surveyed, for most of the last ten years.[2] Historically, the main challenges for the media have been the unchecked power of the authoritarian state and political patronage involving/co-opting media owners.

In recent years, conservative forces within the state and among non-state actors, including selected media, have increased pressure on civil society groups, activists and netizens who express their views regarding issues of liberal Islam and broader human rights standards that affect freedom of expression, women's rights, LGBT rights and discrimination. The alliances between the different factional groups are constantly drawn and redrawn, making analysis of media freedom a lot more complex. Freedom to report is at risk of being reduced to the impunity with which the media can incite hatred towards vulnerable groups. To what extent will Mahathir Mohamad's coalition government honour its manifesto pledge to respect press freedom? Will Malaysians finally see reversals in their country's dismal record and ratings when it comes to respect for civil and political liberties? Could this be a moment of awakening for the media, albeit a delayed one as Malaysian voters demanded change after the 1998 Reformasi and the 2008 political shock, when the Barisan Nasional suffered a serious setback in the elections for the first time in over three decades (Kee 2008)?

This chapter addresses some key developments related to the media sector in Malaysia, and is presented in four sections. It begins with a discussion on the legal environment that affects press freedom, followed by an overview of ownership structures, including the changes taking place in the digital spheres. The third section introduces some of the informal pressures from the state and the invisible hands that direct editorial decisions. The chapter ends with a reflection on whether the media can regain public confidence after years of declining trust, and if the media community is well placed to reclaim and defend its rights.

Legal and regulatory environment

There are no specific media laws in Malaysia. Instead, what exists is a 'package' of laws and regulations that affect media operations and content regulation. Many of the laws were introduced during British rule, while others were amended or introduced by the independent state after 1957. Article 10(1) of the Federal Constitution of Malaysia guarantees freedom of speech, but it also allows for Parliament, as the highest lawmaking body, to legislate restrictions on a range of issues including national security, foreign relations, public order and morality, parliamentary privileges, contempt of court, defamation and incitement to any offence. Legal experts say the constitutional provision on freedom of speech can be interpreted as including freedom of the press, even though it is not explicitly stated, but it does not cover the right to information (Faruqi 2008). This section highlights five laws that are particularly problematic in terms of press freedom: the Printing Presses and Publications Act 1984 (PPPA), the Official Secrets Act 1972 (OSA), the Communications and Multimedia Act 1998 (CMA), the Defamation Act 1957 and the Anti-Fake News Act 2018.

Printing Presses and Publications Act 1984 (PPPA)

The PPPA has been through several revisions since it was first introduced under the British in 1948, and it has been used selectively and notoriously to control the print industry. Until 2012, newspapers and periodicals had to renew their permits annually and were denied avenues for judicial review. Amendments in 2012 were only minor, as publications were still subject to government-imposed conditions, leading to many media outlets choosing to toe the line to avoid suspension or outright closure (Shukry 2015). In 2015, the law was used against two newspapers owned by The Edge Media Group over their reportage about the 1MDB scandal, which involved the country's top leaders misappropriating public funds. That year, *The Edge Weekly* and *The Edge Financial Daily* were suspended for three months. The Home Ministry, which oversees national security and enforces the law, said in the letter of suspension that the reports were prejudicial to public order, national security and the national interest. At that time, the media in general were prevented from pursuing the story, but post-GE14, key individuals involved in the scandal have been brought to trial for money laundering and abuse of power. *The Edge* has won its challenge against the government over the suspension and has since been awarded damages. The harsh action against *The Edge* in 2015 reminded many of the 1987 closure of three media outlets (*The Star*, *Sin Chew Jit Poh* and *Watan*) during 'Operasi Lalang,' a government crackdown on opposition politicians and activists. In the mass arrest of dissenters, the three newspapers were accused of stoking racial sentiments against the backdrop of an already tense political situation between ethnic Malays and Chinese. Other publications that have suffered reprisals under the law include the now-defunct *The Heat*, which was suspended indefinitely in 2013 over its front-page report on the extravagant spending of the then prime minister's wife, Rosmah Mansor. Such reports were particularly thorny for the government as they raised questions about corruption at the highest levels. In 2014, the online news portal Malaysiakini was denied a publishing permit under this law, even after the courts declared the government's refusal unconstitutional. But partisan agendas are often conflated with other interests that could get the media into trouble. Media outlets that publish any images that could be interpreted as offensive to religious sensitivities and could be used as a political tool have received show-cause letters, suspension orders or have suffered actions against their editors (Southeast Asian Press Alliance 2007). This was the case when *The Star* published a photo of singer Erykah Badu exposing her tattoo of the word Allah (Asian Correspondent 2012), or when the Tamil language *Makkal Osai* published a front-page caricature of Jesus holding a cigarette and a beer can with a positive message about redemption (Kent 2007). *The Star* received a show-cause letter and it suspended two of its editors, while in *Makkal Osai*'s case, the suspension was believed to be tied to the newspaper's critical stance against an Indian political party that was part of BN, then the ruling coalition (Kent 2007).

Communications and Multimedia Act 1998 (CMA)

In the last ten years, digital platforms, including social networking sites, became the preferred platforms for alternative and independent media, as the CMA does not require the registration of websites. Yet, the risks faced by journalists and media outlets operating online have become more obvious since 2016, as the authorities began targeting individuals on social media and online media that reported on the 1MDB scandal. Among websites blocked by the authorities were The Malaysian Insider (and its mirror site), the London-based Sarawak Report and Asia Sentinel, as well as other political blogs. Even the US-based online publishing platform Medium.com was blocked because The Sarawak Report, which covered the 1MDB issue extensively, had used it to reach Malaysian audiences after its domestic site became inaccessible. The bans were lifted soon after the newly formed government took office in May 2018. The more controversial sections that relate to freedom of expression in the CMA are Sections 211 and 233, which prohibit 'annoying' and 'offensive' speech online. These sections have the overall effect of restricting what journalists can report on and the voices that can be represented. Both the former and current government want to further regulate online spaces for what they claim are attempts to spread hatred and insults to Islam and the royal families. Although the internet provides opportunities for community or advocacy journalism as alternatives to the mainstream media, challenges linger in terms of the freedom to report and the potential abuse of online civic spaces (Nain and Venkiteswaran 2016).

Official Secrets Act 1972 (OSA)

An important element of press freedom is the right of journalists and the public to access information. However, news media in Malaysia have their hands tied when it comes to reporting on public interest or governance-related issues. Like other laws, the OSA is broadly worded so that the sort of information that can be considered as state secrets is potentially unlimited. Interpretation of what is a state secret is often arbitrarily decided by the authorities. Since the conviction of a *New Straits Times* journalist in the 1980s, the law was tightened to make imprisonment mandatory if those accused under its terms are found guilty. Journalists who possess secret documents can be charged under the law even if they don't publish the content, complicating the coverage of corruption exposed by whistleblowers or when pursuing other investigative stories. Only two of Malaysia's states have freedom of information laws, Selangor and Penang, but these are only applicable for information created and held by public bodies in those states. The OSA has been used by the government to avoid public scrutiny regarding contractual obligations on infrastructure development, water supply and healthcare reforms, among others. Newsrooms are generally averse to reporting on materials classified under the OSA due to the risk of arrest even if they recognize the public interest value of the disclosures. Meanwhile, journalists who have used the freedom of information laws in the two states say that the costs are prohibitive in Penang and public officials are not adequately trained to respond to media requests (Mayuri 2015). The Pakatan Harapan government promised to enact a federal law on access to information, but like other pledges in their election manifesto, the announcements are vague and do not include clear timelines and processes.

Defamation Act 1957

For most in the media, traditional or digital, civil defamation is what affects their interests the most; it is a costly affair, and for those attempting critical reporting, defamation suits are a form of censorship. Anyone can initiate a defamation case to defend his or her reputation, and the outcomes have been mixed. Most importantly, there has been a significant reduction in the amount of damages awarded to claimants. The 1990s witnessed a trend of mega defamation suits filed by corporations, the most significant being the case by business tycoon Vincent Tan, who sued journalist MGG Pillai and seven others, and was awarded a whopping US$2.5 million in damages (Article 19 and Suaram 2005). There have been, however, some positive outcomes for press freedom and freedom of expression in recent years. For example, the courts recognized that the media had qualified privilege (citing the Reynolds principle on the conduct of responsible journalism)[3] in the defamation case filed by a private corporation, Raub Australian Gold Mining, against Malaysiakini. The online media outlet had reported on the affected residents' concerns about the health and environmental threats of one of the corporation's mining projects (Bernama 2019a). Courts have also indirectly supported press freedom by recognizing source protection in a case in which a journalist, who was called in as a witness in a defamation suit by a former legislator, Tiong King Sing, against a federal minister, Ong Tee Keat, was asked to reveal his sources (Malaysiakini 2016). The highest court upheld a decision that the journalist, JJ Sipalan, who was at the time of the suit working with the *New Straits Times*, had the right to protect the identity of his source as a matter of public interest.[4] However, the decision is only applicable in defamation cases involving private parties (Dipendra 2014). On the other hand, defamation is sometimes the only recourse for those who say they have been deliberately targeted and unfavourably portrayed by the media. PH politicians have won cases against the pro-BN media or agreed to settle with them out of court. The sheer number of media settlements with PH politicians is testimony to the impunity with which the pro-BN media operated and to the degree to which they were willing to toss aside professional ethics for political expediency.

Rulings in defamation cases have provided crucial lessons for the media if they want to raise their standards. For instance, the lack of journalistic professionalism was the subject of a 2007 ruling in a case involving the late human rights activist Irene Fernandez, whose organization Tenaganita works on migrant and labour rights. Fernandez successfully filed for libel against the Malay-language and pro-BN newspaper *Utusan Malaysia* in relation to reports about her exposé on alleged abuses at detention centres (*Irene Fernandez v Utusan Melayu (M) Sdn Bhd & Anor* 2008). In delivering the judgement, the high court judge acknowledged that the newspaper had failed to get her side of the story, was dishonest, presented claims as facts and had sensationalized the content (Beh 2007). In another example, the *New Straits Times* had to publish an apology to four civil society organizations in 2013 over a defamatory article that accused them of receiving foreign funds with the intent of destabilizing the government (Yong 2013). The apology was a condition set by the four groups to drop the defamation suit against the newspaper.

Anti-Fake News Act 2018

In the lead up to the 2018 elections, newsrooms were told to avoid reporting on the 1MDB scandal that involved the former prime minister. When still in government, the Barisan Nasional coalition had announced that any reporting on the 1MDB that was not sanctioned by the authorities would be treated as fake news. While there was little evidence that fake news was a problem in Malaysia, the government used it as a broad catch-all phrase to allow politicians to delegitimize any forms of criticism, much like the skewed narrative by US President Donald J. Trump in his attacks against the US media. Malaysia's Anti-Fake News Act – the first in the world – was introduced a month before the 2018 elections. It lacked clarity regarding the meaning or parameters of fake news, but criminalized a wide array of speech online and offline, raising concerns among media practitioners that they could be easily targeted under its terms (Venkiteswaran 2018a). The law had the potential effect of turning members of society against each other over frivolous allegations of spreading allegedly false content. Fake news became a campaign tool used by the BN to run down Pakatan Harapan's call for voters to reject Najib Razak over the 1MDB scandal. Since the elections, the new Parliament has repealed the law in the Lower House, but BN senators in the Upper House rejected the repeal. Both houses will have to vote on the repeal again in 2019.

Media ownership: histories and new challenges

Analysis of the Malaysian media and press freedom would not be complete without a look at the political economy of media ownership (Ding, Koh, and Surin 2013). The state-run Radio Television Malaysia (RTM) operates four television stations and 33 radio stations nationwide, while the largest media conglomerate, Media Prima Bhd, owns four free-to-air commercial television stations, three newspapers, radio stations, production houses and outdoor advertising assets. Media Prima's majority owner was aligned to the previous government through nominee shareholding and government-appointed editors. Two BN political parties have majority ownership in the media. UMNO has owned the Malay-language *Utusan Malaysia* since 1961, the first political takeover of a newspaper, which many argue was the start of its decline in terms of independence and credibility (Zahari 2001). The Malaysian Chinese Association (MCA) bought *The Star* newspaper in 1977, and in 2001, took over ownership of two Chinese-language newspapers, which were subsequently sold to another media conglomerate (Rimbunan Hijau). Meanwhile, Astro, a satellite television service, operates more than 160 television channels, radio stations and internet protocol television (IPTV) stations. It is owned by business tycoon T. Ananda Krishnan, who benefitted significantly from the country's privatization policy in the 1980s, and from government patronage during Mahathir Mohamad's first administration (Gomez 2018). The bulk of the Chinese-language newspapers, as well as those in the two Borneo states, are owned by logging and business tycoons, also with ties to political elites. Dependence on government patronage – even among public-listed media companies – has led to newsrooms taking partisan positions, made particularly challenging because owners can influence appointments of top-level editors and impose censorship.

The financial losses suffered by the media industry in recent years have resulted in layoffs and internal restructuring that have left many journalists out of a job. Media Prima reported losses of more than US$170 million in 2017, while *Utusan Malaysia* has recorded losses since 2012 and was subject to the regulator's scrutiny after it defaulted on loan repayments. *Utusan* reduced its workforce by half, while Media Prima and *The Star* have significantly downsized their operations. Top executives at *Utusan* and Media Prima have also been replaced, largely because of the political shifts after the 2018 elections (Azman 2018). The political party UMNO disposed of the majority of its shares in *Utusan* in early 2019, mainly due to its dire financial situation. It is unlikely that the media's political owners will give up all of their shares or influence because of the government change, but there is a heightened awareness and discourse among the public about the impact of political ownership on press freedom and the ability of the media to offer fair and balanced coverage.

The outliers, or media outlets that are relatively more independent, have grown in terms of influence over the last 20 years. The media landscape became particularly vibrant as online media began to set up, with Malaysiakini being at the forefront in terms of technological adoption and editorial independence. The others include Agenda Daily, Merdeka Review, The Nut Graph, The Malaysian Insider (now known as The Malaysian Insight), and Free Malaysia Today among many others, although some have since shut down. In the print sector, *Sinar Harian* has grown popular mainly with Malay-language readers. It is owned by the publishing house Kumpulan Media Karangkraf, which has a long history in niche magazines and novels. The group launched its newspaper in 2006 targeting the east coast of peninsula Malaysia before establishing a national presence, making it only the fifth Malay daily with significant national coverage. In the broadcast sector, the launch of Astro Awani news and business radio station BFM, with their talk shows and political discussions, has added to the diversity of news and current affairs.

Since the launch of the Multimedia Super Corridor (MSC) in 1998, the digital sphere has become simultaneously more diverse and empowering, as well as crowded and disruptive. The last decade witnessed the growth in social media use among Malaysians, with Facebook being one of the most popular platforms. Together with WhatsApp and Instagram, which it owns, Facebook is used by almost 70 per cent of Malaysia's population of 32 million (Wong 2018). Social media is often the only way people communicate and convey messages, replacing emails, static websites and blogs, making it easier for users but also problematic when access is moderated by the platform owners or regulated through internet service providers. The Malaysian news media, like their counterparts elsewhere, depend on these social networking platforms to reach their audiences, while journalists see these as tools and sources for their data gathering and interviews. There are no successful models for digital news media as such, but the lower costs and relatively less regulated platform, as well as the shifting consumer choices, are motivating the move into fully digital products. One notable example was the decision by The *Malay Mail*, which started in 1896, to go digital and cease its print version in December 2018.

State pressure: those phone calls and preferential treatment

Whether state-owned or private, newsroom routines and decision-making have been subjected to direct and indirect government interference. Prior to the 2018 election, editors received calls from the Home Ministry or the Prime Minister's Office to censor certain issues or to dictate the tone of reporting. But the sources making these calls became more pervasive over the years, as any officer or spokesperson for a minister or a politician would try to wield his or her influence to shape or block news reports (Hwai 2016). Government meetings with editors have included 'advice' on how to cover certain topics, or were outright instructive. On many occasions, editors complied with the requests in order to keep their licences and to avoid any form of reprimand. In conversations, journalists say these phone calls have dwindled post-GE14.

There is also preferential treatment by political parties in office and by public bodies in allocating advertising budgets for subscription newspapers. During electoral campaigns, the BN coalition allocated their advertising budget to friendly media outlets (Anuar 2010). When the internet became more popular around the time of the 2013 general election, the coalition shifted its resources to online advertising in a bid to win over online users who largely supported the opposition in 2008. The opposite occurred with the Pakatan Harapan governments in Selangor and now at the federal level, which issued instructions to their agencies to cancel subscriptions of the pro-BN newspapers, namely *Utusan Malaysia* and *Berita Harian*. In Selangor, the state government also stopped placing advertisements in these two newspapers. Financial support has therefore been weaponized by both sides of the political divide. The practice of either rewarding or punishing media outlets for their political loyalties undermines their integrity and reduces them in the eyes of the public, to propaganda channels.

Media outlets are sometimes blocked from government events or press conferences, either due to lack of accreditation (which is government regulated) or as a way to protest the media's political affiliations. Online news outlets such as Malaysiakini have been prevented from covering official BN press conferences, as online outlets were not eligible for government accreditation until about ten years ago (Pang 2006). Non-BN parties have blocked access to their opponent's media such as *Utusan Malaysia*, *New Straits Times* and TV3 where they hold power.

But newsrooms are active sites of negotiation and contestation; while many of the traditional media have been supportive of the BN, individual editors and journalists do challenge the restrictions when they can and do so, even at considerable risk. Freedoms are enjoyed through the use of columns and special pages to circumvent restrictions, as well as through the strategic use of sources to push stories that would otherwise not be published. Journalists cover events even when they know stories about certain issues, such as political protests, will be pulled, but they force the editors to make that call. At times, issues regarded as controversial may be flagged on social media using the journalists' personal accounts to draw public attention when they are unable to get their stories out via their employers.

Challenges from non-state actors

The power of the media is well established, and scholars have argued that the media often shape ideas and perpetuate existing hegemonic structures, most evident in the way they portray groups of people who have been made vulnerable or disadvantaged (Bleich, Bloemraad, and de Graauw 2015). But the prevailing sense among journalists is that their roles are merely to report 'what's out there,' or to reflect society. They tend not to see themselves performing an agenda-setting role. This intellectual gap in understanding means that pressures from state and non-state actors representing dominant positions are prioritized, especially by media targeting the Malay-Muslim population when reporting on freedom of religion. Islam or Malay rights are often conflated with the interest of certain political parties and the monarchy. Media outlets that express dissenting views on religious freedoms or LGBT rights are threatened with legal action, as in the case of the *Oriental Daily News*, which was warned over coverage that was deemed as 'promoting a "subversive culture" of homosexuality' (Malaysiakini 2018: para. 6). On the contrary, the language used by conservative media echoes that of the authorities in referring to non-conformists (whether based on faith, gender or political viewpoint) as infidels, deviants, ultra-liberals and even terrorists, subjecting the targets to harassment online and offline (Venkiteswaran 2017).

Can the media regain public trust?

Public trust and the credibility of the media suffered especially after the 1987 'Operasi Lalang,' when private newspapers were cowed into self-censorship as editors avoided coverage of issues that could be perceived as challenging the government at the risk of suspension orders. Meanwhile, the use of laws and political ownership meant journalists had to work within the boundaries set by those in power. The 1998 Reformasi further led to public disillusionment with the mainstream media. The shift to online sources for independent and uncensored information grew and was soon reflected in how Malaysians used digital technologies and platforms for political expression. After 2008, polls conducted on public perceptions of media independence showed that while Malaysians got their information from the news media, they did not necessarily have much trust in them, whether about political news or corruption (Centre for Independent Journalism 2008). In its recent survey of online users, the Reuters Digital News Report showed low rates of trust in news among Malaysians, making the country one of the lowest scoring in this global survey, due to perceptions of a lack of media independence (Nain 2018). Despite the relatively open environment post-May 2018, the news media are still constrained in reporting stories of public interest that might prove divisive. This agenda was pushed by the right wing in the former administration and by those in the current one seeking to appease a wider Malay voter base eager to maintain a system of preferences favouring them vis-a-via other ethnic groups (The Malaysian Insight 2019; Hew 2018).

In the aftermath of the 14th general elections, selected media outlets quickly embraced the new mood of renewal in the slogan *Malaysia Baharu* (New Malaysia). Overnight, media outlets began featuring politicians who were excluded from coverage in the past, and private broadcasters added political content into their weekly and daily shows. Radio stations that predominantly aired music introduced segments to discuss news headlines and interviews on current affairs, essentially pushing the boundaries of what their licensing conditions allow. However, television and radio hosts acknowledged that they were still bound by the rules and conditions prescribed in the Communications and Multimedia Act, which has not been amended. For many journalists, the change may not be so quick or easy. Senior journalists in pro-establishment outlets said the mainstream media had been used by the government in the past to create myths and alternative realities (Westbrook and Geddie 2018). The state news agencies have maintained the status quo by pledging allegiance to the government of the day, as they view themselves as civil servants rather than autonomous watchdogs serving the public good. With independent online media, the pressure is on them to raise their standards of reporting. Malaysiakini's Gan says they have to be on the alert and to carve out their unique role because in the new political environment, every media outlet can report relatively freely, which is good news for consumers who today have more choices (Venkiteswaran 2018b).

But there is a long way to go in raising the bar for quality journalism, which should be the priority of media outlets if they want to regain public trust. At the same time, the media community needs to demonstrate that it can come together to defend press freedom in the interest of upholding democracy. In his memoir, the late Said Zahari (2001), a well-known journalist who fought the UMNO takeover of *Utusan* in 1961, lamented the lack of commitment among editors in the print media and journalists' associations to defend press freedom. Malaysia's divided media landscape, due to partisanship, regional differences and the niche language communities, has made it difficult to achieve broad-based collective action, although there have been pockets of resistance. In 1999, journalists submitted a petition with more than 1,000 signatures calling for the repeal of the Printing Presses and Publications Act, and for the introduction of media self-regulation. Media non-governmental organizations have advocated for media law reforms and press freedom since the early 2000s. These organizations include ALIRAN-Charter 2000, the Centre for Independent Journalism, Kumpulan Aktivis Media Independent and the Writers Alliance for Media Independence. Since 2013, a journalists movement for free media, called Gerakan Media Merdeka (GERAMM) and the Institute of Journalists have also joined the fray to represent journalists' interests against threats and harassment. Some of the notable initiatives involving journalist groups and civil society that transcend the boundaries listed earlier, include the campaign against the takeover of two Chinese-language newspapers by the MCA in 2001, solidarity for journalists sacked by *The Sun* in 2002, public calls for media reforms post-elections in 2008, protest against the suspension of the news weekly *The Heat* in 2013 and support for the Malaysian Insider and *The Edge* against government investigations and reprisals in 2015. In early 2019, the media community has been engaged in discussions to establish an independent media council (Bernama 2019b). This is a longstanding agenda that has been co-opted by past governments many times to retain control over the media. In contrast, the current media-led process is expected to push for self-regulation and an independent mechanism that will be guided by ethical and professional standards. If successful and done in a transparent manner, this will be a major milestone for press freedom in Malaysia, especially if Parliament repeals the many problematic laws discussed in this chapter.

Conclusion

The media in Malaysia are still waking up to the new realities since the 2018 general elections, and to some extent, to the changes that have taken place over the last ten years. With the exception of several taboo topics, there is a general sense of opening up for the media, although many still operate on the basis of cue journalism, where journalists respond to signals from or follow the agendas set by official or political sources (Anuar 2006). Only a few pursue original and groundbreaking stories. In 2008, a senior newspaper editor, Chong Cheng Hai, commented that the political shock that year had not opened up space for the media, even though there were opportunities to push the boundaries:

> You think it is less restrictive, so you push the envelope a little further until there is a tug (in the form of action against other publications or a gentle reminder) and you start checking yourself again. The leash may be loosened, but the noose remains.
>
> *(Kee 2008: 272)*

The initial post-election euphoria in 2018 has been tempered by the reality that unless there are substantial changes to the laws or the ways in which the state controls the media, we may only see the loosening of the leash rather than a lifting of curbs on press freedom. Legal changes are political acts, but they can also represent society's aspirations and show how Malaysians wish to express their values and freedoms vis-à-vis the media. Meanwhile, societal forces have increased pressure on the media either to endorse the dominant narratives that relate to religious and ethnic identities, or to suppress any challenges and dissent. The reconfiguration of elite power and the jostling for traditional ethnic-based identity politics in this new political environment could end up preserving the structural and institutional barriers to press freedom, especially in the absence of strong public scrutiny and the inclinations of leaders like Mahathir Mohamad, who in the past mostly resisted press freedom and subverted democratic ideals (Wain 2009). Yet, public trust in the government has gone up considerably since the elections (Cheah 2019), raising hopes that generate momentum for the promised reforms. But equally important is whether public confidence and trust in the media will be restored and for that, the media must adapt to the new environment, adopt new ways of reporting and insist on defending its freedom and rights. If the proposed ideas to self-regulate succeed and the media is governed by ethics and professional standards, we could very well be seeing the start of a real improvement in Malaysia's press freedom.

Notes

1 At the time of the elections in May 2018, the Pakatan Harapan coalition was made up of four political parties – Parti Pribumi Bersatu Malaysia (Bersatu), the Democratic Action Party (DAP), Parti Keadilan Rakyat (PKR) and Parti Amanah Nasional (PAN) – which formed the federal government, together with the Sabah-based Parti Warisan Sabah. PAN is a splinter of the Islamic party PAS. Pakatan Harapan's predecessor was known as Pakatan Rakyat, formed in 2008 and comprising PKR, DAP and PAS, but it disbanded in 2015. Barisan Nasional was a coalition of 14 political parties, but it was left with three after its defeat at the federal level in the 2018 elections.
2 In the 2019 press freedom index, RSF raised Malaysia's ranking by 22 spots to 123 from 145 in 2018, following the promise of opening after the 2018 elections (Reporters Without Borders, 2019).

3 The Reynolds principle or defence stems from the decision in a defamation case, *Albert Reynolds v Times Newspapers Ltd*, in which the House of Lords in the United Kingdom established that the defence of qualified privilege for publication of defamatory statements in the public interest extended to the mass media. It established that a journalist had a duty to publish an allegation even when it turned out to be untrue. As Malaysia draws heavily from the common law tradition, the principle has been applied by the courts in the country (Kenyon and Ang 2010).
4 In the 2009 case, *Datuk Seri Tiong King Sing v. Datuk Sri Ong Tee Keat* at the High Court of Malaya (Kuala Lumpur), Tiong, a former lawmaker, sued Ong, who was then a federal minister, and the *New Straits Times* for defamation over a news story that alleged collusion involving Tiong in a development project. Tiong later dropped the suit against the newspaper but sought to compel the journalist, JJ Sipalan, who was a witness, to disclose his source.

References

Anuar, M.K. (2006) '"Cue journalism": Media should stop playing Follow-the-leader', *Asia Pacific Media Educator*, 1(17): 97–101.

Anuar, M.K. (2010) 'Packaging the PM: The art and ideology of political advertising', in Y.S. Guan (ed.) *Media, Culture and Society in Malaysia*, Routledge: New York.

Article 19 and Suaram. (2005) *Freedom of Expression and the Media in Malaysia*. Part of a series of baseline studies on seven Southeast Asian countries. Available HTTP: <www.article19.org/data/files/pdfs/publications/malaysia-baseline-study.pdf> (accessed 23 March 2019).

Asian Correspondent. (2012) 'Malaysian daily suspends editors over Erykah Badu "Allah" pics'. Available HTTP: https://asiancorrespondent.com/2012/03/after-ban-on-erykah-badus-concert-editors-in-malaysian-english-paper-suspended/> (accessed 23 March 2019).

Azman, S. (2018) 'Four directors resign at Utusan as part of restructuring plan', *The Edge Markets*. Available HTTP: <www.theedgemarkets.com/article/four-directors-resign-utusan-part-restructuring-plan> (accessed 7 November 2018).

Beh, L.Y. (2007) 'Irene wins libel suit, awarded RM200,000', *Malaysiakini*. Available HTTP: www.malaysiakini.com/news/74034 (accessed 17 October 2018).

Bernama. (2019a) 'Federal Court dismisses Raub Australian gold mining's appeal in defamation suit'. Available HTTP: <http://www.bernama.com/en/news.php?id=1694078> (accessed 13 February 2019).

Bernama. (2019b). 'Positive progress in setting up Malaysian media council'. Available HTTP: <http://www.bernama.com/en/news.php?id=1701261> (accessed 13 February 2019).

Bleich, E., Bloemraad, E., and de Graauw, E. (2015) 'Migrants, minorities and the media: Information, representations and participation in the public sphere', *Journal of Ethnic and Migration Studies*, 41(6): 857–873.

Case, W. (2009) 'Electoral authoritarianism in Malaysia: Trajectory shift', *The Pacific Review*, 22: 311–333.

Centre for Independent Journalism. (2008) *Media Independence Survey 2008*. Available HTTP: <https://merdeka.org/pages/02_research.html> (accessed 25 February 2019).

Cheah, B. (2019) 'Malaysian now trust their government, survey shows', *The Star*. Available HTTP: <www.thestar.com.my/news/nation/2019/03/05/malaysians-now-trust-their-government-survey-shows/> (accessed 5 March 2019).

Committee to Protect Journalists. (2000) *Awardee Speeches 2000: International Press Freedom Awards*. Available HTTP: <https://cpj.org/awards/2000/awardee-speeches.php> (accessed 3 January 2019).

Ding, J., Koh, L.C., and Surin, J.A. (2013) 'Mapping digital media: Malaysia', *Open Society Foundations*, London. Available HTTP: <www.opensocietyfoundations.org/sites/default/files/mapping-digital-media-malaysia-20130617.pdf> (accessed 3 January 2019).

Dipendra, H.R. (2014) 'Malaysia and Southeast Asia: Freedom of expression and information', *Global Freedom of Expression*, Columbia University. Available HTTP: <https://globalfreedomofexpression.columbia.edu/publications/malaysi a-and-south-east-asia-freedom-of-expression-and-information/> (accessed 7 November 2018).

Economist Intelligence Unit. (2018) *EIU Democracy Index 2017.* Available HTTP: <https://infographics.economist.com/2018/DemocracyIndex/> (accessed 3 January 2019).

Faruqi, S.S. (2008) *Document of Destiny: The Constitution of the Federation of Malaysia*, Berhad: Star Publications.

Gomez, E.T. (2018) 'Minister of Finance incorporated: Ownership and control of corporate Malaysia', *Institute for Democracy and Economic Affairs* (IDEAS), Palgrave Macmillan & Strategic Information and Research Development Centre.

The Guardian. (2018) 'The Guardian view on the Malaysian election: A second chance to put things right'. Available HTTP: <www.theguardian.com/commentisfree/2018/may/10/the-guardian-view-on-the-malaysian-election-a-second-chance-to-put-things-right> (accessed 3 January 2019).

Hew, W.W. (2018) 'Malay anxiety, exclusion, and national unity', *New Mandala.* Available HTTP: <www.newmandala.org/malay-anxiety-new-malaysia/> (accessed 14 September 2018).

Hwai, L.S. (2016) 'Former senior editor at Malaysia's New Straits Times says he quit after soul-searching over 1MDB scandal', *The Straits Times.* Available HTTP: <www.straitstimes.com/asia/se-asia/former-senior-editor-at-malaysias-new-straits-times-says-he-quit-after-soul-searching> (accessed 23 March 2019).

Irene Fernandez v Utusan Melayu (M) Sdn Bhd & Anor (2008) 2 CLJ 814.

Kee, T.C. (2008) *March 8: The Day Malaysia Woke Up*, Shah Alam, Malaysia: Marshall Cavendish Editions.

Kent, J. (2007) 'Anger at Malaysia "Jesus cartoon"', *BBC News.* Available HTTP: <http://news.bbc.co.uk/2/hi/asia-pacific/6960220.stm> (accessed 23 March 2019).

Kenyon, A.T. and Ang, H.L. (2010) '*Reynolds* privilege, common law defamation and Malaysia', *Singapore Journal of Legal Studies*: 256–281.

Malaysiakini. (2016) 'Federal Court dismisses Tiong's appeal over confidentiality of sources'. Available HTTP: <www.malaysiakini.com/news/333094> (accessed 23 March 2019).

Malaysiakini. (2018) 'Ministry warns Chinese daily over pro-LGBT article?'. Available HTTP: <www.malaysiakini.com/news/447088> (accessed 14 October 2018).

The Malaysian Insight. (2019) 'Majority of Malays unhappy with Pakatan but have hope, says study', Available HTTP: <www.todayonline.com/world/majority-malays-unhappy-pakatan-have-hope-says-study> (accessed 31 January 2019).

Mayuri, M.L. (2015) 'Citing operational hiccups, Selangor Speaker says state FOI law needs improvements', *Malay Mail.* Available HTTP: <www.malaymail.com/news/malaysia/2015/06/10/citing-operational-hiccups-selangor-speaker-says-state-foi-law-needs-improv/913047> (accessed 23 March 2019).

Nain, Z. (2018) 'Malaysia', in N. Newman, R. Fletcher, A. Kalogeropoulos, D.A.L. Levy and R.K. Nielsen (eds.) *Reuters Institute Digital News Report 2018.* Available HTTP: <http://media.digitalnewsreport.org/wp-content/uploads/2018/06/digital-news-report-2018.pdf?x89475> (Accessed 25 February 2019).

Nain, Z. and Venkiteswaran, G. (2016) 'Local media and digital frontiers: The Malaysian conundrum', *Media Development*, 3: 14–17.

Pang, A. (2006) 'Managing news in a managed media: Mediating the message in Malaysiakini.com', *Asia Pacific Media Educator*, 17(1): 71–95.

Reporters Without Borders. (2019) 'World Press Freedom Index 2019'. Available HTTP: <rsf.org/en/ranking> (accessed 25 August 2019).

Shukry, A. (2015) 'Malaysia's brief, rich history of suspending newspapers', *The Malaysian Insider*. Available HTTP: <www.theedgemarkets.com/article/malaysia%E2%80%99s-brief-rich-history-suspending-newspapers> (accessed 23 March 2019).

Southeast Asian Press Alliance. (2007) 'Newspaper suspended for one month for "offending" religious sensibilities', *IFEX*. Available HTTP: <www.ifex.org/malaysia/2007/09/04/newspaper_suspended_for_one_month/>.

Venkiteswaran, G. (2017) '"Let the mob do the job": How proponents of hatred are threatening freedom of expression and religion online in Asia', *Association for Progressive Communications*, South Africa. Available HTTP: <www.apc.org/en/pubs/%E2%80%9Clet-mob-do-job%E2%80%9D-how-proponents-hatred-are-threatening-freedom-expression-and-religion-online> (accessed 3 January 2019).

Venkiteswaran, G. (2018a) 'All the news that's fit to fake', *New Mandala*. Available HTTP: <www.newmandala.org/news-thats-fit-fake/> (accessed 25 February 2019).

Venkiteswaran, G. (2018b) 'Malaysia: Promise of a change', *IFEX*. Available HTTP: <https://ifex.org/malaysia/2018/06/14/election-media-reforms/> (accessed 25 February 2019).

Wain, B. (2009) *Malaysian Maverick: Mahathir Mohamad in Turbulent Times*, London: Palgrave Macmillan.

Weiss, M.L. (2015) *Routledge Handbook of Contemporary Malaysia*, Oxon and New York: Routledge.

Westbrook, T. and Geddie, J. (2018) 'Telling truth to power still no easy task for Malaysia's revved up media', *Reuters*. Available HTTP: <www.yahoo.com/news/telling-truth-power-still-no-easy-task-malaysias-100713096.html> (accessed 17 October 2018).

Wong, C.K. (2018) 'Top instant messaging apps in Malaysia: WhatsApp vs WeChat vs FBMessenger', *SilverMouse*. Available HTTP: <https://blog.silvermouse.com.my/2018/10/top-chat-apps-malaysia-whatsapp-wechat-fb-messenger.html> (accessed 3 January 2019).

Yong, L. (2013) 'NST to apologise for 'plot to destabilise gov't' report', *Malaysiakini*, Available HTTP: <www.malaysiakini.com/news/246512> (accessed 23 March 2019).

Zahari, S. (2001) *Dark Clouds at Dawn: A Political Memoir*, Kuala Lumpur: Insan.

12

MEDIA FREEDOM IN MYANMAR

One step forward, two steps back

Tina Burrett

In politics today, heroes are few in number. For decades, Aung San Suu Kyi's principled stand and personal suffering in resisting Myanmar's military dictatorship made her a rare global icon. In November 2015, election victory for her National League of Democracy (NLD) offered the world a welcome ray of hope in dark political times. But optimism quickly turned to disappointment at home and abroad. As de facto national leader from March 2016, 'The Lady' – as Aung San Suu Kyi is known domestically – is failing to protect the rights and freedoms she long demanded of Myanmar's generals. Her refusal to condemn or fully acknowledge mass atrocities against Myanmar's Rohingya Muslim minority perpetrated by the military – over which constitutionally she has no control – has drawn widespread criticism, including from the UN (Ellis-Petersen and Hogan 2018). Rather, The Lady has reserved her censure for journalists exposing human rights violations (Goldberg 2018). Herself a prisoner of conscience for 15 out of 21 years from 1990, Myanmar's journalists expected State Counsellor Aung San Suu Kyi to dismantle the military-era machine of media repression. But in government, The Lady is proving intolerant of personal criticism and unwilling to denounce the harassment of journalists by military leaders, who retain substantial political power and exclusive domain in the security sphere.

Over almost half a century in government, Myanmar's military assembled a virtually unrivalled apparatus of media control, including one of the world's most restrictive censorship regimes. Seizing power by coup in 1962, military leaders brought much of Myanmar's media under direct state ownership, intimidating and, in many cases, incarcerating journalists and pro-democracy activists opposing junta rule. In 2010, facing multiple armed insurgences, an effective opposition movement and crippling Western sanctions that deepened economic dependence on China, Myanmar's generals initiated a top-down liberalization process aimed at controlling the direction of political change. In March 2011, the military handed power to a new nominally civilian government, led by former general President Thein Sein. The new president introduced a series of reforms, including allowing Aung San Suu Kyi and her National League for Democracy (NLD) to contest parliamentary by-elections in April 2012, following her release from house arrest in November 2010. Reforms also included releasing hundreds of political prisoners, reaching preliminary peace agreements with the majority of armed ethnic groups and in August 2012, abolishing the Ministry of Information's pre-publication censorship regime (Harris 2013). Previously prohibited topics such as endemic corruption, ethnic conflicts and government land grabs began to feature on the front pages. In March 2016, the reform process culminated in the NLD's Htin Kyaw became Myanmar's first civilian president since 1962, a role denied to Aung San Suu Kyi by the 2008 junta-drafted Constitution because she married a foreigner.[1]

Disappointingly, the development of media freedom is stalling under the NLD. Many of the 50 Myanmar journalists, editors and media owners interviewed for this chapter lament that their industry enjoyed more freedom in the twilight years of Thein Sein's presidency than today. The forces undermining media freedom in Myanmar are multiple. First, the legal framework in which the media operates provides state authorities with a choice of methods for silencing their critics. Restrictive colonial- and military-era media and security laws remain in place, with journalistic freedom granted at the discretion of the government, rather than by legal statute. Instead of repealing these draconian laws, NLD politicians – as well as military figures – use them to harass their detractors and to deny reporters freedom of speech, movement and access to information. Second, Myanmar's current political culture is deeply scarred by decades of dictatorship and by the military's continuing influence on politics. Despite the NLD's 2015 election victory, Myanmar is not a full democracy. Before handing power to a civilian government in 2011, Myanmar's generals drafted a new Constitution guaranteeing the military 25 per cent of parliamentary seats, giving them a controlling stake in who is appointed president and an effective veto on constitutional amendments.[2] In battles between Myanmar's multiple power centres, the media are frequently caught in the crossfire. Third, the popularity of social media as a news source is exacerbating social divisions by facilitating the spread of fake news and by encouraging echo chamber effects (Iyengar and Hahn 2009; Jamieson and Cappella 2008; McNair 2018; Clark 2017). Facebook has approximately 20 million users in Myanmar, representing almost all the country's internet users and nearly 40 per cent of the population (Russell 2018). Myanmar's military and militant groups use social media to incite religious and racial violence as a means of expanding their support base (Mozur 2018). Fourth, journalists' lack of training and experience undermines the application of internationally recognized professional standards in Myanmar's newsrooms. Working in the context of political polarization and religious conflict, many journalists eschew their neutral watchdog role to become attack dogs engaged in the fight to determine Myanmar's future. Others self-censor to avoid falling foul of warring factions. Finally, operating in a poor country generating only modest advertising revenues, despite marketization, Myanmar's media remain financially beholden to the state or to wealthy cronies of the former military regime. Economic dependence on the state or on business elites with state connections entails editorial compromise at best. The search for profits in an increasingly crowded media market, meanwhile, is encouraging tabloidization and an emphasis on human interest and entertainment stories over political news.

This chapter analyzes the obstacles to establishing media freedom in Myanmar. A free media is essential to the democratization process. It allows democracy to flourish by providing a forum for public debate, guarding against abuses of power and mobilizing public learning and participation in the political process (Norris 2000). Correspondingly, a free media is an indicator of successful democratic transition. But the end of official censorship, diminishing direct political control and the overall pluralization of the media does not guarantee its positive contribution to the democratization process. The media's ability to facilitate democratization paradoxically depends on the degree to which other political actors and institutions embrace democratic procedures (Gross 2002; Jakubowicz 2006). The quality of democratization in general determines the media's democratic performance (Voltmer 2008). This chapter argues that Myanmar's stalled media transition is a product and an indicator of the country's wider failure to democratize.

In exploring the challenges undermining the development of a free media in Myanmar, this chapter draws on face-to-face interviews with 50 journalists, editors, media owners and trainers working in the Myanmar-based media. Interviews conducted by the author took place during several periods of fieldwork spanning December 2013 to November 2018. Naturally, a potential problem with interview data is deliberate distortion. Given the volatility of the political situation in Myanmar, it may be professionally or legally helpful to censor one's views, or to hide knowledge of any wrongdoing. To mitigate this problem, interviewees were offered anonymity. Furthermore, multiple sources from different organizations were interviewed, and in several cases re-interviewed, to alleviate the effects of embellishment or misinformation.

The following discussion is divided into five sections. The first section analyzes how Myanmar's legal framework inhibits media freedom. Section two examines political competition and the media's ties to political interest groups as a constraining factor. Section three looks at the role of social media as an influence on journalistic procedures as well as on audience opinion. Section four analyzes journalists' professionalism, defined as the media's professional norms and practices (Benson 2004). The final section investigates the impact of economic factors shaping the media market.

Legal framework

President Thein Sein began easing legal restrictions on the media after his military-backed Union Solidarity and Development Party (USDP) took office in

2011. Journalists celebrated when pre-publication censorship was abolished on 20 August 2012. April 2013 saw the publication of the first independent daily newspapers since 1964. In 2015, the USDP government passed a new broadcasting law relaxing ownership of radio and television. But while liberalizing some media functions and operations, the USDP preserved a variety of legal means to silence journalists. Vague national security laws – such as the 1923 Official Secrets Act, the 1950 Emergency Provisions Act and the 2000 Internet Act – ensured that censorship could continue and journalists punished for non-compliance (Crane 2014). In a clear step backwards for media freedom, Parliament in 2014 passed the Printers and Publishers Regulation Act, giving the Ministry of Information ultimate power over what news was permissible to print. The controversial legislation, similar to the previous junta's censorship guidelines, banned the publication of materials that 'insult religion,' 'disturb the rule of law,' 'violate the Constitution,' 'incite unrest' or 'harm ethnic unity' (Crispin 2014). It also created a new registrar position with sole authority to withhold or revoke publishing licences. Fear of losing their licences inevitably encouraged self-censorship among editors, especially in reporting on sensitive topics such as ongoing inter-ethnic tensions and land development (Interview, *The Chronicle* editor, 2014).

Journalists hoped that the new NLD government, in office from 2016, would repeal or amend illiberal media laws and enact legislation to protect newsrooms from state intervention and intimidation. But under the NLD, the military-controlled Ministry of Home Affairs is taking a harder line against journalists than during the USDP administration. Section 66(d) of the 2013 Telecommunications Act is being used to prosecute individuals for criticizing the authorities online. Section 66(d) provides for up to three years in prison for 'extorting, coercing, restraining wrongfully, defaming, disturbing, causing undue influence or threatening any person using a telecommunications network' (Human Rights Watch 2017). At least 106 people have been charged under the law for online defamation, with 90 per cent of cases brought since the NLD took office (Free Expression Myanmar 2017). In May 2016, for example, poet Maung Saungkha was sentenced to six months in prison for posting a poem online that implied he had a tattoo of President Thein Sein on his penis (Hein and Kean 2017). In October 2016, a member of the NLD's Central Executive Committee made a complaint under 66(d) against a Monywa-based party member who unknowingly reposted a fake NLD announcement concerning the committee member's resignation. The NLD defendant received a six-month prison sentence. The same month, a Bago-based USDP member was arrested and later convicted for posting online that Myanmar's people had become dogs since Aung San Suu Kyi took power. A local NLD activist brought the complaint, as 66(d) allowed third parties, as well as those allegedly defamed, to file a case (Free Expression Myanmar 2017). In August 2017, Parliament amended the Telecommunications Act to stop third parties from registering defamation complaints and to increase the likelihood that those charged under the law would receive bail (Shoon and Yimou 2017). But despite widespread protests by civil society groups, the government did not repeal Section 66(d), and amendments to the law were only minor.

Journalists are also being arrested using more obscure laws, adding to concerns that the NLD government is restricting rather than expanding media freedom. In June 2017, Ko Lawi of The Irrawaddy and Democratic Voice of Burma (DVB) reporters Ko Aye Naing and Ko Pyae Bone Aung were arrested for covering an event to raise awareness of drug abuse and illegal trafficking held by members of an armed ethnic group. After facing a possible five-year sentence under the 1908 Unlawful Association Act, charges against the trio were eventually dropped in September 2017. Four reporters working for Turkish state broadcaster TRT World were arrested in October 2017 for attempting to fly a drone near Myanmar's Parliament in Naypyitaw. They were sentenced to two months in prison under the 1934 Myanmar Aircraft Act for flying the drone. They were also charged under the 2012 Export and Import Law for illegally bringing the drone into Myanmar, which carries a penalty of up to three years prison time (San 2017). In December 2017, two Reuters journalists, Wa Lone and Kyaw Soe Oo were arrested under the Official Secrets Act for possessing leaked documents relating to the conflict between government forces and the Arakan Rohingya Salvation Army (ARSA) in Rakhine[3] (See Kingston, Chapter 13, Lakhdhir 2018). Cases such as these undoubtedly create anxiety within the media community and influence what journalists do and do not report.

Government-imposed travel restrictions further impede what journalists are able to report, especially from Myanmar's conflict zones. Journalists are typically barred from areas of ethnic unrest. The government strictly prohibits reporters from visiting northern Rakhine, from where over 700,000 Rohingya refugees have fled military violence into neighbouring Bangladesh since 25 August 2017 (Crispin 2018). ARSA attacks on security-force outposts that day set in motion a cycle of violence. Since then, only a small number of handpicked reporters have been allowed to tour the area, and only under military supervision (Interview Kyaw Min Swe, editor-in-chief of The Voice, 2017). Most reporting on allegations of rape, summary executions and other abuses comes from victim interviews conducted by international reporters in refugee camps in Bangladesh. Journalists based in Rakhine face considerable barriers to reporting on the state's ethnic politics. In December 2017, Kyaw Lin, a local reporter who worked for the Roma Time news service, was stabbed in the back by an unknown assailant while riding on a motorcycle in Rakhine's Sittwe township (Toe 2017). Kyaw Lin says he continues to receive threats by telephone and on social media, forcing him to flee with his family to Yangon (Crispin 2018).

Myanmar's government is also clamping down on foreign journalists' access. In February 2014, the Ministry of Information reduced the duration of foreign reporters' visas from three months with multiple entries to one month with a single entry. The move likely came in response to international media criticism of government treatment of Rohingya refugees displaced following ethnic clashes in Rakhine in 2012. In some cases, international reporters were denied entry altogether. In March 2014, for example, *Time* journalist Hannah Beech was refused a visa, probably in response to her cover story the previous year featuring extremist monk Ashin Wirathu with the headline 'The Face of Buddhist Terror' (Crispin 2014). Since the latest round of violence erupted in Rakhine in August 2017, international journalists report facing greater scrutiny and surveillance when working in Myanmar. Foreign reporters complain of being followed and filmed, and of being asked to sign official declarations stating that they will not visit restricted areas (Reed 2018). The Myanmar authorities are also filing lawsuits against journalists working for international news outlets. In February 2018, the Rakhine state government announced it would sue the US-based news agency The Associated Press (AP) for reporting on the discovery of five mass graves in a Rohingya village in Buthidaung, northern Rakhine (Thiri and Gerin 2018).

In Myanmar, democratization has not included a new freedom of information law. Journalists complain that government ministry information bureaus are under-staffed and difficult to contact (Interview, Irrawaddy editor, 2016). Given the brutal and secretive culture of the junta that ruled Myanmar for 50 years, despite a change in government, officials continue to fear getting into trouble if they talk to the media. Like the rest of society, bureaucrats are traumatized from living under a dictatorship (Interview, Kyaw Min Swe, editor-in-chief of The Voice, 2017). The vague wording of official secrets and other laws means that bureaucrats are often unsure what information they can release to the public. Rather than getting into trouble for releasing restricted information, bureaucrats prefer to release nothing, even when the information requested by journalists is mundane (Interview, *Myanmar Freedom Daily* journalist, 2017). A culture of secrecy, distrust and fear within government ministries impedes journalists' reporting on important news stories in the public interest.

Political culture

The junta's legacy of violent repression, as well as the military's continuing centrality in national politics is warping Myanmar's political culture and undermining the establishment of democracy. Decades of government harassment and attempts at infiltration by state agents have left the NLD and its leaders suspicious of strangers. Journalists complain that getting access to The Lady and her ministers is difficult for reporters not already part of the NLD's inner circle:

> It takes a long time to win the trust of NLD press officers. Even today, military informers try to get inside the party. It is not surprising that they are paranoid, but it makes it hard to get information. Only trusted journalists are invited to interview the Lady.
>
> *(Interview, Yangon-based Reuters correspondent, 2016)*

Journalists who criticize the NLD government, even with the aim of helping improve the party's policies, find themselves ostracized:

> If I criticise the NLD I will be the common enemy of everyone. Sometimes I am more afraid of the NLD than of the military. If I attack the military, my colleagues and readers will approve. They hate the military and are ready to believe the worst of them. But if I criticise the NLD, their supporters will punish me.
>
> *(Interview,* 7 Day News *editor, 2017)*

Myanmar is not a normal democracy and Aung San Suu Kyi is not a normal political leader. For years, The Lady symbolized resistance to oppression. Now in office, her bond with the public remains rooted in emotion, complicating the media's task of holding her and her government accountable:

> People in Myanmar are not like people in other democracies. The experience of dictatorship left us prone to strong emotions. When we love, we love too much. When we hate, we hate too much. People love the Lady, even after many disappointments. There isn't a big market for objective reporting.
>
> *(Interview, Kyaw Min Swe, editor-in-chief of The Voice, 2017)*

Suspicion of outsiders has led to over-centralization of decision-making within the NLD, hampering the flow of information to the media:

> Inside the NLD, the Lady decides everything. Icons do not necessarily make good managers. Maybe her style was necessary when she was running an opposition movement, but it is unsustainable in government. Decisions get bottlenecked, and that includes about what information to make public.
>
> *(Interview, Myint Kyaw, director of the Myanmar Journalist Network, 2018)*

A lack of government experience exacerbates NLD leaders' tendencies towards secrecy and suspicion. When composing her de facto government, Aung San Suu Kyi appointed her close associates, trusted friends who shared her struggle against military rule and who bear the same scars (*The Myanmar Times* 2016). The majority of ministers do not have experience or expertise in the areas they oversee, making them dependent on ministry officials. Journalists suggest that under the influence of junta-trained bureaucrats, NLD ministers regularly reject media requests for information and interviews (Interview, Irrawaddy editor, 2016).

Many interviewees for this chapter argue that the nation's 'two governments' situation is the main reason for the NLD's reluctance to engage with the media. Adopting a realpolitik approach, The Lady and other NLD ministers avoid condemning or confronting the military – Myanmar's 'other government' that operates independently, even setting its own budget that in 2017 totalled US$2.14 billion, almost 14 per cent of state expenditure (Samuels 2018). As the military still control the means of violence, civilian politicians tread softly (Interview, Ma Thida, writer and activist, 2018). Aung San Suu Kyi's failure to denounce the military's ethnic cleansing in Rakhine, or to speak up for journalists investigating these crimes, underscores her compromise strategy.

How much to compromise with the military is an issue that divides Myanmar's media professionals. Kyaw Min Swe, editor-in-chief of The Voice, argues that a negotiated political settlement with the military is the only way to protect Myanmar's political reforms:

> A lasting change can only be built slowly and will have to involve the military. I'm not pro-military, but they are a fact of life. A permanent settlement requires a compromise on all sides.
>
> *(Interview, Kyaw Min Swe, editor-in-chief of The Voice, 2017)*

Others in the media disagreed, believing that political reforms are aimed at strengthening the military's hold on power rather than a genuine transition to democracy. A presenter for satellite broadcaster the DVB summed up the views of many of journalists, stating that:

> The military undertook reforms to protect themselves. If you are in any doubt, look at how they have guaranteed themselves 25 per cent of seats in parliament. The military won't give us democracy. We must fight for it.
>
> *(Interview, DVB presenter, 2016)*

Writer and activist Ma Thida concurs, arguing that the military have already achieved what they intended in initiating political reform:

> What the military always thirsted for was legitimacy. And with the 2015 election they got it. They don't need to stage another coup to take back power – they never gave it up.
>
> *(Interview, Ma Thida, writer and activist, 2018)*

As journalists and activists argue over how to deal with the military, Myanmar's generals continue to operate largely unchecked.

By sacrificing her principles to compromise with Myanmar's generals, Aung San Suu Kyi is forfeiting her two biggest advantages over the military – her domestic popularity and her international support. As director of the Yangon Journalism School, Ye Naing Moe, argues:

> The Lady focuses too much on political issues, like changing the constitution [to allow her to be president] rather than on the concerns ordinary

people. The generals were very clever. By putting the NLD in government, they could shift the blame for failing policies and deflect international criticism of the country's flawed democracy.

(Interview, Ye Naing Moe, director of the
Yangon Journalism School, 2017)

In allowing herself to become a fig leaf for the military, including downplaying their ethnic cleansing in Rakhine, Aung San Suu Kyi has lost her international icon status, with some questioning whether she should be stripped of her 1991 Nobel Peace Prize (Monbiot 2017; Samuels 2018). Along with her international support, The Lady has lost much of her leverage over Myanmar's military. As the generals' hostage, she has little ability or incentive to fight for media freedom. Her capitulation is well symbolized by her decision to retain President Thein Sein's chief media spokesman, Zaw Htay, better known by his Facebook handle Hmuu Zaw (Moe 2016). As director of the president's media operations when ethnic violence erupted between Arakanese Buddhists and Rohingya Muslims in Rakhine in 2012, Zaw Htay uploaded photos to Facebook fuelling tension between the two communities (Moe 2016). His presence at The Lady's side is a blot on her reputation for Press Council member Myint Kyaw, who accuses Zaw Htay of 'fomenting civil unrest' (Interview, Myint Kyaw, director of the Myanmar Journalist Network, 2018). As Aung San Suu Kyi's spokesman in September 2017, Zaw Htay advocated shooting Rohingya fighters (who he called Bengalis[4]) if they displayed threatening behaviour (Nyan 2017). But Zaw Htay is far from the only one in Myanmar using Facebook to spread hate and misinformation. The popularity and pervasiveness of social media as a news source is a significant factor polluting Myanmar's political culture and jeopardizing its democratization.

Social media

The internet and its extensions, such as mobile technology and social media, are transforming communications by facilitating instantaneous, horizontal connections. This potential for connectedness created optimism among scholars that the internet would encourage greater political engagement, participation and awareness (Di Gennaro and Dutton 2006; Zhang, Johnson, and Seltzer 2010). In the case of democratizing countries, there is some evidence of social networking platforms being used to organize civic activism (Loveless 2008; Voltmer and Schmitt-Beck 2006). The role of social media in the Arab Spring is generally perceived positively. The uprisings in the Arab world are often labelled the 'Facebook/Twitter Revolutions' in recognition of the prominent role played by social media in the coordination of mass protests and the release of real-time images to the international community (Cottle 2011; Lim 2012). In Myanmar, despite enabling similar activist coordination and dissemination of information, the influence of social media is largely negative.

In 2013, President Thein Sein's government deregulated Myanmar's telecommunications industry, opening the sector to foreign companies in a bid to expand access to cellular and other advanced technologies. As a result, the price of SIM cards dropped by 99 per cent, from approximately US$200 to US$2, heralding a communications revolution (Ferrie 2013). The simultaneous lifting of junta controls on free expression and a rapid uptake of cellular phones allowed the mobilization of a populist, hard-core Buddhist nationalism that has deep roots in Myanmar's political history. Social media became a tool for stoking fears that Buddhism – practiced by approximately 90 per cent of Myanmar's population – was under siege from the forces of modernity, globalism and Islam. Facebook provided the perfect platform to popularize and spread nationalist, hate-loaded narratives that unleashed a wave of anti-Islamic violence across the country, beginning in Rakhine in 2012. In September 2018, Facebook was singled out in a United Nations (UN) report accusing the Myanmar military of genocide in Rakhine, for the ease with which the platform allows hate speech and misinformation to spread (Safi 2018).

Bordering Bangladesh, Rakhine is home to a long-held national myth that Buddhism in Myanmar is in danger of being overrun by millions of Bengali Muslims. Nationalist Buddhist organizations and their allies in the military began using social media to heighten these fears as a means of boosting their support in a society undergoing rapid political change. Attacks by the ARSA in August 2017 tapped into the deep-seated Islamophobic fears of nearly all Myanmar's Buddhists, resulting in a rallying around the military as defenders of the nation and its majority religion (Callahan 2018: 251). The spread of xenophobic nationalism serves the interests of the military and of extremist Buddhist movements such as 969 and Ma Ba Tha, leading to a coalition between Myanmar's monks and generals. An example of this union came on 30 October 2017, when one of the country's most revered monks, Sitagu Sayadaw, delivered a sermon to military officers at their garrison in Kayin State that was live-streamed on the internet and watched by more than 250,000 people (Mratt 2017). Clips of the sermon, preaching unity between the military and monkhood, and justifying the use of violence to defend the faith against non-Buddhists deemed 'not fully human,' went viral on social media (Callahan 2018: 251).

After much criticism for their slow reaction in dealing with inflammatory material, in August 2018, Facebook removed the accounts of 18 individuals for encouraging human rights abuses, including General Min Aung Hlaing, commander in chief of Myanmar's armed forces (Mozur 2018). But the Myanmar military also uses sham accounts to spread anti-Muslim propaganda and fake news on Facebook. Often posing as fans of popular celebrities, the military dedicates hundreds of personnel to creating troll accounts and news pages that are then flooded with incendiary comments. The impact of this propaganda project is immense. In December 2018, Facebook removed 135 accounts, 425 pages and 17 groups that together had 2.5 million followers (Russell 2018). The military's shadowy operation also collects intelligence on popular accounts and criticizes posts unfavourable to the armed forces (Mozur 2018). Accounts are also used to defame and undermine the credibility of the generals' enemies. One hoax used a genuine photo of Aung San Suu Kyi in a wheelchair and paired it with false suggestions that she had gone to South Korea for Botox injections (Mozur 2018).

The military's anti-Rohingya propaganda on Facebook weakens media freedom in Myanmar in a number of ways. Most obviously, by posting sham photos of corpses said to be evidence of Rohingya-perpetrated massacres, the military are polarizing communities and fuelling extremist views (Clark 2017). Myanmar's mainstream media are reluctant to publish stories contradicting or condemning disinformation about the crisis in Rakhine for fear of provoking a backlash from sectarian audiences. An editor at *7 Day News* explains:

> Whenever we write about the conflict in Rakhine we get a lot of angry letters. Following criticism of our reporting on the violence in Rakhine, we decided to give the issue less prominence.
>
> *(Interview 2017)*

Journalists attempting to expose fake news face the prospect of violent retribution. When one journalist criticized Ashin Wirathu, the charismatic monk who leads the 969 movement, the group attempted to have him prosecuted (McPherson 2017). In another example, a human rights activist who cooperated with the UN panel investigating genocide in Rakhine was subject to a Facebook post labelling him a 'national traitor.' One comment under the post read, 'If this animal is still around find him and kill him.' Facebook told the UN panel that the post did not contravene their guidelines, and it was only removed after several weeks (Safi 2018).

Unsurprisingly, there is a lot of journalistic self-censorship when it comes to reporting about the conflict in Rakhine. Self-censorship by journalists can lead to a dearth of balanced information about the causes of inter-ethnic violence. When balanced reporting is scarce, biased accounts go unchallenged. Several journalists interviewed for this study complained of calculated pro-Buddhist coverage of the Rakhine conflict by much of Myanmar's media. As one journalist at Eleven Media said of his colleagues:

> Most reporters are Buddhists and they are patriotic. Their personal nationalism is reflected in what they write.
>
> *(Interview 2017)*

Although patriotic fervour is not uncommon among journalists in other places at times of national crisis – for example in the United States following the terrorist attacks on 9/11 – it is particularly dangerous in the context of volatile inter-ethnic tensions (Levy and Bugingo 2001). One-sided reporting not only obscures audiences' understanding of the issues, but also increases the probability of further violence.

Other interviewees in this study attribute biased coverage of ethnic conflict to low educational standards among media professionals. Some argue that biased reporting stems from journalists' poor understanding of media framing (Interview, Myint Kyaw, director of the Myanmar Journalist Network, 2018). Framing theory contends that the media focus audience attention on certain events and then place them within a field of meaning (Goffman 1974; Scheufele and Tewksbury 2007; Entman 1993). In Myanmar, by using loaded nouns such as 'Bangladeshi' or 'immigrant' to describe the Rohingya, journalists frame the Rakhine conflict in nationalist terms.[5]

The generals who seized power in Myanmar in 1962 justified their rule as necessary to hold together a country fractured by ethnic strife. Several interviewees for this study raised suspicions that military provocateurs are behind recent outbreaks of sectarian violence. Fresh sectarian violence adds credence to the military's insistence on remaining a prop to Myanmar's civilian government. But despite harbouring strong suspicions that the military are stoking inter-ethnic tensions to justify retaining a prominent role in government, the majority of journalists are too afraid to publish such concerns (Interview, Street View Journal journalist, 2014). Reporters brave enough to expose misinformation receive little support from the NLD government. Aung San Suu Kyi has dismissed reports of abuses against the Rohingya as exaggerated, blaming 'terrorists' for 'a huge iceberg of misinformation' (Warren 2017).

Journalistic professionalism

In Myanmar, as in other authoritarian states, government persecution of the press led journalists to join pro-democracy groups. During military rule, journalists languished in the country's 43 prisons. After decades of harassment by the state, it is difficult for journalists in democratizing states to become neutral observers of political events. Many of Myanmar's journalists are members of the NLD or the '88 movement.[6] This is especially true of many of the former media in exile who began returning to Myanmar following the start of reforms in 2011 (Interview, Press Council member, 2018). Today, journalists continue to eschew their neutral watchdog role to act as guard dogs protecting the interests of their economic and political masters.

Interviews for this study reveal that poor education and the influence of social media, as well as political factors, undermine the application of internationally recognized professional standards in Myanmar media. Journalists in democratizing states often poorly understand the norms expected of their profession, as for years state censors externally imposed standards on the media. In many democratizing societies, media organizations are young and inexperienced, since older, more seasoned journalists are often associated with the state-controlled media of the former regime. When the reform process began in 2012, the average Myanmar journalist was 25 (IMS 2012). Even chief editors are unlikely to be much older than 30. In 2016, only 21 per cent of journalists had seven or more years of professional experience, while 28 per cent had less than two years (UNECO 2016: 84). The inexperience of many Myanmar journalists is compounded by a relative lack of professional training opportunities. Journalism schools are few in number, and places remain scarce (Interview, BBC Media Action trainer, 2018). There are not enough qualified media professionals to fill the demands of Myanmar's expanding media market. 'Anyone who wants to can get into the media,' says a reporter at Sky Net News, herself one of the few at the satellite channel with a degree in journalism (Interview, Sky Net News reporter, 2016). State-owned media often pay better salaries than their commercial competitors, and therefore attract a larger share of journalism school graduates. Competition for qualified journalists and editors increased following the government's decision to allow private newspapers to resume publishing daily editions from 1 April 2013.[7] A senior editor at *7 Day News* explains:

> When we decided to run a daily newspaper, we advertised for new reporters. But in most cases the applications we received were not suitable. Some applicants admitted they didn't even read the newspapers. We couldn't find enough qualified candidates, so we have to edit our daily newspaper with the same number of editors who previously worked on our weekly edition.
>
> *(Interview 2017)*

Finding qualified media trainers is another challenge, as is accessing training materials in Burmese language. International media training organizations like BBC Media Action and Internews are helping to cover the shortfall in training opportunities by providing professional development courses for Myanmar's journalists, both domestically and overseas. But these courses are oversubscribed and usually only last a few months at most (Interview, media trainer, 2016). Courses provided by international organizations are generally more accessible for journalists in urban centres and/or with English-language ability (UNECO 2016). Training opportunities, however, are expanding, with several international organizations targeting courses at journalists from Myanmar's ethnic minority media (Interview, representative of Burma News International, 2014).

In states like Myanmar where foreign media were taboo, journalists lack access to foreign colleagues from whom they could learn international professional norms. By 2012, this situation was improving, as more international journalists began to receive permission to work in Myanmar. But despite growing exposure to international professional standards, ethical norms remained underdeveloped among Myanmar's media professionals. A journalist at *7 Day News* estimates that only half of her colleagues understand the meaning of ethical journalism:

> In my opinion, 50 per cent of journalists behave ethically and 50 per cent do not. Many of my junior colleagues confuse fact with opinion. Sometimes this is not deliberate, but a fact of their poor education. But in other cases, journalists deliberately distort the truth to make their reports more

sensational. These journalists are more interested in getting a lot of Facebook followers than in accurate reporting.

(Interview 2017)

Pursuing financial gain, as well as popularity and fame, can lead journalists to abdicate their professional responsibilities. Several interviewees in this study acknowledged bribery as a persistent problem in Myanmar's newsrooms. For example, an editor at Eleven Media admits:

> When a new business opens a reporter might receive money to write a positive review. As an editor, I read 12 to 16 stories a day. I don't have time to check every fact.

(Interview 2017)

The ethical and professional dilemmas confronting Myanmar's editors are compounded by reliance on citizen journalists with no formal ties to their news organization. In the current Myanmar market, few private media organizations can afford to establish bureaus outside of major cities. As a result, Yangon-based newsrooms often rely on citizen journalists to report on events in remote parts of the country. Lacking any professional education, citizen journalists often fail to record the information necessary to make a story verifiable (Interview, Chin World News editor, 2016).

Journalists' poor training and inexperience means that both deliberate and unintended inaccuracies are commonplace in the Myanmar media. Inaccuracies can undermine public confidence in the mainstream media (IMS 2018). Myanmar audiences are more likely to trust information posted by their friends on Facebook than news appearing in the professional media:

> The media have a bad reputation. For decades there was only the state media and they were propaganda organs for the government. In post-authoritarian states like Myanmar people tend to trust their friends over institutions, including the media.

(Interview, media trainer, 2016)

During the junta period, when reliable information was difficult to access, communities shared news as a form of social engagement (IMS 2018: 12). This sharing culture means that information from social media spreads beyond the online realm, reaching the approximately 60 per cent of citizens who do not have Facebook accounts (IMS 2018: 19). Despite its popularity, navigating social media can be tricky and not everybody understands that Facebook can be used to disseminate fake news. Audiences' ability to assess the reliability of online information is a problem everywhere, but it is particularly acute in democratizing societies like Myanmar, where authoritarian governments discourage the teaching of critical thinking skills (Interview, Ma Thida, 2018). Given the societal preference for sharing news, Myanmar's journalists could help improve media literacy and trust in their profession by being present in local communities. For many, the media are elitist and concerned only with Yangon-related matters. More reporting from outside Myanmar's big cities would improve audiences' assessment of the media. But reporting from Myanmar's far-flung regions is beyond the financial means of most newsrooms.

Media market

In Myanmar, the state continues to dominate the media industry despite marketization. The independent media that appeared after licensing laws were relaxed depend largely on business elites with state connections for their economic survival. Despite a change in government in 2016, state authorities show few signs of giving up their economic influence over the media. The state retains majority control in the television sector, the most popular source of news among urban dwellers (IMS 2018). The NLD government has thus far failed to transform state media MRTV into a public service broadcaster. As a state-owned entity, MRTV is by definition not independent from the government, or free from political interference. The news it provides presents a positive view of the government, while avoiding controversial issues such as land grabs, military operations and corruption (UNECO 2016: 64). Explaining why the new government has retained state control of MRTV, veteran journalist and Director of the Yangon Journalism School Ye Naing Moe argues that:

> The NLD see the value in keeping MRTV as a propaganda machine. MRTV news hasn't changed its style at all. They have just substituted the Lady for President Thein Sein, following her around as she visits hospitals etc. There is no analysis, no attempt to make it interesting. It is still boring shit.
>
> *(Interview 2017)*

Despite its lacklustre style, MRTV remains Myanmar's most popular and trusted broadcaster (IMS 2018). Its privately owned rivals do not have the financial resources or broadcasting infrastructure to compete. Furthermore, Myanmar's two current private networks, MRTV-4 (Forever Group) and Sky Net (Shwe Than Lwin Company) are government joint ventures owned by allies of the former military regime. In a move aimed at improving pluralism in the broadcast media, in February 2018, Myanmar's government issued licences to five additional television companies, including the formerly exiled broadcaster DVB that was a major critic of the junta. The companies will use MRTV's broadcast infrastructure, but will have control over content. It is unclear, however, whether the five new broadcasters will survive. Initial investment, including MRTV rental fees, is over US$4 million. The companies plan to recoup their investment by selling TV commercials, but will likely face difficulties for the foreseeable future due to Myanmar's limited advertising market (Nitta 2018).

State-owned outlets also continued to dominate in Myanmar's print sector. The country's three state-run dailies – which operate as mouthpieces for the government – have a circulation of more than 320,000, while the more popular private newspapers sell only about 80,000 copies per day (Interview, Myint Kyaw, director of the Myanmar Journalist Network, 2018). Private publications cannot compete in terms of distribution networks or cover price. Advertisers often preferred to work with higher-circulation state-run outlets than with the private-owned media. In 2014, financial difficulties forced three privately owned dailies to close within a month (Cunningham 2014). A lack of business acumen among those running private newspapers is another factor hampering their success. Trained managers are scarce, and many editors are former political prisoners or exiled activists with no experience in business (Interview, *Sun Ray* editor, 2014). Financial backers willing to suffer losses while a newspaper establishes a foothold in the market are hard to find. As in other democratizing states, those with the deepest pockets were often cronies of the former regime (Becker 2014; Porto and Hallin 2009). Depending on business elites with connections to the state necessitates major editorial concessions. Private media owners used their political leverage to extract economic and regulatory favours from state benefactors in exchange for turning a blind eye to corruption and failed policies (Interview, *People's Age* reporter, 2016). A few lucky outlets, such as DVB and *The Chronicle* have secured funding from international NGOs, but such sources of finance are limited (Interview, *The Chronicle* editor, 2014). Today, international funding is even more difficult to secure than at the start of Myanmar's reform process, partly as a consequence of the conflict in Rakhine (Aung 2018).

Ties to financial and business interests have restricted what Myanmar's journalists can report about economics, as well as politics. Traditionally, the watchdog role of the media is defined as behaviour that reveals abuses in the exercise of state power and ignores the role of the press as a defence against exploitation in the private sphere – most notably with regard to the economy (Chomsky and Herman 1988). Clearly, the media should act as a source of redress against the abuse of all forms of power. But in Myanmar, privately owned media outlets have refrained from investigating the activities of the conglomerates to which they belong. At Sky Net, for example, a journalist reports being instructed by editors to refrain from investigating misdemeanours by businesses within the same holding company (Interview, Sky Net News reporter, 2016).

When company profits are not in jeopardy, Myanmar's media have shown a predilection for sensationalism and scandal. Growing competition, especially from social media, is encouraging tabloidization of the press. Myanmar is not alone in this regard. In the West, the search for profits in an increasingly crowded market has led to a decline in news quality (Barnett 1998; Postman 1986). In democratizing states like Myanmar, where scandal and gossip were previously forbidden, audiences have become transfixed by 'yellow journalism' (Interview, *Myanmar Times* editor, 2014). When tabloid newspaper *The Sun Rays* (*Thuriya Nay Wun*) hit the newsstands in 2013, its mixture of colourful cover pages, scandal and sensationalism quickly made it one of the highest circulation weeklies in Yangon (Weng and Zaw 2013). Journalists interviewed for this study, however, were critical of Myanmar's tabloids for bringing their profession into disrepute:

> Their unethical behaviour damages public confidence in the media and allows the government to say we need restrictions on what journalists can report.
>
> *(Interview, Irrawaddy journalist, 2016)*

Other journalists expressed concern that the success of tabloids would encourage more newspapers to adopt a sensationalist style.

Some interviewees expressed suspicions that more sinister motives lay behind the tabloidization of the press. Although it appears that by exposing state corruption, tabloids are living up to their watchdog role, such stories concealed political biases, as a member of the Press Council explains:

> Look closely and you will realise that some newspapers only attack members of a particular faction within the military. Their victims are carefully chosen.
>
> *(Interview, Press Council member, 2018)*

Press exposure of corruption is often a byproduct of intra-elite conflict, rather than the result of a commitment to the public interest. Similar 'information wars' between competing elites in post-Soviet Russia severely damaged public confidence in the media, and strengthened support for President Putin's increase in state control of the media from 2000 (Burrett 2011).

Conclusion

Myanmar's historic transfer of power to the NLD in March 2016 has been a tragic disappointment. In office, those who fought so long for democracy are undermining media freedom. Aung San Suu Kyi's suspicion of the independent media and unwillingness to condemn military abuses against the Rohingya, or against journalists exposing these atrocities, are exacerbating a culture of media self-censorship. In Myanmar's dual-power political environment, journalists seeking to hold both the NDL and military to account are often ostracized and harassed by both sides. The state retains significant legal means to coerce the media that are frequently invoked by civilian and military leaders to stifle critical reporting.

Although the NLD have not improved conditions for Myanmar's journalists, significant factors impeding media freedom are beyond the new government's control. Many media challenges are a legacy of Myanmar's military past, while others are a product of the democratization process. The long-simmering conflict in Rakhine, widespread ethnic nationalism and a poor capacity for critical thinking among Myanmar's journalists and audiences are all consequences of the former regime's deliberate stoking of societal divisions and suffocating of civil society. The inexperience and limited education of those drawn into Myanmar's rapidly expanding media market have negative consequences for professional standards and ethics. These ethical challenges are intensified by the accessibility and anonymity afforded by social media that has become a useful tool for military trolls intent on spreading fake news and inter-ethnic discord. In the presence of civil conflict, ethnic loyalties are encouraging journalists to abdicate their professional responsibilities. The tabloidization unleashed by marketization is also curtailing the media's ability to encourage societal reconciliation and present political alternatives, important functions in an emerging democracy. After taking a tentative step forward on the path to freedom, Myanmar's media has taken two steps back, placing in peril the country's journey towards democracy.

Notes

1 President Win Myint replaced President Htin Kyaw when the latter retired in March 2018.
2 Myanmar's president is not directly elected by the public, but nominated by parliamentarians. Three committees, known collectively as the Presidential Electoral College, are formed from upper and lower house parliamentarians. One of the three committees is made up entirely of military-appointed lawmakers. Each committee nominates one candidate for the presidency. Members of the Electoral College then vote for one of the three to become president. The candidate with the most votes takes the presidency, and the unsuccessful candidates become vice-presidents. Constitutional amendments require the backing of more than 75 per cent of Parliament ('FACTBOX – Myanmar's New Political Structure' 2015).
3 The Reuters pair were subsequently sentenced to seven years in jail, but were later pardoned and released in May 2019.
4 Bengali is a term commonly used by government officials and many people in Myanmar to refer to the Rohingya population of Rakhine State to deny their status as a national ethnic minority.
5 The Rohingyas' exact roots are debated, but many likely settled in Burma in the nineteenth century, having migrated from modern-day Bangladesh following expansion of the British Empire. Today, the Rohingya are excluded from the 135 ethnic groups the government recognizes as Myanmar citizens.
6 In 1988, demands for an end to the military dictatorship in Myanmar spilled out from university campuses onto the streets, led by a group known as the '88 Generation Students' Group. The movement was brutally suppressed, and those who were caught were sentenced to decades in prison. Some of those who escaped overseas went on to work in the media in exile.
7 All private dailies in Myanmar were shut down in 1964. Until 2013, the authorities allowed publication of state-run dailies, but only permitted the private media to publish weekly editions.

Works cited

Aung, S. (2018) 'Dying Myanmar media face great challenges', *Myanmar Times*. 27 July. Online. Available HTTP: <www.mmtimes.com/news/dying-myanmar-media-face-great-challenges.html> (accessed 5 March 2019).

Barnett, S. (1998) 'Dumbing down or reaching out: Is it tabloidisation wot done it', in J. Seaton (ed.) *Politics and the Media: Harlots and Prerogatives at the Turn of the Millennium*, Oxford: Blackwell.

Becker, J. (2014) 'Russia and the new authoritarians', *Demokratizatsiya*, 22: 191–206.

Benson, R. (2004) 'Bringing the sociology of media back in', *Political Communication*, 21: 275–292.

Burrett, T. (2011) *Television and Presidential Power in Putin's Russia*, London: Routledge.

Callahan, M. (2018) 'Myanmar in 2017: Crises of ethnic pluralism set transitions back', *Southeast Asian Affairs*, 243–263.

Chomsky, N. and Herman, E.S. (1988) *Manufacturing Consent: The Political Economy of the Mass Media*, New York: Pantheon Books.

Clark, D. (2017) 'Myanmar's internet disrupted society – and fueled extremists', *Wired*. 28 September. Online. Available HTTP: <www.wired.com/story/myanmar-internet-disrupted-society-extremism/> (accessed 3 March 2019).

Cottle, S. (2011) 'Media and the Arab uprisings of 2011: Research notes', *Journalism*, 12: 647–659.

Crane, B. (2014) 'Burma backtracks on press freedoms', *American Interest*. 5 December. Online. Available HTTP: <www.the-american-interest.com/2014/12/05/burma-backtracks-on-press-freedoms/> (accessed 5 March 2019).

Crispin, S. (2014) 'Burma's clampdown gather's pace as legislation passes', *Committee to Protect Journalists* (blog). 14 March. Online. Available HTTP: <https://cpj.org/blog/2014/03/burma-clampdown-gathers-pace-as-legislation-passed.php> (accessed 17 March 2019).

Crispin, S. (2018) 'Threats, arrests, and access denied as Myanmar backtracks on press freedom', *Committee to Protect Journalists*. Online. Available HTTP: <https://cpj.org/blog/2018/02/threats-arrests-and-access-denied-as-myanmar-backt.php> (accessed 5 March 2019).

Cunningham, S. (2014) 'Third daily Burmese newspaper shuts down, but more to come', *Forbes*. 5 April. Online. Available HTTP: <www.forbes.com/sites/susancunningham/2014/04/05/a-third-daily-newspaper-shuts-down-in-myanmar> (accessed 5 March 2019).

Di Gennaro, C. and Dutton, W. (2006) 'The internet and the public: Online and offline political participation in the United Kingdom', *Parliamentary Affairs*, 59: 299–313.

Ellis-Petersen, H. and Hogan, L. (2018) 'Aung San Suu Kyi stays silent on UN report on Rohingya genocide', *The Guardian*. 28 August. Online. Available HTTP: <www.theguardian.com/world/2018/aug/28/aung-san-suu-kyis-response-to-un-report-on-rohingya-genocide-silence> (accessed 17 March 2019).

Entman, R.M. (1993) 'Framing: Toward clarification of a fractured paradigm', *Journal of Communication*, 42: 51–58.

'FACTBOX – Myanmar's new political structure'. (2015) *Reuters*. 31 January. Online. Available HTTP: <http://in.reuters.com/article/2011/01/31/idINIndia-54526820110131?pageNumber=1> (accessed 5 March 2019).

Ferrie, J. (2013) 'N Myanmar, cheap SIM card draw May Herald Telecoms revolution', *Reuters*. 25 April. Online. Available HTTP: <www.reuters.com/article/us-myanmar-telecoms-draw/in-myanmar-cheap-sim-card-draw-may-herald-telecoms-revolution-idUSBRE93N1AX20130424> (accessed 5 March 2019).

Free Expression Myanmar. (2017) '66(d) no real change', *Yangon: Free Expression Myanmar*. Online. Available HTTP: <http://freeexpressionmyanmar.org/wp-content/uploads/2017/12/66d-no-real-change.pdf> (accessed 5 March 2019).

Goffman, E. (1974) *Frame Analysis: An Essay on the Organization of Experience*, New York: Harper and Row.

Goldberg, J. (2018) '"Jailed reporters" wives "devastated" by Aung San Suu Kyi response', *The Guardian.* 5 September. Online. Available HTTP: <www.theguardian. com/world/2018/sep/04/jailed-reporters-wives-devastated-aung-san-suu-kyi-response?CMP=Share_iOSApp_Other> (accessed 3 March 2019).

Gross, P. (2002) *Entangled Evolutions: Media and Democratization in Eastern Europe*, Baltimore, MD: John Hopkins University Press.

Harris, M. (2013) 'Burma: Freedom of expression in transition', *Index on Censorship.*

Hein, K.S. and Kean, T. (2017) '66(d): The defamation menace', *Frontier Myanmar.* 13 January. Online. Available HTTP: <https://frontiermyanmar.net/en/66d-the-defamation-menace> (accessed 5 March 2019).

Human Rights Watch. (2017) 'Burma: Repeal section 66(d) of the 2013 Telecommunications Law', *Human Rights Watch.* Online. Available HTTP: <www.hrw.org/news/2017/06/29/burma-repeal-section-66d-2013-telecommunications-law> (accessed 5 March 2019).

IMS. (2012) 'An assessment of media challenges and opportunities in Myanmar: Change is in the air', *International Media Support.* Online. Available HTTP: <www.i-m-s.dk/files/publications/changeisintheair_january2012_IMS.pdf> (accessed 3 March 2019).

IMS. (2018) 'Myanmar's media from an audience perspective', *Myanmar: International Media Support.* Online. Available HTTP: <www.mediasupport.org/wp-content/uploads/2018/11/Myanmar-audience-study-2018_online.pdf> (accessed 5 March 2019).

Iyengar, S. and Hahn, K. (2009) 'Red media, blue media: Evidence of ideological selectivity in media use', *Journal of Communication I*, 59: 19–39.

Jakubowicz, K. (2006) *Rude Awakening: Social and Media Change in Central and Eastern Europe*, New York: Hampton Press.

Jamieson, K.H. and Cappella, J. (2008) *Echo Chamber: Rush Limbaugh and the Conservative Media Establishment*, Oxford: Oxford University Press.

Lakhdhir, L. (2018) 'A dark anniversary for press freedom in Myanmar', *Reuters.* 12 December. Online. Available HTTP: <www.hrw.org/news/2018/12/12/dark-anniversary-press-freedom-myanmar> (accessed 5 March 2019).

Levy, A. and Bugingo, F. (2001) 'Between the pull of patriotism and self-censorship', *Reporters Sans Frontières.* Online. Available HTTP: <www.rsf.org/article.php.3?id_article=2533> (accessed 5 March 2019).

Lim, M. (2012) 'Clicks, cabs, and coffee houses: Social media and oppositional movements in Egypt, 2004–2011', *Journal of Communication*, 62: 231–248.

Loveless, M. (2008) 'Media dependency: Mass media as sources of information in democratizing countries', *Democratization*, 15: 162–183.

McNair, B. (2018) *Fake News*, London: Routledge.

McPherson, P. (2017) '"We must protect our country': Extremist Buddhists target Mandalay's Muslims', *The Guardian.* 8 May. Online. Available HTTP: <www.theguardian. com/cities/2017/may/08/buddhist-extremists-anti-muslim-mandalay-ma-ba-tha> (accessed 5 March 2019).

Moe, M. (2016) 'Inflammatory spokesman Zaw Htay promoted within president's office leadership', *The Irrawaddy.* 7 April. Online. Available HTTP: <www.irrawaddy.com/news/burma/inflammatory-spokesman-zaw-htay-promoted-within-presidents-office-leadership.html> (accessed 5 March 2019).

Monbiot, G. (2017) 'Take away Aung San Suu Kyi's Nobel Peace Prize: She no longer deserves it', *The Guardian.* 5 September. Online. Available HTTP: <www.theguardian. com/commentisfree/2017/sep/05/rohingya-aung-san-suu-kyi-nobel-peace-prize-rohingya-myanmar> (accessed 5 March 2019).

Mozur, P. (2018) 'A genocide incited on Facebook, with posts from Myanmar's military', *The New York Times*. 15 October. Online. Available HTTP: <www.nytimes.com/2018/10/15/technology/myanmar-facebook-genocide.html> (accessed 17 March 2019).

Mratt, K.T. (2017) 'Tatmadaw, Sangha and government must work together, Sitagu Sayadaw says in sermon to officers', *Frontier Myanmar*. 1 November. Online. Available HTTP: <https://frontiermyanmar.net/en/tatmadaw-sangha-and-government-must-work-together-sitagu-sayadaw-says-in-sermon-to-officers> (accessed 20 March 2019).

The Myanmar Times. (2016) 'Daw Aung San Suu Kyi to join government as NLD reveals cabinet', *The Myanmar Times*. 22 March. Online. Available HTTP: <www.mmtimes.com/national-news/19591-daw-aung-san-suu-kyi-to-join-government-as-nld-reveals-cabinet.html> (accessed 3 March 2019).

Nitta, Y. (2018) 'Myanmar to get five more TV channels', *Nikkei Asian Review*. 21 February. Online. Available HTTP: <https://asia.nikkei.com/Politics/Myanmar-to-get-five-more-TV-channels> (accessed 20 March 2019).

Norris, P. (2000) *A Virtuous Circle: Political Communications in Post-Industrial Societies*, Cambridge: Cambridge University Press.

Nyan, H.L. (2017) 'U Zaw Htay: "If they are going to harm you, you can shoot them"', *Frontier Myanmar*. 5 September. Online. Available HTTP: <https://frontiermyanmar.net/en/u-zaw-htay-if-they-are-going-to-harm-you-you-can-shoot-them> (accessed 5 March 2019).

Porto, M. and Hallin, D. (2009) 'Media and democratization in Latin America', *The International Journal of Press/Politics*, 14: 291–295.

Postman, N. (1986) *Amusing Ourselves to Death: Public Discourse in the Age of Show Business*, London: Heinemann.

Reed, J. (2018) 'Hate speech, atrocities and fake news: The crisis of democracy in Myanmar', *The Financial Times*. 22 February. Online. Available HTTP:<www.ft.com/content/2003d54e-169a-11e8-9376-4a6390addb44> (accessed 5 March 2019).

Russell, J. (2018) 'Facebook purges more "bad actors" in Myanmar but it still won't commit to a local office', *Tech Crunch*. 18 December. Online. Available HTTP: <https://techcrunch.com/2018/12/18/facebook-purges-more-bad-actors-in-myanmar/> (accessed 20 March 2019).

Safi, M. (2018) '"Tied to trees and raped": UN report details Rohingya Horrors', *The Guardian*. 18 September. Online. Available HTTP: <www.theguardian.com/world/2018/sep/18/tied-to-trees-and-raped-un-report-details-rohingya-horrors> (accessed 17 March 2019).

Samuels, L. (2018) 'Is Nobel Peace Prize winner Aung San Suu Kyi guilty of Muslim genocide?', *Newsweek*. 31 May. Online. Available HTTP: <www.newsweek.com/2018/06/08/myanmars-aung-san-suu-kyi-human-rights-icon-now-being-condemned-mistreating-950054.html> (accessed 5 March 2019).

San, Y.A. (2017) 'Timeline: Journalists under attack', *The Irrawaddy*. 15 December. Online. Available HTTP: <www.irrawaddy.com/specials/timeline-journalists-attack.html> (accessed 5 March 2019).

Scheufele, D. and Tewksbury, D. (2007) 'Framing, agenda setting, and priming: The evolution of three news media effects models', *Journal of Communication*, 57: 9–20.

Shoon, N. and Yimou, L. (2017) 'Myanmar retains tough clause in communications law despite calls for repeal', *Reuters*. 18 August. Online. Available HTTP: <www.reuters.com/article/us-myanmar-media-idUSKCN1AY13J> (accessed 5 March 2019).

Thiri, T. and Gerin, R. (2018) 'Interview: The associated press "needs to apologize to Myanmar and correct the report"', *Radio Free Asia*. 7 February. Online. Available

HTTP: <www.rfa.org/english/news/myanmar/interview-the-associated-press-needs-to-apologize-to-myanmar-and-correct-the-report-02072018153358.html> (accessed 17 March 2019).

Toe, W.A. (2017) 'Journalist in critical condition after attack in Rakhine's Sittwe', *Myanmar Times*. 28 December. Online. Available HTTP: <www.mmtimes.com/news/journalist-critical-condition-after-attack-rakhines-sittwe.html> (accessed 5 March 2019).

UNECO. (2016) 'Assessment of media development in Myanmar', Myanmar: UN Education, Scientific and Culture Organisation and International Media Support. Online. Available HTTP: <www.mediasupport.org/wp-content/uploads/2016/06/Myanmar-MDI-report-June-2016.pdf> (accessed 3 March 2019).

Voltmer, K. (2008) 'Comparing media systems in new democracies: East meets south meets west', *Central European Journal of Communication*, 1: 23–40.

Voltmer, K. and Schmitt-Beck, R. (2006) 'New democracies without citizens? Mass media and democratic orientations—a four country comparison', in K. Voltmer (ed.) *Mass Media and Political Communication in New Democracies*, London: Routledge.

Warren, R. (2017) 'Aung San Suu Kyi once called for a free press. Now, the dead are used for fake news', *The Guardian*. 23 December. Online. Available HTTP: <www.theguardian.com/commentisfree/2017/dec/23/aung-san-suu-free-press-fake-news-rohingya> (accessed 5 March 2019).

Weng, L. and Zaw, H.N. (2013) 'Tycoon sues journal on defamation charges', *The Irrawaddy*. 26 November. Online. Available HTTP: <www.irrawaddy.org/burma/tycoon-sues-journal-defamation-charges.html> (accessed 5 March 2019).

Zhang, W., Johnson, T. and Seltzer, T. (2010) 'The revolution will be networked: The influence of social networking sites on political attitudes and behavior', *Social Science Computer Review*, 28: 75–92.

13

PRESS REPRESSION IN MYANMAR

Aung San Suu Kyi, the Reuters reporters and the Rohingya

Jeff Kingston

Two Reuters reporters, Wa Lone and Kyaw Soe Oo, were arrested in December 2017 and subsequently charged with breaking the colonial-era Official Secrets Act (OSA) for obtaining documents about the killing of ten Rohingya boys and men in Myanmar's western Rakhine state (Reuters 2019). Their conviction and sentencing to seven years in prison had a major impact on international perceptions about press freedom in Myanmar, a nation widely denounced around the world for the military's expulsion of some 730,000 Muslim Rohingya in 2017–2018. Their saga illuminates the nexus of ethno-religious nationalism, Islamophobia, continued military repression and the pathologies of destitution in a nation that seemed, not long ago, to be on an upward trajectory of democratization that would open the spigots of international development assistance and foreign investments. The jailing of the Reuters reporters, and the atrocities against Rohingya they reported, exemplify the democratic backsliding that has quelled the domestic and international euphoria and accolades that greeted Aung San Suu Kyi in 2015 when she led her party to a landslide election victory. It is important to understand this broader political context to assess the implications of this miscarriage of justice on press freedom and Myanmar's fragile democratic transition (Brooten, McElhone and Venkiteswaran, 2019). As the economy stagnates, tourism recedes and foreign investment sags, political and military leaders are coming to understand that it is not only democracy that withers in darkness.

Expectations that press freedom would improve with the election of the National League for Democracy (NLD) in 2015 have given way to disappointment, largely because democracy icon and Nobel Peace Prize laureate Daw Aung San Suu Kyi has been at war with the media, prosecuting and jailing far more journalists than the former military-linked regime (Athan 2018). When she was under house arrest and in opposition, The Lady, as she is known, embraced the free press and benefitted enormously from media scrutiny of the military regime that denied the results of the 1990 elections that gave her a comprehensive victory and subsequently inserted a provision in the 2008 Constitution that barred her from becoming president based on her marriage to a foreign national. In the post-2012 process of democratization, the media was lopsided in her favour, pulling out all the stops and abandoning objective reporting (Interview, Wai Moe, November 2018). The NLD's assumption of power in 2016 owed most to her unassailable moral integrity and the potential for delivering Myanmar and its long-suffering people from the abuses and negative consequences of a half-century of military misrule. The media's cheerleading during the election campaign was not essential to her victory, but certainly helped raise expectations about democratization. Apparently, she expected the media to continue offering unconditional praise, and has proven to be remarkably thin-skinned for someone who spoke truth to power for a quarter of a century, and in consequence lived under house arrest for much of that time.

Ethno-religious nationalism and the Rohingya problem

The Lady doesn't have a magic wand to dispel the intractable problems that plague her nation, and democratization has not provided a long enough ladder to climb out of the deep hole the military left as its poisonous legacy. This is a multi-faceted hole featuring endemic poverty, political repression, corruption and ethnic conflicts. It would be churlish to blame Aung San Suu Kyi for the mess she inherited, but it is fair to say that she has made limited progress on this agenda. Poverty has not abated significantly, government critics are still subject to arbitrary enforcement of the law, land grabs go unpunished, corruption flourishes and various ethnic conflicts have flared anew despite efforts towards reconciliation. She declared that ethnic reconciliation was her priority, the unfinished family business of Aung San the founding father of Burma (now Myanmar). But the scars of the military's brutal counterinsurgency campaigns and the unresolved grievances of ethnic minorities, have made progress difficult. For the military, demands for a federal system with greater autonomy are anathema.

Under Myanmar's hybrid governing arrangement of cohabitation between a civilian government and the security forces, the latter retain de facto power and authority, and are not subject to civilian oversight. This context is crucial for understanding what happened to the Rohingya and why Aung San Suu Kyi's government was powerless to intervene and has not pushed for military accountability or an international inquiry. It is also essential to appreciate the emergence of a glowering ethnic Bamar (Burmese) nationalism in Myanmar that favours majoritarian rule at the expense of ethnic minorities, nurturing a hothouse of Islamophobia that ensures little domestic sympathy for the Rohingya (Kesavan 2018). This nationalism has deep roots, extending back to the colonial era and the independence movement lead by ethnic Burmese, and grew exponentially under the military regime of General Ne Win (1962–1988), serving as the military's ideological fig leaf for ongoing repression of minorities (Nemoto 2016; Kingston 2019). In the process of the post-2012 democratic transition, there has been an abrupt explosion of social media coinciding with the rollout of the nation's mobile telecommunications network. Facebook is the most popular platform by far and is the main source of news and opinion for most Myanmarese, with the inherent drawbacks, especially the potential for fake news. Facebook has also been an important channel for the military and its supporters to ramp up nationalism, engage in hatemongering and to spread disinformation aimed at refuting criticism over the Rohingya issue (McLaughlin 2018).

The military has played a key role in instigating a rise in nationalism to bolster support for its 'patriotic' actions and institutional interests. It has engaged in concerted 'othering' to channel public anger towards vulnerable, sanctioned targets that diverts attention away from military excesses and festering socio-economic problems while hyping an imagined Muslim menace (Winn 2013). Much is made of the invented Islamic demographic time bomb, asserting without credible evidence that sometime in the not-too-distant future, Myanmar will no longer be the land of Buddhists owing to polygamous Muslim men; currently about 4 per cent of the nation's population is Muslim. It is this fabricated threat that gave momentum to 2015 legislation aimed at preventing the imagined nightmare scenario by imposing restrictions on who women can marry, banning polygamy and giving authorities power to curb family size (Marriage Law 2015; Mon 2019).

There is also a subnationalist wrinkle to the situation in Rakhine state, where the Buddhist ethnic Rakhine recall the glories of Arakan kingdoms and resent both Burmese control and the presence of Muslim Rohingya. Communal tensions are longstanding, and outbreaks of violence between ethnic Rakhine and Rohingya began during World War II. Rakhine were pleased by the exodus of Rohingya in 2017–2018, but renewed hostilities between the Arakan (Rakhine) Army and the military since then complicate any plans for repatriation of Rohingya refugees and suggest dim prospects for ethnic reconciliation amidst a swaggering Burmese nationalism of majoritarian impulses. While democracy is supposed to be based on majority rule, with the majority ostensibly ruling for the collective interest without fear or favour, nationalism accentuates majoritarian instincts and the use of political power supposedly for the majority's benefit, without regard for minorities. The military is whipping up nationalist sentiments in the mainstream media and on Facebook to justify its praetorian abuses and to fend off international criticism concerning the Rohingya. In addition to this concerted othering, the military has been vigilant about denying press access to the zones of ethnic clearing operations in northwestern Rakhine to sustain its version of events.

MaBaTha, the notorious hardline Buddhist organization, also embraces and stokes this ethno-religious nationalism, cloaking their Islamophobia and hatemongering in saffron robes that confer moral authority (Wirathu 2017). U Wirathu, the angry voice of MaBaTha, has been a key monk inciting religious tensions with his invective against Muslims and harping on the imagined threat they represent to Myanmar's Buddhist culture and heritage. He has been a cheerleader for the anti-Rohingya campaign, reinforcing the military's narrative (Hookway 2017).

In this febrile atmosphere of fear and hatemongering, by contradicting the military's narrative of events in Rakhine, the Reuters reporters were quickly depicted as traitors rather than as diligent professionals taking significant risks to get the story. Inside Myanmar it doesn't appear many people are losing much sleep over the plight of the Rohingya, and there is little enthusiasm for their repatriation. According to Wai Moe, the *New York Times* correspondent in Myanmar, Islamophobia is a shared blind spot among the former pro-democracy activists and liberal intelligentsia predisposing them to believe the worst about the Reuters reporters (Interview, November 2018). Back in 2007, shortly after the Saffron Revolution, a monk in Rakhine explained to me, 'They are like gypsies, nobody wants them around' (Interview, December 2007). A decade on, a pro-democracy intellectual actually attributed the mass exodus of hundreds of thousands of Rohingya to collective homesickness, blasting the international press for spreading ill-informed lies (Interview, December 2017). This rather bizarre explanation highlights the cognitive dissonance that prevailed, even as the military's operations were still under way. Despite lingering anti-Rohingya sentiments, however, public sympathy for the Reuters reporters has gained some momentum as the judicial travesty has created a degree of separation between their plight and that of the Rohingya.

Awakening: freedom of expression on trial

In a series of interviews and conversations in late 2017, I was struck by how many liberals I met in Yangon who had a blind spot about the Rohingya issue. Activists and intellectuals who had been ardent critics of the military, rallied in support of Aung San Suu Kyi and bought the military's line that what happened in Rakhine was purely retaliation for a terrorist attack on state security forces by ARSA (Arakan Rohingya Salvation Army). No matter that ARSA was a lightly armed, poorly organized ragtag band posing little real threat to the government, or that the military's operations were vastly disproportionate. The alleged atrocities were brushed off as anti-Myanmar propaganda, while the bad press and stripping of awards only enhanced the embattled Lady's stature.

Not everyone was fooled (ICG 2018). As one local lawyer told me regarding pro-democracy activists and intellectuals in 2017, 'They swallowed it hook, line and sinker. It's amazing they were so easily fooled by their enemy' (Interview, November 2017). Or perhaps they were just protective of The Lady and found solace in denial; after just gaining power following such a long struggle, they were despairing that their moment of glory and vindication had been so fleeting and suddenly indelibly tarnished. The resplendent renaissance of Myanmar vanished, and the ill-starred nation was back in the international doghouse, a hero-to-zero scenario that many found frustrating, especially in the context of a strident Burmese nationalism.

But perceptions evolved considerably by late 2018 as the liberal constituency of activists, intellectuals, journalists, lawyers, and politicians supporting the ruling National League for Democracy (NLD) became deeply disillusioned (Interview, Wai Moe, November 2018). The Wizard of Oz moment was the trial of the two Reuters reporters in 2018. They were arrested in December 2017 for possessing secret documents related to the military's campaign in Rakhine against the Rohingya. During the 2018 court proceedings, however, the reporters' lawyer proved that the documents were not secret. Then a police captain testified that he was ordered to plant the information on the reporters and frame them. The military's narrative depicting these reporters as traitors blackening the name of the nation collapsed. It became difficult to deny that the military was guilty of atrocities and a concerted cover-up, even managing to bamboozle many pro-democracy activists who had grown up sceptical of and hostile to the military.

Matthew Bugher, regional director of Article 19, a global freedom of expression lobbying organization, condemned the conviction of the Reuters reporters, asserting that the verdict was a 'farcical miscarriage of justice' that exposes the judiciary's lack of independence and undermines the rule of law (Interview, November 2018). In his view, the judiciary is complicit in the government's longstanding efforts to block reporting on the Rohingya crisis and the military's cover-up. Bugher added that the reporters, 'deserve praise, not persecution, but face longer sentences than the soldiers who committed the crimes they were reporting about.'

Jailing the reporters on specious grounds did not solve the problem, because Myanmar antagonized a tenacious and influential organization. Reuters ensured that the judicial sham and military atrocities remained prominent on the global radar screen and mobilized pressure to seeing justice done. In terms of shaping international discourse about the Rohingya and the business operating environment in Myanmar, Reuters enjoys the commanding heights with access to business and political leaders, and a vast global readership. As one of the most powerful media organizations in the world, Reuters is well positioned to promote awareness while generating momentum for international accountability. It cannot be intimidated or silenced, and ensured that Myanmar paid a steep price for locking up the reporters for more than 500 days. Given the flagging economy, sagging investments and a plunge in tourism after the Rohingya pogrom, alienating Reuters proved massively counterproductive, at least in terms of the national interest. As one local editor told me, 'They [the military] picked the wrong enemy' (Interview, November 2018). That is why, he says, top brass advised The Lady to pardon the reporters, a damage control strategy that she rejected, perhaps because she thought it would make her look fallible. But the mounting economic and diplomatic costs of her intransigence ratcheted up pressures for a solution.

Freedom of expression and press freedom are considered key barometers of the business operating environment and good governance. Trying to hush up reporting about gross human rights violations makes Myanmar a risky investment for any international company. In terms of overall country risk issues, the sentencing of the Reuters reporters sent a chilling message. Suddenly, the international scramble to jump on the Myanmar bandwagon gave way to an unseemly scrum at the exits, prompted by fears of reputational damage associated with charges of ethnocide and concerns about the operating environment in a nation jailing the messengers. Impunity and injustice fester in the absence of a free press and the rule of law, an off-putting combination for most investors, although this has not dimmed Chinese enthusiasm.

In April 2019, the final Supreme Court appeal of the two Reuters reporters was rejected, a decision with far-reaching consequences for Myanmar's reputation, press freedom and the rule of law (Ellis-Petersen 2019). This ruling conveyed a determination to bury the truth about the ethnic clearance operations that drove 730,000 Rohingya into refugee camps in Bangladesh from the end of August 2017. Since then, Aung San Suu Kyi's fall from grace continues due to her ongoing failure to speak out for the human rights of these refugees or to condemn the military for its actions. In contrast to her silence, in August 2018, the United Nations determined that the circumstances surrounding the mass exodus amounted to genocide warranting prosecution (UNHRC 2018).

Several activists, lawyers and journalists told me the real problem was that the reporters had been investigating military and police atrocities in Rakhine against the Rohingya, gathering testimony and photographic evidence. So essentially, state security was hoping to intimidate other journalists from doing their jobs by going after the Reuters reporters. Their lawyer, Than Zaw Aung, said that during the 2018 trial, a military court martialed seven soldiers for the execution of ten Rohingya based on the evidence produced by the Reuters reporters, inadvertently lending credibility to their case (Interview, November 2018). Oddly, the seven-year sentences handed down to the Reuters reporters were longer than the six-year jail terms the soldiers face for executing unarmed civilians.

How could the judges all the way up the judicial hierarchy endorse a guilty verdict for the reporters, given the damning testimony exonerating them? The lawyer complained that The Lady should have been held in contempt of court because she influenced the verdict by three times publicly stating that the reporters had violated the Official Secrets Act (OSA) and insisting the case was not about press freedom (Interview, Than Zaw Aung, November 2018). However, under the OSA, the prosecution must prove that the accused was trying to abet enemies of the nation by providing the secret information to them. This was problematic since the Reuters reporters were trying to disseminate the information to a global readership. Thus, to make such a case, police raided the homes of the reporters and seized old notebooks, computers and mobile phones, and apparently found that one of the reporters had the phone number of a leader of an ethnic insurgency, an 'enemy' that would make OSA prosecution viable. It turned out, however, that this 'enemy' had attended a conference by government invitation, and it was in connection to that event that the reporter had the phone number. It gets better. The alleged 'enemy' announced that in fact they had the wrong number and that he had never been in contact with either reporter. All of this information about a sham prosecution is in the case files, so their lawyer was taken aback when The Lady announced, while the appeal was pending, that her cabinet had reviewed the case files and found nothing untoward. The planted fake secrets, an exposed frame job and no enemy, yet inexplicably nothing untoward. This comment also put pressure on the judges involved to go along with the judicial charade, part of a troubling pattern that highlights major challenges in realizing the rule of law in Myanmar (Interview, Than Zaw Aung, November 2018).

Finally, on 7 May, the reporters were pardoned and released by order of President U Win Myint, along with 6,520 other prisoners during Myanmar's New Year celebrations. Missing was any government admission of wrongdoing or apology for this gross injustice and assault on the free press. Since the reporters exposed the role of state security forces in committing atrocities targeting the Rohingya, their release is potentially awkward given the military's propaganda campaign of denial and downplaying of violent excesses.

Freedom of Expression Myanmar (FEM) Director Yin Yadanar Thein, welcomed the pardon but also pointed out, 'we should not forget that this has been a test of Myanmar's new democracy that it failed.' She added,

> Today, the government has stepped in to rescue these brave journalists. But where were the judges that in a democracy are supposed to protect our constitutional rights? Even though Wa Lone and Kyaw Soe Oo were pardoned by the president, they are still criminals according to the state. This needs to be a wake-up call for the judiciary that they need to change, and fast.
>
> *(email, 8 May 2019)*

And there still are many other less high-profile journalists and bloggers in jail, while government intimidation silences many more (Brooten 2019).

Democratic backsliding and press freedom

I spoke with Ma Thida, former director of Pen Myanmar, who wrote about her life as a political prisoner in *Prisoner of Conscience: My Steps Through Insein* (Thida 2016). In her view, there was no legitimate reason to imprison the reporters (Interview, October 2018). She blames the military for destroying the country and its political system, saying that the revival of democracy and civil liberties will be a slow and difficult process. As a member of the NLD and a former close aide to Aung San Suu Kyi, she was arrested and given a 20-year sentence in 1993 for her political views, but released in 1999 on humanitarian grounds, spirits unbowed.

She feels great empathy for the fate of the reporters who languished in Insein Prison – where she spent several years of her youth – merely for doing their job, and thinks The Lady has lost her way, shrinking press freedom being a symptom of a broader problem of democratic backsliding. Thida has longed warned against a cult of veneration and thinks that we are seeing the consequences of Aung San Suu Kyi being a 'prisoner of applause.' Back in 2017, Thida was cautious about the Rohingyas' explusion, but when we spoke about a year later, she was forthcoming and highly critical of the ethnic clearance operations and Aung San Suu Kyi, for not speaking out (Interview, October 2018). Although disappointed, Thida believes that The Lady has been unfairly singled out for something the military did and she was powerless to prevent. Thida remains pessimistic about prospects for repatriation of the Rohingya refugees and freedom of expression under the current government. Regarding the Reuters reporters, she believes that The Lady has been misinformed and doesn't know the real story, relying too much on a small inner circle with military ties. 'That is why her thinking is exactly the same' as the military, she said, referring to the Rohingya crisis overall and the arrest of the Reuters reporters. She also condemned the reliance on colonial-era laws like the OSA to clamp down on press freedom (see Burrett, Chapter 12). Yin Yadanar agrees, and also argues that the OSA should only be applied to officials, not to sideline reporters (Interview, November 2018).

Both of these activists assert that freedom of expression is undermined by the concentration of media ownership among former military oligarchs and their cronies who remain sympathetic to the military, meaning there is little criticism of the junta's lingering influence. Private sector media licences are awarded as a way to control the media and compromise press freedom. Moreover, market competition forces the popular media to cater to the taste for sensationalism and the upsurge in ethno-religious nationalism. Overall, Thida contends that the private media has limited resources, so can't risk defamation charges or cuts in advertising revenues. The mindset of reporters employed by the state media, meanwhile, is also risk averse because they don't want to confront the wrath of powerful players, while editors engage in self-censorship to avoid losing revenues or endangering privileged access. In this context, the Rohingya story is too risky. In her view, 'there is not enough media courage' (Oct 2018, interview) and younger journalists don't know enough to do their jobs well. She laments that politicians too have been reluctant to speak out for press freedom or to defend the Reuters reporters.

Tha Lun Zaung Htet, who joined the state-sponsored Protection Committee for Myanmar Journalists in late 2018, is a firebrand who will certainly change perceptions of what has been a sleepy and compliant watchdog (Interview, November 2018). I spoke with him the night before he was due to meet The Lady and present her with a letter from the families of the two Reuters reporters. It must have been quite a meeting as he bluntly asserted, 'They were framed by the police and military, but she still stands on their side.' He criticized the security forces for pumping up nationalism and hyping the ARSA threat to generate support for expelling the Rohingya in order to undermine the NLD and tarnish her image. In his opinion, her hopes for reconciliation with the military are misplaced. Instead they are using her as a puppet and shield. 'What is she thinking?' he asked rhetorically. 'We believed in her for 20 years but what we fought for has been lost in just three years. We lost hope.'

Another twentyish freedom of expression activist, referencing the title of a book Aung San Suu Kyi wrote, lamented that, 'Power destroyed her. Whatever happened to freedom from fear?' (Interview, November 2018). He added that her dismissal of concerns about the shrinking space for press freedom indicates that she is isolated and out of touch. By transforming the Rohingyas into 'enemies of the state' and 'intentionally committing human rights violations,' he thinks the military has gained strong public support and cowed The Lady into silent acquiescence while making her look weak and complicit.

Htet drew attention to the military's long track record of human rights violations against other ethnic groups to suggest that what happened to the Rohingya is part of a longstanding pattern of violent conduct carried out with impunity because the media has been censored and engages in self-censorship as a survival strategy (also see Annan 2017). The averted-eyes approach to the military's misconduct against Reuters and Rohingya is in his eyes a 'survival strategy that betrays journalistic ethics for which everyone pays a price,' alluding to ongoing democratic backsliding. He also thinks reporters know more than what they write about the military's involvement in illicit drug trafficking and smuggling in Rakhine. Another journalist agrees that the brisk business in methamphetamine production and smuggling in Rakhine has been a cash cow for the military, and for that reason, it is a taboo topic. The Reuters fiasco is a reminder of what can happen to brave reporters who ignore the red lines.

Maung Saungkha, a young democracy activist, maintains that press freedom is receding dramatically under Aung San Suu Kyi, asserting that the previous military-linked government was far more media-friendly precisely because it knew that it lacked credibility, whereas The Lady has been very aggressive in going after critics (Interview, November 2017). He was the first person prosecuted under Article 66(D) of the 2013 Telecommunications Law for defamation due to his posting a poem on Facebook suggesting that he had a tattoo of the President's image on his penis and that on his wedding night, his wife was inconsolable. Apparently, prosecutors didn't have a sense of humour or understand poetic licence. And nobody bought the defence that if such a tattoo existed, it would be a vivid gesture of patriotic loyalty.

While on trial, the Penis Poet spent seven months in the notorious Insein prison before the judge set him free for time served. He was, however, convicted of defamation and sentenced to six months imprisonment, despite not actually naming President Thein Sein in his Facebook posting. Although not required to present evidence in court, he assured me that he has no tattoos and that he is unmarried. He subsequently established Athan (Voice) to monitor press freedom in Myanmar and found that the previous military-backed government only prosecuted 11 reporters while the NLD had gone after more than 160 as of November 2018 (Athan 2018). He was incredulous when in October 2018 The Lady gave an interview in Tokyo scoffing at international allegations of a press crackdown in Myanmar. Ironically, on the night she returned from Japan, three local reporters were jailed for 'defaming' the head of the Yangon regional government, her protégé, over a shady bus contract (Slodkowski 2017). They were subsequently released, but the tactics of intimidation usually associated with repressive authoritarian governments are now embraced by the NLD (Interview, November 2018).

Out of touch

The NLD and The Lady seem to have forgotten that freedom of expression was once a core value during their struggle for democracy. Why doesn't Aung San Suu Kyi criticize the military for its outrages? Her dwindling number of defenders suggest she is doing so to safeguard Myanmar's fragile democracy, raising the prospect of a military coup; she calculates that the fate of her nation of over 52 million is more important than that of the 1 million Rohingya. Others say she hopes to get the military's agreement to amend the Constitution to remove the proviso that bans her from becoming president. Critics scoff at the prospects of either scenario, and grumble that she even vets what issues NLD members can raise in Parliament, rarely delegates and relies on a small inner circle of advisers, mostly with military ties. Others assert that she shares the general antipathy toward Muslims, while some argue that she doesn't want to be exposed as powerless if she calls the military to account and it ignores her.

The common refrain about The Lady is that she is 'isolated and out of touch,' overly reliant on a small circle of 'yes men' with military backgrounds and reluctant to rock the boat of democratic transition. Former supporters believe she has become increasingly authoritarian, isolated and intolerant of criticism. Rather than promote press freedom, she has been dismissive of complaints and has done nothing to promote freedom of expression, instead siding with those persecuting journalists and issuing public comments that compromise judicial independence in cases like the Reuters reporters. Western diplomats said they raise the issue of press freedom at the outset of every meeting with her and persistently lobbied for the reporters' release, reminding her of the costs of international isolation.

There is a widespread sense that The Lady's pride was a major obstacle to gaining justice for the Reuters reporters because this effectively entailed her admitting being wrong, something for which she has not demonstrated considerable capacity. As one Western journalist observed regarding her handling of the Reuters case, 'She is a surprisingly bad politician. She stood for tolerance and freedom, but since 2017 when history called on her to take a stand, it is clear those principles were not there' (Interview, November 2018). He thinks that the drubbing of NLD politicians in October 2018 by-elections, especially in Yangon strongholds, is a barometer of discontent with her betrayal of the values and hopes she once represented, including freedom of expression. He adds that her drift towards authoritarianism and significant democratic backsliding by the NLD government are:

> eroding trust as she is not showing confidence and drawing non-negotiable lines. Instead she has propagated the military's falsehoods regarding the situation in Rakhine and hasn't gotten anything in exchange from the military for soft-pedalling of human rights violations. She has not exercised leadership and has left her moral authority to wither, avoiding risks and taking a stand.
>
> *(Interview, November 2018)*

Another journalist observed that, 'She has played a strong hand remarkably badly and been badly outmaneuvered by the military on the Rohingya and Reuters. She is clueless about social media and how it is consumed' (Interview, November 2018). Many interviewees believe that by not calling out the military, she has called into question the nature of the democratic transition by conceding too much without any reciprocal concessions from the generals. Her government has also closed access to Rohingya IDP camps in Rakhine from earlier clashes, a powerful tool to 'disappear these people' inconsistent with promoting transparency and accountability.

The central government leans on the press to kill certain stories that reflect badly on the NLD, such as the dubious bus contract implicating the head of the Yangon government – not the first allegation of corruption involving him. Corruption is endemic – 'pigs at a table,' as one critic described it – but rather than cracking down on this scourge, the NLD discourages reporting about the venality and some members are apparently not shy about thrusting their snouts into the trough (Interview, November 2018). This critic calls the NLD 'incredibly arrogant,' jailing journalists, intimidating the media and rather than advocating for freedom of expression 'draws lines establishing taboos and no-go zones.' Despite all the hoopla about releasing political prisoners when the NLD swept into power, the institutions of the police state remain intact and are part of the current apparatus of intimidation. According to a journalist, one of the positive developments of the Reuters case is that 'the domestic media has rallied in solidarity' and the trial and framing of the reporters received extensive coverage, a major blackeye for the military and its NLD enablers (Interview, November 2018). This coverage helped draw public attention to the perilous situation of press freedom, and also highlighted the professionalism of the jailed reporters who went to great lengths at considerable risk to uncover the military's misdeeds.

Nyo Nyo Thinn, a politician and lawyer, says that the Reuters case was a colossal travesty of justice and that 'The judge totally violated the law. The verdict was wrongheaded' (Interview, November 2018). There was no evidence, in her opinion, to convict the reporters, so it was a political decision that undermines the rule of law. She is also worried about The Lady's authoritarian inclinations, banning NLD members from raising issues in Parliament that she has not vetted first. In terms of freedom of expression, Aung San Suu Kyi is denying this even to her party members. Thinn laments, 'The real problem is that she doesn't trust many people and those she does are not trustworthy.' She also dismisses concerns that calling out the military might provoke a coup d'etat, saying there is no going back to military rule and everyone knows that, including the generals; currently, they can control politics without taking responsibility for bad outcomes, so have no incentive to mount a coup. Problematically, The Lady is not learning from her mistakes, because she doesn't admit making any, and she refuses to change her mind even when it is clear she has made the wrong decision. Regarding the Rohingya, The Lady and military share a siege mentality due to international condemnation reported by the media, but Thinn also thinks that, 'Most Burmese are happy they are gone and don't want them back. The public rallies to her side even though it knows the military committed abuses' (Interview November 2018). In her view, Aung San Suu Kyi's reputation 'has been destroyed by the military, deliberately, by committing human rights abuses.' Although some human rights activists and pro-democracy groups knew the military was guilty of extensive abuses, they mistakenly hoped to salvage The Lady's reputation through denial, but this strategy clearly backfired. Yet, Thinn notes, outside of Yangon, the emotional attachment to Aung San Suu Kyi remains powerful. Efforts to promote press freedom and freedom of information in rural areas confront the more pressing needs to put food on the table and maintain a roof overhead. Trying to explain the indirect benefits is an uphill battle. Ironically, Thinn says, 'Many in the NLD now reject the need for a freedom of expression law as key to democracy because now they are in power and thus see no need.' She adds, 'the NLD now sees the media as its enemy.'

The future of freedom of expression

The costs of undermining the rule of law, muzzling the media and whitewashing the Rohingya problem are clear as the economy stagnates and Myanmar is again an international pariah. Sonny Shwe, editor of *Frontier*, regarding the Rohingya crisis, says, 'We lost a lot especially the face of the nation. It's a brand problem that has driven FDI down across the board' (Interview, November 2018). In his view, Aung San Suu Kyi embraces 'blind nationalism' and in doing so further isolates the nation, adding that Thein Sein, her much-maligned military-backed predecessor, deserves more credit for boosting press freedom 'while she has pushed things backward.'

Freedom of expression activists told me that advocating for press freedom prompts pushback from the government and military, and indifference in rural areas where most Myanmarese live. The authorities downplay allegations about curbing press freedom, arguing that they are promoting responsible journalism and trying to fight fake news. The problem with this narrative is that top military leaders have had their Facebook accounts blocked for disseminating fake news and hate speech, especially regarding the Rohingya. They have not faced any charges for such actions, while militant monks engaged in similar abuses of social media, spouting Islamophobia, have also not been held accountable. At the same time, critics and civil society activists advocating for transparency, exposing corruption or mocking the government are at far greater risk of prosecution. While it is sometimes argued that Facebook's decision to close the accounts of top brass came too late, a year after the Rohingya exodus, others have asserted that by closing down entire accounts rather than removing offending posts, the senior generals' right to freedom of expression has been compromised. Yet given that the military owns television stations and newspapers, it is able to disseminate its views, meaning the generals have the ability to express their opinions, a key factor suggesting that their rights have not been violated (Spencer and Thein 2018).

Organizations such as Pen, Article 19 and Freedom of Expression Myanmar hold freedom of expression (FOE) workshops for parliamentarians at the national and state level, but these tend to attract a small number of participants, usually fewer than 15, so momentum for building understanding and support is limited. Article 19's Bugher calls Myanmar a tough advocacy environment for FOE, 'because all decision-making authority is centralized under The Lady and it's difficult to get access' (Interview, October 2018). Thida expressed disappointment with the NLD's lack of support for FOE, but maintains that such engagement is helpful in trying to incrementally expand the political space for FOE. In her view, it is essential to raise awareness and avoid counterproductive confrontation about government shortcomings. She pins hope on grassroots activism, and points out that Pen sponsors numerous literary festivals around the nation that attract good crowds and provide an opportunity to spread awareness about FOE and why it matters. That is the crux of the problem. Officials find it inconvenient, while most people can't grasp what it has to do with improving their circumstances. Transparency and freedom of the press are a hard sell because there is only an indirect connection to improving the welfare of ordinary people living in desperate conditions. Here the key is to connect economic conditions with foreign investments and markets and how these can be influenced by limiting FOE and arresting reporters on groundless charges.

International advocates stress it is important not to lecture officials about what they should be doing, but rather to share international best practices and let them draw their own conclusions. FEM Director Yin Yadanar maintains that the NLD doesn't like international non-governmental organizations meddling in Myanmar's domestic matters, so for civil society groups, having such connections reduces their effectiveness (Interview, November 2018). In her view, freedom of expression is something that depends on strong local leadership and should focus on new media, digital rights, gender and LGBT rights, and right to information. Her organization vigorously supported the Reuters reporters and is very critical of Aung San Suu Kyi, saying, 'she doesn't understand that FOE is the foundation of democracy' and has become too old and isolated, with a dysfunctional cabinet. Before 2012, the press was heavily censored by the military, feeding the public propaganda about what they should think. Initially in the post-2012 period, there was harsh criticism of the military, but now there is more self-censorship and the media has extolled the military's role in keeping the nation safe in the context of rising religious and racial tensions. In this sense, she argues that the Rohingya pogrom was a brutally effective strategy for the military to burnish its image and regain the public trust. It controlled the flow of information and thus shaped the narrative by closing off Rakhine to journalists and scrutiny. Thus, the Reuters reporters were guilty of undermining this positive narrative by evading the ban and independently gathering damaging information, including photographs, that implicated the military in executions of Rohingya. This is precisely why freedom of expression is anathema to those who are in control. The military vilified them as traitors betraying the nation by spreading disinformation, but over time, the public came to understand that the military was still up to its old tricks – and the trial was a key factor in this awakening.

Conclusion

Despite the belated pardon and release from prison, the wrongful conviction of the Pulitzer prize-winning Reuters reporters highlights the lack of press freedom and judicial autonomy in Myanmar, critically important foundations of democracy. Advocates call for patience and warn that the process of promoting press freedom and the rule of law will be slow because the still-dominant military is opposed and has managed to co-opt Aung San Suu Kyi and undermine her moral authority. It is also a tough space for challenging the cocoon of impunity enjoyed by the military for its actions against the Rohingya. By stoking the passions of ethno-religious nationalism through a sustained campaign of disinformation, tolerance for the nation's ethnic minorities has ebbed considerably, dimming prospects for repatriation of the displaced and justice for the wronged, while heightening risk of communal tensions. Owing to the horrible ordeal endured by the Reuters reporters, shared by many other journalists and bloggers, there is far greater awareness about the ongoing assault on freedom of expression in a nation haunted by the legacies of military repression.

Sources

Annan, K. (2017) 'Towards a peaceful, fair and prosperous future for the people of Rakhine', *Advisory Commission on Rakhine State*. Available HTTP: <www.rakhine commission.org/the-final-report/> (accessed 13 March 2019).

Athan. (2018) *Mid-Term Report on Freedom of Expression*, Yangon: Athan (Freedom of Expression Activist Organization).

Brooten, L., McElhone, J.M. and Venkiteswaran, G., eds. (2019) *Myanmar Media in Transition: Legacies, Challenges and Change*, Singapore: Yusof Ishak Institute, ISEAS.

Brooten, L. (2019) 'The dangers of Reuters' celebratory media moment in Myanmar', *East Asia Forum*, June 12. Available HTTP: <https://www.eastasiaforum.org/2019/06/12/the-dangers-of-reuters-celebratory-media-moment-in-myanmar/>

Ellis-Petersen, H. (2019) 'Myanmar Court Rejects Appeal by Jailed Reuters journalists', April 23. Available HTTP: <https://www.theguardian.com/world/2019/apr/23/myanmar-court-rejects-appeal-by-jailed-reuters-journalists>

Hookway, J. (2017) 'Buddhist leader spreads hatred of Muslims in Myanmar: With army's blessing, the Ven: Wirathu stokes public support for purge of ethnic Rohingya', *Wall Street Journal*. Available HTTP: <www.wsj.com/articles/buddhist-leader-spreads-hatred-of-muslims-in-myanmar-1507806002> (accessed 13 March 2019).

ICG. (2018). 'The long road ahead for Myanmar's Rohingya refugee crisis', *International Crisis Group*. Available HTTP: <www.crisisgroup.org/asia/south-east-asia/myanmar/296-long-haul-ahead-myanmars-rohingya-refugee-crisis> (accessed 12 March 2019).

Kesavan, M. (2018) 'Murderous majorities', *New York Review of Books*. Available HTTP: <www.nybooks.com/articles/2018/01/18/rohingya-murderous-majorities/> (accessed 13 March 2019).

Kingston, J. (2019) *The Politics of Religion, Nationalism and Identity in Asia*, Boulder, CO: Rowman & Littlefield.

Marriage Law (2015) 'The Myanmar Buddhist Women's Special Marriage Bill' (translated). Available HTTP: <http://www.burmalibrary.org/docs21/2015-Myanmar_Buddhist_Women_Special_Marriage_Bill.pdf>

McLaughlin, T. (2018) 'How Facebook's Rise Fueled Chaos and Confusion in Myanmar', *Wired*. Available HTTP: <www.wired.com/story/how-facebooks-rise-fueled-chaos-and-confusion-in-myanmar/> (accessed 13 March 2019).

Mon, Y. (2019) 'Fees and frustration: Myanmar's mixed marriage law in practice', *FrontierMyanmar*, May 30. Available HTTP: <https://frontiermyanmar.net/en/fees-and-frustration-myanmars-mixed-marriage-law-in-practice>

Nemoto, K. (2016) 'Burma's (Myanmar's) exclusive nationalism', in J. Kingston (ed.) *Asian Nationalisms Reconsidered*, Abingdon, UK: Routledge.

Reuters. (2019) 'Imprisoned in Myanmar'. Available HTTP: <www.reuters.com/subjects/myanmar-reporters> (accessed 13 March 2019).

Spencer, O. and Thein, Y.Y. (2018) 'Has Facebook censored Myanmar's commander-in-chief?', *Frontier Myanmar*. Available HTTP: <https://frontiermyanmar.net/en/has-facebook-censored-myanmars-commander-in-chief> (accessed 12 March 2019).

Slodkowski, A. (2017) 'Suu Kyi's man in Yangon under fire over transit deal with China', August 6. Available HTTP: <https://www.reuters.com/article/us-myanmar-suukyi-yangon-insight/suu-kyis-man-in-yangon-under-fire-over-transit-deal-with-china-idUSKBN1AM01D>

Thida, M. (2016) *Prisoner of Conscience: My Steps Through Insein*, Chiangmai, Thailand: Silkworm Books.

UNHRC. (2018) 'Report of the independent international fact-finding mission on Myanmar', *United Nations Human Rights Council*. Available HTTP: <www.ohchr.org/EN/HRBodies/HRC/MyanmarFFM/Pages/ReportoftheMyanmarFFM.aspx> (accessed 13 March 2019).

Winn, P. (2013) 'Do "rapidly breeding" Rohingya Muslims really threaten Myanmar's Buddhist identity?', *Agence France-Presse*. Available HTTP: <www.pri.org/stories/2013-10-14/do-rapidly-breeding-rohingya-muslims-really-threaten-myanmars-buddhist-identity> (accessed 13 March 2019).

Wirathu, U. (2017) 'Daw Aung San Suu Kyi a threat to national religion and identity', *Irrawaddy*. Available HTTP: <www.irrawaddy.com/in-person/u-wirathu-daw-aung-san-suu-kyi-threat-national-religion-identity.html> (accessed 13 March 2019).

14

PRESS FREEDOM IN THE PHILIPPINES

Sheila S. Coronel

Introduction/overview

Press freedom in the Philippines is strong and enduring. The role of the press in the struggle against colonial rule and the tyranny of authoritarian regimes partly accounts for this strength. It is also bolstered by robust constitutional protections and a community of journalists who guard their power and prerogatives. But at the same time, the independence – and freedom – of the press has been continually undermined by political and business elites, the demands of the market and the news media's own professional and ethical lapses. Thirty years since the restoration of democracy, press freedom in the Philippines remains a work in progress.

The fall of President Ferdinand Marcos in a 'people power' uprising in 1986 gave rise to a freewheeling press that fed the public appetite for news, entertainment, sleaze and scandal. Breaking free after 14 years of authoritarian rule, news organizations took advantage of their freedoms to cater to a public hungry for uncensored news. Watchdog reporting thrived, and so did political commentary. For most of the post-Marcos era, the press was noisy, rowdy, often critical of authority and – despite its shortcomings – widely seen as a check on the excesses of power.

But that is only part of the picture. At the local level, the collapse of centralized rule and the devolution of power to provincial and municipal governments empowered local bosses and political clans. Elections held after Marcos's fall allowed powerful families to monopolize public office in their strongholds and operate with impunity. In those places, journalists were easy targets (Aguilar, Mendoza, and Candelaria 2014). The most egregious example is Maguindanao province on the southern island of Mindanao. In 2009, nearly 200 armed men attacked a convoy of vehicles on a stretch of lonely highway there, killing 58 people, 32 of them journalists. Members of the Ampatuan clan and their private militia led the assault – the family at that time held the governorship, several mayoralties and various other levers of political power in the province.

This is the Philippine paradox: the country's Constitution, crafted in the afterglow of people power, provided broad guarantees of press freedom. The press as an institution is powerful and influential. Newspaper columnists and radio talk show hosts have loyal followings, and are famous for bloviating and opinionating on all things political. Television news anchors have credibility and authority, which is why some of them have been elected to public office. Moreover, the press is a watchful guardian of its freedom and knows how to fight back. Yet it is far from safe from the predations of power.

Nowhere is this more apparent than in the aftermath of the election of Rodrigo Duterte in 2016. Duterte exposed the vulnerability of the press to political pressure, regulatory harassment and online threats. Other presidents who faced criticism had tried to silence the press by putting the squeeze on media owners and advertisers, but Duterte went farther than his predecessors in deploying the courts and state regulators against critical news outlets (Stephens 2019). The president and his allies have also created an alternative information – or disinformation – space, unleashing fake news sites, trolls, state-sponsored bloggers, newspaper columnists and radio commentators to attack and drown out the work of critical journalists (Ghitis 2018).

Whether this toxic information space is the new normal remains to be seen (Ghitis 2018). Dire predictions have been made before, but the Philippine press has been remarkably resilient. Duterte, however, comes at a time when the press is the weakest it has been since the end of authoritarian rule. Like most everywhere else, newspapers – the traditional home of accountability journalism – are shrinking in size and influence, their business models upended by the internet and mobile phones. Online news media are feistier, but being smaller and not as well-resourced, they are also more vulnerable to intimidation and regulatory threats.

In the past decade, the rise of Facebook and other social media platforms, and the ubiquity of mobile phones, have eroded the power and influence of traditional media and their hold on their audience. The use of these platforms for propaganda and disinformation, especially since the 2016 election campaign, left the press scrambling to assert control over the news agenda. This erosion of media power is taking place during a presidency that is flouting democratic norms and the rules of democratic discourse. Duterte is ending the third year of his six-year presidential term with substantial popular support, and has thus far succeeded in stoking popular discontent with political elites. He has also thumbed his nose at the press for defending an elitist democracy that has failed the country.

Like other populist leaders, Duterte's strategy is as much about controlling what comes out in the news as it is about flooding the information space with disinformation and propaganda. In the past, Filipino journalists have defined press freedom as the absence of undue restrictions on the right to report and to publish. As the second decade of the twenty-first century drew to a close, the

Philippine press found itself having to fend off attacks not just on its fraying freedoms, but also its bottom line. The current media environment suggests the need to rethink what constitutes press freedom and how best to defend it.

The road to freedom (and unfreedom)

In 1972, President Ferdinand Marcos, then on his second presidential term and barred from seeking a third one, declared martial law, abolished Congress, shuttered the media and sent scores of journalists to prison. The Philippine press, then considered to be among the freest in Asia, was put under strict control. Draconian measures, including jail terms for offences like sedition and 'rumour-mongering,' were enforced. In the beginning, a military censor sat next to editors in the newsroom (Pinlac 2007), and though that practice ended, control was exercised through ownership as the major newspapers and broadcast networks had been handed over to the president's kin and cronies. In addition, the information ministry churned out propaganda and a mass media council sent out guidelines on what stories were not conducive to 'an atmosphere of tranquility' (Pineda-Ofreneo 1984: 2).

In the early 1980s, a handful of journalists braved the restrictions and set up independent papers that published stories and photographs banned in the Marcos-controlled media. Their audience grew as the ageing dictator lost his grip on power. By the mid-1980s, what Marcos once referred to as the 'mosquito press' was challenging the dominance of the big, pliant newspapers and helping mobilize citizens for protests. In 1986, a three-day popular uprising ousted Marcos and propelled to power Corazon C. Aquino, the widow of an exiled senator who was Marcos's arch-rival.

The press's role as a midwife of democracy gave it prestige and power. In one of her first acts as president, Aquino dissolved the information ministry. The framers of the new Constitution, men and women who had been active in the anti-Marcos movement, enshrined press freedom in the Bill of Rights, borrowing language from the First Amendment to the US Constitution. The new government loosened controls on media ownership and transferred broadcast stations and publishing houses once owned by Marcos cronies to their previous owners, or kept them under state management.

With democracy, the anti-Marcos press flourished, displacing the stodgy newspapers of the old regime. Radio and television exploded, feeding the public hunger for news and entertainment. The media market boomed and became extremely competitive, with media owners in a mad race to peddle newspapers and TV and radio programmes. Crime and scandal sold, as did exposés on the abuses of power. Commentary, particularly in newspapers and on radio, was lively and often strident. The press jealously defended its prerogatives, and pushed back on legal and regulatory attempts to suppress critical reporting.

Until recently, drastic measures were resorted to only in emergencies. In 1987, Aquino temporarily shut down two radio stations broadcasting messages in support of an attempted coup. President Gloria Macapagal-Arroyo, amid worries of a military-backed attempt to unseat her in 2006, issued a short-lived proclamation warning against 'subversive' news and commentary, and ordered soldiers to raid the *Daily Tribune* newspaper. The Supreme Court later ruled that raid illegal (Center for Media Freedom and Responsibility 2007).

Libel remains a criminal offence, however, and politicians and businesspeople sued journalists in the hope of silencing or punishing them. Many of these lawsuits didn't prosper, and when they did, journalists raised a howl. The courts have also mostly ruled in favour of the press. Corazon Aquino sued a columnist in 1987 for reporting that she 'hid under her bed' during an attempted coup d'etat. She lost (UPI 1995). Joseph Estrada, the former movie star who was president from 1998 until his ouster in a popular revolt in 2001, sued *The Manila Times* for saying he was the 'unwitting godfather' of a questionable government contract. The president withdrew the suit but only after he had engineered the sale of the paper to a business ally (Teodoro 2016).

Estrada's successor, Arroyo, and her husband were the subjects of corruption and other exposés during her ten-year presidency that ended in 2010. Jose Miguel Arroyo filed over 50 libel cases against journalists who accused him of taking bribes and peddling influence. These were largely seen to be harassment lawsuits and so several media groups sued him in turn, demanding damages for the anxiety, loss of income and other problems the suits caused journalists (GMA News 2006). In 2007, the First Gentleman, as he was called, withdrew all the lawsuits 'as a gesture of peace' (Philippine Center for Investigative Journalism 2007).

Still, the increasingly embattled Arroyo government continued to use criminal libel to rein in the press. In 2008, Ninez Cacho-Olivares, the publisher of the strident, anti-Arroyo *Daily Tribune*, was sentenced to a jail term for a report that accused a law firm close to the president of corruption. She appealed and has not served her sentence. The same year, the publisher of the *Malaya* paper was detained briefly for libel (Center for Media Freedom and Responsibility 2008).

In 2012, Congress passed a cybercrime prevention law that extended criminal libel to the internet and allowed the executive to block or take down content without a court order (Romero 2012). Journalists, bloggers and internet activists opposed the measure in protests online, on the streets and in petitions to the Supreme Court. The hacker group Anonymous joined the fray by launching denial-of-service attacks on government websites (Malig 2012). In 2014, the high court struck down the provision on takedowns but affirmed the 'cyberlibel' provision that would punish offenders with up to 12 years in prison, double the length of the terms for those found guilty of offline libel (Freedom of the Net 2014; Caliwan 2018).

The law has given rise to a growing number of frivolous cyberlibel suits, mostly by private individuals against people they know (San Juan 2018). But there were a few exceptions. In 2017, a court sentenced a former city administrator to up to four years in prison for his blog and social media posts accusing a senator of being involved in irregularities in public works projects (Burgos 2017). The same year, the agriculture secretary sued a reporter for a Facebook post that said the official had accumulated millions while in office (Lagrimas 2017). And in 2019, Maria Ressa, the CEO of the news site Rappler, spent a night in jail before posting bail for a cyberlibel charge filed by a controversial businessman (Stevenson 2019).

Pressure from the top

Since the Philippines won independence from the United States in 1945, the biggest and wealthiest media houses have mostly been in the hands of business families for whom a newspaper or broadcast station is a source of prestige and influence (Rosario-Braid and Tuazon 1999, 300). Some newspapers and broadcast stations don't turn a profit, but continue to be subsidized by their owners. A media asset is, in the words of a former newspaper publisher, 'a gun in the holster,' a weapon to be wielded against opponents should the need arise (Coronel 1999). But ownership has also been the chink in the armour of the Philippine press, and some presidents have exploited that vulnerability, in both subtle and overt ways.

The country's media moguls have always had an uneasy relationship with political power. They are part of elite families that wield political and economic clout. Some press proprietors have in fact openly aligned themselves with elite factions. But this is a perilous path. In an unstable democracy where elite factions rise and fall with regularity, it's risky for media houses to hitch their wagons to the fortunes of even the most popular politicians. Media owners who run profitable media businesses know they may lose prestige, credibility and market share if they are seen to be craven in the face of unaccountable power (Coronel 2001).

News proprietors, therefore, must be nimble in their calculations. They can resist political – especially presidential – interference, they can submit or they can adapt by playing a cat-and-mouse game with the authorities, calibrating critical and timid reporting depending on their threat assessment. These guerrilla tactics were perfected during authoritarian rule. In the last years of the Marcos era, journalists folded when Marcos was feeling besieged and under threat, but probed the limits of what they could publish or air when there were small openings (Forbes 2015).

As protests rocked the country in the early 1980s, the Marcos-controlled press lost its readership. Citizens flocked to the opposition press and launched boycotts of media houses associated with the dictator. With regime change, the startup press thrived and the old-regime newspapers that survived were those that were seen to be independent or neutral during the upheaval.

There are other, more recent, cautionary tales. Estrada, the popular action movie star elected in 1998, was upset by exposés about his multiple mistresses and the gambling and partying friends who made up his 'midnight cabinet.' He put pressure on media owners by threatening lawsuits and tax audits. The president also told his friends to withdraw advertising from the *Philippine Daily*

Inquirer and kept the country's largest broadcaster in line because his daughter was married to a member of the family that owned the network.

A series of exposés about the president's corruption was largely ignored by the cowed media, prompting readers to find alternative outlets in the nascent internet and *Pinoy Times*, a tabloid whose circulation peaked to several hundred thousand within a few months. Media owners took notice. As more scandals rocked Estrada and popular outrage burst out into the streets, editors defied their owners' interventions and soon, the once-cautious dailies and broadcasters changed their tune (Teodoro 2016: 80–81). In 2001, Estrada was ousted after an uprising on the streets of Manila.

Local power and the killing of journalists

The Philippines is among the deadliest countries in the world for journalists. The National Union of Journalists of the Philippines tallied 185 journalists killed in the 32 years since the fall of Marcos (International Federation of Journalists 2018). There were only a few journalist killings during the authoritarian regime, as the press was firmly under state control (Teodoro 2016: 98).

The Committee to Protect Journalists, which counts only those killed because of their work, lists 142 Filipino journalists and media workers slain since it started counting in 1992. These journalists were mainly covering corruption, crime and human rights. They were not reporting on conflict, war, disaster or civil strife. Instead, they were deliberately targeted for murder and the suspected masterminds were mostly government officials and criminal groups (Committee to Protect Journalists n.d.). Many of the assailants were hired assassins and off-duty or former policemen or soldiers.

There are various explanations for this high casualty count, including the proliferation of firearms and the high level of political violence in the country, from which journalists are not exempt. The vast majority of the victims were working for newspapers and radio stations in the provinces and so did not have the prestige and protection of big media houses in the capital. Manila is a sprawling city of nearly 12 million. Local reporters operate in much smaller spaces with thin-skinned officials unaccustomed to criticism.

The impunity with which journalist killers have been able to get away with murder helps account for the continuing death toll. The Philippine justice system is hobbled by many problems, including inefficiency, corruption and heavy caseloads. Conviction rates are low, and it can take 15 years or more to resolve a lawsuit (Lopez 2018). So far, the courts have successfully tried the killers of only 17 journalists, and in only one of these cases has the mastermind been charged (International Federation of Journalists 2018).

But there are other structural factors that help explain both the violence and the impunity. To begin with, the killings are perpetrated by local power holders for reasons related to corruption and political competition at the local level. Filemon Aguilar et al. (2014) studied 68 journalist murders between 1998 and 2012, and concluded that the murdered journalists did not target the central state. Instead 'these local killings are associated with moves to protect, consolidate, or expand the political and economic interests of local power-holders' (Aguilar et. al. 2014: 659)

The study traced the rise of journalist killings to the devolution of power to local governments after Marcos fell. The first free local elections in the post-authoritarian era were held in 1988. In 1991, Congress passed the Local Government Code, which gave local governments more power and more money. Local political office became a lucrative source of corruption, as local government units now had control of contracts for basic services, as well as regulatory and licensing powers. Their share of taxes also rose dramatically. Moreover, mayors were given the power to nominate police commanders, and have sway over the deployment of police units.

For all these reasons, local office is hotly contested, and local journalists often found themselves caught in the rivalries among competing political families. The Maguindanao massacre is the bloodiest example. The 32 journalists who were killed in 2009 were targeted because they had joined the convoy of vehicles led by the wife and two sisters of gubernatorial candidate Esmael Mangandudatu, who were filing a certificate of candidacy on his behalf. Mangandudatu had received death threats for challenging the incumbent governor, Andal Ampatuan Sr. The Ampatuans held a number of the mayoralties in the province and commanded a private militia that had been linked to the killing of at least 56 other people over land and political rivalries (Human Rights Watch 2010). But guns alone do not explain their dominance. Local political clans derive their power in part from their ability to deliver votes to those vying for national office. The Ampatuans were supporters of then President Arroyo, who aided their rise (Human Rights Watch 2010).

A decade after the Maguindanao massacre, the trial of 188 men accused of the crime is still ongoing, and the end is not in sight. In the meantime, three witnesses to the massacre have been killed, including one whose body was found dismembered by a chainsaw in 2012 (Merueñas 2012). In local elections held in 2013, 74 members of the Ampatuan clan ran for office in Maguindanao, even though the clan's patriarch and several family members were then in jail, awaiting trial for the massacre (Santos 2012).

That massacre aside, local journalists who expose malfeasance by local power holders are often the targets of assassination. The classic example is the 2002 killing of Edgar Damalerio, editor of a weekly newspaper and radio commentator in the southern Philippine city of Pagadian. Damalerio had exposed corruption in the local government and police. On 13 May 2002, he was shot by a motorcycle-riding gunman. Two witnesses identified the assassin as a police officer. Despite this, the local police refused to arrest the suspect. Instead, the witnesses were threatened, and Damalerio's wife, who pursued the case, went into hiding. Eventually one witness was killed, as was a potential witness who had not yet surfaced. Progress was made only after sustained pressure from the media. The police officer 'surrendered' to his commander and was tried in another city where witnesses and family members felt safe. He was convicted of murder in 2010, eight years after the killing (Center for Media Freedom and Responsibility 2010).

One thing worth noting is that many of murdered journalists were radio commentators who ranted against politicians, crime lords and the police and local officials they accused of protecting gambling and drug bosses. Many of them were blocktimers – that is, they were not regular employees but bought air time from radio stations. Radio has wide reach and a mass audience, as stations broadcast in many local languages (Committee to Protect Journalists 2005). In contrast, newspapers are mostly in English, and TV is mostly in Tagalog, the language of the capital.

Many broadcasters build a following through loud and strident on-air commentary that often borders on insult (Rosales 2006). Some of them are suspected to be the mouthpieces of politicians or other vested interests. Paying off reporters is a common practice and many radio journalists are described as 'AC/ DC,' meaning 'attack, collect; defend, collect' (Committee to Protect Journalists 2005). All these make them vulnerable to violent reprisal in places where political families have a monopoly of power and rule with impunity (Rosales 2006).

The emblematic example of this is Jun Porras Pala, a radio host who became famous in Davao City in the 1980s, when he was the rabid spokesman of an anti-communist propaganda campaign that encouraged citizens to kill suspected communists on sight (Arguillas 2003). Pala later took on Rodrigo Duterte, who was Davao City mayor for more than 20 years. As mayor, Duterte presided over an anti-crime campaign that left nearly 1,500 dead, mostly petty criminals (Picardal n.d.). Pala lambasted what he called Duterte's 'reign of terror' and accused the mayor and his son of malfeasance.

In 2003, the broadcaster was killed near his home by masked gunmen riding pillion on motorcycle. His assailants were never found. In 2017, a Davao City police officer confessed that he had planned Pala's assassination at Duterte's behest (ABS-CBN News 2017).

Davao journalist Carolyn Arguillas (2003) chronicled the tragedy of Jun Pala, who started out as an idealist but started hanging out with the AC/DC journalists who inhabited the netherworld of Davao media. With a powerful voice and the gift of gab, he was made for talk radio, and soon became the highest paid broadcaster in the city. In addition, he extorted money from politicians and businesspeople. 'Pala and his highly questionable ways were tolerated by the industry because he made money for the stations,' wrote Arguillas. 'And he allowed himself to be used by anyone – station owners, media handlers, politicians, military and police, businessmen – anyone who could either afford his price or get others to pay him.'

Pala's killing divided Davao's media community, said Arguillas. Many journalists thought that framing his murder as an assault on press freedom was a stretch. At the same time, his execution-style killing was abhorrent, no matter what kind of journalist he was. Asked about the slain broadcaster, Duterte said in

May 2016, shortly before he was sworn into office, 'I do not want to diminish his memory, but he is a rotten son of a bitch. He deserved it' (Agence France-Presse 2016). The authorities have so far not investigated allegations of the president's complicity in his murder.

Ethics and professionalism

No discussion of press freedom can ignore the ethics and professionalism of journalists. Corruption and unprofessional behaviour make journalists vulnerable to both verbal and physical attacks. They also open up the news media to charges that they are in pursuit of private gain rather than a public mission. They erode the legitimacy of the press as an institution, and provide fodder for officials like Duterte who argue that some journalists deserve to be killed.

Corruption in the press is so endemic that there is a whole vocabulary for press corruption. 'Envelopmental' journalism, referring to envelopes of cash discreetly given to reporters during press conferences, is a fairly routine practice. In 1998, the Philippine Center for Investigative Journalism surveyed 100 beat reporters: 71 had been offered money by their sources and 33 admitted they took the money, with 22 keeping the cash for themselves and the rest turning it over to their editors (Chua and Datinguinoo 1998).

Salaries in the media business are generally low, and that partly explains why many journalists accept bribes. The public relations industry is also complicit as it has made payoffs a standard practice. The refusal of many editors and publishers to enforce ethical standards abets the corruption. In some cases, financially strapped newspapers and broadcast stations encourage their staff to solicit advertisements, for which they earn commissions (International Federation of Journalists 2018).

The precarious financial position, particularly of small news organizations outside Manila, encourages practices that put journalists in harm's way. Soon after he graduated from college, Rey G. Rosales (2006) was hired as news director and talk show host of a radio station in central Philippines. The show did not do well because it used formal language and a subdued reportorial voice. But ratings rose when the programming shifted to using 'informal street language and some biting and stinging accusations about misdeeds by public officials.' As Rosales recounted:

> At various points during the commentary, the manager expected this radio show host to strike a large bass drum found at the side of the anchor table so as to attract attention and to add more zing to the points raised during the commentary. This tactic seemed to have worked because the show showed an increase in ratings. The combative language and aggressive style of the commentary, however, which often bordered on name calling, came with a price: death threats. The threats caused this author to abandon a budding career in radio completely.
>
> *(Rosales 2006: 149)*

In 2015, media scholar Edson C. Tandoc (2017) asked 350 Filipino journalists to identify their most important problems. The respondents cited the intertwined issues of low pay, violence against media workers, difficulties in information access and lack of professionalism. These problems have hobbled the press since the end of the Marcos era. A 2018 survey revealed an expanded landscape of threats unique to the Duterte presidency. Journalists identified cyberattacks, poor wages and working conditions, censorship and government attacks on the workplace (International Federation of Journalists 2018: 39).

Duterte: game changer

Duterte was a game changer who breached the boundaries of presidential power over the press. Not since Marcos has a president been so unrelenting in his attempts to muzzle critical voices. Duterte set the tone during the 2016 presidential campaign when he replied, in answer to a question about the killings of journalists: 'Just because you're a journalist, you are not exempted from assassination if you're a son of a bitch' (Gavilan 2019).

Less than a year into his presidency, he accused the owners of one of the largest newspapers, the *Philippine Daily Inquirer*, of owing billions in taxes on government property it had leased and developed. The paper had been critical of the president's anti-drug campaign and had kept a 'kill list' of the campaign's casualties (Rauhala 2018). The *Inquirer's* owners eventually negotiated its sale to a businessman close to the president, although the sale never went through. Duterte also threatened to sue the owners of the largest broadcast network, ABS-CBN, for allegedly refusing to run campaign ads he had already paid for because they were supporting a rival candidate. He said he would object to renewing the network's broadcast franchise when it expires in 2020 (ABS-CBN News 2018); ABS-CBN's reporting has since become more cautious.

The government then unleashed a full-blown attack on multiple fronts against Rappler, a feisty news site that had reported on the president's troll army and police abuses in Duterte's war on drugs. Government lawyers sued the company for tax evasion and for violating the ban on foreign media ownership. In 2018, the Securities and Exchange Commission revoked the company's registration and threatened it with closure. That case is under appeal. In 2019, the justice department charged Maria Ressa, Rappler's CEO, and several members of its staff and board with cyberlibel for a story the site ran in 2012, four months before the cybercrime law was passed. The multiple lawsuits were widely seen as part of Duterte's attempts to silence Rappler (Rey 2019), which has continued to report critically on the president despite the threats and legal harassment.

Like Donald Trump in the United States, Viktor Orban in Hungary and many others who came to power in recent years, Duterte sees the press as the enemy and has accused news organizations of being biased and elitist. He says they are purveyors of fake news and sensationalism, and in one speech shortly before he assumed office, he described journalists as corrupt fabulists who 'pretend to be the moral torch of the country' (*Philippine Daily Inquirer* 2016).

Beyond questioning the legitimacy of the press as watchdog, Duterte has carved out an alternative media space with the help of trolls, bloggers, and social media 'influencers.' During and after the election campaign, he deployed a 'keyboard army' that propagated fake news, most famously by inventing an endorsement of his candidacy by Pope Francis (Ressa 2016; Etter 2017; Ong and Cabañes 2018). This online army also generated insults and threats of violence against the president's enemies, including journalists (Etter 2017; BBC News 2016). Bloggers with large followings were enlisted to disseminate the campaign line, and after Duterte was elected, were put on the government's payroll (Gutierrez 2017).

Duterte, a provincial boss in his 70s, seemed the least likely person to be the Philippines' first social media president. But he had a savvy communications team that took full advantage of the shift in media consumption among Filipinos. While his rivals in the 2016 presidential race spent heavily on television ads, the Duterte team seeded Facebook and YouTube with propaganda and propagated online memes that went viral (Ressa 2016).

For most Filipinos, Facebook is the internet. Most do not own a computer, but mobile phone ownership surpassed 100 per cent in 2012 (*BusinessWorld* 2017). In 2015, Facebook introduced Free Basics to the Philippines, allowing millions to get onto the social media platform and a few other sites even if they did not have a data plan on their mobile phones (TechinAsia 2015). Duterte and his team tapped into Facebook's popularity and ubiquity, using the platform to generate buzz for his candidacy, and once he was in office, for rallying public support for the killing of drug suspects and attacks on the press, while waging a disinformation campaign against his critics.

Since late 2016, when they first reported on how Duterte and his allies were 'weaponizing the Internet' through false news, fake accounts, and fake sites, Ressa and Rappler were targeted by a barrage of hate messages, including death and rape threats (Priest 2019). They were not the only ones. Trolls went after other journalists, including photographers, who provided critical coverage of the president's bloody anti-drug campaign. Two Reuters reporters who reported that Duterte had likened himself to Hitler also faced a troll attack, including calls for 'violent punitive action' against them (Rappler 2016). In 2018, a survey undertaken by the International Federation of Journalists (2018) showed that 'cyberattacks and online harassment/trolling' were among the worst threats faced by Filipino journalists.

The press was not used to such a toxic online space. Before Duterte, the internet was a haven for activists and their causes. There was a samizdat quality to the early Philippine internet. It was a space where Filipino bloggers engaged audiences in conversations they could not have in the mainstream press. Rappler itself started out as a Facebook page in 2011, and its early success was due to its ability to use social media platforms to engage a millennial audience (Johnson 2018).

As media scholars Jonathan Ong and Jason Vincent Cabañes (2018: 12) wrote, the 'toxic incivility' of current online political discussions was 'clearly a marked departure from the middle-class norms of respectability and cultural norms of circumspection and civility' that had previously prevailed in the country's online spaces. Duterte's rancour, they said, struck a chord among many Filipinos who associated such civility with the effete elite that had failed to address crime and corruption. Social media influencers stoked this rancour. 'Drawing on their expertise in Filipino-style snark, wit, and indignation, they fan people's feelings of anger, resentment, and powerlessness towards the state of Philippine democratic politics,' wrote Ong and Cabañes (2018: 55).

Other politicians have used the same playbook of fake accounts and influencers to manipulate political discussions, although they did not smear or threaten journalists in the way Duterte has. He has also mainstreamed the deployment of 'digital black ops' in Philippine politics. Ong and Cabañes (2018: 53) found that longstanding public relations practices, especially political spin, have 'paved the way for political disinformation to thrive unregulated in a digital underground.'

The road ahead

Despite all these challenges, exemplary and courageous journalism continues to be produced. Investigative reporting still commands a following. Many journalists have taken advantage of new technologies to tell stories in novel ways and to engage audiences across multiple platforms. Rappler, the thorn in Duterte's side, is a bright example of how online news organizations can excite and engage younger audiences who have tuned out newspapers and mainstream broadcasters.

Despite the increasing incivility of online discourse, the internet continues to provide spaces for robust discussion and for mobilizing citizens for collective action, including in support of the press. Journalists have undertaken fact-checking and media literacy efforts to help deal with the allure of fake news. They have exposed the vectors and techniques of disinformation, including the possible links of local actors to the Internet Research Agency, the Russian government-backed troll farm (Rappler Research Team 2019). Months before the 2019 midterm elections, news organizations and academic institutions set up a fact-checking consortium in the hope of countering the hoaxes and propaganda that marked the 2016 presidential campaign (Macasero 2019).

Press associations remain robust, and journalists have stood up to the attacks. An informal democracy and disinformation network composed of journalists and academics has organized forums and research on the challenges of the current media landscape. In addition, citizens march in support of press freedom and the international media community has supported Filipino journalists under fire.

For sure, there is a strong strain of timidity and opportunism in the Philippine press. But, as the International Federation of Journalists (2018: 45) noted:

> Today's journalists, besieged though they may be, remain as jealously protective of their rights and freedoms. They also have the added benefit of

strong professional organizations and support systems, as well as extensive international networks they can count on when push comes to shove.

The Philippines under Duterte is one of many battlegrounds around the world where the press has found itself pitted against populist strongmen. Duterte has attacked where the press is weakest: its ownership, the corruption within its ranks, the sensationalism of its news coverage and the elitism of its practitioners. The current media environment perpetuates the divide between English-language and local-language audiences, between the cities and the rural areas, and between the privileged and educated and all the rest. Duterte has exploited those cleavages. His followers in both online and in mainstream news media have encouraged a populist backlash against the press. A fighting tradition helps, but Filipino journalists also need new tools to navigate the treacherous waters of the information deluge. Marches, protests and petitions are defensive tactics, and they are necessary to protect existing freedoms, but they do not address the institutional weaknesses of the Philippine press.

References

ABS-CBN News. (2017) 'Duterte ordered Jun Pala's death, says alleged DDS leader'. Available HTTP: <https://news.abs-cbn.com/news/02/20/17/duterte-ordered-jun-palas-death-says-alleged-dds-leader> (accessed 28 February 2019).

ABS-CBN News. (2018) 'Duterte to "object" to ABS-CBN franchise renewal'. Available HTTP: <https://news.abs-cbn.com/news/11/08/18/duterte-to-object-to-abs-cbn-franchise-renewal> (accessed 28 February 2019).

Agence France-Presse. (2016) 'Media groups condemn Rodrigo Duterte comments on corrupt journalists', *The Guardian*. Available HTTP: <www.theguardian.com/world/2016/jun/01/media-groups-condemn-rodrigo-duterte-comments-journalists-philippines> (accessed 28 February 2019).

Aguilar, F.V. Jr., Mendoza, M.P., and Candelaria, A.K.L. (2014) 'Keeping the state at bay: The killing of journalists in the Philippines, 1998–2012', *Critical Asian Studies*, 46: 649–677.

Arguillas, C. (2003) 'The saga of Jun Pala', *I Magazine*. Available HTTP: <https://pcij.org/wp-content/uploads/2017/02/PCIJ-20031001-09-The-Saga-of-Jun-Pala-i-magazine.pdf> (accessed 28 February 2019).

BBC News. (2016) 'Trolls and triumph: A digital battle in the Philippines'. Available HTTP: <www.bbc.com/news/av/magazine-38226402/trolls-and-triumph-a-digital-battle-in-the-philippines> (accessed 28 February 2019).

Burgos, N.P. Jr. (2017) 'Drilon critic sentenced to up to 4 years in prison for libel', *Philippine Daily Inquirer*. Available HTTP: <http://newsinfo.inquirer.net/873485/drilon-critic-sentenced-to-up-to-4-years-in-prison-for-libelsentenced-to-up-to-4-years-in-prison-for-libel> (accessed 28 February 2019).

BusinessWorld. (2017) 'PHL has "high level" of mobile access, download speeds in urban areas – report'. Available HTTP: <www.bworldonline.com/phl-high-level-mobile-access-download-speeds-urban-areas-report/> (accessed 28 February 2019).

Caliwan, C.L. (2018) 'SC sets rules on issuance of warrants for cybercrime law', *Philippine News Agency*. Available HTTP: <www.pna.gov.ph/articles/1046058> (accessed 28 February 2019).

Center for Media Freedom and Responsibility. (2007) 'Back to the past: A timeline of press freedom'. Available HTTP: <https://cmfr-phil.org/media-ethics-responsibility/ethics/back-to-the-past-a-timeline-of-press-freedom/> (accessed 28 February 2019).

Center for Media Freedom and Responsibility. (2008) 'Publisher jailed for libel, libel conviction of another affirmed'. Available HTTP: <https://cmfr-phil.org/press-freedom-protection/press-freedom/cmfr-philippines-alert-publisher-jailed-for-libel-libel-conviction-of-another-affirmed/> (accessed 28 February 2019).

Center for Media Freedom and Responsibility. (2010) 'Killer of radio broadcaster-witness found guilty'. Available HTTP: <https://cmfr-phil.org/uncategorized/killer-of-radio-broadcaster-witness-found-guilty/> (accessed 28 February 2019).

Chua, Y.T. and Datinguinoo, V.M. (1998) 'The media as marketplace', in C.F. Hofilenna (ed.) *News for Sale: The Corruption of the Philippine Media*, Quezon City: Philippine Center for Investigative Journalism.

Committee to Protect Journalists. (2005) *Philippines: On the Radio, Under the Gun*. Available HTTP: <https://cpj.org/reports/2005/08/phil-05.php> (accessed 28 February 2019).

Committee to Protect Journalists. (n.d.) 'Online database of journalists killed since 1992'. Available HTTP: <https://cpj.org/data/killed/?status=Killed&motiveConfirmed%5B%5D=Confirmed&type%5B%5D=Journalist&start_year=1992&end_year=2019&group_by=year> (accessed 28 February 2019).

Coronel, S.S. (1999) 'Lords of the press', in *From Loren to Marimar: The Philippine media in the 1990s*, Quezon City: Philippine Center for Investigative Journalism.

Coronel, S.S. (2001) 'The media, the market and democracy: The case of the Philippines', *Javnost-The Public*, 8: 109–126.

Etter, L. (2017) 'How Duterte turned Facebook into a weapon', *Bloomberg Businessweek*. Available HTTP: <www.bloomberg.com/news/features/2017-12-07/how-rodrigo-duterte-turned-facebook-into-a-weapon-with-a-little-help-from-facebook> (accessed 28 February 2019).

Forbes, A. (2015) 'Courageous women in media: Marcos censorship in the Philippines', *Pacific Journalism Review*, 21: 195–210.

Freedom of the Net. (2014) *Philippines*. Available HTTP: <https://freedomhouse.org/report/freedom-net/2014/philippines> (accessed 28 February 2019).

Gavilan, J. (2019) 'From Marcos to Duterte: How media was attacked, threatened', *Rappler*. Available HTTP: <www.rappler.com/newsbreak/iq/193882-threats-attacks-philippines-media-timeline> (accessed 28 February, 2019).

Ghitis, F. (2018) 'As Duterte Ramps Up His War on the Media, Many in the Philippines Cheer', *World Politics Review*. Available HTTP: <https://www.worldpoliticsreview.com/articles/24053/as-duterte-ramps-up-his-war-on-the-media-many-in-the-philippines-cheer> (accessed 21 August, 2019).

GMA News. (2006) 'Journalists fight back, file P12.5M libel suit vs. Mike Arroyo'. Available HTTP: <www.gmanetwork.com/news/news/nation/24801/journalists-fight-back-file-p12-5m-suit-vs-mike-arroyo/story/> (accessed 28 February 2019).

Gutierrez, N. (2017) 'State-sponsored hate: The rise of pro-Duterte bloggers', *Rappler*. Available HTTP: <www.rappler.com/newsbreak/in-depth/178709-duterte-die-hard-supporters-bloggers-propaganda-pcoo> (accessed 28 February 2019).

Human Rights Watch. (2010) *They Own the People: The Ampatuans, State-Backed Militias, and Killings in the Southern Philippines*. Available HTTP: <www.hrw.org/report/2010/11/16/they-own-people/ampatuans-state-backed-militias-and-killings-southern-philippines> (accessed 28 February 2019).

International Federation of Journalists. (2018) *Underneath the Autocrats: South East Asia Media Freedom Report 2018*. Available HTTP: <www.ifj.org/fileadmin/user_upload/

Underneath_the_Autocrats_-_IFJ_SEAJU_2018_-_SP_HR.pdf> (accessed 28 February 2019).

Johnson, E. (2018) 'Memo from a "Facebook nation" to Mark Zuckerberg: You moved fast and broke our country', *Recode*. Available HTTP: <www.recode.net/2018/11/26/18111859/maria-ressa-rappler-facebook-mark-zuckerberg-philippines-kara-swisher-recode-decode-podcast> (accessed 28 February 2019).

Lagrimas, N.A. (2017) 'Piñol sues newsman over "libelous" FB post', *GMA News*. Available HTTP: <www.gmanetwork.com/news/news/nation/627553/pinol-sues-newsman-over-libelous-fb-post/story/> (accessed 28 February 2019).

Lopez, E. (2018) 'Decaying justice system aiding crime, corruption in PH–lawyers', *Rappler*. Available HTTP: <www.rappler.com/nation/197813-decaying-justice-system-crime-corruption-philippines-forum> (accessed 28 February 2019).

Macasero, R. (2019) 'Academe, media launch Tsek.ph for collaborative fact-checking', *Philippine Star*. Available HTTP: <www.philstar.com/headlines/2019/02/11/1892791/academe-media-launch-tsekph-collaborative-fact-checking> (accessed 28 February 2019).

Malig, J. (2012) 'Global "Anonymous" attack Philippine Government websites', *ABS-CBN News*. Available HTTP: <https://news.abs-cbn.com/lifestyle/10/02/12/global-anonymous-attack-philippine-govt-websites> (accessed 28 February 2019).

Merueñas, M. (2012) 'Chainsaw murder of Maguindanao massacre witness meant to terrify', *GMA News*. Available HTTP: <www.gmanetwork.com/news/news/nation/260399/chainsaw-murder-of-maguindanao-massacre-witness-meant-to-terrify/story/> (accessed 28 February 2019).

Ong, J.C. and Cabañes, J.V.A. (2018) 'Architects of networked disinformation: Behind the scenes of troll accounts and fake news production in the Philippines', *Newton Tech4Dev Network*. Available HTTP: <https://newtontechfordev.com/wp-content/uploads/2018/02/Architects-of-Networked-Disinformation-Executive-Summary-Final.pdf> (accessed 28 February 2019).

Philippine Center for Investigative Journalism. (2007) 'Journalists welcome, criticize Mike Arroyo's dropping of cases'. Available HTTP: <https://pcij.org/blog/2007/05/03/mike-arroyo-drops-all-libel-cases-vs-journalists> (accessed 28 February 2019).

Philippine Daily Inquirer. (2016) 'Duterte hits media for sensationalism, bias'. Available HTTP: <https://newsinfo.inquirer.net/784772/duterte-hits-media-for-sensationalism-bias> (accessed 28 February 2019).

Picardal, A. (n.d.) 'The victims of the Davao Death Squad: Consolidated report 1998–2015', *CBCP News*. Available HTTP: <www.cbcpnews.com/cbcpnews/?p=76531> (accessed 28 February 2019).

Pineda-Ofreneo. (1984) *The Press Under Martial Law*, Quezon City: Cacho Hermanos. Available HTTP: <www.scribd.com/document/84775518/The-Press-Under-Martial-Law> (accessed 28 February 2019).

Pinlac, M.Y. (2007) 'Marcos and the press', *Center for Media Freedom and Responsibility*. Available HTTP: <https://cmfr-phil.org/media-ethics-responsibility/ethics/marcos-and-the-press/> (accessed 28 February 2019).

Priest, D. (2019) '"Seeded in social media": Jailed Philippine journalist says Facebook is partly responsible for her predicament', *The Washington Post*. Available HTTP: <www.washingtonpost.com/technology/2019/02/25/seeded-social-media-jailed-philippine-journalist-says-facebook-is-partly-responsible-her-predicament/?noredirect=on&utm_term=.fe86b2c561cc> (accessed 28 February 2019).

Rappler. (2016) 'NUJP condemns threats against Reuters reporters'. Available HTTP: <www.rappler.com/nation/148098-nujp-condemns-threats-against-reuters-reporters> (accessed 28 February 2019).

Rappler Research Team. (2019) 'Exclusive: Russian disinformation system influences PH social media', *Rappler*. Available HTTP: <www.rappler.com/newsbreak/investigative/221470-russian-disinformation-system-influences-philippine-social-media> (accessed 28 February 2019).

Rauhala, E. (2018) 'Duterte takes aim at the press, testing the foundations of Philippine democracy', *The Washington Post*. Available HTTP: <www.washingtonpost.com/world/asia_pacific/duterte-takes-aim-at-the-press-testing-the-foundations-of-philippine-democracy/2018/03/16/a7d3f6f4–26d3–11e8-a227-fd2b009466bc_story.html?noredirect=on&utm_term=.0450bf72c558> (accessed 28 February 2019).

Ressa, M. (2016) 'Propaganda war: Weaponizing the internet', *Rappler*. Available HTTP: <www.rappler.com/nation/148007-propaganda-war-weaponizing-internet> (accessed 28 February 2019).

Rey, A. (2019) 'Rappler CEO Maria Ressa arrested for cyber libel', *Rappler*. Available HTTP: <www.rappler.com/nation/223411-maria-ressa-arrested-for-cyber-libel-february-2019> (accessed 28 February 2019).

Romero, P. (2012) 'The Road to the Cybercrime Prevention Act of 2012', *Rappler*. Available HTTP: <https://www.rappler.com/rich-media/13901-the-road-to-the-cybercrime-prevention-act-of-2012> (accessed 21 August 2019).

Rosales, R.G. (2006) 'Shooting the messenger: Why radio broadcasting is a deadly profession in the Philippines', *Journal of Radio Studies*, 13: 146–155.

San Juan, J.R. (2018) 'Cyber-libel cases rising, as friends turn into foes via online platforms', *Business Mirror*. Available HTTP: <https://businessmirror.com.ph/2018/03/19/cyber-libel-cases-rising-as-friends-turn-into-foes-via-online-platforms/> (21 October 2019).

Rosario-Braid, F. and Tuazon, R.R. (1999). 'Communication Media in the Philippines: 1521–1986', *Philippine Studies*, 47(3): 291–318. http://www.jstor.org/stable/42634324.

Santos, R. Jr. (2012) '74 members of Ampatuan clan running in 2013', *Rappler*. Available HTTP: <www.rappler.com/nation/politics/elections-2013/16486-74-members-of-ampatuan-clan-running-in-2013> (accessed 28 February 2019).

Stephens, H. (2019) 'In the Philippines, Duterte's Drug Crackdown Has Been Followed by a Crackdown on the Free Press', *World Politics Review*. Available HTTP: <https://www.worldpoliticsreview.com/insights/25707/in-the-philippines-president-dutertes-drug-crackdown-has-been-followed-by-a-crackdown-on-the-free-press> (accessed 21 August 2019).

Stevenson, A. (2019) 'Maria Ressa, Philippine Journalist Critical of Duterte, Is Released After Arrest', *The New York Times*. Available HTTP: <https://www.nytimes.com/2019/02/13/world/asia/maria-ressa-arrested.html?module=inline> (accessed 21 August 2019).

Tandoc, E. (2017) 'Watching over the Watchdogs: The problems that Filipino journalists face', *Journalism Studies*, 18: 102–117.

TechinAsia. (2015) 'Facebook's internet.org apps bring free mobile Internet to the Philippines'. Available HTTP: <www.techinasia.com/facebook-internet-org-app-smart-philippines> (accessed 28 February 2019).

Teodoro, L. (2016) *Divide by Two*, Quezon City: University of the Philippines Press.

UPI (1995). 'Manila Court Rejects Aquino Libel Suit'. Available HTTP: <https://www.upi.com/Archives/1995/11/14/Manila-court-rejects-Aquino-libel-suit/4614816325200/> (accessed 21 August 2019).

15

PRESS FREEDOM CHAINED IN THAILAND

Pavin Chachavalpongpun

The name 'Thailand' is proudly translated by Thais as the 'Land of the Free.' This translation reflects that Thailand is the only country in Southeast Asia not to have been formally colonized by Western powers. Yet, the concept of freedom is highly contested in the Thai context (McCargo 2003: 15). While the Thai Constitution guarantees freedom of speech, the Thai press is in chains. Thailand has joined a number of countries in Southeast Asia where freedom of the press is being compromised by a myriad of factors, mostly pertaining to the consolidation of the power of the state. The return of authoritarianism in many Southeast Asian states has stirred up concern regarding the lack of press freedom in the region. Attacks against the press have been normalized. This chapter examines the case of Thailand and the current situation of the Thai press. It discusses two important points. First, political leaders, whether they preside over democratic or repressive regimes, have increasingly become threats to press freedom. By discrediting the media, berating journalists and threatening to impose restrictions, these political leaders are driven by the need to protect their interests in the face of the media's scrutiny. Second, regime change in Thailand in recent decades has affected the state of press freedom. Thailand experienced military coups in 2006 and 2014. The control of the state by the military has exacerbated the dire state of freedom of expression, most evidently through the enactment of a series of laws designed to restrict media freedoms. This chapter examines the legal measures and other tactics utilized by the Thai state against the press. It also investigates the emergence of social media as a platform for competing information and the recent phenomenon of fake news as an instrument to undermine political adversaries.

Threats to press freedom: then and now

Thailand was once known as a 'haven of free expression' and for its reputation as one of the freest media environments in the region. In 1997, Thailand became the first country in Southeast Asia to institute a freedom of information law (Hays 2014). But the advent of the Thaksin Shinawatra administration in 2001 imperilled press freedom in Thailand. Like any populist leader, Thaksin publicly dismissed the role of the media as a foundation of democratic rule. During the Thaksin era, the Thai media was depicted as the foe of the government, and Thaksin openly displayed his hostility towards the press (Phongpaichit and Baker 2008). He cracked down on critical media sources, ordering investigations of anti-government journalists and media organizations, as well as blaming the media for inaccurately reporting on his war on drugs and aggravating threats from Muslim insurgents in the Deep South. He also used the government's Anti-Money Laundering Office to intimidate reporters. Some foreign journalists were branded as dangers to national security and threatened with expulsion from the country because they reported on the rift between Thaksin and the late King Bhumibol Adulyadej.[1] The *Far Eastern Economic Review* and the *Economist* were occasionally banned. Some local journalists were threatened with defamation lawsuits that could bankrupt them – a practice also frequently seen in Singapore. Moreover, the operation of certain media companies was suspended, such as in the case of the *Siam Rath Weekly* because of its critical reporting on Thaksin's mishandling of the bird flu outbreak in 2003. In 2002, the Nation Multimedia Group stopped covering politics on its 24-hour cable network in protest against a forced shutdown of its radio news programme by the Thaksin government. In 2005, the *Nation* published this scathing indictment:

> [The] Thai Journalists Association (TJA) issued a strong statement criticising government hypocrisy, particularly the pledge made by Thaksin at the beginning of his second term that he would respect press freedom and democracy. The TJA is succinct in assessing that the government has failed to keep its promises and has instead been using every trick in the book to meddle with news reporting. The government has even threatened to pull out advertising and buy up shares in media companies. And then there are the expensive defamation lawsuits. The National Press Council of Thailand has also condemned the defamation laws that make criminals of journalists.
>
> *(Chongkittavorn 2005)*

Backing up this assessment, in 2005, Reporters without Borders ranked Thailand 107th out of 167 countries in its Press Freedom Index (Reporters sans Frontieres 2019). A year later, in September 2006, Thaksin was overthrown in a military coup, but his ouster did not improve press freedom (Streckfuss 2014: 116). From 2006–2019, press freedom in Thailand deteriorated under the rising influence of militarism in politics. The country's ranking fell to 153th out of 178 in 2010 – the year that saw the massacre of the pro-Thaksin 'Red Shirts' on the streets of Bangkok, where they were protesting the machinations of the political elite against them.[2] The ranking rose slightly from 2011 to 137th following the electoral victory of the Pheu Thai Party headed by Thaksin's sister, Yingluck Shinawatra, who reclaimed the premiership for the family, briefly ending military rule. In the 2014 index, Thailand ranked 130th out of 180 nations, but dropped to 140th in 2018 (Reporters sans Frontieres 2019). Following a military coup in 2014, Thailand has been ruled by General Prayuth Chan-ocha. Tracking Thailand's press freedom ranking indicates that it suffers most under authoritarian regimes. On 24 March 2019, the military government organized an election, the outcome of which brought Prayuth back into power. But the return of the Prayuth government does not solve the political conflict at home. Hence, nothing guarantees that the situation of the country's press freedom will drastically improve.

The critical turn for press freedom in Thailand occurred in the aftermath of the 2014 coup. Hundreds of people, mostly critics of the old establishment, were harassed. They included politicians, political activists, academics and civil society organizations, as well as reporters and journalists. They were summoned to attend military-instructed sessions to 'adjust' their attitudes. Some were detained in army camps, while others were charged with lèse-majesté, the crime of insulting the monarchy. Article 112 of the Thai Criminal Code states that defamatory, insulting or threatening comments about the king, queen and regent are punishable by 3–15 years in prison. Those who refused to be summoned face severe consequences. The junta issued a warrant for their arrest and revoked their passports (Campbell 2014). Some journalists became the victims of the state. The 2014 case of Pravit Rojanaphruk, an outspoken journalist from the *Nation*, demonstrated that freedom of speech was no longer guaranteed by law. He was ordered to attend attitude adjustment sessions conducted by military officers at local Thai army bases. Sometime after he was released from detention at one of these military camps, Pravit was pressured to resign from his job at the *Nation*. Pravit's attitude didn't change, however, as he continued to criticize the National Council for Peace and Order (NCPO), the governing body of the coup makers, for undermining checks and balances, failing to abide by the rule of law, refusing to hold elections and suppressing dissent ('*La Croix*' 2018). The draconian lèse-majesté law and the Computer Crime Act are powerful tools of the state in silencing the media. They prescribe harsh sentences for anyone making critical comments of the country's monarchy or the junta.

Apart from Pravit, some other Thai and foreign journalists encountered similar harassment by the junta. The column of outspoken political commentator Voranai Vanijaka was abruptly dropped by the *Bangkok Post* following the 2014 coup. Scottish journalist Andrew Marshall MacGregor is on the wanted list for lèse-majesté charges. His book, *A Kingdom in Crisis: Thailand's Struggle for Democracy in the Twenty-First Century*, which examined the interventionist role of the Thai monarchy in politics, was banned in Thailand. He was one of three individuals, alongside academics-turned-exiles Somsak Jeamteerasakul and Pavin Chachavalpongpun (Chachavalpongpun 2014), who were declared persona non grata online. Thais were warned not to follow us on Facebook, click like or share our posts, or face serious consequences, including jail time (Holmes 2017). Recently, the editor of the *Bangkok Post*, Umesh Pandey, was allegedly forced to step down over what he claimed was his anti-junta stance. 'When asked to tone down [the negative coverage of the regime] I did not budge and was blunt in letting those who make decisions know that I would rather lose my position than bow my head,' Pandey wrote in a statement ('*La Croix*' 2018). These cases exemplify how the space for press freedom has shrivelled, and what the consequences are for critical journalists.

Harassment against the media

Harassment of the media, including the detention of journalists and suspension of media operations, were deemed short-term measures. After the 2014 coup, a tight grip on the media has been maintained more systematically via junta laws and decrees. As this chapter argues, the intensifying restriction of press freedom in Thailand is a result of both regime change and the rise of militarism of politics. Authoritarian rule in itself does not permit public scrutiny. The role of the media as a watchdog overseeing the government, vital to the functioning of democracy, is largely circumscribed. Furthermore, under authoritarian rule, differences of opinion with the government are forbidden. The only way the media can escape harassment is by promoting the government's policies rather than questioning them. Harassment and reform of the media are both used by the junta to control the free flow of information. Reforms included new laws purportedly to promote ethical standards among media professionals. Restrictive laws such as the Computer Crime Act were not reformed. In 2017, the Computer Crime Act defined computer crimes offences and punishments for computer-related and cybercrime that prevents Thais from criticizing certain institutions deemed important to national security. Since the 2014 coup, the NCPO has issued more than 800 orders and announcements, later transforming these into laws, that significantly constrain media freedom ('Not 'iLaw' 2017).

Legal instruments

The military government of Prayuth began its war against critical media by issuing orders and announcements to curtail press freedom. Four of these decrees stand out as noteworthy (Thavevong 2018):

- NCPO Announcement No 97/2014 prohibits the media from presenting information that 'threatens national security or instigates disorder or conflicts.'
- NCPO Announcement No 103/2014 bans criticism of the NCPO that is made in a 'dishonest way or aims to discredit it.'
- NCPO Order No 3/2015 authorizes military officers to enforce bans on media outlets if their content 'instigates public fear or causes misunderstanding

through distortion which could affect national security or lead to social disorder.'

- NCPO Order No 41/2016 empowers the National Broadcasting and Telecommunications Commission to enforce Announcements No 97/2014 and No 103/2014. It states that media outlets in violation risk fines of Bt50,000–Bt500,000 (US$1,600–$16,000), licence suspension or closure.

These orders and announcements have been used to close TV stations critical of the junta and the government, either temporarily or permanently. Among those targeted were Voice TV, Peace TV, TV24, DMC and Fah Hai TV (Thavevong 2018). Some of these TV stations are linked to the pro-Thaksin Red Shirts, and are thus considered enemies of the state. Voice TV is owned by Thaksin's son, Panthongtae, and has remained a megaphone for Thaksin's party. It has been subject to temporary suspensions several times. The junta has also censored news websites by blocking access to them (Macan-Markar 2017). To avoid being suspended or closed down, the mainstream media engages in self-censorship. For example, leading newspapers, including *Thai Rath* and *Daily News*, never publish any report deemed critical of the army or the monarchy.

Another of the junta's tactics has been the control of community radio stations that spread different political views and mobilize support against the coup makers. They have been closed down, forcing them to either go underground or to broadcast from outside the country. However, the military government finds it more difficult to deal with the urban-based news media, including online media outlets like the Standard and the Matter, as well as Thailand-based international media, such as the BBC, whose content is sometime critical of both the junta and the monarchy. The BBC once published a critical biography of the new king, Vajiralongkorn, on the eve of his enthronement. Although the biography is based on facts, it was considered insulting to the king because it reported on his unconventional lifestyle. A young Thai political activist from Khon Kaen, Jatupat Boonpattararaksa — also known as Pai Daodin – was imprisoned for sharing the BBC article on his Facebook page (BBC 2016). The arrest conveyed a chilling message to the rest of society not to discuss issues related to the monarchy in public, and this has intimidated citizens into silence on this taboo.

In sum, the harassment of the media has escalated and now includes making threats against the liberty of reporters with the deployment of laws to silence them. The regime often relies on 'Strategic Litigation Against Public Participation' (SLAPP). SLAPPs are lawsuits intended to silence critics by burdening them with the cost of a legal defence ('Human Rights Watch' 2018). The government also resorts to laws such as Article 116, which prohibits inciting the public through speech, books or other forms of media. Although cases rarely result in convictions, they are still useful to the government. Those involved in court are forbidden from giving public comment throughout their trial. This creates a vacuum of accountability, as the media are unable to continue their work.

Mounting state pressure on foreign journalists

In tandem with applying legal tools to limit press freedom, the military government has also placed immense pressure on the media through other means. Local journalists and reporters perceived to hold antagonistic views towards the junta can be suspended or expelled due to state pressure on their companies, as in the case of Pravit and Umesh (Charuvastra 2018). The situation for foreign journalists is no less threatening. Foreign media have faced great difficulty, not only in reporting the political role of the junta and the monarchy, but also in making any direct criticism of the gross human right violations perpetrated by the military government. In 2009, the entire board of the Foreign Correspondents Club of Thailand (FCCT) was accused of criticizing the monarchy, and hence threatened with charges under the lèse-majesté law. Threats against foreign journalists range from the possibility of their visas not being renewed to being charged with lèse-majesté. The author's discussions with a number of Thailand-based international journalists revealed that the process of visa renewal has become more difficult, strict and time-consuming. To be able to report from within Thailand, foreign journalists have to adopt a cautious approach and take into account the sensitivities of issues related to the monarchy, its defenders and the lèse-majesté law. From 2009–2019, the situation has not greatly changed. In recent years, the FCCT has been forced to cancel a number of talks. In September 2018, the Thai authorities shut down an FCCT event on Myanmar, stating that it could be used by 'third parties' to cause unrest and endanger national security ('Voice of America' 2018). Earlier, in February 2018, police summoned representatives of the FCCT after an activist was accused of planning an allegedly illegal assembly at the club demanding that a national election be held in November ('The Nation' 2018).

Harassment against the foreign press has reached an unprecedented level. In 2010, an Italian photographer, Fabio Polenghi, and a Japanese cameraman, Hiro Muramoto, were killed during the months of violent confrontations between the Red Shirts and the state's security forces. At least seven foreign or local reporters were wounded. Many reporters who covered the demonstrations told the author that they believed they were deliberately targeted. In the cases of Polenghi and Muramoto, the Thai state has never unravelled the mysteries surrounding their deaths. The lack of sufficient investigation strained Thai-Japanese relations, but Tokyo has refrained from public criticism for the sake of bilateral relations ('AFP' 2012). At a meeting at the FCCT in June 2010, foreign journalists expressed their anger at the government for the deaths of their colleagues and demanded an independent probe into the attacks on reporters. They also complained about the widespread allegation that the foreign press was biased. An illustrative incident took place in November 2013 when German journalist Nick Nostitz was assaulted as he reported from within the anti-Yingluck camp in the centre of Bangkok. The anti-Yingluck protesters demanded that Yingluck step down, owing to allegations of her committing corruption. Nostitz was accused of being sympathetic towards her and the Red Shirts, hence upsetting the pro-establishment protesters in the camp (Farrelly 2013).

Normalization of self-censorship

Owing to the harsh legal measures, the enormous pressures from the state and the attacks on the lives of journalists, the press community has been compelled to practice self-censorship in order to survive in the era of military rule. The media has been forced to carry out self-censorship in two key domains – one concerning royal affairs, and the other in relation to the junta. Reports on the Thai monarchy, while extensively published in foreign media outside the Thai borders, are non-existent in Thailand. For example, reports on the current king, Vajiralongkorn, strolling in Munich wearing a skinny tank top and displaying temporary Yakuza-style tattoos on his torso attracted international media attention, but was missing from the Thai press as a result of self-censorship (Kentish 2016). Other issues related to the monarchy were also buried from public view, including the king taking over of the wealthy Crown Property Bureau and the mysterious deaths of three men who once worked for him. Typically, cases of lèse-majesté have never been reported in the Thai mainstream media. In 2015, the editor of Prachatai, a web-based alternative media outlet, was found guilty for failing to delete lèse-majesté comments on its now-defunct web forum. The editor was convicted under Article 12 of the 2007 Computer Crime Act (CCA) for allowing an allegedly offensive comment about the monarchy to remain on the web board for 20 days. In the end, she was sentenced to eight months imprisonment and a Bt20,000 (US$630) fine, with her jail term suspended for one year ('Prachatai' 2015). This case set a new standard for the editors of online media outlets, suggesting they must monitor their pages 24 hours a day. Should they find insulting comments about the monarchy, they must delete them immediately. Other media websites, like the BBC, even forewarned their users to exercise extra care when writing comments about the monarchy. In many ways, the case also deepened the necessity for self-censorship, both for the media and for news consumers.

Self-censorship is mostly detected in cyberspace. David Streckfuss argues that the new digital landscape has both enlarged the space for political speech and transformed what might be defined as criminal speech – meaning that self-censorship has taken on new importance for actors wishing to protect themselves. He explains how digital technologies have affected those wanting to voice criticism of the military government and shows how they must navigate through a weaponized digital landscape that provides the dictatorship with various mechanisms to silence their critics, either directly or via self-censorship (Streckfuss 2019). In other words, digital technologies create new spaces for discussion, but can also restrict the scope for criticism of the state by encouraging self-censorship.

Voluntary self-censorship represents another kind of compliance to state pressure. Some reporters and journalists have chosen to forge ties with the junta, not only for the sake of avoiding persecution or harassment, but also for personal or professional gain. As part of this practice, journalists avoid criticizing the junta or the monarchy, and refrain from reporting on administrative irregularities or corruption cases. Some have gone further by serving as de facto PR representatives for the junta. For example, a well-known *Bangkok Post* reporter has earned a reputation as an informal spokesperson for the military government due to her close relationship with the army. In return, she has exploited this relationship to enrich herself, by publishing a series of books based on her exclusive interviews with military elites, helping her build a reputation as one of the most knowledgeable reporters on the military ('Manager Online' 2017).

Scant public support for press freedom

The Thai media possesses some distinctive characteristics. The drawn-out political crisis in Thailand, now more than a decade long, has led to a deep polarization between those aligning themselves with the political elites and those in marginalized regions. Often, this deep division is crudely called a colour-coded conflict, between yellow and the red, respectively. The conflict between the yellow and the red has ramifications for the media (McCargo 2017: 4140). Each faction has its supporters in the media. For example, the Yellow Shirts have their own media outlet, the Blue Sky channel. They have also gained solid support from some print media including the *Manager*, the *Thai Post*, *Naew Na* and the *Nation*. Meanwhile, Voice TV, supported by the Red Shirt backers of Thaksin, has maintained its mission to promote Thaksin's political parties and, in the present situation, to criticize the policies of the military government. Leading newspapers, like *Matichon* and *Khaosod*, are known to be sympathetic towards the Red Shirts. Unsurprisingly, Red Shirt-supported media outlets are frequently harassed by the junta. Polarized political ideologies and loyalties mean that harassment against Voice TV, for instance, is cheered by the Yellow Shirts. Public support for press freedom is undermined by these deep factional divisions within Thai society.

Putting aside Thailand's colour-coded politics, since the coup of 2014, the Thai state has successfully created a climate of fear. At one level, the climate of fear has been built up to protect the military government. At another level, such fear has become a new reality under the new reign of King Vajiralongkorn (Sopranzetti 2017). While the reign of previous King Bhumibol Adulyadej was firmly underpinned by his unassailable moral authority, the present King Vajiralongkorn is ruling Thailand by fear. In these circumstances, the press on both sides of the Thai political divide have to take extra care when reporting either on the junta or the monarchy. Public fear is demonstrated by a reluctance to openly endorse the anti-junta media and by rejection of media outlets – mainly foreign – that are critical of the monarchy. While critical reports on the Thai monarchy can be accessed freely outside the country, as seen in the *Economist*, Al Jazeera or in academic blogs like New Mandala, they can be blocked by the Thai state.

The public is extremely careful not to share the content of these publications online. Not only does the problem with press freedom in Thailand derive from the growing culture of self-censorship, but also from a lack of public support for a critical free press.

Recent developments

The current state of the Thai media is worrying. In this section, some recent developments are explored. Some of these developments may further undermine the freedom of the Thai media. Others offer hope for greater press freedom in a country intermittently ruled by the military. The transfer of power from the military to a civilian administration in 2019 sparked some hope for the Thai media. But as shown in this chapter, not all civilian governments in the past cherished press freedom. Media reform can only flourish under the conditions of general democratization in the country.

Fake news

The fake news phenomenon poses a danger for the Thai press. The Thai state has claimed to be the sole arbiter of truth, while those who challenge their edicts are said to spread "lies." Meanwhile, in the Thai conflicts, both sides, including their allies in the media, have relied on fabricated "facts" to undermine the credibility or "dehumanize" the other side" (Sombatpoonsiri 2019). While the Computer Crime Act was introduced to detect fake news and to prosecute those disseminating it, the military government has itself engaged in spreading fake news. Long before the implementation of the Computer Crime Act, the military used fake news to identify elements that were supposedly threatening national security. One of the tactics employed by the military was to create an anti-monarchy chart based entirely on false information. Called *Phang Lom Chao* in Thai, this fake anti-monarchy chart accused certain individuals of having an anti-monarchy agenda, considered by many Thais to be the most severe treason (Chachavalpongpun 2011: 1031). In Thai politics, whereby the monarchy is a key fault line, an anti-monarchy accusation could justify a lengthy jail term as well as physical and psychological abuse by the public.

Fake news undermines serious media coverage and makes it more difficult for journalists to cover significant news stories. Sometimes, it is intended to divert public attention from the real issues. It is used to identify and create internal enemies, which remains a useful tactic in a society like Thailand where there is strong adherence to tradition and the status quo. In the period leading up to the 2019 elections, rising politician Thanathorn Jungrungruangkit of the Future Forward Party was consistently accused of disrespecting the monarchy (Chachavalpongpun 2018). In addition, fake news about Thanathorn disparaging Thai traditional values became virulent on the social media. He was accused of, for example, making fun of Thailand's reputation of being the 'Land of Smiles' and of propagating the abolition of *Wai Kru*, an annual ritual in which students pay respect to their teachers ('Thai Post' 2019). The intention was to damage Thanathorn by branding him as an anti-traditionalist, if not anti-monarchist. Conversely, some political figures have popularized the term 'fake news' to describe negative press coverage of themselves. The Prayuth government often dismissed critical reports as fake news, despite the fact that these reports were based on facts.

The emerging social media

As the space for public opinion and political debate has shrunk under military rule, Thais have moved their political discussions to cyberspace. The media, too, have followed this trend of reporting events on social media networks, as the internet plays a growing role in promoting political discussion. The rise in use of social media platforms such as Facebook, Twitter and Instagram has transformed the way information is distributed and shared in Thailand. For the first time, the people can have direct and even equal access to political information from different sources, made possible by emerging social media networks. They can compare content and make decisions based on these various sources, examine the issues from alternative viewpoints and even challenge the information controlled by the military state. Among Thailand's population of 67 million people, 49 million are on Facebook, 12 million are on Twitter and 13.6 million are on Instagram (Leesa-nguansuk 2018). Noting the rise of social media in Thailand, Matthew Phillips, a British scholar, argues: 'The act of going to a ballot box and casting your vote is obviously something that is being regulated through current political discourse. That being said, you cannot really see the current discourse without understanding the role of social media' (Interview, 15 December 2014). Leading politicians, agents of civil society organizations, representative of independent institutions and a large number of academics have turned to social media as their main platform to engage the public (Chachavalpongpun 2014: 59). For instance, both former Prime Ministers Yingluck Shinawatra and Abhisit Vejjajiva actively use Facebook and Twitter to convey their messages. Yingluck's official Facebook page has received more than 6 million 'likes,' while Abhisit's has almost 2.2 million.

How have social media contributed to opening up society at a time when the country is under military rule? First, the nature of social media, which is relatively free and unrestrained, decentralizes sources of information, making the controlled Thai media increasingly irrelevant as a news source. Second, social media are increasingly used as stages for political campaigns, seen in the establishment of numerous new political groups with specific agendas and clienteles, such as the New Democracy Movement (NDM) and the Network of Relatives and Victims of the Lèse-majesté Law, as well as serving as key platforms during the election campaigns of 2019. Third, social media reintroduces a participatory element that is fundamental to the process of democratization. Participating in politics no longer exclusively means going to the polling station or joining street protests – which are illegal in Thailand under the current military rule. But participation and protest can be done online and possibly more effectively. Fourth, social media has become a forum for critical discussions, dealing with contentious issues that are unable to be discussed in the mainstream media. It has provided a useful platform for alternative media, which today offers different information from that provided by the state.

To be sure, the internet is not an entirely safe zone for debate. The military government has sought to censor certain websites that could be destabilizing to its regime. Content critical of the government's performance, involving the monarchy or highlighting human rights violations – such as the Human Rights Watch website – has been blocked in Thailand. But it is impossible for the government to shut down all social media in the country, as it has effectively inserted itself in a domain previously occupied by mainstream media. Undoubtedly, it has played a pivotal role in providing a space for political debate – a much-needed exercise at a time when Thailand has fallen deeply into political crisis. And this role is ever more significant, now that freedom of speech is lacking under military rule.

Finally, a fascinating recent development on social media in Thailand has been the emergence of political arts in the form of cartoons and music. The proliferation of online artworks and music unleashes optimism in regards to freedom of expression in an era of authoritarianism. A popular cartoonist using the pseudonym Khai Maew (cat's testicles) regularly publishes his cartoons satirizing the political situation of the day, mostly to sarcastically condemn the junta (Khai Maew 2019). He has attracted almost 355,000 followers on Facebook and has organized exhibitions of his artwork both inside and outside the country. Headache Stencil is another artist publishing his works mainly on Instagram. He became known mostly for his artwork on the corruption case against General Pravit Wongsuwan, Deputy Prime Minister in the military government, who was accused of taking bribes in the form of expensive watches. His stencil technique is to reproduce an image or pattern by applying pigment to a surface over an intermediate object, such as his image of a large clock, which appeared on a flyover in Bangkok to publicly expose the corruption case. In the area of music, a pro-democracy group, Rap against Dictatorship, in October 2018, released an online single called '*Prathet Ku Mee*,' or 'What My Country's Got,' detailing what went wrong with undemocratic Thailand. The song went viral on YouTube and at the time of writing had reached almost 60 million views (Rap against Dictatorship 2019). The group used the latest technology to evade government censorship, employing encryption to protect its song on YouTube. Earlier, the deputy national police chief, Srivara Ransibrahmanakul, warned that the video may be breaking the law and the artists were summoned to testify before the NCPO. In an attempt to prevent the video from being lost to censorship, an unknown individual placed 'Rap against Dictatorship' in the Zcoin blockchain using an IPFS link embedded in a transaction on the blockchain. Zcoin is a privacy coin, which is the first full implementation of the Zerocoin Protocol. As a result, the video now has a permanent and indelible copy in the IPFS link on the Zcoin blockchain at block number 111089 (Hundeyin 2018).

Conclusion

The Thai press has long struggled to preserve its freedom. When the political atmosphere is democratic, the media celebrates its freedom of speech. But as the case of Thailand has demonstrated, not all democratic regimes are champions of press freedom. The Thaksin administration prioritized protecting its own agenda at the expense of the media. The situation went from bad to worse following regime change in Thailand in 2006, and once again in 2014. In both cases, elected governments were overthrown paving the way for the return of the military in politics. Regime change had a massive impact on press freedom as the resurgence of authoritarianism has undermined freedom of the press. Democratic backsliding has eroded civil liberties, including the freedom of expression

Since the 2014 coup, the junta has issued a number of orders and decrees that restrict press freedom, on top of the existing draconian lèse-majesté law and the 2017 Computer Crime Act. These legal measures range from prosecuting journalists critical of the military government or the monarchy to suspending or shutting down media companies on the pretext of national security. In addition to such legal measures, the military government deploys other methods to pressure the press, in particular foreign journalists working in Thailand. These tactics include delays in granting and renewal of visas and even expulsion from the country. The situation has become so dangerous that the media have chosen to practice self-censorship in order to survive under the growing climate of fear. Some reporters go further, acting as propagandists for the military in order to avoid being targets of the state and to reap certain benefits from their relationship with the generals.

The political landscape of Thailand, divided along ideological lines, contributes to a lack of public support for press freedom. The pro-military and pro-monarchy Yellow Shirt camp refuses to stand up for the freedom of media outlets close to its enemies in the Red Shirt faction. The situation has perpetuated discrimination and injustice within the press community as a whole. And as fake news emerges onto the political scene, it has the potential to widen the rift between the two political factions. But there is not just bad news when it comes to press freedom in Thailand. The arrival of social media has opened up a space not only for the media, but also for ordinary Thais to engage in politics in a freer manner, despite the existence of laws restricting free expression. Social media allows Thais to voice their criticisms of the government without having to go to the streets to protest. It also helps redirect the flow of information, from being one way and top-down, to becoming more decentralized and participatory, thus indirectly fostering democracy – at least in cyberspace.

Notes

1 On the throne since 1946, King Bhumibol Adulyadej passed away in October 2016. Bhumibol remains a much revered figure even today.
2 Red Shirts are supporters of former Prime Minister Thaksin Shinawatra. The movement first emerged on the political scene in the aftermath of the 2006 coup that overthrew Thaksin. Its initial objective was to protest against the military intervention in politics.

References

BBC. (2016) 'Profile: Thailand's new King Vajiralongkorn', *BBC News*. Online. Available HTTP: <www.bbc.com/news/world-asia-38126928> (accessed 5 April 2019).

Campbell, C. (2014) 'The Thai Junta wants to force critics living abroad to return home', *Time*. Online. Available HTTP: <http://time.com/2856169/the-thai-junta-wants-to-its-force-critics-living-abroad-to-return-home/> (accessed 21 March 2019).

Chachavalpongpun, P. (2011) 'The necessity of enemies in Thailand's troubled politics', *Asian Survey*, 51: 1019–1041.

Chachavalpongpun, P. (2014) 'The politics of social media and information in Thailand', *Global Asia*, 9: 54–60.

Chachavalpongpun, P. (2018) 'Is Thailand ready for its youngest prime minister?', *The Diplomat*. Online. Available HTTP: <https://thediplomat.com/201/03/is-thailand-ready-for-its-youngest-prime-minister> (accessed 26 February 2019).

Charuvastra, T. (2018), 'Editor removed for mismanagement – Not Junta pressure: Bangkok Post'. Online. Available HTTP: <www.khaosodenglish.com/politics/2018/05/15/editor-removed-for-mismanagement-not-junta-pressure-bangkok-post/> (accessed 21 March 2019).

Chongkittavorn, K. (2005) 'The withered state of Thailand's press freedom', *The Nation*. Online. Available HTTP: <https://forum.thaivisa.com/topic/295997-thaksin-wheres-press-freedom/> (accessed 17 August 2019).

Constant, M. (2010) 'Who killed Italian photographer Fabio Polenghi?', *New Mandala*. Online. Available HTTP: <http://asiapacific.anu.edu.au/newmandala/2010/08/17/who-killed-italian-photographer-fabio-polenghi/> (accessed 26 February 2019).

'Dr Seree Yok Pad Hedpol Obrom Tee Thanathorn Min Khonthai Chobyim Proahrai Choodyuen' [De Seree raises 8 reasons why Thanathorn was considered insulting Thais just because of their smiling faces]. (2019) *Thai Post*. Online. Available HTTP: <www.thaipost.net/main/detail/29480> (accessed 5 April 2019).

Farrelly, N. (2003) 'Assault on Nick Nostitz', *New Mandela*. Online. Available HTTP: <http://asiapacific.anu.edu.au/newmandala/2013/11/29/assault-on-nick-nostitz/> (accessed 26 February 2019).

Hays, J. (2014) 'Media in Thailand: Censorship, Thaksin, television, and newspapers gull of gory pictures', *Facts and Details*. Online. Available HTTP: <http://factsanddetails.com/southeast-asia/Thailand/sub5_8e/entry-3267.html> (accessed 26 February 2019).

Holmes, O. (2017) 'Thailand bans online contact with three critics of regime', *The Guardian*. Online. Available HTTP: <www.theguardian.com/world/2017/apr/13/thailand-bans-online-sharing-of-articles-by-three-critics-of-regime> (accessed 26 February 2019).

Hundeyin, D. (2018) 'Activists use crypto to protect "Rap against dictatorship" from government censorship', *CCN*. Online. Available HTTP: <www.ccn.com/activists-use-crypto-to-protect-rap-against-dictatorship-from-government-censorship> (accessed 25 February 2019).

'Joint statement on Strategic Litigation against Public Participation (SLAPP)', *Human Rights Watch*. Online. Available HTTP: <www.nationmultimedia.com/detail/opinion/30337470> (accessed 26 February 2019).

Kentish, B. (2016) 'Crop-tops, mistresses and flying poodles: Meet the next King of Thailand', *The Independent*. Online. Available HTTP: <www.independent.co.uk/news/world/asia/thailand-new-king-crown-prince-maha-vajiralongkor-bangkok-poodle-tattoo-a7361021.html> (accessed 21 March 2019).

Khai Maew. (2019) March 21. Available HTTP: <www.facebook.com/cartooneggcatx/> (accessed 21 April 2019).

Leesa-nguansuk, S. (2018) 'Thailand makes top 10 in social media use'. Online. Available HTTP: <www.bangkokpost.com/tech/local-news/1420086/thailand-makes-top-10-in-social-media-use> (accessed 21 March 2019).

Lui, S. (2019) 'How Thailand's ruling general could stay in the prime minister's seat', *The Diplomat*. Online. Available HTTP: <https://thediplomat.com/2019/02/how-thailands-ruling-general-could-stay-in-the-prime-ministers-seat/> (accessed 26 February 2019).

Macan-Markar, M. (2017) 'Thai Junta steps up internet censorship drive', *Nikkei Asian Review*. Online. Available HTTP: <https://asia.nikkei.com/Politics/Thai-junta-steps-up-internet-censorship-drive> (accessed 21 March 2019).

McCargo, D. (2003) *Media and Politics in Pacific Asia*, London and New York: Routledge.

McCargo, D. (2017) 'New media, new partisanship: Divided virtual politics in and beyond Thailand', *International Journal of Communication*, 11: 4138–4157.

Phongpaichit, P. and Baker, C. (2004) *Thaksin: The Business of Politics in Thailand*, Copenhagen: NAIS.

Phongpaichit, P. and Baker, C. (2008) *Thaksin*, Chiangmai: Silkworm Books.

'Police pressure FCCT over #MBK39election meeting', (2018) *The Nation*. Online. Available HTTP: <www.nationmultimedia.com/detail/politics/30338009> (accessed 24 February 2019).

Rap against Dictatorship – ประเทศกูมี (2019) Youtube video added by Rap against Dictatorship. Online. Available HTTP: <www.youtube.com/watch?v=VZvzvLiGUtw<> (accessed 21 April 2019).

Reporters sans Frontieres. (2019) 'Thailand'. Online. Available HTTP: <https://rsf.org/en/thailand> (accessed 6 April 2019).

Sombatpoonsiri, J. (2019) 'Fake news and Thailand's information wars', *The Diplomat*. Online. Available http: <https://thediplomat.com/2019/07/fake-news-and-thailands-information-wars/> (accessed 17 August 2019).

Sopranzetti, C. (2017) 'From love to fear: The rise of King Vajiralongkorn', *Al Jazeera*. Online. Available HTTP: <www.aljazeera.com/indepth/opinion/2017/04/thailand-junta-king-vajiralongkorn-170411102300288.html> (accessed 26 February 2019).

Streckfuss, D. (2014) 'Freedom and silencing under the neo-absolutist monarchy regime in Thailand, 2006–2011', in P. Chachavalpongpun (ed.) *'Good Coup' Gone Bad: Thailand's Political Developments since Thaksin's Downfall*, Singapore: Institute of Southeast Asian Studies.

Streckfuss, D. (2019) 'Repression and self-censorship under Thailand's military dictatorship', in P. Chachavalpongpun (ed.) *Coup, King, Crisis: Time of a Dangerous Interregnum in Thailand*, Singapore: NUS Press.

'Supreme court rules against Prachatai in internet intermediary liability case'. (2015) *Prachatai*, Online. Available HTTP: <https://prachatai.com/english/node/5725> (accessed 24 February 2019).

'Thailand to offer compensation for slain Japanese'. (2012) *AFP*. Online. Available HTTP: <www.google.com/hostednews/afp/article/ALeqM5iKayQxTk5cKkU0p5

9t3ODwd8l1Xw?docId=CNG.cb10f0d0d9e1040731189773f7f0cf95.761> (accessed 26 February 2019).

'Thai police shut down journalists' discussion about Rohingya'. (2018) *Voice of America*. Online. Available HTTP: <www.voanews.com/a/thailand-police-intervene-in-rohingya-talk/4566369.html> (accessed 24 February 2019).

'Thai reporters, editors axed as press freedom declines'. (2018) *La Croix*. Online. Available HTTP: <https://international.la-croix.com/news/thai-reporters-editors-axed-as-press-freedom-declines/7687#> (accessed 26 February 2019).

Thavevong, K. (2018) 'Media freedom takes beating under Junta', *The Nation*. Online. Available HTTP: <www.nationmultimedia.com/detail/big_read/30346296> (accessed 26 February 2019).

'Three years of the NCPO and its reinforcement of "stable, prosperous and sustainable" powers'. (2017) *iLaw*. Online. Available HTTP: <https://ilaw.or.th/node/4506> (accessed 5 April 2019).

'Wassana Nanuam Oh Sappakhun Prawit konchuayjang Pom Nalika Hloo Pen Khong Pheungsee' [Wassana Nanuam praises prawit before helping to explain the controversy surrounding the Watches Scandal]. *Manager Online*. Online. Available HTTP: <https://mgronline.com/onlinesection/detail/9600000126854> (accessed 5 April 2019).

16
VIETNAMESE MEDIA GOING SOCIAL

Connectivism, collectivism and conservatism

Giang Nguyen-Thu

Introduction

June 2018 was an intense time in Vietnam when one saw the role of social media in revealing and facilitating the (dis)congruity between connectivism, collectivism and conservatism. On 12 June, the National Assembly of Vietnam passed the controversial Cybersecurity Law by a landslide of 86 per cent in favour despite widespread public dissent, including an online petition signed by more than 65,000 people. The new Cybersecurity Law was said to further restrict the already limited freedom of expression in Vietnam and grant too much power to the police in monitoring and punishing online citizens.

The adoption of the Cybersecurity Law happened just three days after the Assembly postponed its vote for the Special Economic Zone Law, another contentious bill that would allow foreign investors to obtain up to 99-year land leases in selected areas. This delay appeared to be an effort to soothe public anger, which had been fervidly manifested on Facebook in the previous weeks despite government assurances that the Special Economic Zone Law would only enable China to encroach on Vietnamese land in the name of economic development.

Despite the postponement, protests driven by an anti-China sentiment erupted across the nation on 10–11 June, including a violent riot in the southern province of Binh Thuan. Mainstream media in Vietnam provided minimal information on these events, using carefully selected terms such as 'gathering' or 'traffic congestion' to downplay any significant social instability. Censorship of the mass media, however, could no longer prevent people from knowing what was happening. The protests were covered on a real-time basis on Facebook thanks to constant updating of statuses, photos and livestream videos. Anyone connected to social media during those days could feel as if they were witnessing the event live and irresistibly engaged in a collective mixture of anger, anxiety, curiosity and enthusiasm. Thanks to the facilitating role of social media, political disruptions in Vietnam were literally a few clicks away.

The passing of the Cybersecurity Law on 12 June, right after the ebbing of the demonstrations, provided a dispiriting end to a cascade of spirited online and offline public activism. While some activists continued to lament the intensified restrictions on freedom of expression, most Facebook users gradually returned to their banal routines. The World Cup opened on 14 June, soon marginalizing political debates, reminding us how Facebook has been first and foremost a platform for ordinary pleasure and concerns. But on 25 June, when the graduation examinations for high school students commenced, Facebook postings again erupted, albeit with less intensity, when people took the opportunity to share their views on the quality of the tests while cleverly mocking the state's consistent failure to make any meaningful change in the educational system. The constant coming and going of Facebook-based public debates remind us that dissenting discussion on social media, whether subtly expressed in a sarcastic tone or frankly manifested in an activist message, never completely disappears, but is always latent in the banality of the everydayness, where ordinary people constantly surf through the trending information endlessly fed to their digital 'walls.'

There are several things one can learn about the Vietnamese media landscape from the unfolding of multiple Facebook-based social movements in June 2018. Most clearly, social media increasingly play an essential role in driving public opinion in Vietnam. The case of collective resistance against controversial legislation in June 2018 was just one among multiple examples in which Facebook served as a platform to defend the perceived public good. But the adoption of a restrictive and conservative Cybersecurity Law in June 2018 indicates how the internet and social media have become urgent concerns for the Vietnamese party-state, allowing it to justify the escalation of political oppression in the name of national security. The fact that the Special Economic Zone Law was postponed under intense public pressure while the Cybersecurity Law was adopted despite significant dissent reminds us that the party-state regards this as a crucial battleground. Whatever social media means to the public and the party-state, it is an undeniable fact that the Vietnamese media landscape is complicated, if not significantly transformed, by the surging expansion of social media in the last ten years.

This chapter provides a broader context to help understand the current dynamics of the Vietnamese media. This task requires a review of how the Vietnamese media system operates, including its censorship mechanisms, its commercial impulse and its struggle to balance between the state, the market and the public demand for quality information. Against this background, I provide a short history of social media (predominantly Facebook, as it had over 45 million Vietnamese users by 2019) in Vietnam and how it is driven by an escalating sense of political and social precarity. In so doing, I hope to engage readers in a more nuanced description of mediated activities in Vietnam beyond the state-centric view, and to diagnose the governing rationality of the party-state behind the adoption of the Cybersecurity Law.

The 'traditional' media landscape

In Vietnam, the mass media are state institutions by law, meaning that there is strictly no private ownership of newspapers, magazines or broadcasting services. The media system is regulated by two main regulatory bodies: the Ministry of Information and Communication (*Bộ Thông Tin và Truyền Thông*) and the Central Propaganda and Education Commission (*Ban Tuyên Giáo Trung Ương*). The former mainly governs legal, technical and economic aspects of the media industries, while the latter deals exclusively with ideological gatekeeping. Operating directly under the Communist Party, the Central Propaganda and Education Commission is the top media censor, working hard to ensure that despite extensive changes in media technology and economy, media practitioners remain committed to the party's agenda.

Although censorship, by nature, operates in secrecy, there is at least one publicly known censoring mechanism in Vietnam: the weekly and mandatory meetings in Hanoi between the Central Propaganda and Education Commission, the Ministry of Information and Communication, and leaders of all media institutions (Tuyên 2008). These meetings provide a review of media activities in the previous week and deliver specific guidance on what should and should not be published in the coming week. The most visible effect of these weekly closed-door meetings is the concerted and uniform coverage of many politically important events. For example, in March 2018, after decades of collective silence, all major newspapers in Vietnam ran extended features with elaborate infographics to commemorate the fallen soldiers in the naval battle between Vietnam and China at Gạc Ma Island 30 years before. In the context of heated territorial disputes in the South China Sea, the fact that this topic returned so boldly in mainstream media after a few years of simmering Facebook-based commemoration indicated that the state had finally given a green light for a public review of this muted trauma. But the boundary of what can be said was also clearly indicated. All mainstream stories honoured the forgotten martyrs without any critical discussion of contemporary Vietnam-China relations, showing how the stories about Gạc Ma Island were permitted but not allowed to get too hot or fan latent anti-Chinese flames, which are commonly coupled with anti-state sentiments. Just as anti-Japanese protests in China are handy vehicles for voicing anti-government sentiments because the authorities are relatively tolerant of such expressions of patriotic loyalty, anti-Chinese protests in Vietnam are one of the few ways that people can express their grievances with the Vietnamese state.

A possibly more insidious mechanism of media governance in Vietnam is self-censorship. Silently embedded in journalistic anecdotes, editorial processes, and lessons at journalism schools, political censorship is a naturalized part of media production. Very early in their careers, journalists learn to imagine and anticipate the censor's reaction for almost everything they produce. The taboos for mainstream media are well remembered: no critical review of socialist history, no defaming of national heroes and socialist leaders, no encouragement of political pluralism, no promotion of democracy and no criticism of human rights abuses. Grey areas include, for example, stories about major corruption cases, environmental pollution and land disputes, as well as critical reviews of important policies. This does not mean that Vietnamese journalists only write what they are told to, but that an essential part of their job is to identify risk, to avoid being negatively listed and to be creative in the grey area that is expanding or shrinking depending on different political situations. Crossing the censorship boundary requires strategic calculation and, in many ways, exposing oneself to the risk of being punished. Taking this risk, however, is necessary for maintaining a media outlet's professional pride and public credibility. Working with and against censorship is thus an art, resulting in a constant tension between journalists, editorial teams, and the governing system.

Regarding media reception, one of the key consequences of blunt political propaganda is that it could never fully convince the audiences. An average reader in Vietnam would know that most news stories are politically monitored. Instead of being passive receivers of propagandist messages, many readers master the skill of reading between the lines, in line with audiences in other communist states. Mocking mainstream narratives is highly common, being a pervasive form of cultural intimacy in both urban and rural areas. Readers or viewers today often share their political concerns on Facebook, comparing news sources and highlighting their sceptical interpretation of official information, and many times inventing their own conspiracy theories based on inputs from both the state-run media and alternative sources.

It would be misleading, however, to talk about media governance in Vietnam with a sole focus on political restrictions, a topic that is central to most international discussions of Vietnamese media. Extensive commercialization is another key feature that significantly shapes the post-reform media landscape. Since the 1990s, the market has steadily permeated all aspects of the media system and fundamentally transformed the way practitioners conduct their professional life. Journalists certainly feel disappointed by restrictive rules imposed from above, but what makes them most anxious is actually the market. Top-down surveillance, after all, is relatively stable and, in many ways, predictable. The market, on the contrary, is volatile and getting more competitive each year. Turning to the market as a source of funding and agency, media practitioners are inevitably trapped between their profitmaking duty and their political obligations.

Regarding its relationship with the market, the party-state is more responsive than repressive. Soon after the 'doi moi' market-oriented reforms launched in the 1980s, the party-state actively outsourced the burden of funding the media to the market. In the television industry, for example, producers started providing viewers with a daily dose of popular entertainment in the 1990s after decades of cultural hunger. Soon these programmes generated a stable source of income from advertisements, creating a strong inducement to produce more. Within less than a decade, foreign and domestic dramas, game shows, talk shows and reality programmes quickly saturated broadcasting time, turning the television industry into a major profitmaking platform. Producers are encouraged, if not forced, to make self-funded shows, almost entirely for entertainment purposes, without much restraint from above. In 2009, the state officially allowed television stations to collaborate with private partners in production activities, with the exception of news and current affairs (Ministry of Information and Communication 2009; Vietnamese Government 2016). The result is that private ownership of television is strictly banned, but private production of television content is quite common. A similar process also happens in the production of lifestyle magazines and many newspapers. In 2018, advertisement and commercial sponsorship served as key sources of funding for many free-to-air television stations, and all major newspapers and lifestyle magazines, putting media practitioners in an intense competition for profits. The defining characteristic of the contemporary Vietnamese media is thus not just political censorship, but the raw combination of political surveillance and commercial pressures.

Businesspeople increasingly have influence over the media, many times acting as hidden censors of nonpolitical content. Market-based power relies on an intricate and flexible network of financial incentives, collaborative partnership, informal friendship and political investment. Commercial sponsorship is extremely common in the television industry, which is easily detected by pop-up logos on the backdrops of almost all popular shows, sometimes even in news and current affairs. Securing a commercial sponsor is one of the key criteria to grant permission for a new programme while rewriting the content to fit the taste of the sponsor has become a norm. Consider, for example, the case of Oppo, a Chinese smartphone brand recently gaining a significant presence in Vietnam. Since 2015, the green logo of Oppo has appeared on many top-rated game shows, comedy shows and reality shows on the national airwaves, where participating celebrities are intentionally chosen to be the brand's ambassadors. VOV, the national radio system, also regularly announces its 'partnership' with major businesses, such as a major milk company or a giant real estate group (Lưu 2016; Phương 2017). It is now a poorly kept secret that the media in Vietnam relies on its relationship with firms for funding, either through direct sponsorship or more concealed forms of public relations.

Drawn into a rapid process of marketization, Vietnamese media practitioners increasingly choose to detour from 'sensitive' topics to focus on commercially rewarding – but politically benign – content. Soon, the commercialized content gained more popularity than politically laden messages, inevitably lessening the dominance of political propaganda. The market thus adds more distraction and fragmentation than significant reformation to the Vietnamese media landscape. Overall, the media remains committed to the political interest of the party-state, while is also inclined to provide a voice for rising business elites and to represent the tastes of the middle class. In many ways, the combination of state and the market further marginalizes radical voices and genuine political debates, redirecting the audience away from critical awareness of structural oppression in both political and economic aspects.

Social media and the new dynamics of Vietnamese media

In 2009, when Yahoo! 360 officially closed, Vietnamese bloggers flooded into Facebook, then an unfamiliar medium of digital connectivity, to continue their online interactions. It took a couple of years until users could access Facebook without expecting technical hindrances, although the Vietnamese government never admitted to establishing a firewall targeting this global social network. Facebook experienced a major surge in 2012, with an increase of nearly 300 per cent from 2.9 million to 8.2 million users within just a year, officially surpassing Zing Me, the largest indigenous social media platform in Vietnam (Mueller 2013). In early 2015, when the number of Facebook users reached 30 million, Vietnamese Prime Minister Nguyễn Tấn Dũng declared that 'it is impossible to ban or prevent people from posting information on the Internet,' urging the government to provide timely and accurate information for the public on social media (Hoàng 2015). This announcement was delivered at a time when there had been a widespread rumour in the blogosphere and on social media that Nguyễn Bá Thanh, the former party secretary of Đà Nẵng City, was poisoned to death by his political rivals (Duong 2017: 382). By July 2018, Vietnam had about 64 million active Facebook users, serving as one of the most thriving digital markets in the world (Hà 2017). Within less than a decade, Facebook has become a ubiquitous digital platform in a country with strict censorship over the media.

In the first few years after its arrival in Vietnam, Facebook was mainly used for benign online interactions, but from around 2015, when it became a dominant platform, Facebook has increasingly acted as a dynamic and disruptive element in the Vietnamese media system, significantly destabilizing and undermining the traditional forces from the party-state and the market. Proving itself to be a potent medium for agenda setting, Facebook directly competes with mainstream media outlets in attracting public attention and framing a salient perspective on social and political controversies. The most valued transformation from the perspective of civil society has been the emergence of multiple dissenting movements that were previously marginalized by both the state and the market. In the wake of social media's surging popularity, as Thiem Hai Bui (2016) argues, the space of civil society in Vietnam has been significantly thickened by more critical voices with stronger influence over elite politics. A culture of protest was formed, against which the party-state felt compelled to respond or repress. There have been a number of cases in which social media provided a public forum for collective resistance against government policies and directives. The successful campaign to protect 6,700 trees from being chopped down on the order of Hanoi's authorities in March 2015 was one of the earliest and most discussed examples (Bui 2016; Le et al. 2015). Another well-known event was the 'I choose fish' movement in June 2016 in response to the environmental crisis caused by Formosa, the Taiwanese steel company based in the central province of Ha Tinh (Reuters 2016). In July 2017, Facebook continued to serve as a vital channel for publicizing a political scandal related to a land dispute, something the party-state would certainly have concealed in the past. In the Dong Tam commune of Hanoi, dozens of police officers and officials were taken hostage for more than a week by a group of villagers, who risked their lives to protect their land from being appropriated by Viettel, a military telecommunications group. As the hostage crisis escalated, leaked information, mainstream news, and casual commentaries were liberally shared on Facebook, connecting social media users into an acute imagined community of vicarious citizenship. The case was resolved peacefully when the villagers reached a satisfactory settlement with Hanoi's authorities. This relieving 'happy ending' largely resulted from intense public pressure for a non-violent solution, which was collectively expressed on social media by activists and common people alike (Ives 2017; BBC 2017). In June 2018, as mentioned earlier, Facebook once more set the nation on fire when the proposals for the Special Economic Zone Law and the Cybersecurity Law sparked widespread opposition. After the disappointing adoption of the Cybersecurity Law, Facebook users continued to update their walls, knowing that their online activities were officially regulated. In this context of a contested digital future, social media users curiously wait for a new political scandal to test the waters and assess the oppressive intentions of the government.

Narrowly focusing on political dissent, however, risks overlooking the dispersed and amorphous power of Facebook, driven more by a techno-economic mechanism than a shared political rationality. Facebook operates in a far more complex way than being an automatic and organized instrument of political resistance. Its algorithm gives prominence to all trending messages, politically driven or not. On a daily basis, Facebook constantly facilitates public awareness and social interpretation of numerous economic, social and cultural issues without an explicit political implication. The repertoire of meanings, feelings and tensions within which Vietnamese people navigate is broadened and thickened, ceaselessly drawing its symbols, myths, significance and contradictions from the contemporary landscape of globalization and the historical depth of collective glories, yearnings, and sufferings. This expanding repertoire is archived, indexed, categorized, and disseminated in a many-to-many model, interwoven into and contaminating the traditional one-to-many model of the mass media. Almost unnoticeably, citizens have become more alert, more informed and less cautious in raising their critical voice and in expressing their sentiments about virtually all aspects of collective and private living. As a result, the space for civil society expands with Facebook, but uncivility, mere banality, blatant sentimentality, viral populist messages and the hegemonic power of the market are also on the rise. At the micropolitical intervention of Facebook, public life becomes more observable and political criticism seems more synchronized, but living itself becomes more tangled, overwhelming, constantly changing and filled with precarity.

There are plenty of examples of how Facebook stirs up social life and amplifies collective sentiments at the level of ordinary living. Consider, for instance, the story of the Vietnamese U23 football team that made history by winning second place at the Asian Football Confederation Youth Championships in January 2018. Vietnamese people have always been ardent football lovers, but this time, Facebook added much more emotional intensity and symbolic substance to existing sports fandom. Each match was turned into a striking collective event, as watching was inseparable from Facebooking. The contagion of popular nationalist sentiments was unprecedented for a sports event when the U23 team was welcomed home by massive traffic congestion right from the airport and by more than 40,000 people waiting at the national stadium to meet their overnight idols. Possibly all Facebook walls in Vietnam during those days were flooded by images of the young team, news and editorials, memes and comics, flags and quotations, and, many times, clever ambush advertising messages. Facebook's principles of connectivity, narrativity and intimacy had allowed this platform to exceedingly amplify the youthful spirit of the team, helping to elevate the whole country, at least for a few days, at a time of pervasive social pessimism. Similar cases of Facebook-based social events are countless: a housewife-led boycott against a top singer for her love affair with a married man, the problematic deaths of vaccinated infants, a food safety crisis related to arsenic-laced fish sauce, a #MeToo story of celebrity sexual abuse, a multi-million-dollar divorce between the owners of a national coffee brand, a British royal wedding, the World Cup, and so on. People increasingly make use of Facebook as a place to express their emotions, most predominantly the feelings of anxiety and disappointment, while also to cultivate new hopes and fantasies commonly driven by a neoliberal impulse.

Predictably, the power of social media in framing the public agenda in Vietnam creates an escalating pressure on the party-state, not only when there is a radical political event, but also at the level of daily regulation. For the first time, the party-state completely lost its ownership and direct control over a media platform. The prolific, borderless, and technologically sophisticated nature of social media increasingly eluded existing mechanisms of media governance. Already busy with the task of monitoring the mass media, which never fully obey the rules, the government now spends even more time responding to viral events on Facebook. In the first six months of 2018, there were multiple cases in which public debates on social media directly shaped the outcome or impact of a social event, forcing the authorities to join the discussion. In March 2018, for example, the Ministry of Health had to spend a week of intense investigation just to confirm that the widely shared story of a young woman dying at home after giving 'natural' birth to her child was just a pure hoax (Lê 2018a). In May, a clip of an English teacher verbally abusing an adult student fuelled heated debates about educational ethics in Vietnam, forcing the Department of Education and Training in Hanoi to comment on the case and then to permanently close the teacher's English centre (Hùng 2018). At that time, Facebookers were also outraged when a child molester managed to gain a reduction of his sentence from three years in jail to a suspended sentence of 18 months. What infuriated the public even more was that this shortened sentence was justified by the man's old age, his previous position as a director of a bank and, most ironically, his Communist Party membership. An online petition to demand a review of the case was launched and immediately went viral, gaining 50,000 signatures within a week (Lê 2018b; Change.org 2018). In an effort to calm public anger, the Supreme Court in Ho Chi Minh City revoked the commutation and reinstated the original sentence.

Media practitioners and journalists tend to add more fuel to the fire, seeing social media as an essential source of information, but also a key rival. Mainstream outlets often follow up and elaborate on viral content on Facebook in order to attract more viewing traffic and to assert their relevance to public life, significantly participating in and intensifying the debates on social media, and consequently increasing the coordination of information circulated online. Anytime it is possible, the mainstream media rely on the public momentum facilitated by social media to expand the boundaries of political discussion, pushing the authorities to comment on the case and take responsibility. Many journalists also choose to directly express their views – often unorthodox ones – on Facebook to boost their personal brands or to draw more attention to their official stories on mainstream outlets. The practice of writing for mainstream media in one voice and explaining the same story in another voice on Facebook with more nuances and criticism is now quite common among media workers.

The rise of Facebook has added new dynamics to the existing blogosphere that has long served as an alternative source of political news and opinion in Vietnam (Duong 2017). In comparison to previous forms of non-mainstream discourses, Facebook is the only medium that can effectively mobilize and mass-customize public sentiments at the capillary level of ordinary life. While dissenting blogs and alternative publishing mainly rely on the aura of unique political voices to assert their influence over the Vietnamese public sphere, hence promoting the logic of rarity, Facebook works by synchronizing elite voices with the abundance of mass political dissatisfaction embedded in the ordinary sphere of daily life. Facebook thus generates an unprecedented amount of banal social debates, putting an end to the scarcity of engaged political and social discussions in Vietnam. Precisely thanks to the voluntary formation of more plural, alert, and vocal publics through Facebook's constant and contingent feeds of the quotidian, intimate and controversial stories of a common life, the collective momentum of political disruption is greatly strengthened. In other words, what is important about the impact of social media in Vietnam is not just the will to resist, but that social media has enabled an organic connection between radical political agendas and mass grievances. Such a connection was significantly missing in the former blogosphere occupied mainly by a few high-profile activist writers. Facebook and the blogosphere thus well complement each other, albeit with different political functions and effects. In the age of social media, the greatest challenge in censoring digital discourses, if that is the party-state's ambition, is thus no longer about punishing a few activists or settling specific political protests, but rather about distracting and diluting the negative sentiments over a range of issues that have become much thicker and more articulable due to the thorough penetration of social media into everyday life.

The Cybersecurity Law and the problem of fear-based censorship

The adoption of the Cybersecurity Law in June 2018 was the culmination of the party-state's escalating campaign against social media. In the preceding year, different strategies to cope with new digital challenges were announced in preparation for the passing of the bill. In early 2017, the government banned major Vietnamese firms from advertising on YouTube in an effort to pressure Google to remove 'toxic content' from its global video-sharing platform. This campaign was considered successful, as the Ministry of Information and Communication later claimed that Google had removed 6,423 videos and Facebook had terminated 159 accounts for 'defaming Vietnamese leaders' (Luân 2017; Trân 2018). In December 2017, the Ministry of Defense declared its 'cyberwarfare' against the negative impact of the internet, proudly introducing a unit of 10,000 members named 'Force 47' that works 'every hour, every minute, every second' to fight against 'erroneous views' online (Mai 2017). In this increasingly hostile discourse against social media and the internet, terms such as 'fake news,' 'trash information,' 'toxic content,' 'erroneous views' and 'hostile voices' are used interchangeably without any clear definition or differentiation. It is quite obvious, however, that the party-state simply equates these terms with any content that violates the censorship taboos traditionally applied to the mass media.

There are two points in the Cybersecurity Law that activists find particularly worrisome. First, the law requires online citizens to comply with an ambiguous and lengthy list of forbidden behaviours, many of which directly restrict the right to raise a critical voice. People are banned from using online platforms to, for instance, 'insult great men, national leaders, historical figures, and national heroes,' to 'distort history, negate revolutionary achievements, and undermine the national solidarity' or to disseminate 'untrue information that stirs obfuscation among the people' (Ministry of Defense 2018). Second, all digital platforms must store Vietnamese users' data within the country, provide users' data upon request, and remove all content that violates the law. The police, the military and other authorities are invested with the power to audit, collect data, block, terminate and prosecute any online platform that poses a danger to national security. The Cybersecurity Law demonstrates that ideologically, the party-state wants to control social media by relying on the same political restrictions long imposed on the mass media. Technically, the party-state aims at turning global platforms into more or less subordinate units under its command, trying to use the 'carrot-and-stick' strategy similar to the way it treats domestic media outlets. Overall, the Cybersecurity Law manifests an unconcealed thirst for digital sovereignty, highlighting the party-state's key concerns and strategies in the digital age.

But it is precisely because the Cybersecurity Law is so absolute in its protection of digital sovereignty that this new bill allows us to identify a major problem of internet governance in Vietnam: the party-state does not seem to understand the difference between mass media and social media. There is no paradigmatic shift in the ideological and technical vocabulary that the party-state uses to talk about social media. In other words, the 'what' and the 'how' of digital control in Vietnam still adhere to the old model of mass media discipline, which is performed primarily through direct determination between right and wrong, and immediate punishment upon detectable faults.

A comparative view from the case of China is useful to explore the implications of the Vietnamese Cybersecurity Law. In her study of the Chinese censorship system, Margaret E. Roberts (2018) convincingly demonstrates that the resilience of authoritarianism in the digital age relies on the capacity to govern online data beyond the traditional mechanism of punishment-based censorship. Internet control requires a clever amalgamation of ideological ambition and technological sophistication. Regarding China's desire for digital sovereignty, the 'what' of authoritarian censorship remains, but the 'how' has significantly grown beyond the old model. In addition to its fear-based control, China has systematically and effectively deployed two new forms of digital control: friction and flooding, resulting in a model of 'porous censorship' that allows the government to eschew the wholesale application of visible oppression (Roberts 2018: 1).

The strategy of friction involves the extensive blockage by the Great Firewall. In the last ten years, one by one, China has blocked almost all major online Western platforms: Google, Facebook, YouTube, Wikipedia, Instagram and Pinterest. Almost all international news sources are banned, and many take an extremely long time to load. The strategy of friction can be easily circumvented by tech-savvy users and politically concerned citizens – hence, it is incomplete – but it works well by depending upon 'the impatience and indifference' of the majority, who are generally too busy to sacrifice their time and energy to be informed about what is missing from mainstream media (Roberts 2018: 224). The key impact of the friction strategy is that it intensifies the disconnection between the dispersed momentum of the masses and the politically active elites in China, and consequently 'prevents coordination of the core and the periphery, known to be an essential component in successful collective action' (Roberts 2018: 8). It is only when a wedge is driven between the masses and the elites that the targeted punishment of a few high-profile activists becomes effective. Thus, at the heart of Chinese internet censorship is the capacity to customize its digital control over different political segments of the population.

The strategy of flooding is performed by the constant production and circulation of hundreds of millions of politically neutral and misleading messages to mould the results of algorithm-based information flows. It is estimated that the Chinese government employed as many as 2 million people, the so-called

'50-cent-party,' to post a massive amount of distracting and confusing messages, about 448 million social media comments a year (King, Pan and Roberts 2017). This results in a diluted online environment without strong coordination of politically controversial information, making it less likely for the algorithm to identify and amplify collective grievance or negative voices. The flooding strategy also makes it more time-consuming for readers to differentiate between valuable information and spam, which again discourages impatient readers and further disconnects the few politically sophisticated people from the politically inactive masses.

Most importantly, the two techniques of friction and flooding are applied in a thriving and self-sustaining nationalized world of Chinese apps and platforms, which provides sufficient online services for a population of 1.4 billion people without having to rely on any Western platform. Internet control in China has thus significantly grown out of the traditional model that seeks merely to threaten, remove or punish violators. This system uses multiple clever and costly methods of data manipulation and digital nationalization that aim to alter the possibility for data production and coordination. Such power to govern at the environment-setting level demonstrates how digital control in China has structurally departed from traditional forms of media censorship.

The Vietnamese Cybersecurity Law is commonly criticized as a duplicate of its Chinese counterpart. Indeed, this is a valid argument if one looks at the party-state's ambition to impose ideological discipline on online discourses. But this might be a misleading diagnosis if we consider the technological reality on the Vietnamese side. The key strategy of digital governance in Vietnam is still punishment based. Punishment can only be performed upon detectable targets, which is useful to terminate radical resistance and high-profile dissenters. But given the daily production and coordination of an immense amount of data online, it is impossible for this strategy to alter the formation and amplification of collective grievance and ordinary dissent. Blatant fear-based censorship can actually backfire in the age of digital freedom, because it only intensifies the desire to resist and to circumvent the concealing techniques, which is precisely what has been happening in Vietnam. The more the government tries to block and punish specific cases of dissent, the more people become curious to find out what actually happened, and come up with conspiracy theories that cast the party-state in an unflattering light.

Regarding the flooding strategy, the so-called 'Force 47' in Vietnam is hardly comparable to its Chinese counterpart. The Vietnamese team (10,000 members compared to 2 million in China) seems to work by engaging in polemics to defend the party-state, rather than by diluting the information environment using neutral or misleading comments. As far as Facebook's algorithms work, the more engagement on a certain topic, regardless of its ideological tendency, the more likely the topic starts trending. The strategy of directly fighting against 'toxic content' by Force 47 might backfire and fuel the anti-state flames by thickening the information flows into the debates. The facts that Facebook still powerfully frames public discourse in Vietnam and provides a platform for anti-state views despite the expansion of Force 47 indicate that this team is not effective at distracting Vietnamese users from public discussions of politically sensitive topics.

Regarding the friction strategy, the Vietnamese party-state is much less likely to block all global platforms due to a severe lack of domestic alternatives. Whereas Baidu and Weibo, launched in 2000 and 2009, remain respectively the dominant search engine and social media platform in China, as of 2017, the Vietnamese authorities only promised that they would build indigenous platforms to replace Google and Facebook 'in the next five or seven years' (Nguyen 2017). Currently, Vietnam blocks many dissent blogs, particularly the ones using the Vietnamese language, but major global platforms with a significant role in promoting knowledge, entertainment and social and economic connectivity, such as Google, Wikipedia, YouTube, Facebook and Instagram, are accessed freely. The young and tech-savvy population in Vietnam has enjoyed the benefits of global communication since the inception of the internet in the country in 1997 and are keen on fighting for these benefits. The economic, social and developmental cost of blocking Vietnam from the global world of digital flows is too high because it can undermine economic growth, social stability and global engagement – all key indices to maintain the party-state's already shaky legitimacy. A technologically weak country like Vietnam is not in a position to resist digital globalization in the same ways as China has been doing. The passing of the Cybersecurity Law thus indicates an oppressive tendency in the ways the party-state handles online discourses, but this does not mean that the party-state is actually capable of preventing online platforms from dispersedly mobilizing social dynamics.

Conclusion

The immense world of big data appears as mysterious as the concealed world of authoritarian censorship. It is thus difficult to predict the future of either, in Vietnam or elsewhere. But there are several things we can conclude about the Vietnamese case by drawing from our understanding of the post-reform media settings, as well as the unfolding of public discourses related to social media in Vietnam and the recent adoption of the Vietnamese Cybersecurity Law. First, the media landscape in Vietnam has long been destabilized by market forces, and in recent years, further transfigured by new pressure from the internet and social media. In order to grasp the nuances of mediated activities in Vietnam, it is important to go beyond the simplistic view that tends to reduce the complexity of the Vietnamese media landscape to a simple problem of direct political antagonism. Second, while the party-state is responsive to the market and the internet, it stays committed to its centralized model of censorship, and is getting more repressive toward online discourses. The adoption of the Cybersecurity Law demonstrates the determination of the party-state to govern the digital world through the application of direct surveillance and punishment. This worrying fact confirms recent international concerns regarding the intensification of the party-state's discipline of political dissenters (Reuters 2018; Washington Post Editorial Board 2018). But the persistence of fear-based censorship also indicates that the party-state largely fails to recognize the sheer impossibility of monitoring online data by direct punishment. The party-state has done little, at least as evinced in the content of the Cybersecurity Law and its recent history of digital control, to governmentalize its traditional mechanism of censorship, as seen in the case of China.

During the first week of July 2018, about 100,000 Vietnamese registered their new accounts on Minds, a self-acclaimed 'decentralized' social network, out of concerns about Facebook's potential co-optation by the party-state (Giang 2018). Within less than a month, Facebook had lost a bit of its symbolic valence as a liberating tool of bottom-up activism in Vietnam, while Minds emerged as a new trend among those with an activist agenda, at least for a couple of weeks. While the party-state has done nothing particularly threatening to the future of Facebook since its adoption of the Cybersecurity Law, online Vietnamese citizens are already prepared for negative effects by looking around for other online platforms as alternatives to Facebook. As we are all waiting to witness the unfolding future of social media in Vietnam, there are two things that we are sure about: first, the speed of technological change is much faster than legislative and political adjustment in Vietnam, and second, Vietnamese internet users are keen on surfing new technological trends and are eager to use their tech-savvy skills to circumvent the party-state's ambition to turn Vietnam into a land of digital isolation. Failing to alter the conditions for the production and coordination of digital content, the party-state is trapped between its technological and financial inadequacy and its ideological ambition to build its world of digital sovereignty.

Acknowledgement

This research is funded by the Vietnam National Foundation for Science and Technology Development (NAFOSTED) under grant number 508.04–2018.02.

References

BBC. (2017) 'Dân Đồng Tâm không chống phá chính quyền' [Đồng Tâm people are not going against the government], *BBC Vietnamese*. Available HTTP: <www.bbc.com/vietnamese/vietnam-39642540> (accessed 6 April 2019).

Bui, T.H. (2016) 'The influence of social media in Vietnam's elite politics', *Journal of Current Southeast Asian Affairs*, 35: 89–111.

Change.org. (2018) 'Ask for a review of unsatisfied penalty regarding Nguyen Khac Thuy's sex crime on minors', *Changer.org*. Available HTTP: <www.change.org/p/vietnam-ask-for-a-review-of-unsatisfied-penalty-regarding-nguyen-khac-thuy-s-sex-crime-on-minors> (accessed 6 April 2019).

Duong, M. (2017) 'Blogging three ways in Vietnam's political blogosphere', *Contemporary Southeast Asia*, 39: 373–392.

Giang, T.H. (2018) 'CEO Bill Ottman Nói Gì Về Minds.com?' [What did CEO Bill Ottman say about Minds.com?], *BBC*. Available HTTP: <www.bbc.com/vietnamese/vietnam-44679954> (accessed 2 July 2018).

Hà, P. (2017) 'Vietnam climbs to seventh worldwide for number of Facebook users: Report', *VnExpress*. Available HTTP: <https://e.vnexpress.net/news/business/data-speaks/vietnam-climbs-to-seventh-worldwide-for-number-of-facebook-users-report-3614034.html> (accessed 10 June 2018).

Hoàng, T. (2015) 'Thủ Tướng: Không Thể Cấm Đưa Thông Tin Lên Mạng' [Prime Minister: It is impossible to prohibit online information], *VnExpress*. Available HTTP: <https://vnexpress.net/tin-tuc/thoi-su/thu-tuong-khong-the-cam-dua-thong-tin-len-mang-3134245.html> (accessed 10 June 2018).

Hùng, T. (2018) 'Chửi học viên là "lợn": Phạt cô giáo 5 triệu, giải thể trung tâm tiếng Anh' [Calling student "a pig": Teaching under a penalty of 5 million VND and the English center closed], *Vietnamnet*. Available HTTP: <https://vietnamnet.vn/vn/giao-duc/hoc-tieng-anh/co-giao-chui-hoc-vien-bi-phat-5-trieu-dong-va-dung-toan-bo-hoat-dong-giang-day-449896.html> (accessed 20 July 2019).

Ives, M. (2017) 'Vietnamese villagers release 19 officials held hostage in land dispute', *The New York Times*. Avaiable HTTP: <www.nytimes.com/2017/04/22/world/asia/vietnam-hostages-land-dispute.html> (accessed 7 April 2019).

King, G., Pan, J., and Roberts, M.E. (2017) 'How the Chinese government fabricates social media posts for strategic distraction, not engaged argument', *American Political Science Review*, 111: 484–501.

Lê, T. (2018a) 'Đề nghị xử lý người loan tin mẹ và con chết vì đẻ "tự nhiên"' [Suggestion of criminalizing those who spred information about mother who died after 'natural birth'], *Zing*. Available HTTP: <https://news.zing.vn/de-nghi-xu-ly-nguoi-loan-tin-me-va-con-chet-vi-de-tu-nhien-post826340.html> (accessed 20 July 2019).

Lê, K. (2018b) 'Tại sao giảm án cho ông Nguyễn Khắc Thủy vì "là Đảng viên"?' [Why shorten Nguyễn Khắc Thủy's sentence just because of his "Party membership"?], *Tuổi trẻ*. Available HTTP: <https://tuoitre.vn/tai-sao-giam-an-cho-ong-nguyen-khac-thuy-vi-la-dang-vien-20180514112749348.htm> (accessed 5 April 2019).

Le, Q.B., Đoan, T.H., Nguyen, T.T.N., and Mai, T.T. (2015) *Report on Movements to Protect #6700 Trees in Hanoi*, Hanoi: Hong Duc Publishing House. Available HTTP: <http://isee.org.vn/Content/Home/Library/472/reports-on-movements-to-protect-6700-trees-in-hanoi.pdf> (accessed 15 April 2018).

Luân, D. (2017) 'Gỡ Bỏ 159 Tài Khoản Facebook Nói Xấu, Bôi Nhọ Lãnh Đạo, Tuyên Truyền Chống Phá' [Removal of 159 Facebook accounts for insulting leaders and sabotaging the state], *Tiền Phong*. Available HTTP: <www.tienphong.vn/xa-hoi/go-bo-159-tai-khoan-facebook-noi-xau-boi-nho-lanh-dao-tuyen-truyen-chong-pha-1223389.tpo> (accessed 15 June 2018).

Lưu, H. (2016) 'VOV Ký Kết Hợp Tác Truyền Thông với Tập Đoàn TH' [VOV signed collaborative contract with TH group on communication], *Voice of Vietnam*. Available HTTP: <https://vov.vn/xa-hoi/vov-ky-ket-hop-tac-truyen-thong-voi-tap-doan-th-553381.vov> (accessed 1 June 2018).

Mai, H. (2017) 'Hơn 10.000 Người Trong 'Lực Lượng 47' Đấu Tranh Trên Mạng' [More than 10,000 members of 'Force 47' fighting for cybersecurity], *Tuổi Trẻ*. Available HTTP: <https://tuoitre.vn/hon-10-000-nguoi-trong-luc-luong-47-dau-tranh-tren-mang-20171225150602912.htm> (accessed 15 June 2018).

Ministry of Defence (Vietnam). (2018) 'Dự Thảo Luật An Ninh Mạng' [Proposal of cybersecurity law], *Dự Thảo Online*. Available HTTP: <http://duthaoonline.quochoi.vn/DuThao/Lists/dt_duthao_luat/View_Detail.aspx?ItemID=1382&LanID=1533&TabIndex=1> (accessed 10 June 2018).

Ministry of Information and Communication (Vietnam). (2009) 'Quy Định Về Việc Liên Kết Trong Hoạt Động Sản Xuất Chương Trình Phát Thanh, Truyền Hình' [Regulation on the collaborative production of television and radio programmes]. Available HTTP: <http://moj.gov.vn/vbpq/lists/vn%20bn%20php%20lut/view_detail. aspx?itemid=12016> (accessed 5 June 2018).

Mueller, C. (2013) 'Tech industry Vietnam going global', *Asia Life Magazine*. Available HTTP: <www.asialifemagazine.com/vietnam/tech-industry-vietnam/> (accessed 1 June 2018).

Nguyen, V. (2017) 'Bộ Trưởng Trương Minh Tuấn: Việt Nam Cần 5–7 Năm Để Thay Thế Facebook, Google' [Minister Trương Minh Tuấn: Vietnam needs five to seven years to replace Facebook, Google], *VnEconomy*. Available HTTP: <http://vnecon omy.vn/bo-truong-truong-minh-tuan-viet-nam-can-5-7-nam-de-thay-the-face book-google-20171117152029732.htm> (accessed 5 June 2018).

Phương, H. (2017) 'VOV Hợp Tác Truyền Thông Với Tập Đoàn FLC' [VOV collaborates with FLC group on communication], *Voice of Vietnam*. Available HTTP: <http:// vov.vn/xa-hoi/dau-an-vov/vov-hop-tac-truyen-thong-voi-tap-doan-flc-675833. vov> (accessed 10 June 2018).

Reuters. (2016) 'Vietnamese rally outside Taiwanese steel plant that spread toxic waste', *Reuters*. Available HTTP: <www.reuters.com/article/us-formosa-vietnam-protest/ vietnamese-rally-outside-taiwanese-steel-plant-that-spread-toxic-waste-idUSKCN 1220BB> (accessed 7 April 2019).

Reuters. (2018) 'Two more activists jailed in Vietnam amid widening dissent crackdown', *Reuters*. Available HTTP: <www.reuters.com/article/us-vietnam-dissidents/ two-more-activists-jailed-in-vietnam-amid-widening-dissent-crackdown-idUSK BN1HJ0SF> (accessed 10 June 2018).

Roberts, M.E. (2018) *Censored: Distraction and Diversion Inside China's Great Firewall*, Princeton, NJ: Princeton University Press.

Trần, B. (2018) 'Google Cam Kết Tuân Thủ Pháp Luật, Bảo Vệ Người Dùng Việt Nam' [Google committed to abide by the Vietnamese laws and protect Vietnamese users], *Sài Gòn Giải Phóng Online*. Available HTTP: www.sggp.org.vn/google-cam-ket-tuan- thu-phap-luat-bao-ve-nguoi-dung-viet-nam-494762.html (accessed 12 June 2018).

Tuyên, Đ. (2008) 'Quy chế phối hợp cung cấp thông tin cho báo chí' [Regulations on the collaboration to provide information to the media], *Ministry of Justice*. Available HTTP: <https://moj.gov.vn/qt/tintuc/Pages/van-ban-chinh-sach-moi.aspx?ItemID=499> (accessed 20 July 2019).

Vietnamese Government. (2016) 'Nghị Định Số 06/2016/NĐ-CP Của Chính Phủ: Quản Lý, Cung Cấp và Sử Dụng Dịch vụ Phát Thanh, Truyền Hình' [Decree No. 06/2016/NĐ-CP of the Government: Regulation, delivery, and utility of radio and television services]. Available HTTP: <http://vanban.chinhphu.vn/portal/page/ portal/chinhphu/hethongvanban?class_id=1&_page=1&mode=detail&document_ id=183193> (accessed 6 June 2018).

Washington Post Editorial Board. (2018) 'Vietnam is systematically snuffing out voices of dissent', *Washington Post*. Available HTTP: <www.washingtonpost.com/opinions/viet nam-is-systematically-snuffing-out-voices-of-dissent/2018/04/14/38ae9dae-3f3f- 11e8-8d53eba0ed2371cc_story.html?noredirect=on&utm_term=.c2178918fbea> (accessed 5 June 2018).

17

PRESS FREEDOM IN BANGLADESH

How to kill the Fourth Estate in 48 years or less

Ikhtisad Ahmed

Prime Minister Sheikh Hasina is never surer of herself than when she addresses her country's media. For its part, at every interaction with her, Bangladesh's grateful press corps repays the self-styled People's Leader and Mother of Humanity's confidence by prefacing questions designed to elicit self-congratulatory responses, with paeans to her leadership and apparent achievements. Two common refrains of Hasina's, always uttered with smiles, are to encourage journalists to work with her government, in service of development, God and country, and remind them to practise responsible journalism. The underlying message is the same, the repetition placing greater emphasis on the diktat: Bangladesh's compliant media is a prop, existing solely to serve the ruling class. Despite this clear assertion of control, the Awami League government and its sycophants insist that the press is completely free and independent, citing the 2,800 newspapers in circulation, the 35 television channels (of which 31 are privately owned) broadcasting daily and nationwide internet proliferation as proof (Hammadi 2019). If the farcical strawman equating volume to an unrestricted pursuit of the truth – in order to distract from the ways in and extent to which the qualitatively toothless media is hamstrung – is difficult to believe by those peddling the lie every day, it is even less likely to fool Bangladesh's citizens. To them, the media is a cruel joke rather than an institution to be trusted. They are under no illusions that they are the oppressed subjects in an autocracy, where neither the press nor they are free to speak.[1]

In this autocracy, it is possible for a draconian law (Digital Security Act 2018) passed to place unfettered restrictions on freedoms of speech, expression and the press to be presented by Hasina's heir apparent, Sajeeb Wazed Joy, as protecting free speech without a hint of irony (Wazed 2018).[2] In 1975, the patriarch of Bangladesh's first political royal family, Sheikh Mujibur Rahman, closed all but four nationalized newspapers in a bid to control absolutely what was said, months before his assassination. In 2019, his daughter has ensured more than the survival of their now-flourishing political dynasty. Hasina has outlawed dissent, dissidence and the truth entirely, succeeding where her father failed by subjugating all state institutions and subsuming the elite class into the ruling class, so that the private sector operates as yet another instrument of an authoritarian state. Worryingly, the capitulation of freedoms of speech and expression, and the collapse of a free press, have long been foregone conclusions. The various political actors – including Islamists, an opportunistic military and a politicized, ambitious and self-serving civil society – have conspired to put Bangladesh on track towards a slow, inevitable surrender of these fundamental rights since independence. In the universal intention of the ruling class to bring the Fourth Estate to heel, the Awami League government and its untouchable holy trinity are currently the chief beneficiaries of a victory won over decades in the country, brought to fruition by the complicity of foreign and domestic participants. News management is no longer required, since the news is manufactured and dictated by the state.

Birth of a national media

A free and radical press existed in Bangladesh before it became an independent nation, not because of the universality of human rights or international law and conventions, but because of the nature of self-determination. The legitimate anti-West Pakistani establishment and pro-East Pakistani autonomy views manifested as a local media fully supportive of the movement that led to independence in 1971 (Bass 2013: 51). The corollary to this is that the press was living up to the ideals of being a real opposition to the ruling class, and giving a voice to intellectuals from a large political spectrum unified by a common enemy. That this freedom had developed organically is particularly significant, since it existed not only in defiance of an oppressive military regime, but also of the dominant global superpower: the United States. When war broke out, the Pakistani military junta took direct action to silence journalists. For the Bengali media, this meant death; for its foreign counterparts, intimidation had to suffice (Bass 2013: 51).

Once the common enemy was vanquished, national unity frayed along ideological lines. A media groomed to dissent took aim at the new authorities who were trying not to be crushed by the enormous burden of building an independent state, set against the unquiet backdrop of Cold War and UN realpolitik, and the Pakistan and Islamist projects. Repressive laws, including the colonial-era Penal Code 1860, Code of Criminal Procedure 1898 and Official Secrets Act 1923, and the Pakistan-era Printing and Publication Ordinance 1960, had been inherited by the newly independent state, and called upon when needed. Therefore, from the outset, the relationship between the new state and the media was defined as one whereby the former had dominance over the latter, as had its defunct predecessors the British Raj and the Pakistani state.

The will to allow free speech, expression and press – instrumental in the independence movement – may have been there, but it constantly came up against a desire to limit. The latter, increasingly ravenous, forced the former into sub-mission. This was reflected in the legislative measures enacted in the country's first half a decade. The Printing and Publication Ordinance 1960 was repealed in 1973, but its replacement, the Printing Presses and Publication Ordinance 1973, reaffirmed rather than reformed its predecessor (Riaz 1993: 205). The second amendment to the Constitution was passed shortly thereafter, legalizing the suspension of fundamental rights, including freedoms of speech and expression, as an emergency action. To this day, these freedoms have not been rescued from their constitutionally mandated conditionality. Crucially, this leeway of making absolute rights conditional upon 'reasonable restrictions' (Constitution of Bangladesh Article 39[2]) formed the legal basis of further laws designed with the sole objective of silencing.

The next year, 1974, was a watershed year in the unhindered development of state censorship. The Special Powers Act (SPA), in effect and expanded on since, became law, severely curtailing freedoms. The Press Council Act, passed a week later, ostensibly stood for freedom of the press, but a combination of the SPA and its spawn – and the partisan politicization of the media along party rather than ideological lines – has diluted this principle and ensured that the press has been controlled in the decades that have followed. Suppression of the media under the Mujib government peaked in 1975. A totalitarian state was founded on the fourth amendment to the Constitution. While it dissolved all political parties except the Awami League, rebranded as the Bangladesh Krishak Sramik Awami League, a Newspaper Declaration implemented the closure of 29 daily and 138 weekly publications, and the nationalization of the remaining four (Mohaiemen 2013).

When the country was further destabilized in 1975 by the assassinations of Mujib on 15 August and four jailed prominent Awami League leaders on 3 November, the leash that had already been put on the press was tightened once Ziaur Rahman took the reins of the country following a series of coups and counter-coups. He personally headed the Ministry of Information and Broad-casting, and martial law decreed that criticism of the regime or reporting on matters that could 'cause fear or alarm' were criminal offences (Alam 2008: 221). For the first time in independent Bangladesh, the foreign press was not spared. Lawrence Lifschultz – the South Asia Correspondent of the *Far Eastern Economic Review* – was arrested, detained for three days and deported for his reporting on the kangaroo court that was conducted for Abu Taher and 11 others (Lifschultz 2018). Zia put a velvet glove on his iron fist. In addition to being the head of state to pay the most visits to the National Press Club to date, he beseeched the media in private to give positive coverage, and brought senior sharp-tongued journal-ists marginalized by the previous Awami League regime into the government fold (Mohaiemen 2013). The media owing fealty to the ruler thus became com-mon practice, the weakening of the Fourth Estate exacerbated by the dual blow of party allegiances of publications and pliable personal interests of individuals.

Zia's successor was Bangladesh's second military dictator, H.M. Ershad. He resumed the existing combative relationship with the media when he assumed office. Building on it, his tenure gave birth to the practice of regular press advisories being issued, warning editors about what not to print (Ullah 1991). Directives were issued to kill any news or investigation that could be embarrassing or dangerous for the authorities. Different foreign newspapers were banned at various stages of Ershad's eight-year rule, with Indian publications specifically targeted throughout. The Customs Act 1969 became a suppression mechanism, used to stop the circulation of international outlets. However, Ershad's brutality notwithstanding, he was viewed as the weakest of the country's three autocrats until then. The media developed subversive means of undermining and criticizing him through cyphered missives that an engaged readership easily decoded and enjoyed. It was aided by the hapless, charmless usurper belonging neither to Mujib's Awami League nor to Zia's Bangladesh Nationalist Party (BNP). Once more, there was a common enemy, and the bipartisan efforts to topple him afforded the press a degree of reassurance, if not protection. Writers and journalists confidently took it upon themselves to transgress and be punished, only to transgress again, energizing the populace to join the resistance. The year 1990 saw 67 individual instances of harassment, 24 attacks on media organizations, 12 arrests, eight ban orders enforced and two deaths (*Nirikkha* 1991), but the journalism remained relentless.

If there was an imperfect red-letter day for the Bangladeshi media, it was during the months of activism, building a groundswell of opposition to Ershad which eventually bore fruit with his resignation and imprisonment, unfolding as the Cold War came to an end. The initiation of democracy in the aftermath could have seen the press's newfound zeal firmly establish its fearlessness and freedom. Unfortunately, the opportunity was squandered. The state machinery for repression retreated to the shadows in the 1990s, but was not dismantled, and editors and journalists spent the decade responding to state and party patronage, prizing personal profit over principles. Politicization of the press has been particularly destructive to the development of human and democratic rights in Bangladesh, since it turned outlets into vehicles of party agitprop with the complicity of the press, rendering it wholly ineffective in holding power to account. This dereliction of duty has at once robbed the country of the clear-sightedness and objective opposition of an independent press, and engulfed the press in the volatility of political partisanship and its consequences. The full force of this has been felt in the twenty-first century, as the BNP, the military, the civil society and Awami League have colluded to take democracy apart, taking turns to emerge victorious as a one-party state has taken shape.

Twenty-first century democracy

By the time the BNP formed a coalition government with the rehabilitated agents of the Pakistani military junta, Jamaat-e-Islami (Jamaat), in 2001 and took a hard right, Islamist turn in its policy and governance, the press unions had relinquished advocating for and defending their profession. The Dhaka Union of Journalists and Bangladesh Federal Union of Journalists were already divided along party lines, fighting one another rather than the authorities who were curbing their rights (Ahmed 2009: 62–63). The advent of new media on the internet and private television brought fresh challenges to its dedication to control. Ekushey Television (ETV), the country's first private alternative to the state channel, BTV, expanded the horizons for journalism and injected a degree of liberalism to the stale state-controlled televisual landscape. Its success in reaching a wide audience owed to its formation coinciding with greater and easier availability of television sets across the country, especially in rural areas. Two-thirds of the population is rural at present, and the proportion was higher when ETV was launched at the turn of the century (Jong 2018). Engaging with this group beyond the standard party rallies and outreach events could change the socio-political landscape. The inverse relationship between urbanization and illiteracy meant television was considerably more effective in shaping minds than the print media nationwide.

ETV soon became a victim of circumstance. Launched in the last days of the Awami League government in 2000, the BNP-Jamaat saw its liberalism as a threat, but couched its objections in claims of unfair partisan bias of the new channel upon taking office. After a persistent campaign against it, ETV was promptly shut down in 2002, and Managing Director Simon Dring, who had been deported for his reporting on Pakistani military aggression in 1971, was expelled once more (Lawson-Tancred 2002). The BNP-Jamaat government was assisted in this attack on freedom of the press by the press itself. Journalist and editor Shafik Rehman, once a strong critic of the Ershad regime and presumed defender of the freedom of speech, had found a political home in the far-right government, and led media sympathizers in a vicious smear campaign against ETV. Framing the matter as a political rather than a human rights issue re-energized the government's base – then in the majority, fresh from the BNP's and Jamaat's largest-ever electoral victory – and made the unpalatable desirable for enough of the populace to make the closure of the channel easy. The media had definitively proved its bona fides as the chief vehicle for government propaganda – creators of lies, not guardians of the truth.

Once taken off air, Bangladesh Telecommunication Regulatory Commission (BTRC) was key in keeping ETV there. Birthed by the Bangladesh Telecommunication Act 2001 (BTA), appointments to the Commission were political, thereby impairing its sworn mission to be independent. The BNP-Jamaat capitalized on the vacuum created by the removal of ETV by granting licences for private television channels to party members. Where once the aim had been to control the media via the state, sustained exposure to the global trends of capitalism and neoliberalism, coupled with a public more wary of state ownership, made controlling via the market a more prudent strategy. A servile print media was achieved over decades. Television was loyal to power from the inception of BTV. Newly licensed Channel 1 and Diganta Television, affiliated with the BNP and Jamaat, respectively, reaffirmed that private ownership would not change this. State institutions corrupted by politicization to silence speech could be used effectively by those in power. The BNP-Jamaat added this arrow to the quiver at the onset of pseudo-democracy, and the incumbent Awami League government has perfected its usage.

The BNP-Jamaat government's greatest success was in laying the groundwork for the complete erasure of democratic institutions and rights. The twenty-first century thus saw Bangladesh commit to authoritarian rule. The short-lived civil society-backed military regime that toppled the BNP-Jamaat in 2007, and its Awami League successor since 2009, have reaped the seeds sown by the coalition's utter rejection of democracy. The BNP-Jamaat deployed the autocrat's favourite sleight of hand of concealing oppressive laws within statutes that trumpeted socio-economic progress. State surveillance was made law by BTA, amended in 2006 (Bangladesh Telecommunication Act [Amended] 2006), granting law enforcement agencies the supreme power to monitor citizens' private communications, at the behest of the government. This was one of two major blows to freedoms dealt in the BNP-Jamaat's last year in office. The other parting gift was the Information and Communication Technology Act 2006 (ICTA), passed to ostensibly oversee the technological strides being made by Bangladesh. Buried inside it was the dreaded Section 57, a conveniently ambiguous legal basis for unfettered restrictions to speech and journalism that could exist due to the allowances made by the Constitution. There was now legal cover for punishing defamation of the state, individuals and religion with heavy prison sentences and fines.

The civil society-backed military regime that wrested control from the BNP-Jamaat did so with the blessing and complicity of the West (Khalil 2016: 125). The overt political actions of the civil society at a time of fundamental, if qualified, rights granted by the Constitution being suspended under a state of emergency was the death knell of an independent and effective Fourth Estate in Bangladesh. In order to justify the undemocratic takeover, a populist message of fighting corruption was concocted. The civil society and the elite class were the staunchest proponents of an anti-corruption drive that was a direct, more brutal descendent of the BNP-Jamaat's Operation Clean Heart and the formation of Rapid Action Battalion (RAB) (Khalil 2016: 125). The *Daily Star*, the largest circulating English-language newspaper in the country derived from the elitist civil society firmament, took the lead in producing propaganda and repeating controversial, unverified information as gospel (Ahmed 2018: 915). Any hesitation lesser outlets may have had to follow suit was put paid to by editors and owners not being immune to totalitarian oppression, with the largest number of editors being imprisoned by any one government since independence, at a time when influential politicians and foot soldiers alike from all major parties were being detained on a regular basis (AFP Correspondent 2007). In a nation where the various factions of the ruling class demand cultic devotion, the *Daily Star* composed hagiographies for the civil society elites – the saviours who were above the law and beyond reproach. Nobel laureate Muhammad Yunus, whose global claim to fame and fortune lay in entrapping society's most vulnerable in a neoliberal cycle of debt and poverty, was the most favoured of the new favoured sons, as he was preparing to take the reins of governance, to extend the rule of the interim government (Boustany 2007). Furthermore, the advent of Wikileaks and the revelation of unflattering diplomatic cables about Bangladesh's ruling class spawned a collective yearning for schadenfreude. The government took advantage of this to garner populist support for the anti-corruption drive by leaking coerced confessions of the rich and powerful to the media, to meet that demand (Mohaiemen 2013). The current Awami League government has taken this further. It has exponentially increased its surveillance capabilities, and unleashed it on the population, often leaking raw and doctored audio to the conventional and through the social media, to display opposition leaders and regime opponents in compromising positions (Privacy International Correspondent 2018).

For once, the international media's general lack of knowledge and nuance about Bangladesh, coupled with the West's role in attempting to create an unelected technocratic government aligned with its interests, resulted in largely positive coverage of the civil society's machinations and the military's suspension of human rights and brutal actions. For instance, *The Economist*'s condescending view on Bangladesh in 2018 disparaged the Liberation War, but during the interim government's tenure, its sexist tone – reducing the country's politics to 'two battling begums' – and tokenistic orientalism underpinned a tacit approval of technocratic governance. Its regular dispatches became popular among the Bangladeshi elite class, and at times bore an eerie resemblance to *The Daily Star*'s reporting (*The Economist* Correspondent 2007; Halder 2007). In 2012, *The Economist* framed an interview with the fugitive Ishraq Ahmed as a defence and promulgation of his views. His attempted coup d'état against Sheikh Hasina's Awami League relied on Hizb-ut-Tahrir and Islamists in the army, including Major Ziaul Haque, a member of Al-Qaeda in the India Subcontinent (AQIS) (Habib 2012). *The Economist* did not include any of this relevant information or diligently scrutinize Ahmed's unsupported claims in its reporting, in which he appeared as a principled patriot opposing India's clientelism – an ever-present factor in the nation's far-right ideology (*The Economist* Correspondent 2012). Nor did it publish a corrective or a follow-up to this piece of irresponsible and dangerous journalism. These cautionary tales of the foreign media lacking essential context and neither being free of agendas nor being virtuous to a fault in pursuit of the truth, fall on deaf ears to urban Bangladeshis. To them, the international press has integrity.

A lasting impression of the civil society-backed military government's repressive denigration towards a free press was left by the case of Tasnem Khalil. A journalist whose work on exposing RAB's abuses of power had resulted in harassment from the security agencies, Khalil was taken without a warrant from his home to a military camp (Human Rights Watch 2008: 10–13). Although the domestic media were silent on the matter, certain sections of the foreign media had picked up the scent of the military running several illegal detention and torture centres across the country (Lloyd 2007), despite Yunus and civil society leaders publicly – and to the world at large – heaping unqualified praise on the men in uniform (Boustany 2007). Khalil's arrest and subsequent torture centred primarily on his coverage of due process and human rights abuses in the conduct of the law enforcement and security agencies, their practices of torture, enforced disappearances and extrajudicial killings, and their links to Islamist groups and militants (Human Rights Watch 2008: 19–20). An investigative feature he wrote on the latter, outlining the nefarious network of senior members of the usurped BNP-Jamaat government, including the BNP's scion, Tarique Rahman, and the army and its intelligence unit, the Directorate General of Forces Intelligence (DGFI), which cultivated and nurtured Islamist militant organizations, drew the ire of the authorities enough to force the magazine that published it, *Forum*, to withdraw that particular issue. It remains the only issue missing from its archives to this day. Khalil gave a false confession under duress, taking responsibility for his anti-state and anti-military criminal activities with the aim of destabilizing Bangladesh (Human Rights Watch 2008: 19–20). Preparations were under way to kill him extrajudicially, but he was saved from this fate in part due to a concerted international campaign (Human Rights Watch 2008: 25).

Progressivism in the age of digital blasphemy

An Al Jazeera investigative report published on 20 March 2019 – on the collusion for personal gain between Prime Minister Sheikh Hasina's security adviser and relative, Tarique Ahmed Siddique, and the DGFI that he previously worked for – resulted in a nationwide block of the website (Patraker 2019). A local news website, The Joban, suffered the same fate for repeating Al Jazeera's claims with attribution (RSF Correspondent 2019). In 2017, The Wire website was similarly blocked for publishing an article, co-authored by Khalil, on the enforced disappearance and secret detention of academic Mubashar Hasan by the DGFI (The Quint Desk 2017). While in the latter case, the BTRC complied with a government and law enforcement agency order, to enforce the block (The Quint Desk 2017), in the former case, the advances made by the Department of Telecommunications (DOT) and the National Telecommunication Monitoring Centre (NTMC) have led to a new system that no longer requires the involvement of the BTRC for agencies to centrally block websites (Khalil 2019). Section 8 of the Digital Security Act (DSA) is the legal basis for such blocks. This is the face of present-day Bangladesh, averse to the truth and developing evermore perfect ways to stifle it. Criticizing or exposing the misdeeds of the Awami League government and the military is one of the three chief blasphemies in this digital nation. The other two are unfavourable elucidations about Islam or Islamism, and attacking the elite class, chiefly the exploitative garments industry at the heart of the Awami League's much-vaunted economic development. While an oppressive Broadcast Law, ratified by cabinet in 2018, awaits implementation, the DSA has taken the rapier of the Section 57 of the ICTA and forged it into a broadsword, in service of ending blasphemy.

Admitting the misuse of the ICTA, the Awami League moved to repeal it. Section 57 – under which over 1,000 people exercising freedoms of speech and press had been arrested since its inception – was broadened into an entire act that would replace the ICTA. The DSA is a de facto anti-blasphemy and anti-speech law, with severe punishments for arrests, search and seizures without warrant, and for which bail is discretionary rather than an absolute right when charged. One of the first to fall victim to the newly minted law was journalist Hedait Hossain Molla of the *Dhaka Tribune*, for reporting that 22,419 more votes than voters had been cast in a constituency in Khulna, as an example of rigging during the January 2019 general election (Tribune Desk 2019) – an election whose incredible result of the incumbent Awami League winning 96 per cent of the seats is largely accepted as having been manufactured. Ironically, the same newspaper had earlier published an op-ed penned by Joy, speciously advocating for the DSA (Joy 2018). In February 2019, the government's newfound zeal, granted by the statute, saw it use the pretext of a crackdown on pornography to officially ban over 20,000 websites, Google Books and the popular blogging site, Somewhereintheblog, among them (Nabi 2019). In December 2018, ahead of the general election, 54 news sites apparently sympathetic to Awami League's opposition were blocked, to stop the spread of 'rumours' – the Bangladeshi equivalent of 'fake news' (RSF Correspondent 2018).

The government's fraught relationship with Facebook had shifted from several attempts to block it to recognizing its potency as an outlet and seeking to wield it. Nevertheless, while the government had the domestic narrative under tight control, Facebook suspended nine pages and six accounts, and Twitter suspended 15 accounts, for spreading lies targeting the opposition (Locklear 2018). Pro-government websites pretending to be legitimate news outlets, including BBC Bangla, *The Dhaka Tribune* and bdnews24, mushroomed during the election campaign, as part of the strategy to control the narrative at home (Locklear 2018). The social media accounts that had come under scrutiny were tied to these sites. There has been an escalation of both volume and activity of questionable online media outlets. Highlighting the selective application of the DSA and government censure, they repeat propaganda, and run smear and disinformation campaigns, to discredit dissenters and dissidents, and cloud the collective judgement of all others. The *Weekly Blitz*'s sustained attacks on Khalil and Al Jazeera in 2019 evolved from the 2018 social media-led campaign to paint the internationally renowned photographer and journalist Shahidul Alam, then in custody, in an unfavourable light. The deliberate convolution of the truth, to justify the unjustifiable acts of oppression, is often endorsed by reputable media outlets – as bdnews24 did in Alam's case – thereby enhancing the effectiveness of defamatory profiles. However, known offenders such as the prominent pro-Jamaat Islamist social media account, Basherkella, have not only escaped the notice of the companies' imperfect monitoring systems, but have been rewarded with verified account status. In 2013, Basherkella was the leading Facebook voice calling for and justifying the slaughter of freethinkers, echoing its sister concern in the mainstream print media, *Amar Desh*, whose editor was notable BNP leader Mahmudur Rahman, and the Hizb-ut-Tahrir associated right-wing BNP intellectual Farhad Mazhar (Allchin 2015). Once a faux leftist Ershad critic, Mazhar's Islamist bona fides were reaffirmed when he encouraged terrorist attacks against journalists – whom he held solely responsible for terrorism by masking hate speech as social justice – on live television ('Farhad Mazhar encouraging bombing on ETV: Subtitled' 2013). In 2018, Basherkella was being quoted by British MP Rupa Huq on Twitter as a trustworthy source of news on Bangladesh (Huq 2018), and Mahmudur Rahman was releasing incendiary videos on Facebook ('Mahmudur Rahman's Speech' 2018), calling for military, Islamist and Western intervention, for the sake of democracy in Bangladesh.

In fact, Islamist online media is entirely exempt from the government's iron-fisted purview. A proliferation of websites and associated Facebook pages[3] espousing Salafism and affiliated to the madrassah network are the fastest-growing media in Bangladesh, operating with relative freedom. The blocks on freethinking sites Mukto-Mona and Istishon (Tribune Desk 2016) are not replicated for these outlets, nor do the 'rumours' monitoring committees established by the government (Human Rights Watch 2018) pay them any heed. A close reading of the contents not only reveals hate speech, lies and propaganda amidst the fundamentalism, but, more worryingly, also shows a carefully coordinated messaging that readily seeps into the mainstream. Hefazat-e-Islam (Hefazat) is an organization of extremist clerics rooted in the country's madrassahs and mosques that benefits from Awami League patronage, and holds considerable sway over the party (Khalil 2018) The mission to denounce Ahmadiyyas as non-Muslims – a staple of Islamist politics in the subcontinent that was last summoned by Jamaat when in government – is the first step towards an attack on all minorities. This tactic is now deployed by Hefazat (Hussain 2019). In early 2019 its chief, Ahmed Shafi, incited violence against the community (Sazzad 2019), but vitriolic rhetoric was already widespread in Islamist online media for months prior to his statement. It is reminiscent of how intolerance was stoked and Islamism disseminated efficiently and with impunity by Hefazat, AQIS and ISIS from 2013 onwards, to outlaw freethinking by targeting key individuals, and having the Awami League government blame the victims and invoke the legal instruments that restrict free speech to hold them, rather than the perpetrators, accountable under the law (Allchin 2015). As Islamist media grows and gains space in conventional media, with the able assistance of the government and the military, freethinkers and progressives retreat from the virtual and real pages, and are thus forced to look for refuge beyond Bangladesh's borders.

Islamists are not the only group to receive Awami League's magnanimity vis-à-vis freedom of speech. The elite class, particularly those involved in the garments industry, is another, and like the Islamists, its members are deeply embedded in the ruling class. In the wake of protests by garments workers in January

2019, within weeks of the fraudulent general election, it was not a worker that the media turned to, but Rubana Huq, owner of one of the largest garment corporations in Bangladesh. Whether she parroted the government's position on the industry and labour, or vice versa, their comments are near verbatim accounts. Summed up in a half-hour sit-down with the country's only English-language talk show, Straight Talk, Huq ran the gamut of defences for the industry, ranging from commending the government for its handling of the protests and a patronizing attitude towards workers, to absolving the industry of blame and placing it squarely on the shoulders of foreign brands, insinuating without proof that third parties had incited workers – since they neither have agency and intelligence, nor rights or the will to fight for them – and stating that abuse of any form is impossible ('Straight talk with Zafar Sobhan: Dr. Rubana Huq' 2019). Huq was not challenged as she presented a utopian image entirely at odds with the views of the average worker, because for long she has been presented by the media as an unimpeachable liberal intellectual and reformer ('Straight talk with Zafar Sobhan: Dr. Rubana Huq' 2019).

She is a columnist for *The Daily Star* and is sought out by the foreign press whenever the issue of the Bangladeshi garments industry is deemed newsworthy. This has allowed her the unique opportunity to take contentious – at times provably false – claims global. Among them have been stating that it is only possible to offer safe workplaces or fair wages, not both (Safi and Rushe 2018), and wrapping exploitation of cheap labour in euphemisms about resilience and women's empowerment ('Bangladesh's top woman entrepreneur' 2016). So in thrall to the industry is the press that a fallacious *Forbes* article mired in false equivalences, misplaced orientalism and the panacea of capitalist greed, written by Tim Worstall (2016) – member of the British far-right UKIP – was reprinted by several major newspapers, glossing over the disproportionate tax breaks and unfair trade advantages granted to the garments industry by the government. The message of development is the feel-good narrative pole on which Awami League has pitched its autocratic tent, one that has resonated abroad (Robinson 2018). The garments industry is indispensable in contributing to the economic growth necessary for the government to maintain this façade. Huq's polished regime and entrepreneurial apologia has seen her ride the public relations wave to becoming president of the undemocratic, opaque and unscrupulous Bangladesh Garment Manufacturers and Exporters Association (BGMEA) (Hammadi 2019).

The labour protests of 2016 and 2019 were covered in the same manner as the student protests in 2018 by a pliant media. Cautious reporting of facts that supported the workers was disrupted by suppression of the media – legal action under the ICTA Section 57 or the DSA, and physical violence at the scene – giving way to vehement defences from industry and regime insiders, and the major outlets waxing lyrical about the industry after the protests were violently crushed by law enforcement. While garments workers are cast aside as unwanted outsiders by systemic classism in the urban centres, students are recognized as a crucial part of urban life and are largely drawn from the middle and upper-middle classes (Haque 2018). In addition to not facing prejudice, they also have social media proficiency. Containing them and controlling the narrative during the protests in 2018 that marked their political awakening was, hence, more difficult (Haque 2018). Shahidul Alam, a conscientious member of the elite class who documented the violent and unlawful actions of the police and RAB working in conjunction with armed militia drawn from Awami League's student-wings, was taken away by warrantless law enforcement officials from his residence in a manner that recalled the horrors of Khalil's abduction (Islam 2018). The international attention it received forced the government to belatedly charge him under Section 57 of the ICTA to make his arrest official. He was not the only one detained under the section for reporting on or sharing information about the protests, nor were journalists spared from the beatings meted out indiscriminately to end the nascent movement (BBC Desk 2018). His profile, however, meant he was ideal to make an example of and to send a clear message that no individual breaking silence on the three sacred subjects was safe (Sarwar 2018).

Alam's 100-day incarceration woke up the international media. The state of freedoms of speech and the press in Bangladesh came into sharp focus, and, by extension, discussions about the nation's slide towards authoritarianism. The foreign press remains the only safe space to detail oppression without repercussions. Wise to this, the government has taken measures to negate its effects. For one thing, the Awami League has sown mistrust of those outside Bangladesh belligerently, allied with apologists flooding the domestic mainstream and social media with neo-nationalism and counter-narratives, and bans where appropriate. For another, the geopolitical recalibration to an India-China axis has seen considerations for Western perspectives diminish as the West's significance and influence wane. Beyond raising awareness of atrocities, foreign media's attention is of little consequence to exerting pressure on the government or preventing further violations of fundamental freedoms. When international media and human rights organizations fulfilling their mission statements are lambasted as enemies of the state by the Awami League, there remains very little leverage to reason or influence. Furthermore, the political benefits of opening the doors to the Rohingya community facing genocide in Myanmar includes adding this favourable caveat to any conversation about human rights in Bangladesh.

In the end

The media business in Bangladesh is largely a losing venture, due to the economy of receding private advertising revenues in a market where the government remains the largest advertising client, lack of literacy and education among the population, and its general apathy (Ahmed 2018: 909). Therefore, only the richest can afford to effectively write off the large investments necessary for the operations of newspapers and television channels, in a country where ownership and economic structures have historically been used by those in power to control the media. Awami League's cronyism is in its 11th year now, meaning the richest are either card-carrying members of the party or vociferous supporters of it. Domestic media outlets are, thus, almost entirely owned by individuals like serving MP Salman Rahman (*The Independent* newspaper and Independent Television), or Awami League-affiliated conglomerates like Gemcon Group (*Dhaka Tribune* and *Bangla Tribune*) and Bashundhara Group (*The Daily Sun*, *Kaler Kantho*, *Bangladesh Pratidin*, Channel 24, et al). A direct consequence of this is that censorship of journalism begins at the source, before the need for persecution and the application of draconian laws. Die-hard sycophants, with qualifications to lend misplaced credibility to their chest-beating and bare-faced lying, rule the roost. Nadeem Qadir exemplifies this coterie. Having been a *Dhaka Tribune* columnist while serving as the press minister at the High Commission in the United Kingdom, he seamlessly transitioned into the senior position of consulting editor at *The Daily Sun*, blurring the lines between the state and the Fourth Estate, and passing off his personal biases as facts by having op-eds devising and propagating falsehoods run on the front page of the newspaper (Qadir 2019).

Unlike Qadir, the majority of people working in the profession to which he does a disservice are drawn from the middle and lower-middle classes. Protecting a meagre livelihood and aspiring to supplement a humble income with generous inducements or the ruling and elite classes' patronage are reasons enough to be dissuaded from upholding the principles of independent journalism. The few who insist on their independence prove to be anything but. Veteran journalist-cum-public intellectual Afsan Chowdhury – a victim of an ICTA Section 57 case in 2017 (Rabbi 2017) – is a standard bearer of this shrinking group. Chowdhury uses his multiple weekly columns to repeatedly laud the political acumen of Prime Minister Sheikh Hasina as being peerless, in lieu of laying bare her regime's brutality ('Straight talk with Zafar Sobhan ep 1' 2018). Additionally, he blames the victims of political retribution and oppression for their plight ('Straight talk with Zafar Sobhan ep 1' 2018), and reports as fact misinformation downplaying the threat of Islamism (Chowdhury 2018a) and state terror (Chowdhury 2018b), while wilfully ignoring their collusion with the government and law enforcement agencies. His journalism propagates ethno-nationalism and nativism for a conservative parochial outlook that benefits Awami League (Chowdhury 2019). Conclusions are drawn at the outset, and facts are manoeuvred or dismissed to fit the conclusions, rather than letting facts lead the way to the truth as a conclusion. Qadir's direct approach and Chowdhury's indirect approach are two means to the same end: eroding freedoms of speech and the press, eroding intellectualism and progressivism, and augmenting authoritarianism.

The absence of freedom of the press has become a cornerstone of autocracy in Bangladesh. There is a crisis of credibility, exacerbated by a pervasive climate of fear and an overwhelming antagonism towards facts within the corridors of power and media. This poses the twin threat of pushing the populace towards Facebook – as an outlet and publisher of news – and other dubious sources that are readily manipulated, and a complete control over what is news. When inconvenient truths occasionally surface against insurmountable odds, the only consequences are faced by those bringing them to light, not the wrongdoers. If there is a reticence to speak and report, it is because doing so comes at a heavy cost and achieves no return. Thus, the principle strictly adhered to is one of news as propaganda, where the West has corroded it as entertainment, and idealism demands it to be a pursuit of the truth. The compliant press in Bangladesh exists as collaborators of the state, to launder lies for the elite and ruling classes, until they are clean enough to plausibly pass for the truth, for a population whose majority has been conditioned to range from ignorant to indifferent. Deprived of this vital component of holding power to account, the people survive in a distorted reality, forced into submission and silence – an unconscionable mirror image of the state of dignified journalism in the country, and indicative of the damning indictment of an antipathetic public's trust in the media being non-existent.

Notes

1 Due to risks to personal safety, numerous experts and relevant professionals were unwilling to provide information pertaining to this chapter, even anonymously. Of the handful who did, the majority did so on condition of anonymity. Without exception, all insisted on the absence of freedoms of speech, expression and the press in Bangladesh.
2 Citations for Wazed and Joy all refer to the same author: Sajeeb Wazed Joy. However, as bylines credit him differently, the citations reflect this.
3 In the interest of avoiding the promotion of these outlets and their views, they are not listed in the text. Noteworthy examples are ourislam24, insaf24 and Qawmi Barta, and associated Facebook pages.

Bibliography

AFP Correspondent. (2007) 'Bangladesh to unveil new graft suspect list', *Agence France-Presse*.

Ahmed, A.M. (2009) 'Media, politics and the emergence of democracy in Bangladesh', *Canadian Journal of Media Studies*, 5: 50–67.

Ahmed, K.A. (2018) 'In Bangladesh: Direct control of media trumps fake news', *The Journal of Asian Studies*, 77: 909–922.

Alam, R. (2008) *Military-Media Relations in Bangladesh: 1975–1990*, Dhaka: Palok Publishers.

Allchin, J. (2015) 'Where atheism can get you killed', *Politico*. Online. Available HTTP: <www.politico.com/magazine/story/2015/05/ananta-bijoy-das-bangladesh-atheist-murder-118223> (accessed 25 April 2019).

'Bangladesh's top woman entrepreneur'. (2016) 'Youtube video, added by CNBC-TV18'. Online. Available HTTP: <www.youtube.com/watch?v=tT27TP-2K40&feature=youtu.be> (accessed 25 April 2019).

Bangladesh Telecommunication Act 2001. Available HTTP: <http://www.btrc.gov.bd/telecommunication-act-2001-english> (accessed 27 August 2019)

Bangladesh Telecommunication Act (Amended) 2006. Available HTTP: <http://www.btrc.gov.bd/amendment2006-telecommunication-act-2001-bangla> (accessed 27 August 2019)

Bass, G.J. (2013) *The Blood Telegram: Nixon, Kissinger, and a Forgotten Genocide*, New York: Knopf.

BBC Desk. (2018) 'Bangladesh protest turns violent with journalists beaten', *BBC*. Online. Available HTTP: <www.bbc.com/news/av/world-asia-45074388/bangladesh-protest-turns-violent-with-journalists-beaten> (accessed 25 April 2019).

Boustany, N. (2007) 'Nobel Laureate eyes election as next prize', *The Washington Post*. Online. Available HTTP: <www.washingtonpost.com/wp-dyn/content/article/2007/03/14/AR2007031402624.html??noredirect=on> (accessed 25 April 2019).

Chowdhury, A. (2018a) 'Lessons learnt, lessons ignored since Holey', *Dhaka Courier*. Online. Available HTTP: <www.dhakacourier.com.bd/news/Column/Lessons-learnt-lessons-ignored-since-Holey/364> (accessed 25 April 2019).

Chowdhury, A. (2018b) 'Goom and limits of law enforcement in network capitalism', *New Age*. Online. Available HTTP: <www.newagebd.net/article/33264/goom-and-limits-of-law-enforcement-in-network-capitalism> (accessed 25 April 2019).

Chowdhury, A. (2019) 'The speech of 7th March: The politicians and the peasant', *Dhaka Courier*. Online. Available HTTP: <www.dhakacourier.com.bd/news/Column/The-speech-of-7th-March:-The-politicians-and-the-peasant/1131> (accessed 25 April 2019).

Constitution of the People's Republic of Bangladesh. Available HTTP: <http://bdlaws.minlaw.gov.bd/pdf_part.php?id=367> (accessed 27 August 2019)

Digital Security Act 2018 Bangladesh. Available HTTP: <https://www.cirt.gov.bd/wp-content/uploads/2018/12/Digital-Security-Act-2018-English-version.pdf> (accessed 27 August 2019)

East West Media Group Ltd. 'About us'. Online. Available HTTP: <www.ewmgl.com/about-us> (accessed 4 May 2019).

The Economist Correspondent. (2007) 'Battered begums', *The Economist*. Online. Available HTTP: <https://www.economist.com/asia/2007/04/12/battered-begums> (accessed 27 August 2019)

The Economist Correspondent. (2012) 'Turbulent house', *The Economist*. Online. Available HTTP: <https://www.economist.com/asia/2012/01/28/turbulent-house> (accessed 27 August 2019)

'Farhad Mazhar encouraging bombing on ETV: Subtitled'. (2013) 'YouTube video, added by Shahbagupdate'. Online. Available HTTP: <www.youtube.com/watch?v=JTXKIUncKsg> (accessed 25 April 2019).

Habib, H. (2012) 'Lessons from the coup that failed', *The Hindu*. Online. Available HTTP: <www.thehindu.com/opinion/lead/Lessons-from-the-coup-that-failed/article13386286.ece> (accessed 25 April 2019).

Halder, C.C. (2007) 'Hasina, Nizami, their top leaders charged', *The Daily Star*. P. 1

Hammadi, S. (2019) 'World Press Freedom Day: Freedom of expression is good for business', *The Daily Star*. Online. Available HTTP: <www.thedailystar.net/lifestyle/perspective/news/world-press-freedom-day-freedom-expression-good-business-1737730> (accessed 4 May 2019).

Haque, A. (2018) 'August Petite revolution', *Shuddashar*. Online. Available HTTP: <https://shuddhashar.com/asheque-haque-august-petite-revolution-2/> (accessed 25 April 2019).

Human Rights Watch. (2008) 'The torture of Tasneem Khalil', *Human Rights Watch*. Online. Available HTTP: <www.hrw.org/reports/2008/bangladesh0208/> (accessed 25 April 2019).

Human Rights Watch. (2018) 'Bangladesh: Crackdown on social media', *Human Rights Watch*. Online. Available HTTP: <www.hrw.org/news/2018/10/19/bangladesh-crackdown-social-media> (accessed 25 April 2019).

Huq, R. (2018) 31 December. Available HTTP: <https://twitter.com/RupaHuq?ref_src=twsrc%5Egoogle%7Ctwcamp%5Eserp%7Ctwgr%5Eauthor> (accessed 25 April 2019).

Hussain, A. (2019) 'Hefazat chief Shafi: Declare Qadianis as non-Muslims', *Dhaka Tribune*. Online. Available HTTP: <www.dhakatribune.com/bangladesh/nation/2019/03/19/shafi-calls-ahmadiyyas-infidels-urges-followers-to-boycott-them> (accessed 25 April 2019).

Independent. Online. Available HTTP: <independent24.com> (accessed 4 May 2019).

The Independent. Online. Available HTTP: <theindependentbd.com> (accessed 4 May 2019).

Information and Communication Technology Act 2006 Bangladesh. Available HTTP: <http://www.icnl.org/research/library/files/Bangladesh/comm2006.pdf> (accessed 27 August 2019)

Information and Communication Technology Act (Amended) 2013 Bangladesh. Available HTTP: <http://www.bdlaws.minlaw.gov.bd/bangla_pdf_part.php?act_name=&vol=&id=950> (accessed 27 August 2019)

Islam, K. (2018) 'Shahidul Alam: Eyewitness to an abduction', *Himal Southasian*. Online. Available HTTP: <https://himalmag.com/shahidul-alam-eyewitness-to-an-abduction-khademul-islam-bangladesh-nepal-bimstec-august-2018/> (accessed 25 April 2019).

Jong, A. (2018) 'Bangladesh's incomplete revolution', *Jacobin*. Online. Available HTTP: <www.jacobinmag.com/2018/04/bangladesh-pakistan-partition-revolution-maoism> (accessed 25 April 2019).

Joy, S.W. (2018) 'In defence of the Digital Security Act', *Dhaka Tribune*. Online. Available HTTP: <www.dhakatribune.com/opinion/op-ed/2018/10/01/in-defense-of-the-digital-security-act> (accessed 25 April 2019).

Khalil, T. (2016) *Jallad: Death Squads and State Terror in South Asia*, London: Pluto Press.

Khalil, T. (2018) 'India is backing Sheikh Hasina's autocratic government for own interest: Ex Bangladesh Chief Justice', *The Wire*. Online. Available HTTP: <https://thewire.in/south-asia/india-bangladesh-modi-sheikh-hasina> (accessed 25 April 2019).

Khalil, T. (2019) 'Bangladesh blocks access to Al Jazeera news website', *Al Jazeera*. Online. Available HTTP: <www.aljazeera.com/news/2019/03/bangladesh-blocks-access-al-jazeera-news-website-190322083809377.html> (accessed 25 April 2019).

Lawson-Tancred, A. (2002) '"Hero" journalist expelled from Bangladesh', *The Telegraph*. Online. Available HTTP: <www.telegraph.co.uk/news/worldnews/asia/bangladesh/1408933/Hero-journalist-expelled-from-Bangladesh.html> (accessed 25 April 2019).

Lifschultz, L. (2018) 'A long road in search of truth: August 15, 1975', *Dhaka Tribune*. Online. Available HTTP: <https://www.dhakatribune.com/bangladesh/2019/08/15/a-long-road-in-search-of-the-truth-august-15-1975-2> (accessed 27 August 2019)

Lloyd, P. (2007) 'Evidence mounts of Bangladesh mass torture', *Australian Broadcasting Corporation*. Online. Available HTTP: <https://www.abc.net.au/news/2007-06-11/evidence-mounts-of-bangladesh-mass-torture/64948> (accessed 27 August 2019)

Locklear, M. (2018) 'Twitter and Facebook target fake accounts ahead of Bangladesh election', *Engadget*. Online. Available HTTP: <www.engadget.com/2018/12/20/twitter-facebook-target-fake-accounts-bangladesh-election/?guccounter=2&guce_referrer_us=aHR0cHM6Ly90LmNvLzZyYYkNUSWpuQ28&guce_referrer_cs=Rktk7-BdvzNRfxF-8KSIEw> (accessed 25 April 2019).

'Mahmudur Rahman's Speech | 15 September 2018'. (2018) 'YouTube video, added by Hokkotha'. Online. Available HTTP: <www.youtube.com/watch?v=UcyGjlYL_zg> (accessed 22 April 2019).

Mohaiemen, N. (2013) 'We wish to inform you: A history of censorship in Bangladesh (1972–2012)'. Online. Available HTTP: <http://blogs.cuit.columbia.edu/nm2678/2013/04/01/censorship-1972-2012/> (accessed 25 April 2019).

Nabi, S. (2019) 'Major Bangla blog, google books on BTRC porn list', *Dhaka Tribune*. Online. Available HTTP: <www.dhakatribune.com/bangladesh/nation/2019/02/21/major-bangla-blog-google-books-on-btrc-porn-list> (accessed 25 April 2019).

Nirikkha. (1991) March 28 issue. Dhaka: Press Institute of Bangladesh.

Patraker, C. (2019) 'The disappearing act', *Himal Southasian.* Online. Available HTTP: <https://himalmag.com/the-disappearing-act-bangladesh-al-jazeera-block-2019/> (accessed 25 April 2019).

Privacy International Correspondent. (2018) 'Amid crackdown in Bangladesh, government forces continue spytech shopping spree', *Privacy International.* Online. Available HTTP: <www.privacyinternational.org/feature/2226/amid-crackdown-bangladesh-government-forces-continue-spytech-shopping-spree> (accessed 25 April 2019).

Qadir, N. (2019) 'Al Jazeera and Bangladesh: Thoughts on a talk whow', *Daily Sun.* Online. Available HTTP: <https://www.daily-sun.com/printversion/details/377597/2019/03/14/Al-Jazeera-and-Bangladesh:-Thoughts-on-a-Talk-Show> (accessed 27 August 2019)

The Quint Desk. (2017) 'Bangladesh blocks The Wire for an article against the government', *The Quint.* Online. Available HTTP: <www.thequint.com/news/world/bangladesh-blocks-the-wire-for-an-article-against-government> (accessed 25 April 2019).

Rabbi, A.R. (2017) 'Afsan Chowdhury sued under Section 57 of ICT Act', *Dhaka Tribune.* Online. Available HTTP: <www.dhakatribune.com/bangladesh/crime/2017/06/07/afsan-chowdhury-sued-sec-57> (accessed 25 April 2019).

Riaz, A. (1993) *State, Class and Military Rule: Political Economy of Martial Law in Bangladesh,* Dhaka: Nadi New Press.

Robinson, G. (2018) 'The rise and rise of Bangladesh', *Nikkei Asian Review.* Online. Available HTTP: <https://asia.nikkei.com/Spotlight/Cover-Story/The-rise-and-rise-of-Bangladesh> (accessed 25 April 2019).

RSF Correspondent. (2018) 'RSF decries blocking of 54 Bangladeshi news sites before election', *RSF.* Online. Available HTTP: <https://rsf.org/en/news/rsf-decries-blocking-54-bangladeshi-news-sites-election> (accessed 25 April 2019).

RSF Correspondent. (2019) 'RSF decries brazen censorship of Bangladeshi news websites', *RSF.* Online. Available HTTP: <https://rsf.org/en/news/rsf-decries-brazen-censorship-bangladeshi-news-websites> (accessed 25 April 2019).

Safi, M. and Rushe, D. (2018) 'Rana Plaza five years on: Safety of workers hangs in balance in Bangladesh', *The Guardian.* Online. Available HTTP: <www.theguardian.com/global-development/2018/apr/24/bangladeshi-police-target-garment-workers-union-rana-plaza-five-years-on> (accessed 25 April 2019).

Sarwar, B. (2018) 'Here's why the Bangladesh government made a huge mistake by jailing Shahidul Alam', *The Washington Post.* Online. Available HTTP: <www.washingtonpost.com/gdpr-consent/?destination=%2fnews%2fdemocracy-post%2fwp%2f2018%2f08%2f20%2fheres-why-the-bangladeshi-government-made-a-huge-mistake-by-jailing-shahidul-alam%2f%3f> (accessed 25 April 2019).

Sazzad, S.R. (2019) '50 Ahmadiyyas injured in co-ordinated attack on the community in Panchagarh', *Dhaka Tribune.* Online. Available HTTP: <www.dhakatribune.com/bangladesh/nation/2019/02/13/sunnis-attack-ahmadiyyas-in-panchagarh> (accessed 25 April 2019).

Special Powers Act 1974 Bangladesh. Available HTTP: <http://bdlaws.minlaw.gov.bd/print_sections_all.php?id=462.> (accessed 27 August 2019)

Star Business Report. (2019) 'Rubana climbs BGMEA summit', *The Daily Star.* Online. Available HTTP: <www.thedailystar.net/business/news/rubana-climbs-bgmea-summit-1726054> (accessed 25 April 2019).

'Straight talk with Zafar Sobhan: Dr. Rubana Huq'. (2019) 'YouTube video, added by Ekattor TV'. Online. Available HTTP: <www.youtube.com/watch?v=tT27TP-2K40&feature=youtu.be> (accessed 25 April 2019).

'Straight talk with Zafar Sobhan ep 1'. (2018) 'YouTube video, added by Ekattor TV'. Online. Available HTTP: <www.youtube.com/watch?v=0dHRqP9AxLY> (accessed 25 April 2019).

Tribune Desk. (2016) 'Istishon blog blocked for Bangladesh users', *Dhaka Tribune*. Online. Available HTTP: <www.dhakatribune.com/bangladesh/2016/09/26/istishon-blog-blocked-bangladesh-users> (accessed 25 April 2019).

Tribune Desk. (2019) 'Dhaka Tribune journalist arrested under Digital Security Act', *Dhaka Tribune*. Online. Available HTTP: <www.dhakatribune.com/bangladesh/nation/2019/01/01/dhaka-tribune-journalist-arrested-under-digital-security-act> (accessed 25 April 2019).

Ullah, M. (1991) *Press Advice*, Dhaka: Anindya Prakashan.

Wazed, S. (2018) 'Bangladesh Digital Security Act protects free speech and minorities', *Modern Diplomacy*. Online. Available HTTP: <https://moderndiplomacy.eu/2018/03/11/bangladesh-digital-security-act-protects-free-speech-and-minorities/> (accessed 25 April 2019).

Worstall, T. (2016) 'Nonsense about the minimum and living wages in Bangladesh', *Forbes*. Online. Available HTTP: <www.forbes.com/sites/timworstall/2016/12/28/nonsense-about-the-minimum-and-living-wages-in-bangladesh/#55caabaa19a2> (accessed 25 April 2019).

18
KILLING PRESS FREEDOM IN INDIA

Siddhartha Deb

On 5 September 2017, Gauri Lankesh, the editor and publisher of a Bangalore-based weekly, the *Gauri Lankesh Patrike*, was shot dead as she returned home from work. As Lankesh got out of her Toyota car to open a gate to the parking area, a man approached Lankesh, his face obscured by a motorcycle helmet. He fired at her, possibly three times, as she ran toward her house, about 10 feet away. She collapsed before she made it inside (NDTV 2017). Post-mortem reports suggested that Lankesh had been shot twice in the chest and once in the abdomen, two of those shots fired from the front and one from behind. A fourth shot had perhaps missed or misfired. And although examination of the footage from cameras revealed only two men on a motorcycle, including the helmeted shooter, a man about 5 feet tall, the police suggested that two other men had also been involved, following the first pair on a second motorcycle (The News Minute 2017a).

Lankesh was an outspoken left-wing journalist working in an India that, since the election of Narendra Modi as prime minister in 2014, has been run by the right-wing Bharatiya Janata Party (BJP). But the BJP is only the visible, political and overt face of over 30 organizations of the Hindu right, some loosely affiliated to it, others nominally independent (Jha 2017: 2). Together, they all subscribe to the virulent brand of Hindu nationalism known as Hindutva, and they have in recent years been associated with activities ranging from lynchings, riots and bomb blasts to threats of rape, dismemberment, incarceration and hanging of anyone critical of them and their sectarian idea of India.

Although the southern state of Karnataka, of which Bangalore is the capital, is run not by the BJP but by a centrist coalition that includes the Congress Party, it remains a hotbed of activity of the Hindu right. This often manifests itself in violent forms. Two years before the killing of Lankesh, the scholar M.M. Kalburgi was gunned down in his living room in Dharwad, a small city 260 miles northwest of Bangalore (Johnson 2015). Before that, in the neighbouring state of Maharashtra, Govind Pansare, an author and a left-wing trade unionist, and Narendra Dabholkar, a doctor and an activist, had been murdered (Nandgaonkar 2015; Byatnal 2013).

Like Lankesh, all three were critics of Hindutva and wrote in local languages (Lankesh and Kalburgi in Kannada and Pansare and Dabholkar in Marathi). All were killed in a similar manner, shot by motorcycle-borne, helmeted men who had used a 7.65 mm pistol of the kind referred to in India as 'improvised' in recognition of their local, illegal manufacturing origins (*India Today* 2017). Nevertheless, there were some efforts at the beginning to suggest that Lankesh's violent death was sui generis, with the police claiming that the men they suspected of the crime were contract killers. K. Siddaramaiah, chief minister of Karnataka at the time of Lankesh's killing, initially suggested that her death was the work of 'organized crime' but that his government was 'confident of nabbing the culprits and bringing them to book at the earliest' (The News Minute 2017b).

The arrests that unfolded over the coming months, the first of them in March 2018, pointed to sources far more shadowy than organized crime. Eighteen people were named by the Karnataka police in the charge sheet filed in November 2018, 16 of those in police custody. But although this investigation, conducted by an agency in a state not controlled by the BJP, was relatively swift, the stalling of the investigations into the murders of Kalburgi, Pansare and Dabholkar – the latter was assassinated in August 2013 – as well as the ongoing intimidation in India of the media, public intellectuals, activists and ordinary citizens, raises the question of whether this larger climate of violence against journalists will change any time soon, or at all.

But who was Gauri Lankesh? Her assassination certainly made her briefly, startlingly visible everywhere, a slender figure with short, cropped hair, sometimes looking animated and sometimes deeply introspective. Protests and vigils broke out throughout India, under posters and giant, colourful puppets proclaiming, 'I am Gauri.' Within a month of her death, her work had been posthumously granted the Anna Politkovskaya award by a British charity (*The Hindu* 2017a). By December 2017, Navayana, a progressive publishing house in Delhi, had brought out a collection of Lankesh's writings (Navayana 2018) and a Bangalore-based singer, Aarti Rao, released 'Song for Gauri' (Indian Cultural Forum 2017).

Yet the fact remains that while Lankesh's work was known to, and admired by, those connected to progressive politics and causes in India – people critical of Hindu nationalism, crony capitalism, sexism and casteism – it was largely invisible beyond those realms. This was particularly true in the domain of large television and print media, outlets that seesaw between tawdry consumerism and virulent nationalism, between retreating into strategic silence on controversial matters of the day and actively cheering on the right-wing politics of the BJP and its various vigilante armies. *The Times of India*, the nation's largest daily typically exhibits a political headline praising Modi and the BJP in its 'news' mail ('Why link Ram temple with 2019 election? PM hits out at Cong') (Times Headlines

2017), while a salacious question about sex usually opens the second, 'lifestyle' mail ('Should I tell my wife that I had 'drunk sex' with a colleague?') (Times Lifestyle 2017).

Lankesh, who grew up in Bangalore, had in fact, worked for *The Times of India* in the mid-1980s, first in her home city and then in Delhi. She returned to Bangalore in 1989 and began reporting for *Sunday,* a now-defunct English-language magazine, before switching to Kannada-language television in the late 1990s. Kannada was not a language she was initially comfortable in, according to her friends and associates, a detail of some significance because her father Palya Lankesh was a well-known figure in the world of Kannada letters.

A polymath who was an English professor, poet, playwright and filmmaker, he also published a weekly tabloid called *Lankesh Patrike.* The *Lankesh Patrike* did not accept advertisements, and it expressed what the Kannada-speaking journalist Krishna Prasad, former editor of the English newsmagazine *Outlook* and writer of the incisive media and politics blog, Churumuri, described, in an interview, as an 'eclectic world view,' erudite and literary while also being political and punchy (Prasad 2017b).

When Lankesh's father died in 2000, she and her brother, Indrajit, took over *Lankesh Patrike,* the editorial duties going to the former while the latter became the publisher. (Their third sibling, Kavita, a filmmaker, was unconnected to the running of the weekly). This new responsibility involved a significant transition for Lankesh, from English print journalism to Kannada, but also, Prasad notes, a shift in focus from the urban, fluffy issues dominating corporate, English media to rural questions that involved a more critical, engaged kind of journalism.

Lankesh's own comments, in an interview given shortly after she took over *Lankesh Patrike,* support such an interpretation. 'I kept myself deliberately away from the publication because it is such a strident, hard-hitting paper, and I was working for the mainstream English media' (Riti 2000), she said of her father's weekly. She added that she had been stagnating in English-language journalism, while her slightly cryptic references to 'being alone' and 'personal confusions' also seemed to hint at the difficulty of being a single, independent-minded woman – she had been married to the journalist Chidanand Rajghatta, but they divorced in the early 1990s – in a patriarchal, conservative milieu.

Toxic nationalism

By all accounts, Lankesh embraced the transformation. She took an increasingly critical position on what Prasad calls 'the upsurge of Hindutva forces of polarization' around the country and in particular in Karnataka. In 2002, she protested the Hindu right's attempt to claim that the eleventh-century Sufi shrine of Baba Budan Giri, 170 miles west of Bangalore, where both Hindus and Muslims had worshipped for centuries, belonged exclusively to Hindus (Gowda 2017). 'She courted arrest on the streets during the protest,' her former husband Rajghatta, who remained friends with her and is now a Washington, DC-based columnist for *The Times of India*, said in an interview 'She was taking an increasingly leftist stand, always siding with the underdog' (Rajghatta 2017).

As Lankesh became more involved in such political questions, she travelled in June 2004 to the southwestern region of Malnad to attend a press conference held by members of the Indian ultra-left movement variously referred to as Naxalites or Maoists. One of the Naxalites she met there was Saket Rajan, a former Bangalore classmate and the son of an army officer, a radical who had written histories of Karnataka and had worked as an environmentally conscious, muckraking journalist before he grew so disillusioned with the media that he became a guerrilla (Srivatsa 2005). Eight months after the meeting with Lankesh, Rajan was dead, shot down in the kind of extrajudicial execution that the police in India refer to as 'encounters' (Prasad 2017a). Lankesh wrote an article about the killing. Her brother Indrajit, an occasional filmmaker and television personality who, in 2018, cited Modi as the inspiration behind his decision to join the BJP (*New Indian Express* 2017), refused to publish the article, apparently for being much too sympathetic to the Naxalites. Lankesh claimed that he threatened her with a gun (Roy 2017).

Lankesh decided to move on and start her own paper, the *Gauri Lankesh Patrike*. The seemingly minor adjustment in name had a wider significance. It brought into even sharper focus her status as a woman, someone who had positioned herself against the dominant currents in India. Instead of denigrating the Naxalites, she attempted to get the government into dialogue with them. An op-ed in the *New York Times*, translated from the original in her tabloid, talked about the commonality and mutual curiosity of Indians and Pakistanis staring at each other across the heavily militarized border of two nations (Lankesh 2017c). Younger activists often split along the lines of identity and ideology spoke of Lankesh's successful attempts to mediate between them – leftists, Muslims, Dalits, women, the indigenous – on the basis of their common antipathy to Hindutva and its dystopian blueprint for the future (Mondal 2017). Rana Ayyub, an independent journalist whose book *Gujarat Files* is an account of her undercover investigation of the bureaucrats and police officials involved in the anti-Muslim pogroms of 2002, when Modi was the chief minister of Gujarat, talked of the steady support she received from Lankesh. 'She published my book *Gujarat Files* in Kannada despite the threats and intimidation she was subjected to,' Ayyub recalled in an email about her friendship with Lankesh, support especially significant in light of the horrifying abuse Ayyub herself had been subjected to on social media (Ayyub 2017).

All of this made Lankesh dangerous to a Hindu right that, in spite of its vigorous claims to represent a majority, is keenly aware of how recent its widespread dominance remains. A coalition of the marginalized that chooses to confront Hindutva with ideas of pluralism and diversity, while focusing on the economic, social, and environmental problems that plague India, could begin a process of wresting the country from its death grip. That, clearly, could not be allowed to happen.

In recent years, Lankesh's opposition to right-wing Hinduism had taken the form of claiming that the Lingayats, the Karnataka community to which she belonged, should be given the status of a separate religion. In an English article for the non-profit news site The Wire on 5 August 2017, published less than a month before she was killed, Lankesh had reiterated her point that Lingayats were not Hindus but 'followers of Basavanna, the 12th-century social reformer who rebelled against Hindu society and established a new *dharma*.' Her arguments would have angered the powerful, conservative faction of the Lingayats, the Veerashaivas, who saw themselves and, by extension, all Lingayats, as part of the Hindu fold (Lankesh 2017a).

'Lingayats have been recruited as the BJP's largest voting bloc, and that's at stake, and with it the BJP's political future in the state,' Raghu Karnad, an editor at The Wire and a friend of Lankesh's, told me in an email. 'A declaration that Lingayats are a minority religion is the single worst thing that could happen to the BJP before the 2018 Assembly election, when it was planning to eliminate the Congress in Karnataka, its final bastion' (Karnad 2017a). Kalburgi, the scholar assassinated in August 2015, and at whose vigil in Bangalore Karnad first met Lankesh in person, had also been a Lingayat. A scholar of the twelfth-century texts central to the Lingayat movement, Kalburgi too had made a similar argument about Lingayats being quite distinct from caste-based Hinduism. He had been threatened, provided with police protection, and killed 15 days after he asked his bodyguards to be withdrawn (Nagaraj 2017).

Karnad thinks that it was this nexus of local and national politics that led to Lankesh's death. Yet whatever specific combination was involved, the broad finger of suspicion points, inexorably, to members of the Hindu right, people determined to eliminate those it considers its ideological enemies, stubbornly standing in the way of India as a Hindu nation.

Connected killings

Pansare and Dabholkar, who had been assassinated in the neighbouring state of Maharashtra, were not involved specifically in the Lingayat question. They were, in fact, part of what is referred to as the rationalist tradition of southern and western India, a tradition strongly committed to a scientific temperament, to debunking superstition and the power of godmen and gurus, and adamantly opposed to both the political violence of Hindu majoritarianism, as well as its social practice of enforcing caste and gender hierarchies. Pansare had promoted inter-caste marriages, while Dabholkar had been attempting to get the state government to introduce a law to ban superstitious practices. Dabholkar's death finally provoked the government into action and in December 2013, it passed the astonishing-sounding 'Maharashtra Prevention and Eradication of Human Sacrifice and Other Inhuman, Evil and Aghori Practices and Black Magic Act' (Jha 2017: 24).

Yet the investigation of the killings of Dabholkar, Pansare and Kalburgi remained tardy, often at cross-purposes. The inquiry into Dabholkar's killing, the oldest of the four cases, was botched by the Maharashtra Police and transferred, through the orders of the Bombay High Court, to the Central Bureau of Investigation, a federal agency. The Maharashtra Police continue, however, to investigate the Pansare killing, while the Karnataka Police handle the Kalburgi and Lankesh killings. The National Investigation Agency, a federal counter-terrorism body, is also involved (Nevagi 2017). The involvement of different police agencies, with coordination required across bureaucratic boundaries, may be one of the factors responsible for the slow pace of the investigations. Abhay Nevagi, who has been representing the Dabholkar, Pansare, and Kalburgi families pro bono in Bombay High Court in a public interest litigation urging the court to demand accountability from the investigating bodies, said in an interview in January 2017 that there had been 24 hearings in court to date (Nevagi 2017).

And yet, in spite of the lack of coordination, cross-communication and perhaps even unwillingness of the investigating bodies to dig too deep or too far, certain patterns have emerged that connect all four killings. According to the ballistic report of the Karnataka Police, which looked at the bullets fired in the assassinations, two 7.65 mm pistols were used in the killing of Pansare in February 2015. One of those pistols matched with the single weapon used to kill Dabholkar in August 2013, while the other matched with the weapon used to kill Kalburgi in August 2015. 'The CBI laboratory has confirmed these matches,' Nevagi told me.

Reports from the forensic labs in Bangalore in the aftermath of Lankesh's killings appeared to confirm that the weapon used to kill Pansare and Kalburgi was also the weapon used to murder Lankesh. A Bangalore-based reporter who did not wish to be identified told me, a few months after Lankesh's death, that his own sources in the Karnataka police had confirmed this match in weapons and were proceeding from there (Interviewee A 2017).

The suspects around these linked pistols are members of a shadowy Hindu organization called the Sanatan Sanstha (SS), with headquarters in Goa, a state bordering Maharashtra and Karnataka. Two members of the SS, Vinay Pawar and Sarang Akolkar, are suspected of being the gunmen in the Pansare and Dabholkar cases. They are also wanted in connection with a bomb blast in a Goa marketplace in 2009 where two members of the SS died – this explains the involvement of the counter-terrorism NIA – but the government so far has, apparently, been unable to trace them (*The Hindu* 2017b). Two other SS members were also arrested for involvement in the Dabholkar and Pansare murders, a doctor named Vinay Tawade and a man named Samir Gaikwad (Nevagi 2017).

The SS responded to the charges against it by parading 31 lawyers at a court hearing and carrying out its own media blitz (Haygunde 2015). It has threatened, on social media, to sue media organizations reporting critically on its activities (Saradka 2017). 'Hindu Dharma is under constant attack,' one of its websites says, claiming that it 'exposed (sic) corrupt practices of Comrade Pansare and Dr Dabholkar' (Hindu Janajagruti Samiti 2017). Dabholkar's son, Hamid, noted in his affidavit to the Bombay High Court that his father's photograph had been displayed on the SS website before the murder with a 'red cross across his face' (Dabholkar 2015).

Murdering freedom of expression

It is tempting, even on the part of those who were her friends and allies, to think of Lankesh as an exceptional case. Her life lends itself easily to the dramatic, illustrating magnificently through a single, individual portrait the tectonic shifts of a vast, populous country. It lends itself easily to a biopic, a novel, a narrative. Yet it is important to remember that her struggle was connected to a larger reality, in life and in death, beyond even the apparent serial assassination of critics of Hindutva.

There is a reason why India ranks 138th out of 180 countries in the press freedom index of Reporters without Borders, a position even worse than its rankings in world soccer and quite out of keeping with its image as the most populous democracy in the world (Reporters without Borders 2018). Syria, in the middle of a brutal war, ranks 177th. Since 1992, according to the Committee to Protect Journalists, 50 journalists have been killed in India (Committee to Protect Journalists 2019). The number is far higher, according to the International Federation of Journalists, with 84 journalists killed since 2005 (Hearne 2019). The killings have increased in frequency since the coming to power of Modi. Nine journalists were killed in 2015, one of them allegedly set on fire by policemen working for a politician accused of rape (International Federation of Journalists 2016). At the time of Lankesh's killing, the non-profit Indian media watchdog The Hoot, which has been tracking the cases of 30 journalists killed since 2010, reported that there had been a conviction in exactly one case (Seshu and Ninan 2017).

Lankesh was the third journalist killed in 2017 and still not the last – the total would rise to 12 by the end of the year (Thakuria 2017). Even as I spoke to Prasad about Lankesh's death on the phone, he was on his way to Agartala, capital of the northeastern state of Tripura, to prepare a report on the murder of a cable television reporter who had been killed while covering a political demonstration. Like Karnataka, Tripura was due for an assembly election at the time; contrary to Tripura's history as a left-leaning state, the BJP would go on to triumph in a violent, sectarian campaign.

In other states on the front line of armed conflicts between the government and the local population, such as Chattisgarh and Kashmir, it is dangerous to be a journalist even when there are no elections on the horizon. Under cover of serving national security, soldiers, police personnel, gangsters and vigilantes appear to function with complete impunity in these states in their intimidation of media personnel critical of government policies (Reporters without Borders 2017). In Chattisgarh, where mining companies encouraged by the state and paramilitary forces are facing off against indigenous populations and Naxalite guerrilla forces, journalists face dangers ranging from threats and being denied rooms by hotel owners to phones being tapped and arbitrary arrests by the police (Kumar 2016).

In Kashmir, social media, television channels and newspapers are regularly shut down by the government (Lakshmi 2016). Twenty-one journalists have been killed there since the beginning of an armed conflict in 1990 (International Federation of Journalists 2017), and of the 45 attacks on journalists in India recorded in 2017 by The Hoot, six were in Kashmir (Seshu and Ninan 2017). On 14 June 2018, Shujaat Bukhari, a much-respected editor of the independent English daily *Rising Kashmir*, was gunned down outside his office, along with the two policemen assigned to protect him. Modi's government, meanwhile, issued an official warning to foreign journalists based in India about travelling to 'certain areas' without asking for permission. '[W]e all knew it was referring to Kashmir,' Annie Gowen, India bureau chief of *The Washington Post* at the time, wrote in response, noting that this coincided with Modi's open contempt for mainstream media and a rise of attacks on her on social media as she reported on the rise of Hindu extremism (Gowen 2018).

Journalists, however, are not the only people under threat, as the killings of Kalburgi and the rationalists make clear. Sometimes, it appears as if the enemy is information itself, along with transparency, exposure, critical thinking – anything and everything that might be seen as characteristic of a free, open society. By March 2018, 67 citizens and activists seeking information under the Right to Information Act – a transparency law that became operational in 2005 – had been killed (Nayak 2018). Meanwhile, in the central Indian state of Madhya Pradesh, in a scam involving admission to medical colleges that implicated the top BJP officials in the state, including the chief minister Shivraj Singh Chouhan, more than 40 whistleblowers, accused and witnesses – doctors, medical students, police officers and civil servants – turned up mysteriously dead over a period of three years (Sethi 2015).

Ironically, national media attention turned to the case, known as the Vyapam scam, only in 2015 when Akshay Singh, a television reporter investigating the death of a 19-year-old medical student – a death that had been passed off by the police as a suicide in spite of the strangulation marks on her body – himself died in mysterious circumstances in the middle of interviewing the woman's family.

The Vyapam deaths, at least, sparked off a brief phase of outrage within India's mainstream media. But this was an exception, as borne out by the refusal of the national media to touch two stories that involved the paunchy, jowly figure of Amit Shah, president of the Bharatiya Janata Party and Modi's consigliere. In October 2017, The Wire published a story stating that a company owned by Shah's son, Jay Shah, had increased its turnover by 16,000 in the year following Modi's election. From revenues of approximately $780 in 2014–2015, it had gone to $12.5 million the year after. A year later, the company had ceased business altogether (R. Singh 2017).

The English and Hindi media refused to report this story. The same was true of an article carried by the Delhi-based *Caravan* magazine in November 2017 about the suspicious circumstances surrounding the death of a 48-year-old judge named Brijgopal Harkishan Loya. Apparently a healthy man, Loya was said to have died suddenly of a heart attack on 1 December, just weeks before he was scheduled to try Amit Shah, who was implicated in an extrajudicial execution that had taken place in Gujarat under his watch as home minister (Takle 2017). An unknown functionary of the Rashtriya Swayamsevak Organization (RSS), the mass organization that serves as the fountainhead of the Hindu right, helpfully turned up out of nowhere to contact Loya's family and explain that the body was being sent to them for funeral rites. Less than a month later, Shah had been acquitted by the judge who took over the case from Loya.

The caution of the national media can in part be explained by the pressure and intimidation it can expect. The Wire was served with a criminal defamation suit by the lawyers of Jay Shah, with the court obligingly issuing a gag order until the trial was complete (Committee to Protect Journalists 2017). A CBI raid was ordered in June 2017 on the residence of the owners of NDTV, a television channel perceived as being critical of the BJP (Hindu Business Line 2018). The same channel was forced off air for 24 hours in November 2016 as 'punishment' for allegedly revealing strategic details about an anti-terror operation (The Hindu 2016).

Yet external pressure is only a partial explanation for the complaisance of the national media, which from the owners down to editorial staff often seems to be a willing participant in promoting Hindu nationalism. Many of the journalists I interviewed had been forced out from previous jobs when articles they wrote or published ran afoul of the Hindu right. Prasad stepped down from *Outlook* in 2016 because a report he had published had resulted in a defamation lawsuit filed by a BJP functionary. He left voluntarily, he told me, out of respect for the owners, who had come under immense pressure. The story, a five-part investigation painstakingly reported over three months by an independent journalist named Neha Dixit, details the trafficking of 31 indigenous girls, their ages ranging from 3–11, by the RSS, ostensibly for the purpose of Hinduizing them (Committee to Protect Journalists 2016). Hartosh Singh Bal, political editor of *Caravan* magazine, which published the Loya story – a story brought to him by a journalist who had it turned down at the magazine he originally worked for – was fired from his previous job in *Open* magazine just before the 2014 election that brought Modi and the BJP to power. He was seen as being too critical of the BJP, he told me, and has since taken his previous employers to court for being dismissed without being given a reason.

Media on the ropes

Lankesh's work and life take on even greater significance against this wider context. By most accounts, she and her tabloid were struggling by the time of her death. Its circulation was low, somewhere between 10,000 and 15,000. She published textbooks and non-fiction to finance her paper, and her own English writing subsidized her Kannada journalism. In November 2016, her column for the English-language *Bangalore Mirror* was cancelled, reducing her income even further.

Friends and associates of Lankesh mention her calls, often connected to efforts to raise money for the paper. She had stopped paying her insurance premiums, Karnad wrote in a tribute published shortly after her death (Karnad 2017b). The house she lived in, Lankesh's sister Kavita told me, had been a gift to her from their mother. 'People were her property,' she said (Lankesh 2017). Prasad, who blogged about Gauri Lankesh in the immediate aftermath of her killing, wrote that Lankesh had called him in April 2017 and said that she had only enough money left to cover a month's expenses. The demonetization move by the Modi government in November 2016, which involved the sudden cancellation of certain banknotes, had devastated the newsstand sales her publication depended on, especially since her readers were middle class or below and used cash to purchase copies. 'When her end came, the ignition was on in Toyota's cheapest offering in India,' Prasad wrote (Prasad 2017c).

Aside from the steady erosion of the material conditions of her journalism, there was also the cascade of lawsuits, threats and character assassination. In 2016, Lankesh was found guilty by a lower court in a defamation case filed by two BJP politicians who had been accused, in an article published in 2008, of defrauding a jeweller. 'Hope other journos take note,' the head of the BJP IT cell tweeted after the verdict. Lankesh believed that she was being targeted for her politics and intended to challenge the verdict (Sen 2017).

The virulence did not ease up after her death. Because she was buried rather than cremated, in keeping with Lingayat practices, there were attempts to argue that she was Christian (S. Singh 2017). A man from Gujarat describing himself as a 'garment manufacturer' and 'Hindu Nationalist,' one of 1,779 accounts followed by Modi, tweeted the following comment on Lankesh's killing: 'One bitch dies a dog's death all the puppies cry in the same tune' (Gettleman 2017). Another man posted on Facebook, 'Not an iota of sympathy for Lankesh, and the killers should have shredded her body with bullets and even blasted apart her apartment.' He also issued a hit list demanding that Shobha De, Arundhati Roy, Sagarika Ghose, Kavita Krishnan, and Shehla Rashid – all prominent women with liberal to left-wing politics – also be killed (A. Singh 2017).

There is no reason to believe that these comments, and the people who make them, are anomalies. The Hindu right, in the run-up to the 2014 elections, popularized the term 'presstitute,' a word that captures perfectly its loathing of a free press as well as the underclass, marginalized women who make a living as sex workers (*The Times of India* 2015). It remains a depressingly popular hashtag on Indian social media, along with demented rants that come from that alternative universe inhabited by the Hindu right, where attacks on 'presstitutes' are accompanied by fake news that attempts to incite violence against its enemies.

Lie factories exposed

The final issue of *Lankesh Patrike* had, in fact, been called 'In the Age of False News,' with an editorial by Lankesh that called out the Hindu right and its 'lie factories' (Lankesh 2017b). She had noted the proliferation of rumours and right-wing abuse, and the deliberate stoking of violence, including by troll farms that in particular target women, religious minorities and people of opposing ideologies. There is no doubt that the Hindu right led by the BJP, with Modi as its figurehead, is at the forefront of this, with its combination of legal intimidation and draconian powers.

Yet the possibility that the Sanatan Sanstha, a relatively recent entrant into the fold of right-wing Hinduism, might have been behind the murders of Lankesh and the others, raises an even more disturbing possibility. It suggests that under the tutelage of the BJP, a model of entrepreneurial Hindutva has been unleashed, with new organizations that carry out independent acts of violence, although with the tacit support and encouragement of establishment Hindutva. The rise of Adityanath, from leader of the Goraknath temple in the northern state of Uttar Pradesh to becoming its chief minister, captures this dynamic perfectly. He is a member of the BJP, chief minister of a state, spiritual leader of a religious order and head of his own organization, the Hindu Yuva Vahini.

Dhirendra Jha, a political journalist with the news site Scroll and author of the book *Shadow Armies*, a study of Hindu right groups, including the Hindu Yuva Vahini and the SS, notes that they are connected to their parent organization and yet not 'direct projections' (Jha 2017a: 5). The SS, set up as a charitable trust in 1991, was founded by Jayant Balaji Athavale. Beginning as a hypnotherapist in Britain in the 1970s, Athavale transformed himself first into the founding guru of the SS before achieving, in 2015, an even more remarkable transformation. He became, Jha's book notes, a living god as manifested by his 'hair turning golden; divine particles falling from his body; the symbol of OM appearing on his fingernails, forehead and tongue; and various fragrances from his body' (Jha 2017a: 21). The seizure of psychotropic drugs from an SS ashram complex in Maharashtra in September 2016 – enough, Dabholkar's son, a psychiatrist, noted in his affidavit to the Bombay High Court, to be 'only required by a mental hospital' (Dabholkar 2015) – adds to the perception that the group has many of the characteristics of a cult.

The larger ambitions of the SS, however – that of establishing a Hindu Rashtra or Hindu Nation by 2023 – suggests the point where cult and Hindutva converge, and where the shadow world of assassinations meets the realm of electoral politics. 'The choice of the date,' Jha told me over the phone, 'seems to be connected to the assumption that Modi will win the election in 2019 and give them another five years to achieve their target, around 2023 or 2024' (Jha 2017b).

This is a sobering reminder of the reality that while the Karnataka police may be nearing closure when it comes to Lankesh's killing, solving the case will not offer answers to the larger societal questions about information and freedom in India. Because whoever the killers turn out to be, Lankesh's death has to be attributed to more than the men who pulled the trigger and rode the motorcycles, or even those shadowy figures who planned the assassination. She was killed by the culture of impunity promoted by the Hindu right wing in India, and that goes not just all the way up to the heads of states and political leaders, but also includes the complaisant mainstream media and the talking heads who rationalize Hindutva, as well as, most distressingly, a broad swathe of Hindu society – mostly well-to-do, urban, professional, upper caste – that gives this violence its wider base, whether by choosing to ignore it, or by actively cheering on the violence or quietly condoning it.

There is no police force in the world that can address such widespread social and political malaise. Perhaps, all that is available is what Lankesh herself did, the forging of connections with and between people, and giving importance to politics and ideas and words. Kavita Lankesh, in an interview with me soon after her sister's killing, recalled that she had asked her sister to act a small part in *Summer Holidays*, a Kannada children's film she was directing. 'She played an activist,' Kavita said, laughing. 'She was very good at it.'

Acknowledgement

An earlier version of this piece was originally published in *Columbia Journalism Review*.

Bibliography

Ayyub, R. (2017) 'Interview'. Email. 14 December.

Bal, H.S. (2017) Interviewed by Deb, S. 20 December.

Byatnal, A. (2013) 'Rationalist Dabholkar shot dead', *The Hindu*. Available HTTP: <www.thehindu.com/news/national/other-states/rationalist-dabholkar-shot-dead/article5041138.ece> (accessed 27 February 2019).

Committee to Protect Journalists. (2016) 'Indian journalist, magazine face criminal complaint for investigative report'. Available HTTP: <https://cpj.org/2016/08/indian-journalist-magazine-face-criminal-complaint.php> (accessed 1 March 2019).

Committee to Protect Journalists. (2017) 'Indian court bars The Wire from publishing stories on businessman Jay Shah'. Available HTTP: <https://cpj.org/2017/10/indian-court-bars-the-wire-from-publishing-stories.php> (accessed 1 March 2019).

Committee to Protect Journalists. (2019) '50 journalists killed in India'. Available HTTP: <https://cpj.org/data/killed/asia/india/?status=Killed&motiveConfirmed%5B%5D=Confirmed&type%5B%5D=Journalist&cc_fips%5B%5D=IN&start_year=1992&end_year=2019&group_by=location> (accessed 1 March 2019).

Dabholkar, H. (2015) Writ Petition No. 3512, High Court of Judicature at Bombay, Criminal Appellate Jurisdiction.

Gettleman, J. (2017) 'India's modi criticized for following Twitter feed tied to nasty post', *The New York Times*. Available HTTP: <www.nytimes.com/2017/09/08/world/asia/india-modi-twitter.html?_r=0> (accessed 1 March 2019).

Gowda, C. (2017) 'Gauri Lankesh arrived as an activist by protecting Baba Budan Giri Shrine from hindutva brigade', *Outlook*. Available HTTP: <www.outlookindia.com/website/story/gauri-lankesh-arrived-as-an-activist-by-hurting-sangh-parivar/301332> (accessed 28 February 2019).

Gowen, A. (2018) 'Dangerous Times for the press in Kashmir', *Columbia Journalism Review*. Available HTTP: <www.cjr.org/watchdog/journalism-kashmir.php> (accessed 1 March 2019).

Haygunde, C. (2015) 'Pansare killing: Gaikwad was in Thane around time of murder, phone records suggest complicity: Prosecution', *The Indian Express*. Available HTTP: <http://indianexpress.com/article/cities/mumbai/pansare-killing-gaikwad-was-in-thane-around-time-of-murder-phone-records-suggest-complicity-prosecution/> (accessed 28 February 2019).

Hearne, A. (2019) 'Interview', Email. 19 February.

The Hindu. (2016) 'NDTV India ordered to go off air for a day', *The Hindu*. Available HTTP: <www.thehindu.com/news/national/NDTV-India-ordered-to-go-off-air-for-a-day/article16436631.ece> (accessed 1 March 2019).

The Hindu. (2017a). 'Gauri Lankesh honoured with Anna Politkovskaya Award'. Available HTTP: <www.thehindu.com/news/cities/bangalore/gauri-lankesh-posthumously-honoured-with-anna-politkovskaya-award/article19802238.ece> (Accessed 28 February 2019).

The Hindu. (2017b) 'Margao blast: Four members of Hindu group held two killed'. Available HTTP: <www.thehindu.com/news/national/Margao-blast-four-members-of-Hindu-group-held-two-killed/article16887287.ece> (accessed 28 February 2019).

Hindu Business Line. (2018) 'Broadcasters' body voices concern over CBI raids on NDTV'. Available HTTP: <www.thehindubusinessline.com/news/broadcasters-body-voices-concern-over-cbi-raids-on-ndtv/article9723745.ece> (Accessed 1 March 2019).

Hindu Janajagruti Samiti. (2017) 'We shall prove, in court, innocence of Sanatan Seeker Sameer Gaikwad and Dr Vierndrasingh Tawade!'. Available HTTP: <www.hindu jagruti.org/news/106482.html> (accessed 28 February 2019).

India Today. (2017) '7.65 MM pistol used to kill Gauri Lankesh, same as Pansare, Kalburgi & Dabholkar'. Available HTTP: <www.youtube.com/watch?v=O6Vu8iNMxV8> (accessed 28 February 2019).

Indian Cultural Forum. (2017) 'Song for Gauri: They'll try and crush us, they cannot hush us . . .'. Available HTTP: <https://indianculturalforum.in/2017/12/05/song-for-gauri-theyll-try-and-crush-us-they-cannot-hush-us/> (accessed 28 February 2019).

International Federation of Journalists. (2016) 'End impunity in India'. Available HTTP: <https://samsn.ifj.org/end-impunity-in-india-2016/> (accessed 1 March 2019).

International Federation of Journalists. (2017) 'Clampdowns and courage: IFJ South Asia freedom report 2017–2018'.

Interviewee A. (2017) Interviewed by Deb, S. 16 December.

Jha, D. (2017a) *Fringe Organizations and Foot Soldiers of Hindutva*, 1st ed., New Delhi: Juggernaut.

Jha, D. (2017b) Interviewed by Deb, S. 20 December.

Johnson, T.A. (2015) 'Former Karnataka University vice-chancellor M M Kalaburgi, who had run-ins with hardliners, shot', *The Indian Express*. Available HTTP: <http://indianexpress.com/article/india/india-others/ex-vc-m-m-kalaburgi-who-had-run-ins-with-hardliners-shot/> (accessed 27 February 2019).

Karnad, R. (2017a). Email. 13 December.

Karnad, R. (2017b) 'Indian Liberals Must Die', *N+1*. Available HTTP: <https://npluso nemag.com/online-only/online-only/indian-liberals-must-die/> (accessed 1 March 2019).

Kumar, R. (2016) 'Why journalists are leaving India's Chattisgarh', *BBC*. Available HTTP: <www.bbc.com/news/world-asia-india-36386258> (Accessed 1 March 2019).

Lakshmi, R. (2016) 'Authorities in India shut down newspapers in strife-torn Kashmir', *The Washington Post*. Available HTTP: <www.washingtonpost.com/news/worldviews/wp/2016/07/18/modi-government-shuts-down-newspapers-in-strife-torn-kashmir/?utm_term=.034183e415f3> (accessed 1 March 2019).

Lankesh, G. (2017a) 'Making sense of the Lingayat versus Veerashaiva debate', *The Wire*. Available HTTP: <https://thewire.in/167389/karnataka-lingayat-veerashaive-debate/> (accessed 28 February 2019).

Lankesh, G. (2017b) 'Gauri Lankesh's final editorial: "In the age of false news"', *The Wire*. Available HTTP: <https://thewire.in/175643/gauri-lankesh-final-editorial-fake-news/> (accessed 1 March 2019).

Lankesh, G. (2017c) 'The girl from Pakistan', *The New York Times*. 25 September. Available HTTP: <www.nytimes.com/2017/09/25/opinion/gauri-lankesh-the-girl-from-pakistan.html> (accessed 28 February 2019).

Lankesh, K. (2017) Interviewed by Deb, S. 20 December.

Mondal, S. (2017) 'Why was Gauri Lankesh killed?', *The New York Times*. Available HTTP: <www.nytimes.com/2017/09/13/opinion/gauri-lankesh-india-dead.html?_r=0> (accessed 28 February 2019).

Nagaraj, S. (2017) 'Gauri Lankesh and Kalburgi Bound by common thread of Lingayat', *The Quint*. Available HTTP: <www.thequint.com/voices/blogs/gauri-lankesh-murder-mm-kalburgi-similarity> (accessed 28 February 2019).

Nandgaonkar, S. (2015) 'Govind Pansare succumbs to injuries', *The Hindu*. Available HTTP: <www.thehindu.com/news/cities/mumbai/govind-pansare-succumbs-to-injuries/article6917451.ece> (accessed 27 February 2019).

Navayana. (2018) 'Navayana | the way I see it: A Gauri Lankesh reader', *Navayana.org*. Available HTTP: <https://navayana.org/products/the-way-i-see-it-a-gauri-lankesh-reader/> (accessed 28 February 2019).

Nayak, V. (2018) 'As number of murdered RTI activists rises to 67, it is the Modi government that needs to "Act Rightly"', *The Wire*. Available HTTP: <https://thewire.in/rights/as-number-of-murdered-rti-activists-rises-to-67-it-is-modi-government-that-needs-to-act-rightly> (accessed 1 March 2019).

NDTV. (2017) 'CCTV shows Gauri Lankesh being shot', *Youtube*. 6 September. Available HTTP: <www.youtube.com/watch?v=fglWVKKru20>

Nevagi, A. (2017) Interviewed by Deb, S. 16 December.

New Indian Express. (2017) 'Politics is a new responsibility, but cinema forever: Indrajit Lankesh', *The New Indian Express*. Available HTTP: <www.cinemaexpress.com/stories/news/2017/jul/09/politics-is-a-new-responsibility-but-cinema-forever-indrajit-lankesh-1026.html> (accessed 28 February 2019).

The News Minute. (2017a) 'Gauri Lankesh murder: Postmortem report says three bullets hit her, damaging lungs and heart', *The News Minute*. Available HTTP: <www.thenewsminute.com/article/gauri-lankesh-murder-postmortem-report-says-three-bullets-hit-her-damaging-lungs-and-heart> (accessed 27 February 2019).

The News Minute. (2017b) 'Gauri Lankesh murder: SIT to be constituted to bring culprits to book, says Siddaramaiah', *The News Minute*. Available HTTP: <www.thenewsminute.com/article/gauri-lankesh-murder-sit-be-constituted-bring-culprits-book-says-siddaramaiah-67984> (accessed 28 February 2019).

Prasad, K. (2017a) 'India's brain-dead TV channels should get a quote from Saketh Rajan on Gauri Lankesh', *Churumuri*. Available HTTP: <https://churumuri.blog/2017/09/09/indias-brain-dead-tv-channels-should-get-a-quote-from-saketh-rajan-on-gauri-lankesh/> (accessed 28 February 2019).

Prasad, K. (2017b) Interviewed by Deb, S. 4 December.

Prasad, K. (2017c) 'Narendra Modi's #demonetisation had felled Gauri Lankeshi before the bullets did'. Available HTTP: <https://churumuri.blog/2017/09/08/narendra-modis-demonetisation-had-felled-gauri-lankesh-before-the-bullets-did/> (accessed 1 March 2019).

Rajghatta, C. (2017) Interviewed by Deb, S. 11 December.

Reporters without Borders. (2017) 'India: Death threats against journalists by Hindu nationalists'. Available HTTP: <https://rsf.org/en/news/india-death-threats-against-journalists-hindu-nationalists> (accessed 1 March 2019).

Reporters without Borders. (2018) '2018 World Press freedom index'. Available HTTP: <https://rsf.org/en/ranking/2018?> (accessed 1 March 2019).

Riti, M. (2000) 'The rediff interview/ Gauri Lankesh', *Rediff.* Available HTTP: <www.rediff.com/news/2000/may/03gauri.htm> (accessed 28 February 2019).

Roy, N. (2017) 'Gauri Lankesh, journalist and activist, 1962–2017', *Financial Times.* Available HTTP: <https://www.ft.com/content/961c5e1c-93b5-11e7-83ab-f4624cccbabe>

Saradka, A. (2017) 'How media tried to pin Gauri Lankesh's murder to Sanathan Sansta', *Readoo.* Available HTTP: <www.readoo.in/2017/10/how-media-tried-to-pin-gauri-lankeshs-murder-to-sanathan-sansta> (accessed 28 February 2019).

Sen, T. (2017) 'The right to dissent is being threatened, says Gauri Lankesh', *The Wire.* Available HTTP: <https://thewire.in/84674/gauri-lankesh-defamation-bjp/> (accessed 1 March 2019).

Seshu, G. and Ninan, S. (2017) 'Impunity Prevails, but what is the solution?', *The Hoot.* Available HTTP: <www.thehoot.org/free-speech/media-freedom/impunity-prevails-but-what-is-the-solution-10369> (accessed 1 March 2019).

Sethi, A. (2015) 'The mystery of India's deadly exam scam', *The Guardian.* Available HTTP: <www.theguardian.com/world/2015/dec/17/the-mystery-of-indias-deadly-exam-scam> (accessed 1 March 2019).

Singh, A. (2017) 'Police identify man who issued "hit list" after Gauri Lankesh killing', *The Indian Express.* Available HTTP: <http://indianexpress.com/article/cities/delhi/police-identify-man-who-issued-hit-list-after-gauri-lankesh-killing-4965266/> (accessed 1 March 2019).

Singh, R. (2017) 'The golden touch of Jay Amit Shah', *The Wire.* Available HTTP: <https://thewire.in/185512/amit-shah-narendra-modi-jay-shah-bjp/> (accessed 1 March 2019).

Singh, S. (2017) 'Gauri Lankesh murder of Patricks and Hindu burials', *The Times of India.* Available HTTP: <https://blogs.timesofindia.indiatimes.com/sanjeev-singh-blog/gauri-lankesh-murder-of-patricks-and-hindu-burials/> (accessed 1 March 2019).

Srivatsa, S. (2005) 'A brilliant student and a good human being', *The Hindu.* Available HTTP: <www.thehindu.com/2005/02/08/stories/2005020808490500.htm>. <https://sites.google.com/site/sakethrajan/gauri-lankesh-saketh-rajan> (accessed 28 February 2019).

Takle, N. (2017) 'A family breaks its silence: Shocking details emerge in death of judge presiding over Sohrabuddin trial', *The Caravan.* Available HTTP: <www.caravanmagazine.in/vantage/shocking-details-emerge-in-death-of-judge-presiding-over-sohrabuddin-trial-family-breaks-silence> (accessed 1 March 2019).

Thakuria, N. (2017) 'Journo deaths and arrests in 2018: How free is Indian Press, really?', *The Quint.* Available HTTP: <www.thequint.com/voices/opinion/press-freedom-journalists-killed-in-2017-india-gauri-lankesh#gs.ENIew6c5> (accessed 1 March 2019).

Times Headlines. (2017) 'Top headlines: "Why link Ram temple issue to 2019 election?" PM hits out at Cong', Email. 6 December.

Times Lifestyle. (2017) 'The Times of India lifestyle', Email. 6 December.

The Times of India. (2015) 'V.K. Singh in new row, calls media "presstitutes"'. Available HTTP: <https://timesofindia.indiatimes.com/india/VK-Singh-in-new-row-calls-media-presstitutes/articleshow/46844032.cms> (accessed 1 March 2019).

19

MUZZLING THE PRESS

Military control and journalism in Jammu and Kashmir

Farrukh Faheem

Editors' Note: Farrukh Faheem, our contributor from Kashmir, was unable to update or revise the copyedited version of his chapter because the Indian government pulled the plug on the internet after it revoked the region's special status in August 2019. The government anticipated that its unilateral action to abrogate Article 370 of the Constitution would spark an angry and possibly violent backlash and thus moved to make mobilization of protests more difficult. The shutdown of mobile phone networks, cable links and internet communications also draw a veil around what Indian security forces are doing in Kashmir, preventing the dissemination of accurate news and making a mockery of press freedom. Under the lockdown, New Delhi decides what is reported about Kashmir. The state of press freedom in India is so compromised that the Press Council of India supports this muzzling of the media in the name of the national interest which apparently no longer extends to constitutional rights and civil liberties. It is important that readers know the context and why it has not been possible for the author to cover these developments. He was able to view and approve the final page proofs.

In the state of Jammu and Kashmir in northern India, the ongoing efforts of the Indian central government to stifle aspirations for self-determination has created a situation where press freedom is a mere chimera. This chapter examines the nature and extent of curbs on press freedom and how they reflect the contested nature of the region's relationship with the Indian state. Such a relationship required nurturing an ersatz democracy to serve as a tool of the state to control dissent in the region, an imperative that mandates a muzzling of the media. Thus, the history and politics of the Indian subjugation of Kashmir are inseparable from an assessment of freedom of expression and press freedom in the troubled region.

Background

During the British colonization of the Indian subcontinent, the state of Jammu and Kashmir, commonly called Kashmir, was one of the 500 princely states of British India. Similar to Travancore in the south, bigger states like Kashmir were almost like countries in their own right (Copland 1997). As the British began hastily planning for the end of colonial rule after World War II, they declared that the princes would decide whether the princely states like Kashmir would accede to the newly imagined nation-states of India or Pakistan. This decision triggered intense political manoeuvering by Kashmiri Muslim subjects who had already been opposing the autocratic rule of an ethnically Hindu prince.

As early as the 1930s, Muslim subjects of Kashmir began rallying behind their leader Sheikh Abdullah against the oppressive regime of the Hindu-Dogra Prince Hari Singh. The Hindu monarchy prohibited formation of associations and banned the press in the state. In order to circumvent this ban, news items and articles were sent outside the state to Lahore for publication. Newspapers like *Inquilab* (*The Revolution*), *Kashmiri Mazlum* (*Oppressed Kashmiri*) and *Kashmiri Musalman* (*Muslim Kashmiri*) published news reports about the oppression Kashimiri Muslims suffered under Hindu-Dogra kings (Bazaz 2002).

In 1946, Sheikh Abdullah launched a people's movement called the Quit Kashmir movement to oust the monarchy of Hari Singh. On the designated day of the transfer of power to the new dominions of India and Pakistan, the monarch, Hari Singh, did not declare his intentions of acceding to either of the dominions. Instead, he offered to maintain the status quo by asking the two dominions to sign an agreement to permit the continuation of various essential services even if their constitutional authority over the affairs of the state was uncertain. While the offer was accepted by Pakistan, India rejected it. In a significant political development, the Muslim population of the Jammu region revolted against the monarch, who was held responsible for carrying out large-scale killings of his Muslim subjects around the time of partition of the subcontinent. The revolt was supported by the co-religionists from the adjoining tribal regions that fell under the control of Pakistan in the aftermath of the partition. To contain the revolt that threatened the monarchy, Hari Singh sought military help from India. India argued that it required accession of Jammu and Kashmir to the Indian Union as a pre-condition for military assistance. Despite confusion about whether the prince finally agreed, India staged a strong claim that Jammu and Kashmir is now a part of the Indian nation-state. In a move that sowed further confusion and tensions, the monarch appointed the popular Kashmiri Muslim leader Sheikh Abdullah as prime minister of the interim government.

To gain control over the region, India and Pakistan went to war. The fighting resulted in the United Nations intervention and a call for a ceasefire, asking both parties to reduce the strength of their troops in the region. The United Nations also proposed a plebiscite under its supervision to decide the future status of the Jammu and Kashmir in accordance with the will of the people. This proposal confronted the reality of the erstwhile princely state of Jammu and Kashmir divided into two – one part being under the control of India and the other under Pakistan. After prolonged negotiations with Indian Prime Minister Jawaharlal Nehru, Abdullah was able to secure maximum autonomy for the region with Indian central government exercising control over defence, foreign affairs and communications.

Over the years, by diluting the autonomous status enjoyed by the region under the menacing shadow of 700,000 Indian troops stationed in Jammu and Kashmir, the Indian state has increased its stranglehold over the territory. The high military presence makes Jammu and Kashmir one of the most militarized regions in the world, with almost one Indian soldier for every ten Kashmiris (Mishra 2000; Junaid 2013).

Since 1947, the region of Jammu and Kashmir has witnessed unrest in the aftermath of its division and subsequent control of its two parts by the newly created dominions of India and Pakistan. In the early 1990s, the demand for self-determination sparked a popular uprising and militant resistance against the Indian state's repressive occupation. Despite the praetorian military presence and reduction in the number of militants to a few hundred, the demand for self-determination remains powerful, periodically erupting into cyclic civilian protests involving demonstrations by large numbers of people. Over the years, clampdowns on press and civil liberties are a regular feature of the Indian state's response to such protests. Crackdowns on reporters, revoking curfew passes, blocking communication lines and confiscating films and notebooks have become part of everyday life for journalists in the region (Coll 1990). In recent years, with an increase in popular mobilizations against the Indian state, there has been an increase in internet shutdowns and the banning of newspapers and local television networks, in addition to violence targeting journalists.

Everyday politics and democracy in Kashmir

Much of the region's history has been dominated by India's efforts to manipulate elections and suppress dissent. In 1953, Sheikh Abdullah, the first Prime Minister of Jammu and Kashmir, was arrested during a military coup, triggering a series of cyclic protests demanding a plebiscite in the region. He was charged with illegally seeking Kashmir's independence and was imprisoned for 11 years except for a break of few months in 1968. During this brief respite from jail, Abdullah lamented that, 'Indian democracy stops short at Pathankot,' the last outpost that separates India from Jammu and Kashmir (Bose 2013).

After Abdullah's arrest, a series of Kashmiri politicians were installed by New Delhi. They actively collaborated in extending the Indian state's control over Jammu and Kashmir. During this period, under Bakshi Ghulam Mohammad, who was installed as the Prime Minister in 1953, the press was subject to tremendous state repression. During the 1960s and 1970s, newspapers struggled to survive under the intensified press curbs. One of the most popular vernacular newspapers in the region, *The Srinagar Times*, was banned for two months in 1970 for being critical of the Indian government's policies and of its collaborators in Kashmir. As many as 11 newspapers were banned during the 1970s (Ahmad 2018). Bakshi's regime banned those newspapers that were allegedly displaying pro-Pakistan leanings or were questioning Kashmir's accession to the Indian Union. Newspapers that supported Kashmir's accession to India were permitted to publish and were promoted with financial support through placement of government advertisements (Department of Information 1955a). The Department of Information monitored newspaper publications, only allowing them to publish the official positions of the state. Many newspaper editors at that time were arrested for being too critical of the regime (Kanjiwal 2017).

Scholars studying state-media relations argue that curbs on press freedom track shifting government incentives for information control. Governments tend to harass the media more during episodes of major public protests and outbreaks of civil conflict (Young 2012). In the context of Kashmir, after the arrest of the popular leader Sheikh Abdullah, a free press posed a clear threat to the Indian state and its collaborators in the region. For example, massive demonstrations demanding plebiscite were embarrassing for an Indian government that was eager to retain control of Kashmir for nationalist and geopolitical reasons. In response to these protests, the Bakshi regime developed close ties with the Indian and international media and made efforts to 'bring them into line with state's narrative on socio-political developments' (Kanjiwal 2017: 78). Indian and international media personnel who wanted to cover Kashmir were required to obtain prior permission to enter the region (Department of Information 1955b). Following the pattern established under Bakshi's regime, subsequent governments in the region were allowed to run a corrupt and 'un-representative government in return for Jammu and Kashmir's integration with India' (Bose 2013: 68).

This quid pro quo has influenced electoral democracy in the region, with massive vote rigging and other dubious practices to ensure that New Delhi's wishes prevailed (Lone 2018: 258; Widmalm 2002: 50). This systemic corruption of democracy has acted as a catalyst to spark cyclic protests demanding the right to self-determination. Although 'democracy' was intermittently revived through the ritual of rigged elections, civil liberties and freedom of speech remained elusive. The Indian state's polices, and overall engagement in the region, have been dominated by subversion of democratic institutions, including a free press (Behera 2006).

In 1987, the Muslim United Front, a coalition of opposition parties, contested and lost a massively rigged election (Snedden 2015), triggering a series of protests demanding the right to self-determination. There were reports that the Indian military compelled people to go to the polling stations and return with a proof of having voted (Pillai 1996). Thousands of people marched to the headquarters of the United Nations Military Observer Group in Srinagar protesting the vote fraud and demanding a plebiscite. Even top Kashmiri bureaucrats joined in. Nearly 100,000 government employees went on strike against the Indian occupation (Sidhu 1990). Given the situation of turmoil and lack of credibility of Indian electoral processes in Jammu and Kashmir, the Indian state could not hold elections for the next nine years, until 1996. In these nine years, the leaders of the All Party Hurriyat Conference (The All-Party Freedom Conference, APHC), a coalition of parties demanding self-determination, were arrested and newspapers were directed not to report their press statements or interviews (Gautam Navlakha 1996). There was complete press censorship. In one instance, copies of the largest selling local English-language newspaper, *The Kashmir Times*, were confiscated for four consecutive days, as were copies of the Chandigarh-based *Tribune*. In Kashmir, democracy and press freedom exercised at gunpoint has become a reality that reproaches India's posturing as the world's largest democracy.

Relying on military might, the Indian state consolidated its power in the region and has been able to repeatedly enforce its authority on the streets of Kashmir. This consolidation coincided with military operations and the imposition of exceptional laws depriving Kashmiris of fundamental civil and human rights, including freedom of expression (Kazi 2007). The Jammu and Kashmir Armed Forces Special Powers Act (AFSPA) of 1990 and Public Safety Act (PSA) of 1978 serve to ensure that state security forces can act with immunity and impunity in imposing New Delhi's writ. A precursor of AFSPA called the Armed Forces (Special Powers) Ordinance, 1942 was introduced by the British colonial government to crush the anti-colonial Quit India movement. In 1958, the post-colonial nation-state of India decided to continue with the law rechristened as AFSPA to bestow powers and immunity on state security forces in the northeastern regions of India. This Act was invoked in 1990 in Kashmir to crush the armed uprising against Indian rule in the region. This law grants the armed forces the power to search, arrest and execute any individual with impunity. Under the provisions of this act, even a non-commissioned officer can shoot to kill on the basis of mere suspicion. The armed forces enjoy complete legal immunity for their actions. In 2012, the United Nations Special Rapporteur on Extrajudicial, Summary or Arbitrary Executions published a report observing that retaining a law like the AFPSA runs counter to the basic principles of democracy and human rights (Prakash 2013).

Similarly, the Public Safety Act (PSA) was first introduced in the region in 1978. Since its introduction, at least 10,000–20,000 people have been detained under its terms. In 2011, Amnesty International observed that the act poses a threat to certain basic and fundamental rights of the people: the rights to life and liberty, freedom of speech and expression, and freedom of movement. It described the PSA as a 'Lawless Law.' The law has been designed to curb participation in protests (Manecksha 2016; Peer 2013).

Since 2003, violence in the region has declined considerably. However, the Indian state's engagement with the region reflects contradictions between its articulated ideals of 'normalcy' and its actual policy on the ground. The core democratic values of access to justice and freedom of expression have both suffered from the contradiction 'between the status-quo and political demands in contemporary Kashmir' (Staniland 2013: 951). The control of the Indian state over the everyday life of Kashmiris suppresses their individual freedom, and they have very few alternatives to check or question the power of the Indian armed forces.

Cyclic protests and curbs on press freedom

In 2008, the state government decided to transfer 98 acres of land to the Shri Amarnath Shrine Board (SASB), a trust that looks after a popular Hindu shrine. This controversial decision attracted a strong reaction in Kashmir, where land ownership is a very sensitive issue. In the region, non-residents are barred from owning land. Over 500,000 people assembled in a playground in Srinagar and later marched to the United Nations Military Observer Group's office, demanding a peaceful resolution of the dispute in accordance with the aspirations of the people. Protesters accused the Indian state of planning to build Hindu settlements in a Muslim-majority area in an effort to change the demographic balance in the region. A blockade imposed by Hindu nationalists prevented essential supplies from flowing into Kashmir and blocked the shipment of apples, the state's main cash crop, from being shipped to markets in India during the peak harvest season. A march by traders, farmers and ordinary people to the Line of Control (LOC) that divides the two Kashmirs was foiled by the Indian armed forces, resulting in the killing of a prominent APHC leader. Fourteen people were killed and hundreds injured during the 61-day-long agitation (Gk 2008; TOI 2008; *The New York Times* 2008). More than 30 journalists were beaten up by the Indian armed forces, while local TV stations were not allowed to broadcast and newspapers were unable to publish because of the day-and-night curfew. The advocacy group Reporters without Borders observed that 'the government in New Delhi cannot continue to ignore the fact that the press in Kashmir has been subject to a state of exception that violates the Indian constitution' (Reporters without Borders 2008). The advocacy group also urged the Indian government to investigate police violence and the killing of a photojournalist.

Similar to 2008, the cyclic protests of 2009 and 2010 challenged the dominant discourse that 'normalcy' and 'peace' is being restored in the region. The 2009 protests were triggered by rape and murder of two women by the Indian Armed forces in the Shopian district of Jammu and Kashmir. The Shopian case represented the intrusion of state violence into the private lives of the population over the years (Duschinski and Hoffman 2011). At least four people died and hundreds were injured across Kashmir in this round of protests (*The Indian Express* 2009).

The 2010 protests were triggered by the killing of a 17-year-old student Tufail Mattoo who was killed in cold blood by Indian armed forces on 10 June. 'As crowds poured into the streets to protest his death, Indian paramilitary forces responded with a "bullet for a stone" policy amidst an atmosphere increasingly charged with restrictive curfews, arbitrary arrests, stone pelting, and increasingly violent protests' (Varma 2010). Text messaging and cellular services were blocked on 30 June, and curbs were imposed on local print and televised news reports. In addition, curfew passes of local journalists were not honoured, and several media professionals were assaulted by the Indian police. To protest against the harassment and assault on journalists, the Press Guild of Kashmir unanimously decided to suspend local newspaper publications for a day (Varma 2010). A local photojournalist, Bilal Bahadur, was injured while he took pictures of Indian police assaulting mourners carrying the dead body of Muzzafar Bhat, another 17-year-old schoolboy killed by the Indian forces (Peer 2010). Indian police also used pump-action shotguns that fire metal pellets as a means of crowd control. These inherently inaccurate shotguns fire hundreds of metal pellets that spread over a wide area, causing severe eye injuries and sometimes blinding the victims. One hundred and twelve people were killed, and thousands were injured during these protests (Ganai 2013).

The year 2010 has been dubbed as the year of 'media emergency.' The state government withdrew the curfew passes of local journalists. Even as there was a clampdown on local journalists, the government allowed Delhi-based television channel's ready access and movement on the curfew bound streets of the region. Before the protests broke out, close to 50 newspapers hit the stands in Srinagar every day. On 8 July, newspapers stopped publications for four consecutive days to protest the government's decision to withdraw the curfew passes of local journalists. In response, at least 15 journalists were roughed up by the Indian police (Motta 2010).

In a democracy, it is expected that all groups and individuals should be able to express their views and interests through a process of rational deliberation. Through such dialogue, democracies seek to render violence unnecessary. Yet, as is evident from the history of Jammu and Kashmir, this is not always the case. From 2003, Kashmir witnessed a significant decrease in the incidents of militant attacks on the Indian army, officially proclaimed as the 'return of normalcy.' To shift away from the repressive narrative of the early 1990s, the Indian state – at least in in its public posturing – supports free and fair elections, free speech and non-violent protests. Between 1996 and 2016, four assembly elections were held in Jammu and Kashmir and the rhetoric of 'peace and development' and free elections dominate the Indian state's version of its engagement in Kashmir. Yet this has not led to a tangible difference on the ground, and in reality, the situation has only gone from bad to worse (Faheem 2018). As is evident from the previous discussion, India's illiberal democracy has made full use of the tools of repression to stifle Kashmiri voices and deny them basic liberties. Freedom of the press can't be allowed in Kashmir, because it would expose the hypocrisy of the Indian state and leave it open to ridicule and condemnation for extensive human rights abuses that are stoking local demands for accountability.

Sword of Damocles

What passes for normalcy in Kashmir hangs by a fragile thread. The 2016 protests were triggered by the killing of a 22-year-old rebel commander Burhan Wani. He was killed in an encounter with the Indian armed forces in a small village in the southern part of Kashmir on 8 July. He was extremely active on social media, and would often post his video messages about the Indian state's oppression in Kashmir and the need to resist it. It is believed that Wani became a militant at the age of 15, quickly growing into an internet sensation and a vexing enemy of the occupying forces. Early in the morning on 9 July, Wani's body was handed over to his family. By 9 a.m., tens of thousands of people had joined the funeral prayers. A remarkable 22 rounds of funeral prayers were held for him as the day progressed, an outpouring of grief and expression of defiance.

In response to the protests triggered by Wani's killing, the government clamped down on the media. For the first time since the early 1990s uprising, the Indian police prevented operation of the printing presses, seized any published newspapers and detained the publication's staff. As well as these extraordinary curbs on newspaper publication, internet and cellular communications were also cut (Masood 2016). Suddenly, the narrative of normalcy evaporated. The newspaper *Kashmir Reader* was banned for three months. The *Kashmir Reader* was launched in May 2012. Its owner ran a successful advertising business in Srinagar. He stopped publication of its popular monthly magazine *Conveyor* to enter the newspaper business. The English daily rapidly rose to prominence, making a place for itself in Kashmir's crowded newspaper scene. A government order dated 30 September 2016 directed the publisher to 'abstain from printing and publishing so that the disturbance of public tranquillity is prevented' (The CARAVAN 2016). The state information department issued a statement saying that before the order was issued, they had served a notice to the newspaper asking them to explain its 'position on a series of items [by *Kashmir Reader*] disturbing public tranquillity and notwithstanding the principles of rules governing the subject' (Mir 2016). A statement quoting the district magistrate of Srinagar also declared that the decision to ban the *Kashmir Reader* was taken 'after a series of reports from various agencies and credible inputs,' providing sufficient grounds for censorship (ibid). The editor of the *Kashmir Reader*, Hilal Mir questioned the state's decision and the justification given by the information department in an opinion piece he wrote for a popular Indian daily, asking:

> Since when did the perusal of a newspaper's content become the job of unnamable 'agencies?' What does 'credible inputs providing sufficient ground for the decision' mean? Every government institution in the thick of the raging uprising, especially police, army, CRPF and the civil administration, has its own PR cell. Reporters regularly talk to them for information and comments. We have not received a single complaint from the information department on any report/article so far. What then made the government act on the reports of 'various agencies?'
>
> *(Mir 2016)*

In a place like Kashmir, the extent of breathing space that the media enjoys depends on reading the shifting signs of 'national security' concerns. Fearing reprisals from the state, journalists work on a razor's edge, testing the limits while engaging in a degree of self-censorship. The ban on the *Kashmir Reader* was lifted after three months. By that time, the newspaper had already laid off 50 per cent of its staff. Mir also lost his job with the *Kashmir Reader* during the 2016 ban. He informed me that the government has used its financial leverage over the media by banning advertisements in the two largest circulating newspapers in the region: the *Greater Kashmir* and the *Kashmir Reader*. Presently working for *Greater Kashmir*, Mir observes that 'the state's control over the media exists at multiple levels. One that is seemingly very innocuous but very effective is the government's advertisements. These are completely under the control of the Indian state and its collaborators in Kashmir' (Interview, 20 March 2019).

In the absence of big corporate accounts, the local newspapers in the region are completely dependent on revenue from state advertisements. The International Federation of Journalists' 2017 report observes that:

> some publications receive advertisements disproportionate to their circulation (some print a token hundred copies for the record, while raking in large advertisement revenue). Pro-government publications are favoured with government houses, land, and other 'privileges' for propagating the official line. Those who do not play the game, pay a price.
>
> *(International Federation of Journalists 2017)*

Amnesty International notes that in October 2017, the government of India's Ministry of Home Affairs sent a letter to senior officials of the Jammu and Kashmir government and police, stating that:

> It is understood that some newspapers in J&K are publishing highly radicalized content . . . publishing of anti-national articles in the newspapers of the state should be strictly dealt with. Such newspapers should also not be given any patronage by way of advertisements by the state government.
>
> *(Amnesty International 2018)*

During ordinary times, the state may be indifferent to the press; however, during periods of unrest, the state deploys direct methods of controlling the media. Recalling his experience of working at the *Kashmir Reader*, Mir reflects:

> Kashmir Reader was a fairly independent newspaper. It was owned and run by a businessman. Initially, there were no government advertisements at all. Whatever private advertisements he would get, he managed to run the newspaper from that. He hired the best of the talent and he paid them well. But during 2016, when so much was happening around, it was the only newspaper which reported things the way they were unfolding. And then it was banned for three months. After that most of us left the newspaper. We were forced by circumstances. We understood that the owner is

being harassed by the state; we thought it wise that if this newspaper is to survive, we'd better leave. We had no other option.

(Interview, 20 March 2019)

Showkat Motta, presently the owner and the editor of the magazine *Kashmir Narrator*, believes that in Kashmir, the state continues to be the main threat to press freedom. He observes that the 'state is like a Damocles' sword hanging over the heads of newspaper publishers. In our part of the world it is the state that decides how much breathing space the press should enjoy and for how long' (Motta 2019). Motta expressed this concern for good reason. On 14 August 2018 at around 11 p.m., his 30-year-old assistant editor, Asif Sultan, was taken away from his house in Srinagar by police. Just one month before his arrest on 1 July 2018, the *Kashmir Narrator* had published 'The Rise of Burhan,' Sultan's feature on the popular underground youth leader Burhan Wani. On 31 August 2018, the police announced the arrest of Sultan; he was booked under an anti-terror law and accused of harbouring militants.

The monthly magazine *Kashmir Narrator* was first published in 2016, and before Sultan's arrest, the magazine would hit the newsstands on time. With his assistant editor behind bars, the magazine only managed its release after a delay of three months, as Motta now divides his time between the courtroom and his office.

In Kashmir, the fear of reprisals leads to self-censorship, but sometimes the passion of journalists gets the better of their self-preservation instincts. Commenting on Asif Sultan's arrest, Motta explains:

> We had decided that if we are doing a story on Burhan Wani two years after his death it should be different. So we decided to dig into the story. . . . We decided that we would like to investigate how did he manage to evade an encounter with Indian army for five long years? Who offered him food and shelter? Asif [Sultan] did a fine job. He interviewed young people, his former associates. He also met his childhood friends. So it was an exclusive story with exclusive pictures.

(Interview, 15 January 2019)

Fifteen days after the story appeared in the *Kashmir Narrator*, Motta received an email apparently from the local office of the Central Investigation Department (CID), seeking an explanation regarding the story and threatening him with action in case he did not respond to the email. Motta says that the email in question was not sent from the department's official email, but from an unofficial Gmail account (Interview, 15 January 2019).

In a highly militarized place like Kashmir, if a journalist has to cover a story on an ongoing encounter between Indian armed forces and militants, they often do not get access to the site of the encounter. As mentioned earlier, they are either detained or their curfew passes are not honoured. The lack of access to such sites also denies them access to independent sources. In the absence of independent sources, news reports tend to reproduce police press briefings and official accounts. As one Kashmiri journalist observes:

> I remember when I started my work as a journalist in a local newspaper. Every evening we used to get a police press note. Ten militants killed today. . . . What I and my colleagues used to do is just change the names of the place and the number of the militants, 'we got a report and encircled the house, they opened up fire, we retaliated and then such and such militant was killed.' That is it. We just had to change the name of the places and the militants and only the numbers change. So nothing has changed since the 1990s. We are now in 2019 you have the same story, you have the same information and also the source of information remains the same: the Indian police and the army.
>
> *(Interview, 20 March 2019)*

The state adopts a carrot-and-stick policy towards the media. In Kashmir, local journalists 'are often the targets of violence by soldiers acting with the [Indian] government's tacit consent' (Reporters without Borders 2008). This creates an atmosphere of intimidation that encourages self-censorship. The content of newspapers is also influenced by the economic vulnerability of the media and their dependency on government advertising. The banning of newspapers, beating, arresting and disappearing of journalists, and the channelling of advertisements to pro-government newspapers, is how the game is played. As Motta observes:

> The state has achieved whatever it wanted to achieve by arresting Asif [Sultan]. You see one of my reporters just completed an assignment on the infamous torture center Papa Two. This assignment was given to him last year. It is a brilliant story . . . an account of people who have survived Papa Two. Recently a young school teacher, Rizwan, who was picked up by Indian police was killed in one of the torture centers. So for a moment I thought this is the right time to publish the story. But with my assistant editor still languishing in the prison. . . . I have to think twice before I decide to do so.'
>
> *(Interview, 15 January 2019).*

Regions of conflict are also battlefields of contested narratives. In the context of Kashmir, the official Indian narratives of 'normalcy' and 'democracy' promote images of beautiful landscapes and tourists flocking to the region. However, at times these aspirational narratives are contested and subverted by Kashmiri photojournalists and cartoonists. Images of young boys being dragged off into police vehicles, or shot dead by Indian police, indict the official versions of the incidents. Similarly, Kashmiri cartoonists have presented some of the most scathing criticisms of the Indian state's response to cyclic protests in the region. Unsurprisingly, incidents of Kashmiri cartoonists are harassed, and photojournalists being arrested or injured by pellets fired by Indian police, have increased (The Wire 2018; Zargar 2016).

The difficult choices that journalists have to make about remaining silent or speaking out reveals something about the perceived inequality of power that exists between the media and the state in the region. Overt censorship by the state involves the banning of newspapers, denial of state advertisements, arrests, assaults, killings and maiming of journalists, while the practice of self-censorship in the form of muted discussions regarding state oppression and extrajudicial killings of civilians is the goal of this explicit censorship and intimidation – one that is not always achieved.

Conclusion

Although hyper-nationalist regimes are commonly seen as the worst threat to press freedom, under Indian rule, it doesn't seem to matter in Jammu and Kashmir. A free press in Kashmir is perceived to be an enemy of the state and is treated as such. Through democratic contrivance and military control, the Indian state manages the news and tries to stifle the yearning for self-determination. However, the inherent contradiction in the Indian government's 'normalcy' discourse is reflected in cyclic uprisings that have time and again erupted in the region. The heavy-handed approach of New Delhi has been counterproductive as new generations of Kashmiris experience the bitterness of occupation and repression. Press censorship sends an unmistakable message that the state fears transparency and accountability, whetting popular desires. Bland press releases can't disguise the harsh reality that Kashmiris face on a daily basis.

As the state curbs media freedoms, the pretence of Indian democracy in Kashmir confronts popular support for self-determination. In periodic clampdowns, Kashmiri journalists are far more vulnerable than those from outside the region. A recent report by the International Federation of Journalists (2017) suggests that by denying them curfew passes the local journalists face discrimination by the state. The local journalists believe that they are perceived as 'anti-national,' while the parachute journalists from New Delhi, who propagate positive images of Kashmir palatable to the Indian nationalist discourse, get privileged access and treatment. They influence popular Indian perceptions of the Kashmir 'problem,' one that is attributed to Pakistani machinations far more than local grievances. So, when there are attacks against Indian forces, the Indian media stokes demands for retaliation against Pakistan. There is little space for reflecting on the Kashmiri problem separate from this geopolitical rivalry, as Indian nationalism dictates narratives of victimization and revenge. Thus, in assessing prospects for press freedom in Kashmir, the peculiar politics of contested sovereignty remain a critical factor.

Bibliography

Ahmad, K.B. (2018) 'Journalism in Kashmir: Origin and evolution', *Rising Kashmir.* 9 March. Online. Available HTTP: <http://risingkashmir.com/news/journalism-in-kashmir-origin-and-evolution> (accessed 1 March 2019).

Amnesty International. (2018) 'JK Deteriorating space for freedom'. Online. Available HTTP: <https://amnesty.org.in/news-update/jk-deteriorating-space-for-freedom-of-press/> (accessed 1 April 2019).

Ashiq, P. (2019) 'Many journalists barred from R-Day function in Sringar', *The Hindu.* 27 January. Online. Available HTTP: <www.thehindu.com/news/national/many-journalists-barred-from-r-day-function-in-srinagar/article26102060.ece> (accessed 1 April 2019).

Bazaz, P.N. (2002) *Inside Kashmir,* Srinagar: Gulshan Publishers.

Behera, N.C. (2006) *Demystifying Kashmir,* Washington, DC: The Brookings Institution.

Bhinda, N. (1994) 'The Kashmir conflict', in M. Cranna (ed.) *The True Cost of Conflict,* London: Earthscan.

Bose, S. (2013) *Transforming India: Challenges to the World's Largest Democracy,* Cambridge: Harvard University Press.

The CARAVAN. (2016) 'Two months into the ban on the Kashmir reader, its journalists stand with the newspaper'. 27 November. Online. Available HTTP: <https://caravan magazine.in/vantage/two-months-ban-kashmir-reader-journalists-stand-with-news paper> (accessed 1 April 2019).

Coll, S. (1990) 'India clamps down on press in Kashmir', *The Washington Post.* Online. Available HTTP: <www.washingtonpost.com/archive/politics/1990/01/27/india-clamps-down-on-press-in-kashmir/b0196195-e0f6-4053-92bb-50a718f8fcc0/?utm_term=.835b3be79754> (accessed 31 March 2019).

Copland, I. (1997) *The Princes of India in the Endgame of Empire, 1917–1947,* Cambridge: Cambridge University Press.

Department of Information. (1955a) 'Correspondence of the information minister with press', Department of Information, Srinagar State Archives. File 152 NF/C-35/55.

Department of Information. (1955b) 'Permission sought by the local and foreign correspondents', Jammu.

Duschinski H. and Hoffman B. (2011) 'Everyday violence, institutional denial and struggles for justice in Kashmir', *Race & Class,* 52: 44–70.

Faheem, F. (2018) 'Understanding student protests in Kashmir', *Kashmir Narrator.* 27 July. Online. Available HTTP: <http://kashmirnarrator.com/understanding-student-protests-in-kashmir/> (accessed 31 2019).

Ganai, N. (2013) 'National Conference blames the army for 2010 unrest in Kashmir Valley', *India Today.* 2 January. Online. Available HTTP: <www.indiatoday.in/india/north/story/jammu-and-kashmir-national-conference-blames-army-for-2010-unrest-150579-2013-01-02> (accessed 3 April 2019).

Gautam Navlakha, R.M. (1996) 'Political situation in Kashmir: Duped by media and government', *Economic and Political Weekly,* 31: 1927–1931.

GK. (2008) 'Memorandum submitted', *Greater Kashmir.* 18 August, p. 1. Srinagar, GK Communications.

Hoffman, B.A. (2013) 'Contestations over law, power and representation in Kashmir Valley', *Interventions: International Journal of Post-Colonial Studies,* 16(4), July: 501–530.

The Indian Express. (2009) '100 injured as protests Paralyse Kashmir', *Indian Express.* 3 June. Online. Available HTTP: <https://archive.indianexpress.com/news/100-injured-as-protests-paralyse-kashmir-val/470714/> (accessed 1 March 2019).

International Federation of Journalists. (2017) 'Kashmir's media in peril: A situation report', Communications and Campaigns Department. 30 November. Online. Available HTTP: <www.ifj.org/media-centre/reports/detail/kashmirs-media-in-peril-a-situation-report-2017/category/asia-pacific.html> (accessed 29 March 2019).

Junaid, Mohamad. (2013) "Death and Life Under Occupation: Space, Violence, and Memory in Kashmir." in Kamala Visweswaran (ed.), *Everyday Occupations: Experiencing Militarism in South Asia and the Middle East*, Philadelphia: University of Pennsylvania Press. 158–190.

Kanjiwal, H. (2017) 'Building a new Kashmir: Bakshi Ghulam Muhammad and the politics of state-Formation', Un-published Thesis, The University of Michigan, Detroit.

Kazi, S. (2007) *Between Democracy and Nation: Gender and Militarization in Kashmir*, London: Un-published Doctoral dissertation, London School of Economics.

Lone, F.N. (2018) *Historical Title, Self-Determination and the Kashmir Question: Changing Perspectives in International Law*, Leiden: Brill Nijhoff.

Manecksha, F. (2016) 'The public safety act is a political weapon for the government in Kashmir', *The Wire*. 28 December. Online. Available HTTP: <https://thewire.in/government/public-safety-act-kashmir> (accessed 15 March).

Masood, B. (2016) 'Kashmir gagged: Newspaper presses raided, editors say staff held', *The Indian Express*. 29 April. Online. Available HTTP: <https://indianexpress.com/article/india/india-news-india/kashmir-violence-protest-burhan-wani-killing-media-blockade-newspaper-raid-staff-held-2918852/> (accessed 25 March).

Mir, H. (2016) 'Kashmir: By banning our newspaper, government is only looking for scapegoats', *The Indian Express*. 29 April. Online. Available HTTP: <https://indianexpress.com/article/opinion/columns/jk-govt-bans-valley-newspaper-kashmir-reader-3065628/> (accessed 9 March 2019).

Mishra, P. (2000) '"Death in Kashmir" New York Review of Books', September 21. Available HTTP: <https://www.nybooks.com/articles/2000/09/21/death-in-kashmir/> (accessed 28 August 2019).

Motta, S.A. (2010) 'The gag bites the selective media muzzling has the local Kashmiri press furious', *Outlook*. 26 July. Online. Available HTTP: <www.outlookindia.com/magazine/story/the-gag-bites/266278> (accessed 2 March 2019).

The New York Times. (2008) 'Land transfer to Hindu site inflames Kashmir's Muslims'. 28 June. Online. Available HTTP: <www.nytimes.com/2008/06/28/world/asia/28kashmir.html> (accessed 10 April 2019).

Peer, B. (2010) 'Tear gas over Batamaloo', *The National Interest*. 20 October. Online. Available HTTP: <https://nationalinterest.org/article/batamaloo-4242> (accessed 2 March 2019).

Peer, G. (2013) 'Preventive detentions in Kashmir: Still a Lawless law', *The Journal of Indian Law and Society Blog*. 9 March. Online. Available HTTP: <https://jilsblognujs.wordpress.com/2013/03/09/preventive-detentions-in-kashmir-still-a-lawless-law/> (accessed 5 March 2019).

Pillai, A. (1996) 'Vote Marshalled', *Outlook*, 9: 10–15.

Prakash, P. (2013) 'Armed forces special powers act: India' mediaeval law in Kashmir and its northeast', *Open Democracy*. Online. Available HTTP: <www.opendemocracy.net/en/armed-forces-special-powers-act-india-mediaeval-law-in-kashmir-and-its-northeast/> (accessed 2 January 2019).

Reporters without Borders. (2008) *Black Month for Press Freedom in Kashmir*, Paris, France: RSF.

Reporters without Borders. (n.d.) 'India'. Online. Available HTTP: <https://rsf.org/en/india> (accessed 31 March 2019).

Sidhu, W. (1990) 'With the arrest of Top JKLF leaders, security forces gain ground in Kashmir'. 31 August. Available HTTP: <www.indiatoday.in>. <www.indiatoday.in/magazine/indiascope/story/19900831-with-arrest-of-top-jklf-leaders-security-forces-gain-ground-in-kashmir-812969-1990-08-31> (accessed 30 March 2019).

Snedden, C. (2015) *Understanding Kashmir and Kashmiris*, London: Hurst and Company.
Staniland, P. (2013) 'Kashmir since 2003: Counterinsurgency and the paradox of "normalcy"', *Asian Survey*, 931–957.
TOI. (2008) 'Kashmiris play to UN gallery', *Times of India*. 19 August. Online. Available HTTP: <https://timesofindia.indiatimes.com/india/Kashmiris-play-to-UN-gallery/articleshow/3378701.cms> (accessed 1 April 2019).
Varma, A.A. (2010) 'Curfewed in Kashmir: Voices from the valley', *Economic and Political Weekly*. 28 August. Online. Available HTTP: <www.epw.in/journal/2010/35/commentary/curfewed-kashmir-voices-valley.html> (accessed 3 April 2019).
Widmalm, S. (2002) *Kashmir in Comparative Perspective: Democracy and Violent Separatism in India*, New York: Routledge Curzon.
The Wire. (2018) 'Want to be a journalist? The NIA will now tell you how'. 16 Feberuary. Online. Available HTTP: <https://thewire.in/culture/nia-kamran-yusuf-real-journalism> (accessed 2 April 2019).
Young, P.V. (2012) 'Assaults on the Fourth Estate: Explaining media harassment in Africa', *The Journal of Politics*, 75(1): 36–52.
Zargar, S. (2016) 'How Kashmir cartoonists are telling the stories of Kashmir killings', *Scoopwhoop.com*. 26 July. Online. Available HTTP: <www.scoopwhoop.com/This-Is-How-Kashmiri-Cartoonists-Are-Telling-The-Stories-Of-Kashmir-Killings/#.2e6rzxz1e> (accessed 1 April 2019).

20

CHALLENGES OF PRESS FREEDOM IN NEPAL

Dharmendra Jha and Narayan Ghimire

Under exceptionally hostile circumstances, the Nepali press has played a watch-dog role and kept the public informed. It has exposed numerous social evils, including corruption and administrative malfeasance, thereby holding the state apparatus and public officials accountable and pressuring them to enact reforms. But this is only part of the story.

Press freedom in Nepal faces a critical watershed as the government has made a series of moves in recent years to constrain the media and limit the freedom of expression. In May 2019, the government proposed new legislation that would greatly undermine the right of press freedom guaranteed in the 2015 Constitution (Nepal Law Commission 2019) and subject journalists to more extensive government control and political meddling. This bill has drawn widespread criticism from within Nepal, and also from international advocates of press freedom. For example, Steve Butler, Asia programme director with the Committee to Protect Journalists (CPJ), contends the new law would constrict press freedom in Nepal and urges, 'the administration to engage in a dialogue with media members and other stakeholders and amend the bills so that journalists can work in Nepal safely and without fear of prosecution' (Committee to Protect Journalists 2019b).

Prime Minister KP Sharma Oli maintains, however, that the government is committed to democracy, press freedom, and human rights (*Kathmandu Post* 2018). He also claimed that because the Nepal Communist Party (NCP) he leads, 'is the father of democracy . . . it would be unimaginable to think that the very government led by NCP has been violating democracy, press freedom, and human rights' (*Kathmandu Post* 2018).

Not everyone agrees. Former prime minister Sher Bahadur Deuba, head of the opposition Nepali Congress Party, slammed the new Media Council Bill, suggesting that the government was staging a coup against press freedom. 'Journalists themselves fought for press freedom. It is not something that is gifted by communists' (Himalayan News Service 2019b). He has threatened to lead protests inside and outside the Parliament to stop the erosion of press freedom. It is argued that the bill grants the Nepal Media Council excessive powers to punish journalists, and essentially places it under the Ministry of Communications and Information Technology, limiting its power to defend the media from state intervention. The previous Press Council Act granted it greater autonomy and limited its punitive powers. General Secretary of the Federation of Nepali Journalists Ramesh Bista also demanded withdrawal of the bill for sowing fear among journalists by authorizing heavy fines on them while Nepal Press Union President Badri Sigdel is also opposed, arguing the bill will curtail freedom of the press (Himalayan News Service 2019c).

The proposed reform of Nepal's media regulator would permit the government to appoint more of the body's members and empower the regulator to levy fines ranging from 25,000–1 million Nepalese rupees (US\$233–\$8,927) against journalists and media outlets deemed to have damaged a person's reputation (Committee to Protect Journalists 2019b).In addition, a proposed Information Technology Bill would replace the current Electronic Transaction Act 2006 and empower authorities to restrict social media access and impose penalties for posting 'improper' content on social networks. The bill states that citizens can only use social networks approved by the Nepalese Department of Information and could be fined for posts made on those networks (Committee to Protect Journalists 2019b). Individuals could be fined up to 1.5 million Nepalese rupees (US\$13,390) and sentenced to up to five years in prison for posting defamatory content on social media or information harmful to national security. The bill's broad definition of 'social network' potentially grants it control over private chat apps, such as WhatsApp and Viber, in addition to public social networks like Facebook and Twitter.

Political and legal context

Nepal is a federal democratic republic based on the 2015 Constitution of Nepal. The Constitution is the most progressive national charter the country has ever had, guaranteeing several fundamental rights in a nation that until recently was a monarchy, where civil rights have been limited and the democratic transition has been fitful. Perhaps the most salient development was the end of the civil war in 2006 after a decade of conflict, extrajudicial killings, arbitrary arrest, torture and disappearances. This dark era was a difficult and dangerous time for the media. Since then, Nepal has embarked on a democratic transition, but the antagonists remain powerful and influential. The Maoist insurgents now control Parliament while the security forces remain key institutions of the state.

The legacy of this conflict looms over the polity and some issues remain unresolved and represent taboo topics that hamper freedom of expression, transitional justice chief among them. The media have to be careful about how they cover the range of human rights abuses inflicted in that era, contributing to the impunity enjoyed by the still powerful perpetrators. Moreover, the intense competition between rival actors over resources distributed through the political system in a society that experienced prolonged violence creates a volatile situation where journalists face significant risks just for doing their jobs (International Crisis Group 2006).

The International Federation of Journalists (IFJ) observes that:

> Nepal witnessed a stable government under the premiership of KP Sharma Oli, though the same cannot be said for freedom of the press. The government, buoyed by the two-third majority in the parliament, has largely ignored freedom of the press and unnecessarily criticized the media and journalists to tarnish the public image of the media. Alongside that, it has also introduced laws or drafts of laws that could eventually degrade the state of press freedom in the country.
>
> *(International Federation of Journalists 2019)*

In the preamble of the 2015 Constitution, press freedom is guaranteed, although realizing that ideal has been difficult. Other articles prohibit prior censorship of any print, broadcast or digital materials (Freedom House 2016). However, the Constitution also provides for 'reasonable restriction' of media content that is determined to undermine national unity, stoke ethnic tension, or damage public morality. The vague wording bestows sweeping discretionary powers on the government that enable it to limit press freedom.

Article 27 of the Constitution specifies the 'Right to Information,' stating that: 'Every citizen shall have the right to demand and receive information on any matter of his or her interest or of public interest.' But, 'provided that no one shall be compelled to provide information on any matter of which confidentiality must be maintained *in accordance with the law*' (emphasis added).

The phrase 'in accordance with the law' needs to take into account the fluid context of federalism, in which many new laws are being made at the provincial level that may restrict citizens' access to information, impede the right to information, and grant authorities considerable discretionary power to undermine constitutional guarantees. Rather than protecting press freedom under central government legislation, 'Provinces are drafting media-related laws arbitrarily and most of them are against the constitutional provisions, press freedom and freedom of expression,' according to Tara Nath Dahal, chairman of Freedom Forum, an NGO that advocates democracy, human rights, press freedom and equitable development of society (*Kathmandu Post* 2019a).

The 2007 Right to Information Act exemplifies the widespread problem in Nepal's mediascape whereby good laws are undermined by artful implementation and there is no recourse. The government requires that applicants furnish reasons for their requests, even though that is not stated in the law, and the government routinely flouts the information law and the transparency it is supposed to promote by not acceding to requests (Freedom House 2015).

Despite the constitutional guarantee of press freedom, violations are rampant and justice for past victims and their families remains elusive. Given the power dynamics in society, perpetrators of attacks targeting the media enjoy a cocoon of impunity. And, new regressive laws on cybercrime and freedom of expression have been deployed to arrest journalists and muzzle the media. The Federation of Nepali Journalists (FNJ) recently launched a national campaign to protect and promote press freedom, demanding the government amend existing draconian laws and that it adopt press-friendly provisions and enact new laws to uphold constitutional commitments (Himalayan News Service 2019a). Similarly, a national daily, the *Kathmandu Post*, recently observed that:

> This government's penchant for controlling information and muzzling the press is particularly disappointing, since the KP Sharma Oli-led administration has repeatedly touted its commitment to transparency. The tendency to suppress the free press often has unforeseen consequences, and if the state continues to do so, whatever achievements Nepal as a country has achieved so far will be offset by this seemingly precipitous slide towards authoritarianism.
>
> *(Kathmandu Post 2019a)*

Those unforeseen consequences include a lack of accountability, abuse of power, impunity for the powerful and well connected, an uneven commitment to the rule of law and a deterioration in the business operating environment that deters investors and limits economic development.

Unfinished democratic transition

The media atmosphere during the civil war was very harsh, and there has been no peace dividend for the press. During the decade-long armed insurgency from 1996–2006, over two dozen journalists were killed. Expectations for significant improvements in a democratic Nepal have not been realized as the killing, arrest and intimidation of journalists continues. As Freedom House (2015) notes:

> In practice, media workers frequently face physical attacks, death threats, and harassment by armed groups, security personnel, and political cadres, and the perpetrators typically go unpunished . . . in 2014 Maoist groups repeatedly tried to block the publication of several leading newspapers that they viewed as unflattering in their coverage of their party. In December, the five Maoist insurgents arrested for the high-profile and brutal 2004 killing of Radio Nepal journalist Dekendra Thapa were convicted, though each were sentenced to two years or less in prison.

Such light sentences for murdering a journalist reinforce perceptions that perpetrators enjoy considerable impunity.

The rhetorical commitment of political parties and those in power to respect press freedom has not been implemented in practice. Typically, political leaders across the political spectrum hail the Nepali press, and extol its role in promoting democracy. Yet, their words are not backed up with commensurate action. The current leftist coalition government has a two-thirds majority in Parliament, but has not used its power to protect or promote media freedom, opting instead to impose legal and regulatory constraints that impede press freedom.

While political rivalries have flourished during the post-conflict democratic transition, journalists have been targeted by various political actors who want to use the media to promote their own agendas, thwart others and clamp down on transparency. During 2016, many reporters were attacked while covering protests and political unrest, some of it targeting the new 2015 Constitution, presumably by the government because it didn't want anti-government actions or state security abuses to be covered and perhaps sow greater unrest. Powerful individuals often deploy goons to convey their displeasure over news stories exposing their misdeeds and illegal or dubious activities. Exposés about human trafficking or poor labour conditions for overseas Nepalese workers spark death threats, while beatings of journalists over small matters are a common professional risk (Freedom House 2016). For example, reporter Ramesh Rawal was threatened for publishing news about the misuse of a city vehicle by a rural municipality chairperson (Freedom Forum 2019a). In Nepal, the bar is set low for death threats when even such minor exposés provoke such strong reactions.

In this threatening atmosphere, it is not surprising that the media has engaged in self-censorship as a survival strategy and succumbed to a system of sticks and carrots that has eroded freedom of expression. During elections, journalists are most vulnerable, and the number of press freedom violations increases because the stakes are high for political actors. For example, from May 2018 to April 2019, a period that includes the national 2018 election campaign, there were 104 recorded incidents of press freedom violations involving 158 journalists (Freedom Forum 2019b).This report paints a grim picture of press freedom in contemporary Nepal due to harsh laws and regulations, manipulation of information, the targeting of investigative reporters and continued impunity for crimes against journalists.

It is troubling that:

> In Nepal, journalists are induced to take sides with political parties. This political engagement undermines objective reporting, institutionalizes bias and erodes professionalism and public trust in the media. Most of the major political parties maintain media wings for public relations, agenda setting and electioneering, thereby compromising media freedom. The media outlets run by such party media wings provide access and income, but also coopt journalists and thus undermine press autonomy and freedom.
>
> *(Bhuwan 2014)*

Impunity relating to crimes perpetrated against journalists is endemic and leaves them vulnerable and fearful. Thus, the media's ability to expose various social ills, financial irregularities and corruption is compromised, facilitating illiberal democracy and little progress on good governance. Families of journalists killed and disappeared during the armed insurgency, and even after the beginning of the peace process since 2006, are desperately waiting for justice. A total of 24 journalists were killed in Nepal between 1996–2006, but the perpetrators from both sides remain free (IFEX 2018).Transitional justice mechanisms – such as the Truth and Reconciliation Commission and the Commission on Investigation of Enforced Disappeared Persons – have not been effective, and are now without standard bearers. It is worrying that these commissions formed to look into conflict era cases have failed to provide justice to the families of those who were killed or disappeared, largely owing to the unwillingness of the political parties and governments to pursue accountability. These commissions were left in limbo, and although complaints were lodged for some cases of killed and disappeared journalists during the armed insurgency, there was no meaningful response from the commissions. Violence meted out against journalists was ignored in the name of maintaining political consensus because pursuing accountability might implicate powerful actors and institutions. This failure to seek justice foments fear among journalists and media houses, and thus poses a serious challenge to press freedom. Journalists' evident courage to expose the vicious cycle of corruption and high-level illegal deeds that derailed development and defiled democracy has been betrayed by feeble laws and an indifferent political system. The journalists who thrive in such a system are loyal sycophants and lapdogs, rather than press-freedom fighters and watchdogs, fuelling public scepticism.

Hostility towards journalists is triggered by their exposure of misdeeds, corporate interests, low professional ethics, insufficient training, a lack of self-regulation among journalists and a culture of media houses being more committed to profits than to professionalism. This antagonism poses a threat to journalists' physical, financial and professional security.

It is also important to understand that Nepal is a nation suffering from post-traumatic stress disorder, and after a decade of gruesome atrocities, barriers to violence have eroded. Disputes are still settled by intimidation, beatings and murder. Media owners along with reporters face such risks because those who are embarrassed or exposed seek retribution. In 2013, there was a series of murders of owners who had angered the wrong people (UN News 2013).

Social media

Social media provide a convenient platform for common people to express their views and to monitor and comment on local and national issues of public concern. There are often allegations of corruption and irregularities involving politicians and officials, and to some degree, this promotes accountability, shaming some officials to abide by the law. Similarly, people's updates on social media can help journalists find news sources. The popular print media have extensively utilized these platforms to boost their visibility.

Social media comes under the 2007 Electronic Transaction Act (ETA), which is used frequently to arrest and harass journalists merely for doing their jobs (Nepal24hours.com 2019).These provisos are so vague and subjective that they grant authorities a carte blanche for harassing journalists and muzzling the media. Many journalists have been detained and charged with cybercrimes, but later released by the court. However, there is only one court in Nepal that deals with cybercrime, meaning that journalists could be held in detention for enough time to convince them to modify their professional conduct. This sows fear among journalists and deters them from writing news on irregularities and corruption, or about the involvement of bigwigs in such activities. Ordinary citizens are also at risk for sharing awkward information on social media about elite corruption or other crimes.

In April 2019, a journalist was arrested and charged with a cybercrime under the ETA. Journalist Arjun Giri, editor of the local *Tandav* weekly, had written a news story about a businessperson and posted it on the eponymous news portal in Pokhara city (Committee to Protect Journalists 2019a). After the business-person complained about Giri at a local police station, Giri was detained and charged with initiating a cybercrime. The businessperson, Bipendra Batas, filed a defamation case against Giri after he published a story detailing a land fraud case implicating Batas. Giri was arrested by security officials of the Kaski district and brought to the capital city Kathmandu and arraigned in the Kathmandu District Court, Nepal's only court that deals with cybercrime. Giri was released after four days in jail, a harrowing experience that sends a chilling message to all reporters and editors about the risks involved in reporting about malfeasance.

With government at all three tiers – federal, provincial and local levels – held by the Nepal Communist Party, the largest political party in the country, the normal checks and balances of democracy are not robust. Under these circum-stances, political intervention in how the media functions is rampant, and no more so than in the hotly contested digital space. Here the desire to suppress anti-government views is manifest and the pressure is escalating. On social net-working sites such as Facebook and Twitter, journalists and writers who criti-cize government activities are castigated by a slew of ardent party members and sympathizers. Such harassment of journalists in the digital commons spreads fear, thereby causing self-censorship. Self-censorship is detrimental to professionalism and undermines press freedom. As such, legions of internet trolls are stifling democracy by muzzling the media to protect their leaders. They also spread dis-information that fuels confusion and tarnishes the image of journalism. This is a global problem, but an especially grave assault on Nepal's nascent democracy, with cyber literacy and awareness of the dangers not yet well developed.

Social media removes the gatekeepers, enabling citizen journalism, but as in other countries, this is a mediascape in which trolls and propagators of fake news often dominate. Fact-checking has become more common to counter false claims and misinformation, but the fires keeps outpacing the firefighters, and the arsonists enjoy impunity. Those who dislike journalists and opinion makers for expressing critical views or divulging damaging information react aggressively, involving digital bullying and surveillance. Debate about the 2019 Media Council Bill is especially contentious, and critics of it are targeted by pro-government trolls trying to counter the criticism.

Internet penetration and the use of smart phones is increasing, creating a new battleground. With internet penetration nearing 60 percent in Nepal, the number of Facebook users has reached around 10million, while those using Twitter are about 1million. This has created a vibrant space for freedom of expression, and citizen journalism that contends with those trying to dominate the same space for antithetical aims. The proposed Information Technology Bill (ITB) would enhance the government's monitoring powers over social media in ways that could potentially impede citizen journalism and increase risks for government critics (Committee to Protect Journalists 2019b). That is why the ITB enjoys the support of political actors who want to hide their illicit activities from the media, but have found it difficult to do so.

This antagonism towards freedom of expression poses a threat to democracy. Threats on social media have escalated as a way to deter anyone from posting awkward news, creating a chilling atmosphere for anyone trying to keep the public informed. A recent issue of the Freedom Forum newsletter, *Free Expression*, highlights how hopes for greater freedom of expression in democratic Nepal have been crushed and how hope is in short supply as reporters and citizens are subject to various abuses and threats (Freedom Forum 2019c). Social media has become a hothouse of intimidation and fake news aimed at confusing readers, complicating the job of journalists. They also face other legal challenges.

Criminalizing journalism

Chapter 1 under Part 3 of the 2017 Criminal Code, 'Crimes against Privacy,' is a serious threat to journalists' right to free reporting (Committee to Protect Journalists 2018). Taking photographs of public officials or recording their conversations is prohibited without prior consent, thereby shackling investigative journalism. There are several other legal impediments that prevent journalists from doing their jobs. Section 293 prohibits recording and listening to conversations between people without prior consent, while Section 294 prohibits making private information public without prior consent. In addition, Section 306 criminalizes satire that disrespects an individual.

Regarding this legal minefield, the Committee to Project Journalist's (CPJ) Asia programme coordinator, Steven Butler, observed that:

> Nepal's new criminal code marks a giant step backward for press freedom. . . . Legislators need to go back and scrub the law of these overly-broad

provisions that effectively criminalize the normal newsgathering activities of journalists.

(Committee to Protect Journalists 2018)

To avoid stifling free expression on social media and online news sites there is a need for reform, but the authorities have shown little interest in ceding their current powers.

The *Kathmandu Post* commented:

> The criminalisation of legitimate journalistic activity should not be taken lightly. Cybersecurity is necessary, but authorities should not use safety as a weapon to gag the press. Any cybercrime legislation that possesses a threat to press freedom must be revised. Fear is a critical component of curtailing freedom, and recent studies on press freedom have shown a worldwide downward trend in access to unbiased media, along with an increase in attacks on journalists.

(Kathmandu Post 2019b)

Manipulating the news

According to Freedom House (2015), there is a lack of transparency about media ownership in Nepal and scant autonomy from political influence:

> The media generally offer a broad spectrum of political views and appear to have diverse owners, though there is no reliable information on media ownership in the country. The government owns several of the major dailies as well as the influential Radio Nepal and the Nepal Television Corporation. Political parties have also come to own an increasing share of newspapers in recent years. It is not unusual for the selection of editors at national newspapers to be governed by political deals and bargaining.

Private media companies are mostly run as private companies, rather than public enterprises, so unlike with listed firms, there is little public disclosure. This prevents critical examination of business practices that might undermine media ethics. Owners want to make a profit and to wield influence, motivations that tend to undermine journalistic standards and concede press autonomy. Getting licences often depends on having connections that owners are loath to risk just to promote the media's credibility. Often such owners have other corporate interests that are vulnerable to political whims, another reason to tone down controversial coverage. In some cases, they are cronies of political leaders or other powerful actors, and thus keen to demonstrate their loyalty in the expectation of a quid pro quo. This situation kills the neutrality of the press, tarnishes its image and credibility while shortchanging transparency. A co-opted media cannot act as a watchdog.

Prajapati (2012) argues that the press cannot play its watchdog role effectively under these circumstances. Based on news content analysis of four newspapers, Prajapti finds a significant influence of ownership on how the news is or is not reported. The findings suggest that privatization of the media over the past two decades has loosened the state's once exclusive control over the media, but it does not appear that this has unshackled the media, instead providing entry for new influence seekers among corporations and political parties. Privatization of the media accompanied the 1990s political transition from a 'party-less Panchayat System to a multiparty democratic system' (Prajapati 2012). This study finds that as a result of privatization, the wall between editorial and business operations has collapsed, and news content is influenced by owners' and advertisers' preferences, violating basic media ethics. Journalism is now subject to the pressures of investors and advertisers that involve killing some stories or slanting content. The insidious influence of commercialism on news content is a global phenomenon (Altschull 1984). Mainali (2006) contends that owners and editors nurture networks of influence and are therefore reluctant to offend and eager to please in order to secure favourable decisions affecting their wider business interests. And as Freedom House (2015) notes, 'Since the government is a major source of advertising, journalists are often forced to self-censor in order to avoid conflict with the ruling party.'

Prajapati (2012) examines how newspapers reported about a labour dispute with media firms, and confirms that the media framed this issue in ways prejudicial to the union and favourable to the owners. The reporters were making basic demands regarding poor employment conditions and various irregularities, but the media portrayed their demands as part of a political campaign by the Maoists to influence news reporting and impinge on press freedom. Thus, journalists saw their interests somehow sacrificed on the altar of press freedom while the conspiring media owners accused the Maoists of political machinations.

There was another case when the media criticized the quality of a large conglomerate's juice products. As one of the leading advertisers, Dabur Nepal used its leverage to reward and punish media depending on their coverage (Prajapati 2012).The Indian Ambassador also got involved by condemning the criticism of Dabur Nepal, a joint venture involving Indian business interests, leading to a backlash from certain newspapers against his meddling. This then morphed into allegations that *Kantipur* newspaper in particular was anti-Indian and the Indian government took steps to retaliate, including cutting its ads and getting Indian joint ventures to cut their ads to *Kantipur*, reducing such revenues by 20%, while disrupting imports of newsprint through the port of Calcutta. Media groups who took a more favourable view about India and the juice products were rewarded. Prajapati (2012: 26) found that:

> those who received advertising from Dabur Nepal, ignored the news about the allegation that the Dabur Nepal products were substandard, whereas

those who did not get advertisements highlighted and extensively covered incidents that proved the Dabur Nepal products to have been of low quality.

He concludes, 'these practices of biases are evidences of how Nepali media are violating the fundamental ethical principles of objectivity and neutrality' (Prajapati 2012: 26). Furthermore:

> ownership of media, helps to set the agenda in favour of those who own the news media. The use of headlines, lead, tone of article and sources has shown that media ownership interest is visible in framing the news content.
>
> *(Prajapati 2012: 30)*

The one-sided coverage of issues important to owners and advertisers is not unique to Nepal, but has a great impact on public attitudes due to low media literacy and is not subject to any effective oversight.

China also seeks to influence the Nepalese media, pressuring the government to quell reporting about the Dalai Lama. Reporters without Borders (RSF) called on the Nepalese authorities to drop an investigation targeting three journalists with the state-owned national news agency Rastriya Samachar Samiti (RSS) for publishing a report about the Dalai Lama's health in April 2019 (France 24 2019). Reporters without Borders called on the government to resist Chinese embassy pressure to intimidate Nepal's media (France 24 2019). The story in question reported that the Dalai Lama had been released from hospital and returned to Dharamshala, the northern Indian city that is the Tibetan exile community's capital. The information and communication minister, Gokul Baskota explained, 'dissemination of this report by the state-run agency, particularly during the president's state visit to China, is against Nepal's commitment to One-China policy' (Kathmandu Post 2019). Located between two large rivals, Nepal and its media have to tread carefully, but this need to not offend puts freedom of expression at risk even over small matters.

Professionalism

Financial insecurity is a paramount factor undermining media professionalism. Most journalists in Nepal are underpaid and irregularly paid. Job hopping is common, and many reporters quit the media because of financial insecurity. Publishers' reluctance to invest in professional development is another major problem impeding improvement in professionalism, and media standards. The government has asked the media houses to pay a minimum wage of Rs 19,500 (US$177) a month to its journalists, but private media groups have not complied; only 38 percent of journalists actually receive the minimum wage (Kathmandu Tribune 2018). Owners are focused on the bottom line and don't worry about retaining reporters or nurturing their skills, encouraging high turnover and low levels of professionalism. Due to financial insecurity, journalists are under pressure to compromise professional ethics, and thereby bring the free press into disrepute.

Shortchanging professional development for journalists harms the public interest because it limits their capacity. Only trained and capable journalists can ensure professional integrity and demonstrate the value of a free press. Nearly 100 colleges, including Tribhuvan University – the oldest university in Nepal – and Purbanchal University are offering academic programmes, including graduate degrees, in mass communications and journalism. In addition to these academic courses, there are various vocational training programmes run by journalists' activist organizations. The FNJ has long done so. It is estimated that there are some 13,000 FNJ members in Nepal, with an estimated 1,500 female journalists among them. Similarly, Freedom Forum is another frontline organization that for the past decade has been working for journalists' rights, capacity building, freedom of expression and the right to information. It continuously monitors press freedom violations, provides training, conducts research and prepares reports on prevailing conditions. The Centre for Investigative Journalism (CIJ) also nurtures relevant skills, and its alumni have played a key role in bringing to light irregularities, scams and corruption. The Nepal Press Institute (NPI) is another institution providing journalism training for several years. It has produced thousands of journalists who are working actively for various media. There are other organizations focusing on specific issues, such as the environment or gender. They, too, are providing training necessary to enhance journalists' capacity. These organizations' contributions are essential to promoting good governance, an informed citizenry and democratic values.

Despite these efforts, training for Nepali journalists remains insufficient, as hundreds enter the profession each year while many quit the profession for the reasons cited previously. Journalism and the skills required have evolved considerably in the digital age. Keeping pace with these technological developments is a major challenge. Reporters need to be equipped with modern technology and digital literacy, so that they can embrace global best practices, but owners focus on profitability and don't invest in upgrading skills. As a result, Nepalese democracy suffers.

Conclusion

The Nepali press is at crossroads. Fear among journalists has deepened in response to growing threats, hostility, limited protections and press freedom violations across the country. Legal reforms affecting the media are aimed at limiting rather than protecting freedom of expression. However, the free press is crucial to advancing Nepal's democratic transition. While various stakeholders in the media, academia, civil society organizations and the judiciary are working together to protect and promote press freedom and to expand the space for democracy, they confront powerful actors that have much to lose from greater transparency and accountability. These champions of authoritarianism have promoted a dysfunctional democracy by stifling press freedoms – and thus imperil the nation's future.

References

Altschull, J.H. (1984) *Agents of Power: The Role of the News Media in Human Affairs*, New York: Longman.

Bhuwan, K.C. (2014) 'Political inclination of journalists & it's influence on news', *Centre for Media Research-Nepal*. Online. Available HTTP: <http://research.butmedia.org/wp-content/uploads/2017/02/PoliticalInclination.pdf> (accessed 2 June 2019).

Committee to Protect Journalists (CPJ). (2018) 'New Nepali criminal code threatens press freedom'. Online. Available HTTP: <https://cpj.org/2018/08/new-nepali-criminal-code-threatens-press-freedom.php> (accessed 2 June 2019).

Committee to Protect Journalists (CPJ). (2019a) '*Tandav News* editor Giri investigated under Nepal's cybercrime act'. Online. Available HTTP: <https://cpj.org/2019/04/tandav-news-arjun-giri-nepal-cybercrime.php> (accessed 2 June 2019).

Committee to Protect Journalists (CPJ). (2019b) 'Nepal government proposes bills that endanger press freedom'. Online. Available HTTP: <https://cpj.org/2019/05/nepal-government-proposes-bills-that-engender-pres.php/> (accessed 2 June 2019).

Freedom Forum. (2019a) 'Death threat to journalist for publishing news'. Online. Available HTTP: <http://nepalpressfreedom.org/main/issue-single/1057> (accessed 2 June 2019).

Freedom Forum. (2019b) 'Regressive laws, mounting violations'. Online. Available HTTP: <http://freedomforum.org.np/download/press-freedom-may-3-report-2019/?wpdmdl=3676> (accessed 2 June 2019).

Freedom Forum. (2019c) 'Free expression'. Online. Available HTTP: <http://freedomforum.org.np/download/free-expression-45/?wpdmdl=3649> (accessed 2 June 2019).

Freedom House. (2015) 'Nepal'. Online. Available HTTP: <https://freedomhouse.org/report/freedom-press/2015/nepal> (accessed 2 June 2019).

Freedom House. (2016) 'Nepal'. Online. Available HTTP: <https://freedomhouse.org/report/freedom-press/2016/nepal> (accessed 2 June 2019).

Himalayan News Service. (2019a) 'FNJ announces national campaign for press freedom', *The Himalayan Times*. Online. Available HTTP:<https://thehimalayantimes.com/kathmandu/fnj-announces-national-campaign-for-press-freedom/> (accessed 2 June 2019).

Himalayan News Service. (2019b) 'Bill on Nepal Media Council draws mixed reactions', *Himalayan Times*. 12 May. Available HTTP:<https://thehimalayantimes.com/kathmandu/bill-on-nepal-media-council-draws-mixed-reactions/> (accessed 4 June 2019).

Himalayan News Service. (2019c) 'Govt planning coup against media: Deuba', *Himalayan Times*. 13 May. Available HTTP:<https://thehimalayantimes.com/kathmandu/government-planning-coup-against-media-nepali-congress-president-sher-bahadur-deuba/> (accesses 4 June 2019).

IFEX. (2018) 'Documentary on two decades of media killings in Nepal'. Online. Available HTTP: <https://ifex.org/documentary-on-two-decades-of-media-killings-in-nepal/>(accessed 2 June 2019).

International Crisis Group (ICG). (2006) 'Nepal's political rites of passage', *International Crisis Group Asia Report*, Kathmandu and Brussels. Online. Available HTTP: <www.

crisisgroup.org/asia/south-asia/nepal/nepal-s-political-rites-passage> (accessed 2 June 2019).

International Federation of Journalists (IFJ). (2019) 'Nepal: Legal Stranglehold', *IFJ Press Freedom Report 2018–2019*. Online. Available HTTP: <www.ifj.org/fileadmin/user_upload/IFJ_SAPFR_-_NEPAL.pdf> (accessed 2 June 2019).

Kathmandu Post. (2018) 'Media plays crucial role in making people aware: PM Oli'. 12 August. Available HTTP: <http://kathmandupost.ekantipur.com/news/2018-08-12/media-plays-crucial-role-in-making-people-aware-pm-oli.html> (accessed 4 June 2019).

Kathmandu Post. (2019) 'Three journalists are under investigation over publishing news about the Dalai Lama'. Available HTTP: <https://kathmandupost.com/national/2019/05/12/three-journalists-face-probe-over-publishing-dalai-lama-news> (accessed 25 Sept 2019).

Kathmandu Post. (2019a) 'Provincial media bills will curtail press freedom, experts warn'. Available HTTP: <https://kathmandupost.ekantipur.com/news/2019-02-11/provincial-media-bills-will-curtail-press-freedom-experts-warn.html> (accessed 4 June 2019).

Kathmandu Post. (2019b) 'The criminalisation of legitimate journalism should not be taken lightly'. Online. Available HTTP: <https://kathmandupost.ekantipur.com/news/2019-04-19/intimidation-game.html> (accessed 2 June 2019).

Kathmandu Tribune. (2018) 'Only 38% journalists get minimum wages in Nepal'. 28 January. Available HTTP: <https://kathmandutribune.com/38-journalists-get-minimum-wages-nepal/> (accessed 4 June 2019).

Mainali, M. (2006) 'Kantipur publications: The perils of concentration', in J. Son, S. Sivaraman and S. Pradhan (eds.) *Asia Media Report: ACrisis Within*, Quezon City: IPS Asia-Pacific Centre Foundation.

Nepal24hours.com. (2019)'Scrap Electronics Transactions act', Online. Available HTTP: <www.nepal24hours.com/scrap-electronic-transaction-act-federation-of-nepali-journalists/> (accessed 2 June 2019).

Nepal Law Commission. (2008) 'Electronic Transaction Act'. Online. Available HTTP: <www.lawcommission.gov.np/en/archives/category/documents/prevailing-law/statutes-acts/the-electronic-transactions-act-2063-2008> (accessed 2 June 2019).

Nepal Law Commission. (2019) 'Constitution of Nepal', Online. Available HTTP: <www.lawcommission.gov.np/en/archives/category/documents/prevailing-law/constitution/constitution-of-nepal> (accessed 2 June 2019).

Prajapati, U. (2012) 'Safeguarding public Interest in the era of corporate media: Case studies on impact of ownership on news content', Policy Discussion Paper. *Kathmandu: Alliance for Social Dialogue*. Online. Available HTTP: <http://research.butmedia.org/wp-content/uploads/2013/09/safeguarding_public_interest_in_the_era_of_corporate_media_UjjwalPrajapati.pdf> (accessed 2 June 2019).

UN News. (2013) 'Nepal: UNESCO chief deplores killing of Nepalese media owner'. Online. Available HTTP: <https://news.un.org/en/story/2010/03/331362-unesco-chief-deplores-killing-nepalese-media-owner> (accessed 2 June 2019).

21

PAKISTANI MEDIA UNDER SIEGE

Syed Javed Nazir

It is tempting to imagine Pakistan's media landscape as a surreal and uneven battlefield. Those defending press freedoms from within are fewer in number, but they hold on steadfastly to notions of freedom and critical thinking. Arrayed against them are forces of the status quo and of social conservatism. A third force, representing religious extremists and subnationalists of the most virulent kind, is encamped in close proximity. They have in their crosshairs both the enlightenment seekers and the status quo enthusiasts. This scenario of ever-growing religious and nationalist extremism adds to the country's image in the popular imagination as the world's 'most dangerous place' (Moreau 2007), and to expectations of an imminent 'descent into chaos' (Rashid 2008). Declan Walsh added a somewhat redeeming dimension to his 2010 book *Insha'Allah Nation* in identifying elements of modernity in contention with religion and mediaeval custom. The picture has become even murkier since these accounts of Pakistani society were penned almost a decade ago.

Growth and resilience

Pakistan, however, also has layers of resilience. This is what the outside world neglects to see, given its predilections for the dramatic and stereotypical. Media in Pakistan are especially vibrant and increasingly assertive. Of course, there exists a phalanx of tough challenges. Challenges have always existed, and are confronted with courage, fortitude and optimism. That's what makes the narrative around media in Pakistan particularly inspirational. Alas, 22 journalists have died in the line of duty in the last decade in Pakistan (Committee to Protect Journalists 2018). This toll is mind-numbing, but also reflects the irrepressible spirit of those who pay the ultimate price for just a bit more freedom. It is also encouraging that Pakistan is enjoying an unprecedented media expansion. Well-heeled entrepreneurs are jumping on the media bandwagon because it endows them with power and an ability to influence society. For instance, in October 2010, Mian Amer Mehmood, a prominent entrepreneur, who owns the largest education business in Pakistan, launched a TV news channel Dunya. Since then, he has consolidated his position as Pakistan's newest and strongest media mogul. His media empire includes a successful daily Urdu-language newspaper, which goes by the same name as his TV news channel. In addition, in 2018, Pakistan's biggest confectionary maker, Gourmet, started a news channel called the Gourmet News Network, appealing to the mainstream audience and, of course, the bourgeois foodie demographic.

For a country that has witnessed remarkable media growth since the turn of the century (until the early 1990s, Pakistani media were overshadowed by a single state-owned TV channel, the PTV) one would think the decades-long culture of control and censorship would recede, but freedom remains a quest and a struggle. The optimists' enthusiasm, as they watch the number of private TV channels vault from one to close to 100, might seem like irrational exuberance.

The growth – both in its vertical and horizontal dimensions – has not meant an easing of restrictions on freedom of expression. Not that limits placed around articulation of independent opinion have not been challenged. Courageous journalists continue to push back against a culture of prior restraint, taboo subjects, acquiescence before the state's security narrative and, especially, impunity. Retribution for their hunger for truth has been swift, and daunting for others.

Freedom of expression

Dawn, Pakistan's respectable English-language daily, in a defiant editorial published on 3 May 2019, captures the essence of this struggle, opining:

> When governments legislate to muzzle the media, when they discredit journalists and sow confusion in the public by promoting false narratives, often through third parties on social media, it signals their intention to prevent the scrutiny of their policies and actions. Journalists who threaten this impunity do so at the cost of their lives.
>
> (Dawn *2019*)

The newspaper goes on to argue rather chillingly that the situation in Pakistan cannot be gauged by the number of body bags alone. There is a whole range of other serious issues confronting the media. Liberalization of the media in Pakistan has mainstreamed it as a stakeholder, almost on a par with the judiciary and Parliament. However, the country's transitional and fragile democracy has prevented it from playing a watchdog role for society (Pintak, Bowe and Nazir 2016). Much more important is the fact that in the absence of an independent judiciary, enterprising journalists feel vulnerable. Unlike some democracies in South Asia, where judges have been extending a protective umbrella to investigative journalists, Pakistanis definitely miss having a matching institution. Moreover, Pakistan's long history of dictatorship (since gaining independence from the British in 1947, the country has been ruled by Pakistan's powerful military for nearly half of its history) casts a long shadow over democratic aspirations across the social and political spectrum. Most of the societal distortions witnessed today owe their existence to prolonged military rule, including the radicalization of Pakistani society.

The campaigners for freedom of expression, whether they represented political parties, the media or civil society, paid a steep price during three eras of martial law (1958–1969, 1977–1988 and 1999–2008). Even so, publications such as *Herald, Newsline, Friday Times, Frontier Post, The Muslim* and the Urdu-language daily *Naw-e-Waqt* refused to bend, unlike the situation in Singapore or the Gulf states where the media has been effectively tamed. The advent of a 24/7 news media has also brought the CNN effect to Pakistan, whereby real-time news updates generate public pressure for government action (Belknop 2002). The CNN effect is a double-edged sword for governments: it can be a strategic enabler, helping policy makers to build public support for specific policies and operations. But it can also bring risks, as real time reporting and journalist embeds can expose information that may compromise operational security. In the case of Pakistan, the presence of CNN has provided some impetus for other networks to upgrade their news-gathering standards. In addition, the presence of a vibrant Indian media just across the border exerts a hugely significant influence. Pakistani journalists, especially those working in the print media, yearn for more freedom, and cross-border rivalry is an inspiration for nurturing professional excellence. Since the 1990s, the BBC and other satellite TV networks likewise have offered models of change and transformation. Thus, Pakistan's media landscape has not been hermetically sealed and has benefitted from various external influences and the propagation of global norms and industry best practices. Perhaps it is most encouraging that independent voices in the media proved their resilience even during the darkest periods of censorship in Pakistan (1977–1988).

Co-opted and vulnerable

It is ironic that while Pakistani media have evolved since liberalization in 2002, all other state institutions are caught in the hardened concrete of tradition and of an authoritarian mindset. The military is no exception.

Pakistan is currently described (Pintak et al. 2016) as a transitional democracy with a media system that reflects some aspects of the Polarized Pluralism Model (Hallin and Mancini 2004). According to this model, the media are an integral part of party politics, but the state remains the dominant player in the sector. This dominance has to do with the weak and spasmodic growth of commercial media in the previous decades. Almost all media entities in Pakistan depend disproportionately on the state for generating their finances. This means that private TV channels, hundreds of radio stations, newspapers and magazines continue to rely on government advertisements to stay viable. This is the media's Achilles heel. This vulnerability to co-optation has existed for decades, and may well persist until the private sector develops, enabling the media to tap into financial markets for support and survival. Currently, there is no constraint on the state's ability to coerce, manipulate and ultimately stifle independent voices in the media. The threat to choke off financing for an offending or non-conforming media entity is a given. This means that newspapers and TV stations must navigate carefully between their own agendas and the state's imperatives.

Take the case of *Dawn* newspaper, which published a news story in April 2017 entitled 'Act against the militants or face international isolation, civilians tell military.' Since the publication of this controversial news story, the newspaper has borne the brunt of the state's coercive apparatus. Its quota of government advertisements has been slashed, along with alleged efforts to restrict its distribution in major towns and cities (*Dawn* 2019). Moreover, Geo, Pakistan's largest TV news channel, had its broadcasting licence revoked for 15 days following its face-off with the military authorities (Jon 2014).

Situating the media in its present-day political and cultural context is essential before one can grasp the extent of the challenges journalists face in their day-to-day work. The system of checks and balances in Pakistan remains beholden to military power, despite the constitutional roles of Parliament and the Supreme Court. An intense polarization defines political parties, and in some cases, they conduct themselves as militarized outfits. Media entities have no qualms in seeking alliances with one of Pakistan's parties – a structure called political parallelism (Hallin and Macini 2004). Research undertaken in recent years indicates that this parallelism has the potential to intensify polarization of the media-political environment prior to elections (Carkoglu, Baruh, and Yildirim 2014). It is common knowledge that militant organizations hold sway in parts of Khyber Pakhtunkhwa and Balochistan, existing as a 'state within a state.'

A phenomenon known as clientelism also permeates Pakistan's political and social organizations. This is an environment in which patronage firmly connects social and political actors to the state (Curran 2002: 231). In the media sector specifically, clientelism manifests itself when owners use their influence to leverage economic power. The no-holds-barred support of GEO TV network for former Pakistani prime minister Nawaz Sharif can arguably be viewed through this prism. In fact, this is what mostly drives media ownership as evident in the growing fortunes of cross-platforms within the Pakistani media landscape. The cost of such a focus is the decline in professional standards, as media owners don't invest in training journalists. Proximity to power creates other avenues for revenue generation; for example, the granting of permission to start new industries or favourable bank loans. Investment in the training of journalists, on the other hand, is a long-term strategy for professional excellence with no immediate dividends.

The media are also influenced by the diversity of a nation of 200-plus million people riven by some major fault lines based on ethnicity, subnationalism, and religious sectarianism. These varying identities often collide, and local, ethnic and cultural identity can take precedence over notions of national cohesion (Jalal & Snellinger n.d). Violence increasingly defines life as groups remain locked in a mortal fight along religious, ethnic and political lines. The military is fighting the Islamist militants, and the confrontation with rival India is always simmering and is sometimes at risk of boiling over. All of this makes Pakistan the most dangerous place for journalists to work (*The Nation* 2018). Reporters and editors are routinely intimidated, harassed and sometimes killed by fanatical groups or those who position themselves as patriotic saviours of the nation. Pakistan's deep state, too, is implicated in stifling contrarian voices in the media. The fact that Pakistani journalists are poorly paid and poorly trained adds another layer of complexity to the situation.

This overview of the broader context in which the media operates raises some important questions. How has the media traversed the last decade and half of incredible growth, especially in the electronic media (close to 40 TV news channels operate in the country)? To what extent has the media impacted society and politics? Can a case for the mediatization of society and politics be made in Pakistan? Mediatization is a concept describing the extent of the media's influence over a society and its culture. Why is journalism increasingly regarded as a dangerous profession? Why are Pakistan's best and brightest not attracted to this profession? What is the role of media laws? The right to information is recognized, but has it been implemented? To what extent is speculation about the stifling role of the country's intelligence agencies true? And most importantly, how do militant organizations affect critical voices in the media? Does the so-called jihadi media exist? And, finally, do international media watchdog organizations like Committee to Protect Journalists (CPJ) and Reporters without Borders (RSF) exert any restraining influence on those elements in Pakistan whose government wields an authoritarian sledgehammer? This chapter seeks answers to some of these questions – and indeed others.

Legal landscape

Let's consider Pakistan's media laws and regulations and study their impact in slowing down the pace of growth of an independent media. Media enthusiasts may argue that notwithstanding these prohibitive laws, Pakistani media now enjoy relative freedom in comparison with other countries in South Asia. However, the fact that these laws have the potential to block an 'offending' publication or TV channel cannot be disputed. The Press and Publications Ordinance Law (1860) is a carry-over from the colonial era, while other undemocratic laws were put in place by military dictators to control the media and, as a consequence, public discourse. The Constitution of Pakistan is explicit in reaffirming the fundamentals of democracy and premise of media freedom, but these principles are often observed in the breach. The military went about dismantling the Constitution and democratic dispensations three times. Naveed Butt, a former reporting editor at the *Frontier Post*, an intrepid newspaper that some media critics credit for heralding the age of investigative journalism in Pakistan in the 1980s and 1990s, wrote (2019):

> In those dark and dystopian times, it was Pakistan's media that insisted on lighting the candle and keeping the country together and providing a sense of the road ahead. No other state institution, no political party, not even the judiciary – the idea of a civil society hadn't taken root yet – had the gumption to resist. The media took on the opposition's role and asked a shocked and passive citizenry to come out and resist the dictators.

There is a raft of legislative and regulatory measures in place designed to 'discipline' the media. These include the Press and Publication Ordinance (PPO), Printing Presses and Publication Ordinance (1988), the Freedom of Information Ordinance (2002), the Pakistan Electronic Media Regulatory Authority (PEMRA) (2002), the Defamation Ordinance (2002), the Contempt of Court Ordinance (2003), the Press-Newspapers-News Agency and Books Registration Ordinance (2003), the Press Council Ordinance (2002), the Intellectual Property Organization of Pakistan Ordinance (2005) and the Access to Information Ordinance (2006).

Let's look at the colonial-era Press and Publication Ordinance. The law oversees the registration and licensing process of newspapers and periodicals, which can be quite a slippery slope. Along with this law, Pakistan also inherited other media-specific legislation from the British era of colonial rule when the focus was on restraining rather than promoting the press. The PPO was used as a guillotine to suppress dissent and social unrest. After the partition of colonial India into Pakistan and India in 1947, almost all subsequent civilian and military governments in Pakistan embraced expediency and spurned democracy. They threw their weight behind these retrogressive laws in order to protect their power base and class privilege (Clingendael 2010). The PPO was used as an instrument of oppression, and efforts were made to revive some of the most stringent aspects of the colonial-era regulatory mechanisms.

The most insidious efforts were launched in 2002 to control and regulate the electronic media. These efforts came hard on the heels of liberalization sweeping the media landscape. The Pakistan Media Regulatory Authority (PEMRA) was set up and presented as a major step towards reforming the media. Media observers soon discovered to their dismay that PEMRA actually masked a sharp regulatory ploy (IMS 2009). The rationale behind the establishment of PEMRA was to improve standards of information, education and entertainment; expand the choices available to the people of Pakistan for news, current affairs, religious knowledge, art, culture, science, technology, economic development, social sector concerns, music, sports, drama and other subjects of public and national interest; facilitate the devolution of responsibility and power to grassroots by improving access to the mass media at the local and community level; and finally, to ensure accountability, transparency and good governance by optimizing the free flow of information. These are nice-sounding words, but totally vacuous, given the way PEMRA has been used by the government in recent years. Media practitioners, however, view PEMRA as a licence-issuing office that mostly involves erecting regulatory hurdles in the way of broadcasters. The four-point foundational agenda for PEMRA, on first reading, appears thoroughly in keeping with a democratic ethos. How it conducts its actual business, however, is a different matter. Pakistani military dictators have a gift for turning a perfect idea on its head. PEMRA laws were exploited by the Musharraf regime to browbeat the media. A number of stations were shut down and some faced harassment.

Bureaucrats and ex-police officers have been on the 12-member board that runs PEMRA. In recent years, PEMRA has been tilting at those TV channels that had the temerity to fall out of line. The country's most popular TV channel 'GEO' has been smarting from suppressive PEMRA diktats. It was essentially targeted over the way it covered the lawyers' movement and its criticism of the government in power (IMS 2009). It finds itself, at the time of this writing, in a similar predicament, albeit lesser in severity. It had been supporting the Pakistan Muslim League-Nawaz government, which lost the 2018 election to the Pakistan Tehreek-e-Insaf-led coalition.

It is ironic that among the documents required for a permit or 'declaration' for publishing a newspaper is a written assurance by the editor to conform to an ethical code of practice. The infamous PPO demands it. Imagine the hypocrisy on the part of Pakistan's autocratic rulers: they hold their high office after usurping power, and demand ethical standards from editors and thought leaders, a situation complicated by the lack of a universally acceptable code of conduct for media stakeholders.

The country's defamation laws too have attracted criticism because of their capacity for squeezing the space for independent comment. Defamation in Pakistan is a criminal act. The Defamation Ordinance (2002) specifies two kinds of defamation: libel and slander. Defamation lawyers maintain that the law is still untested in court. However, the International Media Support (IMS) Report is quite damning about the consequences of intimidation:

> The defamation Ordinance 2002 is meant to protect people's reputation from unfair attacks. In practice, it has become a tool to hinder free speech and powerful people from scrutiny. The ordinance ignores the standard set for freedom of speech and slaps a straight-jacket on the press.
>
> *(IMS 2009)*

Militant influence

Perhaps the most formidable existential challenge to freedom of expression, and those working in the media, comes from elements who represent Pakistan's infamous fringe of ideologues and fanatics. The latter brook no tolerance for a contrary point of view and regard all objective discussions of taboo subjects like blasphemy laws as off limits. There is simply no room for disagreement, and those who disagree risk being shot.

Since 9/11, the international media have seen Pakistan as a centre stage for extremist religious violence, support for the Taliban and terrorist organizations, sectarian schisms and growing intolerance towards non-Muslim minorities. How soon Pakistan might fragment with hundreds of nuclear weapons falling into the hands of terrorists is part of the dismal narrative. How are journalists in Pakistan faring in their search for truth? There are no easy answers.

A climate of fear impedes media coverage of abuses by militant groups. Journalists increasingly practice self-censorship due to threats and attacks from militant groups (HRW Report 2018). Indeed, violence by radical extremists has exposed the media's shortcomings. Mainstream media have made little effort to explain what helped trigger the surge of extremism in Pakistan, while it has also made no attempts to counter extremism (IFP/Clingendael 2010). There are suggestions that some part of the mainstream media in Pakistan might itself be sympathetic to such extremist sentiments, but this is not documented (Fair, Malhotra, and Shapiro 2014). However, one could characterize Pakistan's English-language media as more open and liberal in outlook as opposed to the vernacular press and TV networks that are steeped in conservative tradition.

Investigations by the IMS group speak of the leverage radical organizations might have with the mainstream media. It turns out that threats and intimidation work, and some journalists acquiesce. Strong-arm tactics work in many ways. For instance, it has been observed that when reporters are working on their stories in the field in the frontier provinces, militants shadow them and stop them from getting close to local people. There is an escalation ladder of threats and violence. If some pesky reporter insists on chasing his story, threats to kill him and his family follow as a matter of course. A survey focused on editors and reporters conducted by the Pakistan Institute for Peace Studies, as cited by the IMS report, found that free expression was under attack because of the radicalization of society (IMS 2009). Intriguingly, the latest Committee for the Protection of Journalists Report (Committee to Protect Journalists 2018) says that the decline in the number of deaths among journalists in Pakistan the previous year was linked to a reduced space for freedom of expression in Pakistan. In simple translation, it means that journalists are not taking the risks that they should be taking. Prior restraint is the order of the day as a survival strategy.

On balance, it would appear that mainstream newspapers regularly challenge the extremist agenda in their opinion pages. Their voice is heard by the decision-makers and thought leaders in Pakistan. Take the recent case of forced marriages involving Hindu women and Muslim men in Sindh province. These young girls were forced into marriage and later compelled to embrace Islam. Thanks to social media activists, the issue made headlines across the country, compelling the government to order punitive action against the perpetrators. Obviously, the radicalized elements were incensed, for they believe every convert to Islam comes as a blessing. However, they could not do much against a groundswell of sympathy for the victims. Thinking Pakistanis believed they were on the moral high ground for the first time in a long while.

Military influence

The military in Pakistan has behaved much more professionally in recent years: the country has allowed two democratically elected governments to complete their terms in office, and the third one is in its first year of tenure. By choosing not to infringe on civilian turf, the military has had a chance to put its own house in order.

That said, the Pakistani military has a track record of intervening extensively in the media realm. Following the first military coup, in 1958 by General Ayub Khan, successful efforts were launched to buy the political allegiance of senior journalists. These trends were reinforced when General Muhammed Zia-ul-Haq imposed martial law in the country, leading to sharp divisions across the journalistic community throughout the 1980s. The main journalist organization, the Pakistan Union of Journalists, was split into two rival factions, one representing those who supported the dictator and the other his opponents. The trend continued in subsequent years and, according to some media activists in Pakistan, this divisive strategy persists (Clingendael 2010). Arguably, the most significant pieces of military legislation having serious implications for media autonomy was the establishment of a media regulatory entity in 2000 called the Regulatory Authority for Media Broadcast Organizations (RAMBO), the sinister precursor to PEMRA.

While civilian governments in Pakistan have tended to view independent media through an adversarial lens, the military does not engage directly with journalists. If he military had its way, it would rather like to be left alone. It generally regards reporters as interlopers. Just how far are military commanders willing to accommodate reporters in Pakistan's troubled areas? The answer is: as little as possible; ideally, not at all. This attitude is also common among the militaries of other countries. America's wars in Iraq and Afghanistan shed light on media-military antagonism. Pakistan's troubled areas are mainly the Khyber Pakhtunkhwa (KP), formerly the frontier province and its adjoining tribal belt, home to militants of all stripes. The Pakistan army has been fighting an intense war against terrorists here and the war shows little signs of abating any time soon. The army has taken thousands of casualties and successfully faced down terrorists in KP. In the process, it has also upended the lives of a large number of people living in the area. Hence, the media are naturally interested in covering this situation – and that has proved to be highly contentious.

The Pakistani army is also engaged in suppressing an insurgency in Balochistan. The insurgency is ostensibly supported by some foreign powers in what is considered to be a replay of the 'Great Game,' this time involving China, the United States and India (Murkert 2015). The Chinese and Pakistanis are building a modern port at Gwadar on the Arabian Sea. The port is an important hub along the China-Pakistan Economic Corridor (CEPC), a part of China's Road and Belt project. The mineral and gas-rich Balochistan is Pakistan's largest province in terms of territory; it has been a hotbed for militants, too. It is currently witnessing a bizarre confluence of forces, including anti-Iran elements and the Baloch separatists. The Pakistani army is spread thin here, and obviously engaged on many fronts. Its sensitivities regarding freewheeling journalists looking to embarrass it by reporting 'the stuff that happens' are understandable. However, Pakistan's modern and democratic media insist on seeking the truth.

The Pakistani media have two choices: go into these troubled areas as military 'embeds,' or operate unilaterally. Pakistani journalists have opted for both approaches. Unless the preponderance of news coverage originates from independent and sustained contacts in the affected areas, journalists are always going to get the story wrong (King 2013).

The Pakistani army has restricted avenues for reporting. Access to regions including Balochistan is denied. Officers encourage self-censorship by subtle and overt intimidation, including making calls to editors to complain about unwelcome coverage. In addition, there have been accusations against the security forces for inciting violence against reporters (Committee to Protect Journalists 2018).

Political influence

Where do politicians figure into the debate about media freedom in Pakistan? While the Pakistani media have been careful not to attack the military, they have enjoyed a free hand in lambasting politicians and the government. Politicians also demonize particular newspapers or broadcasters, just like they favour sympathetic media outlets. Before we reflect more on this phenomenon, it would help to understand the health of Pakistani democracy and politics. While the international research community views democracy in Pakistan as fragile, the British newspaper *The Guardian* employs a better term: semi-democracy. According to the newspaper, the growth of 'semi-democracy across the world, where elections are held but are rigged by the state power holders, has brought into ever sharper focus how much a country's media system conditions the quality of its democracy' (*The Guardian* 2018). It would be fair to remark that media and politicians enjoy a symbiotic relationship in Pakistan, barring some aberrations. Imran Khan, the present charismatic prime minister, has a visceral dislike, bordering on disgust, for the country's largest newspaper and broadcasting network 'Geo.' While campaigning he would often vent his anger at the manner in which Geo and the network's newspapers were portraying him. GEO was supportive of Khan's nemesis, ousted prime minister Nawaz Sharif.

The media-politicians nexus goes back some decades. Both the Pakistan Peoples Party and Muslim League governments bent over backwards to win over journalists. The Nawaz government offered all kinds of inducements ranging from bank loans to residential plots to unspoken lavish perks (*Dawn* 2017). Governments formed by both parties encouraged a culture of patronage. The military governments also promoted sycophancy and patronage. Vernacular media emerged as a green pasture for government politicians. Those journalists who refused to be 'bought' and who maintained integrity and professionalism were recognized for their integrity by their organizations. Also, the ones who opted for the path of truth and ran exposés on the regime's corrupt practices were ostracized first, chased and intimidated later. The Intelligence Bureau (IB) was used frequently to torment independent journalists. The same trends continue today to a lesser extent. In a sense, parts of the media did lose credibility for allowing themselves to be bought, igniting a sense of alienation among citizens, particularly among the young. Pakistan's youth are increasingly distrustful of the media. When asked if they read newspapers, most students respond in the negative. The phrase '*Lafafa*' journalism (money-filled envelope) was coined in the 1980s and has stuck ever since. That is the sordid side of the media in Pakistan. Along with inspiring examples of courage and defiance, crassness is in evidence. If watchdogs in the media are tightly tethered or tamed with 'threats,' they relinquish their essential role. Self-seeking politicians thrive in the absence of a strong media focus. Frontline leaders in Pakistan's last two semi-democratic governments are now in the dock facing accusations of enriching themselves at the expense of impoverished Pakistani citizens. The leaked and widely publicized 2016 Panama Papers implicated then Pakistani prime minister Nawaz Sharif in property-related corruption charges. The last 30 years of Pakistani history speaks of limitless greed on the part of politicians and their cronies, undermining democracy and morality.

Judicial negligence

It is important to critique the massive but indirect role the courts have played in blocking media freedom in Pakistan. Until the robust judicial activism that has defined the Supreme Court in the last five years, the higher judiciary has mostly played a subservient role to the military and to civilian autocrats. Most Pakistanis responded with disbelief and surprise as they internalized the fact of a radically transformed judiciary, occurring almost overnight. It was perplexing and counter-intuitive: generations of judges have been sleeping on their haunches and rubber-stamping the sacking of civilian governments and imposition of martial law in the country. The doctrine of necessity was used to usher in the country's controversial and universally abhorred dictator, General Zia-ul-Haq in the late 1970s. For instance, in the case *Malik Ghulam Gilani vs. the Province of Punjab* (PLD 1979, Lahore 546J), the appointment of General Zia-ul-Haq as president of Pakistan was called into question. It was upheld by the Lahore High Court that the appointment promoted the good of the people and was valid: 'The imposition of martial law stands validated on the doctrine of necessity and this principle would apply to the appointment of the president also as, in the present situation, there is no guidance in the Constitution. Resort to extra-constitutional measures is not only justified but is necessary.' This verdict has had cascading consequences. The doctrine of necessity paved the way for the successive martial laws in the country, each causing a bigger disaster than the previous one (*The News* 2017). Other than representing the grossest act of betrayal by the defenders of the Constitution and the rule of law, this verdict altered the psychology of the country, opened the floodgates of extremist ideologies and produced an environment where journalists were abandoned to their fates.

The judiciary's indifference to media freedom is what journalists rue most in Pakistan. The protective role the judiciary has played in India, even in the darkest days of the Indra Gandhi-imposed emergency, presents a contrast. 'The media owes a lot to the Supreme Court of India for the freedom it enjoys,' affirms Kuldip Nayer, the doyen of Indian media in an article published in *Tribune Express* ('Kuldip Nayar, Indian Supreme Court and the Media' 2012). In a landmark case, *Indian Express Newspaper* vs. Union of India, the Supreme Court of India observes: 'There can not be any interference with the freedom of press in the name of public interest. The purpose of the press is to enhance public interest by publishing facts and opinions, without which a democratic electorate can not take responsible decisions.' Pakistani journalists have had their necks on the line without protective judges or supportive verdicts.

Pakistan's contempt laws are problematic. A Human Rights Watch report says that judges in Pakistan are using contempt of court laws to prohibit the media from criticizing the judiciary. If judges do so, they risk being seen as an instrument of coercion and censorship (HRW World Report: Pakistan 2012). Legal experts believe that a contempt of court case can be made if the media cast aspersions on the character of a judge or proceedings of the court. Human Rights Watch's perspective is that once a judgement is made, it becomes part of the public domain, and can be critiqued. The outgoing Pakistani chief justice, Saqib Nisar, remained very proactive until his retirement in early 2019. In a shocking departure from the established practice, demeanour and gravitas associated with his office, he put on the mantle of a government politician. He would arrive impromptu at public places in a bizarre cavalcade of cars and security officers and pronounce orders: 'transfer this hospital chief, that CEO.' People loved his activism. But he had his detractors, including in the media. Two TV networks were shrill in their criticism until they were told that they might be subject to contempt of court proceedings.

Professionalism?

It is important to examine the academic formation, training and working environment of journalists. Most public and private universities across the country now offer journalism as a subject at the undergraduate level. There are multiple post-graduate programmes as well. Since the liberalization of broadcast media in Pakistan, interest in media-related studies has spiked. The University of Punjab boasts the oldest department of journalism in the country, going back to 1941. It is interesting that the founder P.P. Singh was a graduate of the University of Missouri. His vision made room for American influence in both Pakistani and Indian journalism programmes. Professor Singh moved to India after the partition in 1947 to pursue his journalism ideals. The University of Karachi established its own journalism department in 1955. Since then, almost all Pakistani universities have their well-developed journalism curricula. Pakistan's two elite universities, IBA at Karachi and LUMS in Lahore, have also started programmes in journalism. Students have responded enthusiastically in what is predominantly a corporate environment. The demand and supply chain is stable for the first time, although the perception is that about half of the journalism graduates find their way into careers in fields other than journalism. No credible research is available yet to determine the trajectory of graduates emerging from these programmes. Most editors, however, choose to hire individuals not on the basis of their degrees or discipline, least of all based on whether they studied journalism, but rather on how well they can write.

The working conditions of journalists depend on the kind of media (electronic, print), the audience and the size of operation, and the usual rural-urban binary. There is a stark gap between what journalists employed in the electronic media earn and those who work for the traditional print media. Except for some leading newspapers, remuneration for journalist is low, even by Pakistani standards. Most journalists work on a contract basis. The TV journalists earn far more, and the anchors take home astronomical pay packages and perks. For the first time, more women have come on board to work as journalists, breaking stereotypes and patriarchal barriers. In recent years, some of the audacious and most respected professionals have been women editors. This has added to the vibrancy of the media landscape.

Watching TV anchors and news presenters on the broadcast media feels as if we have entered an era of shouting in Pakistan. Speed-talking is the norm, where guests, experts and pundits are stopped in mid-sentence. 'Show me a TV channel where you are allowed to complete a decent sentence,' says an academic working alongside the writer of this chapter. The quality of language – and indeed, the social discourse – has deteriorated in favour of provocative soundbites. These of course represent some of the teething problems of broadcast journalism in Pakistan. Maturity will surely follow in some years, and reporting standards will have to be improved, along with news-gathering standards. One only has to tune into the old PTV news and view its programmes to savour the refined Urdu accent, and to sense the decline. There is considerable room for journalism students to embrace ethics and adopt best practices, but this requires the unlikely prospect of reversing the decline of a media discourse that is engulfed by superficial sensationalism.

Alongside mainstream media, social media has grown significantly in Pakistan. About 22 per cent of Pakistan's population now has access to the internet, which means 44 million people are online (Pakistan Social Media Stats and Research Summary 2018). The growth in mobile internet users has been remarkable, as well. Social media has emerged in Pakistan as a preferred platform for the mobilization of social and political causes (Khilji 2018). Online, there is space for citizen journalism, which is very welcome in a society riven with discord. As elsewhere, the spread of the internet in Pakistan has led to contradictory developments for free speech and the right to information. Social media platforms allow citizens to highlight and discuss the multiple instances of systemic failure in the functioning of state hospitals, universities, airlines and highways, but the prevalence of social media also offers an unparalleled opportunity for the propagation of destructive ideologies. Banned militant outfits are using social media to radicalization and recruit Pakistani youth. According to *Dawn*, of the 64 militant organizations outlawed by the interior ministry, 41 are represented online by 700 Facebook pages and groups using their names. Upwards of 160,000 users like these pages (*Dawn* 2019). Self-radicalization is not a recent phenomenon in Pakistan. Abundant radical literature is available on the internet, which has recently prompted the Pakistani government to take punitive action against militants and groups seeking to influence vulnerable individuals. Social media is the stomping ground for swarms of trolls produced by militant religiosity and extremism. Can the state police the internet with an honest face? Libertarians in Pakistan scoff at efforts aimed at controlling the internet. They think the state has its own agenda.

There is, of course, a positive side to the advent of social media in Pakistan. It lies in its potential for reforming society. Sexual harassment in the workplace, in the public domain and at home has attracted huge attention in recent times, and so has the physical and sexual abuse of children. So-called taboo subjects like homosexuality and discrimination against transgender people have been at the heart of social media debates. In May 2019, there was a groundswell of anger and disquiet over a case of forced marriage involving a marginalized Hindu minority girl and a Muslim man (*Dawn* 25 March 2019). The girl was forced to undergo conversion to Islam following the nuptials. The mainstream media did not get a whiff of the scandal until voices on social media blew the lid off the episode. The resulting public outrage forced the government, both at the provincial and federal levels, to arrest the perpetrators and provide justice. Extremists love the spectacle of conversion, but their voices were drowned out in the face of what seemed like a perfect storm. Pakistan is transforming because of social media, and the drumbeat of social awakening. On a light note, two years ago, a young man with rakishly handsome looks became a social media star on both sides of the subcontinental divide. He was employed at a wayside restaurant in Islamabad pouring tea for customers – until a young woman photographed him and put his mug shot on Facebook. Fashion designers swooped in on him and he became the talk of the town (BBC 2016). Of course, there is another dark side to social media: psychopaths and pedophiles stalk the internet for prey. We see new kinds of crimes originating from social media platforms.

Finally, there is no doubt that Pakistani media are thriving and, in some cases, helping to drive democracy, however imperfect. Questions are being asked, and answers are being sought. The media's public service efforts are helping to enlighten Pakistani citizens. Those who inhabit the corridors of power have developed a dependency syndrome with regard to the media. Among its finest practitioners are a small band of devoted democracy-inspired journalists who keep up the average for their peers.

That being said, the media's enhanced societal role, if history teaches us anything, is unlikely to go unchallenged in Pakistan. Pakistan's deep state – its security agencies, both civilian and military, including the infamous Inter-Services Intelligence (ISI) – would need to abandon their culture of intimidation and arrogance for one of tolerance and openness. That would be the only way for them to coexist with a democratic media. Politicians, too, are begrudgingly aware of the growing influence of the media. However, the main worry is about the health of Pakistan's fractious democracy and the vulnerabilities of its economy. Independent media need an enabling environment in terms of an independent judiciary and stable Parliament. Both are missing from the equation in Pakistan. The ride ahead for the media is bumpy, unless the real power institutions are reformed to become more transparent and accountable. Thanks to the media, Pakistani citizens' hunger for information and truth has reached critical mass. It is difficult to imagine that some despot in Pakistan, now or in future, can again ride roughshod over media freedom. Pakistan's media sector has become too big and diverse to totally silence. But the importance and prominence of the media in Pakistani society comes at a price.

> A loosening of controls on the Pakistani media in recent years has meant the influence of Pakistani journalists is increasingly being felt in the country's tumultuous internal politics and in its relations with the West. That has sparked a backlash, which has made Pakistan among the most dangerous place for journalists in the world.
>
> *(Pintak and Nazir 2013)*

Although the press survived authoritarian and corrupt leaders, now the existential threat to freedom of expression and civil society comes from Pakistan's fringe of extremists.

Bibliography

BBC. (2016) *Pakistan Chaiwala Turns Model after Finding Fame.* 19 October. Available HTTP: <www.bbc.com/news/world/asia-37704029>

Belknop, M.H. (2002) 'The CNN effect: Strategic enabler or operational risk', *Parameters.* Online. Available HTTP: <https://ssi.armywarcollege.edu/pubs/Parameters/articles/02autumn/belknap.pdf> (accessed 26 May 2019).

Butt, N. (2019) 'Interview with former Frontier Post reporting editor', 5 May held in Lahore bureau of the newspaper.

Carkoglu, A., Baruh, L., and Yildirim, K. (2014) 'Press-party parallelism and Polarisation of news media during an election campaign: The case for the 2011 Turkish elections', *The International Journal of Press/Politics*, 19: 295–317.

Clingendael. (2010) 'IFP/Clingendael report'. Online. Available HTTP: <www.Clingendael.org/sites/default/files/pdfs/20101109_CRU_publicaties.mmezzera.pdf>, page 9 (accessed 26 May 2019).

Committee to Protect Journalists (CPJ). (2018) 'Report'. Available HTTP: <https://cpj.org/reports/2018/09/acts-of-intimidation-pakistan-journalists-fear-censorship-violence-military.pfp>

Curran, J. (2002) *Media & Power*, London/New York: Routledge.

Dawn. (2017) 'Diminishing freedom'. Online. Available HTTP: <http://epaper.dawn.com/page=03_05_2019_008> (accessed 26 May 2019).

Dawn 11. (25 March 2019) *Protest against Forced Conversion of Hindu Girls.* Available HTTP: <www.dawn.com/news/1471638>

Fair, C., Malhotra, N., and Shapiro, J. (2014) 'Democratic values and support for Militant Politics: Evidence from a National Survey of Pakistan', *The Journal of Conflict Resolution*, 58(5): 743–770.

Hallin, D.C. and Mancini, P. (2004) *Comparing Media Systems: Three Models of Media and Politics*, Cambridge: Cambridge University Press.

HRW Report. (2018) 'Pakistan'. Online. Available HTTP: <www.hrw.org/asia/pakistan> (accessed 26 May 2019).

HRW World Report: Pakistan. (2012) Available HTTP: <www.hrw.org/world-report/2012/country-chapters/pakistan> (accessed 2 June 2019)

IMS. (2009) 'In an unfolding conflict: Media in Pakistan', *International Media Support Report*. Online. Available HTTP: <www.mediasupport.org/wp-content/uploads/2012/11/ims-media-pakistan-radicalisation-2009.pdf>

Jalal, A. and Snellinger. (n.d.) 'Pakistan: A political history', *Asia Society*. Online. Available HTTP: <http://asiasociety.org/agha-muhammad/pakistan-political-history> (accessed 15 May 2019).

Jon, Boone (2014) 'Geo TV's face-off with ISI spy agency: A snapshot of a larger tussle in Pakistan', *The Guardian*. Online. Available HTTP: <www.theguardian.com/world/2014/apr/27/geo-tv-isi-spy-agency-pakistan-military> (accessed 26 May 2019).

Khilji, U. (2018) 'Polls & social media', *Dawn*. 25 July.

King, L. (2013) 'The media and the military in Viet Nam and Afghanistan', *Reuters Institute*. Online. Available HTTP: <https://reutersinstitute.politics.ox.ac.uk/our-research/media-and-military-vietnam-and-afghanistan> (accessed 26 May 2019).

'Kuldip Nayar, Indian Supreme Court and the Media', Tribune Express. (2012) May 7. Online. Available HTTP: <https://tribune.com.pk/story/374878/indias-supreme-court-and-the-media/> (accessed 26 May 2019).

Moreau, R. (2007) 'Pakistan: The most dangerous?', *Newsweek*. Online. Available HTTP: <www.newsweek.com/pakistan-most-dangerous-102955> (accessed 26 May 2019).

Murkert, M. (2015) 'Pakistan in the new great game: On Gwadar Port', *E-International Relations*. Online. Available HTTP: <www.e-ir.info/2015/10/26/pakistan-in-the-new-great-game-on-gwadar-port/> (accessed 26 May 2019).

The Nation (2018) '26 journalists killed in Pakistan in last five years'. Available HTTP: <https://nation.com.pk/01-Nov-2018/26-journalists-killed-in-last-5-years-in-pakistan> (accessed 2 June 2019).

The Guardian (2018) Available HTTP: <https://WWW.Theguardian.com/commentsisfree/2018/jan/21/democracy> (accessed 2 June 2019).

Pakistan Social Media Stats and Research Summary. (2018) Available HTTP: <https://alphapro.pk/pakistan-social-media-stats-2018/> (accessed 2 June 2019).

Pintak, L., Bowe, B.J., and Nazir, S.J. (2016) 'Mediatization in Pakistan: Perceptions of media influence on a fragile democracy', *Journalism: Activism in Crisis*, 19: 934–958.

Rashid, A. (2008) *Descent into Chaos: The United States and the Failure of Nation-Building in Pakistan, Afghanistan and Central Asia*, New York: Viking.

Walsh, D. (2010) *Insha'Allah Nation: A Journey Through Modern Pakistan*, London: Bloomsbury Publishing.

22

FREE AND FAIR MEDIA

A distant dream for Sri Lanka

Rajan Hoole and Elijah Hoole

Historical origins of discrimination, terror and censorship

The arc of Sri Lanka's post-independence history is short, but it bends toward injustice, impunity and peril.

Ceylon, as it was then known, gained its independence from Britain in 1948, a few months after India. The Soulbury Constitution, given at the time of independence, did not have a chapter on fundamental rights and left qualifications for citizenship unspecified. Six months after independence, the government passed the Citizenship Act 'de-citizenizing' the bulk of the Plantation Tamils (ethnic Tamils brought from colonial India by the British to work on the tea plantations). This was a clear violation of Section 29 of the Constitution, which afforded protection to minorities by making 'communities' equal before the law regarding privileges and disabilities. However, the Supreme Court upheld the Citizenship Act in contravention to Section 29's implied guarantees against discrimination. The bench engaged in semantic nit-picking to justify its stance: it ruled that the Citizenship Act, which did not reference any 'community' but simply specified that anyone wishing to be recognized as a citizen must submit proof of his father's birth in Ceylon, was not discriminatory. In effect, the highest court of the country betrayed the inclusive spirit of the Constitution and did not concern itself with the consequences for a vulnerable minority, the Plantation Tamils.

It was a defining precedent that facilitated the power elite to make laws that could be interpreted and applied adversely to the disadvantaged.

The next major discriminatory legislation was the Official Language Act of 1956, which rendered Tamil, the language of more than a fourth of the population at the time, unofficial and unfit for official purposes. However, a more courageous judge in 1964 held that the Language Act was in violation of the constitution. From this time, a majority of ethnic Sinhalese (about 75 per cent of the island's population) politicians came to view Section 29 as a hazard. By late 1960s, Sinhalese political leaders were publicly arguing that the country must do away with Section 29 as it was, as the Minister for Constitutional Affairs declared in 1971, 'an entrenched clause which safeguarded minorities against discriminatory legislation' (de Silva 1977: 318). The first republican Constitution of 1972 omitted the offending section, with little opposition. The 1972 Constitution also structurally politicized the judiciary by giving the executive a direct say in the appointments of judges in the higher courts.

In April 1971, disaffected with the elite ruling class and a deepening economic crisis, rural Sinhalese youth led an armed insurgency aimed at toppling the government. The government, in a sign of things to come, after initial panic brutally crushed the militants, who were poorly trained and poorly equipped (Kearney 1977).

The next government that came to power in 1977 introduced the executive presidency which aggregated enormous powers in the hands of an individual. By this time, youth unrest among the Tamil minority in the northeast was also gathering momentum. Some took to violence in search of self-determination and a separate state. The state had become entrenched in Sinhala-Buddhist majoritarianism and enacted policies which overtly discriminated against the Tamil minority. The Tamil militant struggle, jolted by the 1983 communal violence into a civil war, lasted 26 years. In the late 1980s, there was yet another episode of insurgency led by rural Sinhalese youth, also brutally crushed with tens of thousands killed (Hoole 2001: 257). There have also been, particularly since late 1980s, numerous episodes of severe violence targeting the ethnic Muslim minority.

This bloody history and political leaders' utter disregard for the law has had a profound impact on media freedom in the country.

Media freedom and media accountability

On 26 October 2018, President Maithripala Sirisena sacked Prime Minister Ranil Wickremasinghe and appointed former President Mahinda Rajapaksa to the office. The ten years that Rajapaksa functioned as president, from 2005 to 2015, were among the darkest days for media freedoms in the country. Media institutions critical of the regime were stoned, raided and set ablaze. Journalists who thought and wrote independently were abducted, tortured and murdered. Sri Lanka was among the most dangerous countries to be a journalist, ranking 165th out of 170 countries in the Reporters without Borders' World Press Freedom Index in 2014. The most high-profile journalist to be murdered during this period was Lasantha Wickrematunge, the editor of *The Sunday Leader*; Rajapaksa's brother, Gotabaya Rajapaksa, then Secretary of Defense, is a prime suspect in the crime (Wickrematunge 2019). Other notable cases include the disappearance of the cartoonist Pradeep Eknaliyagoda, the abduction and torture of journalist Keith Noyahr and the assault on Poddala Jayantha, general secretary of the Sri Lanka Working Journalists' Association. *Sudar Oli* correspondent S.S. Rajan was murdered three weeks after publishing incriminating photographs of the five Tamil students from Trincomalee shot dead at point blank range by the Special Task Force on 2 January 2006.

The present Sri Lankan government under President Sirisena and Prime Minister Wickremasinghe came to power by defeating the incumbent Rajapaksa in 2015. They campaigned on a platform that promised widespread democratic reform – including a new Constitution, greater press freedoms, investigation into the excesses of the Rajapaksa regime and good, corruption-free governance. With the 'October Coup,' Sri Lankan politics had come full circle.

The two months of utter chaos that ensued following Sirisena's illegal sacking of Wickremasinghe and the appointment of Rajapaksa as prime minister brought into focus the two themes that dominate Sri Lanka's media discourse: media freedoms and media accountability.

On the one hand, we were reminded that the free press, amidst pervasive political instability, is constantly poised on the verge of acute danger. As the secret swearing in of Rajapaksa as prime minister on 26 October 2018 drew to a close, trade unions aligned with Rajapaksa's political party took over the state-owned Lake House press. Several high-profile editors and journalists were forced under duress to cede their positions to Rajapaksa stooges. Mobs threatened the staff at the Independent Television Network to vacate their offices or face violence (Reporters without Borders 2018).

Moreover, we also saw that media institutions themselves are politically biased and unethical, and can often be a threat to the public good. When it became apparent that Rajapaksa did not command the majority in the house, Sirisena prorogued the Parliament. Media aligned to the instigators ignored clear evidence of phenomenal financial bribes the Sirisena-Rajapaksa camp offered to entice opposition support. When protesters questioned the privately held Capital Maharaja Networks' biased coverage of the coup-induced political turmoil, the network singled out the protesters' faces in its telecast and warned them not to 'force its hand' (News First Sri Lanka 2018).

Even though Wickremasinghe was eventually restored to his office through a combination of democratic protest and string of strong rulings in the higher courts, the country is still reeling from the aftereffects of the coup. There is an imminent danger of a retreat from what little progress has been made since 2015 while ambitious reforms have stalled. Prospects for constitutional revision to address minority grievances are dim, the perpetrators of mass atrocities and murder of journalists still roam free and corruption remains rife among politicians.

Economic and political turmoil looms large. The likelihood of a chaotic future casts a cloud over Sri Lankan citizens' efforts to nurture a press that is free as well as fair.

Threats to free media

Media law in Sri Lanka

The 1978 Constitution of Sri Lanka, in Articles 14 and 15, grants freedom of expression (including publication) to citizens and residents, but places pro forma restrictions subject to national security. As such, the Constitution does not extend the freedom of expression to organizations, including media companies. The interpretation of what constitutes a threat to national security has expanded considerably through subsequent legislation and practice.

Moreover, successive Sri Lankan governments have also relied on Emergency Regulations – imposed continuously for nearly 40 years, starting in 1971 – and the Prevention of Terrorism Act (PTA) to seal printing presses, censor publications and broadcasts, and threaten journalists into revealing their sources (Secretariat for Media Reforms 2016). Under the PTA, the state tried journalist J.S. Tissainayagam and sentenced him to 20 years of imprisonment for causing 'communal disharmony' based on a few sentences critical of the state's military operations during 2008 that he wrote as part of two editorials in the *North-East Herald* magazine (Anketell and Gunatilleke 2011).

Perhaps the only positive development in the last decade vis-à-vis media law reform is the enactment of the Right to Information Act. After assuming power in 2015, The Sirisena-Wickremasinghe government introduced the 19th Amendment to the Constitution. After decades of pressure on different governments by activist groups, this amendment included the recognition of the Right to Information (RTI) as a fundamental right. Since its passage in Parliament, independent international bodies have recognized the Sri Lankan RTI Act as one of the strongest across the world, at least on paper, and the Act has been used by a wide range of actors, primarily ordinary citizens, to hold the government accountable. Since its establishment in 2016, the Right to Information Commission, the final authority over RTI claims, has ruled on more than 1,000 cases of the government's denial of information requests. The Commission has largely adopted a progressive outlook and encouraged proactive disclosure from government institutions, including the security establishment. For example, the RTI Commission ruled in favour of the Tamil journalist Dileep Amuthan's RTI request to the Sri Lanka Army regarding the details of hotels, shops and stores security forces operate in the Northern Province (Right to Information Commission 2018). Even though it is unlikely that a new government would repeal the act, in the absence of sustained civil society pressure, future governments may undermine the legislation by simply refusing to disclose information.

In addition, aside from a few notable exceptions, journalists have not pursued the potential of the RTI Act. As Ranatunga (2019) points out, the bulk of RTI-based reports that have appeared in the local media since the Act's enactment have been compiled by a few select journalists, and no media house has so far set up a dedicated RTI desk.

Other major deficiencies in the legal landscape particular to the media are the lack of laws ensuring editorial independence and journalists' right to protect their sources, the absence of an independent media and broadcasting regulatory system, and the state being a large player in the media space, as well as its only – and often arbitrary – regulator (Media Ownership Monitor 2018c).

However, rather than the existence or absence of specific laws relating to media, what matters is the evolution of law enforcement at large into its current predatory self, particularly as regards the poor and vulnerable, and the arbitrariness with which the state selectively applies or ignores parts of it. For instance, given the entrenchment of discrimination against minorities within the state, it is unsurprising that journalists from minority ethnic and religious groups have faced the brunt of the state's crackdown on media personnel (Between 2005 and 2015, 14 of the 20 journalists killed in Sri Lanka were Tamil. Perry 2017). Similarly, it is not surprising that the country's law enforcement and judiciary, which have for long colluded with the powers that be, have done little towards delivering accountability and justice on crimes against journalists.

Compromised judiciary

While there is extensive literature regarding the shortcomings concerning the letter of Sri Lanka's Media Law, the historical role the country's compromised judiciary has played in suppressing truth and media freedoms is not as well studied.

Judicial officers who obfuscate truth in the service of those in power are richly rewarded within the country's legal system. The most recent example is the appointment of former Deputy Solicitor General Yasantha Kodagoda as the president of the Court of Appeal in February 2019. Kodagoda served as the lead counsel for the attorney general at the Udalagama Commission of Inquiry which probed 16 different grave crimes and human rights violations committed in the period spanning 2005–2009. Among them was the massacre of 17 Tamil aid workers functioning under the French organization Action Contra la Faim on 4 August 2006.

In the latter case, evidence collected at the time of the incident, as well as the weaponry used, pointed to the state security forces as the primary suspects (UTHR (Jaffna) 2009a). Kodagoda, whose job as the attorney general's lead counsel was to assist the commission in establishing the truth, instead 'aggressively cross examined the witnesses who came before the commission, in a vigorous attempt to protect state agents against whom these witnesses were giving evidence' (Asian Human Rights Commission 2016). During the proceedings, Kodagoda dismissively introduced the crucial affidavit of a key eyewitness implicating the state security forces that contradicted his original exculpatory statement made to the commission's investigating team (*UTHR* 2009a). But the eyewitness, a Tamil police officer, had clearly stated the reason why he did so in the affidavit itself: a senior police officer involved in the inquiry had threatened the Tamil officer's family's safety in unmistakable terms. The commission, in the end, ignored his testimony, exonerated the security forces and implicated the Liberation Tigers of Tamil Eelam (LTTE) for the crime. The International Independent Group of Eminent Persons (IIGEP), who monitored the proceedings of the Udalagama Commission of Inquiry, specifically highlighted the negative role played by Kodagoda in this travesty of justice.

When the judicial culture is fundamentally one of political expediency, it can directly prevent truth from surfacing and pervert justice. Take the case of the Matale mass graves in the Central Province (Somadeva 2013). In 2013, a team of leading archaeologists dated the 154 skeletons and other artefacts excavated from a mass grave at the Matale General Hospital premises to the late 1980s. The press soon began filling in circumstantial facts linking the discovered mass grave to the security forces' large-scale killing of People's Liberation Movement (JVP) Sinhalese militants during the same period. For instance, the Disappearance Commission appointed a few years after the quelling of the JVP insurgency in 1989 had identified 450 disappearances in the Matale District. Moreover, Gotabhaya Rajapaksa, the brother of President Mahinda Rajapaksa as well as the secretary of defense at the time of the discovery of the skeletons, had functioned as the district coordinating officer of the Army in the area in 1989 (Abeywickrema 2013). President Rajapaksa appointed a Commission of Inquiry headed by a retired Supreme Court judge. Radio-carbon test results on bone samples sent by the police concluded that the skeletons belonged to an era prior to the 1950s. Two years after the discovery of the mass grave, the commission ruled that it had no connection with the JVP insurgency of the late 1980s. Crucially, however, the commission failed to point to any other historical event accounting for the large collection of skeletons which bore evidence of 'severe torture prior to death, making the grave a site of mass murder' (*Sunday Times* 2015). The truth about the mass grave, as with so many grave violations in Sri Lanka, will likely never surface and the mainstream press media miserably failed at keeping such issues fresh in public discourse.

Culture of self-censorship

The roots of the systematic use of state terror may be attributed to the United National Party (UNP) government of J.R. Jayewardene that defeated Sirimavo Bandaranaike's Sri Lanka Freedom Party (SLFP) in 1977. Within three weeks, mobs attacked Tamil civilians countrywide, leaving little doubt that they received their sanction from the newly elected regime. It became clear to journalists and their editors that they had to be circumspect in what they said. A burden was placed on editors, who received calls from government functionaries about particular items in their papers. Some, like the editor of *The Island* in the mid-1980s, got away with reporting facts regarding the dirty ethnic war that commenced during the time without editorializing about them. It was often in the Hansard (official record of parliamentary debates) that one could find some frank criticism of the government. One such example is the Communist MP Sarath Muttetuwegama's speech in Parliament in May 1985, soon after the LTTE's massacre of Sinhalese civilians in Anuradhapura:

> Now I want to ask the Government this. I have been reading *The Hindu* regularly the last few days. It reported the Anuradhapura attack as a retaliatory measure I want to ask the Government is it true that after the death of Lt. Mendis in Valvettiturai 79 boys from the ages of 12 to 20 were rounded up, taken and shot or blown up in cold blood?
>
> *(Tamil Information 1985)*

The speaker's objective was to decry the one-sided reporting of events. He was typically asked by a minister which side he was on. It was a time when reading the foreign media became obligatory for those who sought objective reporting.

During the civil war years, from the mid-1980s until 2010, the governments of the day enforced prior censorship on news relating to national security. In 2006, the Rajapaksa government set up the Media Centre for National Security and tightly controlled the dissemination of all news related to national security and defence (Secretariat for Media Reforms 2016). Successive Sri Lankan governments have also blocked various websites within the country by issuing instructions to local internet service providers. An RTI request to the Telecommunication Regulatory Commission revealed that the process for blocking websites is ad hoc at best: often, it just takes the form of a verbal request from someone in power (Wickrematunge 2017).

While overt regulatory censorship by the state largely ceased after 2009 with the end of the war, other more subtle forms of censorship continue to pervade Sri Lanka's media and intellectual landscape. Legal scholars (Anketell and Gunatilleke 2011) have identified the culture of intimidation and the threat of arrest under the PTA and Emergency Regulations as a major reason for the widespread practice of self-censorship within the press.

The discourse and deliberations on censorship, unfortunately, tend to be centred on its effects and not its roots and fail to take a comprehensive view of the subject. Particularly when it comes to the threats to the freedom of speech of minorities, the focus is often squarely on the state as the predator. This is but a skewed representation of the reality.

The LTTE, the dominant Tamil militant group, was a perpetrator of grave atrocities against dissident activists and journalists. Even today, ten years after the organization's military defeat, global networks of influential LTTE sympathizers continue to demonize alternative voices calling for critical reflection on the permanent harm the LTTE's political ideology inflicted upon the Tamil community. Those advocating coexistence with the Sinhalese on equitable terms are assailed as traitors. These stifling forces dominate the Tamil press and Tamil academic milieu.

For instance, in October 2018, academics from the University of Jaffna, the foremost Tamil-majority academic institution in the country, were party to banning the screening of *Demons in Paradise* at the Jaffna International Film Festival (Colombo Telegraph 2018). *Demons in Paradise* is an internationally acclaimed documentary film by the Tamil filmmaker Jude Rutnam that describes the LTTE's brutal decimation of other Tamil militant groups and Tamil dissident voices starting in mid-1986 in its bid to become the 'sole representative of the Tamil people'. Those Tamils who were vicariously complicit in the LTTE's terror are eager to preserve the status quo by monopolizing the collective memory of the Tamil community. Days after their success in banning *Demons in Paradise*, which they censured as one-sided, the same actors, including senior university academics in Jaffna, led the laudatory commemoration of Mylvaganam Nimalrajan of the BBC Tamil Service. He was shot on 19 October 2000 by a Tamil group affiliated to the state's military intelligence. His well-documented (Hoole 2001: 439) complicity with the LTTE's terror, however, is never mentioned. Deliberately censored from public memory are Tamil academics such as Dr. Rajini Thiranagama, who was killed by the LTTE in 1989. She courageously questioned all forms of terror and violence, including the supposedly emancipatory variety espoused by Tamil militant groups – including the LTTE. Her commemoration in 2014 was disallowed in the very university where she had been employed (Klodawsky 2005).

Such ideological self-censorship and homogenizing narratives can also be observed in the Sinhalese media and Sinhalese academia. They, too, were bitterly polarized during the second JVP insurgency of the late 1980s, when death stalked many because of their views. The JVP that was once part of the broad left turned viciously on those who opposed its drive for power. It killed many activists, including Vijaya Kumaratunge and George Ratnayake, and media figures such as the eminent radio and television broadcasters Thevis Guruge and Premakeerthi de Alwis (*The Island* 2009). Every May – the month in which the LTTE was militarily defeated in 2009, marking the end of the civil war – the Sinhalese media is filled with jingoistic veneration of the Sri Lankan security forces. Hardly a thought is spared for the thousands of Tamil civilians who were killed during the final phases of the war. The University of Peradeniya, a venerable institution of higher education located in the Central Province, banned in October 2018 a photographic exhibition covering issues such as the ongoing torture of Tamil political prisoners and violence targeting minorities in postwar Sri Lanka. The ban was the result of intensive pressure from sections of the student body that characterized the exhibition as pro-LTTE propaganda (Sri Lanka Brief 2018).

In this atmosphere, the wounds of the civil war fester in orchestrated silence, censorship and denial. The media refrains from interrogating this taboo, a lingering legacy of survival instincts honed during the conflict.

Commercial survival

In line with global trends, the Sri Lankan print media is currently struggling to operate profitably. This has resulted in a string of shutdowns. Sinhala-language newspapers such as *Janayugaya* and *Saththanda*, and English newspapers such as *The Sunday Leader* and *The Nation*, have stopped operating in the last few years. Between 2016 and 2017, overall annual circulation figures for national dailies fell by roughly 3–5 per cent across the three languages – Sinhala, Tamil and English (Economy Next 2018). In December 2015, the media house Express Newspapers shut down its three-and-a-half-year-old Tamil political magazine *Samakaalam*, citing non-profitability. This was a rare recent Tamil print publication that provided a space for alternative political views and long-form writing.

While emerging media platforms such as Roar Media focus entirely on online text and video content, the older media houses have struggled to adapt to the reality of the internet. Most newspapers have poorly laid out, non-responsive websites. While most make their print versions available online as e-papers, their user interfaces are poorly designed, making the least of this potential lifeline. Major media houses' slow digital transition and their stale and uncreative content has unfortunately left a vacuum that is, for the most part, filled by gossip sites.

Moreover, advertising accounts for a significant part of the revenue of media companies. But businesses now increasingly advertise online on social media platforms which often facilitate greater customer engagement and better response rates. This has led to falling advertisement revenues for traditional media. The state controls 70 per cent of the economy, and is also the single largest advertiser. As such, state-owned media receive a large chunk of the state's advertising spending (Manobuddhi, Ranawana, and Ranawana 2014). There have also been instances where the state has stopped advertising in certain privately held media houses in retaliation for critical coverage (Secretariat for Media Reforms 2016). Moreover, government actors also often pressure large private conglomerates into not advertising in media outlets that question the state's authority and conduct, a loss that privately held media outlets can ill afford.

Journalism pays poorly, and many journalists work part-time elsewhere to supplement their income or engage in transactional journalism, trading their ethics for cash. The training provided to journalists in the country is lacking in many respects, particularly with respect to the use of digital tools. All of this has led to a situation whereby journalists are viewed not as a bastion of the Fourth Estate, but rather as stooges of those in positions of power and influence.

Obstacles to fair media

In early January 2019, an alliance of artists, activists, and progressive civil society organizations held silent protests opposite print and electronic media institutions in Colombo. They submitted a letter to each of these media organizations, reminding them that a fair media reports truthfully, stays independent of commercial and political interests, discourages discrimination and racism, and remains accountable to the public.

This protest highlights the eroding public trust in the local media. However, this not an entirely new phenomenon: even during the war years, many relied on the BBC Tamil-language and Sinhala-language services, and regionally dominant Indian newspapers such as *The Hindu*, for objective coverage.

Particularly, in moments of crises when impartial and objective reporting is essential, Sri Lankan media assumes a partisan flavour. For example, the sooner an election is declared, state-owned press, television and radio start functioning as the incumbent government's propaganda machinery. Transparency International Sri Lanka (2015) monitored state television coverage in the run-up to the January 2015 presidential election and found that the incumbent received disproportionate air time. Moreover, the incumbent ran an unprecedented number of advertisements (around 40 commercials per hour during the last few days of the campaign) without paying fees, and had his final rally broadcast in violation of the directives issued by the Commissioner of Election. This deference to power is a hard habit to break.

Language enclaves and ethnic polarization

A defining feature of the Sri Lankan media landscape is its polarization along ethno-linguistic lines. Often, the front pages of the vernacular press could be mistaken for reflecting the news of two different countries, with zero overlap in content. Moreover, the same incident may be covered in the Tamil and the Sinhala media with entirely different tone and nuances. Every news item gets sifted through and coloured by the dominant political ideologies of each language medium – Tamil nationalism and Sinhala-Buddhist nationalism, respectively. Moreover, the politics of mainstream English media largely aligns with Sinhala-Buddhist nationalism, while there are Tamil language publications such as *Vidivelli* that focus exclusively on Muslim affairs.

In February 2018, anti-Muslim riots broke out in Ampara, in the Eastern Province of Sri Lanka. The alleged source of the conflict was the claim that a Muslim-owned eatery was mixing sterilization pills into the food served to Sinhalese customers. Sinhalese mobs roamed the streets of Ampara, setting ablaze the town's mosque and vandalizing Muslim-owned businesses. Even though oral sterilization pills do not exist, almost all leading Sinhala-language newspapers reproduced the allegation without disputing it (Verité Research 2018). While the Tamil press identified the perpetrators of the ensuing violence as Sinhalese mobs and the victims as Muslim inhabitants of the town, the Sinhalese press was entirely ambivalent on these questions. None of the mainstream Sinhala-language papers ran the image of the burnt mosque. Within days, the rioting spread from Ampara to Digana in the Central Province. A chief instigator was a Buddhist monk, who was recorded on video expressing inflammatory, racially charged sentiments against the Muslim minority living in the area. Again, Sinhala-language newspapers completely left out this element in their reportage.

It is common to find downright racist remarks in the vernacular press. In the aftermath of the anti-Muslim riots, in March 2018, the Jaffna-based Tamil newspaper *Valampuri* ran three separate editorials targeting Muslims living in the Northern Province. The editorials warned the Tamil community that their existence was imperilled by Muslims, taking jibes at the alleged high fertility rates of Muslim women and warning about the portents of Muslim businesses 'expanding without limits' in Tamil areas. The media watchdog Ethics Eye has regularly exposed the Sinhala press's selective invoking of a subject's minority ethnic identity in the context of negative stories, such as drug smuggling, and the resulting perpetuation of ethnic stereotypes (Groundviews 2019).

The effect of such polarization is a deeply fragmented national polity. Each ethno-linguistic group, and its respective media stronghold, is unable to even begin to grapple – let alone empathize – with the problems faced by the 'other.' For example, the Sinhala media is still unable to articulate the Tamil demand for federalism without invoking the language of separatism. But following the LTTE's defeat in 2009, mainstream Tamil politics has expressly denounced the demand for a separate state: the Tamil National Alliance (TNA), the single largest minority political party in Parliament, has repeatedly stated that it stands for a federal power-sharing arrangement within a united, undivided and indivisible country. Similarly, week in and week out, the continued struggle of victims of enforced disappearances, the ongoing struggle of the war-displaced to return to military-held land, and the unresolved question of political prisoners arrested under the PTA only receive marginal coverage in the Sinhala media. Conversely, Tamil media outlets pay little attention to the struggles of ordinary Sinhalese. In 2013, when the Rajapaksa government quelled a protest demanding access to clean drinking water in Rathupaswala by sending in the Special Task Force and gunning down three civilians, the Tamil press was largely ambivalent. Moreover, even though many Sinhalese families are also victims of enforced disappearances from two insurgencies in the south (1971 and 1987–1990), there has been little effort on the part of the Tamil press to build solidarity.

Media ownership, audience concentration, and politicization

The state itself owns key print and electronic media outlets. It has a publishing house that is home to half a dozen national newspapers, owns two television channels and two radio stations, and has dedicated news websites. The state also regulates the entire media landscape: specific authorities have been established to register and regulate newspapers, issue licensing and allocate spectra to radio and television channels, as well as control access to the internet. State-owned media function chameleon-like, as the mouthpiece of the government of the day.

On 29 October 2018 – two days after the illegal sacking of Wickremasinghe as prime minister – the editorial of the state-run English-language *Daily News*, affirmed President Sirisena's illegal move as 'the need of the hour' and hailed it as having presented the country with a fresh opportunity to correct course (*Daily News* 2018a). On 17 December 2018, the editorial in the same newspaper described Wickremasinghe's restoration to the office of Prime Minister via a

Supreme Court ruling as a 'triumph for democracy' (*Daily News* 2018b). The same pliant editor wrote both the pieces.

A recent study (Media Ownership Monitor 2018b) by Verité Research and Reporters without Borders assessed 46 popular media houses across print, television, radio and online domains. A key finding was that high audience concentration across a few major media players is a threat to pluralism. For instance, the top four owners of print media institutions account for 75 per cent of the countrywide readership, while the top four owners of television networks account for 77 per cent of the viewership. Further, the study also established that a vast majority of private media house owners have known political affiliations. Owners with political affiliations have 79 per cent of the press readership share, while politically affiliated television media owners hold a 54 per cent audience share (Media Ownership Monitor 2018a).

These incestuous political connections run deep. The chairperson of the country's largest radio network is the brother of a former minister who was sentenced to death for the murder of a parliamentarian. The daughter of a current minister heads the most-watched television channel in the country. A Tamil parliamentarian owns the largest Tamil regional newspaper in the Northern Province. Prime Minister Wickremasinghe's extended family owns the country's most widely read newspaper while his cousin serves as the country's (non-cabinet) Minister for Mass Media. Partisanship is thus in the DNA of Sri Lanka's mainstream media, highlighting the importance of social media.

Social media, fake news and real consequences

In times of national crisis, social media platforms have served to counter the state's monopoly on information. During the anti-Muslim riots in Aluthgama in 2014 and Ampara and Digana in 2018, the presidential and parliamentary elections of 2015, and the coup of October 2018, independent journalists used their Twitter handles and personal Facebook accounts to provide real-time updates to the general public. Their reporting often ran counter to the government's narrative. Activists have used the freedom of social media to highlight, inter alia, police inaction against mobs attacking minorities, the nexus between prominent politicians and underworld drug lords, corruption within state institutions and the subversion of language rights within government institutions. Former Secretary of Defense Gotabhaya Rajapaksa, in recognition of the freedom of social media, once remarked that it served as the 'final threat to Sri Lanka's national security' (Gunatilleke 2016). Facebook and Twitter have also enabled citizens to hold their elected officials to account. There have been numerous instances in the recent past when politicians have been made to retract their statements or rectify their actions after facing a social media backlash. For instance, in February 2019, against a backdrop of severe social media criticism for using a publicly funded project for self-promotion, a government minister removed a massive billboard containing his portrait announcing the opening of a newly constructed swimming pool. Conversely, in the face of false reporting by mainstream media, politicians have used social media to engage the public directly and provide their versions of the truth. This is often the case for minority politicians who are regularly covered in a negative light by the Sinhala media.

However, social media platforms, particularly Facebook and WhatsApp groups, also function as fertile breeding grounds for fake news and hate speech (Samaratunge and Hattotuwa 2014). The Sri Lankan government openly blamed Facebook's failure to take down posts that users flagged as hate speech as one of the primary reasons for the spread of the 2018 anti-Muslim riots in Ampara and Digana. For instance, Facebook responded to a lodged complaint against a Sinhala-language post calling on Sinhalese to 'kill all Muslims, don't even let an infant of the dogs escape' by saying the post did not violate its definition of hate speech (Tribune News Service 2018). In fact, the government eventually blocked access to Facebook, WhatsApp and Viber for nearly a week as part of the state of emergency enforced to quell the riots. The blocking drew a keener response from Facebook, which has since intensified the policing of vernacular content on its platform.

Whereas Facebook and WhatsApp are largely the domain of vernacular languages and ethno-linguistic nationalists, Twitter has a significantly smaller user base and essentially functions as an outpost for the urban living and ever shrinking group of English-speaking Sri Lankan liberals. This is not to say that Sri Lankan Twitter is not without its problems. An in-depth study by Groundviews revealed that Namal Rajapaksa, a member of Parliament and son of former president Mahinda Rajapaksa, had created for himself an army of Twitter bots – accounts that are often just software designed to execute a particular function. These bots collectively and strategically publish content vilifying those who criticized the Rajapaksa family, as well as amplify the reach of Namal Rajapaksa's own content through viral retweeting (Hattotuwa 2018).

Fake news, in and of itself, is nothing new to Sri Lanka. However, the addition of smartphones, cheap internet access and social media to existing inequalities and shortcomings in media literacy has created fertile conditions for the weaponization of the fake news phenomenon. More and more Sri Lankans are coming online and consuming news from all kinds of sources. The number of active mobile connections in the country outnumber the population, and there are close to 6 million Sri Lankan Facebook users (Enfection 2018) – nearly a third of the population. The internet and social media are great equalizers that can make everyone and everything seem credible (Ball 2018). Internet users often have trouble distinguishing between the source and the platform: i.e., many on Facebook view it as a source of news as opposed to merely a platform on which multiple players, including hate groups, feverishly message.

The absence of a responsible digital citizenry leads to situations like Ampara's anti-Muslim riots. A Sinhalese customer at a Muslim-owned restaurant found a small ball of dough in his food and made phone calls. The Muslim owner was soon made to confess on video by a mob that the dough was, in fact, a sterilization pill. This video was widely circulated on Facebook and WhatsApp, rousing communal sentiments and sparking violence against Muslims (Bohram and Attanayake 2018). To this day, the perpetrators have not faced legal consequences for their actions.

Established media outlets, too, engage in deliberate false reporting on sensitive matters and are increasingly relying on the virality of the internet to advance and sustain dangerous narratives. Recently, Captial Maharaja Networks ran a story on its website claiming that a leading Tamil parliamentarian heavily involved in the ongoing constitution-making process told a Tamil audience in Jaffna, Sri Lanka, that the country could face division (News First Sri Lanka 2019). Maharaja television channels repeatedly aired a 10-second clip to this effect, misleadingly taken out of context to suggest he supported separatism. This was a deceitful spin on an hour-long speech that strongly urged Tamils to stop entertaining separatism. The title of a recent Sri Lanka Mirror piece accused the same Tamil parliamentarian of 'trying to change the name of the country.' In fact, all that had happened was the parliamentarian in question merely suggesting an alteration to the official name of the country from 'Democratic Socialist Republic of Sri Lanka' to either 'Republic of Sri Lanka' or plain 'Sri Lanka' (Sri Lanka Mirror 2019). Such deliberately false reporting severely undermines the country's reconciliation efforts, as well as the process of enacting a new Constitution, both of which remain fragile and in need of fair and balanced media coverage.

Distant dreams in dire straits

The Sri Lankan media, in a reflection of the perils engulfing the country at large, is also characterized by the same impasse. Many of the prominent media personalities and columnists across the language divide are self-proclaimed ethno-religious nationalists. Similarly, politicians who espouse extreme views account for a giant share of media content. Together, they continue to perpetuate and advance the very ideas and myths that led the country to a calamitous, decades-long civil war. As we saw in the preceding sections, there is little room for genuine reflection about our past in a media landscape charged with nationalist fervour and deep-rooted biases.

Mainstream media in Sri Lanka, thus, are victims of political processes overdetermined by ethnicity at the expense of urgent issues, such as the suppressed and unresolved class conflict that led to two Sinhalese youth insurgencies in the south, caste divisions in the northeast, and growing economic and educational inequalities across the board. A political middle ground, where both the Tamil and the Sinhalese media can converge, is completely absent and shows no sign of emerging. In such a context, the prospects for a free and fair media in Sri Lanka are negligible.

Bibliography

Abeywickrema, M. (2013) 'Justice sought for the fallen comrades', *The Sunday Leader.* Available HTTP: <www.thesundayleader.lk/2013/04/07/justice-sought-for-the-fallen-comrades/> (accessed 21 April 2019).

Anketell, N. and Gunatilleke, G. (2011) *Emergency Law in the Context of Terrorism: Sri Lanka*, Colombo: South Asia for Human Rights. Available HTTP: <www.southa sianrights.org/wp-content/uploads/2009/10/SL-Terrorism-and-Emergency-Laws_ Draft1.pdf> (accessed 15 February 2019).

Asian Human Rights Commission. (2016) *Objection to the Designation of Mr. Yasantha Kodagoda, Deputy Solicitor General (DSG) as the Chairperson of the Government's Steering Committee on 'Torture Prevention and the Law' of the National Human Rights Action Plan.* Available HTTP: <http://srilankabrief.org/2016/09/appointment-of-yasantha-koda goda-to-torture-committee-of-hrc-sl-inappropriate-ahrc/> (accessed 21 April 2019).

Ball, J. (2018) *Post-Truth: How Bullshit Conquered the World*, London: Biteback Publishing.

Bohram, M. and Attanayake, D. (2018) 'Tension in Ampara after fake "sterilization pills" controversy', *Sunday Observer.* Available HTTP: <www.sundayobserver.lk/2018/03/04/ news/tension-ampara-after-fake-%E2%80%98sterilization-pills%E2%80%99-con troversy> (Accessed 8 April 2019).

Civil Rights Movement. (2012) 'Attempt to remove the Chief Justice', *Daily FT.* Available HTTP: <www.ft.lk/article/120159/CRM-on-the-attempt-to-remove-the-Chief-Justice> (accessed 21 April 2019).

Colombo Declaration on Media Freedom and Social Responsibility. (2008) Available HTTP: <www.pccsl.lk/sites/default/files/Colombo%20Declaration%20of%201998%20% 28English%29.pdf> (accessed 1 March 2019).

Colombo Telegraph. (2018) *Larger Questions of Responsibility for the Failure to Screen Demons In Paradise in Jaffna.* Available HTTP: <www.colombotelegraph.com/index.php/ larger-questions-of-responsibility-for-the-failure-to-screen-demons-in-paradise-in-jaffna/> (accessed 21 April 2019).

Daily News. (2018a) *Need of the Hour.* Available HTTP: <http://archives.dailynews.lk/ epaper/?id=10&tday=2018/10/29> (accessed 8 April 2019).

Daily News. (2018b) *A Triumph for Democracy.* Available HTTP: <http://epaper.dailynews. lk/News.aspx?tday=2018/12/17> (accessed 8 April 2019).

de Silva, K.M. (1977) *Sri Lanka Survey*, Honolulu: University Press.

Economy Next. (2018) 'Sri Lanka newspaper circulation down in 2017'. Available HTTP: <https://economynext.com/Sri_Lanka_newspaper_circulation_down_in_2017-3-11730.html> (accessed 1 March 2019).

Enfection. (2018) 'Sri Lanka: the land of the mobile'. Available HTTP: <http://www. enfection.com/sri-lanka-land-mobile-2/> (accessed 30 August 2019).

Groundviews. (2019) 'Reporting on identity in the Sri Lankan media: Ethics and errors'. Available HTTP: <https://groundviews.org/2019/01/12/reporting-on-identity-in-the-sri-lankan-media-ethics-and-errors/> (accessed 1 March 2019).

Gunatilleke, G. (2016) 'Survivalist and irrepressible: The two faces of the Sri Lankan media', in S. Ududpa and S. McDowell (eds.) *Media as Politics in South Asia*, London: Routledge.

Hattotuwa, S., Wijeratne, Y., and Serrato, R. (2018) *Weaponising 280 Characters: What 200,000 Tweets and 4,000 Bots Tell Us about State of Twitter in Sri Lank*, Colombo: CPA. Available HTTP: <https://groundviews.org/wp-content/uploads/2018/04/ Weaponising-280-characters.pdf> (accessed 28 February 2019).

Hoole, R. (2001) *Sri Lanka: The Arrogance of Power: Myths, Decadence, and Murder*, Jaffna: UTHR.

Hoole, R. (2015) *Palmyra Fallen: From Rajani to War's End*, Jaffna: UTHR, Chapter 8.

Hoole, R., Somasundaram, D., Sritharan, K., and Thiranagama, R. (1990) *The Broken Palmyra*, Jaffna: UTHR.

Human Rights Watch. (2007) 'Sri Lanka and Burundi human rights defenders win 2007 Martin Ennals Award'. Available HTTP: <www.hrw.org/news/2007/05/04/sri-lanka-and-burundi-human-rights-defenders-win-2007-martin-ennals-award> (accessed 28 February 2019).

The Island. (2009) 'Foxes watching over poultry'. Available HTTP: <www.island.lk/2009/01/13/editorial.html> (accessed 8 April 2019).

Jayaweera, N. (2017) *The Vavuniya Diaries: Recollecting the First JVP Uprising 1971*, Colombo: Ravaya Publishers.

Jayawickrema, N. (2016) 'Healing the nation: A question of leadership', *Colombo Telegraph*. Available HTTP: <www.colombotelegraph.com/index.php/healing-the-nation-a-question-of-leadership/> (accessed 21 April 2019).

Kearney, R.N. (1977) 'A note on the fate of the 1971 insurgents in Sri Lanka', *The Journal of Asian Studies*, 36(3), Cambridge: Cambridge University Press, 515–519.

Klodawsky, H. (2005) *No More Tears Sister: Documentary Film on the Life and Times of Rajani Thiranagama*, Montreal: National Film Board of Canada.

Manobuddhi, R., Ranawana, A., and Ranawana, K. (2014) 'Sri Lanka's media five years after the end of war', Groundviews. Available HTTP: <https://groundviews.org/2014/05/13/sri-lankas-media-five-years-after-the-end-of-war/> (accessed 30 August 2019).

Media Ownership Monitor. (2018a) 'Greater stake, greater say?'. Available HTTP: <https://sri-lanka.mom-rsf.org/en/findings/political-affiliations/> (accessed 1 February 2019).

Media Ownership Monitor. (2018b) 'Indicators of risks to media pluralism: Media audience concentration'. Available HTTP: <https://sri-lanka.mom-rsf.org/en/findings/findings/#!9fed61067e34232006ff7dcd0ed479d0> (accessed 1 March 2019).

Media Ownership Monitor. (2018c) 'Who watches the watcher?' Available HTTP: <https://sri-lanka.mom-rsf.org/en/findings/state-run-media/> (accessed 30 August 2019).

News First Sri Lanka. (2018) 'News 1st reporters verbally abused at a peaceful candle lit vigil organized by the UNP youngsters'. Available HTTP: <www.youtube.com/watch?v=ZD6In58w9sw> (accessed 29 February 2019).

News First Sri Lanka. (2019) 'The possibility of a divided nation'. Available HTTP: <https://www.newsfirst.lk/2019/01/13/the-possibility-of-a-divided-nation/>

Perry, D. (2017) 'Conviviality vs censorship: On media freedom in Sri Lanka', *Groundviews*. Available HTTP: <https://groundviews.org/2017/12/14/conviviality-vs-censorship-on-media-freedom-in-sri-lanka/> (accessed 20 February 2019).

Ranatunga, S. (2019) 'A law for journalists: Not churanalists', in K. Pinto-Jayawardena (ed.) *Reflections on Sri Lanka's RTI Act & RTI Regime*, Colombo: RTI Commission.

Reporters without Borders. (2018) 'Sri Lankan political crisis threatens media independence'. Available HTTP: <https://rsf.org/en/news/sri-lankan-political-crisis-threatens-media-independence> (accessed 25 February 2019).

Right to Information Commission. (2018) *G. Dileep Amuthan v. Ministry of Defence: RTICAppeal/70/2018*. Available HTTP: <www.rticommission.lk/web/index.php?option=com_content&view=article&id=480:dileep-amuthan-v-ministry-of-defence-rticappeal-70-2018&catid=46&Itemid=186&lang=en> (accessed 1 March 2019).

Samaratunge, S. and Hattotuwa, S. (2014) *Liking Violence: A Study of Hate Speech on Facebook in Sri Lanka.* Colombo: CPA. Available HTTP: <www.cpalanka.org/liking-violence-a-study-of-hate-speech-on-facebook-in-sri-lanka/> (accessed 15 February 2019).

Secretariat for Media Reforms. (2016) *Rebuilding Public Trust: An Assessment of Media Industry and Profession in Sri Lanka.* Colombo: SMR/IMS.

Somadeva, R. (2013) *Human Skeletal Remains Found at the District General Hospital Premises in Matale: The Report on Forensic Archaeology.* Available HTTP: <www.jdslanka.org/images/documents/disappearances_executions/matale_forensic_archaeology_report.pdf> (accessed 8 April 2019).

Sri Lanka Brief. (2018) *CPA Condemns Censorship of 'Unframed' at the University of Peradeniya.* Available HTTP: <http://srilankabrief.org/2018/10/cpa-condemns-censorship-of-unframed-at-the-university-of-peradeniya/> (accessed 8 April 2019).

Sri Lanka Mirror. (2018) 'Sumanthiran tries to change the country's name'. Available HTTP: <https://srilankamirror.com/news/12646-sumanthiran-tries-to-change-the-country-s-name> (accessed 8 April 2019).

Sunday Times. (2015) *Skeletal Remains Have no Connection to 1989–1990 Disappearances: PCI.* Available HTTP: <www.sundaytimes.lk/150510/news/skeletal-remains-have-no-connection-to-1989-1990-disappearances-pci-148375.html> (accessed 8 April 2019).

Tamil Information. (1985) *Anuradhapura and after: What Sri Lanka MP Said in Parliament,* Colombo: Tamil Information. Available HTTP: <http://padippakam.com/document/tamilinfomation/tamilinfomation_07_85.pdf> (accessed 8 April 2019).

Transparency International Sri Lanka. (2015) *Electoral Integrity: A Review of the Abuse of State Resources and Selected Integrity Issues during 2015 Presidential Election in Sri Lanka,* Colombo: TISL. Available HTTP: <www.test.tisrilanka.org/wp-content/uploads/2015/02/PPPR_2015_ENG_Final.pdf> (accessed 1 March 2019).

Tribune News Service. (2018) 'Kill all Muslims, don't let even one child of the dogs escape': In Sri Lanka, Facebook struggles to curb hate speech', *South China Morning Post.* Available HTTP: <www.scmp.com/news/asia/south-asia/article/2139811/kill-all-muslims-dont-let-even-one-child-dogs-escape-sri-lanka> (accessed 8 April 2019).

UTHR (Jaffna). (2007) 'Special report no.27: A bullet for a fig leaf'. Available HTTP: <www.uthr.org/SpecialReports/spreport27.htm> (accessed 21 April 2019).

UTHR (Jaffna). (2009a) 'Special report no.33: Third anniversary of the ACF massacre'. Available HTTP: <www.uthr.org/SpecialReports/spreport33.htm> (Accessed 21 April 2019).

UTHR (Jaffna). (2009b) 'Special report no.34: Let them speak: Truth about Sri Lanka's victims of war'. Available HTTP: <www.uthr.org/SpecialReports/Special%20rep34/Special_Report_34%20Full.pdf> (accessed 22 April 2019).

Verité Research. (2018) 'Unsubstantiated facts riddle Ampara coverage', *The Media Analysis,* 8(9): 8–9.

Verité Research and Reporters without Borders. (2018) *Media Ownership Monitor,* Colombo: VR/RSF. Available HTTP: <https://sri-lanka.mom-rsf.org/en/findings/state-run-media/> (accessed 1 March 2019).

Wickrematunge, A. (2019) 'What they did to my father and why they did it', *DailyFT.* Available HTTP: <www.ft.lk/opinion/What-they-did-to-my-father-and-why-they-did-it/14-670330> (accessed 8 April 2019).

Wickrematunge, R. (2017) 'Blocked: RTI requests reveal process behind blocking of websites in Sri Lanka', *Groundviews.* Available HTTP: <https://groundviews.org/2017/12/08/blocked-rti-requests-reveal-process-behind-blocking-of-websites-in-sri-lanka/> (accessed 1 March 2019).

PART 4
Internet freedom

23

THE POLEMICS OF INTERNET FREEDOM IN ASIA

Reality, perception and attitudes

Chuanli Xia and Fei Shen

Freedom of speech and information rights are recognized as fundamental human rights in many international covenants. Many argue that the rights individuals enjoy offline should also be protected online (Clarke et al. 2002; Papacharissi 2002). This standpoint, however, is not always accepted by the authorities in Asian countries,[1] where political and media restrictions are deeply rooted (Abbott 2013). The most notable case is China, where the government employs a large variety of tools and resources to constrain citizens' personal expression and online activities based on claims of national security, political stability and state sovereignty concerns (Lessig 2009; Shen 2014). Others are following China's lead.

Although internet freedom in Asia is limited by state authorities, do Asian citizens support or tolerate restrictions on freedom internet? How do Asian citizens respond to limits on free speech on the net? Many may mistakenly assume that internet users in Asia consent to limits to their online freedom. However, evidence suggests otherwise. For instance, a 2017 worldwide survey by the BBC World Service reveals that more than 70 per cent of internet users in three Asian countries – China, India and Indonesia – attach much importance to free access to the internet. Around 50 per cent of them strongly oppose government regulation of the web (BBC 2017a).

Given the sharp divide between individuals' expectations and the reality of internet freedom in Asia, it is valuable to explore the current status of internet freedom, regulation of the web and people's perceptions of related issues.

Internet freedom in Asia

Not only is internet freedom a universal right, but it is also an important indicator of democratic development in a society (Best and Wade 2009). However, there are very few projects dedicated to tracking and recording levels of internet freedom globally. The Freedom on the Net (FOTN) report by Freedom House is one of the few projects that focuses on tracking freedom of expression on the internet. Each country receives a score on a 100-point scale ranging from 0, which denotes 'most free,' to 100, which denotes 'least free.' The status of internet freedom in each country is further classified into three categories: 'free' (0–30 points), 'partly free' (31–60 points) and 'not free' (61–100 points) (For methods, see Freedom House 2018a).

It is important to point out that the FOTN score is not without limitations. First, not every country is included in the scoring system. Only 17 Asian countries are included. Second, some argue that the indices used by Freedom House are politically biased, because better ratings are received by countries with stronger political ties to the United States (Mainwaring, Brinks, and Pérez-Liñán 2001; Steiner 2016). Despite these constraints, the FOTN report is by far the best existing resource for obtaining an overview of internet freedom cross-nationally.

As expected, the survey indicates that very few Asian societies enjoy a free internet environment, because many Asian governments maintain tight control over the internet (Endeshaw 2004; Gainous, Wagner, and Abbott 2015). Common practices by governments to constrain individuals' freedom on the internet include network shutdowns in the times of political or security crises, temporary or permanent blocking of citizen journalism websites and social media sites, the deletion of content criticizing the authorities and arbitrary and disproportionate purges targeting journalists and other government critics. According to the FOTN 2018 report, three of 17 Asian countries (including Eurasia) were rated as 'free,' and Japan is the only Asia-Pacific country with 'free' internet. A total of nine countries were rated as 'partly free': Bangladesh, Cambodia, India, Indonesia, Malaysia, Singapore, Sri Lanka, South Korea and the Philippines. The remaining five countries were rated as 'not free': China, Myanmar, Pakistan, Thailand and Vietnam (Freedom House 2018b). Compared with countries in other continents listed in the report, there are far fewer Asian countries with free internet, signifying a gloomy reality for internet freedom in Asia (Table 23.1). The status and scores of internet freedom and the five-year changes from 2013 to 2018 for 17 Asian countries are presented in Table 23.1.

In recent years, there has been a downward trend in internet freedom all over the world, but the trend is more obvious in Asia because governments in this region have become more sophisticated in controlling the internet. Compared with the FOTN scores back in 2013 (Freedom House 2013), in 2018, 11 of 17 Asian countries declined, whereas only four countries made progress. In the last five years, Cambodia has suffered an 8-point increase since 2013. In 2018, the Cambodian government issued an inter-ministerial proclamation restricting online news outlets and social media sites, which paved the way for stringent censorship of online content (Dara and Kimsay 2018).

As shown in Table 23.1, scores also increased in the Philippines and Thailand. In 2018, the Philippines went from 'free' to 'partly free' because content distortion and cyberattacks have caused serious problems for online communication.

TABLE 23.1 The status and total scores of internet freedom in Asian countries in 2018 and 2013

	Freedom on the Net 2018 status	Freedom on the Net 2013 status	Freedom on the Net 2018 total score	Freedom on the Net 2013 total score	Five years change of internet freedom
Georgia	free	free	25	26	↑
Japan	free	free	25	22	↓
Armenia	free	free	27	29	↑
Philippines	partly free	free	31	25	↓
South Korea	partly free	partly free	36	32	↓
Singapore	partly free	–	41	–	–
India	partly free	partly free	43	47	↑
Malaysia	partly free	partly free	45	44	↓
Indonesia	partly free	partly free	46	41	↓
Sri Lanka	partly free	partly free	47	58	↑
Bangladesh	partly free	partly free	51	49	↓
Cambodia	partly free	partly free	55	47	↓
Myanmar	not free	–	64	–	–
Thailand	not free	partly free	65	60	↓
Pakistan	not free	not free	73	67	↓
Vietnam	not free	not free	76	75	↓
China	not free	not free	88	86	↓
On average	–	–	**49**	**47**	↓

Note: Data come from the Freedom on the Net 2018 report. Singapore and Myanmar were not included in the Freedom on the Net 2013 report. Up arrow in the last column indicates improvement of internet freedom from 2013 to 2018, and down arrow indicates decline of internet freedom from 2013 to 2018.

Additionally, the government-ordered shutdown of mobile phone networks and the increasing number of libel cases against journalists and opinion leaders for their criticism of the government, further aggravated the problem (Ballaran 2018). For example, reporter Rambo Talabong from Rappler, a news website often critical of the authorities, was sued in 2017 by John Castriciones, an under-secretary of the Department of the Interior and Local Government (DILG), for a series of reports about DILG officials petitioning President Duterte to sack Castriciones (Rappler 2017). In Thailand, there is intensive censorship of online news. Critics of the government and monarchy face arrest and prosecution. Threats to social order or national security are also used as grounds to harass the authors of online content (Prachatai 2016).

Despite the overall decline of internet freedom in Asia, it is worth noting that a few countries have improved their internet freedom. The largest improvement occurred in Sri Lanka. Regardless of temporary national blocks of social media sites such as Facebook, WhatsApp and Instagram, detainments and prosecutions for online activities have become less frequent in Sri Lanka (Freedom House 2018b).

The extent to which people perceive the internet environment to be free may differ from the reality of internet freedom because of the influence of social and political culture (Shirky 2011). People's perceptions and attitudes towards internet freedom are not well understood, since few relevant cross-national opinion polls have been conducted in Asia. One recent attempt was a large multinational survey of internet users in 11 East Asian societies conducted by Shen and Tsui in 2015 (Shen and Tsui 2016). A total of 7,357 internet users from 11 Asian societies were asked their opinions on a range of issues related to internet freedom in an online survey conducted between 29 July and 24 August 2015.

What do internet users think of the state of internet freedom in these 11 Asian societies? According to the results of the survey, on average, 71 per cent of the respondents believed that the internet environment was not free, and that online censorship existed in their countries or regions. The percentages of respondents who held such opinions in each country or region are listed in Table 23.2. Overall, the perceptions of internet freedom were generally consistent with the Freedom House assessments.

Government tactics to control the internet

Almost all governments in the world have exercised some form of control over the internet since its inception (Morozov 2011). Governments usually invoke concerns over national security, public order and government stability to legitimize internet control. The need for control has become more pertinent as a result of concerns about the volume of misinformation online.

TABLE 23.2 Perceptions of internet freedom in 11 Asian societies

	The perception that censorship of the internet exists and internet environment is not free (%)
Hong Kong	73.3
India	73.0
Indonesia	83.3
Japan	43.5
South Korea	76.0
Malaysia	72.8
Pakistan	68.2
Singapore	85.5
Taiwan	68.6
Thailand	54.0
Vietnam	78.9
Overall	**70.8**

Note: The percentage is the sum of the percentage of respondents who strongly agree with the statement and the percentage of respondents who agree with the statement.

In recent years, with the proliferation of the internet and the expansion of social media use, misinformation or fake news has become a global issue. This phenomenon has drawn much more attention from scholars, politicians and the general public since the 2016 US presidential election in which many voters' political preferences were believed to have been manipulated by a 'military-grade' disinformation campaign organized by Russia (Bovet and Makse 2019). Intentional dissemination of misinformation and fake news can induce severe social consequences, such as ethnic tensions, mass violence and political confrontation (see Kingston, Chapter 13). In order to quell misinformation and fake news on the internet, nations around the world are taking different actions. Countries' approach to dealing with fake news draws on methods previously used to control the internet.

Online platforms blocking and content filtering

Governments can tackle the problem of fake news by identifying and removing misinformation. Alternatively, they can block certain online platforms that often feed users with low-quality content and fake news (Pennycook and Rand 2019). As a matter of fact, technical blocking and content censorship are two approaches commonly adopted by Asian governments to control the flow of online information – although the motivation behind such censorship is not only to purge misinformation.

In order to stop the spread of misinformation to large audiences, social media platforms are often blocked temporarily. For instance, a fake news story that more than 20,000 sterilization pills had been captured from a Muslim pharmacist helped to spark communal violence between members of the Sinhalese Buddhist majority and the Muslim minority in Ampara in Sri Lanka in early 2018 (Aneez and Sirilal 2018). Hate speech went viral on social media during the confrontation and Facebook posts incited users to 'kill all Muslims, and don't let even one child of the dogs escape' (*South China Morning Post* 2019a). In response, the Sri Lankan state blocked Facebook, Instagram, Viber and WhatsApp for one week in March 2018 to quell communal violence induced by online misinformation (Safi 2018). Although this block was temporary, it caused huge negative consequences in society: ordinary citizens in affected areas lost contact with their friends and family on social media, and merchants and entrepreneurs were not able to connect with their customers (Gross 2018). In Pakistan, YouTube has been blocked for more than three years in reaction to the anti-Islamic video clip 'The Innocence of Muslims' which was considered to include blasphemous content and caused a widespread furor in 2012 (Boone 2015). Social media applications and the websites of most news channels were temporarily blocked nationwide by the Pakistani government in November 2017, due to professed security concerns (Hussain 2017).

Some countries permanently block social media platforms. For example, censorship monitoring website GreatFire.org (2018) found that 185 of Alexa's top

1,000 websites in the world, including Google, Facebook, YouTube, WhatsApp, Instagram and Dropbox, were blocked in China. Such large-scale blocking of social media platforms isolates Chinese people from global networks. In August 2017, India cut off access to the Internet Archive, a longstanding digital archive of the world's publicly accessible web pages based in San Francisco. Although the reason why the Indian government blocked access remained unclear, there is speculation that it had to do with the efforts to block users from the suicide game 'Blue Whale' linked to the Russian social networking site VKontakte (The Wire 2017; Kim 2017). Blocking of social media sites and instant messaging is a common practice to constrain the free flow of information on the internet in many Asian countries (see Table 23.3).

Other than online platform blocking, governments can suppress dissemination of misinformation by filtering, deleting and removing certain pieces of fake news from the web. However, due to the lack of checks and balances in the political system, many authoritarian governments employ severe censorship that targets not only misinformation, but also a variety of politically or socially sensitive messages. Political criticism against the authority constitutes a large portion of these censored messages. For instance, Philippines President Duterte often condemns media outlets that take a critical stance towards his administration as 'fake news websites,' a move seen as an attempt to discredit critical news media (*South China Morning Post* 2019b). In China, internet service providers are required by the authorities to proactively monitor and remove problematic content. Problematic content commonly refers to a range of controversial issues – such as food safety, media censorship, official misconduct, the reputation of the Communist Party or principal officials, and civil society activism – which are perceived by the government as harmful to social stability. Thus, Chinese companies invest significant resources in developing sophisticated self-censorship mechanisms (Shanghaiist 2017).

Similar to China, the Department for Culture and Ideology of the Communist Party of Vietnam (CPV) regularly instructs online media outlets to remove

TABLE 23.3 The list of Asian countries banning popular social media and websites

Social media and websites	Currently blocked	Has been blocked	Has threatened a ban/content interference
Facebook	China, North Korea	Vietnam, Malaysia, Bangladesh, India	–
Twitter	China, North Korea	–	South Korea, India, Pakistan
YouTube	China, North Korea, Iran	Thailand, Pakistan, Armenia, Bangladesh, Indonesia	Malaysia
WhatsApp	China, North Korea	–	–
Wikipedia	China, North Korea	Pakistan	–

Source: Digital Information World (2018), Index on Censorship (2014) and Friends Fort Point (2018).

problematic content through nontransparent and verbal orders. The authorities successfully obliged international internet companies such as Facebook, YouTube and Google to purge a substantial number of fake accounts, videos and posts deemed to be slandering Vietnamese leaders (Peel 2017). Content removal happens frequently under the military leadership in Thailand, as well. Content providers and intermediaries have to follow removal requests because they were subject to prosecution under the 2007 Computer-related Crime Act (CCA) for disseminating information the Thai government considers harmful to national security or public order. To comply with a Thai court decision, Facebook and YouTube in 2017 each removed around 1,000 links deemed to contain illegal information (Tortermvasana 2017). Google's transparency report (2017) revealed that the Thai government sent out 141 requests to the company from July to December 2017 to remove 3,348 items. Many of these items were public criticism of the government. In Malaysia, blog owners and social media users were required by the government to delete content on sensitive issues such as royalty, religion and race in a nontransparent way (Tan 2018).

Deliberate disruption of internet services

More extremely, authorities in some Asian countries sometimes disrupt the whole internet network to combat fake news or during a period of social and political confrontation. In 2018, a series of mob actions was sparked by a piece on WhatsApp news about a 'child-lifting gang' in India. Consequently, the Indian government imposed shutdowns of telecommunication services as a way to interrupt the spread of rumours and misinformation (Bahroo 2018).

Another case in point was the Chinese government's implementation of a ten-month internet blackout in Xinjiang after the massive ethnic riots in the autonomous region. Conflict between the Uyghurs and Han Chinese in Urumqi on 5 July 2009 left more than 140 people dead and hundreds injured (Branigan 2009). Following the deadly ethnic rioting, communication systems in Xinjiang were totally restricted (Wong 2010). Online disruption was not limited to Xinjiang. The Chinese government blocked access to Twitter and search queries containing keywords such as 'Urumqi,' 'Xinjiang' and 'Uighur' throughout the country in order to restrict the flow of negative information about the ethnic unrest (Ward 2009). Xinjiang, as a remote and restive border area, is often subject to stricter internet controls by the government than the rest of the country. More recently, in the hope of blocking information about a violent attack by three assailants that left eight Uighurs dead, internet and mobile networks were temporarily cut off in Xinjiang's Pishan County in February 2017 (Qiao 2017). The Pakistani government also periodically disables internet services during periods of political and religious crises. During the 2017 12th Rabiul Awwal, a religious holiday observed by Sunni Muslins annually on 1 December, mobile internet services were suspended in some major Pakistani cities such as Karachi, Hyderabad, and Sukkur (*The Express Tribune* 2017a).

Lawmaking and legal prosecution

In addition to directly blocking and deleting information that officials would rather their citizens not see, some Asian governments also have used recent concerns about fake news to limit media freedom. For instance, in June 2017 in the Philippines, the government introduced Senate Bill No. 1942 penalizing those who spread fake news both online and offline. According to the bill, any person who is found disseminating fake news and misinformation will be charged with fines ranging from PHP 100,000–5 million (US$1,800–$93,000) and could be imprisoned for one to five years (Tordesillas 2017). In 2018, Cambodia amended its Law on Access to stipulate that anyone found guilty of creating or distributing false information could face imprisonment for up to two years and fines of up to US$1,000 (Asian Correspondent 2018).

State authorities argue that such laws and prosecutions are intended to suppress the dissemination of rumours and to regulate wrongdoing on the internet. In practice, however, many prosecutions were initiated to control online public opinion, to punish political activists and dissidents, and to restrict free expression online. Such judicial harassment is a longstanding problem threatening internet freedom in Asia. In its annual global survey, the Committee to Protect Journalists (CPJ) found that there were at least 63 journalists imprisoned in Asian countries in 2018, some of whom worked for online news websites. As shown in Table 23.4, China, Vietnam and Myanmar are the three countries with the most journalists imprisoned in Asia. Nearly 50 journalists were imprisoned in China in 2018. The large number of journalists jailed is partly the result of the Chinese government's escalating persecution of the Uighur ethnic minority beginning in 2018.

TABLE 23.4 The number of journalists imprisoned in Asian countries in 2018

Country/ Region	Number of journalists imprisoned	Country/ Region	Number of journalists imprisoned
Bangladesh	0	Nepal	0
Bhutan	0	North Korea	0
Brunei	0	Pakistan	1
Cambodia	0	Philippines	0
China	47	Singapore	0
Japan	0	South Korea	0
India	1	Sri Lanka	0
Indonesia	0	Taiwan	0
Laos	0	Thailand	0
Malaysia	0	Vietnam	11
Myanmar	2		

Source: Committee to Protect Journalists (2018).

Legal prosecutions are not only launched against professional journalists who work for online or offline media platforms, but also against ordinary internet users. Two illustrative cases took place in Pakistan. In June 2017, a Pakistani man was sentenced to death for blasphemy after he posted content about the Prophet Mohammed on Facebook (BBC 2017b). Three months later, a Christian was sentenced to death for sharing content criticizing Islam with a Muslim friend on WhatsApp (*The Express Tribune* 2017b). In Thailand in 2017, prison terms of over a decade were handed down to two internet users for lèse-majesté, an offense against the dignity of the established authority, or insulting the monarchy. One man was sentenced to 35 years in jail because he posted ten messages using a fraudulent Facebook account (*The Guardian* 2017). Another Thai internet user was given an 18-year jail term for uploading several videos to Facebook that the court deemed insulting to the monarchy (Lefevre and Perry 2017). Although these mentioned legal prosecutions targeted a very small portion of overall internet users, as well as online journalists, they play an important role in undermining online activism and promoting self-censorship by the public.

It remains unclear whether the previously discussed internet controls can successfully battle the problem of fake news. Critics worry that these controls could be used as pretexts by authoritarian governments to stifle freedom of speech and to compromise the free internet environment. In early 2018, the European Commission convened a group of experts to advise on policy initiatives to deal with fake news and misinformation (HLGE 2018). The group advised the Commission against simplistic solutions and cautioned against any form of censorship. Indeed, there are alternatives to censorship in fighting fake news. Promotion of media literacy is one alternative. The California government, for example, passed a law bolstering media literacy education in that US state's public schools (Minichiello 2018). The Danish government distributes brochures with tips on how to avoid misinformation (Funke 2018). Another potential way to tackle fake news is by encouraging fact-checking, a process of verifying statements presented as facts. Fact-checking by journalists can positively contribute to promoting debate and respectful discourse in the public sphere (Skelton 2018). However, these approaches are not widely adopted by governments in Asia.

Asian public opinion towards internet freedom and control

Given the fact that many Asian governments appeal to national security and political stability to legitimize their control over the internet, to what extent do Asian publics support government actions? It is generally assumed that citizens of Asian states do not expect their governments to offer broad internet freedom. Furthermore, it is assumed that they will tolerate a high degree of internet surveillance and censorship due to the political and social cultures in

Asian societies (Barr 2000). Few studies have empirically explored Asian citizens' attitudes towards the internet and internet freedom. One exception is Shen and Tsui (2016), who conducted a large-scale survey of 7,357 internet users in 11 East Asian societies in 2015. Preliminary findings focusing on description of public opinion in each of the 11 Asian countries and regions have been presented in a research report from the Berkman Center (Shen and Tsui 2016). Data from this study are used in the following subsections to compare public opinion on the internet across Asian countries and to further explore the impact of Asian culture on these attitudes.

Support for internet freedom

Almost two decades ago, Asian citizens showed little expectation of internet freedom because the internet was not very common in many Asian states (Barr 2000). However, as internet penetration has accelerated across the region, internet users in Asia have become more supportive of internet freedom. Nearly eight in ten of Asian internet users surveyed (78 per cent) believed that freedom of expression on the internet should be protected. The right to internet access was considered a basic human right by 90 per cent of respondents (see Table 23.5).

In spite of strong overall support for internet freedom, there are large variations between countries. Among the 11 societies surveyed, Pakistani citizens were the least supportive of internet freedom. Only 48.7 per cent of Pakistani internet users responded that free speech should be protected on the internet,

TABLE 23.5 Perception of and support for internet freedom in 11 Asian societies

	Support for internet freedom (%)	
	Freedom of expression online	*Internet access*
Hong Kong	84.6	94.5
India	89.8	88.3
Indonesia	82.8	92.1
Japan	68.2	80.8
South Korea	81.7	95.9
Malaysia	82.4	92.8
Pakistan	48.7	66.7
Singapore	72.0	91.5
Taiwan	78.5	93.4
Thailand	78.0	93.9
Vietnam	76.9	90.5
Overall	**77.6**	**89.2**

Note: The percentage in the second column denotes what percentage of respondents believe that freedom of expression should be guaranteed on the internet. The percentage in the third column denotes what percentage of respondents consider access to the internet as a basic human right.

and only 66.7 per cent considered access to the internet as a basic human right. Surprisingly, Japan turns out to be less supportive of internet freedom than many other Asian countries, despite the relatively free internet environment in Japan. Roughly two-thirds of Japanese internet users favour internet freedom. By sharp contrast, Hong Kong and India are on the higher end of support; almost 90 per cent of respondents expressed strong support for free expression on the internet and for the right of internet access. Demographic backgrounds play a very small role in individuals' support for internet freedom. Male respondents are slightly more supportive of internet freedom than female respondents. Age, income and education are not related to people's support for freedom.

Support for internet censorship

It is important to point out that support for internet freedom is not necessarily the same as being anti-censorship (Shen 2017). Freedom from censorship is defined as negative internet freedom, only constituting part of the concept of overall internet freedom. A comprehensive understanding of internet freedom includes not only negative freedom, but also positive freedom – the universal right to access the internet that enables different voices to be heard (for a discussion on positive and negative internet freedom, see Ross 2010). Internet censorship, within certain established rules, is needed to achieve internet freedom in a broader sense (Clinton 2010). This implies that people who support internet freedom could express support for some form of censorship as well.

Indeed, internet users in the 11 societies surveyed expressed strong support for content censorship. More than two-thirds of internet users believed that some form of censorship is necessary to enhance rather than to restrict overall internet freedom. As with attitudes towards freedom of the web, support for internet censorship varies between societies.[2] Pakistan (54 per cent), Japan (59 per cent) and South Korea (65 per cent) are least supportive of general online censorship, while Indonesia (91 per cent), Taiwan (88 per cent), and India (83 per cent) are most supportive.

One interesting observation is that people's attitude toward general internet censorship is different from their support for censorship of different types of content. In terms of censoring political content, over 50 per cent of internet users in Taiwan, India, Indonesia and Vietnam showed support. By contrast, less than 30 per cent of internet users in Japan, Hong Kong and Malaysia support political censorship. Support for censoring political information might be positively related to support for the governing authorities in each society, because criticism of the government and of politicians accounts for a large portion of political content online. According to the fourth-wave Asian Barometer Surveys (Pan and Wu 2016), a majority of people in Vietnam and Indonesia and many Taiwanese showed strong support for their regimes, while only a few people surveyed in Japan and Hong Kong supported their governments. In addition, political content online also involves issues of public order and national security.

Given the serious security threats resulting from separatist militancy at the border, racial and cultural unrest in the northeast and Maoist threats across the eastern seaboard in India, it is understandable that Indians are more likely to support censoring political content (Singh 2019). The same reason might be applied to Taiwan, which constantly faces potential political and security threats from China (Christensen 2002).

Support for religious censorship seems to correlate with levels of religiosity within a given society. Majority support for religious censorship online was found in Thailand, India and Indonesia, where there are deeply embedded religious cultures. In contrast, internet users from more secular Hong Kong and Japan demonstrate the least support. However, it is surprising to see that only 45 per cent of people surveyed showed support for religious censorship in Pakistan, where Islam is the state religion and most Pakistanis identify with this faith (Toor 2011).

There is a widespread consensus that pornography and online gambling needs to be censored in all the 11 societies surveyed, with the exception of Japan, where the porn industry is strong (Hambleton 2016). The strong support for censorship of this type of content could be a manifestation of the third-person effect which posits that people tend to perceive a more negative effect of 'dangerous content' on others than on themselves (Gunther 1995; Lee and Tamborini 2005; Wan and Youn 2004).

Only about 40 per cent of respondents in Japan and Malaysia believe that it is necessary to censor hate speech. This may suggest that Japanese and Malaysian citizens are more tolerant of hate speech compared with individuals in other Asian countries, or that it is not perceived as a significant problem. It is also possible that lower support for censoring hate speech could stem from the belief that it is better to allow extremists to be exposed on the internet as a means of better combatting their hate and discrimination.

The view that online content threatening national security should be censored is strongest in Taiwan, perhaps understandably, given China's cyber interference in Taiwanese politics (see Huang, Chapter 9; Lim, Chapter 4). Support for censorship in defence of national security is also strong in Indonesia and Vietnam. These arguments receive the least support among internet users in Japan and Hong Kong. One possible explanation why Hong Kong people show low support for censoring content relevant to national security would be the rise of Hong Kong localism and the spread of the 'Hong Kong independence' discourse in recent years. Although this has become more prevalent among youth on the internet, such pro-independence discourse is perceived as undermining Chinese sovereignty by the authorities (Cheung 2017).

All the societies in the survey demonstrated majority support for censorship to protect copyright content, except for Japan and Hong Kong, where fewer than 50 per cent of respondents agreed with this idea. One possible reason is that copyright protection has already been strengthened in Japan and Hong Kong by the means of legislation, good regulation of media and media literacy education.

The Copyright Law of Japan and the Copyright Ordinance in Hong Kong became effective in 1970 and 1997, respectively. Thus, there are relatively fewer cases of copyright infringement, resulting in less motivation for people to call for copyright infringement censorship (Schroff 2019; Yu 2009).

It is not surprising that there is considerable variation across the region in levels of support for these six different types of online censorship (see Table 23.6). Attitudes toward censorship are influenced by a variety of factors; for instance, the level of political liberty in a given political system (Warf 2011). Considering the fact that many citizens in authoritarian societies are inclined to identify with the authorities owing to government propaganda or political pressure, or fear of official wrath, they are more likely to show stronger support for internet control than their counterparts in democratic societies (Chung 2008; Shen and Guo 2013). Or it is possible that respondents in authoritarian countries are too afraid to express their opposition against internet control by the government out of fear of retaliation. Religiosity and social cultures such as conservatism are also related to support for censorship of certain content online (Droubay, Butters, and Shafer 2018). Given the emancipatory potential of the internet, favourable attitudes towards online censorship are found to be weak in states with high rates of internet penetration (Greitens 2013). However, it is important to point out that the assumption of a uniform impact of each societal factor on censorship attitudes oversimplifies the situation. Political, economic and cultural factors interact with each other and further mix together with micro individual factors to shape citizens' attitudes towards internet censorship (Shen 2017).

TABLE 23.6 Support for censorship in 11 Asian societies

	Censorship of general and specific content (%)						
	Censorship in general	*Politics*	*Religion*	*Porn and gambling*	*Hate speech*	*National security*	*Copyright*
Hong Kong	65.9	26.9	25.2	54.2	49.6	48.6	46.8
India	83.4	56.3	67.4	67.5	66.6	76.7	72.3
Indonesia	90.7	64.5	84.7	83.3	89.7	85.4	75.0
Japan	59.0	18.8	28.7	48.5	37.2	47.7	39.2
South Korea	64.5	42.4	37.5	67.7	68.2	65.1	59.2
Malaysia	72.7	29.2	47.1	57.9	41.8	49.3	54.4
Pakistan	54.1	39.7	45.0	51.0	49.7	48.0	59.2
Singapore	78.1	46.1	61.5	56.7	55.5	73.6	52.8
Taiwan	87.9	53.6	37.4	69.7	76.0	81.7	67.3
Thailand	71.7	42.1	59.6	55.8	58.6	73.7	64.0
Vietnam	77.4	65.4	79.2	79.9	81.6	88.9	80.4
Overall	**73.9**	**44.6**	**52.8**	**63.1**	**61.4**	**67.5**	**61.5**

Note: The percentage in each cell denotes what percentage of respondents support censorship of general or specific content.

Perceived consequence of internet control

Although people generally show moderate to strong support for content censorship depending on the topic, Asian citizens have mixed views on the consequences of government censorship (see Table 23.7). The majority of internet users from the 11 societies surveyed tend to agree that strict control of the internet brings less innovation, less variety of content, more surveillance and less freedom of expression. At the same time, a large number see some positive consequences of internet control, such as improved content and a safer internet environment. In addition, internet censorship is an effective approach to combat fake news, a phenomenon that increasingly causes economic damage (DW News 2019). Therefore, many internet users surveyed in the 11 societies also believe that government control of the internet can maintain good economic order and facilitate economic growth.

Asian internet users in general tend to see more negative than positive consequences of government control of the internet. Only citizens of three of the 11 societies believe positive consequences are more prominent. Internet users in Indonesia perceive that government control can improve the quality of online content (81 per cent). Pakistani (73 per cent) and Thai (78 per cent) internet users think that government control can create and maintain a safer internet environment. In most societies, there are strong levels of concern about the possible negative consequences of government actions to control the internet. In particular,

TABLE 23.7 Perceived consequences of government control over the internet in 11 Asian societies

	Positive consequences (%)			Negative consequences (%)			
	Improve content	Grow economy	Increase safety	Stifle innovation	Limit content	Surveillance	Limit freedom
Hong Kong	58.8	44.4	65.5	76.7	79.9	82.3	76.6
India	74.6	72.4	77.9	76.3	79.2	76.6	77.5
Indonesia	81.1	77.5	86.5	42.7	62.9	43.5	50.7
Japan	45	30.4	53	64.7	61.8	64	72.1
South Korea	53.3	33.5	52.5	69.8	75.8	77.5	74.5
Malaysia	57.9	49	69.2	75.9	82.2	83.4	80.5
Pakistan	71.3	55.7	72.5	55	57.1	58.1	61
Singapore	59.3	53.8	75.5	73	83.4	80.3	73.6
Taiwan	72.9	50.4	77.8	68.6	79.6	80.6	70.9
Thailand	72.7	64.1	77.6	55.3	65.1	69.5	61.3
Vietnam	77.6	72.1	81.8	53.4	83	74.7	66.8
Overall	66.3	55.7	72.2	65.5	74.2	72.5	70.3

Note: The percentage in each cell denotes what percentage of respondents agree or strongly agree that government control of the internet will lead to certain consequence.

internet users in Hong Kong, South Korea, Malaysia and Taiwan are worried about surveillance issues, and internet users in India, Singapore and Vietnam are apprehensive about the possible limitation of online content.

Individual freedom through technology empowerment

Internet users in Asia are well aware of the limits to their online freedom resulting from internet censorship and government control. Given this situation, some internet users with relatively high levels of computer and internet literacy turn to alternative tools and software to enhance their individual freedom and privacy protection (see Table 23.8). Overall, about 25 per cent of internet users in the 11 Asian societies surveyed report using circumvention (23.5 per cent), anonymization (25 per cent) and encryption tools (26.7 per cent) in order to access online information that their governments would prefer they did not see.

Willingness to adopt technological tools to circumvent government control of the internet is largely related to individuals' perception of internet freedom in their respective societies. Specifically, in Japan, Singapore and South Korea, where fewer people believe censorship is a major issue, internet users do not often use circumvention tools. By comparison, internet users in Vietnam, India and Indonesia more often employ such means to evade restriction. In addition, certain demographic characteristics were related to technical tool adoption. Young male users with high levels of education and income are generally more likely to use these tools than older people, female users or people with low levels of education or income.

TABLE 23.8 Technical and non-technical means of privacy protection in 11 Asian societies

	Technical means (%)		
	Circumvention tools	*Anonymization tools*	*Encryption tools*
Hong Kong	17.2	13.8	18.9
India	32.3	41.5	43.7
Indonesia	24.1	29	28
Japan	4.3	3.2	3.8
South Korea	17.1	15.7	20.3
Malaysia	20	26.3	27.2
Pakistan	50.8	31.2	33
Singapore	14.7	16.7	16.2
Taiwan	20.9	25.2	29.1
Thailand	18.3	27.3	30.8
Vietnam	33.5	33	30.6
Overall	**23.5**	**25**	**26.7**

Note: The percentage in each cell denotes what percentage of respondents have certain technical or non-technical means of privacy protection.

Comparison across Asian societies

Overall, the cross-sectional survey describes internet users' attitudes towards internet freedom and censorship in the 11 Asian societies (see Table 23.9). In order to make further comparison between these societies, the level of support is categorized into three groups: 'low support' (less than 60 per cent), 'moderate support' (between 60 to 80 per cent) and 'high support' (more than 80 per cent).

As shown in Table 23.9, nine of the 11 societies have high support for internet freedom. The only exceptions are Japan and Pakistan. The widespread high support for internet freedom across societies could be correlated to high rates of internet penetration in the Asian societies. There is abundant evidence showing that frequent use of the internet facilitates demand for democracy and freedom (Stoycheff and Nisbet 2014). The characteristics of the internet – being open, interactive and pluralistic – help citizens better participate in civic and political activities, which in turn cultivates their pro-civic attitudes (Stoycheff, Nisbet,

TABLE 23.9 A summary of support for internet freedom and censorship in 11 Asian societies

	Freedom support	*Censorship support*
Hong Kong	High	Moderate
India	High	High
Indonesia	High	High
Japan	Moderate	Low
South Korea	High	Moderate
Malaysia	High	Moderate
Pakistan	Low	Low
Singapore	High	Moderate
Taiwan	High	High
Thailand	High	Moderate
Vietnam	High	Moderate

TABLE 23.10 Internet penetration rate in 2019

Country/region	*Penetration rate (%)*	*Country/region*	*Penetration rate (%)*
Hong Kong	89.4	Pakistan	21.8
India	40.9	Singapore	84.5
Indonesia	53.2	Taiwan	92.8
Japan	93.5	Thailand	82.2
South Korea	95.1	Vietnam	65.7
Malaysia	80.1		

Note: Data sources: Internet World Stats (2019). Statistics in this table are for 30 June 2019. See www.internetworldstats.com/stats3.htm for detailed information.

and Epstein 2016). This may also explain the low support for internet freedom in Pakistan, since limited technology resources and underdeveloped infrastructure prevent a large portion of the population from accessing the internet (see Table 23.10). However, if there is a positive link between internet use and support for internet freedom, how can we interpret the moderate level of support in Japan? One possible explanation might be that internet freedom is not much of an issue in Japan because there has been a free internet environment in this country for many years, and citizens take this situation for granted. Therefore, citizens may not feel it is necessary to assert their support for internet freedom, although they value their freedom on the internet.

When it comes to support for internet censorship, approval is high in India, Indonesia and Taiwan. In Hong Kong, South Korea, Malaysia, Singapore, Thailand and Vietnam, there is moderate support for censorship, while low support is observed in Japan and Pakistan. One critical factor relating to censorship attitudes is trust in government. Scholars argue that the more citizens trust their government, the more likely they will believe that their government regulates the internet in an impartial and rule-based way, leading to more support for government control of the internet (Margetts 2009). Supportive empirical evidence was found in the survey that there is a positive correlation between government trust and support for internet censorship ($r = .30$, $p < .001$). Asian citizens' experience with authoritarianism might be another explanatory factor. On the one hand, people residing in a society with a long history of authoritarianism tend to emphasize obedience and respect for authority, which invites more support for government regulation on the web (Calingaert 2010). There is a strong relationship between belief in authoritarianism and censorship support ($r = .45$, $p < .001$). On the other hand, it is possible that intensified political pressure in authoritarian states makes people refrain from expressing their opposition to government policy and action, which results in an illusion of high support for internet censorship. Additionally, many other factors such as international relations, foreign policy and the security situation could also impinge upon people's attitudes towards internet censorship. Nevertheless, even following these arguments, one cannot fully explain these findings; for instance, why is there low support for internet censorship in both Japan and Pakistan, which are very different in terms of governance and individuals' trust in their regime? This is a topic which requires further research.

Public opinion towards internet freedom and Asian cultures

According to the Asian values thesis (Barr 2000), one would expect that long-standing Asian cultural norms – such as collectivism, conformity, emotional self-control, family, humility, filial piety and deference to authority (Shen and Tsui 2018) – would have a negative impact on public attitudes towards internet freedom. Such cultural tropes could potentially lead to prioritizing national unity, social harmony and authoritarian politics over liberal democracy and freedom

(Park and Shin 2006; Welzel 2011). But our findings refute such expectations, raising further questions about the validity of the widely debunked Asian values thesis.

In our cross-national survey, Asian internet users do not reject calls for internet freedom. Although authoritarian principles are pillars of traditional Asian cultures, some scholars ague that this does not preclude support for Western-style democratic principles such as individualism, freedom and equality (De Bary 1998). Asian cultures are not homogenous, but contain many subcultures and embrace different values, norms and principles that have a complex impact on people's attitudes towards internet freedom (Acharya 2010). This explains why Asian internet users express varying levels of support for online censorship of different types of content.

Shen and Tsui (2018) provide robust evidence that only two dimensions of Asian culture – emotional control and deference to authority – are negatively related to support for freedom of expression online, while other dimensions such as collectivism and family achievement encourage support for internet freedom. To summarize, people's attitudes towards internet freedom and control are influenced by deeply entrenched Asian cultural norms, but this influence is more nuanced than is often assumed, and subject to state manipulation in order to legitimize authoritarian practices.

Tightening internet control in Asia

Although Asian citizens demand more freedom on the internet, many states in Asia are tightening their restrictions on internet freedom, especially given the widespread recent phenomena of fake news and misinformation. In this regard, China stands out as an important player. For a long time, the Chinese government has implemented extremely strict control over the internet (Shen 2014). Although often criticized by advocates of human rights, some scholars argue that strict internet controls render social and political misinformation a rare issue in China (Repnikova 2018). China's 'successful' experience could become a role model for other Asian societies (for a contrasting view about this success, see Anonymous, Chapter 3).

Seen by other Asian governments as a successful model for purging undesirable information online, the 'Chinese internet governance model' has been gaining popularity in the region. In recent years, the Chinese government has enthusiastically nurtured foreign media professionals and government officials to establish a network of sympathetic professionals all over the world (see Lim, Chapter 4). The Philippines, Thailand and Pakistan have been targeted by China in particular and encouraged to follow its practices of internet governance. Chinese telecommunication companies also participated in infrastructure development in different countries, and some companies even provide high-tech tools of internet censorship and surveillance to other governments (Hong Kong Free Press 2018). As a result, the expansion of the 'Chinese model' is becoming a big obstacle to internet freedom in Asia. Yet this is not an appealing model for netizens around the region.

Within China, the state's censorship of critical reporting and propagation of propaganda that distorts or ignores reality, constitutes Asia's largest wellspring of fake news in service of manufacturing consent and stifling dissent.

Conclusion

Governments everywhere manage the internet to different degrees, but censorship of political content and of criticisms of the state are common in Asia. Moreover, internet governance in Asia often lacks transparency, inputs from grassroots participants and checks and balances, which in turn leads to the potential for abuses of power. The battle between internet freedom and internet control has only just begun. As internet penetration rates in Asia continue to grow, people will increasingly demand a freer information environment. The main challenge is nurturing internet governance in Asia that navigates the demands of the state and the market, respects cultural norms and protects universally recognized human rights.

Notes

1 Given the scope of this book, Asian countries refer to the countries in East Asia, South Asia and Southeast Asia.
2 In the survey, two statements were used to measure people's attitude towards internet freedom: 'Freedom of expression should be guaranteed on the internet' and 'Access to the internet should be considered as a basic human right.' To measure attitudes towards general internet censorship, respondents were presented with the proposition: 'Censorship should exist in some form on the internet.' To elicit attitudes towards censorship of different types of content, respondents were asked if they agreed with the statement, 'The internet needs to be censored for specific content.' For instance, people were presented with the statement, 'The internet needs to be censored for politically inappropriate content' to glean their attitudes towards censoring political content online.

References

Abbott, J. (2013) 'Introduction: Assessing the social and political impact of the internet and new social media in Asia', *Journal of Contemporary Asia*, 43: 579–590.

Acharya, A. (2010) 'Asia is not one', *The Journal of Asian Studies*, 69: 1001–1013.

Aneez, S. and Sirilal, R. (2018) 'Sri Lanka to lift social media ban: Minister', *Reuters*. Online. Available HTTP: <www.reuters.com/article/us-sri-lanka-clashes-socialmedia/sri-lanka-to-lift-social-media-ban-minister-idUSKCN1GP2LO> (accessed 4 February 2019).

Asian Correspondent. (2018) 'Cambodia introduces its own "fake news" law', *Asian Correspondent*. Online. Available HTTP: <https://asiancorrespondent.com/2018/07/cambodia-introduces-its-own-fake-news-law/> (accessed 4 February 2019).

Bahroo, M. (2018) 'India leads the world in the number of internet shutdowns: Report', *Forbes*. Online. Available HTTP: <www.forbes.com/sites/meghabahree/2018/11/12/india-leads-the-world-in-the-number-of-internet-shutdowns-report/#3d7513803cdb> (accessed 4 February 2019).

Ballaran, J. (2018) 'Group criticizes gov't move shutting down cellphone signals during events', *Philippine Daily Inquirer*. Online. Available HTTP: <http://newsinfo.inquirer.

net/963786/group-criticizes-govt-move-shutting-down-cellphone-signals-during-events-signal-jamming-cell-sites-fma-media-group-shutdown> (accessed 3 February 2019).

Barr, M.D. (2000) 'Lee Kuan Yew and the "Asian values" debate', *Asian Studies Review*, 24: 309–334.

BBC. (2017a) 'Fake internet content a high concern, but appetite for regulation weakens: BBC World Service Poll'. Online. Available HTTP: <www.bbc.co.uk/mediacentre/latestnews/2017/bbc-world-service-poll> (accessed 12 March 2019).

BBC. (2017b) 'Facebook blasphemer' given death penalty', *BBC*. Online. Available HTTP: <www.bbc.com/news/technology-40246754> (accessed 4 February 2019).

Best, M.L. and Wade, K.W. (2009) 'The internet and democracy: Global catalyst or democratic dud?', *Bulletin of Science, Technology & Society*, 29: 255–271.

Boone, J. (2015) 'Dissenting voices silenced in Pakistan's war of the web', *The Guardian*. Online. Available HTTP: <www.theguardian.com/world/2015/feb/18/pakistan-war-of-the-web-youtube-facebook-twitter?CMP=share_btn_tw> (accessed 4 February 2019).

Bovet, A. and Makse, H.A. (2019) Influence of fake news in Twitter during the 2016 US presidential election. *Nature Communications*, 10: 7.

Branigan, T. (2009) 'Ethnic violence in China leaves 140 dead', *The Guardian*. Online. Available HTTP: <www.theguardian.com/world/2009/jul/06/china-riots-uighur-xinjiang> (accessed 3 February 2019).

Calingaert. (2010) 'Authoritarianism vs. the internet', *Policy Review*, 160: 63.

Cheung, T. (2017) 'Why all the fuss about Hong Kong independence', *South China Morning Post*. Online. Available HTTP: <www.scmp.com/news/hong-kong/politics/article/2110059/explain-why-all-fuss-about-hong-kong-independence> (accessed 7 May 2019).

Christensen, T.J. (2002) 'The contemporary security dilemma: Deterring a Taiwan conflict', *Washington Quarterly*, 25: 5–21.

Chung, J. (2008) 'Comparing online activities in China and South Korea: The internet and the political regime', *Asian Survey*, 48: 727–751.

Clarke, I., Miller, S.G., Hong, T.W., Sandberg, O., and Wiley, B. (2002) 'Protecting free expression online with freenet', *IEEE Internet Computing*, 6: 40–49.

Clinton, H.R. (2010) *Remarks on Internet Freedom*. Washington, DC: U.S. Department of State. Available HTTP: <www.immagic.com/eLibrary/ARCHIVES/GENERAL/US_DOS/S100121C.pdf> (accessed 16 May 2019).

Committee to Protect Journalists. (2018) '250 journalists imprisoned', Committee to Protect Journalists. Online. Available HTTP: <https://cpj.org/data/imprisoned/2018/?status=Imprisoned&start_year=2018&end_year=2018&group_by=location> (accessed 22 August 2019).

Dara, M. and Kimsay, H. (2018) 'Three Ministries set up web-monitoring group to look out for "fake news"', *The Phnom Penh Post*. Online. Available HTTP: <https://bit.ly/2sN7LhT> (accessed 3 February 2019).

De Bary, W.T. (1998) *Asian Values and Human Rights: A Confucian Communitarian Perspective*. Cambridge, MA: Harvard University Press.

Digital Information World. (2018) 'Banned: 10 popular social networks and websites that are (or were) blocked in other countries', *Digital Information World*. Online. Available HTTP: <https://www.digitalinformationworld.com/2018/10/popular-social-media-sites-that-were-or-are-blocked-in-other-countries.html> (accessed 21 August 2019).

Droubay, B.A., Butters, R.P., and Shafer, K. (2018) 'The pornography debate: Religiosity and support for censorship', *Journal of Religion and Health*, 1–16.

DW News. (2019) 'Economic impact of fake news', *DW News*. Online. Available HTTP: <www.dw.com/cda/en/economic-impact-of-fake-news/av-39323555> (accessed 15 April 2019).

Endeshaw, A. (2004) 'Internet regulation in China: The never-ending cat and mouse game', *Information & Communications Technology Law*, 13: 41–57.

The Express Tribune. (2017a) 'Cell phone services restored in Karachi, other cities', *The Express Tribune*. Online. Available HTTP: <https://tribune.com.pk/story/1573913/1-cell-phone-services-expected-restored-8pm/> (accessed 3 February 2019).

The Express Tribune. (2017b) 'Christian sentenced to death over "blasphemous" WhatsApp text', *The Express Tribune*. Online. Available HTTP: <https://tribune.com.pk/story/1507124/christian-sentenced-to-death-over-blasphemous-whatsapp-text/> (accessed 4 February 2019).

Freedom House. (2013) 'Freedom on the net 2013', *Freedom House*. Online. Available HTTP: <https://freedomhouse.org/report/freedom-net/freedom-net-2013> (accessed 16 May 2019).

Freedom House. (2018a) 'Freedom on the net methodology', *Freedom House*. Online. Available HTTP: <https://freedomhouse.org/report/freedom-net-methodology> (accessed 16 May 2019).

Freedom House. (2018b) 'Freedom on the net 2018 the rise of digital authoritarianism', *Freedom House*. Online. Available HTTP: <https://freedomhouse.org/report/freedom-net/freedom-net-2018/rise-digital-authoritarianism> (accessed 16 May 2019).

Friends Fort Point. (2018) 'Countries where WhatsApp is banned!', *Friends Fort Point*. Online. Available HTTP: <http://friendsoffortpointchannel.org/countries-where-whatsapp-is-banned/> (accessed 16 February 2019).

Funke, D. (2018) 'A guide to anti-misinformation actions around the world', *Poynter*. Online. Available HTTP: <www.poynter.org/ifcn/anti-misinformation-actions/> (accessed 18 March 2019).

Gainous, J., Wagner, K.M., and Abbott, J.P. (2015) 'Civic disobedience: Does internet use stimulate political unrest in East Asia?', *Journal of Information Technology & Politics*, 12: 219–236.

Google Transparency Report. (2017) 'Government requests to remove content', *Google Transparency Report*. Online. Available HTTP: <https://transparencyreport.google.com/government-removals/overview?hl=en&removal_requests=group_by:totals;period:Y2017H1&lu=removal_requests> (accessed 22 August 2019).

GreatFire.org. (2018) 'Censorship of Alexa top 1000 domains in China', *GreatFire.org*. Online. Available HTTP: <https://en.greatfire.org/search/alexa-top-1000-domains> (accessed 12 February 2019).

Greitens, S.C. (2013) 'Authoritarianism online: What can we learn from internet data in nondemocracies?', *PS: Political Science & Politics*, 46: 262–270.

Gross, G. (2018) 'Sri Lankan Shut down of Web Based services creates huge social costs', *Internet Society*. Online. Available HTTP: <www.internetsociety.org/blog/2018/03/sri-lankan-shutdown-web-based-services-creates-huge-social-costs/> (accessed 4 February 2019).

The Guardian. (2017) 'Man jailed for 35 years in Thailand for insulting monarchy on Facebook', *The Guardian*. Online. Available HTTP: <www.theguardian.com/world/2017/jun/09/man-jailed-for-35-years-in-thailand-for-insulting-monarchy-on-facebook> (accessed 4 February 2019).

Gunther, A.C. (1995) 'Overrating the X-rating: The third-person perception and support for censorship of pornography', *Journal of Communication*, 45: 27–38.

Hambleton, A. (2016) 'When women watch: The subversive potential of female-friendly pornography in Japan', *Porn Studies*, 3: 427–442.

HLGE. (2018) 'A multi-dimensional approach to disinformation', *HLGE*. Online. Available HTTP: <https://ec.europa.eu/digital-single-market/en/news/final-report-high-level-expert-group-fake-news-and-online-disinformation> (accessed 16 May 2019).

Hong Kong Free Press. (2018) 'China's high-tech censorship and surveillance tools are inspiring other countries, study says', *Hong Kong Free Press*. Online. Available HTTP: <www.hongkongfp.com/2018/11/01/chinas-high-tech-censorship-surveillance-tools-inspiring-countries-study-says/> (accessed 16 February 2019).

Hussain, J. (2017) 'Pemra, PTA order the restoration of TV channels and social media', *Dawn*. Online. Available HTTP: <www.dawn.com/news/1372997> (accessed 12 April 2019).

Index on Censorship. (2014). '10 countries where Facebook has been banned', *Index on Censorship*. Online. Available HTTP: <https://www.indexoncensorship.org/2014/02/10-countries-facebook-banned/> (accessed 21 August 2019).

Internet World Stats. (2019) 'Internet usage in Asia', *Internet World Stats*. Online. Availble HTTP: <https://www.internetworldstats.com/stats3.htm> (accessed 22 August 2019).

Kim, A. (2017) 'Russian social network VKontakte temporarily blocked in India for Blue Whale threat', *The Times of India*. Online. Available HTTP: <https://timesofindia.indiatimes.com/india/russian-social-network-vkontakte-temporarily-blocked-in-india-for-blue-whale-threat/articleshow/60478655.cms> (accessed 4 February 2019).

Lee, B. and Tamborini, R. (2005) 'Third-person effect and Internet pornography: The influence of collectivism and Internet self-efficacy', *Journal of Communication*, 55: 292–310.

Lefevre, A.S. and Perry, M. (2017) 'Thailand sentences man to 18 years in prison for insulting monarchy', *Reuters*. Online. Available HTTP: <www.reuters.com/article/us-thailand-rights/thailand-sentences-man-to-18-years-in-prison-for-insulting-monarchy-idUSKBN1AP0CJ> (accessed 4 February 2019).

Lessig, L. (2009) *Code: And Other Laws of Cyberspace*, New York: Basic Books.

Mainwaring, S., Brinks, D., and Pérez-Liñán, A. (2001) 'Classifying political regimes in Latin', *Studies in Comparative International Development*, 36: 37–65.

Margetts, H.Z. (2009) 'The internet and public policy', *Policy & Internet*, 1: 1–21.

Minichiello, S. (2018) 'California now has a law to bolster media literacy in schools', *The Press Democrat*. 18 September. Online. Available HTTP: <www.pressdemocrat.com/news/8754461-181/california-now-has-a-law?sba=AAS> (accessed 18 March 2019).

Morozov, E. (2011) 'Whither internet control?', *Journal of Democracy*, 22: 62–74.

Pan, H.H. and Wu, W.C. (2016) *Quality of Governance and Political Legitimacy: Governance-Based Legitimacy in East Asia*, Asian Barometer Surveys Working Paper Series. Online. Available HTTP: <www.asianbarometer.org/publications//96047634fd37cd9b360485a62ea44a56.pdf> (accessed 17 May 2019).

Papacharissi, Z. (2002) 'The virtual sphere: The internet as a public sphere', *New Media & Society*, 4: 9–27.

Park, C.M. and Shin, D.C. (2006) 'Do Asian values deter popular support for democracy in South Korea?', *Asian Survey*, 46: 341–361.

Peel, M. (2017) 'Vietnam targets multinationals in social media censorship drive', *Financial Times*. Online. Available HTTP: <www.ft.com/content/853db6f2-0ae1-11e7-97d1-5e720a26771b> (accessed 3 February 2019).

Pennycook, G. and Rand, D.G. (2019) 'Fighting misinformation on social media using crowdsourced judgments of news source quality', *Proceedings of the National Academy of Sciences*, 201806781.

Prachatai. (2016) 'MDES blocks *Phnom Penh Post* news Cambodia received request to extradite 3 Thais facing *lèse-majesté charge*', *Prachatai*. Online. Available HTTP: <https://prachatai.com/journal/2016/10/68564> (accessed 3 February 2019).

Qiao, L. (2017) 'The telecommunication services were cut off in Xinjiang Pishan County', *Radio Free Asia*. Online. Available HTTP: <www.rfa.org/mandarin/yataibaodao/shaoshuminzu/ql1-02162017115429.html> (accessed 4 February 2019).

Rappler. (2017) 'DILG official files libel complaints vs Rappler reporter', *Rappler*. Online. Available HTTP: <www.rappler.com/nation/189253-dilg-undersecretary-castriciones-libel-rappler-reporter-rambo-talabong> (accessed 18 March 2019).

Repnikova, M. (2018) 'China's lesson for fight fake news', *Foreign Policy*. Online. Available HTTP: <https://foreignpolicy.com/2018/09/06/chinas-lessons-for-fighting-fake-news/> (accessed 22 March 2019).

Ross, A. (2010) 'Internet freedom: Historic roots and the road forward', *SAIS Review of International Affairs*, 30: 3–15.

Safi, M. (2018) 'Sri Lanka blocks social media as deadly violence continues'. Online. Available HTTP: <www.theguardian.com/world/2018/mar/07/sri-lanka-blocks-social-media-as-deadly-violence-continues-buddhist-temple-anti-muslim-riots-kandy> (accessed 4 February 2019).

Schroff, S. (2019) 'An alternative universe? Authors as copyright owners-the case of the Japanese Manga Industry', *Creative Industries Journal*, 1–26.

Shanghaiist. (2017) '1984 meets Silicon Valley: A peek inside China's new censorship machine', *Shanghaiist*. Online. Available HTTP: <http://shanghaiist.com/2017/09/29/censorship-machine/> (accessed 4 February 2019).

Shen, F. (2014) 'Great Firewall of China', in K. Harvey (ed.) *Encyclopedia of Social Media and Politics*, Thousand Oaks: SAGE.

Shen, F. (2017) 'Internet use, freedom supply, and demand for internet freedom: A cross-national study of 20 countries', *International Journal of Communication*, 11: 22.

Shen, F. and Guo, Z.S. (2013) 'The last refuge of media persuasion: News use, national pride and political trust in China', *Asian Journal of Communication*, 23: 135–151.

Shen, F. and Tsui, L. (2016) *Public Opinion toward Internet Freedom in Asia: A Survey of Internet Users from 11 Jurisdictions*, Cambridge: Berkman Center Research Publication.

Shen, F. and Tsui, L. (2018) 'Revisiting the Asian values thesis: An empirical study of Asian calues, Internet use, and support for freedom of expression in 11 societies', *Asian Survey*, 58: 535–556.

Shirky, C. (2011) 'The political power of social media: Technology, the public sphere, and political change', *Foreign Affairs*, 90: 28–41.

Singh, B.P. (2019) 'India's internal security-challenges & solutions', *The Pioneer*. Online. Available HTTP: <www.dailypioneer.com/2019/state-editions/india-s-internal-security-challenges-solutions.html> (accessed 7 May 2019).

Skelton, R. (2018) 'Fact checking in a world of misinformation, disinformation and fakery', *ABC*. Online. Available HTTP: <www.abc.net.au/news/2018-09-11/fact-checking-and-fakery-in-news/10230956> (accessed 19 March 2019).

South China Morning Post. (2019a) 'Kill all Muslims, don't let even one child of the digs escape: In Sri Lanka, Facebook struggles to curb hate speech', *South China Morning Post*. Online. Available HTTP: <www.scmp.com/news/asia/south-asia/article/2139811/kill-all-muslims-dont-let-even-one-child-dogs-escape-sri-lanka> (accessed 11 April 2019).

South China Morning Post. (2019b) 'Explained: Fake news in Asia', *South China Morning Post*. Online. Available HTTP: <www.scmp.com/week-asia/explained/article/2188645/explained-fake-news-asia> (accessed 12 March 2019).

Steiner, N.D. (2016) 'Comparing Freedom House democracy scores to alternative indices and testing for political bias: Are US allies rated as more democratic by Freedom House?', *Journal of Comparative Policy Analysis: Research and Practice*, 18: 329–349.

Stoycheff, E. and Nisbet, E.C. (2014) 'What's the bandwidth for democracy? Deconstructing internet penetration and citizen attitudes about governance', *Political Communication*, 31: 628–646.

Stoycheff, E., Nisbet, E.C., and Epstein, D. (2016) 'Differential effects of capital-enhancing and recreational internet use on citizens' demand for democracy', *Communication Research*, 4: 1–22.

Tan, J. (2018) 'MCMC will be asked to monitor bloggers and social media users', *Marketing*. Online. Available HTTP: <www.marketing-interactive.com/mcmc-will-be-asked-to-monitor-social-media-abuse-says-minister/> (accessed 3 February 2019).

Toor, S. (2011) *The State of Islam: Culture & Cold War Politics in Pakistan*, London: Pluto Press.

Tordesillas, E.T. (2017) 'OPINION: SEA lawyers groups call on Senate not to pass Villanueva bill on fake news', *ABS-CBN News*. Online. Available HTTP: <https://news.abs-cbn.com/blogs/opinions/11/23/17/opinion-sea-lawyers-groups-call-on-senate-not-to-pass-villanueva-bill-on-fake-news> (accessed 12 April 2019).

Tortermvasana, K. (2017) 'Thailand removes illicit webpages', *South China Morning Post*. Online. Available HTTP: <www.scmp.com/tech/article/2105911/thailand-removes-illicit-webpages> (accessed 3 February 2019).

Wan, F. and Youn, S. (2004) 'Motivations to regulate online gambling and violent game sites: An account of the third-person effect', *Journal of Interactive Advertising*, 5: 46–59.

Ward, M. (2009) 'China clampdown on tech in Urumqi', *BBC*. 6 July. Online. Available HTTP: <http://news.bbc.co.uk/2/hi/technology/8136944.stm> (accessed 4 February 2019).

Warf, B. (2011) 'Geographies of global Internet censorship', *GeoJournal*, 76: 1–23.

Welzel, C. (2011) 'The Asian values thesis revisited: Evidence from the world values surveys', *Japanese Journal of Political Science*, 12: 1–31.

The Wire. (2017) 'Access to internet archive's wayback machine blocked in India', *The Wire*. Online. Available HTTP: <https://thewire.in/165988/access-internet-archives-wayback-machine-blocked/> (accessed 4 February 2019).

Wong, E. (2010) 'After Long Ban, Western China is back online', *New York Times*. Online. Available HTTP: <www.nytimes.com/2010/05/15/world/asia/15china.html> (accessed 3 February 2019).

Yu, P.K. (2009) 'Digital copyright reform and legal transplant in Hong Kong'. *University of Louisville Law Review*, 48: 693–718.

INDEX

Note: Page numbers in italic indicate a figure and page numbers in bold indicate a table on the corresponding page.